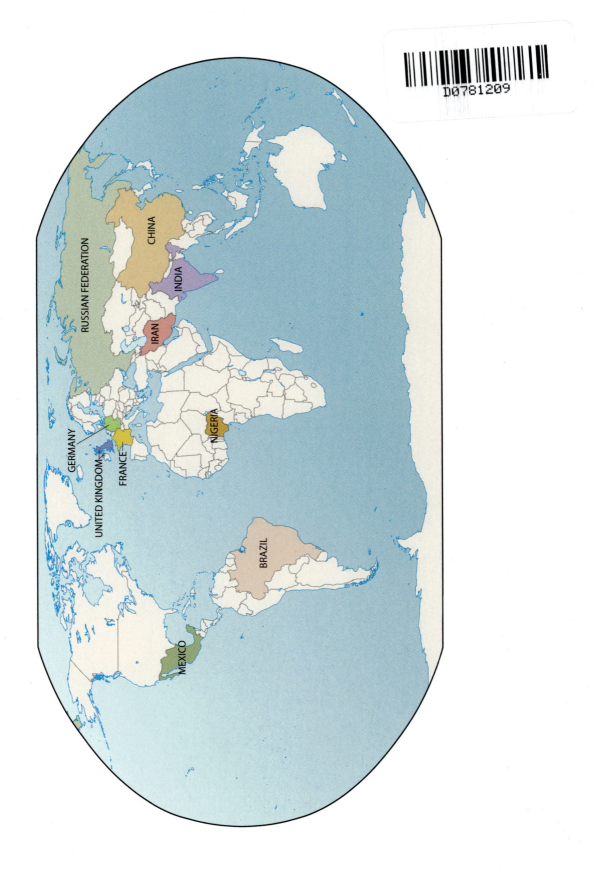

Comparative Politics
Structures and Choices

Lowell Barrington, Marquette University

Michael J. Bosia, Saint Michael's College

Kathleen Bruhn, University of California, Santa Barbara

Susan Giaimo, Marquette University

Dean E. McHenry, Jr., Claremount Graduate University

WADSWORTH
CENGAGE Learning™

Australia • Brazil • Japan • Korea • Mexico • Singapore • Spain • United Kingdom • United States

Comparative Politics:
Structures and Choices
Lowell Barrington

Executive Acquiring Sponsoring Editor:
Carolyn Merrill

Acquiring Sponsoring Editor: Edwin Hill

Development Manager: Jeffrey Greene

Development Editor: Terri Wise

Associate Editor: Katherine Hayes

Editorial Assistant: Matt DiGangi

Media Editor: Laura Hildebrand

Senior Marketing Manager: Amy Whitaker

Marketing Coordinator: Josh Hendrick

Marketing Communications Manager:
Heather Baxley

Content Project Manager: Susan Miscio

Print Buyer: Miranda Klapper

Senior Rights Acquisition Account Manager:
Katie Huha

Text Designer: Janis Owens

Photo Manager: Jennifer Meyer Dare

Photo Researcher: Stacey Dong

Cover Designer: Sarah Bishins

Cover Image: Jeremy Woodhouse, Zocalo,
Mexico City, Mexico © Getty Images;
WIN-Initiative, Communist crowd © Getty
Images

Compositor: Macmillan Publishing Solutions

For product information and technology assistance, contact us at
Cengage Learning Academic Resource Center, 1-800-423-0563

For permission to use material from this text or product,
submit all requests online at **www.cengage.com/permissions**.
Further permissions questions can be e-mailed to
permissionrequest@cengage.com.

Library of Congress Control Number: 2008941130

Student Edition:
ISBN-13: 978-0-618-49319-7

ISBN-10: 0-618-49319-0

Wadsworth
20 Channel Center Street
Boston, MA 02210
USA

Cengage Learning products are represented in Canada by
Nelson Education, Ltd.

For your course and learning solutions, visit **www.cengage.com**.

Purchase any of our products at your local college store
or at our preferred online store **www.ichapters.com**.

Printed in the United States of America
1 2 3 4 5 6 7 12 11 10 09 08

Brief Contents

Contents

Part II   Economic, Cultural, and Identity Structures   62

Part III   Political Structures   189

x   Contents

Part IV   Elites, Masses, and Political Decision Making   321

Chapter 9

Political Participation, Clientelism, and Interest Groups   321

Part V   Using Structures and Choices to Understand Political Outcomes   443

Preface and Acknowledgements

In November 2008, Americans once again went to the polls to help select the president of the United States, Barack Obama. This act of choosing the government's most important leader, in a free and fair setting, is something most Americans take for granted. In other parts of the world, many individuals long for such a chance. In the last decade, a large number of people have taken to the streets, sometimes with tragic results, to demand such a right. It is precisely because much of the world is so different from the United States that an introduction to the field of comparative politics is enormously valuable for American students.

When students come to the end of an introduction to comparative politics, they should have a better understanding of many of the world's largest and most important countries. But the journey toward an understanding of politics outside of the American context should also provide them with a comprehensive introduction to central concepts, important theoretical perspectives, and methods for studying other parts of the world. This textbook was developed to help students of comparative politics on such a journey.

There are two traditional approaches to introductory comparative politics. The first is to spend most of the semester discussing countries, often covering a country per week and attempting to bring in important broader themes along the way. The second is to spend the first half of the semester on these important themes and then turn to specific countries. For professors and students alike, both approaches can be frustrating. The country per week approach can provide a significant amount of information about a set of countries, but too often it becomes primarily a fact-based

exercise, leaving students without a framework to use in comparing the countries. The approach that introduces concepts in the first part of the course and countries in the second part can do a good job of providing conceptual and theoretical frameworks. Yet, early in the course it frequently leaves students thinking "so what?", longing for country-specific examples when the concepts and theories are being discussed. Students may also struggle to recall the thematic information later on when country-specific information is finally presented. This book is designed to address these shortcomings typical of introductory comparative politics textbooks.

Comparative Politics: Structures and Choices provides students with a framework for understanding major political outcomes. It examines different types of structures (economic, cultural, identity, and political), before turning to how individuals are linked to the political system and how they make political choices. Ultimately, students are encouraged to consider how structures and choices interact, including the extent to which existing economic, social, and political structures both constrain decision makers and provide them with opportunities.

In employing this overarching framework, the book ties together concepts, theories, and country-specific information to an extent not seen in any other existing comparative politics textbook. Whenever an important set of concepts is introduced, the discussion promptly turns to how those concepts play out in a set of ten countries. To facilitate comparison, these countries—the United Kingdom, Germany, France, Mexico, Brazil, Russia, China, India, Nigeria, and Iran—are combined into groups of two, three, or four. Although countries from the same part of the world (e.g., Mexico and Brazil) are often grouped together, the specific groupings differ from chapter to chapter, driven by the particular traits of the countries with regard to the broader concepts focused on in a given chapter. After this "Topic in Countries" (TIC) section, the chapter then turns to the next set of important concepts, followed by another TIC section on that set of concepts.

In addition to the TIC approach, the book contains a number of features designed to get students thinking about and discussing the central topics of each chapter. It introduces important comparative politics theories by uniting thematic and country-specific information within "In Theory and Practice" boxes embedded in the discussions of particular countries. These boxes provide both an overview of a theory's basic claims and a discussion of how the theory relates to aspects of one of the TIC cases. Starting with Chapter 2, each chapter ends with a "comparative exercise." These exercises are designed to help students think about how one conducts comparative politics research. They include research questions, hypotheses, data, and findings about a topic related to the main themes of the chapter in which they appear. Other features include "Think and Discuss" boxes, which provide ready-made questions for students to discuss, and "Applying Concepts" sections, which help students think about how issues such as concept measurement affect how one understands important political outcomes.

For the Instructor: Innovative Teaching Tools

In addition to writing much of this book's text, I have been centrally involved with producing a tightly integrated set of instructional materials to accompany the book. They complement the content of the book and offer instructional assistance with all aspects of teaching comparative politics. These materials include:

- **Online Instructor's Resource Manual:** This resource provides instructors with material that relates directly to the framework and organization of the book. To access this manual, visit the password-protected instructor website at **www.college.cengage.com/politicalscience/barrington.**
- **CL Testing:** This CD provides instructors with all the tools they need to create, author, edit, customize, and deliver multiple types of tests. Instructors can import questions directly from the Test Bank, create their own questions, or edit existing algorithmic questions.
- **PowerPoint Slides.** PowerPoint slides, which include figures from the text and brief outlines of chapter content, are available on the password-protected instructor website at **www.college.cengage.com/politicalscience/barrington.**
- **In-Class "Clicker" Quizzes.** Multiple-choice quizzes, delivered in PowerPoint format and compatible with "clicker" technology, are available for download on the password-protected instructor website. **www.college.cengage.com/politicalscience/barrington.**
- **AP NewsNow (powered by The Associated Press)** Bring the news right into your classroom! AP NewsNow PowerPoint slides allows instructors to engage students in events that are shaping the world right now. Use the slides to take a class poll or engage in a lively debate related to these stories, which may be downloaded from our password-protected instructor website at **www.college.cengage.com/politicalscience/barrington.** No in-class Internet connection required! The Associated Press also provides a live news-feed that can be accessed on the Student and Instructor Websites.
- **ComparingGovernments.org:** Encourage in-class discussion through **ComparingGovernments.org.** Correlated to the Table of Contents in the text and fully customizable by instructors, this site

provides online videos; media; and quality writing and homework assignments. The site also helps students stay current with daily headlines from the *BBC*. An online Notebook allows instructors to track which assignments the students have completed. To learn more and to set up a course, visit **ComparingGovernments.org.**

- **Student Website**, accessible at **www.college .cengage.com/politicalscience/barrington,** offers a wide array of resources for students. Included are ACE Practice Tests, flashcards, maps, and an online feature called "Deepening Your Understanding" that can be assigned for additional reading and provides yet another avenue for students to see how key concepts in the chapter play out in the real world.

Acknowledgements

A large number of people played crucial roles in the development of this book. Four scholars made significant contributions to the book, particularly in the discussion of four of the TIC cases: Mike Bosia (who wrote on France), Kate Bruhn (Brazil), Sue Giaimo (Germany), and Dean McHenry (India). Their expertise on these cases and valuable comments and suggestions has made this a much better book than it would have been without them. They were also, simply put, a joy to work with. They met deadlines, accepted suggestions, and provided valuable feedback on the chapters' thematic discussions.

Equally important was the book's developmental editor, Terri Wise. Terri helped fine-tune the book's approach, oversaw reviews of the manuscript, and worked with me and the other contributors on numerous drafts of each chapter. It is impossible to do justice to Terri in describing how helpful she has been. I will, instead, simply say thank you.

An additional thank you goes to the senior editors and sponsoring editors at Houghton Mifflin and Wadsworth/Cengage: Katherine

Meisenheimer, Traci Mueller, Carolyn Merrill, and Edwin Hill. Katherine believed in the project from the start, aggressively pursued me to sign with Houghton Mifflin, and worked closely with me in the early stages of the writing. Traci worked closely with Terri Wise to take the book in new and valuable directions. Carolyn was very helpful and reassuring during the initial period following Cengage's purchase of Houghton Mifflin's College Division. Edwin took on the role of sponsoring editor during this time as well and, along with the help of many others at Cengage, particularly project manager Susan Miscio, played a significant role in guiding the manuscript through the final stages and helping to produce a wonderfully-designed textbook.

A large number of reviewers provided suggestions, criticism, and encouragement. The book would not be anything close to what it is without their input. These reviewers included: Nozar Alaolmolki, Hiram College; Valentine J. Belfiglio, Texas Woman's University; Prosper Bernard, College of Staten Island; Terry Clark, Creighton University; Jane Leftwich Curry, Santa Clara University; Eliot Dickinson, Western Oregon University; Richard Farkas, DePaul University; Julie George, Queens College, City University of New York; Anke Grosskopf, Long Island University—C.W. Post Campus; Jennifer Horan, University of North Carolina, Wilmington; Zachary T. Irwin, Pennsylvania State University—Erie; F. David Levenbach, Arkansas State University; Stephen P. Mumme, Colorado State University; John Occhipinti, Canisius College; Ronald M. Schneider, Queens College, City University of New York; Michael Shepherd, Har-Ber High School, Springdale, Arkansas; Carole Wilson, University of Texas, Dallas.

At Marquette University, many of my colleagues in the department of political science also read drafts of chapters and provided helpful feedback. They included Julia Azari, Janet Boles, Jeff Drope, Michael Fleet, Rich Friman, Ryan Hanley, Larry LeBlanc, John McAdams, Barry McCormick, Duane Swank, Christopher Wolfe, and McGee Young. A number of graduate research assistants—including Brooke Chichakly, Craig Frizzell, Yuliya Humphrey, Ivana Ivanovic, John LeJeune, Anne Mozena, Craig Shockley, and Natalie Worlow—also played important roles throughout the book's development.

Above all, my wife, Therese, and our children, Alex, Colin, Tristan, and Quinn, were extremely supportive. Writing this book involved many late nights (and subsequent grumpy mornings), as well as activities put off and events occasionally missed. Through everything, my family was more than understanding. This book is for them.

It is also, of course, for the students who will use it during their introduction to the comparative study of politics. I hope they find it both helpful and interesting. When they have finished the book, they will have a deeper understanding of many of the world's most important countries. Even more important, they will have improved their ability to analyze and discuss political outcomes outside the United States, not only this semester but also long after their introductory comparative politics course is done.

LB

Part I Comparative Politics: Themes and Approaches

Learning Objectives

After reading this chapter, you should be able to:

- Define key terms covered in the chapter, such as politics, power, legitimacy, science, hypothesis, and variable.
- Discuss the basic steps involved in the scientific research method, including the use of hypotheses and theories.
- Summarize the comparative method and the alternative approaches within it.
- Describe the basic difference between structures and choices.

1

The Comparative Study of Politics

In July 2006, Jarosław Kaczyński became Poland's new prime minister. At first glance, this would hardly strike one as extraordinary. New prime ministers come and go—in some democracies, quite frequently. But Kaczyński was nominated to become prime minister by his identical twin brother, Lech, who happened to be Poland's *president* at the time. For the next year and a half, Poles had the distinction of watching the Kaczyński twins control their national government. A vote in parliament in October 2007 sparked early elections, which Jarosław Kaczyński's party lost. This strange chapter of Polish politics ended (for the time being, at least) the following month. President Lech Kaczyński nominated Donald Tusk to replace his brother and presided over Tusk's swearing in as prime minister. ■

Look for this icon to point you to **Deepening Your Understanding** features on the companion website www.college.cengage.com/politicalscience/barrington, which provide greater depth for some key content.

Comparative politics involves the study of such events—along with others not quite so remarkable—to gain a better understanding of the forces that drive political outcomes around the world. These political outcomes include everything from elections, constitutional reforms, and policy changes, to mass protests, coups, and civil wars. As a result, comparative politics is demanding. As political scientists Mark Lichbach and Alan Zuckerman argue, this field of political science "asserts an ambitious scope of inquiry. No political phenomenon is foreign to it; no level of analysis is irrelevant, and no time period is beyond its reach."[1]

This description makes it seem easier to identify the topics not covered in comparative politics than those that are. Indeed, comparative politics scholars, called **comparativists**, are required to understand the numerous factors that influence politics—the structures that shape political decisions, the process of making those decisions, and the leaders who oversee the process—in a variety of settings. However, comparative politics is not as complex as it might first appear. Comparativists compare and contrast the domestic politics of a country or countries with the domestic politics of another country or in between countries. Comparativists tend not to focus their analysis on foreign policy or international relations, though they certainly consider the role that trends and events outside a country can have on politics within it. They only occasionally concentrate on local politics. They commonly know very well only one country or a small set of countries in the same part of the world. Comparativists in the United States also frequently exclude the American case from their investigations. Instead, in the United States, American politics has the status of its own field in political science (studied and taught by scholars called "Americanists").

Like all political scientists, comparativists engage in research about political behavior and other political phenomena. The study of these political outcomes involves a number of activities: defining key terms, collecting and analyzing data, describing and categorizing these data, understanding and explaining causal relationships within these data, predicting political outcomes, and prescribing policies to address social problems.

Of these activities, the central one is understanding and explaining causal relationships. Understanding causal relationships requires and/or makes possible all of the comparativists' other activities. A set of readily agreed-upon definitions of concepts, empirical data (i.e., observations), and the organization of these data into categories are all necessary steps prior to understanding the political outcomes in which comparativists are interested. Having a grasp on causal relationships in the political arena allows researchers to predict political outcomes. One can, of course, predict an outcome without understanding it by simply extrapolating from an existing trend. Unfortunately, if the driving forces behind that trend are not understood, any prediction based on that trend is fragile. People engaged in this form of prediction will be correct a decent portion of the time, but when they make a mistake, they are likely to be *really* wrong.

Likewise, policy prescriptions require an appreciation for the causes and consequences of the policy in question. Political science has become concerned with making its research "policy relevant"—that is, useful to political leaders and to those in charge of administering public policy. It is tempting to think that this trend requires political scientists to "dumb down" their research, but an effort to make research findings more readable for politicians should not lead political scientists to lose their

Comparative politics is a field of political science that engages in the systematic study of political outcomes through the comparison of different cases.

Comparativists are scholars who generally focus on domestic politics at the national level outside the United States.

own understanding of the causal relationships in question. Doing so helps neither their profession nor the practitioners they seek to advise.

Because of the importance of causal relationships in political science, a good portion of this chapter is devoted to a discussion of how one examines such causal relationships in a systematic manner. This discussion includes the principles of scientific research, the extent to which political science is a science, and how one conducts comparative political research. Finally, the chapter also introduces the notion of "structure versus choice," a framework for sorting out the many causal arguments about political outcomes you will encounter in your comparative politics course.

Just as an actual political science study begins with definitions of the key concepts, it is necessary to open this chapter with the discussion of two crucial concepts, politics and power. Additional key comparative politics concepts— for example, "nation" and "state"—are covered in detail in Chapter 2. Each of the remaining chapters include definitions of other concepts, which are central to the topic of that chapter.

Key Concepts in the Comparative Study of Politics

Like all branches of science, the social sciences rely on a set of central concepts with definitions that most scholars generally accept. Political science is no exception. Thinking through how one defines key concepts is particularly important in comparative politics, since the act of comparing requires the use of terms and categories that are broad enough to be applied to different countries and different cultures without being so vague as to be unhelpful.[2]

Moreover, definitions allow people to "speak the same language." There are few things more frustrating than realizing, after a long debate with someone about an issue, that your differing ways of defining the topic of the debate meant that you were not arguing about the same thing. Unfortunately, there is less agreement on definitions of concepts among political scientists than among natural scientists (chemists, biologists, etc.). Two comparativists' definitions of democracy, for example, may differ significantly. In addition, how comparativists use many terms— such as "nation"—differs from how you likely use these words in conversation with your family, friends, or others who may not have taken a comparative politics course.

This variation in understandings of central concepts is an obstacle to the comparative study of politics, but it is far from insurmountable. Overcoming this potential complication requires those researching political outcomes to do three things: (1) clearly state how they define important concepts, (2) use terms in a manner consistent with their definitions, and (3) not assume that others have the same understanding of those terms. In order to get the most out of this book, you need to become familiar with its definitions of such key comparative politics terms as politics and power.

Politics: Who Gets What, When, and How

If **politics** is the arena of the comparativist, what does this arena look like? The term politics is used in many ways in everyday language, often with a negative implication of self-interest, backstabbing, and trickery, such as in the phrase "office politics." This characterization is not completely unfair; even in the government, politics often involves such intrigue. But

Politics is the set of activities that organizes individuals, systematically resolves disputes, and maintains order in society through the creation and enforcement of rules and government policy. These decisions involve winners and losers; as a result, politics can also be thought of as process of deciding "who gets what, when, and how" in a particular society.

one need not think of politics only as a negative endeavor. In fact, despite the common joke that the word comes from "poly" (meaning many) and "ticks" (blood-sucking insects), politics is an essential activity for any sizeable group of people. As Aristotle put it in *The Politics*, "Man is a political animal." Without cooperation and an ability to enforce the rules established to govern behavior, large groups would be subject to chaos and the will of the strongest to a much greater extent than happens in modern societies.

In light of this discussion, what does the word politics mean to political scientists? There are two aspects to the concept of politics. The first is a relatively hopeful and positive view of politics: that it is a set of activities that *help organize individuals, systematically resolve disputes, and maintain order in society*. These actions include passing and enforcing laws governing individual behavior, mobilizing and channeling mass participation, and socializing individuals to support the political system and the values on which it is based. Activities and institutional arrangements designed to prevent and resolve disputes require decisions to be made. In politics, such decisions are known as **policy**. The individuals and decision-making mechanisms that generate this policy are known as the "government" (see Chapter 2).

The other side of politics is less upbeat. In exchange for the order that government provides, individuals surrender a certain degree of their freedom. They surrender a certain amount of wealth as well, since governmental policies generally cost money. Consequently, the government's ability to extract resources from society and redistribute them through its policy decisions is one of the keys to a successful, stable political system. Because politics generates policies that extract and distribute resources, as well as policies that address grievances and settle disagreements, politics involves winners and losers. The winners "get" something from a governmental decision, while the losers do not—or at least not as much as they give. As political scientist Harold Lasswell described it in the early twentieth century, politics concerns *who gets what, when, and how*.[3] There is little in one's life that is not touched by politics.

> **Did You Know?**   The real origin of "politics" is the Greek word *polis* meaning "city."

Think and Discuss

In this chapter, you are presented with two ideas about politics. The first is a more positive view of politics: an activity that helps organize individuals, systematically resolve disputes, and maintain order in society. The second view—one that looks at politics as a process which decides "who gets what" and thus produces winners and losers—is less encouraging.

1) Which of the two ideas of politics better captures the essence of the concept?
2) Why?

Power: How People Get What They Want

If politics involves "who gets what, when, and how," then when and how people get what they want depends to a large extent on their **power**. It is, therefore, impossible to understand politics without comprehending the concept of power. The products of politics—such as official governmental policies—come from decisions made by individuals. These individuals have certain powers, including the official ability to make these policy decisions, but they are also

> A **policy** is an official decision designed to organize people, resolve disputes, or address other collective problems.
>
> **Power** is defined by political scientists both as influence—A getting B to do something even if B does not want to engage in that activity—and as the capabilities that allow A to get B to do what A wants.

influenced in these decisions by other individuals and groups.

Power as Influence Unlike some of the other important concepts in comparative politics, power is a concept that most people grasp well. Power is influence: *getting people to do what you want them to do*. The concept of **power as influence** includes the idea that one person in a power relationship can overcome the resistance of another. Unfortunately, defining power as influence over others creates problems for comparativists in practice. Seeking to understand power relationships in a particular country, a political scientist who views power as influence would try to observe the influence as it occurs. But how easy is it to observe one person's influence over another? Such influence can manifest itself in numerous ways, some of which are much easier to observe than others.

Though scholars have written about various levels of influence (or "faces of power"), there is a general consensus that influence can vary from aboveboard and understood by all involved to unspoken and not understood by everyone involved. It might help to walk through these alternatives using two people, named Anne and Bob. When Anne openly tells Bob to do something, Bob publicly announces that he does not want to do it, but eventually does what Anne wants. In this case, the influence is upfront and clearly understood by both Anne and Bob. In such cases—for instance, doing the readings for next week after your professor tells you there will be a quiz on them—the influence may be easy to observe. But power relationships between Anne and Bob can be much more complex and certainly more subtle.

As the influence becomes more subtle and complex, it also becomes more difficult for the outside observer—a political scientist searching for power relationships in a particular political system, for example—to detect the influence in practice. For example, Anne may tell Bob to do something in private, with no record of the conversation. Or, hoping to gain from the action, Bob may do something without Anne having said anything. In these situations, the power relationship is understood by the two people involved, but the influence itself is less apparent.

Bob may even do something because Anne has, unbeknown to Bob, convinced Bob that (without any regard to Anne) it is in his interest to do it. In other words, Bob does something that Anne wants him to do because it is something that Bob really wants to do. In this case, Anne may be aware of her power, while Bob may be oblivious to his status as the subordinate member of a two-person power relationship. Being interviewed by a political scientist seeking to understand Bob's actions, Bob would simply report he was acting in his own best interest. In other words, the more complex and interesting power relationships get, the more difficult it is to identify and to understand them.

Power as Capabilities The difficulties of measuring and observing power as influence have led scholars to discuss and study power in a different way: **power as capabilities**. Rather than looking for the influence as it is taking place, one instead looks at the abilities that Anne has that make her able to get Bob to do what she wants him to do. In other words, thinking about power as capabilities allows political scientists to look for more tangible, easier to measure indicators of power.

Of course, thinking about power as capabilities assumes that one can identify tangible and easily measured indicators of power. In the realm of domestic politics, many characteristics that would provide the potential for influence are obvious: official positions in government,

---

Power as influence is the ability of A to get B to do what A wants, even if B does not want to engage in the activity.

Power as capabilities focuses on characteristics that would give one the ability to influence important outcomes.

money, control of armed forces, and so on. However, comparativists would struggle to agree on an exact list of such capabilities. In addition, some capabilities are harder to observe than others. This is particularly true of noncoercive capabilities, the topic of the next section.

Thus, moving from power as influence to power as capabilities solves some problems, but it does not solve all of them. Thinking about, recognizing, and analyzing power are challenges for comparativists. But given the importance of power to the understanding of politics, they are vital challenges for scholars and students of comparative politics to address.

Coercive versus Noncoercive Power

If Anne gets Bob to do something for her that Bob would rather not do, Anne has power over Bob. But why does Bob obey? Broadly speaking, power has two foundations. The first is coercion. With **coercive power**, Anne has rewards and/or punishments at her disposal. For example, if Anne is Bob's boss, she has the ability to reward or punish him for his actions, through a promotion or a raise or with a cut in pay or termination of his employment.

In domestic politics, government leaders can pass laws that prohibit certain actions and come up with punishments for those who break the law. In authoritarian and totalitarian political systems, officials can punish those who threaten their rule, even if they have broken no formal law. Rewards are commonly used instruments of power as well. Many government programs redistribute money. Such financial rewards can lead individuals to behave in ways government officials desire, but, in democracies at least, this is not a one-way power relationship. Citizens also hold some power in their ability to reward and punish government officials at election time. A number of political science studies have addressed the extent to which government officials' decisions take into account the potential for voters to hold them accountable in future elections.

Noncoercive power rests on a different foundation, one that does not involve rewards and punishments. In this case, power results from a sense of **legitimacy**. What does it mean that an individual, a political system, or even the state itself has legitimacy? Unfortunately, political scientists use this term in different ways. One view of legitimacy is to understand it as similar to support. More and more, however, the term is thought of *as the belief in the right to rule*, and that is how it is used in this book. The belief in a right to rule does *not* mean that all government decisions are supported. One does not have to agree with the specific policies that the American Congress produces, for example, to still believe that Congress has the right to make these rules.

In practice, people often follow rules because those making them have both coercive and noncoercive power. Even in systems with a high degree of legitimacy, rules are followed by many citizens at least in part because of a fear of punishment. However, a system that is legitimate will be able to produce policies, and enforce them, more effectively than a system that lacks legitimacy. Rulers of totalitarian, authoritarian, and democratic systems generally all strive to establish legitimacy for their systems. Securing it makes leaders' lives easier.

But how does one observe legitimacy? How can one determine who believes in a system's legitimacy and who follows its rules due to fear of punishment or hope for reward? Surveys can provide a sense of the extent to which people believe in the system's right to rule in democracies, but valid survey data are hard to collect in nondemocratic countries. When a nondemocratic system collapses due to large-scale, violent protests, it is reasonable

---

Coercive power is getting what one wants through the use of rewards and punishments.

Noncoercive power is getting what one wants because of legitimacy.

Legitimacy is the belief by those obeying commands that those making the commands have the "right to rule."

to conclude the system lacked both legitimacy and effective coercive capacity. But what about a stable nondemocratic system that is repressive but whose leaders also work hard—stressing impressive economic performance or socializing the population to accept an official ideology—to develop legitimacy? Identifying whether people are obeying because of legitimacy or because of fear is one of a comparativist's more difficult tasks.

Authority is a concept closely related to legitimacy. While some comparativists use the term authority interchangeably with power, most think of it as *power based on legitimacy*. In other words, authority is noncoercive influence. While legitimacy is the belief among those being ruled that the leader (or system) has the right to rule, authority is the use of that legitimacy.

In a famous 1918 speech, sociologist Max Weber (pronounced "Vayber") linked the concepts of politics and power, stating that politics "means striving to share power or striving to influence the distribution of power."[4] Weber is also well known for outlining three types of authority throughout history. The first is **traditional authority**. Monarchies often hold this form of authority, deriving their legitimacy from the masses' belief that a particular family deserves the throne, or even that the monarch has a "divine right to rule." In the latter case, ordinary people believe that the monarch has been chosen by God to lead. For example, with the help of the Russian Orthodox Church, Russian tsars presented themselves as a link between God and the general population. In such a setting, one can certainly understand why the masses follow the political system's rules. To disobey them would be to disobey God.

The second type of authority that Weber emphasized is **charismatic authority**. In this case, a leader, and perhaps the system as a whole, becomes legitimate because of the leader's ability to inspire or because the people like or feel attached to the leader. The danger of relying on this form of legitimacy is that it is closely tied to an individual leader. If the leader dies, or

somehow falls out of favor with the masses, the system as a whole is in trouble.

Weber's final form of authority is **legal authority**. Here, legitimacy is based on an established constitution—a political system's set of rules for making new rules—to which the political leaders adhere. It can also involve selecting

Sociologist Max Weber, known for his groundbreaking conceptualization and study of power, national identity, and the state.

(©Hulton Archive/Getty Images)

Authority is power exercised through legitimacy rather than through coercion, though some comparative politics scholars use the term interchangeably with power.

Traditional authority, common in monarchies in the past, bases the power of leaders on their family's claim to the throne and/or the belief that God has granted the leader the right to rule.

Charismatic authority is power based on the personal attachment of the masses to a particular leader.

Legal authority is based on an established set of rules in a political system that govern how political leaders are chosen and how they make policy decisions.

leaders through elections. Those who vote for a losing candidate certainly may not like the person who wins, but the process of selecting the leaders through an election adds to the legitimacy of the policies that the resultant government produces.

Think and Discuss

If power is central to understanding politics, and politics is about "who gets what," can the underprivileged in society ever get a fair deal from the government? Explain your answer.

Political Science as a Science

How exactly does one study concepts like power? Political science is one of the few academic disciplines that include the word "science" in its name. But, political science faces difficulties that some of the natural sciences do not. Before considering how scientific political science (and, therefore, comparative politics) can be, it is helpful first to discuss the goals and methods of scientific inquiry.

Scientific Research and Scientific Knowledge

The term science refers to undertaking a particular form of systematic study to better understand events and processes. **Science** pursues general and reliable knowledge as the basis for such understanding. This knowledge is general in that it can be applied to help comprehend a variety of settings. Science seeks regularities or patterns in nature (including in human behavior). It aims to discover how factors relate to one another in order to use that understanding to predict future relations between those factors.

Causality   Scientific research questions are most often "why" questions. Consequently, **causality** is a central consideration in any discussion of science. A causal relationship involves two or more **variables**. Variables are things whose existence or value can vary, such as gross domestic product per capita, type of economic system, or whether a political system is a democracy. Such variables include the result or effect that a researcher seeks to understand. This type of variable is called a **dependent variable**, since its value or existence is dependent on the presence and/or values of other variables. The elements that the researcher examines as possible causes of the presence and/or value of the dependent variable are called **independent variables**. They are given this label because their magnitude or occurrence does not depend on the value or presence of other variables examined in the study. Theoretically, a causal relationship could include only one dependent and one independent variable. Causal relationships, however, are often more complex than this, involving

---

Science is a form of systematic study undertaken to better understand nature and human behavior. Science relies on empirical data (observations), employs a generally accepted methodology to allow others to replicate findings, and focuses on questions about how things are rather than how things ought to be.

Causality is a relationship between two or more variables where changes in the presence or value of one or more of them produces a change in the presence or value of another.

A **variable** is an item, studied in science, whose existence or value is subject to change.

In a causal relationship, a variable can be the outcome the investigators seek to explain, called the **dependent variable**.

A variable can also be something investigators use to explain the outcome, whose value or existence is not affected by the set of factors they examine, called an **independent variable**.

multiple independent variables and multiple stages of causality.

Think and Discuss

Name a type of major political outcome that you think would make an interesting dependent variable.

Theories as "Causal Stories" Observations alone may not provide definitive evidence about causality. In such cases, making causal claims requires more than data collection and analysis. It requires a **theory** to provide the "causal story" behind the patterns in the data. Furnishing the underpinnings of hypotheses, theories are the backbone of scientific inquiry. A theoretical framework which argues that two or more variables are causally related transforms observations of *what* happened into an explanation of *why* it happened.

Thus, it is generally not the data themselves but rather new or existing theories that allow comparativists to make causal claims. The existence of data that are consistent with a theory support that theory, but they cannot "prove" the theory correct. Data that are inconsistent with a theory call it into question. One cannot have confidence in a theory that offers an explanation for something that appears not to have taken place.

At times, comparativists are not trying to test a theory but, rather, seeking to understand a particular political outcome in a given country. In such instances, theories help them to make sense of what has happened. Within many of this book's Topic in Countries sections are boxes labeled "In Theory and Practice." Each of these boxes lays out a key theory related to the topic of the chapter. Consistent with the dual nature of theories in comparative politics, some of these boxes stress how the country lends support for (or challenges) the theory, while others focus on how the theory can help understand an aspect of that country.

The Scientific Method

Having in mind what science seeks to do, what does the practice of scientific inquiry look like? How does one discover general and reliable knowledge? What does it mean to study a topic "scientifically"? Most political scientists believe that engaging in scientific study does *not* depend on the subject of the study. One can study chemistry unscientifically, and, though it may be more difficult than for other topics, one can study politics scientifically. How scientific an endeavor is depends on the *method* of the research. Scientific research involves a generally accepted process of collecting, analyzing, and interpreting data.

Research Questions The research process begins with the identification of a **research question**. This question generally entails some puzzle that the researcher finds interesting and that does not have an obvious answer; if it did, there would be little reason to engage in systematic study of it. The question is also usually a "why" question, such as "Why do some countries become democracies and others do not?"

In the early stages of research on a particular topic, it is necessary first to establish the basic patterns in the variables under study. In these initial stages, the research questions might be "who, what, when, where, or how" questions. For example, early studies of democracy by comparativists centered on questions

> A **theory** is a set of generally accepted information about how and why phenomena relate to one another in a variety of settings. This "causal story" allows researchers to explain why the particular phenomena they examine are causally related.
>
> A **research question** is a puzzle that does not have an obvious answer and forms the basis for a particular research project. These are generally "why?" questions, inquiring about the reason for a particular outcome.

such as "What are the identifiable features of a democracy?," "When did democracy emerge?," and so forth. Once the general patterns have been established, however, researchers turn to *understanding* the reasons for the patterns. Understanding requires answers to "why" questions.

Hypotheses and the Use of Theories as "Hypothesis Generators"   The next step is to develop a **hypothesis.** This is a tentative statement representing an educated guess at the answer to the research question. It is tentative because it is assumed to be correct but will be tested. It is based on existing theories or logic. Thus, in this case, theories serve a role as "hypothesis generators." Through their general causal story about how certain phenomena are related to one another, theories also provide more specific, testable claims. A theory about how historical, economic, and other differences between regions within a country would affect political attitudes, for example, could be used to generate a hypothesis about regional divisions in a specific country—Ukraine, for example—and their impact on particular attitudes, such as support for independence from Russia. In the case of a typical "why" research question, the hypothesis is a statement about a causal relationship between the result the scientist wants to understand (e.g., democracy) and the factors the researcher examines as a cause or causes. In other words, hypotheses include variables.

The hypothesis must be **falsifiable**. This does not mean the researcher must find that the hypothesis is false. Rather, it means that there must be a *possibility* that the statement is false. In other words, the hypothesis cannot be a statement that is true by definition. For example, the statement that large countries have more territory to defend than small countries is nonfalsifiable. It is true by definition. Such a claim is called a **tautology.** (One of the most damaging criticisms that one can make of a particular

study is that the major finding of the researcher is a tautology.)

The researcher then tests the hypothesis or hypotheses. If the data are consistent with a particular hypothesis, the researcher can claim that the research findings provide support for that hypothesis. If the data are not supportive of the research hypothesis, the researcher rejects the hypothesis. Analysis of the data *cannot* prove a hypothesis to be *true*.

Conceptualizing and Operationalizing Variables   Once a hypothesis has been developed, a researcher should clearly define the key terms in the study and how they will be measured. These two processes are called **conceptualization** and **operationalization.**   Conceptualization means making clear what one has in mind by a particular term (i.e., what democracy *means*). Operationalization is laying out how that concept will be captured in practice in the research project (how democracy will be *measured*).

Neither of these steps is as easy as it sounds. Even if two scholars agree on a definition, they may differ greatly about how best to measure the idea in practice. Even when they agree on how

---

A **hypothesis** is a tentative statement by a researcher about the expected relationship between what the researcher is seeking to understand and what the researcher is examining as a potential cause or causes. The researcher tests the hypothesis by collecting and analyzing data about the effect and its suspected cause.

A hypothesis must be **falsifiable**, meaning that it cannot be a statement that is true by definition.

A statement that is true by definition is known as a **tautology**.

Conceptualization is the way that a researcher thinks about a particular concept, including which aspects are most important to consider when studying it.

Operationalization is the establishment of a particular measurement scheme for that concept, allowing one to observe and categorize data about the concept.

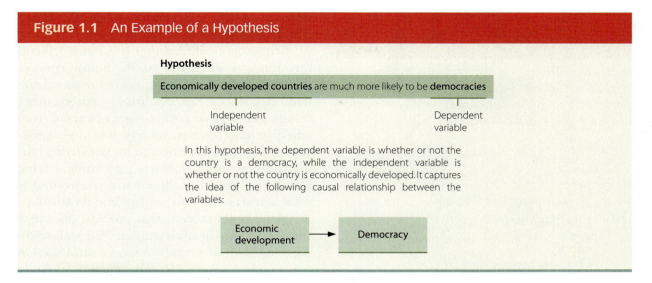

Figure 1.1   An Example of a Hypothesis

Hypothesis

Economically developed countries are much more likely to be democracies

Independent variable   Dependent variable

In this hypothesis, the dependent variable is whether or not the country is a democracy, while the independent variable is whether or not the country is economically developed. It captures the idea of the following causal relationship between the variables:

Economic development → Democracy

to measure it, the measurement scheme they select may prove difficult in the field. (Remember the problems with conceptualizing power in terms of influence, including the difficulties it poses for operationalizing power in a particular research project, discussed earlier in this chapter.) Without agreement about definitions and measurement, and without a realistic way to measure concepts, observations cannot be organized in a meaningful way.

Collecting and Analyzing Data About the Variables The next steps in the scientific method are to *collect and analyze data*. Political scientists seeking to collect data involving people usually require the approval of a board that reviews their proposed research and looks for any potential ethical concerns. The analysis must also conform to certain accepted standards. Statistical analysis, for example, involves procedures that are generally understood—or at least understood by those who use statistical techniques. A researcher also adheres to particular scientific norms in presenting the findings of the research, though the exact norms may differ from discipline to discipline. This openness and use of accepted norms relates to the idea of *transmissibility* of scientific

knowledge. If other scholars cannot determine how one of their colleagues arrived at a particular finding, that finding will be received with skepticism.

How Scientific Is Political Science?

Political science, like other social sciences, is limited in its ability to produce generalizable causal claims because its subject matter involves people. People are more complex, less predictable, and more unruly than chemicals in a laboratory. Some comparativists challenge the idea that definitive causal statements can be made about something as complex and multifaceted as politics. Such comparativists also emphasize the difficulties of measuring important comparative politics concepts in practice. They contend that the most central concepts, like power, also tend to be the most difficult to measure and observe. As a result, they argue that measurement difficulties are not simply research challenges; they strike at the heart of the ability of political scientists to study their subject in a scientific manner.

In addition, skeptics of the ability to study politics scientifically point out that it is often difficult to control for various possible explanations

Figure 1.2 A Diagram of the Research Process

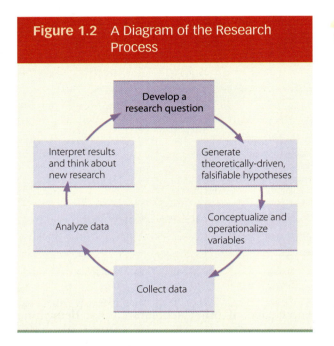

of a political outcome when examining a particular, posited hypothesis. In areas where political science and psychology overlap, researchers commonly use experiments. When political scientists examine the effects of media content on attitudes about political candidates, for example, they sometimes employ experimental methods in their research. But think about how difficult experiments are if one is interested in the effects of economic development on a country's prospects for democracy. As intriguing as it might be, political scientists cannot assign a group of similar small countries into an experimental group and a control group, alter the level of economic development in the experimental group, hold constant everything else the countries experience, and see what happens.

The complexity of politics, difficulty in measuring key concepts, and challenges to controlling for rival explanations lead some comparative politics scholars to reject causality as central to their study of politics. Instead, they tend to focus on "degrees of association" between two or more variables. They examine how certain variables appear to be correlated with one another,

without generating claims about the exact strength, or even the direction, of causality.

Still others contend that it is more difficult for political scientists to be non-normative than it is for other researchers in the social and natural sciences. Since politics is, among other things, about how resources get extracted from and distributed across society, it is not surprising for political scientists to have a strong normative take on the subjects they study. Caring about how social problems are confronted is what attracts many to politics and its study.

None of this means that political science is condemned to be unscientific. Political scientists can and do employ research strategies to make their work *as scientific as possible*. To do so requires an understanding of the goals of scientific inquiry and ideas of the scientific method, as well as the limitations involved when studying politics and the options available to scholars to address these limitations. It also means acknowledging the importance of theory in causal explanations.

Methods of Comparing to Understand Politics

Comparativists face three vital questions when designing a research project: (1) what level(s) of analysis to employ, (2) how many cases to examine, and (3) what form(s) of data to collect and study.

Levels of Analysis

The "level of analysis question" is one researchers in all disciplines face. The term **level of analysis** relates to where one looks for the

A **level of analysis** is a choice from a continuum of options—from the individual to the international system—concerning where a researcher will look for data. In comparative politics, the options include individuals, groups of individuals, regions within states, states, regions of states, or the international system as a whole.

answer to the research question. In comparative politics, there are a number of possibilities. Some comparativists collect data on individuals, including their attitudes or their decision-making strategies. Many comparativists examine groups within a particular society (or compare such groups in more than one society), searching for differences in their collective political behavior and trying to explain such differences. Others study localities or regions within one or more states, making comparisons and seeking to understand variation among them. Still others examine aspects of the political system, looking at the political institutions, their rules, and their outputs. Others prefer to examine and compare regions of states, systems, or societies. A researcher might ask, for example, why the depth of integration is greater in Europe at the present time than in any other region. A comparativist could even compare the international community as a whole at different points in time, though this level is more the domain of an international relations scholar than of a comparativist.

The state level, including its institutions and society, is the most common for comparative politics. Here, different states are compared to one another, though one could also look at a single state at different periods in its history. This is, arguably, the most typical approach of the "comparative method" discussed later in this chapter. It is also the level of analysis generally employed in the "comparative exercises" at the end of a number of the chapters in this book.

The Number of Cases

Comparative politics research can be divided into two categories, **quantitative studies** and **qualitative studies**, based on the number of cases. In comparative politics, a "case" is often a country. It is important to remember, however, that cases can come from any of the levels of analysis in Figure 1.3. Quantitative studies—sometimes called "large N" research,

with the "N" referring to the number of cases—allow statistical analysis of the data. Qualitative studies involve a small number of cases (i.e., "small N" research). The specific research question can drive the decision to engage in qualitative or quantitative research. Some research questions are better answered with a large number of cases, others with a small number of cases.

Case Studies The smallest number of cases examined in a comparative politics research study is one. A research project that looks at only one case is called a **case study** or **single case study**. Here the advantages and disadvantages of small N research are most apparent. A case study allows a deep understanding of the events in question *in that case*. It provides an opportunity for "thick description." Arguably, it can also allow what one might call "thick explanation,"[5] if the in-depth study allows the researcher to see the causal mechanism in progress. In that circumstance, the researcher can *explain* the events based on the observations, reducing the need for theory about why an apparent relationship is causal and in the direction the researcher claims.

Being able to see the causal process in action can give case studies powerful **internal validity**.

Studies that involve a large number of cases, allowing the researcher to analyze the data through the use of statistical techniques, are called **quantitative studies**.

Qualitative studies involve a small number of cases and do not allow the researcher to analyze the data through statistical analysis.

A **case study** is a research project that looks at only one case.

A case study is also sometimes called a **single case study**.

Internal validity is soundness of the claims that the researcher makes based on the data the researcher is using.

Figure 1.3   Possible Levels of Analysis in Comparative Politics

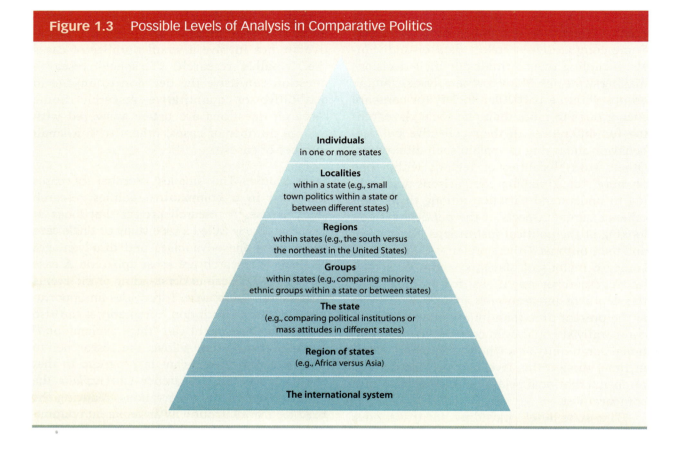

Individuals
in one or more states

Localities
within a state (e.g., small
town politics within a state or
between different states)

Regions
within states (e.g., the south versus
the northeast in the United States)

Groups
within states (e.g., comparing minority
ethnic groups within a state or between states)

The state
(e.g., comparing political institutions or
mass attitudes in different states)

Region of states
(e.g., Africa versus Asia)

The international system

Internal validity is the sense that the claims of the researcher about a causal relationship in the case or cases examined are well founded. This does not mean the finding would hold in all cases, but rather that the researcher appeared to "get it right" in this particular study.

On the other hand, in a case study researchers cannot control for certain variables while looking at the effects of others in the way that they can in, for example, an experiment involving a number of subjects. With only one case, it is impossible to examine the effects of a particular variable while holding the others constant. All variables that might theoretically affect the dependent variable are in play at the same time. Even when "close to the action," judging the relative effects of multiple variables in only one case places a great burden on the researcher. This includes the problem of objectivity, something that can be difficult when one gets too close to the subject of one's study. Institutions or individuals the researcher comes to like personally might appear the most important. The effects of important variables, which the researcher is less attached to, might be missed. The ability to be objective is a challenge for all researchers, but the temptation to "go native" is apt to be greatest for researchers who work only on a single case.

Another, and more obvious, limit of a case study relates to the ability of the researcher to generalize from the findings. After all, how can one know if the findings of the case would hold in other cases if one does not examine any other cases? This means that case studies are, in general, weak on **external validity**. External validity is the sense that the claims of the researcher about a causal relationship would apply to cases the researcher did not examine. The more cases one examines, the more confident one can be that strong patterns found in the data would hold in other cases as well. The fewer cases one examines, the less confident one is that the findings apply generally.

Because of the generalizability problem, case studies are also limited in helping researchers test existing theories about political outcomes. If the theory leads to an *unqualified* hypothesis—"All democracies are the result of high levels of economic development"—a case study could allow a researcher to call the theory into question. India, for example, can do great damage to a theory that claims high levels of economic development are necessary for the development of democracy. However, comparative politics theories are rarely absolute. The more common form of theory is a probabilistic theory, leading to a hypothesis such as "Democracies will be much more likely in countries with high levels of economic development." A single case can do minimal damage to a probabilistic theory.

This does not mean case studies are unhelpful to comparativists interested in political science theories. First, looking at a single case might help a researcher *generate* a new theory that could be examined in other cases. The case study is not a test of this theory, since the case was used to develop the theory. It can add a degree of validity to the theory, however, by showing that it works in at least one case.

Second, comparativists occasionally conduct what are known as **deviant case studies**. This approach examines a case that seems to be an "outlier"—a case that is far from the pattern that one sees looking at a larger number of cases. By understanding how a case could differ so greatly from the rest, the researcher may gain insight into the other cases. Deviant

case studies can lead researchers to consider different explanations that they might have ignored if they had also ignored the deviant case.

The flipside of the deviant case approach is the **critical case study**. A researcher employing a critical case approach seeks a case that provides a particularly powerful example of the research question in practice, such as one that offers a tough test of the study's key theories and hypothesis. Danish social scientist Bent Flyvbjerg, a specialist in case study methodology, claims that the goal is to find a case that leads one to "a generalization of the sort, 'If it is valid for *this* case, it is valid for all (or many) cases.'"[6] Flyvbjerg adds that it is easier to understand in general how the critical case would work than it is to identify such a case ahead of time, but he gives the example of a classic study by Robert Michels, published in 1911. Michels (a student of Max Weber) proposed that all social and political organizations have a tendency to develop an oligarchic leadership structure. According to Flyvbjerg, by choosing a "horizontally structured grassroots organization with strong democratic ideals"—that is, an organization that one would

External validity is the extent to which the findings of a particular study would hold up if data from other cases—not examined in the study—were analyzed. The greater the sense that the findings would apply to a large number of cases, the greater the external validity.

A **deviant case study** is a project that examines a particular research question in a case that exhibits characteristics very different from a generally known pattern. Understanding why such an "outlier" exists may give researchers new insight into the topic of their study.

In a **critical case study**, the case is selected because it provides a tough test of the central hypothesis or hypotheses in the researcher's study. As a result, findings consistent with the hypothesis are more generalizable than those produced from other case studies.

not expect to be ruled by an oligarchy—Michels was able to "test the universality of the oligarchy thesis" through the study of a single case.[7]

Finally, it is important to remember that single case studies can also be valuable because the case itself is important to understand. In addition to testing theories, comparativists are also expected to have a handle on the domestic politics of one or more countries and to use that knowledge to help those in charge of making government policy. To an official in the U.S. Department of State, the generalizability of a particular political science theory is likely to be much less interesting than a deep and convincing explanation of recent political events in a country like Russia, China, or Iran.

Quantitative (Statistical) Analysis At the opposite extreme from the case study is quantitative, large N research. This form of data analysis involves examination of a large number of cases—usually no fewer than fifty; typically well over one thousand—with the help of such software programs as SPSS or STATA. The cases may be events or they may be individuals. Quantitative analysis of data from surveys of mass attitudes is relatively common in comparative politics.

An important advantage of large N studies is that the analysis can incorporate an element of control, similar to that in experiments but absent in case studies. The more cases there are, the more easily a statistical software program can control for the effects of one variable while estimating the effects of another. This is important since it can help prevent researchers from mistakenly believing that two variables are causally related when actually they are not. Take the example of party identification in the United States. Republicans sometimes like to point out that those in the general population who identify themselves as Republicans tend to be more educated than those who see themselves as Democrats. Before one makes a causal claim about this correlation ("Better education leads

to identification with the Republican Party"), it is necessary to control for other factors. One of the most important of these is income. Income and Republican Party identification are also correlated, as are education and income. Having a large number of cases allows one to control for income when looking at the effect of education. Doing so weakens considerably the case for more education leading one to become a Republican.

In addition, large N research possesses a great advantage for generalizability. Sometimes statistical analysis can be performed on the entire group of cases one wants to understand. More often the analysis is performed on a sample of that group. Assuming proper sampling techniques, the larger the number of cases in the sample, the more confident one can be that the sample reflects patterns in the larger group. Thus, the external validity of large N studies is one of their important strengths.

Large N research also has its limitations. The most basic disadvantage is that information about each case is limited. Large N studies lack the depth of knowledge about each case that is the hallmark of case study research. One could, for example, look at how local government decisions tend to favor one group over another in a large number of cases. Doing so might uncover a pattern that holds well across a number of localities. One might also discover that a pattern that holds for large cities does not for small ones. However, there is no opportunity to see the causal relationship in practice, as can sometimes occur in case studies. As a result, quantitative research is also dependent on theory to turn findings of correlation into causal claims.

The Comparative Method A final approach seeks to combine the best of both the case study and large N statistical analysis. Though many comparativists rely on case studies or large N research, this alternative approach, called the comparative method, is widely accepted as the cornerstone of comparative politics research. This book provides a number of examples of the comparative method in practice, including in some of this book's "comparative exercises."

By examining a smaller number of cases, typically between three and ten, the comparative method seeks to bring in some of the rich detail of the case study. At the same time, by examining more than one case, the approach attempts to provide a degree of generalizability and the ability to control for rival explanations that a single case study cannot. Along with combining the best of the case study and large N approaches, the comparative method incorporates their weaknesses as well. The comparative method cannot incorporate statistical control; there are not enough cases. It cannot provide the depth of understanding of each case that a single case study can. Researchers engaged in comparative studies hope that the strengths outweigh the weaknesses, but they also search for other ways to address the limitations.

One important way to address the inability to use statistical control involves the introduction of something similar to statistical control through the *careful selection of cases*. There are two main approaches to this technique, usually called the **most similar** and **most different approaches** to the comparative method. A third approach has also emerged in recent years, which is an intriguing hybrid of the other two. A comparativist's resources and existing knowledge of particular countries, as well as the substantive problem that he or she wants to address, affects which of these approaches the comparativist chooses.

The most similar approach examines cases that are, at first glance, very much alike. A most similar study might include the cases of Canada, the United States, the United Kingdom, Australia, and New Zealand. Although very similar countries, they pose a puzzle for the researcher: the dependent variable—for example, percentage of the national budget spent on the military—differs noticeably across the cases. Yet they share a number of key features, such as "Western" cultures with predominantly English-speaking populations, high levels of economic development, large middle classes, and sizeable native and/or ethnic minority populations.

These similar characteristics allow the researcher to rule out a number of possible explanations for why the dependent variable's values differ across the cases. The shared features (e.g., level of economic development) are essentially constant across the cases, while the dependent variable is varying. There is no correlation between a constant and a fluctuating variable, so no causal relationship can exist between them either. By controlling for these mutual characteristics, the researcher can look for other factors which vary along with the dependent variable. These additional independent variables would be chosen based on existing theories. In Table 1.1, the first independent variable appears

---

The **comparative method** is a research design which seeks to understand the effects of a particular dependent variable by examining a small number of cases. The small number of carefully selected cases improves generalizability and control over single case studies, but also allows one to look more in depth at each case than one can in "large N" studies.

The **most similar approach** to the comparative method examines cases that are very much alike, but the dependent variable in the study varies from one case to the next. Their general similarities allow the researcher to control for a large number of variables, ruling them out as possible explanations for the varying dependent variable.

The **most different approach** to the comparative method examines cases that are very different from one another, but the dependent variable in the study is similar from one case to the next. Their general differences allow the researcher to control for a large number of variables, ruling them out as possible explanations for the dependent variable, which is consistent across the cases.

Table 1.1	An Example of a Most Similar Approach Comparative Study		
Case	Dependent Variable	Independent Variable$_1$	Independent Variable$_2$
1	Low	High	High
2	High	Medium	Low
3	High	High	Low
4	Medium	Low	Medium
5	Low	Medium	High

not to be related to the dependent variable, while the second independent variable appears negatively related to it.

The most similar approach has its strengths and weaknesses. The major strength of the most similar approach is that the findings would seem to apply to countries with very different values of the dependent variable. The main weakness of this approach is that it limits the researcher's ability to generalize from the findings to countries that are quite different from the ones examined in the study. Because the countries studied are similar in so many ways, the results might *only* apply to the certain type of country examined in the study.

The most different approach is the exact opposite, both in the types of countries and the pattern of the dependent variable. A most different comparative study at the state level of analysis might include the countries of Germany, Russia, Costa Rica, Argentina, Thailand, and Israel. Although these countries would appear to have little in common, they pose a puzzle, as the dependent variable in the study, perhaps something like portion of the government budget spent on retirement programs, is essentially constant across the cases. Because so many features of these countries are dissimilar, the researcher is able to rule out a number of possible explanations for the values of the dependent variable. In this case, many possible independent variables are varying, while the dependent variable is not, again producing a lack of correlation and therefore no causal relationship between these variables and the dependent variable.

The task for the researcher in the most different study is to find one or more independent variables that have similar values in these otherwise diverse cases. Again, the researcher would turn to existing theories for guidance about which variables to observe. In the example in Table 1.2, the first independent variable appears to have a strong positive relationship with the dependent variable, while the second independent seems to have no relationship at all.

The major strength of the most different approach is the ability of the researcher to generalize from the findings to a wide range of countries. After all, if the results apply to this diverse group of countries, why would one expect them not to hold in other cases? The drawback of this approach is that the findings apply at best only to countries with roughly the same value of the dependent variable as those in the study. The researcher is unable to generalize to other cases in which this particular dependent variable looks quite different.

The final approach to the comparative method brings together the logic of most similar and most different research designs. The **cross-regional approach** examines sets of countries in different regions of the world. As comparativist Evelyne Huber describes it, the cross-regional approach "is a combination of within- and cross-region comparisons of several cases, which entails the identification of regional patterns and the comparison of these patterns to each

The **cross-regional approach** combines aspects of most similar and most different studies by looking at sets of similar cases—each set coming from a particular region—and then comparing the findings across the different regions.

Case	Dependent Variable	Independent Variable$_1$	Independent Variable$_2$
1	High	High	High
2	High	High	Low
3	High	High	Low
4	High	High	Medium
5	High	High	High

Table 1.2 An Example of a Most Different Approach: Comparative Study

other."[8] Thus, the approach combines aspects of most similar and most different comparative studies.

Within each region, researchers look at similar cases in which the dependent variable varies. Between the different regions, they compare patterns to determine whether the findings hold in different settings. If the findings are consistent across the sets of cases, the researchers would have addressed one of the major limitations of the most similar approach: the question of whether the findings apply to countries different from those examined in the study. The results need not be consistent in the different regions to be helpful. Variation in patterns across the regions—for example, one variable appears important in European countries but another appears important in Asian countries—can encourage comparativists to reconsider the theories used in the study to better take into account contextual details, or even to develop brand-new theories that could be tested through further research.[9] This approach is particularly valuable for providing insights about theories originally developed to explain European cases alone.

Think and Discuss

In your opinion, is the cross-regional approach really an improvement over the most similar and most different approaches? Why or why not?

A Framework for the Comparative Study of Politics: "Structure versus Choice"

An introduction to comparative politics is a little less challenging for you as a student if you are armed with a general framework to help make sense of the various concepts, theories, and empirical discussions you will encounter. (You will find, especially the longer you study comparative politics, that there are many of them to encounter!) This section introduces the idea of "structure versus choice" as such a framework.

The structure versus choice framework combines traditional ideas of comparative politics with emerging new approaches. What is called the **structural approach** in this book has been prevalent in comparative politics for decades and remains popular today. It examines underlying economic, social, and political structures in an effort to understand the political outcomes in which the researcher is interested. Thus, although there are a lot of them, all variants of the structural approach share one feature: they focus on the broader setting

A **structural approach** seeks to explain political outcomes by looking at the effects of the underlying economic, social, or political-institutional setting in a country or set of countries. Scholars using this approach do not focus on the decision-making process and are generally not interested in a specific decision by a single individual.

in which individuals make political decisions rather than on the individuals or decisions themselves.

A second traditional political science approach involves looking at decisions of political leaders. This route has evolved into a focus on the process of decision making among both elites and masses. Thus, what is called the **choice approach** in this text includes the role of individual leaders, ideas of "leadership," and perspectives on political decision making. Decision-making theories often center on how rational individuals act when making political choices.

Consolidating the different comparative politics traditions into two broad categories helps make sense of the array of causal factors examined in comparative politics. This book is far from the first work to employ the structure versus choice framework. It is widely used in disciplines such as sociology and anthropology. Comparativists, particularly those studying democratization, have also frequently utilized the structure/choice dichotomy. Mark Lichbach has stated that "interests, identity, and institutions contend for theoretical primacy in comparative politics."[10] To Lichbach, "institutions" include not only political structures but also underlying socioeconomic ones as well. His "identity" translates into this textbook's focus on identity-based and cultural structures, while his "interests" are a main part of what this book discusses as decisions or choices. Though he uses slightly different terminology from what you will find in this book, his basic point—that these theoretical perspectives are seen as rivals, battling it out for supremacy in comparative politics—is persuasive.

By the time you reach the end of this book, you may come to believe that this "battle" is misguided. In its pure form, structural determinism—the perspective in which underlying structures are seen as ultimately driving all important political outcomes—is incompatible with an argument centering only on individual leadership and choice. But comparativists need

not, and often do not, operate at such extremes. Two rival theoretical approaches can often be placed on a continuum, in the middle of which a gray area exists. Within this gray area, causal theories initially seen as contradictory can, in fact, complement one another. They might even be used together to form a less elegant, but often more honest, explanation of political events. However, before one can bring them together, one must first discuss the issues and theories connected to particular structural and choice variables in their more pure form and thus treat them as distinct from one another.

Understanding Political Outcomes by Examining "Structures"

Scholars who believe politics is best understood through the use of structural approaches feel that paying attention only to decision making is misguided. They believe that structures largely determine how political decisions are made, and an effort to understand political outcomes by looking at decision making is thus incomplete at best and terribly misleading at worst. Greater attention to structures (even perhaps at the expense of examining the decision-making process) provides a better way of answering the most important questions in the comparative study of politics. Put bluntly, for structural theorists, it not only makes little difference who is making a specific decision, but also the decision-making process itself is fundamentally uninteresting.

Structures can be domestic or global. Even among those scholars focusing on domestic structures, some might emphasize the impact of

The **choice approach** seeks to explain political outcomes by looking at the effects of individual political actors and gaining an understanding of their decision-making process. Since it is hard to develop theories about the actions of unique individuals, this approach tends to focus on the general concept of decision making.

economic development on political outcomes, while others might look at the collective identities in a particular society to understand that society's politics. This book puts forward four categories of structure—economic, cultural, identity, and political-institutional—and illustrates their influence on political outcomes.

Understanding Political Outcomes by Examining "Choices"

Choice-based explanations of political outcomes bring together two somewhat distinct ideas. One is that who the particular political decision makers are makes a big difference; comparativists must be aware of the individuals involved in the political process under investigation. It makes sense that leadership should matter in politics. So much of history—at least as it is taught—is about decisions and actions of great leaders. Arguing that familiarity with the person making a particular political decision is crucial to understanding the resultant political outcome, however, can cause a problem. If each individual is unique, how does one develop and test theories that can be useful in analyzing events at different points in time and in varying settings around the world?

The answer is that most scholars taking the "choice" approach anchor themselves to the level of the individual but do not stop there. Their ultimate goal is to understand political action in a general sense. They do this by focusing on the second half of the choice approach's dual nature: the process of individual decision making. While applicable to specific cases of decision making, theories that focus on the decision-making process include general assumptions. A common one is that humans act rationally to maximize their personal utility. Thus, explanations of specific political events—democratization in a particular country, for example—might highlight the role of individual action, but *theorizing* about democratization moves scholars into the more generalizable realm of decision making.

How others decide to act and the need to make similar decisions over time also influence political decisions. Choice arguments can be extended to explain decisions over time, such as voting, and decisions involving other individuals, such as whether to join a political organization. As Chapters 9–11 discuss in detail, these are common topics for arguments which assume rational action.

Structure, Choice, and Levels of Analysis

Whether one leans in the "structure" or "choice" direction has implications for decisions such as which level of analysis to employ. For those taking a choice approach, the level of analysis is often the individual. The "choice" scholar may prefer to interview particular political leaders, organize focus groups with small numbers of participants, or collect survey data involving large numbers of respondents. For those taking a structural approach, the level of analysis is generally the state; the political system; society; a collection of states, systems, or societies; or the international community. The "structure" scholar might turn to data on economic development or assess the extent to which different ethnic groups in a country speak different languages and have different religious faiths.

Those who make structural arguments generally contend that individuals are not autonomous from the structures in which they reside. This view, of course, limits the ability of structural approaches to help understand the political decisions of a single person. Using structural theories to explain a specific individual's actions invites an **ecological fallacy**: an error in explanation due to the assumption that observations that apply to groups also apply to the individuals who make up the groups. This assumption is

An **ecological fallacy** is an error resulting from assuming that general trends or observations of groups are also relevant to particular events or actions of specific individuals.

flawed for two reasons: Rarely does the average value of a group apply to every member of that group, and there are "group dynamics" that do not always translate well to the individual level. For example, just because a researcher discovers that members of the middle class tend to be more supportive of immigration than members of the working class, it does not mean that the researcher could say with certainty how two specific individuals, one middle class and one working class, feel about immigration.

CONCLUSION

The discipline of political science provides researchers, students, and politicians with a better understanding of politics and its impact on society. The field of comparative politics captures all the complexities, divisions, and satisfactions of this discipline. The course you are taking will enhance your appreciation of the importance of politics, while improving your ability to assess political systems and understand political outcomes outside the United States. You will learn about concepts—such as politics and power, introduced in this chapter—that comparativists use in their work. These concepts can be challenging, so it is important to have a solid understanding of them and to use them in a consistent manner.

This introduction was also designed to provide an overview of the scientific study of politics, and the approaches to such study in comparative politics. This included a discussion of the research process—from developing a research question and generating hypotheses to developing new research questions based on the research. It also introduced you to different data collection methods and the issues surrounding the number of cases comparativists examine. You read about the comparative method, an approach to comparative politics research that seeks the depth of understanding of a case study and the control and generalizability of "large N" research.

Finally, the chapter gave you a first glance at the idea of "structure versus choice" as a framework for understanding comparative politics. This framework is used throughout the book. Chapter 3, for example, deals entirely with the topic of economic structure and is followed by a series of chapters addressing cultural, social, and political structures. It is a framework that you can use in other political science (or social science) courses, and in your daily observations of the political world around you.

Key Terms

Authority, p. 7
Case study, p. 13
Causality, p. 8
Charismatic authority, p. 7
Choice approach, p. 20
Coercive power, p. 6
Comparative method, p. 17
Comparative politics, p. 2
Comparativist, p. 2
Conceptualization, p. 10
Critical case study, p. 15
Cross-regional approach, p. 18
Dependent variable, p. 8
Deviant case study, p. 15
Ecological fallacy, p. 21
External validity, p. 15
Falsifiable, p. 10
Hypothesis, p. 10
Independent variable, p. 8
Internal validity, p. 13

LIBERTÉ
ÉGALITÉ
FRATERNITÉ

Learning Objectives

After reading this chapter, you should be able to:

■ Describe the relationship between the concepts of societies, nations, and states.

■ Lay out the basic features of the state, regime, and government in the ten Topic-in-Countries cases.

■ Discuss current tensions surrounding the principle of state sovereignty and the extent to which global trends are weakening sovereignty in practice.

■ Describe the approach taken in this chapter's comparative exercise.

2

The Setting of Politics:
Societies, Nations, and States

In 1991, Croatia, a region of the country of Yugoslavia, declared independence. This triggered violent clashes between ethnic Croats, who supported Croatia's secession from Yugoslavia, and ethnic Serbs, who—with the backing of the Yugoslav military and numerous paramilitary militia groups—sought to prevent Croatia from becoming a sovereign state. That fall, Slavenka Drakulic, a Croat, discussed the consequences of the conflict:

I have to admit that, as with many of my friends, being a Croat didn't mean much to me. . . . I can only regret that awareness of my nationality came to me in such a painful way, through death, destruction, and the suffering of people, and through reduction, accusations, suspicions, and extreme homogenization. Being a Croat in this war makes me an orphan too, because it robbed me of the only possession I acquired in my life—my individuality. . . . So no one is allowed not to be Croatian, and our attackers are to blame, for removing our freedoms to be firstly persons and citizens and then Croats."[1] ■

Look for this icon to point you to **Deepening Your Understanding** features on the companion website www.college.cengage.com/politicalscience/barrington, which provide greater depth for some key content.

Drakulic's statement highlights how many of the main topics of comparative politics, such as national identity and state sovereignty, can affect the lives of ordinary people. Chapter 1 introduced the importance of concepts, highlighting politics and power. This chapter introduces several additional central concepts in the comparative study of politics: society, nation, nationalism, state, government, and regime. All are crucial components of the arena, or "setting," of politics. Additional important concepts—class, political culture, clientelism, and so on—are defined and discussed in subsequent chapters.

This chapter also introduces the Topic-in-Countries ("TIC") approach employed throughout most of this book. The TIC sections discuss in detail how the main topics of each chapter affect ten of the world's most important countries: the United Kingdom, Germany, France, Mexico, Brazil, the Russian Federation, China, India, Nigeria, and Iran. This chapter also includes the book's first comparative exercise, which follows the TIC section. The comparative exercises are short summaries of how one might undertake answering a particular research question. Each exercise uses one of the basic approaches to comparative politics research (large N, case study, and comparative method) discussed in Chapter 1. This chapter's comparative exercise examines a topic that stands at the intersection of society, nation, and state: views about the European Union in a number of European countries.

Society

The starting point for thinking about the arena of politics is **society**. The term society may be one of the most used yet most difficult to define terms in political science. This is partly due to its hidden quality: One can point to particular governmental institutions, but it is difficult to *see* society. Society refers to a generally large collective of people who are connected in some meaningful way. This connection includes interactions and common traits

among members that provide a sense of identity. Physical proximity is usually one of the binding traits—members of a particular society generally do not live in isolation from one another in different parts of the world—though possible exceptions, such as groups with common interests linked together via the Internet, could challenge even this idea. Proximity (or linkage via the Internet) allows the group to function as a relatively closed system. The interactions among members of a particular society create a degree of affiliation and interdependence that does not exist with others who are not part of this society.

Though based on the Latin *societas*, meaning "friendly relations with others," the term is often used to refer to the population of a country, a group that is too large for all members to know each other and whose members certainly do not always behave toward each other in a friendly way. The larger a society, the more subgroups exist within it, and the more complex the society is. As discussed in Chapter 1, this complexity has historically led groups of individuals to organize themselves politically, forming governments to establish official rules regarding the behavior of the members of their society.

Yet, government rules are not the only rules in a society. Unwritten rules or expectations of behavior, called **norms**, can develop through the interactions of individuals in a society. Consider driving a car. A large number of government-created rules regulate driving. Driving, however, is also regulated by norms that emerge over time: flashing one's headlights to warn approaching drivers of the presence of a police speed trap, the

Society is a large group of people connected through interactions and common traits. One key trait is often physical proximity, allowing the group to function as a relatively closed and interdependent system of relations among its individual members.

Norms are unwritten rules or expectations of behavior that help govern the activity of individuals in a society. These norms can be as influential on daily life as governmental laws.

friendly wave from someone when a driver lets him or her enter a lane of traffic, or speeding up to prevent a particularly annoying driver from entering one's lane. In addition, other organizations in society may produce official rules meant to influence society members' behavior. A section later in this chapter focuses on how rules produced by the state generally take precedence over these other rules in society.

Nation and Nationalism

Within the broader society, there is a portion of the population—and sometimes the entire population—that shares a particular form of identity which unites and binds them together. This is called **national identity**, and the group that shares such identity is a **nation**. In everyday language, people use the word nation to mean country. They commonly talk about the "nation of France" or the "nation of Estonia." Even some political scientists—especially Americanists, who tend to refer to the United States as a nation—use the term in this way in their general discussion of countries. However, this is not how people use the word nation in other parts of the world, and it is not how it is used among comparativists. Instead, for comparativists, nation refers to a large group of people, though exactly how large is difficult to say. This group is *self-aware*—it recognizes itself as a group—and is *united by shared cultural features*, especially myths and symbols but often other traits such as language. Its members need not speak a single language, though unilingualism makes group unity easier.

So far, this description depicts many groups in society. A religious group in a particular country, for example, can have a large number of self-aware members united by their religion—a shared cultural feature. Yet this is not enough to make them a nation. Therefore, while size, awareness, and unifying cultural features are necessary components of a nation,

these qualities alone do not distinguish between nations and certain other large social groups. The most important feature distinguishing nations from other large groups in society is a particular belief; members of the nation believe in the group's *right to political control over a certain territory*. In other words, nations have a "territorial referent,"[2] which makes them different from other collective identities such as ethnic groups. Nations believe that they deserve to control their own affairs within a given territory.

The members of the nation often consider this territory to be the national "homeland." This land could coincide with the territory of an existing state. This is particularly common when the state's territorial boundaries were established prior to the emergence of a strong sense of national identity across that territory. Sometimes, nations exist without their own states—for example, the Kurds and Palestinians. In these cases, members of the nation may pursue

A Kurdish family stand together near a tent after fleeing to the mountains in Khalifan, northern Iraq.
(©Patrick Barth/Getty Images)

A nation's self-awareness and sense of unity is called **national identity**.

A **nation** is a large, self-aware segment of society, united by shared cultural features and possessing a belief in the right to political control over a particular territory.

political control of a territory within an existing state or even several states. Many Kurds believe in their right to control Kurdistan, a territory encompassing parts of Iraq, Turkey, Syria, and Iran. The cause of Kurdish nationalism has been thwarted, not only by opposition from elements of the international community, including the four states which contain parts of Kurdistan, but also by disputes between leaders of the Kurdish communities in these four states.

Civic versus Ethnic Nations

Though ethnic groups and nations are distinct concepts, comparativists who study national identity do not ignore ethnicity. In some parts of the world, ethnic identity provides the cultural common ground for national identity, and the nation's membership boundaries coincide with membership boundaries of a specific ethnic group. The ethnic group's criteria for membership become the criteria for national membership as well.[3] (Ethnicity is also a socially and politically important form of identity in its own right, and it is a core topic of Chapter 5.)

Nations whose membership is based on a common ethnic identity are called **ethnic nations**. Ethnic nations are most common in Asia and Eastern Europe. Members of the Estonian nation, for example, are considered Estonian not because they live in, or even are citizens of, Estonia. Rather, they are members of the Estonian nation because they are ethnically Estonian and believe in Estonians' right to control the state of Estonia.

Many other nations, especially in North America, South America, and Africa, are multiethnic. In these cases, the membership boundaries are based primarily on an adherence to a set of political values and by citizenship in an existing state, rather than on a specific ethnic identity. As a result, they are called political nations or, more commonly, **civic nations**. In civic nations, the overarching cultural features may favor one ethnic group over another.

For example, there is often a single national language used in schools and by government, which privileges those who speak it, but membership in the nation is open to those of different ethnic backgrounds.

These two types of nations are best thought of as ideal types. An **ideal type** is a pure form of a concept. As such, ideal types provide a baseline that allows one to compare instances of a given concept even though the concept may never be realized in its pure form. Many social scientists consider Americans, for example, to be as close to the ideal civic nation as any nation in the world. How closely Americans approach this ideal of civic national identity, however, is a matter of debate. In the development of American national identity, membership has historically been open to a variety of ethnic groups. Membership in the American nation has centered on the possession of U.S. citizenship and acceptance of a general set of values about personal liberty and political equality. That said, what those who have had the power to shape American identity have chosen as the particular shared cultural features to unify Americans—for example, knowledge of English—certainly privileges some ethnic groups over others.

Think and Discuss

To what extent are Americans really a civic, as opposed to an ethnic, nation? Do they have enough of a unified sense of identity to be considered a nation at all?

When national identity is based largely on ethnic identity, the nations are called **ethnic nations**.

In **civic nations**, members of the nation are united by multiethnic cultural features and citizenship in the state rather than by shared ethnic identity.

An **ideal type** is a pure form of a concept that may not exist in the real world but is useful in investigations of the concept in practice.

Nationalism

Nationalism is the process of pursuing a set of rights for a nation, including at least the right of territorial self-determination. This pursuit of territorial control need not be successful, nor must the leaders of nationalist movements—called **nationalists**—strive for complete independence and the establishment of an internationally recognized state. The quest for **territorial autonomy** within an existing state is consistent with nationalism. When a group has territorial autonomy, it controls much of the daily happenings of a particular area of the country, but it surrenders authority over some matters (e.g., national defense) to the country's central government. Yet an independent national state is the ultimate goal of nationalists. The term **nation-state** highlights this goal: an independent state existing for a single nation.

In seeking this perceived right to territorial control, nationalists must tell a convincing story about two boundaries. The first is the identity boundary, which marks the membership limits for the nation. This requires explaining *who belongs to the nation*. Second, nationalists must delineate the territorial boundaries of the national homeland. In other words, they must address *what territory the nation should control*. It is mobilization through appeals to these two corresponding boundaries that makes nationalism such a powerful force in modern politics. It unites the passions of belonging to a group with the feeling of connection to a territory. Both of these—belonging to a group and connecting to the land—are arguably among the more powerful emotional triggers in humans. Nationalism combines them, and nationalists exploit them.

Slobodan Milosevic waving to supporters in May 2000.
(©AP Photo/Str)

Did You Know? Estimates vary considerably, but it is reasonable to conclude that there are several thousand distinct ethnic groups in the world. As a result, though the concept of self-determination sounds good in theory, recognizing each ethnic group as an ethnic nation that deserves control over its own territorial homeland would lead to an explosion in the number of states in the world. Imagine the United Nations General Assembly with three thousand members! There would also likely be a dramatic increase in violent conflicts during and after this process.

Who Belongs to the Nation? The response to the "Who belongs to the nation?" question generally takes either a more ethnic or a more civic form. As such, it is possible to talk about ethnic nationalism—also commonly called ethno-nationalism—and civic nationalism. These are simply different strains of nationalism based on different views of the membership boundaries of the nation. Answering the "Who belongs to the nation?" question also typically involves highlighting the differences between those who belong to the nation and those who do

Nationalism is the pursuit of a set of rights for a nation, including the right of political control over a certain territory.

Leaders of nationalist movements, called **nationalists**, define both the membership boundary and the territorial boundary for the nation.

A group with **territorial autonomy** is allowed to control much of what happens in a particular region, but the region is not officially independent. A group accepting such autonomy surrenders authority over such matters as national security to the central government.

The ultimate goal of nationalists is a **nation-state**, an independent state that exists for a single nation.

not. Thus, nationalists may portray the "other" as physically different, culturally inferior, and less intelligent, as well as presenting them as a threat to the nation. This representation of the other as a threat is a common theme in ethnonationalist conflicts, even before the conflict turns violent.

What Territory Should the Nation Control?

Nationalists also have to demarcate the territory that they are pursuing and justify control over it. Nationalists may emphasize historical ties to a region, demographic dominance of it, or some other aspect illustrating the nation's connection to the territory. These traits are presented as evidence that the territory is the nation's homeland. Problems arise when the territory that one nation perceives to be its homeland is claimed in a similar way by another national group. The existence of **overlapping homelands** is one of the key causes of conflict in the world. For example,

the overlapping homelands predicament drives, in part at least, the conflict between Israelis and Palestinians. It is most common in cases of ethnic nationalism, where two ethnic groups have lived in the same area for a long period of time but developed distinct national identities.

Think and Discuss

Although nationalism is often portrayed in a negative light, a core principle of national identity—control over one's own political affairs—is also a core principle of democracy. Are nationalism and democracy complementary or contrasting pursuits?

Overlapping homelands exist when two or more nations lay claim to the same territory as part or all of their homeland. This remains a major cause of conflict in the world.

National Identity in the United Kingdom, Germany, and France

The United Kingdom, Germany, and France have many shared historical experiences. Yet their approaches to national identity have differed. German nationalists chose an ethnic answer to the "Who belongs to the nation?" question, while British and French nationalism was more civic than ethnic. Even these two cases differed, however. The British emphasized individualism as a unifying national value, while French national identity developed around the ideas of universal citizenship and collective sovereignty.

The United Kingdom

Separation from continental Europe, the territorial proximity of the main ethnic groups, and, at least among Protestants in the United Kingdom, religious commonalities have combined to aid the development of an overarching British national identity. The United Kingdom's four main ethnic groups—English, Scots, Welsh, and Irish—make up the heart of the British nation.

Unlike some ethnic majority groups that choose an ethnic approach to national identity that excludes minorities from its membership boundaries, the English sought to foster a multiethnic, British identity. Though in the past this approach sometimes took the form of ruthless repression of minority cultural practices and nationalist movements, in recent years this civic national identity has allowed a revitalization of ethnic minority cultural practices. Whether this new interest in ethnic cultures will lead to significant support for ethnic nationalism among the Scots, Welsh, and Irish remains to be seen.

An additional question is the fate of the immigrant minorities. Among many who accept an overarching, civic British identity uniting English, Scots, Welsh, and Irish, the idea that Pakistanis or Nigerians living in the United Kingdom are actually British is harder to accept. As these groups continue to grow as a percentage of the population, the tensions over the extent to which they belong as members of the nation are likely to increase as well.

Topic in Countries

Germany

German national identity has long been defined in ethnic terms. In the nineteenth century, romantic philosophers conceived of German identity in terms of blood or heritage as a way to compensate for the absence of natural borders and the delayed establishment of politically recognized external boundaries. This notion of "Germanness" took on a particularly insidious form under the Nazi government's conception of the German nation, or *Volk*, as a people of common German blood, and its corresponding persecution and murder of Jews, Slavs, and other minority groups who were not deemed German.

Historically, German citizenship reflected its ethnic national identity. The 1913 citizenship law granted citizenship on the basis of German heritage. Consequently, ethnic Germans (*Aussiedler*) living beyond Germany's borders were granted automatic citizenship in the Federal Republic. They continued to enjoy this privileged status in the years immediately after the fall of the Berlin Wall, but policies have since become more restrictive. However, children of nonethnic German immigrants born on German soil were not considered citizens; they and other immigrants had to undergo a cumbersome naturalization process if they wanted to acquire German citizenship. Such provisions raised serious barriers to the integration of immigrants, especially the foreign workers (*Gastarbeiter*) from Turkey whom Germany had recruited in the 1960s to alleviate a labor shortage.

In an effort to better integrate immigrants and their offspring, the government of Gerhard Schröder enacted a new citizenship law that went into effect in 2000. This law retained the provision of citizenship based on German ancestry, but also conferred automatic citizenship to children born in Germany of immigrant parents who have legally resided in the country for eight years. The law permits dual citizenship for such children only to adulthood; after that, they must choose German or other citizenship, although there have been exceptions made in cases of hardship. The new law also shortened the duration of time one must live in Germany as a legal resident before naturalization.[4] Germany's foreign population is currently 7.3 million persons, or 8.8 percent of its population, with 1.8 million Turks comprising the largest minority group.[5]

France

French culture and an overarching national identity developed through conquest and the obliteration of native languages across the country. The south of France, for example, had a distinct language, *langue d'oc* ("the language of one who says 'oc' for 'yes'"), while Alsatian—a form of German—was the principle language along the Rhine. Strong regional identities still exist in areas such as Brittany (the peninsula in western France between the English Channel and the Bay of Biscay) and the Mediterranean island of Corsica.

With the exception of many Corsicans and Bretons, most of those who were physically and culturally absorbed during the French nation-building project came to accept the French language and the emerging French culture, as well as the universal promise of the French Republic—the rights and duties of the citizen that, in theory, extend equally to all human kind. Napoleon himself, some historians say, altered his birth date to make it appear that he was born after his native Corsica was transferred from Italian to French control. At the same time, the dominant culture, which came to be centered on Paris, adopted practices and attributes from those they conquered. While immigration remains a contentious issue, North African couscous is now a French staple and Afro-Caribbean, Spanish, and Arab music is as popular as traditional French and American rock.

Another important aspect of national identity is the perception that France is a country of major international importance and serves as an alternative model to American cultural and economic development. The perception is not unfounded. French Republicanism—an ideology emphasizing the "general will" and the "common good"—provides an alternative to American individualism. France is a leading economic, diplomatic, and nuclear power, and is a major player in pharmaceuticals, automobiles, technology, and military hardware. France's political influence extends across the globe. Through cultural, political, economic, and sometimes secret military agreements and networks, it has significant authority in its former colonies in French-speaking West Africa, often called *la françafrique*,[6] and exerts influence in English-speaking African countries. The French role in North Africa, also once part of its colonial empire, is greater than any other non-Arab country. Overall, the official "Francophonie" includes twenty-two African countries where French is an official language, and to varying degrees extends to thirty-three other states around the world where French is an official or influential language. Finally, France continues to play a central role in European integration and the evolution of the European Union.

National Identity in Mexico and Brazil

In both Brazil and Mexico, elites overseeing the development of national identity stressed a civic approach to the "Who belongs to the nation?" question. One could argue that these countries' colonial history left them little choice. The ethnic mixture that colonialism fostered drove those looking for ways to unify the population away from aligning national identity with a particular ethnic identity. Yet, in both countries, contradictions surrounding national identity are evident. Of the two, Brazilian elites have struggled more noticeably in their efforts to identify unifying cultural features that link descendents of the native, colonial, and immigrant populations.

Mexico

In large part because of its colonial experience, Mexican national identity contains a number of discordant components. It is anchored in *mestizo* identity, a collective identity that formed through the mixing of native and European peoples in the centuries since the Spanish conquest.[7] Those pursuing a civic Mexican national identity have struggled with how to address native cultural rights, yet there is a deep pride in native Indian civilizations of the past. Like its Canadian counterpart, Mexican national identity is partially "defined by opposition to the United States,"[8] yet many Mexicans have a respect for and even envy what they see as an affluent American lifestyle.

Catholicism, the faith of the vast majority of Mexicans, is the final and arguably most important cultural component of Mexican national identity. Mexican Catholicism strongly embraces the vision story of the Virgin of Guadalupe, whom Mexican Catholics believe was the Virgin Mary who appeared for the first of numerous times in Mexico on a hillside near Mexico City on December 12, 1531. Consequently, the feast day of the Virgin of Guadalupe, December 12, is one of the most celebrated Mexican holidays. The idea that she took the form of a native woman and spoke the indigenous language, while appearing to a native man who had converted to Catholicism, captures in many ways the tensions inherent in Mexican national identity.

Brazil

By the late 1800s, the Brazilian government began to see the development of an overarching national identity as an important goal.[9] Already by then, and even more as time went on, the demographic characteristics of those living in

The *mestizo* group is the vast majority of Mexico's population. It developed following the Spanish conquest through the intermixing of native and European populations.

Topic in countries

Brazil made achieving this goal difficult. As highlighted in the "Territory and Population" section on Brazil later in the chapter, the population is ethnically, culturally, and even religiously diverse. Immigrants and their descendents include both slaves from Africa and those from Western and Eastern Europe, Asia, and the Middle East who chose to settle in Brazil. Like other countries with a history of large-scale immigration, tensions developed between the desire for a coherent Brazilian national identity and the variety of cultural traits carried into Brazil by waves of new immigrants. Such tensions remain today.[10]

One might think such ethnic diversity would make it easier to develop an overarching civic national identity, since no obvious ethnic alternative existed that could unite the majority of the population. Yet the lack of shared cultural features among the population—even in comparison to the Mexican case—can make the already-difficult task of agreeing on a set of unifying national cultural features even more challenging. Consequently, while Brazil is closer to the definition of a civic nation than to an ethnic one, it continues to struggle, like Mexico, to build a unifying civic national identity.

National Identity in the Russian Federation, China, and India

Perhaps even more than in Mexico and Brazil, leaders have struggled to forge an overarching national identity in Russia, China, and India. Russian elites continue to debate the membership boundaries of the nation, while Chinese leaders struggle to contain nationalism among the country's sizeable minorities. In India, national identity is based in large part on valuing diversity, but this approach was solidified only after partition of the country around the time of independence—a step many believed was the only viable option to make possible a unifying national identity among the remainder of the population.

The Russian Federation

Unlike a country such as the United Kingdom, in which the ethnic English majority actively sought to create an overarching British national identity, Russia's ethnic diversity has led to dissonant views of Russian national identity and incongruent nation-building efforts. Many Russian nationalists, including those in the pre-Soviet period, have emphasized an ethnic national identity. In this vision of national identity, ethnic Russians (*russkie* in Russian) form

the nation's membership boundaries, whether they live in Russia or not. Alternatively, other nationalists and most Russian government officials have sought a more civic form of national identity encompassing Russia's minorities. In this variant, citizens of Russia (*rossiiskie* in Russian) constitute the nation.

Likewise, Russian nationalists do not always agree on the territory that constitutes the Russian homeland. Increasingly, many accept the current borders of the Russian Federation as the proper territorial boundaries of the national homeland. Others, however, maintain the view that Russians have the right to control the entire territory of the old Soviet Union, or at least the other "Slavic" areas such as Ukraine, Belarus, and northern Kazakhstan.

Perhaps because of the difficulty in agreeing on the proper membership or territorial boundaries of the Russian nation, Russian nationalists have increasingly looked for an "other"—defining Russians not by what they are but what they are not, and stressing the threat posed by new "friends" like the United States. Such Russians see American foreign policy and dominance of international politics as both a threat to their national culture and their national security. They blame American-led financial aid programs during the 1990s for weakening Russia. They also view the West as failing to show Russia proper respect. This is one reason why many Russian nationalists have lined up to support President-turned-Prime Minister Vladimir Putin, whom they view as both willing and able to reestablish Russia's international standing as a great power.

China

China has the oldest recorded continuous history of any civilization, and the Chinese are proud of their long history. Partly for this reason, many Chinese share a trait with many in the French population: the belief that their country deserves to be even more important in global affairs than some, particularly Americans, believe the Chinese are at present.

While the Chinese government has encouraged this kind of outward-looking national pride, the combination of ethnic diversity and the concentration of minority groups in the country's periphery has made an overarching Chinese national identity difficult to establish. The Communist government is constantly concerned about nationalism by China's minorities, many of whom see themselves as distinct nations deserving control of their own territory. Three regions, Taiwan, Tibet, and Xinjiang, have particularly gained the Chinese government's attention and that of the international community. Of the three, Taiwan is the biggest concern to international observers due to the potential for a large-scale military conflict between the Chinese government and the (American-supplied) Taiwanese government.

Taiwan is an island not far off the coast of mainland China. It is home to an indigenous population, as well as the descendents of the Nationalist leaders of China who fled at the end of the civil war that brought the Communists to power. Taiwan held the seat of China at the United Nations, and was recognized as the legitimate China by countries such as the United States, until the 1970s. At that point, the international community—led by the United States—granted international recognition to the government of mainland China, while stripping Taiwan of its recognition status. As a result, the current Chinese government considers Taiwan to be part of China, a position known as the "one China" policy. Although the United States now recognizes mainland China as the official Chinese state, it continues to provide support to Taiwan to help prevent China from forcibly stripping Taiwan of its de facto sovereignty.

India

The leaders of the Indian independence movement had to accept the partition of imperial India, relinquishing control over territory in the east and the west to what became Pakistan (and, later, Bangladesh). The chaos and bloodshed that followed—with Hindus fleeing Pakistan and Muslims fleeing India, coupled with the subsequent conflict between India and Pakistan for control of the region of Kashmir—added to the difficulties of the independence process. Once sovereignty was secured, the leaders of newly independent India turned their attention once more to fostering an overarching national identity among the people of India.

India's founders realized that its multidimensional diversity could not be ignored during the nation-building effort. Consequently, Indian democracy and national identity were built on the notion of "unity in diversity." Given the country's diverse population, the degree of political and social stability it displays is one of India's notable accomplishments. Though sometimes belatedly, tolerance has often trumped intolerance, and the Indian people have accepted diversity as a key feature of national character. At the same time, the periodic electoral success of the Bharatiya Janata Party (BJP), whose official ideology equates Indian identity with Hinduism, provides evidence that not all accept diversity as Indian national identity's defining trait.

Like a number of other TIC cases, Indian national identity is also increasingly associated with attitudes about India's place in the international community. Unlike France, Russia, and China, however, there is not a sense that India is inadequately respected. Rather, there is a recognition that, with its economic progress, India has gained international respect. Pride in "being Indian" has risen accordingly.[11]

National Identity in Nigeria and Iran

Iran and Nigeria share many features, including oil production as a centerpiece of their economies. They also share the experience of only partial success in their efforts to get all major ethnic groups to buy into the idea that they are part of an overarching national identity. Of the two, Iran has the advantage of a much longer history of political control over its territory and the ability to point to one of the oldest recorded civilizations in the world.

Nigeria

One cannot fully comprehend Nigerian national identity today without examining the country's colonial experience and earlier periods in its history. Around 700 A.D., for example, Islamic traders came into the area of present-day Nigeria converting the populations of the northern part of the country to Islam. Islam did not penetrate to the south, and the resulting religious divide has reinforced ethnic and regional divisions in the country.

These divisions within the broader population have proven to be a challenge to those hoping to build an overarching Nigerian national identity following independence. Like governments of many of the other multiethnic African states, the Nigerian government hoped to foster a sense of national identity to unify the population in the postcolonial period. This effort was hindered by economic difficulties (which tended to pit the ethnic groups against one another), government corruption, and—as discussed in more detail in Chapters 5 and 6—the decision by the postindependence government to create internal political units that reinforced the dividing lines in the population. The result was an ethnically driven civil war in the late 1960s that cost the lives of around a million residents of Nigeria.

Iran

Iranian national identity is deeper and more coherent than most national identities in the Middle East. The Iranian population is both aware and proud of its national culture.[12] This is due in part to the long history of the Iranian (Persian) people, who controlled their own territory for most of that period. Like China, Iran is home to one of the world's oldest civilizations.

At the same time, tensions in Iranian national identity abound. Prior to the Islamic Revolution, efforts to unify the population behind an overarching national identity incorporated a secular, modernizing focus similar to nation-building in Turkey. Since 1979, however, Shi'a Islam has moved to the front and center of nation-building efforts.

In addition, the multiethnic and multilingual nature of the country's population makes civic national identity a necessity, but the Iranian government has always been suspicious of ethnic minorities, and tensions between the government and the largest minority groups remain. In the summer of 2006, Azeris took part in huge demonstrations sparked by a cartoon published in a state-run newspaper. Azeri elites viewed the cartoon as offensive to their ethnic identity and language, and they initially demanded resignations and apologies. In a warning shot to the government about the potential for ethnic minority nationalism, the protestors' slogans and demands quickly grew more radical, including calls for recognition of the Turkic Azeri language as an official language in Iran and the right of Azeris to establish trade unions and political organizations.[13] The Iranian government takes the potential for minority nationalism seriously, particularly since a number of the largest ethnic minority groups—the Azeris, Kurds, and Turkmen—have coethnic populations who control all or portions of neighboring countries.

The State

The **state** is one of the most important concepts in all fields of political science. Many other key concepts in comparative politics, even those already discussed in this chapter, relate to the state. Nationalism, for example, involves the pursuit of political control of a territory. For nationalists, this typically means hoping that, sooner or later, the nation will gain control of its own state. The state is also often the level of analysis in comparative politics. Those who specialize in a particular area of the world—what comparative politics calls area studies specialists—tend to know one or more states very well.

Understanding how political scientists use the term state is a challenge for comparative politics students. This is partly because, as with the term nation, what comparativists mean by the state is different from its meaning in everyday language in the United States. In everyday language, people use the word state to mean a territorial division within the United States: New York, Texas, Wisconsin, and so on. The American politics field of political science also often uses the term state in this way. For American politics, such use is arguably appropriate; the territorial divisions within the United States are indeed called states. Comparativists typically refer to such internal territorial divisions as regions, provinces, or territories.

In addition, as you will see by the end of this section, the term is frustrating because it is complex. The definition of state encompasses a large number of attributes, while scholars and politicians also place states around the world into a variety of categories: democratic states, developing states, rogue states, states in transition, and so on. It requires effort to keep track of both the different components of the state and the different types of states.

With that in mind, how should one define the term state? A state is something like a combination of what Americans in everyday language call a country and what they call a government. The state is *the basic unit of political organization in the world* and the focal point of political power. Its leaders govern—through a set of institutions—a population in a designated territory. Therefore, comparativists generally consider a state to include the following necessary characteristics: *a permanent population, a given territory, governing institutions, sovereignty,* and *international recognition.*

Territory

When a specific state is mentioned, most people think of its territory. It is hard to explain the connection of people to territory, but there is

> **Did You Know?** There are more than twice as many Azeris in Iran as in Azerbaijan, their internationally recognized nation-state. This demonstrates the often poor fit between the members of a particular nation and the territorial boundaries of the state they control.

> The **state** is the basic unit of political organization in the world. It is distinguished from other rule-making bodies by its combination of a permanent population, a defined territory, governing institutions, sovereignty over its territory, and international recognition.

no denying its importance. In many countries, sports teams include the name of their home cities as a way of increasing fan loyalty. A squad is no longer just a team; it is *our* team.

This link between territory and identity is not lost on political elites. As discussed earlier, national identity involves a belief in the right to control a particular territory. Nationalists nurture this belief among the general population in order to gain their support. In addition, people are willing to give up certain freedoms in the name of defending the territory of the state from external and internal threats. The government body that coordinates activities to prevent terrorism in the United States could have been called many things, such as the Terrorism Prevention Department. Instead, it is the Department of *Homeland* Security.

The history of warfare is full of disputes over territory. Some states have small, easily defensible borders, while others have long, contested borders with numerous neighbors. The peaceful acceptance of the border between the United States and Canada should not be taken as typical. International recognition is crucial to a state, yet border agreements with neighbors may be even more important to its stability. Although border agreements do not guarantee peace, they dramatically reduce the chance of combat between neighboring states.

Population

China and India have over a billion people living within their borders, but even the smallest states usually have somewhat sizeable populations. In most states, the vast majority of residents hold a special designation, which marks them as "official members of the state."[14] This designation is called **citizenship**, and those who hold it are known as citizens. An individual is generally a citizen of a single state. Some people, however,

New American citizens take their oath of citizenship at Monticello, the historic home of Thomas Jefferson, in Charlottesville, VA, July 4, 2008.
(©AP Photo/Steve Helber)

hold citizenship in two or more states. This situation, deemed **dual citizenship**, is uncommon, arguably for good reason. Citizenship carries with it not just special rights, but also a set of duties, such as military service, that represent one's loyalty to the state. Persons with dual citizenship, therefore, can have dual loyalties as well, something that the governments of most states find troubling.

It is also possible for an individual not to hold citizenship in any state, a condition known as being **stateless**. When their independence

Did You Know? The Holy See (Vatican City) has the smallest population of an internationally recognized state, with fewer than one thousand residents.

Citizenship is a designation of official membership that a state confers to most of its permanent population. Citizenship carries rights and responsibilities not afforded noncitizens, even if those noncitizens have lived in the state for a long time.

A person who holds more than one official citizenship is said to have **dual citizenship**.

Those with no citizenship are deemed **stateless**.

from the Soviet Union was restored in 1991, Estonia and Latvia had to decide to whom to grant citizenship. Estonia and Latvia chose to exclude from automatic citizenship sizeable portions of their populations, mostly ethnic Russians and other Russian-speaking minorities. The Estonian and Latvian governments justified this action because these individuals arrived during the half century of Soviet rule, a period they considered to be an illegal occupation. This decision created not only distinct bodies of citizens for both countries, but also large bodies of stateless persons. Some of these people ended up taking Russian citizenship, and a small but increasing number were able to become Estonian and Latvian citizens through naturalization, the process by which a noncitizen becomes a citizen. Many, however, remain stateless to this day.

Though the Baltic case is an extreme example of stateless individuals, it is not unusual for individuals to live outside the country in which they hold citizenship. While the bulk of the population of most existing states consists of citizens of those states, a number of other people may live in a state for long periods of time, even their entire lives, without citizenship in that state. There are many labels for such individuals. Those living in a country legally may be called permanent residents, resident aliens, or guest workers. These individuals often, though not always, hold citizenship in another country. Those who live in their country of residence unlawfully are known as illegal aliens or illegal immigrants. In the United States and around the world, the question of what to do with illegal immigrants has become a particularly controversial policy question. But all immigrants are potential targets for persecution, and immigration has become a potent political issue in developed and developing countries alike.

Territory and Population in the United Kingdom, Germany, and France

At different points in their histories, the United Kingdom, Germany, and France all controlled significantly more territory than they do at present. All three are medium-sized states in Europe, though France is noticeably larger than the other two. Their populations are somewhat similar in size as well, though for that category Germany is the largest of the three. Finally, although they have quite different patterns in terms of ethnicity and religion, all three have significant immigrant populations.

The United Kingdom

As a state, the United Kingdom has a long and relatively stable history. It once controlled an incredibly large amount of the world's territory (hence the phrase, "The sun never sets on the British Empire"). Today, almost all of the territory of that former empire belongs to independent countries. What remains of the core of the empire is a medium-sized country.

The term United Kingdom has been used since 1801, when Ireland united with Great Britain. In the early 1920s, Ireland gained its independence, with the exception of six of the counties in the northeast of the Irish island. These counties became known as Northern Ireland and remained in union with the rest of the country. As a result, the country's official name today is the United Kingdom of Great Britain and Northern Ireland.

In its past, the United Kingdom was called the Kingdom of England, and these days many people still use the term England for the country. In reality, England is only a part of the territory of the United Kingdom—one of its four regions. To the north of England is the region of Scotland, Wales is to its west, and Northern Ireland sits across the Irish Sea. The country is also referred to as Britain or Great Britain, though Great Britain technically only applies to a combination of the regions of England, Scotland, and Wales. Though this book uses the term United Kingdom instead of Britain, using United Kingdom as an adjective is awkward. In this book, therefore, the word British is used to refer to the people of the United Kingdom and their government.

At a little over 61 million, the United Kingdom's population is around one-fifth that of the United States.[15] Yet, its territory is less than 250,000 square kilometers, roughly the size of California. Its population density is accordingly ten times higher than that of the United States. Though the image of the rolling Scottish countryside is not completely inaccurate, the United Kingdom is heavily populated. Many people reside in sprawling urban areas. The population is also fairly ethnically diverse, with four main ethnic groups corresponding to the United Kingdom's four regions and a number of smaller groups—mostly immigrants from former British colonies.

Germany

Germany is a crowded, medium-sized country. Its temperate climate has four seasons with largely moderate winters. The exceptions are the southern part of the country, Bavaria, which contains the Alps, and the Harz Mountains to the east, which receive more snowfall than the rest of the country.

Outside of the Alps to the south and the Baltic and North Seas to the north, Germany lacks natural borders separating it from its neighbors. This lack of natural borders has shaped its development as a nation-state and its national identity. Following a series of wars that set its external boundaries, Germany became a nation-state in 1871, a relatively late date compared with most of its European neighbors. Otto von Bismarck established Germany as a nation-state (known as the Second Reich; the First Reich having been the Holy Roman Empire of medieval times). Bismarck was simultaneously the chancellor of Prussia, the kingdom that spanned territory in eastern Germany and

modern-day Poland, and the chancellor of the Second Reich. Known as the Iron Chancellor, Bismarck created the Second Reich by bringing together a number of decentralized principalities under Prussian dominance and by militarily defeating Denmark, Austria, and France in separate conflicts.

Approximately 82 million people live in an area of 357,000 square kilometers. Germany has one of the highest population densities in Europe with 231 people per square kilometer,[16] just behind the United Kingdom among the ten TIC cases. The two largest cities in Germany are Munich and Berlin, the capital and home to almost 3.5 million inhabitants. Germany also has a number of medium-size cities that are centers of regional importance. The heaviest concentration of population is in the northwest of the country, along the Rhine River and in the Ruhr area, Germany's industrial heartland. The territory that comprises the former East Germany is sparsely populated and features enormous farms blanketing the flat plain.

France

France can be thought of as three geographic units. First, there is metropolitan France. At more than 540,000 square kilometers, it is the largest country in Western Europe. It is called "the hexagon" because it has six distinct sides created largely by natural borders, which include the Mediterranean and the Alps in the south and the Rhine and the English Channel to the north. Next are the Overseas Departments of Guadeloupe and Martinique in the Caribbean, French Guyana in South America, and the island of Réunion in the Indian Ocean, each fully integrated into the French Republic. Finally, New Caledonia and Tahiti in the South Pacific and Saint Pierre and Miquelon off Canada's northeast coast, with different degrees of self-government, are part of the French Republic. All together, the Republic spans nearly 675,000 square kilometers with around 65 million inhabitants. Approximately 60 million of these live within the hexagon.

Though many outside observers imagine the French to be a cohesive cultural and ethno-national group, this is only partly true. With a colonial history and territory still spread across oceans, France has a racially diverse society. Almost as soon as France conquered its African and Asian colonies, immigrants began arriving in the hexagon. France was a primary immigrant destination, and few residents of France emigrated to the United States during the period of relatively open American borders in the nineteenth century. Almost one-third of French citizens have at least one great-grandparent of foreign origin, and 20 percent have at least one parent or grandparent who immigrated to France.[17]

With industrialization in the nineteenth century and rapid expansion in the twentieth, employers needed a new pool of urban workers.

Within the hexagon, the combination of a comparatively low birthrate, the transfer of agricultural land to a large segment of the peasantry during the French Revolution, and the promotion of peasant welfare by successive governments meant that these workers had to be found outside France's borders. Consequently, the French government, while not actively courting immigrants, enabled immigration as a way to address the industrial labor shortage. Through family unification policies for guest workers that lasted into the 1970s, new families continued to come to France. Under a principle called *jus soli* (or citizenship based on place of birth, not parentage), children born to immigrant parents in France were automatically granted the right to citizenship, although their parents or grandparents—born in French colonies—had no such right.

Territory and Population in Mexico and Brazil

The territorial and demographic traits of both Mexico and Brazil are, to a large extent, the products of colonialism and repeated waves of European immigration. In contrast to Mexico, the indigenous population of Brazil was historically relatively sparse and lived mostly in remote areas in the Amazon basin, far from the coast.

Mexico

Before the colonial period, Mexico had among the most highly developed civilizations in the world. The two main precolonial groups were the Mayans and the Aztecs. The Mayans had been in the area a long time—they can be traced as far back as 1500 B.C.—but their civilization especially flourished in the period from 300 to 900 A.D. A combination of food problems, invasions, earthquakes, and internal divisions eventually wiped this civilization out.

The Aztecs emerged around 1300 A.D. They had an impressive, urban civilization. Their capital, Tenochtitlan (today's Mexico City), had over 300,000 people, making it larger than any city in Europe at the time. Their last leader, Moctezuma ("Montezuma" in English) ruled from around 1480 until 1520. The Aztec period effectively ended with the arrival of Hernando Cortes and the Spanish on April 21, 1519. Within two years, the Spanish had conquered the Aztecs.

Because Spain took a great interest in Mexico, there were some positives from the colonial period, including one of the first universities in all of North or South America, the University of Mexico in Mexico City. However, there were enough negatives, especially concerning the particular Spanish rulers in power, to create robust discontent by the late 1700s and early 1800s. This set the stage for the struggle for independence and the birth of the modern state of Mexico in 1821.

Today's Mexico has a sizeable population and relatively large territory. The country has a diverse climate, with mountains and arid areas limiting the amount of arable land. Over

110 million people live in the nearly 2 million square kilometers of Mexico. The resultant population density is less than one-fourth that of the United Kingdom. The population density around the capital, Mexico City, is another matter. Estimates of Mexico City's population vary widely. Official government statistics likely underestimate the population. When the surrounding area is included, the best estimate is that around 20 million people live in the urban area of Mexico City, making it one of the largest in the world.

One of the legacies of colonial rule is the ethnic composition of Mexico's population. At least 60 percent of the population is *mestizo*. Another 30 percent is considered native ("Amerindian") or predominantly native. Even in this case, some ethnic intermixing has occurred over the centuries. About 10 percent of the population speaks an indigenous first language. Only 10 percent of the population is made up of white Hispanics.

Brazil

When Portuguese explorer Pedro Álvares Cabral officially claimed the land for Portugal in 1500, the king initially was not impressed. His new territory was a land of rocky coastlines, dense jungles, and few apparent riches. While Jesuits made some efforts to evangelize the indigenous population, it was not until gold was discovered in the central highlands in the late seventeenth century that extensive colonization took place within the country's wild interior.

Today, Brazil is a land of great diversity and startling contrasts. It is one of the largest countries in the world, with 8.5 million square kilometers of land (3.3 million square miles). Only Russia, the United States, Canada, and China are bigger. Brazil shares a common border with every country in South America except for Ecuador and Chile. It is also the fifth largest country in the world in population. Over 80 percent of Brazil's nearly 200 million people live in

Did You Know? The name "Brazil" refers to an indigenous term for a red wood, pau-brasil, native to Brazil and used during the colonial period to produce red dyes for clothing.

cities—some of which are among the largest in the world—and most of its large cities are along the coastline. Vast areas of land in the interior are virtually unpopulated, making its official population density of 22 people per square kilometer misleading. The population density in the region of Rio de Janeiro is 352 people per square kilometer, but only two people per square kilometer in the region of Amazonas.

The land itself is also incredibly varied. On the one hand, the Brazilian Amazon is the largest rainforest on the planet. On the other hand, only 6.9 percent of Brazil's land surface is suitable for farming—less than all of the other TIC countries. Parts of the country are subject to frequent flooding, others to frequent drought. Those areas of the rainforest that have been cleared for farming often produce crops for only a few years. Despite its lush appearance, the rainforest ecosystem requires an incredibly fragile balance among plants and animals that have evolved together for thousands of years. The soil is not especially fertile and, when stripped of its protective canopy of plants, easily washes away in the region's torrential rains.

Finally, Brazil's people are very diverse. According to census information, about 54 percent of the population is white, 39 percent is mulatto (mixed black and white), 6 percent is black, and less than 1 percent is indigenous. However, the category of "white" is made up not only of Portuguese descendants, but also of subsequent waves of immigrants from Italy, Spain, Germany, and Poland. There are even small communities of Japanese and Arab immigrants. Many of these groups are regionally concentrated as waves of immigration went to different places. They are also more diverse religiously than Mexicans. While 74 percent are nominally Catholic, there is a large and growing Protestant community, almost all of them Pentecostal evangelicals. About 4 percent continue to practice traditional African religions.

Territory and Population in the Russian Federation, China, and India

Russia, China, and India share some territorial and demographic features. They cover significant areas of the Asian continent, though much of western Russia is considered to be part of Europe. They also have relatively large populations, though the population size of China and India—the two most populous countries in the world—dwarfs that of Russia. In addition, while the governments of both China and India have worried about their populations growing too quickly, the Russian government has expressed significant concern over its declining population.

The Russian Federation

The history of the Russian Federation as an independent state is a very recent one, but its roots can be traced back to the ninth century A.D. and the establishment of the state of Kievan Rus. As the word Kievan indicates, it was based around the city of Kiev. As a result, Ukrainians and Russians both claim Kievan Rus as their first state, leading to occasional quarrels about which group has a legitimate claim to the present-day Ukrainian territory. Among the most important events of the Kievan Rus period was the choice in 988 by one of its leaders, Vladimir I, to convert to Orthodox Christianity. This decision, and the subsequent forced conversion of the subjects of Kievan Rus, created a religious division that remains today. Among believers, Russians, Belarussians, and most Ukrainians are Orthodox Christian. The populations to their west are largely Catholic and Protestant, while those to their south are predominantly Muslim.

Following a long period of rule by the Mongols, the Russians gained control of a huge portion of Eurasia, beginning in the fifteenth century with the "gathering of Russian lands" under tsar Ivan III (Ivan the Great). Under subsequent leaders—including names with which you may be familiar such as Ivan the Terrible, Peter the Great, and Catherine the Great—Russia became one of the world's largest and most important empires. The Soviet Union occupied much of the territory of the tsarist empire. This meant two things: the Soviet Union was huge, and its population was culturally diverse. The Russian part of the Soviet Union shared these two features with the country as a whole. Russia was a **union republic**, one of what ultimately became fifteen Soviet union republics, the highest level territorial unit below that of the federal government in the Soviet ethno-federal system. But it was the largest and most populous. Consequently, when the Soviet Union collapsed at the end of 1991 along the lines of the union republics, creating fifteen independent countries, Russia was the largest and most populous of these as well.

To say that the territory of the Russian state is expansive is an understatement. Spanning eleven time zones, the country covers more than 17 million square kilometers or approximately one-ninth of the world's land mass. This makes Russia more than eight and one-half times as big as Mexico and almost seventy-six times as large as the United Kingdom. However, with only around 140 million people, its population density is the lowest of the ten countries studied in detail in this book.

This is not because of a lack of large cities. Russia has a dozen cities with more than one million residents; with around 8.5 million inhabitants, Russia's capital city of Moscow is the largest European city. Instead, Russia's low population density is due to its vast expanses of virtually unpopulated land. That such a large swath of Russia is nearly uninhabited has much to do with the climate of the country. Most of the country is north of the 50th parallel, making its climate

A **union republic** was the highest level territorial unit below that of the federal government in the Soviet ethno-federal system. Russia was one of fifteen union republics when the Soviet Union collapsed in late 1991.

more like Canada's than the United State's, and a sizeable portion of it is north of the Arctic Circle. Large shares of the central and eastern parts of the country make up Siberia. Some regions of Siberia are populated by less than one-twentieth of a person per square kilometer.

The Russian population is ethnically diverse. While more than 80 percent of the population are ethnic Russians, and an even larger portion speaks Russian as its first language, there are also more than one hundred ethnic minorities, many of which are concentrated in particular regions. A few of these groups have developed strong nationalist movements, pushing for greater control of the territory in which they reside or even for outright independence.

Low life expectancies, especially among men, in the late Soviet and early post-Soviet period have combined with low birthrates to bring about dramatic declines in population. This trend is expected to continue. Some scholars estimate that the Russian population may decline by tens of millions by the middle of this century. In response, the Russian government has taken steps to encourage its citizens to have more children.

China

China's land, its people, and the interaction between the two have shaped its history. China's land is vast, diverse, and challenging for those who inhabit it. The country is home to one of the world's largest deserts, a number of mountain ranges, and several large rivers. The often harsh climate complicates food production. Only 10 to 15 percent of the land is suitable for farming. Flooding is a common problem, yet irrigation is needed for agriculture.

With more than 1.3 billion people living in roughly 9.5 million square kilometers of land, China's population density is, on average, much higher than that of the United States but still a reasonable-sounding 137 persons per square kilometer. This number is terribly misleading. Like Russia, China has huge areas of open, sparsely populated land. Most of China's people live in less than one-sixth of its area. China is home to more cities of one million or more people than any other country. Ethnic Han Chinese make up over 90 percent of the population. Minority groups, found particularly in the country's border areas, make up a relatively small percentage of the population but in absolute numbers are some of the larger ethnic minority groups in the world.

India

India, a relatively new state, formally assumed its independence from the United Kingdom in 1947. Its birth was traumatic. British sovereignty over India was not uniform, so in the months preceding independence hundreds of agreements had to be worked out for the accession of princely states to the union, and some resisted incorporation.

India is about one-third of the size of China or the United States, though it possesses similarly diverse land forms. These range from desert in parts of Rajasthan in the west to rainforests in parts of Arunachal Pradesh in the east and from the high Himalayas in Uttarankhand in the north to the ocean at Kanyakumari in Tamil Nadu in the south.[18] It has a population of about 1.2 billion people and, at 380 people per square kilometer, it is more densely populated than most other geographically large countries, including Brazil, Russia, China, and the United States.

Indian citizens speak over four hundred languages. Under the 8th Schedule of the Constitution, the government officially recognizes twenty-two languages. The most widely spoken languages may be categorized as Indo-Aryan (spoken by about 74 percent of the population) or Dravidian (spoken by about 24 percent of the population). In 1950, the government declared Hindi to be the national language and set a goal for the phasing out of English in government communications within fifteen years. Although the effort was aimed at fostering nationalism and unity, it led to subnationalism and disunity. Leaders in the Dravidian-speaking south threatened secession. A kind of pragmatic flexibility in the application of the law eased the tensions, and the crisis passed. English remains in wide use, and its popularity has been enhanced by globalization.

Although more than 80 percent of the Indian population is classified as practicing the Hindu religion, there is considerable internal variation among adherents. In addition to Hindus, over 13 percent of the population is Muslim, while Christians constitute over 2 percent, Sikhs almost 2 percent, Buddhists almost 1 percent, and Jains almost 0.5 percent. Two opposing arguments about religion and unity have surfaced in India. *Hindutva* adherents, such as the Bharatiya Janata Party (BJP) and many of its supporters, claim that being Hindu is the same as being Indian. Secularists—leaders of the Congress Party, the Left parties, and many of their supporters—counter that the state must not assume the mantle of any religion. This debate constitutes a major political cleavage, with some leaders using religion as a tool for organizing supporters.

Some of the richest and poorest people in the world live in India. It has produced rich and prosperous farmers in the Punjab and indebted and poverty-stricken farmers in the Vidarbha region of Maharashtra. Certain urban families display immense wealth in a variety of ways, including, increasingly, high-profile philanthropic activity. These include the Tatas, owners of the Tata automobile company, and the Birlas, whose Aditya Birla Group is one of India's most prominent multinational corporations. At the same time, terrible slums exist in most major cities. Between these extremes is the middle class, numbering up to 300 million. The middle class expanded greatly during the twenty-first century's first decade thanks to the Indian economy's take-off.

Territory and Population in Nigeria and Iran

Nigeria and Iran are relatively large countries with large populations—at least when compared with other countries in their respective regions, though not if compared with China and India. They are both ethnically diverse as well. The two also differ, including in the religious traits of their populations. While Islam is important in the northern half of Nigeria, it commands politics and society to a great extent across the whole of the Iranian territory.

Nigeria

With around 150 million people, Nigeria is one of the world's ten most populous countries and the most heavily populated country in Africa. Its population is larger than Russia's yet concentrated in less than 925,000 square kilometers (or around one-eighteenth the size of Russia). The result is a population density figure that is higher than China's. Nigeria's largest city is Lagos. An estimated 15 million inhabitants live in and around the city.

Despite the suitability of much of its land for farming, Nigeria has difficulty producing necessities, including food, for its sizeable population. It is a net importer of food. This is partly the result of limited technology in the country's agricultural sector. While Canada has more than 25,000 tractors per million people, Nigeria has barely more than one hundred.

Nigeria's population is ethnically diverse. The four main ethnic groups are the Ibo (or Igbo), Yoruba, Hausa, and Fulani. These groups comprise more than two-thirds of the population. They also tend to be concentrated in certain parts of the country. The Ibo tend to live in the east; the Yoruba live in the west. The Hausa and Fulani are concentrated in the north. The Hausa and Fulani have many similar traits and are sometimes difficult to distinguish—a legacy

Topic in countries

of the imposition of Fulani rule over the Hausa in the 1800s, which led to significant intermixing. Scholars often treat them as a single group, the Hausa-Fulani. Consequently, from this point on, this book utilizes the Hausa-Fulani label.

Nigeria also contains significant religious diversity. The emergence of Islam in Nigeria's north but not in its south means that the ethnic divisions are reinforced by religion. Around half of the population is Muslim, with another 40 percent Christian, and 10 percent practicing traditional religions. This makes Nigeria home to one of the largest Muslim populations in the world.

Iran

For long periods, the Persians dominated large areas of the Middle East, including the contemporary Iranian territory. At the same time, the area that is today Iran was the target of invasions by numerous groups of people, each of which has had important influences on the development of the Iranian state, society, and national identity. The Arab conquest brought Islam to Persia in the middle of the seventh century A.D. In 1055, the Turks invaded, followed by the Mongols—descendants of Genghis Khan—in the early 1200s.

At more than one and one-half million square kilometers, Iran is one of the largest countries in the Middle East. It borders seven other countries, including its long western border with Iraq. Ironically, given that it is situated between the Caspian Sea to the north and the Persian Gulf and Gulf of Oman to the south, much of the south and east of the country is desert.

Iran is also one of the most populous countries of the Middle East. Estimates of its population vary from 65 to 75 million people.[19] Its population combines with the size of the country to create a moderate population density figure. This is, like some of the other TIC cases, somewhat deceptive. Vast areas of the country are relatively unpopulated. Much of the population is concentrated in the far north and northwest of the country, and most live in large cities. Many people live in the area around Tehran, the capital city in the north-central part of the country. This region contributes more than one-quarter of the country's gross domestic product.

The population is varied in many ways. A little more than half of the population is Persian. The largest ethnic minority, around one-fourth of the population, is the Azeris. Concentrated in the north and northwest of the country, they are the majority group in some areas. There are also nearly one-half million Kurds, making them Iran's fourth largest ethnic group. Nearly 60 percent of the population speaks Persian, while more than one-quarter speak a Turkic language. The great majority of the population is Shi'ite, but Sunni Muslims make up about 10 percent of the population. Indeed, Iran's Islamic population breaks down almost opposite of the global pattern (90 percent of the world's Muslims are Sunnis). Iran also has small Jewish and Christian populations.

Institutions

A state's ruling institutions are the heart of its political organization. Social scientists disagree about the nature of institutions: economists think of institutions as sets of rules, sociologists highlight the importance of unwritten norms, and political scientists see institutions as organizational arrangements.[20] This chapter's section on society mentioned the importance of norms. But, as is common in political science texts, this book places a greater emphasis on the nature of organizational arrangements, including the composition and official roles of legislatures, executives, and judiciaries. Such general patterns of institutional arrangements define the main types of political systems—democracy, authoritarianism, and totalitarianism—as well as categories within these broad types such as majoritarian versus consensus democracy (see Chapter 6).

A state's institutions form its political structure, and later chapters of this book focus on a variety of institutional arrangements in detail. The arrangement of institutions in a particular state can have profound implications for policy creation, tensions between groups in society, and a state's stability. The state's institutions are, therefore, part of the overall structure that influences individuals' political actions but are also, themselves, the result of past choices.

Sovereignty

A state enjoys **sovereignty** when its governing institutions have ultimate control over affairs within the state's territory. While sovereignty is an important part of what makes a state different from other levels of political organization such as local governments or international organizations, not all states have full control over every aspect of their political business at all times. States may choose to surrender a degree of sovereignty to international organizations or other entities. Existing states may also lose control of part or all of their territory to rebel groups or foreign powers. After the first Gulf War in 1991, for example, the United States, the United Kingdom, and France established "no fly zones," which prevented the Iraqi government from using its military as it desired in two large areas of the country. Finally, certain topics seen as international problems, such as the environment, raise questions about the limits of state sovereignty. Does the government of Brazil, for example, have the right to pursue economic development strategies that lead to the destruction of the Brazilian rainforest?

Many noted scholars have emphasized the idea of being "in control of one's own affairs" in their conceptualizations of the state. One of the most important of these is Max Weber. Some consider Weber's 1918 lecture, "Politics as a Vocation," to be the most important talk ever given by a social scientist. Its ideas about

A rainbow arches across a rainforest in Brazil.
(©James L. Stanfield/National Geographic/Getty Images)

the state and power (remember the discussion of Weber's three types of authority in Chapter 1) influence how scholars think about these terms to this day. In his speech, Weber put forth the idea of the state as "a human community that (successfully) claims the monopoly of the legitimate use of physical force within a given territory."[21] Thus, Weber tied his idea of the state to the concept of power. Later in the speech, he called the modern state "a compulsory association which organizes domination."[22]

His idea of successful claims to the monopoly of legitimate use of force raises interesting questions. What is force? When is the use of force legitimate? How does one measure successful claims to the use of such force? Weber's conceptualization of the state is, therefore, problematic. The inclusion of ambiguous terms poses measurement problems for comparativists. It remains, however, one of the most common ways that comparativists discuss the state, and it is one with which all comparative politics students should be familiar.

Sovereignty is the ability to conduct one's own affairs. It is a defining feature of states, though not all existing states have complete sovereignty at all times.

Think and Discuss

The topic of the environment causes problems for the concept of state sovereignty. What other topics create problems for the idea of states in the international system having the right to control their own affairs?

International Recognition

At least in the short run, states can exist without sovereignty as long as they do not also lose **international recognition**. International recognition is the external acceptance, sanctioning, and legal endorsement of a state's sovereignty by other states in the international state system. It is important to note that this recognition can be granted before sovereignty has been achieved, and it can continue after sovereignty has, in reality, been lost. The European and American governments, for example, recognized the independence of several republics of Yugoslavia, Slovenia, Croatia, and eventually Bosnia, before the governments of these republics had complete control over their territory from the Yugoslav military.

After the U.S.-led coalition invaded Iraq in 2003—and even after the return of power to the new Iraqi government in 2004 and elections for a provisional parliament in 2005—the United States and its allies largely controlled the affairs of the Iraqi state. Yet, even with its lack of actual sovereignty, the international community continued to recognize Iraq's status as a state. Thus, international recognition is best thought of as the recognition of the *right* of a state to be sovereign rather than the recognition of actual sovereignty.

When a territory is recognized as a state, it gains more than just a vote in the United Nations General Assembly. International recognition gives those in control of the territory a greater ability, within reason, to use force to maintain order without fear of international intervention. It also increases the likelihood that the new state will gain legitimacy among its own people, making the use of force to maintain order less necessary. Finally, international recognition allows the state to enter into binding agreements with other states, improving its ability to trade, address problems with causes beyond its own borders, and defend itself.

Patriotism

Though not a defining feature of a state, **patriotism** is an important factor in the stability of states. Patriotism is the connection with a given state, including one's loyalty to and pride in that state. Thus, the common way of thinking about patriotism (love of country) is a solid definition to use in the study of politics. Given the tendency to confuse the terms nation and state in the comparative study of politics, it is perhaps not surprising that nationalism is also often confused with patriotism. Since the main goal of most nationalists is control of a state, it makes sense that people would come to see patriotism and nationalism as interchangeable terms. This is especially understandable in countries such as the United States, where the national identity is more civic than ethnic, and many national myths and symbols are symbols of the state.

There are, however, key differences between patriotism and nationalism. Even an overly simple definition of nationalism such as loyalty to the nation is different from loyalty to

---

International recognition is the international community's acceptance of a state's right to sovereignty. This recognition can come before sovereignty is actually attained, and it can remain in place—even for quite a while—after sovereignty has, in actuality, been lost.

Patriotism is loyalty to, pride in, and love of, an existing state.

the state. In addition, nationalism is a deeper, more complex phenomenon than just loyalty to one's nation. Such loyalty is certainly something that nationalists seek to develop in the general population, but only alongside the more crucial beliefs about membership and territorial boundaries.

Government and Regime

Regime

When most people use the word **regime** in everyday language, they often are referring to the particular leaders of a state. But, for political scientists, the word regime means a set of rules that determine the way decisions are made. In comparative politics, a regime is best thought of as the particular political system in a state under which the government operates. The regime includes the official set of rules for making government policy (i.e., the rules for deciding "who gets what"), known as the constitution. It also includes the extent to which the government diverts from the process spelled out in the constitution when it *actually* makes decisions. While most Americans accept the notion of "constitutionalism"—the view that governments must follow the official rules as spelled out in the constitution—the fit in many countries between the official constitutional rules and the actual government practice is poor.

As a system of rules, regimes organize political activities. They provide political structure, which helps shape political behavior. This is not to imply that the regimes themselves fully control the actions of political participants. Rather, they are like a complex web of roads on which citizens and leaders can drive. Political leaders may choose to turn the country in a particular direction, but the options that the political system provides influence the exact route that turn can initiate.

Regime types include the three major forms of government covered in Chapter 6 of this book: democracy, authoritarianism, and totalitarianism. That chapter spells out how these different types of regimes govern in distinct ways. Even two states that are both considered democracies may be organized very differently.

In addition to the broad categories of democracy, authoritarianism, and totalitarianism, comparativists have identified other types of regimes based on particular characteristics. One such regime type is **theocracy**, a political system in which religious leaders control political decisions and religious law provides the basis for policy decisions. The Taliban, who controlled Afghanistan prior to the American-led military action after the attacks of September 11, 2001, represented an extreme form of theocracy. A less extreme case—but one that is very important to the study of comparative politics—is Iran. The discussion of Iran in the Topic in Countries later in this chapter takes account of how theocracy works in practice.

Government

When most people think about politics, their first thought is of government. The term **government** has two meanings in comparative politics. The first is broad: the ruling institutions of a given

A **regime** is the political system of a particular state, including all its rule-making institutions and the "rules for making new rules" known as a constitution.

A **theocracy** is a type of political system in which religious leaders hold the main positions in the government and religious law is used as the basis for policy decisions.

Government is the set of individuals, the roles they play, and the institutions in which they function that produce policy decisions on behalf of the state. A more narrow use of the term associates it with the leading policy-making officials such as a prime minister and cabinet at a given time in a particular country.

state and the people who occupy positions of power in that state. Governments are the instruments of state sovereignty. They make the decisions about how the state conducts its affairs within its borders and in its relations with other states. To borrow language from the previous chapter, governments are the individuals and decision-making mechanisms that generate the collective policy decisions which determine "who gets what." The more narrow meaning refers to a political system's chief executive and cabinet officials, particularly in parliamentary systems. The "Brown government" may mean only United Kingdom Prime Minister Gordon Brown and his ministers. In either meaning, the individuals who comprise the government can change through elections, through the overthrow of a leader, and by other means. Such changes in the government's makeup need not lead to a change in the overall way the political system is organized or the general set of rules that instruct how policy decisions are made and enforced.

Did You Know? From June 1945 to June 2001, Italy formed a new government, in the narrow meaning of the term, nearly sixty times. Even with some individuals serving as prime minister more than once, Italy still had twenty-five different prime ministers during those fifty-six years. By comparison, the United States had eleven different presidents during this period.

Think and Discuss

The section above includes the point that the leaders of a particular country's government can change without a fundamental change in that country's regime. Could a country's regime go through a fundamental change without a corresponding significant change in its government? Why or why not?

Regime and Government in the United Kingdom, Germany, and France

With their colonial histories and prominent role in international politics today, the political systems and governments of the United Kingdom, Germany, and France provide models to many other states. Yet, they are different models. The British system evolved over time into one that concentrates power in the hands of the prime minister and his party, which controls a majority of the seats in parliament. The German approach, combining a federal system with an electoral system that encourages coalition governments, fosters more power sharing. The current French system—the fifth variant of republican government in its history—includes a dual executive arrangement in which a president and prime minister share executive authority.

The United Kingdom

Today, the United Kingdom operates under what is known as the **Westminster political system**. This is a representative democratic regime with a powerful parliament, a strong prime minister, and a first past the post (FPTP) district electoral system. This system serves as a model for many other countries. The parliament is made up of two houses: the House of Commons and House of Lords. As discussed in more detail later in the book, Commons is the much more powerful of the two houses though reforms to the House of Lords are underway to make it more like upper houses found in other countries.

When King John signed the Magna Carta in 1215, it set the tone for a series of changes in the British political system over time. These changes initially limited the power of the monarchy, later restricted the power of the aristocracy, and with the emergence of the House of Commons as the

A **Westminster political system** combines a prime minister, a strong parliament, and a first past the post district electoral system for selecting members of the parliament.

centerpiece of British politics, increased the size of the electorate. Such changes, while dramatic, have generally taken place without the significant levels of political violence often prevalent in the history of other countries. This is due, at least in part, to the evolutionary approach of the British. With each change to the regime, some key elements of the previous political system were preserved. The monarchy was weakened, but not abolished; when the House of Lords became secondary to the House of Commons, the Lords still maintained some real powers and many more ceremonial ones.

Though the central government retains sovereignty over levels of government below it, the United Kingdom's membership in the European Union leads one to question the extent to which the European Union controls British policymaking. Because EU membership requires member states to surrender a certain degree of sovereignty to EU institutions, there are limits on the authority of the British state and the government acting on its behalf.

In the narrow sense of the term, the United Kingdom's government has been in power since

Former British Prime Minister Tony Blair takes questions in parliament in November of 2005, shortly before losing a key vote on an anti-terrorism bill—the first time in his tenure as prime minister that a measure he supported was defeated.

(©AP Photo/PA)

June 27, 2007, when Gordon Brown replaced Tony Blair as prime minister. Hence, one now refers to the "Brown government" rather than the "Blair government" when discussing the most important executive members of the British government. Consistent with the United Kingdom's history of carrying the past into the present, the monarch still has some official duties. In reality, these duties are largely ceremonial. Governing is left to the prime minister and his or her government.

Germany

The current regime in Germany, the Federal Republic, is a parliamentary democracy consisting of a bicameral legislature, a prime minister (known as the chancellor), and a ceremonial president elected by the lower house and the provinces. The lower house of parliament (the *Bundestag*) is directly elected by the voters under a mixed system of proportional representation and single-member districts. Germany is also a federal system with sixteen "states" (*Länder*). The upper house of parliament (the *Bundesrat*) is not directly elected; instead, the *Länder* send their representatives to this chamber. The Federal Republic's institutions of coalition governments, federalism, and incorporation of major interest groups into the formulation and implementation of policy deliberately disperse state power in response to previous authoritarian regimes.[23]

While the Federal Republic is a stable democracy today, Germany had a history of a sometimes violent regime change. The Second Reich (1871–1918) was an authoritarian regime. There were trappings of democratic institutions, but the real power lay with the chancellor and emperor. Following its defeat in World War I, Germany experienced a brief interlude of democracy under the Weimar Republic (1919–1933). The legitimacy of this nascent democracy was undermined by the violent, antidemocratic activities of authoritarian forces on the Right and Communists on the Left, the association of democracy with the humiliating terms of defeat after World War I, and the government's inability to deal with the massive economic suffering of the Great Depression.

These conditions proved to be fertile ground for the rise of the National Socialist (Nazi) Party. Under the leadership of Adolf Hitler, the Nazi Party came to power, legally, in 1933. Hitler then turned on the democratic system, installing a totalitarian dictatorship that sought to order all aspects of society in a one-party state and party-controlled groups, used terror and propaganda to silence all opponents, and embarked on a violent and expansionist foreign policy that culminated in World War II. By 1945, the Nazi regime lay in ruins, destroyed by the Allied forces in that war.

Following the defeat of the Nazi regime, Germany became a focal point of the Cold War between the United States and the Soviet Union. From 1945 to 1949, Germany was under occupation by the four victorious Allies, with the British, French, Americans, and Soviets each responsible for their own zone of occupation, and Berlin was carved up into separate zones among the four powers. By 1949, the Cold War had institutionalized the division of Germany into two separate countries and regimes. The Federal Republic of Germany (FRG, commonly known as "West Germany") was formed out of the American, British, and French zones of occupation and their corresponding sectors in Berlin. The Allies ensured that the FRG had a capitalist economy and the democratic political system sketched on page 49. To the east was the German Democratic Republic (GDR, or "East Germany"), which had been the Soviet zone of occupation. The Soviets imposed a Communist political regime on the GDR.

The end of the Cold War and the fall of the Berlin Wall in November 1989 led to the reunification of Germany. East Germany entered the Federal Republic as five new *Länder* and all-German elections were held in 1990. Germany's current democratic and capitalist regime has applied to both eastern and western parts of the country since 1990. The current government in Berlin, formed in 2005, is a "grand coalition" (see Chapter 7) of the two largest parties, the center-right Christian Democratic Party (CDU) and the center-left Social Democratic Party (SPD). Its chancellor, Angela Merkel, is Germany's first female prime minister and is an East German CDU politician.

France

Similar to how they view the United States, many comparativists consider France's approach to politics to be "exceptional." Despite often competing views of the world, the United States and France share origins in a revolution, the early adoption of a guarantee of civic rights in the eighteenth century, and the idea that their values and norms are "universal," not just appropriate for or applicable to their own citizens.[24] Indeed, the French sense of universalism extends from political values and culture to include global standards for wine, cuisine, and fashion.

Like its national identity development, the French road to a durable democracy has been volatile. Since the first days of revolution in 1789, France has fluctuated among three kingdoms, two empires, a quasi-fascist state, and five republics. This tendency has been fueled by an unyielding conflict between those attached to the legacies of the French Revolution and those who oppose it: the Republican militants who conceived government as the expression of popular sovereignty in an elected assembly dominating a centralized government in Paris and the forces supporting a strong monarchy backed by the church and the aristocracy. Only with defeat at the hands of the Nazis in 1941, and the subsequent victory of the Allies that discredited wartime collaborators in 1945, did a democratic consensus begin to emerge—and only after one more regime change did it become consolidated.

From the early days of the Revolution, both France's traditional and elected representatives often turned to the skills of a talented bureaucracy, and these experts provided continuity while promoting modernization through the various regimes. Specialized schools, such as those for civil and military engineers, began in the eighteenth century. Under the Revolution and Napoleon, these schools were expanded and codified as the elite *Grandes Écoles*, superior to the respected French university system. Today, the pinnacle of bureaucratic training is the École Nationale d'Administration, or ENA. Founded in 1945, the ENA graduates approximately one hundred students each year. Known as *énarques*, ENA alumni have dominated the highest ministerial positions and elective offices, as well as leading corporate offices in France.[25]

The current Fifth Republic was founded in 1959 by Charles de Gaulle, the general who led the official resistance to the German occupation. It is an attempt to reconcile Republicans and anti-Republicans, supporters of a strong executive and of a popular assembly, as well as the power of the elite bureaucrats with representative government. In this semipresidential system, the constitution divides executive authority between a popularly elected president and the prime minister whom he or she appoints. Legislative authority is held primarily by the National Assembly, elected from single member districts. Because of two-stage elections, however, a large number of parties compete in the first round, and typically two or three candidates emerge from the Left and Right for the second round. The assembly is balanced by a less powerful senate, which is not elected by popular vote but instead by a special electoral college. Neither the prime minister nor his or her ministers can hold office in the Assembly, though along with deputies to the Assembly and senators, ministers can be local mayors and municipal or regional councilors. The legal system is organized much like a bureaucracy, and courts have little guaranteed independence and cannot interpret laws. The constitutional court provides advice and guidance to lawmakers before a law is passed.

The network of *énarques* and other graduates of the *Grandes Écoles* have been influential, especially in economic and social policy. Since the end of World War II, successive governments have agreed on the need to promote "modernization" to increase and redistribute wealth in order to ensure stability and reduce conflict between social classes. This "common good" supplants individual interests, and important policies are often made by ministers or bureaucrats and not elected representatives. The initial result was substantial and rapid economic growth, known as the 30 Glorious Years. But a regime dominated by its bureaucratic leadership in Paris has not been without controversy. The role of *énarques* has come under great scrutiny, and some have referred to modern France as a "blocked society" partially because of its inability to incorporate fresh leadership and new perspectives.[26] In 2007, newly elected President Nicolas Sarkozy appointed only one *énarque* to his cabinet.

Topic in countries

Regime and Government in Mexico and Brazil

Today, both Mexico and Brazil are presidential democracies. Corruption, a feature of both countries' political pasts, continues to plague their present democratic systems. They have also shared the experience of enduring a rocky road to democracy, though the roads differed. For much of the twentieth century, Mexico was an authoritarian system centered around a single political party. Brazil experimented with democracy multiple times, with the experiments typically ended by the military's violent intervention into politics.

Mexico

Though many Americans are unfamiliar with Mexico's governing institutions, its political system should look familiar to them. It is a presidential system, and thus the president is both the head of state and the head of government. The legislature, called the Congress, has two houses. The system also has checks and balances, though less so than in the American case, and it is a federal system with thirty-one "states" (*estados*) and the federal capital of Mexico City.

Mexico's regime was forged from the chaos of the end of Spanish rule, external threats to independence, a long dictatorship under Porfirio Diaz (1877–1910), and a revolution ending in 1917. The Mexican Revolution gave rise to some of the more colorful, noteworthy figures in the history of political uprisings, including Emiliano Zapata and Pancho Villa.

A presidential authoritarian system, dominated by a single party—the National Revolutionary Party—emerged from this chaos. The National

Revolutionary Party changed its name to Mexican Revolutionary Party in 1938 and then to the Institutional Revolutionary Party (PRI) in 1946, the name it maintains at present. The acronym PRI is based on the Spanish language name of the party, *Partido Revolucionario Institucional*.

The PRI ruled Mexico for most of the twentieth century. With its combination of fixed presidential terms and one party control, Mexico was among the most stable, predictable political systems in the world. This began to change during the 1980s and 1990s with the slow erosion of PRI dominance, culminating in the election of a non-PRI president in 2000. In this case, the change in government leadership also marked a change in political regime.

President Felipe Calderón heads the Mexican government. Calderón is from the National Action Party (PAN), a right-of-center party that emerged as a challenger to PRI domination. Since the PAN does not have a majority of seats in the Mexican legislature, Calderón has had a difficult time passing legislative initiatives. The legislature's deference to the president, a trait of most of the twentieth century in Mexico, has diminished greatly—something that Calderón's predecessor, Vicente Fox (also from the PAN), found out a number of times. By the opening of the twenty-first century, Mexican legislators seemed to enjoy their ability to frustrate the president.

Brazil

Brazil was unique among Latin American countries in achieving independence without a bloody struggle. To escape Napoleon Bonaparte's invasion of Portugal in 1808, the king of Portugal officially transferred his court to Brazil. Although most of the royal family returned to Portugal in 1821 after Napoleon was defeated, the king's son decided to stay. A year later, he declared Brazil independent of Portugal and became Dom Pedro I, emperor of Brazil.

As a result, the former colonial overlords simply "became Brazilian" and continued to rule for another sixty-seven years. The monarchy ended in similarly bloodless fashion. The emperor's decision to abolish slavery in Brazil in 1888 had led to widespread famines in the northeast, where wealthy plantation owners depended on slave labor. Together with other wealthy oligarchs, the northeastern elites supported a military coup that deposed the monarch (but did not kill him). It would be the first of many military coups that would mar Brazil's political development.

Brazil has had several different constitutions, often interrupted by the violent overthrow of the government. The current constitution dates to 1988. It establishes a formal structure of government that is very similar to that of Mexico and the United States. Brazil has a federal system with twenty-six states (*estados*) and a federal district. There is a president, a vice president, and a bicameral legislature composed of the Federal Senate and the Chamber of Deputies.

The current president is Luiz Inacio Lula da Silva, invariably referred to by his nickname, Lula. Lula started his political career as a labor organizer and later founded the leftist Workers' Party (PT, for its initials in Portuguese). Although he was reelected to a second four-year term in October 2006, Lula's government has been repeatedly criticized for failing to live up to his campaign promises of major reforms in favor of the landless, the working class, and the poor. His difficulties illustrate one of the persistent problems of Brazilian presidents: they rarely have a legislative majority of their own party. In Lula's case, his party controls only 11 of the 81 seats in the Brazilian senate (13.5 percent) and 83 of 513 seats in the Chamber of Deputies (16.2 percent). Thus, to pass any legislation he must get cooperation from the deputies of other political parties. But the two largest parties besides his own are much more conservative and oppose significant land or labor law reform. They control a combined 30 percent of the Chamber of Deputies.

Personalism and corruption also plague Brazilian politics. Most past governments have solved the problem of legislative cooperation by distributing money, favors, or government positions in return for support for the president's bills in the legislature. Lula at first refused to follow this tradition. Instead, he named only supporters of his own coalition to his cabinet and other important positions. The result was that only reforms supported by the conservative parties—and therefore *not* the progressive reforms his own party wanted—could pass the legislature. He soon switched tactics. In 2005, an opposition party deputy accused of taking bribes revealed that he had, in fact, also been taking bribes from the PT to favor the party's initiatives in the legislature, in the form of a monthly allowance of about $12,000. Though Lula himself stayed in power, several deputies and PT leaders were forced to resign as a result of the scandal.

Regime and Government in the Russian Federation, China, and India

Russia, China, and India have had thoroughly different experiences with democracy. Russia had a brief encounter with democratic arrangements in 1917 and a more extensive one in the 1990s, but is moving away from democracy today. China's Communist government continues to work to prevent democratization. In India, democracy accompanied independence, and the country remains solidly democratic at present.

The Russian Federation

The difficulties of governing Russia's vast territory helped generate nondemocratic rule with the aid of a hefty bureaucracy. From Kieven Rus through the tsarist period, the Russian political system had a strong tendency toward authoritarian, at times almost totalitarian, rule. In 1917, the tsarist system collapsed, in part from its poor showing in World War I. An interim authority, called the "provisional government," led Russia for much of 1917. During this time, increasingly important local organizations called workers' councils (or soviets) also issued decrees.

Democracy never had a chance. Under the leadership of Vladimir Lenin, the Bolsheviks seized power late in 1917. Elections for a new legislature, the Constituent Assembly, were held in early 1918, but the Bolsheviks quickly shut the assembly down after failing to win a majority of the seats. For the next three years, the Bolsheviks fought to win control of the lands of the old Russian Empire. In December 1922, the Bolsheviks declared a union of four Soviet republics: Russia, Ukraine, Belorussia, and Transcaucasia. The Union of Soviet Socialist Republics (USSR) was born, and the Bolsheviks became the Communist Party of the Soviet Union (CPSU). The Soviet system survived until the last days of 1991.

As a result, Russia had little experience with democratic politics. With the collapse of the Soviet Union came hope for a democracy. Indeed, the political system appeared quite democratic at times in the 1990s. But concerns among analysts who studied the country lingered, particularly because of the strong powers concentrated in the office of the president (who, during the 1990s, was Boris Yeltsin). These concerns increased dramatically after Vladimir Putin became president. Particularly after 2003, Putin used the significant powers of his office to limit democratic freedoms and governmental accountability. The result was something scholars have called "creeping authoritarianism," a topic examined in more detail later in the book.

From 2000–2008, the Russian government revolved around (then-president) Vladimir Putin. In 2004 and 2005, Putin made a number of dramatic proposals to alter the Russian political system, such as the revamping of the electoral system (see Chapter 10). In 2008, Putin passed the presidential torch to Dmitry Medvedev but maintained his grip on power by becoming Russian prime minister. Putin's political party, United Russia, dominates the lower house of parliament, the *Duma*, the more powerful of the two houses of Russia's bicameral national legislature. After the December 2007 parliamentary elections, United Russia directly controlled 315 of the 450 seats in the *Duma*, with an additional 78 seats controlled by two parties supportive of Putin.

China

One of the many reasons why China is valuable as a comparative case is that it is an officially Communist state. This makes it different from states such as Russia, which have to deal with legacies of the Soviet period but not with being officially Communist. The Communist Party leadership controls a large state bureaucratic apparatus, but the military remains an important actor in the political system. Only relatively recently has holding an official position at the top of the government corresponded to being one of the recognized leaders of the country.

While the Communist Party governs China today, most of the country's recorded history and the development of much of its culture took place under dynastic rule prior to the Communist period. The various dynasties ruled with the help of a civil service that expanded over time. Japan's defeat of China in a war in 1895 convinced many that simply reforming the imperial system was not enough. The 1900 Boxer Rebellion, an uprising against foreign rule, set the stage for the 1911 Nationalist revolution and the overthrow of the imperial system.

Did You Know? Each dynasty in China typically lasted around three hundred years. Key dynasties were the Han (206 B.C. to 220 A.D.), Tang (628 to 907 A.D.), Yuan (the period of Mongol rule from 1279 to 1368), and Ming (1368 to 1643). The final Chinese dynasty, the Qing, in which Manchus took over control of China, lasted from 1644 to 1911.

The Communist's ultimate victory over the Nationalists in the Chinese civil war in 1949 brought an approach to Communist rule that was quite different in many respects from the Stalinist Soviet model. Mao Zedong, the charismatic leader of Communist China for nearly three decades after the civil war, sought a more agrarian, less industrial form of Communism. Events like the Great Leap Forward of the late 1950s and the Cultural Revolution of the mid-1960s (see Chapter 11) caused more harm than good for Chinese economic and cultural development.

In 1976, the death of Mao led to the emergence of Deng Xiaoping, a leader who transformed China as fundamentally as Mao had. Starting in the late 1970s, economic reforms brought market principles into a previously state-run economy and fueled dramatic economic growth. However, the Communist Party did not succumb to pressure to surrender its monopoly control over the political system—epitomized by its crackdown against the Tiananmen Square uprising in 1989 as Communist rule was crumbling in Eastern Europe. Even with Deng's death in 1997, the political system remained largely as it had been—an authoritarian government ruling over a large, heavily populated, and increasingly capitalist country.

The current government, led by President Hu Jintao, represents a new, post-Deng Xiaoping generation of Chinese leaders. Less revolutionary than past leaders, Hu Jintao's government is based more on technical expertise and performance. Government corruption remains a concern, limiting China's ability to attract even more foreign investment than it already has and cutting into the regime's legitimacy.

India

Despite an initially difficult transition to independence from British control, India has built and sustained the world's largest democracy. Citizens choose their leaders in generally free and fair elections; multiple political parties compete in those elections; the press is free and takes diverse stands on national issues; and individuals frequently use their right to demonstrate "in the streets" their support for, or opposition to, policies and events. Indeed, there are few countries in the world where so much time and energy is devoted to the expression of political positions.

Like other former British colonies, independent India adopted a parliamentary system of government—a system only slightly modified by the country's first Constitution adopted in 1950. The directly elected "lower" house of parliament, the *Lok Sabha*, is the center of power, and the prime minister, a member of the *Lok Sabha*, is acknowledged to be the most powerful individual in government. There is an "upper" house, the *Rajya Sabha*, indirectly elected, which formally represents the administrative divisions that make up the country's federal system and other specific interests. A president possesses symbolic functions much like the British Queen.[27]

The country's diversity led to the creation of a federal system, though problems arising from that diversity resulted in the center's retention of most powers. Most of India's administrative divisions are governed by a *Vidhan Sabha* (Legislative Assembly), an institution parallel to the *Lok Sabha*; a few of them also have a second house, a *Vidhan Parishad* (Legislative Council), which parallels the *Rajya Sabha* at the national level. There are also municipal governments in all major cities, and a unique and unevenly developed representative arrangement, known as the *panchayat* system (discussed in Chapter 6), which involves local councils that coordinate village governance in rural areas throughout the country.[28]

Regime and Government in Nigeria and Iran

Nigeria has had several democratic episodes since its independence from British control. Similar to Brazil, Nigeria's brief periods of democratic rule have ended at the hands of the military. In contrast, Iranian leaders have been hostile to attempts to liberalize the political system. While some hoped that the 1979 Islamic Revolution would produce a democratic reaction to the previous authoritarian regime, these hopes faded quickly.

Nigeria

Like other British colonies, Nigeria began independence with a Westminster-style government. This First Republic was brief and ended in failure. The military intervention that ended the First Republic marked the first of several such interventions in Nigeria's postcolonial history. As in other sub-Saharan African countries, the military both ruled for long periods of time and came to believe in its right, even duty, to intervene in politics. The failed attempt at democracy also led to an effort to redesign the system during Nigeria's second experiment with democracy in 1979. The system became a presidential one, a trait that Nigeria has maintained even while making other constitutional changes.

Today, Nigeria is in its Fourth Republic. Its leader is President Umaru Yar'Adua, who replaced Olusegun Obasanjo in June 2007 after winning a controversial election the preceding month. Domestic and foreign election observers criticized the presidential vote as fraught with fraud. A European Union delegation, for example, stated that the election fell "far short of basic international and regional standards for democratic elections."[29] A former military leader, Obasanjo handed over power to give democracy a chance in 1979, and the handover of power from him to Yar'Adua in 2007 marked the first peaceful transfer of power from one elected president to the next in Nigeria's history as an independent country. Prospects for a consolidated democracy in Nigeria remain weak. It will likely take years to determine if the specter of military intervention has been exorcised, and if the tumultuous and internationally criticized 2007 elections were an anomaly or if they signaled Nigeria's move, once again, away from democracy.

Iran

The current Iranian regime is the product of a 1979 revolution, which overthrew the American-supported shah. It combines features resembling a Western-style democracy—including an elected president and legislature—with oversight by religious leaders. These leaders can challenge specific policy provisions of the government or influence the shape of that government by controlling which candidates are allowed to run for political office.

Iran's current political system is a theocracy. As discussed earlier in the chapter, this is a system in which religious leaders control political decisions, and religious law provides the basis for policy decisions. The attempts of the Guardian Council to limit reform by blocking "unacceptable" candidates from running for political office is one example. Later chapters of the book cover in more detail the institutional powers of the religious clerics, and the way in which conservative religious leaders have used their unelected political positions to thwart reform.

For now, consider the role of the **Supreme Leader** in the Iranian system. A second chief executive in addition to the president, the Supreme Leader is the more powerful of the two. He has authority over all political decisions in which he seeks to intervene and works closely with other institutions, such as the Guardian Council, to provide a check on the elected institutions of the Iranian government. Following the 1979 Revolution, the first Supreme leader was Ayatollah Ruhollah Khomeini. The current Supreme Leader is Ayatollah Ali Hoseini-Khamenei.

Iran's president is Mahmoud Ahmadinejad, a conservative and a very different figure from his predecessor, the more moderate Muhammed Khatami. Khatami's attempts to reform the political system and society had made him popular with many in Iran. His election in 1997 and reelection in 2001 created problems for religious conservatives, especially since the legislature alongside him was similarly reform-minded during most of his second term. This changed in 2004 when the Guardian Council, the institution in charge of approving legislative candidates, prevented reform-oriented candidates from running for the parliament. The result was a much more conservative legislature. It was also a sign of things to come. Ahmadinejad's election in 2005 consolidated the control of conservatives and hardliners over the elected institutions of the Iranian government, though cracks in their political dominance began to appear by 2007. The 2009 Iranian presidential election, in which Ahmadinejad is expected to seek reelection, will be a test of the ability of conservatives in Iran to maintain their control over the elected components of the Iranian theocracy.

> In the Iranian political system, the **Supreme Leader** is a chief executive with more powers than Iran's elected president. He has the ultimate ability to rule on political matters, and is a cornerstone of the Iranian theocratic political system.

COMPARATIVE EXERCISE

Support for the EU in Several European States

This chapter's comparative exercise explores the question of attachment to membership in the European Union in a number of European countries, including one of this book's core cases: the United Kingdom. As the project of European integration continues, perhaps toward something like a "United States of Europe," the question of how much the societies of the existing European Union member states support the EU becomes increasingly important. Understanding such support at both the individual and state levels of analysis is a focus of a number of scholars who study comparative and international politics. The study in this chapter uses the state level of analysis by aggregating individual level survey data from a number of EU countries.

As discussed in the previous chapter, a common approach when using the state level of analysis is the "most similar" version of the comparative method. In this approach, a scholar looks at otherwise similar countries (e.g., EU member states) that vary on the dependent variable (support for their state's EU membership). Because of the similar features of EU states (relative economic development; same region of the world, etc.), the researcher seeking to understand support for membership in the EU can control for many possible explanations. Given the less economically developed nature of many of the Eastern European countries that joined the EU in 2004, one would not want to include any of those countries in such an analysis. Thus, the most similar comparative study here includes a number of countries that had been part of the EU when there were only fifteen members: Finland, Ireland, Italy, the Netherlands, and the United Kingdom.

Measuring the Dependent Variable

The decision about how to measure variables is an important one in any research project. In this exercise, two questions from the Eurobarometer 65 survey are used to capture the dependent variable, support for membership in the EU.[30] The Eurobarometer is an ongoing survey of people in EU member states sponsored by the EU. The Eurobarometer 65 survey involved data collected in the spring of 2006.

The two questions are: "Generally speaking, do you think that [OUR COUNTRY]'s membership in the European Union is a good thing?" and "Taking everything into account, would you say that [OUR COUNTRY] has on balance benefited or not from being a member of the European Union?" The measure for the dependent variable is the percentage of respondents answering that membership is a "good thing" added to the percentage answering that the country has benefited from membership. A "high" score is one in which the percentage of respondents giving pro-EU answers is over 120 percent combined (i.e., above 60 percent on average for each question). "Medium" support is 90 to 120 percent. "Low" support is under 90 percent.

It is important to remember that which survey questions researchers use to measure a particular variable can have a large impact on their findings. In the case of this comparative exercise, using different questions would have generated different assessments of the populations' views about the EU. The Netherlands scored very high using the two questions above, while Italy was average. Yet, if one looks at a third question

asked on the survey—whether the EU has a positive or negative "image" for the respondent—Italy scores quite high while the Netherlands is in the average range. Interestingly, the United Kingdom and Finland score low regardless of which of these three questions a researcher might use.

Hypotheses and Independent Variables

To get a sense about what might explain the patterns in the dependent variable, researchers first look to previous research and existing theories. In the case of support for the EU, some scholars stress the relationship between general interest in politics and support for EU membership. As early as 1970, political scientist Ronald Inglehart argued that interest in and knowledge about political circumstances related to European integration were related to support for such integration, the so-called "to-know-it-is-to-love-it" argument.[31] More recently, political scientists Radoslaw Markowskia and Joshua Tucker argued that interest in politics would be related to support for the EU if national governments were active in pushing the European integration project. Those following politics will be more likely to hear the pro-EU message.[32] Most EU member-state governments fall into the category of active proponents of the European integration. According to this hypothesis, *the "political interest" hypothesis*, countries with politically interested populations should be more supportive of their countries' EU membership.

Although the Eurobarometer 65 survey report did not include the results from a question about interest in politics, a report using data from late 2003 data did.[33] This is less than ideal compared with having 2006 data on interest in politics. However, comparativists often must make do with the data available to them, and this is no exception. The 2003 survey question asks about interest in politics in the respondent's country, in other EU countries, and in the rest of the world. An independent variable was created from this question by adding together the percentages who said they were interested in each of these three topics. A "high" score was given to a country where more than 150 percent total—an average of 50 percent for each of the three topics—expressed interest in politics. A "medium" score was given for totals between 120 percent and 150 percent, and a "low" score was assigned to totals under 120 percent.

Another focus of EU analysts is the extent to which EU member-state residents see it as the cause of and/or solution to social and economic problems. As David Miliband, a United Kingdom member of parliament said in 2002, "The EU exists to help nations and regions rise to the challenges of globalisation. The test of EU action is its capacity to add value; where the EU can help tackle problems that would otherwise overcome national governments, and where it can make a constructive contribution, then it should act. Where it cannot add value, it should keep out of the way."[34] If people are concerned with problems the EU is unlikely to solve (or which they think national governments are better able to solve), they will have a less favorable view of the EU.

Such problems include immigration, which many Europeans believe is encouraged rather than discouraged by membership in the EU. Dutch social scientist Claes de Vreese has argued that "anti-immigration sentiments are of crucial importance for understanding popular support for European integration."[35] Thus, a second possible hypothesis, the "immigration hypothesis," is that countries in which the population worries about immigration as a problem will be less supportive of EU membership. The Eurobarometer 65 survey from 2006 includes a question which asks what the respondent believes are the two most pressing problems facing the country. An independent variable was created from this question by looking at the percentage who mentioned immigration. A "low" score was given to a

country where fewer than 10 percent mentioned immigration, a "medium" score for 10 to 30 percent, and a "high" score for over 30 percent.

In addition to immigration, a number of scholars have argued that the general public connects the EU to economic concerns like employment. Thus, the "employment hypothesis" asserts that people who are optimistic about employment in their country would be happy about being in the EU, while those who feel negatively about employment (i.e., those who expected more unemployment) would oppose EU membership.

The Eurobarometer survey includes a question about whether the respondent expects the country's employment situation to improve, get worse, or stay the same over the next twelve months. An independent variable was created from this question by subtracting the percentage who answered worse (i.e., those who expected more unemployment) from the percentage who answered better (expected unemployment to decline). A country in which the difference was between 10 and 25 percent—showing optimism about the coming year—was scored as "high." If the difference was between 10 and –10 percent, the country was coded as "medium," and where the difference was between –10 percent and –25 percent, the country was coded as "low."

Results

The analysis of the patterns of the dependent and independent variables shows strong support for one hypothesis but mixed support at best for the remaining two. The results are presented in Table 2.1. The first column in the table to the right of the countries includes the category rankings for the dependent variable, support for EU membership. The next three columns are the "scores" on the three independent variables corresponding to the study's three hypotheses.

The first two independent variables do not share a clear-cut pattern with the dependent

Table 2.1 Summary of the Results of an Analysis of Support for EU Membership

Country	Dependent Var.	Ind. Var. 1	Ind. Var. 2	Ind. Var. 3
	(Support for EU Membership)	(Interest in Politics)	(Immigration as a Problem)	(Expectations about Econ.)
Ireland	HIGH	MEDIUM	MEDIUM	HIGH
The Netherlands	HIGH	HIGH	MEDIUM	HIGH
Italy	MEDIUM	HIGH	MEDIUM	MEDIUM
Finland	LOW	LOW	LOW	LOW
The United Kingdom	LOW	LOW	HIGH	LOW

variable. The interest in politics variable contains the same categories as support for EU membership for the Netherlands, Finland, and the United Kingdom, but not for Ireland and Italy. Likewise, the immigration variable is the same as the dependent variable for Italy and Finland but not the other three. Based on these results, it is possible to reject the first two hypotheses.

The pattern of the third independent variable, however, is identical to the dependent variable. Ireland and the Netherlands score high, Italy receives a medium score, and Finland and the UK score low. The apparently strong connection between economic expectations and support for EU membership should concern those who support deeper EU integration. If the public's support for the EU is driven by how it views the economy, political elites in Europe who support a stronger European Union must work to improve expectations about the economy and produce lasting economic results. However, as Chapter 13 describes in greater detail, policies that aim to improve the economy in the short run can have negative long-term consequences.

Think and Discuss

Given this chapter's discussion of the state and the results of its comparative exercise, what are the obstacles to the European Union evolving from an international organization of member states to a single state with internal territorial divisions similar to the United States? Is the goal of a "United States of Europe" unrealistic?

CONCLUSION

This chapter presented several more key concepts in the study of comparative politics. These included state and nation, as well as related terms, such as nationalism and patriotism. It is important to keep straight the differences among these various terms. In the case of state and nation, both involve membership and territorial boundaries. But while an actual territorial boundary is a necessary part of a state, it is the national group's *belief in its right* to control a particular region that brings territory into the concept of nation. A nation need not actually control such a territory to exist as a nation. In addition, the membership and territorial boundaries may or may not coincide between nations and states. American national identity, for example, is one in which the territorial and membership boundaries of state and nation correspond closely. But states can exist with more than one nation within them, and nations can be spread across more than one state (such as the Azeris in Azerbaijan and Iran). Finally, states are more than just units marked by borders and possessing permanent populations. They include institutions that make rules over society. These rules generally trump the regulations of other rule-making organizations, giving the state sovereignty over the population within its territory.

Regarding the terms state, regime, and government, reflecting on how likely each is to change and how a change in one of them affects the others, can help one to grasp their differences. Of the three, the state is least likely to change dramatically in the short term, especially in terms of its territorial and population components. There was a noticeable increase in the number of states in the world in the twentieth century, but there were even more government and regime changes. Regime changes are also not incredibly common, but changes to a particular state's political system occur more often than the breakup of existing states. Most common is a government change, especially if one uses the narrow definition of government. One can often see the government change in a parliamentary system (the particular prime minister and cabinet), but the system remains a parliamentary democracy. Remember the "Did You Know?" box on government change in Italy in the second half of the twentieth century!

Government changes do not necessarily result in changes to the regime or state. Changes to the regime, however, will generally coincide with changes in the set of political leaders, though some authoritarian leaders win founding elections and maintain power after a transition to democracy. Regime change does not generally bring changes in the territorial or demographic makeup of the state, but obviously does change its institutional arrangements.

Comparative politics has traditionally devoted far more attention to the state than to society or the nation. But societies craft states, and nationalist ambitions can tear them apart. Because society, nation, and state combine to form the arena of domestic politics, it is impossible to understand one without the others. Therefore, before focusing on political institutions later in the book, the next section examines various structures—economic, cultural, and identity-based—within societies and nations. These economic and social structures interact with the structures of government to produce the conditions under which individuals make political choices.

Key Terms

Citizenship, p. 36
Civic nations, p. 27
Dual citizenship, p. 36
Ethnic nations, p. 27
Government, p. 47
Ideal type, p. 27
International recognition, p. 46
Mestizo, p. 31
Nation, p. 26
National identity, p. 26
Nationalism, p. 28
Nationalist, p. 28
Nation-state, p. 28
Norms, p. 25
Overlapping homelands, p. 29
Patriotism, p. 46
Regime, p. 47
Society, p. 25
Sovereignty, p. 45
State, p. 35
Stateless, p. 36
Supreme Leader, p. 57
Territorial autonomy, p. 28
Theocracy, p. 47
Union republic, p. 41
Westminster political system, p. 48

3

Economic Class, Development, and Globalization

Learning Objectives

After reading this chapter, you should be able to:

- Define key terms such as *class* and *globalization*.
- Describe the social and cultural changes that accompany economic development.
- Discuss globalization, its role in economic development, and whether it helps or hurts the poor around the world.
- Describe the class structures, level of economic development, and degree of globalization in the ten Topic in Countries cases.
- Explain the arguments that globalization (1) strengthens states, (2) weakens states, or (3) has mixed effects.

Reivu Umukoro is a mother of four, who lives near the oil facility in Utorogu, a community in Nigeria's Niger Delta region. This 70,000 square kilometer region produces most of Nigeria's oil. The only benefit Umukoro has received from living in this oil-rich territory, however, is the ability to dry recently harvested cassava (the most important food product in southern Nigeria) in the fires produced by the oil facility as it discharges unused natural gas.[1] Meanwhile, her nearby town lacks electricity and clean drinking water.

Umukoro's story is not unique. The suffering faced by citizens of postcolonial Nigeria comes partly from their government's failure to translate the wealth generated by oil revenues into a diversified economy with a vibrant middle class. In addition to the importance of this story for ordinary Nigerians, Nigeria's economic setting matters for those seeking to understand the country's political outcomes and those of other countries like it. ■

Look for this icon to point you to **Deepening Your Understanding** features on the companion website www.college.cengage.com/politicalscience/barrington, which provide greater depth for some key content.

A considerable number of comparativists view economic structure as the primary factor that shapes newly created political systems, fosters changes in these systems over time, and affects the policies they generate. Such scholars consider it impossible to understand politics in isolation from economics. It therefore makes sense to begin this book's detailed discussion of structural explanations by focusing on economic structure.

Some proponents of the economic structural approach, known as "economic determinists," hold that economic structures *determine* the choices an individual makes in the political arena. Other theorists do not go so far, highlighting economics as a key factor in an individual's political choices but not the entire story. Either way, economic structural arguments are based on the idea that one cannot fully understand individual political decisions by focusing on the decisions themselves. Rather, only by understanding the underlying economic structure can one make sense of important policy decisions or other major political outcomes.

The relationship between economics and politics is not unidirectional. Politics also shapes elements of economics. The interplay between economics and politics is treated by many political scientists as its own field, **political economy**. In addition to studying economic effects on politics and political effects on economics, political economists examine more complex relationships. Chapter 13, for example, explores in more detail types of economic systems distinguished by the extent of government intervention in the economy, as well as the formulation of specific economic policies by governments and the role of the success or failure of these policies in evaluations of government "performance." In contrast, the current chapter centers on the extent to which economic structure influences politics. In other words, this chapter mostly looks at only one part—the economic structure affecting political outcomes part—of the complex relationship

between economics and politics that political economists study in depth.

There are three broad themes in the study of economic structural effects on political outcomes: class, economic development, and economic globalization. Each deserves its own detailed discussion, but these three topics are also related to one another. Developed economies have different class structures from lesser developed ones, and economies that are more interconnected with other economies often develop at a faster rate.

Class and Class Structure

Class is a crucial concept in the study of economic structure. Discussing voting in elections, for example, comparativist Russell Dalton argues, "Social scientists have probably devoted more attention to the relationship between social class and voting than to any other social characteristic. Theoretically, the class cleavage involves some of the most basic questions of power and politics that evolve from Marxian and capitalist views of societal development. Empirically, one's position in the class structure is often a strong predictor of voting choice."[2]

Different scholars define and use the term class in different ways. Many scholars who research political behavior measure class according to an individual's level of wealth and/or income. Scholars who study economic development are much more likely to think of class in terms of occupation, status, property ownership, and the resulting relationship to those with other occupations, levels of status, or ownership circumstances. Sociologist Max Weber brought

---

Political economy is a field of political science that focuses on the connections between economics and politics.

A **class** is a large group of people with similar economic attributes that shape their lifestyles and life chances.

class and status together by emphasizing an individual's present lifestyle and future life chances. Most would agree that ownership of property improves one's life chances, but Weber believed this was far from the only factor. Weber's ideas influence how class is used in this textbook, to refer to a large group of individuals with comparable social and economic attributes and, as a result, broadly similar current lifestyles and future life chances.

Karl Marx also had a profound impact on how many social scientists understand class and class conflict. Part historian and part forecaster, Marx believed that economics provides the "substructure"—think of a house's foundation—for everything else in society. Marx viewed class regarding *how* money was made rather than simply about *how much* money was made. Marx emphasized the **mode of production** as the cornerstone to any understanding of society and government.[3] The mode of production is the structure of an economy based on the methods of production, patterns of property ownership, and relations between workers and owners. Accordingly, different modes of production correspond to different patterns of control over the **means of production**, which are the individual factories and businesses that produce goods and the machines and inputs used to produce them. Marx argued that the wealth capitalist production generates—and, especially, the subsequent inequality in wealth between classes—is the key to understanding economics, social relations, and politics.

Marx emphasized two main classes in capitalist society: the **bourgeoisie**, who own the means of production, and the **proletariat**, who use the means of production in their work but do not own them. Relations between classes flow from this disparity in ownership. The bourgeoisie exploit the proletariat by forcing them to receive far less in pay than the value of their work. This difference, called surplus value, is an important component of the profits that

the bourgeoisie receive from capitalist production. Though Marx saw class relations as real, he also believed that power relationships and other causal processes may be hidden. Marx, and Marxists after him, rejected the idea that if something cannot be observed and measured it cannot be important to understanding patterns of behavior.

Marx's idea of a capitalist class structure with two main classes appeals to many scholars and students, but among comparativists the terms **working class** and **middle class** have generally replaced proletariat and bourgeoisie. Some divide the middle class into the **old middle class** (similar to the small business owners that made up a portion of Marx's bourgeoisie) and the **new middle class** (service, white collar, and civil service jobs). This

---

Mode of production refers to the type of economic system based on methods of production, patterns of property ownership, and relations between workers and owners.

The **means of production** are the individual businesses, factories, and other entities that produce goods, as well as the machines and other inputs used to produce them.

Bourgeoisie is a term used by political economy scholars like Karl Marx to refer to the individuals who own the means of production.

Proletariat is a term used by political economy scholars like Karl Marx to refer to the individuals who use the means of production in their work but do not own them.

The **working class** includes individuals in a variety of occupations, such as manual laborers, who have historically generated relatively low levels of income.

The **middle class** includes individuals in a variety of occupations that generate moderate levels of income, including small business owners and those in the service sector. Some scholars distinguish between the **old middle class** (capitalist owners of the means of production) and the **new middle class** (service workers, white collar managers, and civil servants).

new middle class has grown dramatically in many countries. Already by the 1950s it made up a larger portion of the American workforce than manual laborers. A few decades later, it became a majority of the workforce in many developed countries.

As other scholars considered the complexities of class in more detail, they added additional categories, creating in some cases as many as ten different class categories. Two of these additional categories—the **upper class** (those with the greatest wealth and status in a country) and the **underclass** (the poorest in the country with few prospects for improvement in their fate)—are particularly important for us to consider. While members of the upper class have high levels of status, connections with others in the upper class, and opulent lifestyles, the underclass are those with the fewest life chances (generally the least educated) and worst lifestyles (low income, small living space, poor health). Certain ethnic or racial groups may be disproportionately found in the underclass. African Americans in the United States, for example, are three times more likely than white Americans to fall into the category of underclass.[4]

Measuring Class and Poverty

Some of the debates over class boil down to disagreements over measurement. How to measure poverty and determine who falls into the underclass category, for example, is a matter of particular contention. A typical measure used today calculates the number of people and portion of the population living on less than $1 or $2 per day of income. Though this makes sense in many developing countries, it does not take into account the cost of living in the country. As a result, others have suggested looking at those who earn a certain percentage of the country's **median income**. Median income is one way to think about the average income

Child labor is common in countries with a large underclass. Here, a young girl helps her family pick cotton in China's Xinjiang province.
(©Chien-min Chung/Getty Images)

in a particular country. It is the income level that half of the population falls below and half of the population falls above. It can be stated in terms of either individuals or households. In the United States, for example, median household income in 2006 was estimated to be $48,201.[5] This means that half of the households took in less than this amount, while the other half earned more.

Think and Discuss

The "Applying Concepts" box on page 66 presents a number of criteria that can serve as possible measures of class. Which ones are the most compelling to you? Why?

The **upper class** is the wealthiest and most powerful members of society.

The **underclass** is a term for the poorest individuals in society with few chances for improvement.

Median income is the amount of income above what those in the bottom half of the population earns but below that earned by the upper half of the population.

APPLYING CONCEPTS

Class: Indicators of Lifestyle and Life Chances

Different studies may use one or more of the following features as measures of class:

- Income
- Wealth
- Occupation
- Ownership of the means of production (land, raw materials, tools, etc.)
- Education
- Political connections
- Societal connections
- Family name or reputation

These various criteria can be put into Weber's categories of "lifestyle" and "life chances."

Class Structure

The particular arrangement of the population into different classes is known as a country's **class structure**. Class structure clearly relates to level of economic equality.[6] Countries with high levels of wealth concentration tend to have little to no middle class. Class structure can also give strong hints at the degree of industrialization a country has experienced. In a postindustrial, economically developed country, the majority of the population falls into the middle class. On the contrary, a sizeable middle class is highly unusual in a country that has not experienced significant industrialization.

Think and Discuss

If class structure is related to inequality, how can some countries (including the United States) have such a large middle class and yet such high levels of wealth concentration?

Class Consciousness and Its Decline

The extent to which the members of a class are aware of, or attached to, their identity as members of that class varies. This awareness, **class consciousness**, emerges as individuals become aware of their "location" in a particular class, develop a sense of solidarity with other members of this class, and come to deem important the relationship, usually thought of as conflicting, between their class and other classes.[7] The greater the degree of class consciousness the more important class is as a factor shaping political outcomes.

At the time of Marx's most influential writings, class divisions were fairly clear-cut, and class consciousness, particularly among the lower class, was emerging. It is interesting to note that after 1850 Marx had become more pessimistic about working class consciousness leading to a worldwide workers' revolution. One could argue that this pessimism was premature, given the large number of Communist states that emerged during the twentieth century. On the other hand, since World War II, class distinctions and class consciousness have declined throughout the world.

One of the reasons for the decline of class as a force in politics is the blurring of the line between the middle class and the working class. As Russell Dalton puts it, increased pay for certain manual labor occupations has led to the "embourgeoisement" of the working class, while the growth of the service sector, often with relatively low-paying jobs, has brought a

A particular country's **class structure** refers to the portions of the population that fall into different classes. A country that has experienced high levels of industrialization is likely to have a class structure with a relatively large middle class.

Class consciousness is the combination of awareness of belonging to a particular class, recognition of the relationship between this class and other classes, and a sense of solidarity with members of this class.

"proletarianization" of the middle class.[8] This does not mean that appeals to class—often derided in the United States as "class warfare"—have no effect on political outcomes. (In 2004, for example, John Edwards, a presidential candidate seeking the Democratic Party nomination in the United States, rallied supporters around the theme of the existence of "two Americas": the upper class versus everyone else.) It simply means that one's class is one of many parts of an individual's identity and may not be the primary identity component.

Think and Discuss

To what extent is one's class in the United States determined at birth by the class of the individual's family? To what extent is class the result of effort? How representative is the United States on this point compared with other countries around the world?

Class in the United Kingdom, France, and Germany

The United Kingdom, Germany, and France have similar class structures. Having developed economically long ago, all three have large middle classes. Class divisions have influenced politics in each of the three, but certainly less—particularly in recent years—than earlier political economy scholars such as Marx would have expected. Despite these similarities, their class structures are far from perfectly identical. The United Kingdom is the least economically equal of the three. The lower levels of inequality in Germany and France reflect a greater commitment in those countries to use government policies to level, at least somewhat, the economic playing field.

The United Kingdom

A large and generally poor urban population and early industrialization fostered sharp class divisions earlier in British history. Class no longer drives political behavior in the United Kingdom as it once did, but it remains important to understanding British political outcomes. Despite the country's large middle class, a large portion of the population would identify themselves as working class—certainly a greater portion than would embrace that label in the United States. As in other economically developed countries, the United Kingdom's upper class is small but economically and politically powerful. The top 1 percent controls a smaller portion of wealth than the top 1 percent does in the United States, but some contend that the British upper class has had greater advantages in education and personal connections than its American counterpart.

In the past, these lifestyle and life chance privileges translated into domination of British political life. During the twentieth century, however, reforms weakened the British economic elite's political power. The Conservative Party reached out to the working class, which had previously been the Labour Party's base of support. Several Conservative leaders, including former Prime Minister Margaret Thatcher, came from working or lower-middle class backgrounds.

At the same time, inequality in the United Kingdom remains a problem. From the earliest days of its industrialization, economic inequality has been prevalent in British society. At present, the United Kingdom's population is economically more equal than that of the United States, but the gap between the poorest and wealthiest remains substantial. Like many countries, gaps in income correlate with race, ethnicity, and immigrant status.

Germany

Like the United Kingdom, Germany has a large middle class and a small upper class. However, levels of inequality and poverty in Germany are much lower than in the United Kingdom. This is the product of Germany's generous welfare state, progressive taxation, and wage compression achieved through agreements between industrial unions and employers' associations.[9]

This depiction of German class structure largely describes West Germany since the 1950s and unified Germany today. However, the East German Communist state (1949–1989) had a dichotomous class structure, which consisted of a large working class and a small elite of Communist Party members. Since unification, Germany's eastern region has experienced greater levels of economic hardship than the western part of the country, and regional inequality increased during the 1990s. Privatization of state industries in the eastern *Länder*, coupled with the decision to equalize wages between the eastern and western *Länder* as much as possible, led to massive deindustrialization and unemployment in Germany's east.[10] East German enterprises, less efficient than their western counterparts to begin with, were unable to survive with higher wage costs resulting from the wage parity efforts. The worst of the economic shakeout of the 1990s has now passed. Yet, with unemployment in the east remaining stubbornly high, Germany is a country that has, between its east and its west, distinct class structures.

France

Marx recognized three "social groups" in France—capitalists, workers, and peasants—but considered only workers and capitalists to be distinct classes. For Marx, peasants were no more than a "sack of potatoes" because they could not understand their collective interests.[11] Marx plainly underestimated the importance of French peasants, failing to anticipate that they would become a key constituency of the French Republican state.

In addition, while French laborers have played a significant role in political life, not all workers share the same interests. By the nineteenth century, the French working class was divided between urban artisans—for example, skilled workers in small businesses and factories producing specialty goods such as bread and luxury items like fine porcelain—and unskilled workers in a variety of industrial and mining operations, many in the heavily industrialized north.

Even the peasants have been divided. Those in the region of Provence, for example, traditionally have practiced smaller scale farming because of dispersed land ownership. In the west of France, large concentrations of land have allowed for mechanization and single crop production.

Despite occupational and political differences and recent increases in wealth concentration related to globalization, wealth disparities in today's France are among the lowest in the world. Since the end of World War II, many elites have come to value prestige and status over financial gain, ending the influence and power of private money held by the traditional center of French wealth, the so-called "200 families."[12] The government has correspondingly instituted a variety of programs to reallocate wealth, increase purchasing power, and expand economic activity and opportunities for the working class. Some observers of France's political economy regard the resulting economy—uniting an intrusive bureaucracy, powerful unions, and government subsidized three-hour lunches—as one that is stagnant and unfriendly to innovation. Others, however, point out that these efforts have also produced free university education, universal health care, a thirty-five-hour work week, and at least five weeks of paid vacation every year.

Class in the Russian Federation, China, and India

Russia, China, and India share a legacy of a socialist approach to economic development for much of the latter half of the twentieth century. During this period, class divisions were minimized. All three followed this with a move toward capitalist economic development over the last couple of decades. While this capitalist period has generated significant amounts of wealth, it has also produced economic inequality at levels unseen in the previous period.

The Russian Federation

During the economic stagnation of the late 1970s and early 1980s, a social contract emerged between the Soviet people and the government: Don't speak out about being unhappy, and we won't make you work too hard; life won't be great, but conditions will be okay. This and other Soviet policies created a large lower class, not starving but generally not much better than those in the United States designated as living in poverty. Especially if one takes into account prestige and standard of living, there was also an upper class: the Communist Party elite.

When market economic elements were introduced in the late Soviet and early post-Soviet periods, the ensuing economic collapse hurt many people. Severe inflation meant workers and pensioners' life savings disappeared in short order. Meanwhile, a new upper class emerged. Many who belonged to this new class (called *novie russkiye*, or the "new Russians") had held important state or party positions. A few were true entrepreneurs, but most had ties to the old system's set of privileges, and sometimes ties to or "membership" in organized crime. During privatization, these connections gave them an advantage. A small number of individuals came to dominate segments of the economy and shape political developments in the 1990s under former President Boris Yeltsin. Their role was so prominent that scholars viewed the system as "oligarchic capitalism," relying on market principles to a large extent but ruled by "oligarchs."[13]

In the late 1990s and early 2000s, a small middle class also emerged, primarily concentrated in larger cities and composed of younger residents. The older and rural population remained poor, though the general prosperity of the early 2000s did trickle down a bit even to them, partly in the form of government programs, under then-President Vladimir Putin, designed to rein in discontent. Putin also successfully took on a number of the oligarchs, limiting their economic and political power as he worked to deepen his own hold on the political system.

China

Like Russia, China has seen a dramatic increase in economic inequality with the implementation of promarket economic reforms. Inequality is greater today in China than at any time since the establishment of Communist Party rule in 1949. The divide between rural areas and larger cities is especially sharp. Rural incomes did rise in the late 1970s and early 1980s, but these increases were quickly outpaced by those in large cities, and the gap grew larger as rural income stagnated by the middle of the 1990s.[14] Since more than half of the population of China still lives in the countryside, the Chinese government ignores rural poverty at its peril. Poverty is not only a rural problem. There are poor in the cities as well.

With capitalist development comes a middle class, and China is no exception. Its middle class is small (perhaps as little as 5 percent of the population), but it continues to grow. China's actions to bring former territories back into the country have made the middle class more visible and potentially destabilizing. Hong Kong, which rejoined China in 1997, brought millions of new residents, many of them middle class, to the country. Hong Kong's middle class might favor democracy, but it is less clear that the rest of China's middle class is as supportive. As political scientist An Chen argues, the Chinese middle class is used to political submission, it does not have as much economic autonomy from the state that it can translate into political power as the middle class tends to in Western countries, and many middle-class Chinese have become wealthy through links to corrupt government officials.[15]

India

India's class structure resembles that of states like Russia and China which have shifted from planned toward liberal economies. Like Russia and China, inequality has increased since liberalization. The country also has some unique aspects related to class. India's economic hierarchy corresponds roughly to the country's complex social hierarchy of mostly Hindu-based castes and tribes (see Chapter 5) and "backward classes" as identified by the government for affirmative action purposes. Also, while commentators correctly identify the growing disparity in the income of the richest and poorest, the polity in democratic India remains an arena where solutions to the hardships of those suffering from economic deprivation can be addressed. Unlike the situation in many other countries, the poor in India are more likely to vote than the rich.

At the very top of the class structure is a small group of extremely affluent business people. Three of them were identified by *Forbes* magazine as among the twenty richest people in the world in 2007.[16] Key politicians and bureaucrats might be included in this leading class as well, due to the power they can wield over the economic fortunes of both the rich and the poor.

The significant growth of the Indian economy has produced an enlarged middle class, estimated at over 300 million. It includes individuals in both the public and private sectors. The social critic Pavan Varma has referred to the middle class as a "consumerist predator" and has suggested that members of the class think "the best way to counter the unspeakable squalor and poverty and disease and illiteracy of the vast majority is to take as little notice of them as possible."[17] Surely, such a critique is an exaggeration. The middle class consists of people, including Varma himself, with a wide range of views toward the poor. Yet, Varma's critique highlights an aspect of the middle class that may generate potent political struggles in the future.

Much of the population falls into the lower classes. The poorest in India, members of the underclass living below the Government of India's official poverty line (about 22 cents per day), number about 300 million people; more than twice as many people live on $1 per day or less. They and those whose income is slightly higher live mostly, but not exclusively, in rural areas. They engage in many different economic activities in order to survive.[18] Their lives are in stark contrast to the growing middle class. Farmer suicides are widespread, as many farmers have become so in debt that they see no future and take their own lives.

Class in Mexico, Brazil, Nigeria, and Iran

Compared with countries like the United Kingdom, Germany, and France, the class structures of Mexico, Brazil, Nigeria, and Iran have a pattern more typical of lesser developed countries, with a large working and underclass. Unlike Nigeria, however, the other three do have middle classes that are sizeable enough to be a potentially important factor for understanding the countries' political developments.

Mexico

Of these four countries, Mexico has the most visible middle class, particularly in the industrial north. Estimates of the portion of the population in the middle class vary, but are often above 25 percent. The group has traditionally been politically passive, tolerating political corruption in exchange for their economic well-being. In June 2004, however, the middle class flexed its political muscle in Mexico City. Around 500,000 people—many from the middle class, but joined by those of other classes as well—protested corruption and ineffective law enforcement in the face of a growing number of murders and kidnappings in Mexico's largest cities.

Hundreds of thousands of Mexicans gather around the Independence monument on June 27, 2004, in Mexico City to protest against high levels of crime and pay tribute to victims of violent crime.

(© AP Photo/Pablo Aneli)

Having a noticeable middle class does not mean Mexican society is economically equal. The country contains a sharp division between a small number of quite wealthy individuals and a large number who fall into the working class and underclass. A 2003 report by World Bank Chief Economist François Bourguignon claimed that "(e)xtreme poverty in Mexico today affects 20 percent of the population."[19] Bourguignon stated that improvements in inequality along with economic growth were needed to make a significant dent in Mexico's poverty problem. In addition to the rural poverty in the south, Mexico's capital city, Mexico City, is home to many of the chronically poor. Many residents live in the outskirts of the city, in rundown shantytowns.

Brazil

Such conditions are even more apparent in Brazil, whose economic inequality is severe even by developing country standards. The poorest 10 percent of the Brazilian population captures less than 1 percent of national income, while the richest 10 percent captures nearly 45 percent.[20] Nearly one-third of the population lives below the poverty line; one-fourth lives on less than $2 per day. As a result, Brazil ranks among the five most unequal countries on earth. This inequality is a legacy of colonialism and slavery. Class and race are still strongly associated: white Brazilians and newer Asian immigrants have generally higher levels of education and income than black Brazilians or indigenous peoples. Inequality tends to perpetuate itself. Children of the poor have less access to education, health care, or good nutrition, decreasing future income and life expectancy.

Nevertheless, the industrial and service sectors' growth has fed an emerging middle class. The middle class's size is hard to estimate and fluctuates along with periods of economic crisis or stability, but in good times it may reach as much as 30 percent of the population. Manual workers in the formal sector of the economy make almost as much as the lower ranks of the middle class.

As in other developing countries, where the social system really breaks down is among those who work in the informal sector (see the "Applying Concepts" box on the informal economy later in the chapter). Nearly 10 percent of Brazilians declare that they are unemployed, but as much as 40 percent of the population may work in the informal economy. These workers get no health care, no pension, and no stable income. They frequently work in dangerous conditions, without state protection of their labor rights. They make very little money, often at or below the poverty line. Despite these enormous class differences, class has typically not shaped voter choices outside of the unionized workers who support the Workers' Party (PT).

Nigeria

Nigeria is a country with extreme inequality. Economists Benjamin Senauer and Linda Goetz estimate the Nigerian middle class at considerably less than 5 percent of the country's population.[21] The vast majority of the population falls into the working class and underclass. Unlike many LDCs, poverty in Nigeria is not regionally concentrated; the poor live in all parts of the country and in both rural and urban areas.

Using the $1 or $2 per day income measures of poverty shows the extent of the underclass in Nigeria. During the 1990s, more than 70 percent of Nigerians lived on less than $1 per day, and more than 90 percent lived on less than $2 per day, leading many individuals to search for or grow their own food and exchange goods through barter. Even taking into account the cost of living in Nigeria, these are stunning levels of poverty for a country with the amount of oil wealth that Nigeria has.

Although the government has expressed a commitment to addressing poverty at different times over the last couple decades, economic growth in Nigeria has hardly benefited those in poverty.[22] One of the major difficulties in addressing poverty, in addition to government corruption, is the country's high population growth rate. While the population in 1975 was around 55 million, twenty-five years later it had more than doubled; current estimates put the population at nearly 170 million by 2015.[23]

Iran

In Iran, the prosperity of the late 1960s and early 1970s brought industrialization and an emerging middle class. The expansion of the government bureaucracy under the shah helped to develop a sizeable group of "new middle class" members of the population. By the middle 1970s, however, the economic bubble had begun to burst. Few ordinary Iranians were seeing the wealth trickling down to them. Thus, though the Islamic Revolution of 1979 was clearly political and religious, it was also about transferring some of the country's prosperity to ordinary citizens.

The nature of the postrevolution economic system has prevented that transfer and limited further expansion of the middle class. The middle class is still noticeable in the larger cities, and it has been among the strongest supporters of reform in Iran. This is particularly true of the young, educated, middle-class residents of such cities as the capital, Tehran. Although the reformist former president, Mohammed Khatami, had broad support from across the electorate, his support among members of the middle class was much greater than his support among the other classes.

But there is more to Iran's class structure than its middle class. Iranian President Mahmoud Ahmadinejad was elected in 2005 partly because he expressed concern about Iran's less economically fortunate. Highlighting the extent to which Iran's oil wealth had not reached the working class, Ahmadinejad used populist rhetoric to appeal to Iran's working class and underclass, who display a good deal of class consciousness. It worked. Much of his support came from those living in more rural areas of the country and those not in the middle or upper classes.

Economic Development

The topic of development underscores the way in which economics and politics are tightly linked. Though one can separate the economic components of development from the political ones, political scientists often use the term development to refer to both processes occurring at the same time—for example, the establishment and consolidation of democracy in an increasingly productive and prosperous capitalist society, whose culture is also undergoing change. In this chapter, we focus on economic development and its consequences.

Economic development involves changes in the structure of the economic system, including economic diversification, and increases in overall prosperity due to these changes. One way to summarize a country's economic system is to look at the kinds of goods it produces. Most economies develop by creating new products, using technology to increase production of existing products, and finding ways to improve worker productivity. Some economies change more quickly than others, but a general pattern—moving from agrarian economies based on labor-intensive agriculture to industrial economies based on products made in factories and then to postindustrial, service economies—is common. Moving from an agricultural economy to an industrialized one has economic consequences which in turn affect politics. It is no accident that the poorest countries in the world are those that have failed to industrialize and, at best, rely on the export of raw materials and agricultural products.

Economic Growth and Prosperity

Structural changes to the economy affect economic growth and prosperity. **Economic growth** refers to the increase in a state's economic production over a particular period of time. The standard way to measure economic growth is to look at annual changes in a country's **gross domestic product (GDP)**. A country's GDP is

the sum value of the goods and services in its economy. When researchers (academic or governmental) examine GDP over time, they often measure it in **constant dollars**. This technique controls for the additional value of goods and services resulting from inflation. Although GDP is a measure of economic activity, it measures neither tasks such as housework nor illegal economic activity. Some analysts estimate that goods and services produced or distributed illegally—often labeled the "informal economy" (see the "Applying Concepts" box on page 74)—make up more than $15 trillion globally!

Economic development refers to changes over time in an economy that enhance its productive capacity and improve society's prosperity.

Economic growth is one way of thinking about economic development.

Changes in growth are typically measured by the **gross domestic product (GDP)** over time.

GDP is often presented in **constant dollars**, which controls for increased value due to inflation.

APPLYING CONCEPTS

The Informal Economy

A July 2002 World Bank–sponsored publication describes the **informal economy** as including "unreported income from the production of legal goods and services, either from monetary or barter transactions—hence all economic activities which would generally be taxable were they reported to the state (tax) authorities."[24] It thus commonly includes goods and services provided by domestic workers or street vendors, and illegal exchanges such as prostitution or black market trade. It is difficult to monitor. Because of the elusive nature of the activities involved in the informal economy—and because different scholars have different definitions of what it entails[25]—it is one of the concepts that comparativists struggle to measure accurately. As a result, estimates of the value of goods and services made up by the informal economy vary, though some believe it comprises over 40 percent of the total value of economic activity across Africa and Latin America.[26]

Prosperity refers to the overall wealth and standard of living of a country. One could use GDP alone to get a sense of a country's prosperity, but that would tell little about how the average person in that country is doing. A country might have a GDP five times the size of its neighbor, but if it has ten times the number of people of its neighbor, it is hard to call it more prosperous. One approach to solving this problem is to take population size into account. Thus, overall prosperity of a country is often measured in terms of **GDP per capita**. This is the GDP of the country divided by the number of people in the country.

Using GDP per capita to gauge a country's prosperity is better than GDP alone, but it can still be misleading. A second "correction" to GDP takes into account the cost of living, adjusting for how much one can purchase with the same amount of money in different countries. This adjustment to GDP is known as **purchasing power parity (PPP)**. It can make a big difference in per capita GDP estimates. Luxembourg has the highest per capita GDP in the world. According to the International Monetary Fund's World Economic Outlook database, its unadjusted GDP per capita was estimated to be more than $117,000 in 2008. But goods and services in Luxembourg are so expensive that the PPP correction took this number down to around $83,500. In the case of Norway, GDP per capita in 2008 fell from almost $98,000 without the PPP correction to under $55,500 with it.[27]

Even when correcting for purchasing power, using GDP per capita to gauge prosperity tells an incomplete story. The United Arab Emirates, for example, has a relatively high GDP per capita PPP (around $27,000 in 2007), but has among the most concentrated income and wealth in the world. In such cases, the country may appear prosperous, but most do not share in this prosperity. Thus, economists and other social scientists also look at income and/or wealth inequality. These statistics are typically estimated by considering the percentage of income or wealth controlled by the wealthiest 1 percent, 10 percent, 20 percent, and so on, as well as the bottom 40 percent or 20 percent of the population. Wealth and income inequality relate to the concept of class structure, presented earlier in the

---

The **informal economy** includes the portion of a country's economic activity from illegal undertakings, as well as unreported legal economic activities.

Prosperity refers to the overall wealth and standard of living of a country. It is usually measured by per capita GDP or other similar statistics.

GDP per capita is the gross domestic product of a state divided by the number of people in that state. This number allows researchers to take into account the size of the population when using GDP to get a sense of the level of prosperity in the country.

Purchasing power parity (PPP) is an adjustment to statistics such as GDP per capita, taking into account the cost of living in a given country. In countries such as Japan where the cost of living is high, GDP per capita-PPP may be dramatically lower than GDP per capita.

chapter. The more concentrated wealth is in a country, the less likely that the country has a sizeable middle class.

Types of Countries Based on Economic Development

Comparativists use the label **economically developed countries (EDCs)** for the most economically prosperous states. There are several labels for the countries that do not fall into the EDC category (see Table 3.1 on page 77). The broadest label is **lesser developed countries (LDCs)**. At the extremes of the LDC category are two subsets: the **least developed of the lesser developed countries (LLDCs)** and the **newly industrialized countries (NICs)**. LLDCs are the poorest, least economically developed countries in the world. The NICs, found especially in Asia and Latin America, are countries that have improved their economic development statistics greatly over the last several decades but still retain enough characteristics of LDCs to keep them from being broadly considered as EDCs. Some scholars consider countries such as South Korea or Taiwan as ones that used to be appropriately labeled as NICs, but are today better thought of as EDCs.

The differences in level of overall prosperity between LDCs and EDCs correspond to other differences as well. EDCs generally have a different class structure than LDCs, with sizeable middle classes in EDCs and small (though perhaps emerging) middle classes in LDCs. EDCs also have more diverse economies, while LDCs tend to concentrate their economic activity in agriculture and extraction of raw materials. Countries relying on raw materials, even raw materials like oil that can generate a lot of money, face a problem. **Finished products**, those products that are manufactured from raw materials, cost more money than the raw materials that go into them. Thus, it takes a lot of raw material sales to afford the purchase of finished products. This is even more the case the more complex the technology is that is involved in

APPLYING CONCEPTS

Income Versus Wealth

Many statistics that address economic well-being use income (wages, interest earnings, etc.) rather than wealth (the total value of an individual's assets). This is largely done because valid indicators of wealth are harder to observe. Assessments of inequality can differ significantly, however, depending on whether the measure of prosperity is income-based or wealth-based. Since wealthier individuals use their higher incomes to accumulate assets (such as property) over time, as well as inherit portions of their wealth from family members, the use of income-based statistics tends to underestimate the gap between the wealthiest and least wealthy in a particular population. In the middle 1990s, for example, the U.S. Census Bureau calculated that the top 20 percent of income earners in the country had a median net wealth that was more than twenty-three times that of the bottom 20 percent of income earners.

the finished product. Even as oil reached record highs above \$140/barrel in mid 2008, it still required the sale of a lot of oil to equal the cost of many of today's high-tech consumer goods.

Economically developed countries (EDCs) are countries with high levels of per capita GDP, a sizeable middle class, and diverse economies.

Lesser developed countries (LDCs) are countries with low per capita GDP and a small middle class. Their economic activity is often concentrated in agriculture and raw materials extraction.

The poorest countries in the world are known as the **least developed of the lesser developed countries (LLDCs)**.

The more economically developed LDCs, found particularly in Asia and Latin America, are usually called **newly industrialized countries (NICs)**.

Finished products are goods produced from raw materials. This production adds value, making finished products much more expensive than the raw materials that go into them.

Some countries' development patterns are unique enough to necessitate additional labels. The Eastern European and Eurasian post-Communist states, for example, are often called **countries in transition (CITs)**. On some economic statistics—such as per capita GDP—they resemble LDCs, but in other ways (such as their levels of urbanization and education), they look more like EDCs. In addition, a number of them are now members of the European Union, making the LDC label even more problematic. Thus, though sometimes considered an additional subset of the LDC category, the CITs are often thought of as justifying their own development category.

A large number of the NICs and CITs have attracted a great deal of investment from foreign countries in recent years. This is largely due to the perception on the part of international investors that, while somewhat risky, these countries have the potential to offer a significant return on their investment. As a result, countries as diverse as Brazil, China, Egypt, Indonesia, Mexico, Poland, and Russia also share the label of **emerging markets**.

The "Resource Curse"

For countries with a lot of oil, the incentive to focus on the extraction and export of oil is great, even if it does not encourage economic diversity. Consequently, while such countries may be fortunate to have a commodity to export that is in high demand and commands a high price, the wealth from these exports rarely generates comprehensive economic development. Political economists

Did You Know? According to a United Nations report in 1999, the assets of the world's three wealthiest people exceeded the combined gross national product of the world's forty-three poorest countries. At the time, these countries had a total population of over 600 million people.

Did You Know? In 2007, the sum of the estimated GDP-PPP figures for all the countries in the world, known as the gross world product (GWP), was $69.5 trillion. Of this, the vast majority came from EDCs, with almost $14 trillion from the United States alone!

refer to this situation as the **resource curse**. The resource curse can be thought of a vicious circle (see Figure 3.1). The discovery of oil (or some similar resource) leads a government to place priority on extraction of that resource. Because this extraction can be achieved with low-skill or foreign workers, the economy does not develop a vibrant middle class. The wealth generated by exports of the resource feeds government corruption, but is not invested into other sectors of the economy. Instead, extraction of the resource commands even greater attention from government leaders, increasingly dependent on the resource to prop up the country's economy—and to allow them to line their own pockets.

Think and Discuss

British philosophy professor Leif Wenar has argued that natural resources belong to a country's entire population; consequently, "resource curse" practices amount to theft; purchasing "resource curse" commodities is equivalent to buying stolen property; and thus Western governments should work to ensure that "resource curse" countries' populations share in the wealth from the commodity. Do you agree or disagree? Why?

The post-Communist states are typically referred to as **countries in transition (CITs)**.

The LDCs and CITs that are most desirable to foreign investors are referred to as **emerging markets**.

The **resource curse** is a term used to describe the tendency for developing countries that have the ability to export a commodity such as oil to focus on the extraction of that resource at the expense of broader economic development. The resource curse is associated with government corruption and the failure to develop a middle class.

Table 3.1 Categories (and Labels) of Development

Economically Developed Countries (EDCs)	Lesser Developed Countries (LDCs)
Other Labels: • The North • Developed Countries • More Developed Countries • Industrialized Countries • Postindustrial Countries • Rich Countries **Subcategories:** • Newly Industrialized Countries (NICs) • Countries in Transition (CITs)	**Other Labels:** • The South • Developing Countries • Underdeveloped Countries • Less Industrialized Countries • Poor Countries **Subcategories:** • Least Developed of the Lesser Countries (LLDCs) • Newly Industrialized Countries (NICs) Countries in Transition (CITs) • Emerging Market Countries

Figure 3.1 The Vicious Circle of the "Resource Curse"

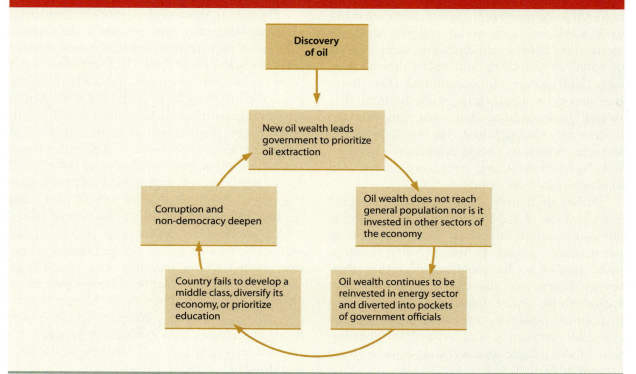

Economic Development in the United Kingdom, Germany, and France

The United Kingdom, Germany, and France are all EDCs, but their development paths differed both in time and approach. As the birthplace of the industrial revolution, the United Kingdom urbanized earlier, maintained a larger portion of its population in cities, and limited the role of the state in economic development more than other major European countries. Both Germany and France developed with the help of significant state involvement, though France's development was more uneven and took place over a longer period of time than Germany's.

The United Kingdom

Urbanization in England followed the development of agricultural practices—such as the seed drill (allowing seeds to be planted into the soil rather than spread across the soil) and crop rotation, which allowed farmers with large land holdings to be much more productive than those with small amounts of land. These developments were aided by the Enclosure Acts, a series of edicts in the 1700s and 1800s that allowed large land owners to consolidate their holdings and drive small farmers off the land. The poorer farmers had no choice but to move to the increasingly swelling cities. The rise of industrial factories, which increased productivity through labor specialization and machinery, contributed to sharp class distinctions.

Although British workers failed to accept Marx's vision of a violent revolution, economic development had important effects on the British political system. British political development tended to be evolutionary rather than revolutionary. But the changes over time—a steady move away from the concentration of political power in the hands of the monarchy and aristocracy and toward its distribution to the middle and working classes—were considerable.

Today, the United Kingdom is one of the more economically developed countries in the world and the most prosperous of the ten Topic in Countries (TIC) cases. Its GDP per capita was estimated at over $48,000 in 2008, but the United Kingdom's comparatively high cost of living dropped the per capita-PPP figure to around $39,000, or $6,000 less than that of the United States.[28]

Germany

Germany's experience of comparatively late and rapid industrialization has profoundly influenced its political development. Germany's economy in the mid-nineteenth century lagged behind that of the United Kingdom and the United States, spurring its economic and political elites to pursue a course of rapid industrial catch-up. The strategy was successful. By the end of the nineteenth century, Germany had become a major economic power pursuing an expansionist foreign policy.

Though it possessed a modern industrial economy, Germany was not yet a democracy. Germany's industrialization was a conservative modernization from above. Industrialists of the Ruhr region and landed nobility (*Junkers*) in the east—the "marriage of iron and rye"—worked in partnership with the authoritarian state bureaucracy.[29] The government disenfranchised and harassed the working class and its Socialist Party. The middle class, having failed in its 1848 liberal democratic revolution, remained politically passive. It was "content to make money" and leave the task of governing to the conservative industrialists and *Junkers*, and it supported the state's nationalist foreign policy.[30] Rapid industrialization created a large working class, which fragmented into a reformist Social Democratic Party and a radical Communist Party. Class polarization survived into the Weimar Republic—the failed experiment with democracy between the world wars—contributing to the rise of the Nazi dictatorship.

Following World War II, economic *and* democratic reconstruction became the new pattern of development in the Federal Republic (West Germany). Out of the rubble of the war, the "economic miracle" of the 1950s and 1960s transformed the Federal Republic into a prosperous country. Growth rates in the 1950s exceeded 8 percent per year and averaged 4.4 percent from 1960 through 1973.[31] These impressive growth rates were matched by low inflation, essentially full employment, and large trade surpluses. Moreover, all classes partook of the prosperity, which helped legitimize the new democratic republic. The economic miracle ended with the oil shocks of the 1970s.

The German Democratic Republic (East Germany) also enjoyed strong growth in the 1960s and 1970s. Its economy was propped up by the combination of cheap oil from the Soviet Union, West German loans, and the shelter of COMECON (the Communist trading bloc). However, economic problems set in by the mid-1970s. Although the Communist system did not officially have unemployment, state enterprises generated underemployment, basic goods were in short supply, and living standards stagnated.[32]

Economically, the first two decades of unification have been difficult. Economic growth has been anemic, averaging a meager 1.5 percent between 1990 and 2000,[33] though it picked up starting in 2006 and stood above 2.5 percent in 2008. Germany's 2008 GDP per capita was around $41,500 (slightly below France), while it's GDP per capita-PPP was roughly $34,300 (slightly above France). Unemployment in 2004 stood at 8.4 percent in the west of the country and 18.3 percent in the east.[34] This led to an overall unemployment rate well above 9 percent, though it had dropped to under 9 percent by 2007. The German economy has also seen low rates of labor force participation by women and men aged fifty-five to sixty-four, and growing fiscal strains on the welfare state.[35]

These economic difficulties have multiple causes. The government financed the reconstruction of the eastern *Länder* with deficit spending and tax hikes, and Germany's welfare state shouldered much of the burden of unification. Generous early retirement pensions and unemployment benefits absorbed unemployment in the east that arose from deindustrialization. Because the German welfare state is financed primarily through payroll taxes, the expansion of these benefits pushed up labor costs of firms throughout Germany, prompting successive waves of layoffs and early retirements, which further reduced labor force participation. A shrinking pool of workers left to finance a burgeoning number of pensioners and unemployed has placed the welfare state under enormous financial strain. Using the welfare state to hide unemployment has led to "welfare without work" that politicians have painstakingly tried to address.[36]

France

From the late seventeenth century to the present, French capitalism developed by using the power of the state to promote certain sectors, protect vulnerable business, and cushion others from economic failure. Scholars call this approach the *dirigiste* state (from the French word *diriger*, "to direct"), in which a central authority oversees economic activity. This development strategy closely resembles a mercantilist political economy, where the state governs the economy in its own interests, although in some periods the *dirigiste* approach also included the goal of social improvement or modernization.[37] Under the Second Empire (1851–1870), a modest experiment in free trade was balanced by the establishment of a system of banking and finance that would remain central to French economic development.[38] During the Third Republic (1870–1941), the economic elite and state bureaucracy agreed on basic principles that limited economic risk and protected the government's key constituencies: capitalists and peasants.[39]

Following defeat at the hands of the Nazis during World War II, however, the government renewed its emphasis on modernizing French society. The post–World War II government confiscated industries and banks, including automaker Renault, and imposed a system of five-year economic plans. The role of bureaucrats expanded, with key industrial sectors and giant firms receiving special attention. While governments of both the Left and the Right emphasized modernization in the decades following the war, they also promoted social welfare. The guiding principle was known as *solidarité* ("solidarity"), the view that society has a collective responsibility to ensure the well-being of all its members.

By the 1970s, France completed three decades of rapid economic growth, now called the "30 Glorious Years," which transformed society. While overall GDP remains lower than that of Germany or the United Kingdom, the French per capita GDP, nearly $43,000 in 2008 (with a per capita GDP-PPP of $34,150), is similar to its European counterparts. Economic growth in the past decade has been consistent, though unemployment was 9.5 percent or higher from 2003 through 2006, before dropping to 8 percent by 2008.

Economic Development in the Russian Federation, China, and India

Russia, China, and India saw significant developments in their economies during the twentieth century, under a system of state control of the economy. In the latter part of that century, all three relaxed state control dramatically. In China and India, the liberalization of the economic system produced dramatic economic growth. In Russia, economic growth in the post-Communist period was uneven—rising and falling in concord with global oil prices.

The Russian Federation

Prior to the collapse of the tsarist system in 1917, Russia was underdeveloped. Heavily agrarian and generally poor, the country had only begun the earliest stages of capitalist development. When the Bolsheviks, led by Vladimir Lenin, seized power, they initially adopted a policy called War Communism. This involved nationalization of industry and seizures of grain from the peasants to fund a long civil war. When this approach proved unsuccessful, the government turned to the New Economic Policy (NEP), which reintroduced elements of capitalism. This policy remained in place until Lenin's death and Joseph Stalin's rise to power. Stalin ended NEP, nationalized many additional industries, and attempted to collectivize agriculture in the countryside. Though he had to make tactical retreats in these efforts, by the mid-1930s the economic system looked much like it would through most of the rest of the Soviet period.

Under the Soviets, the government engaged in socialist development, using an economic planning approach (see Chapter 13). This approach emphasized heavy industry over the production of consumer goods. The result was uneven but rapid economic development before and after World War II. The displacement of World War II—not the least of which involved the dramatic number of casualties suffered during the war—set back Soviet development significantly. Still, by the 1960s and 1970s, many in the West were concerned about Soviet economic advances.

The apparent successes hid problems that grew increasingly acute during Leonid Brezhnev's rule. In the 1970s and early 1980s, economic growth slowed and worker productivity declined. Brezhnev's successor, Yuri Andropov, initially felt that cracking down on absenteeism and alcoholism would solve the problem. Andropov's protégé, Mikhail Gorbachev, continued this approach when he came to power in 1985. In less than two years, however, it was clear to Gorbachev that more substantial changes were needed, and he launched his *perestroika* (restructuring) reforms. The reforms introduced some market principles, while still protecting many inefficient state-run industries. Along with other Gorbachev reforms, *perestroika* sped up the process of Soviet economic collapse. By the end of 1991, the Soviet Union was gone.

The Russian economy has been uneven since 1991, though statistics like GDP point to dramatic growth in recent years. From 1992 through 1994, real GDP declined more than 10 percent annually. The following three years brought signs of hope, but the economy again took a sharp downturn in 1998. Conditions have since improved markedly. In the decade following 1998, Russia's growth was impressive. By 2008, its GDP per capita-PPP figure stood at over $14,600 (around $10,500 without the PPP adjustment). This is a large step up from the previous decade. For much of the 1990s, GDP per capita-PPP had hovered between $6,000 and $7,000.

The economic collapse in 1998 continues to serve as a reminder, however, of the fragile nature of the Russian economy. Russia achieved much of its post-1998 economic success due to the high global price of oil. Like other countries that depend heavily on a single source of revenue, Russia cannot assume oil profits of this sort will last forever. In addition, as economic growth occurred in Russia, inequality rose dramatically. In many respects, therefore, the Russian economy resembles that of an LDC more than an EDC, with a substantial gap between rich and poor in an economy largely dependent on the world price of a single commodity.

China

Until recently, China's history was marked by slow economic development. Its development was held back by a number of factors. These included climatic constraints (e.g., the small portion of the land of China that is suitable for agriculture), a large population that grew dramatically in the nineteenth and twentieth centuries, and efforts to control its vast territory with a centralized and heavily bureaucratized political system. Its potential was also held down by key political decisions during the Communist period, such as the Great Leap Forward and Cultural Revolution (see Chapter 11).

Over the last several decades, however, Chinese economic growth has been sizeable. Reforms following the death of Mao Zedong in 1976 introduced capitalist practices to an economy previously dominated by state planners. The state's control over economic activities declined during the 1980s and 1990s, although the state remained active in overseeing economic progress and taking steps to protect Chinese companies from external competition. The result has been average economic growth of around 9.5 percent per year since the late 1970s. From 1980–2007, China's constant dollar GDP grew at less than 7 percent per year only three times.

Today, China's economy continues to grow at an impressive rate. At less than $3,000, its 2008 per capita GDP figure looked quite low. However, China is a country whose statistics improve with the PPP adjustment. China's GDP per capita-PPP for 2008 was almost $10,000, which is higher than the TIC cases of India, Iran, and Nigeria, and close to that of Brazil and Mexico. It is unlikely that China's economy will grow larger than that of the United States anytime in the near future, though its economy is approaching the size of the American economy if one takes PPP into account. But, because of the size of its population, the goal of catching up with EDCs in figures like per capita GDP, even if one takes PPP into account, is decades away.

In addition, many of its visible and highly positive macroeconomic numbers hide serious economic and financial problems below the surface. Tax revenue as a portion of GDP is quite low, estimated at well under 20 percent in the early 2000s; bad debt in state-owned banks is very large (potentially as high as 50 percent of GDP!); and the consequences of growing unemployment and underemployment, produced by the slow phasing out of inefficient state-run enterprises, continue to concern the Chinese government.[40]

IN THEORY AND PRACTICE

China and Modernization Theory

Modernization theory is one of two main theories that seek to explain differences in capitalist development and its social and political consequences across countries. The other such theory, dependency theory, is introduced in the "In Theory and Practice" box on Nigeria. Modernization theory is based on a belief that Western Europe and the United States provide a model for economic and political development.[41] Like Marx, modernization theorists suggest that economic development follows "stages of growth"; however, these stages are notably different from those detailed in Marx's theories. In modernization theory, capitalist democracy represents the pinnacle of development. Popular especially in the 1950s and early 1960s, modernization theory reemerged with the collapse of Communist rule at the end of the Cold War.

Modernization theory predicts that a number of social, cultural, and political changes take place along with economic development. These include **urbanization**. Bigger cities allow the factories to be situated near a large number of workers. Development is also associated with increases in education and literacy rates. In order for a country to develop economically, it needs **physical capital** and **human capital**. Physical capital refers to the machines and factories workers use to produce goods and provide services. While it is imperative that a factory have up-to-date and well-functioning machinery, human capital is no less important. Workers must be competent and possess relevant skills. Governments invest in human capital through their support of education. Modernization theory also proposes that economic development is related to cultural changes. As people become more prosperous, gain education, and live in larger cities, changes in underlying values, such as the relative importance of freedom versus order, occur. Finally, modernization theorists argue that economic development fosters democratization, largely due to the creation of a large middle class that values political equality.

Proponents of modernization theory point to the economic success of many Asian countries and the political liberalization that has often accompanied it. China is a rapidly growing LDC.

Modernization theory argues that a country's move from underdevelopment to modernization can be understood and modeled after development in the West. Thus, industrialization, urbanization, Western cultural values, and democracy mark a country's move from underdevelopment to modernization.

Urbanization is the dramatic increase in the portion of a country's population that lives in large cities.

Physical capital refers to the means of production used in an enterprise.

Human capital refers to the skills and other productive characteristics of workers in a particular state.

Whether the other aspects of development that modernization theory highlights, especially the establishment of democracy, can be expected to take hold in China is uncertain.

There are several reasons to suspect that China may indeed democratize in the near future. First and foremost, there is the track record of political liberalization in countries that reach the levels of economic development that China is approaching. Second, this growth has fueled continually rising expectations, which have already been met with disappointment in the countryside and could be in the large cities as well if another economic crisis hits Asia. Third, the Chinese Communist Party has almost completely abandoned Marxist ideology and continues to scale back state-run economic activity. This does not guarantee democracy, but the less government controls society the more the door to a potential democratic China is opened. Finally, there is external pressure on China from the United States and other members of the World Trade Organization to be a good member of the international economic community. In order to do so, China must respect such legal agreements as copyrights. As China takes more forceful steps toward adherence to its international economic agreements, it is reasonable for Chinese citizens to expect a similar adherence to the rule of law domestically.

Why might one not expect China to democratize anytime soon? Unlike in many other cases of democratization, the Chinese middle class appears unlikely to push for democracy. For many middle-class Chinese, the costs of political instability outweigh the potential benefits of increased political rights, and connections between the middle class and the state remain strong. Chinese leaders also saw what happened to the Soviet Union. The Chinese government witnessed the collapse not only of Communist Party control but also of the Soviet Union itself under the weight of forces released by Gorbachev's political reforms. Chinese Communist officials may envision greater democracy in the future, but even if modernization speeds up this process, the lesson that the Soviet Union provides to Chinese leaders makes a democratic China unlikely any time soon.

India

Along with China, India has one of the oldest civilizations on earth. Urban settlement and small-scale trade in the Indus River Valley can be traced back as far as 2500 B.C. Over the next three thousand years, portions of the territory of present-day India became united, were torn apart again, and fell under outside control (such as Mongol rule from the twelfth through fourteenth centuries). Still, during the centuries prior to British colonial rule, India had one of the world's largest economies. Estimates are that from the 1500s to the early 1700s, only China's economic production was larger than India's. During the 1700s and 1800s, however, countries such as England, France, and the United States began to emerge as the world's economic powers. India's development was directed to the benefit of the British, who controlled India from the mid-1800s until 1947.

In the postindependence period, India turned to economic planning, relying on Soviet-style five-year plans. In 1991, India began the transition from a planned to a liberal economy. In fact, private enterprise played an important role prior to that date, and state-run enterprises continue to play a role to this day. But in 1991 the country's economy underwent an important change in emphasis, moving away from government planning and toward a greater emphasis on economic liberalization (this policy change is discussed in more detail in Chapter 13).

India's growth rates have varied. During the government's first postindependence economic plan (1951–1956), the average was 3.6 percent. During the fourth plan (1969–1974), growth barely averaged 2 percent. During the seventh plan (1985–1990), growth rates rose to just over 6 percent, approximately the same average in the early stages of the liberalization period that followed the seventh plan. In the last few years, though, growth rates have risen dramatically to between 7 and 9 percent per year. These recent changes have led many to believe that an economic "take-off," similar to that which began three decades ago in China, is well underway in India.

Estimated at just over $1 trillion in 2008, India's GDP places it as the twelfth largest economy in the world. The breakdown of GDP by sector is approximately 51 percent services, 28 percent industry, and 21 percent agriculture. Like many other countries highlighted in this text, India's GDP per capita and GDP per capita-PPP figures differ markedly. While the former was estimated at under $1,100 in 2008, the latter was over $4,500.

Economic Development in Mexico, Brazil, Nigeria, and Iran

The remaining four TIC cases have more traditional LDC features. All have significant poverty (with noticeable regional differences), have historically focused on raw material exports, and to varying degrees have fallen victim to the "resource curse." Compared with the other two, however, Mexico and Brazil are often considered NICs or emerging market countries, partly because their economies manufacture many finished products.

Mexico

Mexico is an excellent example of the way in which economic development can foster political development. During three periods of its post–seventeenth-century history—1770–1799, 1895–1909, and 1933–1981—Mexico experienced significant economic growth. Especially high and sustained growth rates from the 1940s and 1970s fed and were fed by trends such as urbanization and improvements in education. These various periods of economic development each created changes in the social fabric of the country that made pushes for political change possible. These pushes were triggered when an economic downturn created conditions in which the population perceived a threat to their economic well-being.

Many consider Mexico to be an emerging market and even an NIC, but it remains an LDC in many ways. Its per capita GDP for 2008 was nearly $9,000, while its GDP per capita-PPP figure was over $12,300. This is slightly above Brazil and slightly below Russia, but still only around one-fourth that of the United States. Mexico produces a great deal of energy. Much of its oil reserves—the fourth largest in the Western Hemisphere—are exported to the United States, and it has benefited from high oil prices over the last few years. Yet it desperately needs to modernize and reform its domestic energy market.[42] Despite directing government assistance to its poorest states, Mexico's north remains notably more prosperous than its south.

Brazil

Brazil's early economic development revolved around the export of agricultural products and minerals. Following a brief period of trade in timber, the sugar plantation economy emerged in the late sixteenth century. Brazil industrialized by following a strategy very similar to that of Mexico in the 1930–1980 period. The policy, known as **import substitution industrialization (ISI)**, involved government protection of domestic industries from foreign competition and subsidies of key inputs such as energy and steel.

The result, as in Mexico, was a prolonged period of rapid economic growth. Between 1945 and 1973, Brazil could boast a growth rate well above the world average. By the end of the 1970s, however, Brazil's economy slowed down. The debt crisis that erupted throughout Latin America in the early 1980s put the final nail in the coffin.

Brazil still exports many primary products—by 2004 it had become the world's third largest exporter of agricultural products—but it also constructs finished products for export. The share of manufactured goods in Brazil's exports to the United States rose from 48 percent in the early 1980s to nearly 70 percent by the late 1990s. Domestically, agriculture accounts for only 8 percent of Brazilian GDP, compared with 38 percent for industry and 54 percent for services. As of 2008, Brazil's per capita GDP had reached $7,500, and its GDP per capita-PPP was more than $11,000.

Nigeria

At the time of its independence in 1960, Nigeria appeared to have greater economic potential than most postcolonial states. By African standards, it had a solid infrastructure, did not need to import food, and had a moderately diverse economy. The discovery of oil in the 1950s seemed to be a reason for even more optimism. Instead, Nigeria's economic development since independence has been uneven. The country allowed oil to dominate its export sector, making the country vulnerable to fluctuations in global prices, and it did not use its oil wealth to improve its long-term development prospects. With the 1970s oil boom came urbanization and other changes that normally accompany development. The government mandated universal primary education, a goal

that was difficult to meet but did help increase literacy in the country dramatically. Still, as recently as 2001, around 35 percent of the adults in the country were illiterate.

After rising significantly during the 1970s, GDP per capita-PPP actually declined in the early part of the 1980s and again in the early 1990s. From 1994 to 2008, it began a fairly steady rise, finally reaching $1,000 in 2003. By 2008, Nigeria's GDP per capita-PPP had improved to more than $1,350. (Without the PPP adjustment, per capita GDP stood at just under $950.) Despite the impressive growth in its overall GDP over the last fifteen years, Nigeria remains one of the poorest countries in the world. When the PPP adjustment is taken into account, its level of economic development is well below any of the other TIC cases.

In recent decades, changes in Nigeria's GDP have correlated with global oil prices. This is not surprising, as Nigeria is heavily dependent on selling oil, which provides up to 95 percent of the country's export revenue and 80 percent of total government income.[43] Thus, the dramatic rise in global oil prices from 2004 through 2008 had a positive effect on Nigeria's economy. The government could have used this increased revenue to pay down its debt and, even more important, invest in education to improve the country's human capital and bring much needed diversity of production into the economy. But the early signs—along with Nigeria's track record of spending such windfalls on short-term fixes and allowing it to be wasted by corrupt government officials—are not encouraging, appearing instead to follow closely the "resource curse" blueprint.

Import substitution industrialization (ISI) is an economic development strategy emphasizing subsidies of key domestic industries and other protectionist trade policies. It was used by countries such as Mexico and Brazil, particularly from World War II through the 1970s.

IN THEORY AND PRACTICE

Nigeria and Dependency Theory

Modernization theory's main rival is known as **dependency theory**. Dependency theory first developed among Latin American scholars (its proponents labeled *dependencistas* or *dependistas*), but the theory quickly spread across the globe.[44] Dependency theory explains the gap between LDCs and EDCs as a function of the international capitalist system and the efforts of capitalists in the EDCs and their political allies (in both EDCs and LDCs). It holds that the blatant and direct control of LDCs as colonies in the past has been replaced by less transparent conditions of dependency in the present. Dependency theorists contend that EDCs, international organizations, and multinational companies employ a series of strategies to impede LDC development, including:

- Developing trade relationships with LDCs that encourage them to specialize in a small number of raw material exports
- Encouraging LDCs to amass mounting debt, which prevents effective long-term economic planning
- Supporting the role of multinational corporations in controlling new economic development in LDCs
- Supporting repressive political regimes that maintain these conditions

Thus, dependency theory has two implications for the economic and political systems in "dependent" countries: the country stays underdeveloped economically, and it stays corrupt and authoritarian politically.

The Nigerian case supports dependency theory proponents' claims. Nigeria's dependence on natural resource exports, the failure of its oil wealth to trickle down to the general population, and the tendency for Nigeria to be dominated by corrupt, authoritarian leaders since independence are features that dependency theorists blame on the global, capitalist economy. Clearly, Nigeria and many other countries in Africa provide more evidence in support of dependency theory than the NICs in Asia.

At the same time, one can point to changes in Nigeria that are consistent with the assumptions of modernization theory. Urbanization has increased, education has improved, and consolidated democracy has become at least conceivable. Lingering corruption and the failure of the growing economy to reach ordinary citizens remain the largest blemishes against modernization and the strongest arguments in favor of dependency theory. Until Nigeria's class structure begins to resemble that of an NIC, dependency theorists will continue to single out Nigeria to support their arguments.

> **Dependency theory** argues that LDCs have become economically dependent on the EDCs through the system of international capitalism. According to dependency theorists, LDCs cannot follow the path of the EDCs—as modernization theory proposes—because their dependence on the EDCs effectively bars them from this path.

Iran

Throughout much of its history, and despite its challenging climate, Iran was agricultural. During the twentieth century, Iran experienced rapid development fueled by revenues from the sale of oil. Profits from oil exports led Iran's economy to grow sharply in the early 1970s. As often happens in countries at Iran's level of development that suddenly experience an infusion of wealth, the population's expectations of wealth rose alongside the prospering economy. These expectations have, for the most part, gone unmet.

The reasons for this disappointment are both internal and external. Poor relations with the United States have limited its economic potential since the Islamic Revolution. An even larger factor, however, is the war with Iraq during much of the 1980s. This conflict created economic displacement and focused the government on military production and procurement. Another problem is the heavy dependence on the sale of oil, which continued after the revolution. Petroleum exports make up more than 80 percent of Iran's export revenue (and up to half of government revenue). When world oil prices declined in the middle 1980s and again in the late 1990s, Iran's economy suffered.

Another challenge is the population explosion and increase in urbanization—Tehran is one of the twenty largest cities in the world—that have affected Iran's postrevolution development prospects. Urbanization normally accompanies economic development, but the religious government's opposition to birth control and encouragement of population increase also drove Iran's demographic patterns. Although population growth slowed in the middle to late 1980s, the early 1980s "baby boom" in Iran continues to have consequences. With a large percentage of the population recently entering the workforce, the government's ability to provide jobs continues to be tested.

Even more frustrating for Iran's youth, educational opportunities did not emerge alongside other development trends like urbanization. Only around 10 percent of the country's high school students are admitted to universities; many of the best and brightest have sought to leave the country to pursue educational opportunities in the West, causing a "brain drain" that further threatens long-term economic development.[45] Some of those who remain have sought to engage the system through participation in periodic political rallies and protests. Others have withdrawn and turned to drugs, though this is certainly not a problem unique to Iran.

Positive economic statistics hide many of these problems. With the rebound in world oil prices, economic growth was strong in the early part of this decade, averaging almost 6 percent annual real growth from 2002 to 2008. GDP per capita-PPP has risen as well, from just under $6,000 in 2000 to over $9,500 in 2008. Without the PPP adjustment, Iran's GDP per capita figure was around $4,500 in 2008. Significant wealth and income gaps remain. Nearly one out of seven people lives on less than $1 per day.

Economic Globalization

The opening chapter in this book introduced the idea that structures, such as economic development, can be domestic or global. This distinction is particularly pertinent due to the increasing degree of influence that forces outside a state's borders have over the internal decision making in that state. Today, states are more interconnected the ever before—economically and otherwise—both with neighboring states and with those on the other side of the world. They are also increasingly influenced by international organizations (e.g., the European Union) and nonstate economic actors (e.g., McDonalds, Nike, or Microsoft).

Social scientists have dubbed this process of international interconnections **globalization**. Although globalization is anchored by deepening

Globalization is the process of increasing connections in the areas of economics, communications, technology, and politics.

Table 3.2 Topic in Countries Cases, 2007 A.T. Kearney/Foreign Policy Globalization Rankings (of Seventy-two Countries Ranked)

Country	Overall	Economic-Total	Econ.-Trade	Econ.-FDI	Personal-Total	Technological-Total	Political-Total
U.K.	12	18	53	12	21	9	6
Germany	22	45	36	50	34	16	19
France	25	31	58	18	29	24	3
Mexico	49	50	49	43	45	41	37
Nigeria	57	39	34	37	58	65	45
Russia	62	49	54	38	60	46	52
China	66	43	44	35	67	56	65
Brazil	67	69	70	58	71	39	42
India	71	66	62	67	59	63	69
Iran	72	65	55	72	72	54	70

Source: The Globalization Index 2007: Globalization Index Rankings, *Foreign Policy*, no. 163 (November/December 2007), http://www.foreignpolicy.com/story/cms.php?story_id=4030.

economic ties between countries, scholars generally agree that it involves other aspects as well. Most measures of the extent of economic globalization use multiple indicators. Two of the most common are trade as a portion of GDP and **foreign direct investment (FDI)**. Trade includes both **imports** (goods and services produced outside the borders of a state that are brought inside those borders for consumption) and **exports** (goods and services produced inside the borders of a state that are sent outside those borders for consumption). FDI is investment from outside a country into a particular economic entity in that country with the goal of establishing a lasting presence. Because FDI is intended to develop a lasting presence, portfolio investments (such as in stocks of companies in the country) are not considered FDI. The International Monetary Fund (IMF) requires ownership of 10 percent or more of a company before the investment in that company is considered FDI.

The A.T. Kearney/Foreign Policy Globalization Index ranks seventy-two countries on fourteen components in four categories: economics, personal connections/communications, technology, and political ties. In this chapter, the discussion of globalization highlights its economic side, focusing on the way in which economic interconnectedness can shape the domestic economic and political landscape of countries around the world. Other chapters examine globalization's cultural and political manifestations. Table 3.2 summarizes the rankings of the ten TIC cases on the A.T. Kearney/Foreign Policy Globalization Index for 2007.

Foreign direct investment (FDI) is investment from outside a country into a particular economic entity in the country that is designed to develop a lasting presence. A typical guideline is investment of more than 10 percent in a company.

Imports are products and services made outside the borders of a state that are brought inside those borders for consumption.

Exports are produced inside the borders of a state and sent outside those borders for consumption.

Few economists would dispute that globalization improves overall global economic efficiency. How individual countries benefit from globalization, however, is less clear-cut. Some countries benefit from it more than others, and even within a particular country globalization can have positive and negative effects. Some argue, for example, that often only the wealthiest members of developing countries

benefit from globalization. At the same time, countries whose economies have become more integrated with other countries had higher economic growth rates in the 1990s. As a result, the chief economist of the World Bank, Nicholas Stern, proclaimed in 2001 that "globalization often has been a very powerful force for poverty reduction." He added, however, that "too many countries and people have been left out."[45]

Globalization in the United Kingdom, Germany, and France

Because many people associate economic development with globalization, it can be surprising to learn that the United Kingdom, Germany, and France—the most economically developed of this book's TIC cases—have less "globalized" economies than many LDCs. As members of the European Union, their *regional* economic interconnections are substantial. Yet their ties to non-EU members are less substantial, and a substantial portion of their economies are domestically oriented rather than tied to imports and exports.

The United Kingdom

Like residents of other countries, citizens of the United Kingdom benefit from globalization in many ways, yet a number of them express concern over its potential negative impacts. Many imported products are less expensive for British consumers—in some cases, much less expensive—than if they had been produced in the United Kingdom itself. At the same time, the large number of British multinational corporations is a source of concern. Some fear that the United Kingdom's exposure to the global economy pushes down wages at home, since companies can threaten to "outsource" jobs or move the company entirely to another country, and

workers who have lost their jobs to outsourcing have difficulties finding work and often earn less when they eventually do.

But is the United Kingdom really as globalized as British citizens believe that it is? How does it compare with the other TIC cases? Combining the A.T. Kearney/Foreign Policy Globalization Index's four components, the United Kingdom scored in the upper fifth of the seventy-two countries in 2007. Its number 12 overall ranking, however, was somewhat misleading. Although its technological and political rankings were quite high (9 and 6, respectively), its economic ranking was 18. In one of the measures of the economic component, trade, the United Kingdom ranked number 53 out of 72 countries. In an era of global capitalism, the extent to which the birthplace of the capitalist industrial revolution is sheltered from the global economy is somewhat ironic.

How can a member of the European Union be so sheltered from global trade? It is always important to consider how a particular variable is measured. In the globalization index, trade is measured by dividing the value of exports by the country's overall GDP. Including imports in the measure might increase the United Kingdom's openness to global trade, but probably only somewhat. Also, while the United Kingdom trades openly with other EU members, EU rules do not easily allow non-EU countries to penetrate EU markets. Finally, it is important to note that countries with relatively large economies generally rely less on trade. Think about your own life. How many of the things you do on a daily basis actually involve goods and services from abroad or destined for export? As you ponder this, consider that the U.S. 2007 A.T. Kearney score for the trade dimension placed it 71 out of the 72 countries examined, ahead of only Algeria.

Germany

Post–World War II Germany's economic success owes much to its strategy of "diversified quality production," or the export of high-quality, high-valued added goods that required a skilled workforce and that underwrote high wages, a generous welfare state, and extensive vocational training.[47] Regional integration through the European Union has also had important effects on German economic performance. Germany was a founding member of the institutions in 1950 that later evolved into the EU. Unlike the United Kingdom, Germany has also participated in the single European currency, the euro, since 2002. Although Germany played a central role in creating the euro, whether the country has benefited from the EU's centralized monetary policy remains a subject of political debate. Critics of the euro argue that the European Central Bank's exclusive focus on low inflation has yielded a restrictive monetary policy that is at least partly responsible for economic stagnation and unemployment in Germany.

The A.T. Kearney/Foreign Policy Globalization Index ranked Germany number 22 in its 2007 survey of 72 countries. Germany's noneconomic globalization rankings were quite high. It scored high on political integration, especially in the category of participation in international organizations like the UN (where it ranked fifth of the 72 countries examined). Its economic dimension ranking

(45 out of 72), however, put it below France and the United Kingdom. Within the economic category, Germany ranked 36 on trade and 50 on FDI. While its trade ranking was higher than the United Kingdom and France, much of Germany's trade is with other EU member-states. It also lagged well behind the United Kingdom and France on FDI. The low level of FDI has sparked much soul-searching among political and business elites, who worry that Germany's regulatory climate and high production costs continue to discourage beneficial foreign investment.

France

In France, governments of the Left and Right have sought ways to manage globalization to the benefit of French industry. In 1984, France was continental Europe's first state to make significant reforms in response to globalization. Under a Socialist Party majority government, the French began to dismantle financial regulations, denationalizing banks and later other key industries. These neoliberal reform efforts even earned former (Socialist) President François Mitterrand an award from the *Financial Times*.[48]

The 2007 A.T. Kearney/Foreign Policy Globalization index places France at 25 overall, though like many of the other TIC cases, this ranking hides variation across the globalization dimensions. France ranks 3 on the political dimension, 24 on technological connectivity, and 29 on personal contacts, but only 31 on the economic dimension. Like its EU counterparts, the trade component of the economic dimension pulls France's ranking down.

Today, Socialist politicians share the desire of many on the Right to promote a pragmatic engagement with global markets. One manifestation of this desire has been economic reforms that enabled and encouraged firms to invest abroad, making it possible for French companies to compete globally by merging across national borders and penetrating into new markets. Consequently, a French firm, Sodexho, is the largest provider of institutional food services in the United States (including on American college campuses), and Renault owns and controls the Japanese auto giant Nissan. This approach has also led France to have one of the highest levels of foreign direct investment in the world. Although France's overall FDI ranking on the 2007 A.T. Kearney Globalization index was 18, this understates FDI into France. The index's FDI measurement rules control for the size of the country's economy. In absolute terms, France had more FDI inflows from 2001–2004 than all the other TIC cases except the United Kingdom and China.

While the French government has worked both to manage and to encourage globalization, new unions, parties, and movements in France offer another alternative to free market globalization called *altermondialisation* ("alter-globalization").[49] One activist, José Bové, started the Confédération Paysanne, a labor union for peasants, and went to jail after participating in the ransacking of a partially constructed McDonald's in the town of Millau in 1999 to protest the government's support of American trade policies. In 2005, French citizens bucked the government and voted against the approval of a new European Union constitution, which many, particularly on the left, believed went too far in its embrace of American-style free markets at the expense of the French working class. In 2006, students and young people, using the Internet and text messaging, organized huge demonstrations against a government plan to reduce their employment rights as a way to make French labor more competitive on the global market.

Globalization in the Russian Federation, China, and India

Russia, China, and India have a "Jekyll and Hyde" relationship with globalization. The increased economic ties to other countries, particularly in the West, have helped fuel economic expansion over the previous decade. On the other hand, all three countries' efforts at encouraging FDI into their countries have been hampered by corruption, as well as concerns among the elite and masses about the economic, social, and political consequences of increased connections with forces outside their country. These patterns are most apparent in India.

The Russian Federation

Russia's economic ups and downs in the 1990s were driven in part by its increasing connections to the global economy, but it has not become the player in international trade and finance that some had anticipated. Russia faces two significant problems. The first is a legacy of the Soviet period. Much of Russian industry remains inefficient, producing products with little appeal in regions such as Western Europe. Russia exports energy, but Russian finished products are in low demand. The second problem is corruption and the lack of "rule of law." Rule of law involves government holding itself accountable for any illegality of its actions and businesses honoring the terms of contracts (for more on the concept of rule of law, see Chapter 6).

Russia's 2007 A.T. Kearney/Foreign Policy Globalization Index ranking placed it 62 out of the 72 countries. Its economic ranking was 49, its technology ranking was 42, and its political ranking was 52. Its personal contact ranking was 60 of the 72 countries—higher than China, Brazil, and Iran but lower than Nigeria and India. Within the economic dimension, Russia's FDI ranking stood at 38, but its near trade ranking was noticeably lower at 54.

Topic in countries

China

Repeatedly being informed of the large trade deficit that the United States has with China and seeing "Made in China" on scores of products they buy, many Americans view China as the poster child of globalization. They would be surprised to learn that the A.T. Kearney/Foreign Policy Globalization Index ranking for China in 2006 placed it 66 of the 72 countries ranked. Like some of the other TIC cases, China's economic ranking was quite different from its personal, technological, and political rankings. In China's case, however, the economic ranking (43) was much higher than its ranking in the other three categories (67, 56, and 65). Its FDI ranking within the economic category was 35, the third highest of the ten TIC cases.

Despite its desire for FDI and the large increases in imports since its membership in the World Trade Organization in 2003, China remains less open to global connections than many countries. China's long commitment to mercantilist policies—fed by nationalism and the country's historical experience with allowing foreign penetration—prevents closer ties with the global economy. One of the most important questions for the international community is whether China will accept norms, agreements, and "procedural disciplines" from the outside when it fails to accept these practices internally.[50] Domestically, the country has liberalized economically without dramatic political liberalization. Internationally, it is hard to imagine how China can avoid political integration as it continues to pursue additional economic integration.[51]

India

India's reforms in 1991 encouraged connections with the world economy, but India also has advantages over some of its rivals in enhancing such involvement. In contrast to Russia or China, for example, English is deeply embedded in India. A vibrant English-language press exists, education at English-medium schools is in great demand, and it is the language of instruction in most universities. The presence of a workforce relatively fluent in English facilitates EDC outsourcing of information technology work to India. Call centers—handling customer service for a variety of American companies—are located at many sites in India.

Facility in English has fostered emigration. Indeed, Indians constitute one of the largest expatriate communities scattered around the world. The linkages have brought a variety of advantages to India beyond the remittances from incomes earned abroad. Expatriate Indian communities, sometimes known as "Non-Resident Indians" (NRIs), in settings as varied as the United States, the United Kingdom, Tanzania, and the United Arab Emirates, have established business ties to India. The State Bank of India (SBI) has branches across the world. It primarily caters to the expatriate Indian community, though its loans are not confined to that group.

Although these examples—and others such as the Tata Group's purchase of the Corus Group, a British-Dutch steel maker, for over $12 billion in late 2006—signify the aspiration of a part of the Indian business class to involve itself more in the international economy, that involvement remains quite limited. India's 2007 A.T. Kearney/Foreign Policy Globalization Index ranking stood at 71, ahead of only Iran. It ranked 66 in economic integration, with comparatively low ranks on both trade (62) and FDI (67). New FDI is rising sharply, but remained under $10 billion in 2007, far below India's needs according to Prime Minister Manmohan Singh, and well below that received by more globalized Asian countries such as Singapore.

What explains India's modest FDI rates? Elements of the Left remain deeply suspicious and resist moves to open the economy. In parts of the country, for example, Coca-Cola has become a symbol of globalization and has been targeted by political activists. When land is sought for both national and international industries, local political leaders have stimulated peasant opposition to their loss of land. Selling public corporations to international firms has elicited strong opposition by labor unions, though once again such opposition has often been solicited by individual politicians. Thus, India's open political system has allowed politicians to voice the concerns of people who fear the consequences of globalization, thereby placing constraints on other political leaders' efforts to become more fully a part of a globalized world.

Globalization in Mexico, Brazil, Nigeria, and Iran

To varying degrees, Mexico, Brazil, Nigeria, and Iran face a classic LDC problem: they tend to produce commodities for export and rely on imports of finished products. Yet, there are important differences. The four vary noticeably in their economic globalization. Also, while Brazil's exports go to a variety of countries, Mexico's are directed largely at one (the United States). Nigeria and Iran both use oil to generate a large portion of their export revenue, but Iran has been much less open to finding ways to attract FDI to bolster its oil industry than Nigeria.

Mexico

Mexico's economic interconnectedness has been more regional than global. **The North American Free Trade Agreement (NAFTA)**—with the United States and Canada—is Mexico's most important trade agreement, but far from its only regional one. It also participates in trade arrangements with other Latin American countries. NAFTA was launched at the beginning of 1994. Predictions of its effects on Mexico were extreme, and the results have been moderate in comparison. Mexico has not experienced the kind of economic growth that NAFTA advocates had expected, but its trade and foreign investment numbers have improved markedly.[52]

Because Mexico's economic development was quite low and its trade barriers were quite high prior to NAFTA, the agreement did not turn Mexico into a highly globalized economy. Mexico's A.T. Kearney/Foreign Policy Globalization Index ranking for 2007 was 49, with its component rankings ranging from 50 (economic) to 37 (political). Mexico's relatively low trade ranking (49) again points to the danger of assuming that a country's participation in trade agreements (e.g., NAFTA) is a sign of high levels of economic interconnectedness.

> **The North American Free Trade Agreement (NAFTA)** is a trade agreement involving Canada, Mexico, and the United States, launched at the beginning of 1994.

IN THEORY AND PRACTICE

Mexico, NAFTA, and the 'Race to the Bottom'

Over the last few decades, a number of political economy scholars have tackled the question of globalization's political effects. A central issue in these discussions is the impact of economic interconnections and openness on the size and power of national governments. On this issue, a set of globalization theories has emerged that emphasize the state's deterioration in the face of globalization. These can be labeled "**weak state theories.**"

Comparative politics scholars have been more reluctant than antiglobalization activists to propose that globalization weakens states. Yet a number of scholarly works over the last couple decades can be placed in the "weak state" camp, such as former Harvard economist David Korten's book, *When Corporations Rule the World*.[53] Korten argues that globalization encourages a "**race to the bottom.**" Developing countries, seeking to attract multinational corporations, have to compete with one another to lure companies to move production facilities to their country. This competition encourages poorer working conditions and lower wages, reduced government oversight of economic activities, and weaker environmental standards. Standards continue to decline in a race to the bottom—cheered on by multinationals hoping to make as much money as possible.[54] Weak state theory proponents point to the presence of "sweatshops" in developing countries and persistent government corruption in LDCs as evidence of the effects of the global race to the bottom, though much of their evidence is anecdotal.[55]

As NAFTA was debated in the United States in the early 1990s, Mexico was often demonized as the source of a looming "sucking sound" of American jobs being pulled to the south.[56] Arguments against NAFTA were similar to those of "Race to the Bottom" theorists: Mexican workers will work for lower wages, the country has adopted minimal environmental standards, and large American companies will force standards even lower by promising to move factories across the border in return. Did Mexico engage in a race to the bottom after NAFTA? The evidence is mixed. Some problems associated with a race to the bottom, such as corruption and environmental concerns, existed long before NAFTA but have certainly not been solved by it. Environmental conditions have improved in some areas and worsened in others.

A straightforward answer to the question of NAFTA's effects is also complicated by economic problems that coincided with the launch of the trade agreement. A large amount of investment flowed into Mexico in advance of NAFTA's commencement; however, by the end of 1994, the amount of investment leaving the country was reaching a crisis level.[57] In part because of this, the Mexican currency, the peso, fell dramatically against the dollar. The resulting economic downturn had a great effect on real (inflation adjusted) wages in the country, which declined 20 percent. Real GDP declined more than 6 percent in 1995. Thus, NAFTA critics who point to problems such as minimal gains in real wages in the country are correct, but largely because the baseline dropped so much in 1994 and 1995. Since 1996, gains in real wages have been sizeable,[58] challenging the idea that NAFTA fueled a sustained "race to the bottom" in Mexico.

Weak state theories argue that globalization limits the ability of governments to tax, spend, and regulate.

An important component of weak state theories is the concept of a **race to the bottom**, in which states lower standards and reduce regulations in an effort to attract or maintain the presence of large corporations.

Brazil

As in much of the rest of the world, the 1980s and 1990s saw Brazil embarking on a project of economic reform that limited state involvement in the economy, lowered protectionist barriers, and opened the economy up to free trade and globalization. Like Mexico, many of these connections are more regional than truly global. Unlike Mexico, however, Brazilian trade is highly diversified in terms of export partners. By the mid-1990s, only 20 percent of Brazilian exports were destined for the United States, compared with over 80 percent of Mexico's exports. An additional 24 percent of Brazilian exports went to other Latin American countries, primarily its Southern Common Market (Mercosur) partners: Argentina, Paraguay, Uruguay, and Venezuela.

Nevertheless, Brazil ranked well below Mexico and most other countries on the 2007 A.T. Kearney/Foreign Policy Globalization Index. At number 67 overall, Brazil scored higher than just five countries, two of which, India and Iran, are other TIC cases. Brazil's highest ranking (39) was on technological connectivity, and its worst (71) was on personal contact (telephone, travel, and remittances), ahead of Iran but no other country. On economic integration, Brazil ranked 69 of 72. Brazil does attract some foreign direct investment, though this is driven more by the large size of Brazil's population and its abundant natural resources than by government policy or the ease of starting up new businesses. In terms of trade openness, Brazil's number 70 ranking was the lowest of the TIC cases.

Nigeria

Globalization has affected Nigeria significantly compared with many developing countries. Nigeria's 2007 A.T. Kearney/Foreign Policy Globalization Index ranking for economics was 39 of the 72 countries ranked, higher than all but two of the ten countries focused on in this text. Largely fueled by investment in its oil sector, Nigeria's FDI ranking stood at 37, similar to other cases such as Russia, China, and Mexico. This oil-based interconnectedness with other countries has not, however, spilled over to other areas of globalization. The country's overall ranking for 2006 was 57, pulled down in part by its number 58 ranking in personal contacts and its number 65 ranking in technological connectivity.

Nigeria also demonstrates that the relationship between globalization and domestic

Oil traders watch at London's International Petroleum Exchange in July 2004, as violence in Nigeria pushes oil prices close to $50/barrel for the first time.
(©AP Photo/Richard Lewis)

political and social unrest in a given country can be a two-way street. The renewed threat of worker strikes in the oil sector, along with local groups upset at the failure of oil wealth to penetrate into the general population threatening—and acting on these threats—to blow up oil installations and kidnap oil company officials or members of their families, helped drive world oil prices up over $50 per barrel in late 2004, $70 per barrel in early 2006, and $140 per barrel in mid-2008. Thus, while political scientists often focus on ways in which economic globalization can influence politics in a developing country, Nigeria also demonstrates that a single country's political instability can have significant implications for the global economy.

Iran

The Islamic Revolution isolated Iran from the West. Though the government of former President Khatami, a moderate reformer, sought greater openness, even under Khatami the process was slow. Despite Khatami's efforts at reform, Islamic conservatives that dominate key positions in Iran's political system feared dependence on and cultural contamination from the West. Their suspicious nature made closer connections with the United

States impossible. For its part, the United States maintained sanctions on Iran during Khatami's two terms as president.

Iran's overall 2007 A.T. Kearney/Foreign Policy Globalization Index ranking places it last among the 72 countries examined, finishing just below India. Only its technology ranking (54) was not near the very bottom, thanks to a 52 position in the category of Internet users. Its economic, political, and personal rankings were 65, 70, and 72, respectively. The "Law on the Attraction and Protection of Foreign Investment," passed in 2002, has, to date, done little to increase FDI. The FDI component of the economic dimension garnered a number 72 ranking. Iran's total economic ranking was kept out of the 70s only by a number 55 position on trade.

COMPARATIVE EXERCISE

Globalization and Government Spending

As highlighted in the previous section, globalization is a major comparative politics topic. Many comparativists study globalization's domestic political effects. This chapter's comparative exercise does as well, examining a common but critical question: *Does globalization make states stronger or weaker?*

Hypotheses, Measurement of the Dependent and Independent Variables, and Cases

The "In Theory and Practice" box on Mexico discussed "weak state theories." Weak state theorists argue that globalization attacks state sovereignty. The state surrenders an increasing portion of its ability to control its own affairs and turns over more decision making to international organizations and multinational corporations. A testable hypothesis based on these claims is that *there is a negative relationship between increasing economic globalization and state strength.*

In contrast, **strong state theories** suggest increased economic interconnections do not weaken states but rather require a large state apparatus. One group of strong state theorists postulates that globalization leads to greater domestic fear of economic displacement. These fears generate demands for government policies to protect workers from the consequences of economic upheaval, such as unemployment compensation, worker training, and insurance benefits.[59] The government's efforts to compensate for the effects—or at least the presumed effects—of globalization lead to increases in spending, including on social welfare programs.

A second strain of strong state theories focuses on the need for regulation and rule of law as capital becomes more mobile. Simply put, investors want to know that their investments are going to be secure and that contracts are going to be obeyed. To varying degrees, this can lead to a more transparent relationship between governments, corporations, and investors. This transparency allows for greater scrutiny of rules and practices. Though this does not rule out government corruption, making the climate appealing to investors does require understood and enforced rules of the game, which in turn require a strong and functioning government. A testable hypothesis based on strong state theories is that *there is a positive relationship between increasing economic globalization and state strength.*

> **Strong state theories** argue that even with increasing globalization, governments have maintained, and perhaps even enhanced, their ability to tax, spend, and regulate.

A simple, but commonly used measure of the dependent variable (state strength) is the portion of the country's GDP made up of government spending. The main independent variable in this study is globalization. It is measured in two ways: FDI as a percentage of GDP and imports plus exports as a percentage of GDP.

In an ideal comparative politics study of this question, a researcher would collect data on as many countries for as many years as possible, examining the relationship between the globalization measures and the measure of state strength over time while controlling for other rival explanations of state strength. This exercise is more modest, examining the pattern between the measures of the dependent and independent variable in six of the TIC cases (the United Kingdom, Mexico, Russia, China, Nigeria, and Iran) from 1995 to 2002.

Results

Just eyeballing the patterns in Tables 3.3 and 3.4, which present figures for government spending, FDI, and imports plus exports, all as a portion of GDP, seems not to indicate much of a pattern. In the United Kingdom, particularly from 1995 to 1999, government spending as a portion of GDP declined, FDI/GDP increased, and imports and exports divided by GDP generally declined. In Russia, as FDI and trade increased, government spending decreased. In Mexico, FDI and trade figures bounced around a bit over the period examined, but government spending was virtually constant. In China, government spending rose sharply in the second half of the period examined. During that increase, trade also increased, but FDI was flat or even declined. In Iran, spending was fairly consistent, as were the other variables until 2002. Note the large jump in both FDI and trade that year. Looking at whether this affected government spending in 2003 would be an interesting project. Finally,

in Nigeria, all three variables jumped around considerably.

There is no reason, however, to rely on eyeballing the data. In "large N" studies, where one has many observations of the variables in question, one can estimate the correlation between the variables statistically. Correlation does not prove causation, but correlation is one of the necessary conditions of causality. As a result, the absence of correlation allows a researcher to reject a causal claim. To calculate the correlations between government spending and the globalization variables, one can use a statistical software program (in the case of this comparative exercise, it is SPSS).

Running these calculations produces the following correlations. The correlation between government spending/GDP and FDI/GDP between 1995 and 2002 in the six countries examined was 0.09; statistical significance tests for this result indicated that it was not significantly different from 0 statistically. The figure for government spending/GDP and (imports plus exports)/GDP was −0.13 and again lacked statistical significance.

One can also examine these variables in terms of change from the previous year. Looking at China between 1995 and 1996, for example, the change in government spending as a portion of GDP was −0.11 percent. Running correlations using this form of the variables, the correlation between change in government spending/GDP and change in FDI/GDP between 1995 and 2002 in these six countries was −0.07 and statistically indistinguishable from 0. The correlation for change in government spending/GDP and (imports plus exports)/GDP, however, was −0.28 and close to significant at the traditionally used .05 level of statistical significance.

What do these numbers mean? Using the regular spending, FDI, and trade numbers, the correlations support neither the strong state hypothesis nor the weak state hypothesis.

Table 3.3 Government Spending and Globalization in the United Kingdom, Russia, and Mexico

	UK			Russia			Mexico		
Year	Total Gov't. Spending as a % of GDP	Foreign Direct Investment as a % of GDP	Sum of Imports & Exports as a % of GDP	Total Gov't. Spending as a % of GDP	Foreign Direct Investment as a % of GDP	Sum of Imports & Exports as a % of GDP	Total Gov't. Spending as a % of GDP	Foreign Direct Investment as a % of GDP	Sum of Imports & Exports as a % of GDP
1995	41.09%	1.91%	57.09%	19.44%	0.52%	55.18%	15.52%	3.32%	58.06%
1996	40.30%	2.30%	59.13%	20.41%	0.66%	47.92%	15.14%	2.76%	62.10%
1997	37.84%	2.82%	57.34%	19.41%	1.20%	47.26%	15.94%	3.20%	60.64%
1998	36.55%	5.24%	54.59%	15.85%	1.02%	55.77%	14.46%	2.93%	63.48%
1999	35.92%	6.12%	51.60%	13.59%	1.69%	69.39%	15.02%	2.74%	63.11%
2000	36.40%	8.49%	58.19%	13.75%	1.04%	68.09%	15.45%	2.86%	63.94%
2001	36.60%	3.76%	57.44%	15.39%	0.81%	60.46%	15.44%	4.31%	57.25%
2002	37.58	1.87%	55.40%	18.89%	1.00%	58.83%	16.12%	2.28%	55.46%

Table 3.4 Government Spending and Globalization in China, Iran, and Nigeria

	China			Iran			Nigeria		
Year	Total Gov't. Spending as a % of GDP	Foreign Direct Investment as a % of GDP	Sum of Imports & Exports as a % of GDP	Total Gov't. Spending as a % of GDP	Foreign Direct Investment as a % of GDP	Sum of Imports & Exports as a % of GDP	Total Gov't. Spending as a % of GDP	Foreign Direct Investment as a % of GDP	Sum of Imports & Exports as a % of GDP
1995	12.22%	5.12%	45.68%	22.23%	0.02%	35.77%	12.58%	3.84%	86.47%
1996	12.11%	4.92%	39.91%	22.86%	0.02%	38.50%	10.20%	4.51%	75.58%
1997	12.79%	4.92%	41.37%	22.36%	0.05%	34.16%	12.12%	4.25%	82.70%
1998	14.09%	4.62%	39.21%	21.56%	0.02%	40.51%	15.39%	3.27%	71.60%
1999	16.30%	3.91%	41.49%	21.36%	0.04%	43.71%	28.54%	2.89%	78.03%
2000	18.09%	3.55%	49.07%	18.71%	0.04%	43.97%	14.07%	2.21%	90.81%
2001	19.42%	3.76%	48.55%	19.06%	0.05%	39.14%	20.93%	2.30%	77.68%
2002	20.64%	3.88%	54.77%	20.03%	0.24%	52.06%	18.17%	2.74%	81.77%

Looking at the change in these figures from one year to the next, the weak state hypothesis has some support from the correlation between trade and government spending, but neither hypothesis is supported by examining change in FDI/GDP and change in spending/GDP. Thus, this chapter's comparative exercise indicates that there is more to the story of government spending in these six countries than the effects of globalization.

CONCLUSION

This chapter dealt with central concepts and some of the key comparative politics theories regarding the potential influence of economic structure on political outcomes. Economic structure approaches have been prominent in comparative politics for decades. They draw on intellectual work from the last three centuries by scholars such as Adam Smith and Karl Marx, and they continue to be relevant today as the world becomes increasingly economically, culturally, and politically globalized.

This chapter also presented key economic structural features of the ten countries examined in detail throughout this textbook. These cases provide comparativists with different examples of class structure, patterns of economic development, and degrees of economic interconnections with other countries. A study of them also generates common themes about their economic setting and its political consequences.

For many comparativists, an examination of economic structure is the starting point for understanding political outcomes. This does not mean the economic structural approach is beyond criticism. Those who are critical of focusing on economic structure argue that events of the late twentieth century demonstrate that Karl Marx clearly got it wrong, economic factors have at best indirect effects on politics, scholars' economic arguments about politics reflect the normative position of the scholars, and focusing on economics leads comparativists to miss other important factors such as culture, identity, political institutions, and political decision making.

Such criticisms have some validity, but one must be careful not to take a criticism of focusing too much on economics to mean that economics is unimportant. Ignoring economics is certainly no better than focusing on it exclusively. Indeed, economics plays an important role in structuring political outcomes in countries at different levels of economic development and with different types of political systems.

These effects on important political outcomes are both direct and indirect. For example, class structure, economic development, and economic globalization directly influence the likelihood that a country will become a stable democracy. At the same time, economic structural conditions also play a role in shaping other structural features that, in turn, affect a political outcome like democratization. These include political culture and identity, the topics of the next two chapters.

Key Terms

Bourgeoisie, p. 64
Class, p. 63
Class consciousness, p. 66
Class structure, p. 66
Constant dollars, p. 73
Countries in transition (CITs), p. 76
Dependency theory, p. 86
Economically developed countries (EDCs), p. 75

Learning Objectives

After reading this chapter, you should be able to:

- Define culture and political culture.
- Describe, compare, and contrast the political cultures of the ten TIC countries.
- Discuss how socialization, major events, and long-term processes can shape political culture over time.
- Describe the meaning of ideology and distinguish among several major ideological perspectives.
- Explain the findings from the comparative exercise in this chapter on cultural globalization.

4

Ideas as Structure:
Political Culture and Ideology

On November 4, 2007, voters cast ballots for mayor of the village of Santa Maria Quiegolani, in the Oaxaca region of Mexico. The local village council ordered that all of the ballots supporting one of the candidates, Eufrosina Cruz, be ripped up and not counted. According to these officials, because Eufrosina Cruz was a woman, she was not a citizen and therefore could not be a candidate for local office.[1] Santa Maria Quiegolani's residents are members of the Zapotec indigenous ("Indian") group, and the village government is run by men who seek to maintain its traditional values and practices. These practices dictate that women, as well as men over the age of sixty, are prohibited from participating in local politics.[2] Thus, in a country working to consolidate its democracy—and one where women have played a prominent role in national politics—Eufrosina Cruz is unable to seek political office in her own village, because the indigenous group to which she belongs continues to emphasize a traditional, male-dominated social structure. ■

Look for this icon  to point you to **Deepening Your Understanding** features on the companion website www.college.cengage.com/politicalscience/barrington, which provide greater depth for some key content.

As the arguments in Chapter 3 highlight, economics can strongly influence many political outcomes. But how much people expect from government, and how much government people are willing to tolerate, often extends from something deeper than their pocketbooks. The story of Eufrosina Cruz shows how values, beliefs, and ingrained approaches to interpreting events can create and constrain political opportunities. Among a group of people, these embedded beliefs act as a lens through which the group sees the world and judges what it sees. This lens is the group's culture. The portion of that lens that is used to see and judge political events, and consequently helps structure political behaviors, is the group's political culture.

Political culture is not something reserved for individuals who are actively involved in political events; everyone shares in a particular political culture. Individual values and beliefs—which come together with those of others to form a collective culture—are the products of events of the past, life experiences at present, the social institutions that guide individuals through childhood and continue to mold them as adults, and the actions and stances of political institutions and leaders. This chapter provides an overview of how political culture develops, how it is spread among individual members of a community, how it can change, and how it can affect political behavior and other political outcomes. The chapter also examines ideology, the extension of political culture into a political blueprint for society and its governance.

Culture

Although this chapter is primarily about political culture rather than culture in general, it is necessary to discuss broader ideas of culture before considering political culture. Within the social sciences, **culture** is generally defined in two distinct but related ways. The first way of thinking about culture is as the *underlying values* in a society that shape behavior. Note that this is not the same thing as attitudes, which are seen as more at the surface of an individual's hierarchy of views and positions and more susceptible to day-to-day fluctuations. Instead, values are deeper and less vulnerable to sudden changes. These values, in other words, are "sticky."

Other social scientists conceptualize culture as a *system of meaning*. In this view, culture is a frame that shapes how people understand someone or something with which they come into contact (good/bad, like us/different from us, etc.). The idea of culture as a system of meaning makes clear that culture is not only shaped by experiences, but also that it shapes how individuals interpret those experiences. As political scientist Marc Howard Ross puts it, culture "frames the context in which politics occurs."[3]

Though these two views of culture—values versus system of meaning—differ, both conceptualizations understand culture as a collective concept. It takes a group to have a culture. An individual can have deep beliefs and a particular way of interpreting events, but an individual cannot have a culture. In addition, neither of these understandings of culture defines it as behavior. In everyday language, the term often refers to behaviors such as the habits of a particular group. Social scientists who emphasize the importance of culture, however, believe that culture influences behavior. Thus, including behavior as part of the definition of culture becomes potentially tautological: behavior becomes the explanation for behavior.

Culture is defined in two distinct but related ways. Some social scientists define culture as a particular group's values. Others see it as a system of meaning that provides a lens, which helps groups make sense of the people and events they encounter.

This idea of the collective values and systems of meaning for a given group does not mean everyone in the group holds the same values or interprets the world in the same way. Characterizing the culture of a particular group of people is somewhat like using the average of a group of numbers to summarize those numbers. When statisticians look at summary statistics like the average of a set of numbers, they usually look for additional information as well. The standard deviation of the group of numbers, for example, indicates how much a typical number in the set deviates from the average. If all the numbers in the group are very close to the average, the standard deviation is very small. Likewise, when scholars characterize the culture of a group, they also want to know how representative this characterization is. If the vast majority of the population has similar values and a common system of meaning, there is **cultural homogeneity** across the group. On the other hand, if there are many substantial sets of beliefs, some of which contrast with one another, there is a high degree of **cultural heterogeneity**.

One source of cultural heterogeneity is the presence of multiple identity groups, each of which may itself be quite culturally homogeneous. Members of an ethnic group often share similar beliefs, but these beliefs differ greatly from those held by members of other ethnic groups. This type of overall cultural heterogeneity—with sharp cultural differences corresponding to social group boundaries—is more threatening to social stability than when various sets of beliefs are more randomly spread across the population.

Political Culture

Political culture is the underlying set of values and beliefs about politics and the system of meaning for interpreting politics among a given population. Political scientists stress a number

of values as components of political culture. To compare one country's political culture to another's, comparativists can examine these values, by looking at how they combine together and the extent to which the typical combination is dominant (a homogeneous culture) or just the most common of many combinations (a heterogeneous political culture). This chapter highlights five sets of features in order to provide a framework for understanding political culture. Other political scientists may emphasize a different set of features, but these five are among the most commonly examined political culture components.

Components of Political Culture

The first set of beliefs that political scientists emphasize concerns *social relations and authority*. These beliefs address whether the masses accept the authority of a social elite and, consequently, whether social relations are vertical or horizontal. **Vertical social relations** occur in hierarchical societies, with those at the top (including political leaders) having the right to impose their decisions upon those at the bottom. **Horizontal social relations**, on the other hand, emphasize equality and a role for many if not all in society to help shape political and social decisions.

The second set of values concerns *group welfare versus the interests of the individual*. Is

Cultural homogeneity refers to a case where members of a group are relatively unified in their beliefs and system of meaning.

Cultural heterogeneity occurs when other conspicuous sets of beliefs exist alongside the most typical cultural features of the group.

Vertical social relations exist in societies that emphasize an authority hierarchy.

Horizontal social relations highlight equality among members of society to help shape political and social decisions.

society individualistic, or is the fate of the collective more important than that of individuals? **Individualistic political cultures** discourage governments from implementing policies that protect groups or level the economic playing field in society. **Collectivistic political cultures** tend to coincide with government programs aimed at benefiting large numbers of people.

The third set concerns the potential *tradeoff between liberty and security.* Do people accept a strong state that, through rules governing individual behavior, penetrates into society in an effort to maintain order? Or do they value freedom from state action, with the state leaving most decisions to individuals themselves, even if it means less stability and security? Again, different answers to these questions shape the governmental institutions and policies in a particular country. Where freedom is more important than order and security, there will be a strong emphasis on "negative rights"—freedoms from government action or, put another way, things government cannot do to citizens of the state. If security and order are more important than freedom, the state may be highly intrusive in the name of maintaining order.

The fourth set of beliefs centers on the *legitimacy of the political system and its leaders*. Do individuals accept the existing political regime as having the right to rule? Can political leaders generally be trusted, or must society carefully monitor the activities of government?

The final set of beliefs centers on what political scientist David Easton called the "political community." *With what political unit does the population identify most readily?* Does the population as a whole have a strong attachment to an overarching national identity? Other identities within a country can be more powerful than national identity. People's loyalties may lie with other parts of their identity, such as their race, ethnic group, or region of residence.

Several of these cultural features are complementary, such as individualism over collectivism, a belief in liberty at the expense of order, and a general suspicion of government institutions. At the same time, the five components can be combined in many different ways. A society that views social relations as horizontal, for example, could have either individualistic values or collectivistic ones. A comparativist seeking to understand the political culture in a particular state must first characterize that culture. Looking at the particular combination of these five sets of values that seems to be dominant—as well as how dominant that particular combination is—allows one to characterize the structure of a given group's political culture.

Different combinations and different degrees of homogeneity of the political culture add up to different political cultural structures, each with its own array of implications for politics. In a comparative study of Norway and the United States, for example, political scientists Tom Christensen and B. Guy Peters point to such cultural differences, as well as the

Individualistic political cultures discourage government involvement in the protection of groups or leveling of the economic playing field.

Collectivistic political cultures support government action aimed at benefiting large numbers of people.

Table 4.1 The Five Major Components of Political Culture

Component	Questions
1. Beliefs about Authority	1A. Are social elites accepted as legitimate? 1B. Are social relations vertical or horizontal?
2. Group versus Individual	2A. Is the collective more important than the individual? 2B. Is equality more important than personal freedom?
3. Liberty versus Security	3. Do people value freedom from state action, even if it means less stability and less security?
4. Political System Legitimacy	4A. Does the existing political regime have the right to rule? 4B. Can political leaders generally be trusted?
5. The Political Community	5A. With what political unit does the population identify most readily? 5B. Does the population as a whole have a strong attachment to an overarching national identity?

consequences of these differences for political outcomes:

The homogeneity, lack of conflict, egalitarian values, and trust in political institutions in Norwegian culture makes it probably more easy to reach collective decisions and implement them than in the United States, but also creates a centralized system that can have problems with attending to differentiated interests and needs. . . . Trust in political institutions and giving central actors high discretionary influence may secure flexibility and effectiveness in decision-making processes, but also make institutions and central actors insulated from critical and public knowledge about the content of decision-making processes.[4]

Just as a certain combination of the various components of political culture may be unique to a particular society, so too may it be unique to a particular point in time. Political cultures are usually slow to change, but there are circumstances, discussed later in this chapter, in response to which the political culture of a society may undergo a radical shift in a fairly short amount of time.

It is also necessary to distinguish between mass and elite political culture. Elites and masses may value different things. Although political scientists typically use political culture to refer to the values and/or systems of meaning in the general population, some focus on political culture at the elite level, as well as the extent to which it matches mass political culture. In studies of democracy, for example, it is not unusual for comparativists to pay more attention to elites' commitment to democracy than to such a commitment in the general population. Without such a commitment among the ruling elite, democracy is difficult to establish. At the same time, without a commitment to democracy among the general population, maintaining a democracy over the long term becomes a challenge.

Topic in Countries

Political Culture in the United Kingdom, Germany, France, and India

The United Kingdom, Germany, France, and India all have consolidated democratic systems, and many comparativists would argue that the overall political cultures of their societies are, to somewhat varying degrees, consistent with this political outcome. Yet they arrived at these comparable political cultures in quite different ways. The deep-rooted British political culture has combined the political elite's openness to government programs (and eventually political power) for the lower classes with the lower classes' deference to elite authority to help maintain stability and cultivate the tradition of evolutionary progression toward greater democracy. German political culture, however, had been less supportive of democracy—valuing traditional social relations along with order and stability—until dramatically remade after World War II. Consistent with the pattern of alternating democratic and nondemocratic political systems, French political culture has combined the values of the French Revolution (liberty, equality, and "brotherhood") with more traditional elements. India's political culture displays a similar balance between contrasting ideals, blending a respect for authority with a tolerance of inconvenience and acceptance of national "unity in diversity."

The United Kingdom

Consistent with the stereotype of the British as being overly concerned about proper etiquette, British political culture places a great deal of emphasis on *status and the authority of elites*. This holds particularly true among the working class, which over the years has generally respected the authority of economic and political elites. This belief in the authority of political elites is known as **working class deference**, and it has had a number of important consequences. It is part of the reason for the lack of

violent class-based uprisings, the maintenance of the monarchy even as its power was whittled away, and the relative success of the Conservative Party in the United Kingdom among working class voters.

Working class deference is only half of the story. In the past, and arguably still today, the upper class also held an important value about its relationship with the lower classes. Elites saw their economic and social privileges not only as advantages but also as carrying responsibilities to look out for society's less fortunate. This value, known as **noblesse oblige**, has combined with working class deference to promote British political stability. It also played a role in the process of decolonization. Compared with other European powers, the British surrendered control over their colonies more slowly, more cooperatively, and with more of an eye toward leaving the colony with a chance to survive as a politically stable democracy.

When discussing *individualism versus collectivism* in British political culture, it is natural to compare it both to the United States and to the cultural features of continental Europe. In such comparisons, American political culture is typically described as more individualistic (and suspicious of authority) than British political culture.[5] At the same time, British political culture is seen as less collectivistic than the rest of Western Europe. British philosophers (e.g., John Locke) and some British politicians (Margaret Thatcher) have placed a strong emphasis on individual liberty and restraints on government control.[6] But the American experiences of separation

---

Working class deference is the belief by the lower classes, present throughout English and British history, that the British elite have the authority to rule over them.

Noblesse oblige is the belief among the British social, economic, and political elite that their position implies an obligation to enhance the quality of life for those less fortunate than themselves.

from British control and settlement of the frontier had no counterpart for the British. It is likely that these events contributed to the development of a stronger American individualism.

Geert Hofstede, a Dutch professor of business and organizational anthropology, produced a well-known comparative study of culture, initially based on surveys of IBM employees around the world in the 1970s. He was criticized for using these data, and one certainly should not assume that IBM workers have the same values as the rest of a country's population. But comparing workers for the same company in different countries can be informative, and Hofstede has updated his index with more recent and diverse data over the years. Hofstede focuses on five dimensions of culture, one of which is individualism. His score for the British on this component is high (89), behind only Australia (90) and the United States (91). The average for European countries that Hofstede examined is under 60, indicating the British may be much more like the residents of their former colonies than like their continental European neighbors.

The British have participated in a number of wars, but these wars were rarely the result of foreign invasion. Therefore, concerns about security are less central in British culture than in the cultures of most other countries. Hofstede also looks at order and security (which he calls "uncertainty avoidance"). The British score is relatively low on this component (30) compared with a European average of almost 70. It is also noticeably lower than the U.S. score (46).

Even so, the British have a tradition of secrecy in matters related to national security (codified in the country's Official Secrets Act as early as 1911).[7] The idea of a freedom/security tradeoff became more prevalent in the minds of the British public with the terrorist campaigns of the Irish Republican Army in the second half of the twentieth century. Just as concerns about IRA terrorism were finally diminishing, Islamic terrorists attacked the British public transportation system in July 2005. The event had the potential for providing a similar shock to British political culture that the September 11, 2001, attacks had on American political culture. It will be interesting to see how permanent this effect will be.

The tradition of deference and the tendency for changes to be evolutionary rather than revolutionary have combined to create generally high levels of *political system legitimacy* in the United Kingdom. But, as discussed in Chapter 1, system legitimacy does not necessary translate into support for specific leaders or policies. British political culture is marked by a concurrent faith in institutions of government and belief in the individual's right to protest specific government actions. In the fall of 2006, for example, Prime Minister Tony Blair announced that his resignation from the position of prime minister was on the horizon. Blair's decreasing popularity, itself a function of growing mass opposition to the British participation in the War in Iraq, drove his decision. The British people still believed in the political system's "right to rule," but they had enough of the person in charge of that system.

The question of *attachment to the political community* is complex in the case of the United Kingdom. The presence of sharp ethnic divisions, reinforced by territorial boundaries, has made attachment to the overarching British national identity tenuous at times. In recent decades, ethnic politics has rekindled the nationalism of the past, and the central government has made concessions to the Scots, Northern Irish, and Welsh that have increased their control over their own political affairs.

At the same time, the United Kingdom shows a stronger commitment to the national political community than many other countries. As an island country, its ethnic groups have more in common with each other than with other Europeans. In addition, the European integration process has brought the ethnic groups of the United Kingdom together more than it has divided them. The decision by the British government (for now) to opt out of the European Union's European Monetary Union (EMU) program with its requirement to adopt the euro as the official currency, had as much to do with the identity-based emotion connected to abandoning the British pound as it did with rational economic calculations about the costs and benefits of EMU participation.

IN THEORY AND PRACTICE

The United Kingdom and Almond and Verba's Civic Culture Theory

In 1963, Gabriel Almond and Sidney Verba published one of the more influential and controversial books in comparative politics, *The Civic Culture*.[8] Its argument—that the cultural form of a society influences prospects for successful democracy—rests on assumptions common to other political culture theories: that culture can be observed; it is, to a great extent, fixed in a particular setting; and it influences political outcomes. The authors examine five countries: the United States, the United Kingdom, West Germany, Italy, and Mexico. They identify three main political cultures—participatory, subject, and parochial—based largely on an examination of survey data from the countries. The three types of culture differ on the extent to which people follow politics and believe in being active citizens. "Participants" believe that their participation can influence political outcomes, "subjects" are interested in politics but feel disconnected from the political system, and "parochials" have little knowledge of their political system and thus no desire to participate. Almond and Verba state that no country possesses a pure form of one of the three cultures. Rather, each involves a relatively unique mix, the composition of which has substantial political implications.

For Almond and Verba, predominantly subject cultures, like those in Italy and Mexico, have fewer prospects for democratic success than participatory cultures such as the American one. Ultimately, however, they argue that the British mix of participatory and subject culture provides the greatest degree of democratic stability. Up to the time that they were writing, British history seemed to bear out their characterization of the United Kingdom's culture and its political consequences. Shortly after their book was published, however, the United Kingdom was nearly torn apart by the troubles in Northern Ireland, violent crime increased, and the longstanding deference to authority seemed less solid than it had ever been.

This shift points to the potential problem of using a snapshot in time (in the case of Almond and Verba, surveys from 1959–1960) to capture a country's culture and make predictions from it. The Almond and Verba study was also criticized for the design of the specific survey questions used in the study, and some contended it is impossible to capture culture through surveys of individuals. Still other detractors deemed the theory to be ethnocentric and more prescriptive than objective and empirical.

Yet, whether or not one agrees with it, Almond and Verba's **civic culture theory** is an important example of a cultural theory that provides an explanation for a political outcome (democratic stability) on the basis of the type of culture in a particular country. Their characterization of a balance between deference and participation remains a useful summary of British political culture. That the British political system survived numerous challenges supports the vision of a stable British political system flowing from a well-balanced political culture.

Almond and Verba's **civic culture theory** argues that each society's distinctive mix of "participatory," "deferential," and "subject" political cultures influences political outcomes, including the likelihood of successful democracy.

Germany

The Second Reich, which created a single German nation-state in 1871, glorified *traditional social relations and authority*. These values reflected the country's feudal structure and the dominance of the Prussian aristocracy in the military, bureaucracy, judiciary, and education system. Socialists, who promoted a classless society along Marxist lines, challenged this hierarchical social structure, but they were disenfranchised by the regime. The value of hierarchical deference reached its apex in the Nazi regime with the leadership principle, or *Führerprinzip*, which required absolute obedience and devotion of the population to Adolf Hitler. Deferential and authoritarian values eroded during the democratic regime in the Federal Republic (West Germany) after World War II. At the same time, the East German Communist regime promoted the values of a classless society. The rise of the Green Party in West Germany since the late 1970s has posed the most cogent challenge to a hierarchical social order. The party has not only promoted environmentalism but also has championed radical democracy in social and political relations (*Basisdemokratie*) as an alternative to hierarchy.

German culture is largely one that values *collectivism over individualism*. The liberal tradition associated with individual rights in the economy and society has been historically weak: a revolution advocating political liberalism was crushed in 1848, and the Free Democratic Party representing liberalism remains a small party mustering less than 10 percent of the vote. As discussed in detail in Chapter 13, German society is highly organized along corporatist lines, with peak associations representing major sectors of the economy, society, and professions.

Dating from the medieval guild tradition, collectivist organizations and values have also been legitimized by social Catholic doctrine of the nineteenth century. Social Catholicism promotes the idea of **subsidiarity**, which holds that major responsibilities for social provision should remain with the lowest level of social organization possible: first the family, then the group, and finally the state. This has an impact on German approaches to social welfare. The state plays a limited role in the welfare state in Germany, delegating substantial authority to churches, labor unions, and employers' associations to administer social welfare programs.

More oppressive versions of group identity have existed in German history. During the Nazi regime, individuals were expected to subsume their will into the greater good of the German nation. In Communist East Germany, the regime discouraged individual effort or thinking and instead promoted its version of the classless society of Marxism-Leninism.

Security, both national and economic, *has taken precedence over liberty* for much of Germany's history. The lack of natural borders, frequent wars with its neighbors, and late political unification, made many Germans in the nineteenth and early twentieth centuries value the security of the nation ahead of individual liberty. Liberty was all but crushed under subsequent Nazi fascist and East German communist totalitarianism, but the Federal Republic did enshrine individual rights in the constitution. Partly because of two periods of hyperinflation and the Great Depression in the twentieth century, Germans also value economic security and stability. They continue to support a generous welfare state safety-net, a hallmark of the Federal Republic.

System legitimacy under the Weimar democracy (1919–1933) rested on its performance. The humiliation of the Versailles Treaty following Germany's defeat in World War I, plus the economic

> **Subsidiarity** is an idea from Catholic social thought that individuals have a right to make decisions for themselves and that, as much as possible, families and small social organizations should provide economic protection and distribute social goods to individuals rather than the state furnishing such protections.

woes of the Great Depression, turned many against the fragile democracy. In the initial years of the Federal Republic, the population also judged the regime on its performance. Fortunately, the "economic miracle" of the 1950s and 1960s delivered spectacular prosperity, which helped legitimize democratic rule. The passing of the Nazi generation also helped cement democratic values. Today, the democratic institutions of the Federal Republic enjoy broad public support, which has endured despite difficult economic performance and high unemployment in the last two decades.[9] By contrast, in Communist East Germany, the regime's legitimacy was sharply affected by economic downturn. As economic growth stalled in the 1980s, the system's legitimacy faltered, leading to the street demonstrations that brought down the regime in 1989.[10]

The nearly two decades since German unification have been economically difficult for united Germany. The east especially has endured hard times, and support for democracy there is relatively weak. Surveys in 2000 and 2003 showed only one-third of easterners were satisfied with the functioning of democracy, compared with nearly two-thirds of westerners.[11] The association of democracy with poor economic performance helps explain easterners' weaker attachment to democratic rule. But the relative weakness of democratic values in the east may also reflect the decades of Communist Party rule and a yearning—at least among older voters—for the economic security it provided.

Equating the *political community* to the nation came later to Germany than to other parts of Europe. It was forged only in 1871, by elites among a scattering of principalities. The Nazi regime defined the political community, the *Volk*, as composed of ethnic Germans. The country's partition into West and East Germany after 1949 bifurcated this national identity, although the official line in West Germany was that the country remained a single nation-state.

Since World War II, the question of German national identity has been contested. On the one hand, the reunification of Germany in 1990 fulfilled the vision of a single German nation-state. On the other hand, in reaction to their Nazi past, many Germans are reluctant to participate in overt displays of nationalism. Instead, elite and popular opinion tends to subscribe to a European Germany, firmly embedded in the institutions of the European Union. Regional identities and attachment to territorial units of the German federal system have also remained strong, particularly in the case of Bavaria.

France

French political culture was long divided by the competing legacies of the Revolution of the 1790s.[12] Supporters of the Republican approach follow the motto of that revolution—*Liberté, Egalité, Fraternité*—while their opponents have historically emphasized what are considered the more established attributes of French society, including traditional social relationships, religion, and the country's history prior to the Revolution. Like the Napoleonic Empire of the early nineteenth century, the current French political system, the Fifth Republic, represents an attempt to consolidate the social advances of Republican political culture while appropriating the symbols of authority, status, and order important to the Revolution's opponents. The Fifth Republic weakened the legislature (the National Assembly), but French Republicans still consider it to be the institution that should represent the citizens and embody the general will or sovereignty of the Republic. At the same time, the president in the Fifth Republic is meant to embody the nation, while holding the chief responsibility for the security of the state, social order, and the preservation of the principles spelled out in the constitution. Consequently, French presidents are, in most cases, above the law while they hold office. During his two terms (1995–2007), for example, Jacques Chirac refused even to be questioned by investigators looking into corruption scandals that emerged from his years as mayor of Paris.

Broadly speaking, therefore, the French political system today reflects an attempt to find compromise on the core values of *authority, equality, liberty,* and *security*. To a large extent, the endeavor has been successful. The ideals of the Revolution resonate across the political spectrum. French citizens value liberty, as it enables the organized expression of political dissent and partisan debate. *Fraternité* ("brotherhood") includes the principle of universalism as well as that of solidarity, which emphasizes the collective obligation of all citizens to each other. They also value equality. The only legitimate forms of social hierarchy are those based on individual training and merit.

The potential for contradiction in a culture forged by compromise has been most evident in the arena of the French *political community*. In recent years, for example, the government banned students in public schools from wearing a religious emblem, such as a Muslim head scarf, Jewish yarmulke, or Catholic crucifix. The Republicans live by the principle of *laïcité*, a form of secularism where religion is considered a private matter, the expression of which has no place in any public institution. But in a nod to traditional social groups, the Fifth Republic also strongly supports private religious education, with extensive state funding for Catholic and Jewish schools.

This debate over religious expression also illustrates the power of "reason" in French political culture. As the home of the Enlightenment—an eighteenth-century movement that transformed social life through the power of philosophical learning and debate—France considers itself the country that thinks more than any other. In France, philosophers and intellectuals are actual celebrities, the network news broadcasts take place during television prime time, and a significant portion of other prime-time broadcasts consists of issue-oriented or philosophical talk shows, history telecasts, and arts programs. In the debate over religious symbolism in schools, deputies in the National Assembly from both the mainstream

Right and Left argued that religion was in conflict with reason, and that students should have a place free of religious thought where they could explore all realms of knowledge.

India

Recognizing the complexity of Indian values and systems of meaning is a starting point for discussing their political role. Mahatma Gandhi, for example, emphasized the practice of nonviolence, but his assassination and those of Prime Ministers Indira Gandhi and Rajiv Gandhi provide a dissonant view of the values underlying Indian political behavior. Popular deference to the wealthy, such as the Ambani family, which controls the Reliance Industries, indicates that capitalism is culturally accepted, but popular deference to Communist Party of India (Marxist) leaders, such as Jyoti Basu, suggests that it is not. Nevertheless, the fact that cultural heterogeneity is great in India does not mean there are *no* widely disbursed common attributes.

Several Indian scholars have sought to locate such shared attributes. Indian analyst Pavan Varma suggests such components include a high level of tolerance for inconvenience and hardship, a low level of social trust, a desire to achieve ends regardless of the means to achieve them, a "materialistic pragmatism," a "natural amorality," and an "excessive love for the perks of power."[13] Focusing on *beliefs about authority and social hierarchy*, he goes on to say:

> As the legatees of a centuries-old system of hierarchy, Indians have a special weakness for status; power is coveted for the status it guarantees; the state is the highest repository of both status and power; and politics is the highest-yielding path to the resources of the state.[14]

Indian sociologist Dipankar Gupta suggests that Hindu fundamentalism is unlikely to arise because Hinduism is *more individual than congregation-based*. He says, "As fundamentalism does not allow for any differences among the faithful, it will find it very difficult to take root in Hindu India."[15] Commenting on *trust and legitimacy*, he contends that, within Hinduism, "trust is more often placed on individuals and rarely ever on institutions."[16] He is critical of the Indian elite stating, "They adhere to symbols and norms that heighten the distance between people. . . . snob rules continue to be very effective in non-modern societies like India where there is legal equality but little else."[17] And, he claims, "While democracy and elections give the impression of representation" in India, "governance at all levels is oiled by connections."[18]

Echoing these claims, Geert Hofstede's analysis of Indian political culture ranks India well above the global norm on the "power distance" dimension, indicating an acceptance of high levels of social inequality. He also points to the Indian people's individualism, perseverance, and tolerance of "unstructured ideas and situations."[19]

Encompassing the individualism inherent in Indian political culture is the notion of *a political community based on the concept of "unity in diversity."* This concept seems to have been contradicted in practice by the behavior of certain political leaders, who have emphasized divisions within the population to mobilize their political supporters. Nonetheless, it became a basic part of India's political culture—reinforced by the experiences of the Partition in 1947.

In summary, in the midst of the contradictory attributes and great overall complexity, there are identifiable features of Indian political culture: accepting an underlying hierarchical system that places great value in power and status; appreciating the utility of personal connections more than institutional rules; valuing the achievement of ends over adherence to rules guiding means; tolerating inconvenience; and accepting the notion of "unity in diversity." These traits have combined to help maintain democracy, despite the challenges of economic hardship, identity divisions, and social and political corruption.

Political Culture in Mexico, Brazil, and Nigeria

Like other states with developing economies and fragile democratic systems, traditional values and systems of meaning are conspicuous in Mexico, Brazil, and Nigeria. Social relations remain hierarchical, the population—partly because of persistent corruption—is unconvinced about the political system's legitimacy, and the commitment to an overarching political community is relatively shallow. At the same time, all three also have significant heterogeneity in their political cultures, driven to a great extent by the ethnic diversity of their populations.

Mexico

Mexican political culture rests on an interesting tension regarding beliefs about *authority and social relations*. In many ways, it is a highly authoritarian culture, acquiescent to elite rule and emphasizing social hierarchy that includes patriarchy. These values were solidified during colonial rule, through the influence of Spanish culture, strong state control, and the Catholic Church's domination of social institutions. (The Catholic Church came to own a sizeable portion of the land in Mexico by the end of the colonial period.) At the same time, Mexico has had a number of uprisings—against the Spanish, during the Mexican Revolution, and more recently in the region of Chiapas. These uprisings were as much social as political, with many of the great revolutionary leaders acting in the name of land ownership for the impoverished peasantry.

This combination of deference to social authority and admiration of revolutionary spirit would appear, at first glance, to be incongruent. Yet, this combination helps explain the dominance of the Institutional Revolutionary Party (PRI) for much of the twentieth century. As the heirs to the revolutionary victors, and as a party officially representing those in society who had rebelled, PRI leaders could play the "revolution card" when it suited their purposes. Nevertheless, the system that the PRI created was authoritarian and hierarchical, which complemented deeply established social values.

Looking at the component of *collective versus individual orientation*, Mexican political culture is much less individualistic than that of its neighbor to the north. The family is a particularly important social institution, and extended family relations are typically closer than in the United States. The previous section introduced Geert Hofstede's examination of various components of political culture in a number of countries. Mexico was one of those countries, and its individualism score (30) is stark in comparison to the U.S. score of more than 90.

The PRI's name, combining the concepts of revolution and institution, reflects the dichotomy in Mexican culture between an *embrace of freedom and a focus on security*. Mexicans have, until recently, leaned much more in the order and security direction than in the freedom and liberty direction. Hofstede's uncertainty avoidance index score for Mexico was Mexico's highest scoring component in his study (with a score of 82, compared with under 50 in the American case), representing the desire for order and stability. The events of the last several decades—in which democracy, even if it means some instability, appears to be increasingly valued—may signal a shift in this balance. Survey results in the late 1990s and early 2000s indicate some attachment to values associated with democracy, and the recent changes in Mexico's regime have likely fed this shift, by showing that while democracy involves uncertainty, it does not necessarily bring utter chaos.

While perhaps hard for Americans to believe, the PRI-dominant regime had, for many decades, a great deal of *system legitimacy*. Individual party leaders may not have been popular, but the connection to the 1910 Revolution and years of impressive economic growth fed a belief that the PRI regime was the only game in town. This began to change as time wore on, and a cultural shift led an increasing number of people to consider the potential for a more democratic system.

Corruption remains the Achilles's heel of the new democracy's legitimacy. Vicente Fox's victory in 2000 was, in part, a condemnation of corruption by the PRI over the previous decades. Yet, surveys in 2002 indicated that while a majority felt Fox's election would lessen corruption in the office of the president, less than one-third thought corruption had declined in the previous year, a small percentage thought Fox would be able to reduce overall corruption a great deal, and most felt other social institutions like the Catholic Church had a better chance of attacking corruption than the government.[20] If the Mexican people perceive that National Action Party (PAN) leaders like Fox and Mexico's current president, Felipe Calderón, are not able to address corruption effectively, it is not only a threat to the PAN's future electoral prospects, but it could also undercut Mexicans' belief that democracy is a solution to the problems of the past.

Mexico has faced challenges in the *political community* component of its culture but has been relatively successful in addressing them. Building attachment to Mexican national identity has been a long endeavor. At the time of independence in the early 1820s, the Mexican population was sharply divided along ethnic and class lines. The colonial period—during which Spanish men greatly outnumbered Spanish women—resulted in a large portion of the population becoming *mestizo* (part native, part European). At the same time, a significant number of "unmixed" indigenous and European inhabitants remained, as well as a sizeable black population in certain parts of the country who had come to Mexico as slaves.

The Mexican Revolution did little to end these divisions, even reinforcing them in the short run. Thus, along with economic development, a major task of the government that emerged from the Revolution, led by the political coalition that would eventually become the PRI, was nation-building. Through a combination of effort and favorable conditions—the presence of a single, dominant religion and the near universal use of the Spanish language—the PRI by and large succeeded in building an attachment to Mexican identity and the Mexican state.

Brazil

Brazilian political culture is quite heterogeneous, the result of its multiethnic and multicultural population, as well as unresolved economic and social inequalities that render some ethnic groups more marginalized, or more privileged, than others. The life of a black agricultural worker in Brazil's impoverished northwest bears little resemblance to the life of a white banker in São Paulo, whose children attend private schools, shop at upscale malls, and go on vacations abroad in the summer. That said, one can broadly identify general political cultural traits.

Brazilian political culture remains highly, though decreasingly, authoritarian. Despite its deep inequalities, Brazil never produced a major social revolution to counteract the *hierarchical and authoritarian culture* imported from Portugal. Independence was won without a shot being fired or a peasant being mobilized. Brazil is the only Latin American state to have established a successful monarchy—a monarchy that died in a palace coup rather than via mass protests.

Rebellions in Brazil mostly took the form of evasions and escapes rather than direct confrontations with power, perhaps because its vast and largely empty territory provided an easier route to political autonomy than bloody fighting. One example is the *quilombo* communities, founded in Brazil during the 1600s by escaped African slaves and other socially marginalized people. One of the largest communities, Palmares, contained at its height some thirty thousand individuals and lasted nearly a hundred years. Many such communities exist to this day, speaking a mixture of African languages and Portuguese.

Another form of evasion of power is the *jeito*, a nearly untranslatable Brazilian word meaning

a way of getting around formal rules.[21] Brazilians are proud of their ingenuity in circumventing their state's bureaucratic rules, but the *jeito* can also apply to nearly any social or economic interaction. Rules are obeyed in form but not in substance. One does not attempt to overturn an unjust law; one simply sidesteps it. Despite its subversive potential, there is little real equality in the *jeito*. While cleverness is appreciated, connections and money matter more. Some people are better placed to exercise the *jeito* than others, and they are free to extract "gifts" from those they help in this way. When Brazilian president Lula da Silva's party was caught taking kickbacks to finance the party's campaigns, his overall reaction was to shrug and argue that everyone does it. In the 2007 Latinobarometer poll, 66 percent of Brazilians said they knew personally of an act of corruption in the previous twelve months, more than twice the percentage of any other Latin American country.[22]

The *jeito* is also *more individualistic than collective*. Benefits are won not for groups, but for individuals with the clout to get around the system. Accordingly, Brazilian political culture is somewhat more individualistic than the norm in Latin America, with a score of 38 on Hofstede's index compared with the average Latin American score of 21.[23] Nevertheless, as in Mexico, the family remains the most important social unit and tempers tendencies toward individualism.

Brazilians strongly prefer *security over freedom*, a preference even incorporated into the country's flag: across the blue globe in the flag's center is a white band with the words "Order and Progress." This design was adopted for the Brazilian Republic in 1889, and thus precedes the current wave of violence and drug-trafficking that might motivate modern Brazilians to prioritize security. Brazil's highest score on Hofstede's cultural index is for uncertainty avoidance, at 76.[24]

However, most Brazilians do not believe that their political system can deliver security. The *legitimacy* of Brazilian democracy is unusually low. In the last twelve years of Latinobarometer polls, there has never been a year in which a majority of Brazilians agreed that democracy is preferable to any other form of government. In 2007, only 30 percent of respondents supported democracy, one of the lowest figures in Latin America.[25] Brazilians also do not believe that their country is a model of democracy. Fewer than one-third thought Brazil was "very democratic," and only slightly more had confidence in the government.[26] Brazilians tend to like the president more than the Congress, and the Congress more than political parties, which win approval from fewer than one-third of Brazilians. More generally, Brazilians have the lowest level of interpersonal trust of any of the Latin American countries. Only 6 percent of Brazilians thought that you "can trust most people," well below the Latin American average of 17 percent.[27]

Along with these low levels of trust, Brazilians also feel a low level of attachment to *political community.* To the extent that political communities exist, they are based on regional identities. Brazil's historical tradition of federalism puts a lot of power in the hands of regional leaders. Political careers are made first at the regional level, often through governorships, and then projected onto the national stage. Powerful political dynasties use their control of regions to manipulate the selection of national political candidates, especially for the legislature.

Nigeria

Examining political culture in Nigeria is complicated by the diverse nature of its population and the dominant role of religion in society. The country has cultural fissures along religious and ethnic lines. This leads to a heterogeneous political culture, with particularly sharp divisions between the north and south of the country. One Nigerian scholar states clearly the effect: unlike much of the Western world, "Nigeria does not have a 'national culture.'"[28]

On average, however, Nigerians *respect authority and accept vertical social relations.* The British encouraged the precolonial tendency to accept authority and unequal social relations during colonial rule. British rulers needed a stable social hierarchy with which to work, and in places where one did not exist they created it. In rural areas of the country, social position remains very important, and there is little sense of horizontal social relations or acceptance of the idea that one can be socially mobile and move beyond the standing inherited at birth.

Given the deep social divisions in Nigeria, however, it is not surprising that these views differ to an extent among different ethnic groups. The Hausa-Fulani (who are Muslims and are concentrated across Nigeria's north) traditionally valued social hierarchy more than the Ibo (who live mostly in the southeast of Nigeria) and the Yoruba (who live in the southwest). The Yoruba, whose region of Nigeria is highly urbanized and industrial, are also somewhat more inclined to believe in the possibility of social advancement than the Hausa-Fulani.

On the whole, precolonial Nigerian political culture emphasized *collectivism over individualism.* The Ibo have traditionally been more individualistic than the other peoples that came to fall within the borders of Nigeria. The British never seriously set out to develop a spirit of individualism, and thus the overall collectivism and the division between Ibos and others changed little during the colonial period. In the postcolonial period, collectivist values have been encouraged by religious and ethnic elites, who sought loyalty from the masses as the official representatives of the religious or ethnic collectives. Because the ethnic divisions in the country have remained quite sharp, the willingness of Nigerians to make individual sacrifices for the group depends greatly on whether the sacrifices benefit "our" group or "their" group.[29]

In the arena of *freedom versus security,* Nigeria's experiences with democracy have given the population little reason to believe that freedom brings prosperity or that freedom can coexist with stability. The high degree of unrest that has accompanied independence has severely impeded Nigeria's ability to develop both economically and politically. The unstable politics and the economic hardship that the vast majority of the population has faced have in turn reinforced traditional values of order and security.

This is not to say freedom has no value among the Nigerians. Hofstede's political culture studies do not include Nigeria. However, Ronald Inglehart's World Values Survey project includes a dimension he calls survival versus self-expression, which is similar to Hofstede's uncertainty avoidance index. According to Inglehart's analysis, Nigerians fall in the middle of the survival versus self-expression values index. They are less focused on security and order than Russians and slightly less than the Chinese, but they are more concerned with stability and order than Mexicans and much more so than the British.[30] Thus, if the Nigerian government can show that political freedoms can coexist with greater prosperity over a sustained period of time, Nigerians may be willing to tolerate less than complete order and stability. But when disorder accompanies economic despair, liberty typically takes a backseat to concerns about stability.

It is hard for *political system legitimacy* to exist in settings where the legitimacy of the state itself is weak. In the early Nigerian postindependence period, the state's right to exist was in dispute. Only after a violent civil war and the redesign of the Nigerian federal system did the desire to break apart the country begin to erode. Even as the legitimacy of the state increased, however, the legitimacy of the postcolonial political system continued to face hurdles. Two significant attempts at postindependence democracy failed due to the deep social divisions, poor institutional design, and corruption.

In between the democratic periods, the military ruled through a highly authoritarian and highly corrupt system. Despite the acute social cleavages, Nigerians do share certain beliefs regarding government accountability and a strong dislike of corruption. Accusations of corruption and mismanagement of resources, therefore, hurt both the military and democratic governments. Since the reinstitution of democracy in 1999, Nigeria has struggled to unify its population and purge the vestiges of corruption from within its government. But there is much to overcome. The latest attempt to establish a working democracy has grown increasingly fragile. While Nigerians were strongly supportive of democracy in 1999, backing has greatly declined since, especially after the disputed 2007 elections. That year's electoral fraud deepened beliefs that Nigeria's current government had fallen victim to the corruption it had pledged to tackle.

Long before the arrival of European colonizers, which ultimately led to the creation of the present boundaries of the country, the main groups of Nigeria were culturally distinct, with different economic, religious, and political traditions. Thus, there was no overarching attachment to a *political community* beyond the local affiliations of the population in a region. British rule did little to change this. Even British attempts to leave Nigeria with a functioning democracy did as much to reinforce divisions as they did to overcome them, and loyalty to one's ethnic group dominated loyalty to the Nigerian nation.

In postcolonial political struggles, the emerging political consciousness became tied to ethnic and religious groups. The violence that continues to afflict Nigeria today is a result not only of the government's failure to eliminate corruption from within its ranks but also of the sharp ethnic divisions deepened by political power struggles. Adding to this challenge is the internal division between those who wish to codify the rules and regulations of Nigeria into a version of Western law and those who wish to base their decisions upon Islamic Law, or *Shari'a*. This has divided the country along philosophical as well as religious lines and has contributed to the overall sense of distrust and uncertainty that plagues the country.

Political Culture in the Russian Federation, China, and Iran

The political cultures of Russia, China, and Iran highlight the extent to which governments can benefit from a particular set of underlying values at certain times but be greatly constrained by them at other times. Throughout Russian history, collectivism, emphasis on security and order, and deference to strong authority figures benefited successive nondemocratic regimes. Yet the tendency for individuals to desire the collective to take care of them and to view with suspicion those who get ahead caused problems in the late Soviet and early post-Soviet periods for those hoping to reform the economic system to give individuals greater responsibility. In China, the Confucian view of society combined a respect for authority, an acceptance of social hierarchy, and an emphasis on working hard for the good of the collective with an obligation by those in positions of power to act responsibly. This included government, which Confucius believed had a divine right to rule *as long as it ruled responsibly.* This favors continued Communist Party rule, if the economy continues to prosper and daily life remains orderly. Elements of the Iranian political culture are consistent with nondemocracy, but it is less traditional in orientation than many other countries in the Middle East (and less traditional than many Americans believe it is).

The Russian Federation

For centuries before Vladimir Lenin seized power in the name of a workers' revolution, the Russian population had demonstrated deference to authority, collectivist tendencies, and support for security and order at the expense of personal freedom. These beliefs were complemented by a general disconnect from politics, particularly among the country's rural population. Tsarist, Soviet, and post-Soviet Russian leaders have taken advantage of these cultural traits. Other aspects of Russian political culture, however, such as its ambivalent attachment to an overarching national identity and its tendency to connect system legitimacy to economic and military performance, have created challenges for authorities.

The Russian people have a long tradition of emphasizing *the collective over the individual.* Russians are often suspicious of individuals who get ahead, perceiving their success as the result of illegal, or at least unethical, efforts. In many cases, Russians would rather be personally less successful than see someone else be more successful than them. A Russian "God talks to a peasant" joke (of which there are many variants) captures this attitude well:

> One day, God calls out to a peasant working in the field. He says, "My son, I will give you anything you wish for, but your neighbor will get twice of whatever you get." The peasant thinks about it for a little while and then asks God to strike out one of his eyes, leaving his neighbor totally blind.

In the post-Soviet period, suspicions of successful individuals and economic reform's failure to greatly improve ordinary Russians' lives fed negative views about change. The wealthy "new Russians," discussed in Chapter 3, became the subject of disdain. When former Russian President Vladimir Putin attacked the economic and political power of the super-rich "oligarchs" in the early 2000s, the confrontations were largely applauded by the Russian population even if some understood that Putin's efforts were largely about consolidating his own political power.

At the same time, Russians have a commitment to their own individual well-being not always found in collectivistic cultures. During the Soviet period, residents of communal apartments, which had private rooms where families resided and shared areas such as bathrooms, would often take great care of their own areas while the communal areas were left unclean and in disrepair. Thus, the component of Russian culture concerning collectivism versus individualism contains an interesting dissonance. Individuals look out for themselves in some aspects of their private lives, but they also depend on the state to provide for them and lack a commitment to the general idea that individuals with ability who work hard should get ahead.

Centuries of dictatorial rule (by tsars and Soviets alike) reinforced Russians' strong attachment to *security and order at the expense of liberty and freedom.* Major events have added to the cultural aversion to disorder and insecurity. The territory of the present-day Russian Federation has been invaded a large number of times over the centuries—by the Mongols, the Lithuanians and Poles, the French, the Germans, and the Germans again. These invasions have brought economic devastation and led to the deaths of millions of Russians. The current Russian government has taken advantage of the tendency for Russians to defer to a leader who portrays an image of strength. Much of Putin's ongoing popularity is based on the belief that he is a strong leader, who has turned the chaotic situation of the 1990s into one of order, security, and prosperity today.

The combination of deference to authority figures and a desire for security and order has affected views about the *legitimacy of the political system.* The tsarist governments worked to develop the belief that the tsar was the link between God and ordinary people. At the same time, beginning with the tsars and continuing to the present, the population also linked its belief in the right of the system to rule over them to its performance. Defeats in wars, such as the Crimean War in the middle 1800s, the Russo-Japanese War of 1904–1905, and (most devastatingly) World War I, weakened the legitimacy of the system. Military success, on the other hand, boosted legitimacy. Following World War II, the Soviet government continually stressed the country's

victory as an example of the strengths of the socialist system, even though the government had used nationalist themes rather than socialist ones to rally the population during the war. Veterans were encouraged to wear their war medals in public as a symbol of their service in the war. Economic success (particularly under Stalin and Khrushchev, and more recently under Putin) also brought legitimacy, while economic hardship (from Brezhnev through Gorbachev and continuing under Yeltsin) challenged it.

A number of legacies of the past affect the *political community* component of Russian political culture, weakening attachment to Russian national identity and to the Russian Federation, as well as increasing the political culture's overall heterogeneity. Among these is the expansion of the Russian Empire under the tsars, which led to the control of a vast land containing many small ethnic minorities. Many of these minority groups have little in common with Russians culturally. Second, Russians themselves have been conflicted about the meaning of Russian national identity since well before the Soviet period, with some supporting a vision of an ethnic nation that excludes those who are not ethnically Russian and others advocating a civic national identity inclusive of ethnic minorities. Finally, the Soviet decision to create provinces within the Russian union republic that were named for ethnic minorities, and treated by the minorities as national homelands, reinforced the tendency of minority groups to associate more with the region and locality than with the central government.

Thus, attachment to an overarching political community is weaker among Russia's ethnic minorities than it is among ethnic Russians. But even among ethnic Russians, the vastness of the Russian territory and

Did You Know? The Russian word for friend, друг (pronounced "drook"), has a deeper meaning than its English counterpart. In Russian, the word implies a companion who can be counted on to help even if it places him or her in danger. This difference in meaning captures the importance of a small, tight circle of family and friends in Russian life. Particularly in the past, the harsh Russian climate and even harsher authoritarian and totalitarian political systems meant that how loyal a friend turned out to be could mean the difference between life and death.

disagreements about the membership boundaries of the Russian nation have combined to limit an attachment to Russianness and a commitment to the Russian state. The problem even led then-President Boris Yeltsin to convene a special committee to propose a set of ideas about what can unite the Russian population (i.e., defining the Russian national identity). Rather than the unified vision that Yeltsin had hoped for, the report included a large number of different (and conflicting) characteristics. In a telling indication of the disagreements about Russian national identity, the committee ultimately concluded that the effort to find such unifying factors is the most important thing that Russians can do to be unified.

China

Chinese political culture continues to reflect values from **Confucianism** as well as the (often complementary) values stressed by the Communist government. Confucius was an educator in China around 500 B.C. Confucian traditions emphasize *hierarchy and respect for authority* within all major social institutions. These include the family, where males and elders are to be given particular respect. Confucius emphasized a series of dominant-subordinate relationships (leader-subject, parent-child, male-female, and old-young). When the Communists seized power, they selectively emphasized a number of Confucian beliefs about authority while challenging others. Mao was particularly critical of the idea that women should be subordinate to men, although the Chinese Communists did not work actively to abolish that view.

While believing in the general goodness of individuals, Confucianism emphasizes the fate of the entire *society over individual well-being*. Individuals are expected to work hard, but the idea that individuals should look out for themselves is discouraged in Chinese culture much more than it is in political cultures such as those of the United Kingdom and United States. At the same time, education is valued, and according to Confucian thought people are able to improve their social

standing by improving themselves through education. This tendency to value education led the Chinese to develop a merit-based governmental civil service much earlier than most other countries.

The Communist period reinforced the ideas of collective over individual, particularly during the rule of Mao Zedong. With the economic reforms that began under Deng Xiaoping in the late 1970s, however, the Communist government stressed a combination of the Confucian idea of hard work with a newfound toleration of individual gain. In Geert Hofstede's political culture analyses, China still has a very low individualism score (15). Its score is low even in comparison to other Asian countries Hofstede analyzed, which averaged a score of 23 on the individualism component. Thus, an accent on traditional collectivism certainly remains in place, although the introduction of capitalist economic principles will likely continue to weaken it somewhat over time.

Another of the legacies of Confucianism is the emphasis on *order and security at the expense of freedom.* The prominence given to social harmony—through a respect for those in positions of authority and responsible actions by those with authority—left little room for individual freedom. While Confucius encouraged individuals to better themselves through education, he viewed individuals' ultimate responsibility to be their use of skills in a disciplined manner to improve social conditions. Some scholars discuss these values as crucial to the relative long-term stability of Chinese politics (the early to mid-twentieth century being the most notable exception). The government expected individuals to be loyal to their political leaders and the nation as a whole.

As China has developed economically in recent decades, the traditional emphasis on order

> **Confucianism** is a set of beliefs based on the writings of Confucius, which emphasize respect for authority and hard work and an obligation by those in power to rule responsibly and in the interests of society as a whole.

at the expense of freedom has begun to break down. Chinese culture remains far from most Western cultures on the order/freedom continuum, but the Chinese have become more materialistic. They may have even begun to develop what Ronald Inglehart and Christian Welzel call "self-expression values"[31]—orientations championing freedom from control and the importance of human choice—a circumstance that must concern the country's Communist leadership.

Confucian traditions benefited Chinese political systems throughout history, by helping to generate strong beliefs in *system legitimacy*. Yet the leaders of the system were not free to act in any way they wished. Confucianism combines an emphasis on traditional authority with an element of performance-based system legitimacy. According to Confucius, the authority of government officials was to be respected, but the government also had an obligation to act honorably with this authority. Natural disasters in China came to be viewed as displeasure from heaven about corruption or other failures in government performance.

When the Communists seized power, they promoted Marxist-Leninist-Maoist ideology (see the section on ideology later in the chapter) as a source of legitimacy. Arguing that the Chinese Revolution had given China a "blank slate," Mao also pushed Chinese to remake their society. At times, such as during the Cultural Revolution of the 1960s, he even encouraged the population to remake the Communist system. Following Mao's death, fundamental challenges to the legitimacy of the system emerged. Deng's economic reforms simultaneously lessened the relevance of official state ideology and unleashed market-based economic growth. New values blossomed, particularly among the young in the large cities. Many came to see the Chinese Communist system as an illegitimate, authoritarian system.

The immediate result was the Democracy Wall in the late 1970s. Similar to Gorbachev's toleration of mass criticism in the Soviet Union in the hope that it would increase support for his reforms, Deng initially tolerated posters in central Beijing (and other cities) that protested government actions and specific officials. Soon the criticism became too great, and the Democracy Wall was abolished. A decade later, the cause of democracy reemerged. The Democracy Movement of the late 1980s, which culminated with the Chinese government's crushing of the Tiananmen Square uprising in June 1989, was led by university students and older intellectuals who had grown tired of Communist Party authoritarianism and corruption. The crackdown by the government, in which thousands of protesters were killed, succeeded. Yet the uprising proved that system legitimacy was not accepted by all segments of the population, particularly the urban, educated youth.

Within the *political community* component of Chinese political culture, the Chinese people are, for the most part, patriotic and proud of their national identity. Similar to Russia, however, China's size and considerable ethnic minority populations in the periphery of the country create complexities and tensions. As a result, neither the development of unified loyalty to the Chinese state nor attachment to an overarching Chinese national identity has been easy, and the government remains suspicious of identity-based organizations.

The Chinese government has encouraged nationalism among the general population. Occasionally promoting anti-American protests, for example, the government has tried to use nationalism to unite the population while simultaneously deflecting criticism of government policies. Over the last decade, in fact, the Chinese government has pushed the ideals of nationalism significantly more than those of socialism. It has worked for much of the population, but ethnic divisions in the outlying regions pose continuing concerns for the Chinese government.

Iran

Traditional Iranian culture encourages *respect for authority and promotes vertical social relations*. Historically, the leaders of the monarchy were seen as a source of law and largely above the law—at least until the "Constitutional Revolution" of the early 1900s introduced a parliamentary system. Religious leaders enjoyed similar respect. On both respect for authority and vertical social relations, however, Iran is less extreme than many of its neighbors. For example, while there is a high degree of patrimony, women have a greater standing in Iranian society than in many other developing countries, particularly in the Middle East. In addition, one of the components of Hofstede's political culture framework is called the "power distance index" (PDI). A high PDI score indicates a society that accepts inequality in social standing. Iran's PDI score of 58 captures its nature as respecting authority to an extent. Its score places it well below the Middle Eastern average of 80, but it is nearly twice as high as that of the United Kingdom.

In most Middle Eastern countries, the *collectivism versus individualism* aspect of political culture leans sharply toward collectivism. In Iran, the individualistic mindset is somewhat more in evidence and seems to be on the rise, particularly among the urban young. Hofstede's political culture study "scores" Iran at 41 on individualism. This is above the Middle Eastern average, but still well below countries such as the United States and United Kingdom. Hofstede's data on "uncertainty avoidance" point to Iran as having a political culture that *values stability and order at the expense of freedom* but not as much as other Middle Eastern countries. Its score of 59 is well below the Middle Eastern average of 68. Inglehart's survival versus self-expression "score" for Iran also indicates its relatively moderate position, more focused on self-expression than China and much more so than Russia.[32] Writing with Daphna Oyserman, Inglehart argues that Iran "shows a surprisingly pro-democratic political culture," and on the survival versus self-expression component is approaching the "transition zone," in which mass political culture becomes harmonious with democratic approaches.[33]

Of all the dimensions of political culture, it is most difficult to find reliable data about *political system legitimacy*. Since the Islamic Revolution, Iran has remained virtually impenetrable to foreigners wishing to study the beliefs of individual Iranians about their political system. The harsh punishments handed out to dissidents must be taken into account as one attempts to gauge the true feelings of members of the government and local citizens expressing support for the theocratic regime. When on camera and through the government-controlled print media, the Iranian people indeed express great satisfaction with the decisions of their government. Such statements are consistent with their acceptance of the government's legitimacy. They are also consistent with recognition of the government's coercive power. On the other hand, certain behaviors are inconsistent with a belief in legitimacy. The prominent successes in the 1990s of candidates associated with political reform, for example, is hard to understand if the masses had a deep belief that the current system is legitimate.

Attachment to the national *political community* is relatively strong in Iran. In addition to the role played by Iran's long history (mostly as the entity of Persia), prerevolutionary and postrevolutionary governments encouraged a strong national identity. For the most part, these efforts have been successful. Because of the nature of the Islamic Revolution, however, one of the most powerful political units in Iran is the local and regional religious institution. These institutions are of social as well as religious importance and play powerful roles in determining public policy and garnering local support. In addition, like Russia and China, attachment to an overarching national identity is much weaker among ethnic minority groups living in outlying regions of the country than among the rest of the population.

Think and Discuss

What are the similarities and differences among the political cultures in the ten TIC cases?

Where Does Political Culture Come From? Events, Experiences, and Socialization

Political scientists have generally emphasized three factors that shape political culture: defining events, repeated experiences, and socialization. Because political culture is "sticky," life experiences of the individuals whose values and systems of meaning comprise a particular culture do not change that culture easily. Therefore, events must be either dramatic or sustained over a period of time. **Defining events** can provide a shock to society that overwhelms the tendency of political culture to resist change. In situations where people feel threatened, their desire for security will often lead them to support preventive action by governments even if it means restrictions on freedom.[34] The events of September 11, 2001, for example, shocked the American people. Many Americans' values and systems of meaning shifted and, as a result, the collective political culture was transformed as well.

Ongoing or **repeated experiences** may also affect political culture, particularly if they continue for years or decades. The previous chapter included a discussion of how economic development can have cultural consequences. But just as economic development is a protracted process, its impact on culture is gradual as well. In West Germany after World War II, decades of economic success accompanied the reestablishment of democracy. This economic boom eventually undid many of the negative beliefs about democracy that had emerged during the interwar period when the implementation of the Weimar democratic system was followed by an economic depression. Negative experiences can also shape values and beliefs. The Great Depression greatly affected Americans, and many other people around the world, altering their views about the role of government in the economy and the necessity of a social safety net.

"Migrant Mother," a photograph of Florence Owens Thompson and her three children during the Great Depression, by renowned photographer Dorothea Lange.

(©Dorothea Lange/Corbis)

Political culture is also shaped through **socialization**. Socialization is the process of transmitting values and systems of meaning, usually from one generation to the next. This process takes place within the major social institutions that are responsible for laying down beliefs about right and wrong. The most important institution in this regard is the family. Though the correlation is not perfect, a strong predictor of the political beliefs of young adults is the beliefs of their parents. Other important

Defining events are one type of factor that can shape political culture. Such events are dramatic, providing a "shock" to the existing political culture.

Repeated experiences, smaller events that reoccur or are sustained over time, can also shape political culture.

Socialization is the process of transmitting the components of a political culture to the next generation through social institutions such as families, churches, and schools.

institutions in the socialization process include places of worship, the workplace, the media, the educational system, and the government.

Sometimes socialization is more subtle than telling children what is right and wrong. Schools are a powerful venue for socialization through what they do and do not emphasize. One of the most important socialization tasks of schools is to teach the society's history. Events in the past are filtered through the institutions of socialization in the present. Although it is difficult to make up or fully ignore significant historical events, it is certainly possible to highlight certain events more than others, underscore the positive or negative implications of those events, and explore history through the viewpoint of one particular class, race, or gender. Although recent years have seen a movement toward including the perspectives of more marginalized peoples, determining history remains the prerogative of the victor. Thus, while history cannot be made up out of thin air, it can be molded and shaped to suit the interests of those in power.

Taken together, events and socialization are the starting point for a model of political culture and its consequences. This model is captured in Figure 4.1. Note that the model includes both the direct effects of events on political culture and the filtering of events through the socialization process before they shape political culture. The theories discussed in this chapter's

"In Theory and Practice" boxes focus on parts of this model, providing causal stories about why political culture develops and/or influences political behavior.

Globalization, Socialization, and Political Culture

In addition to the important domestic institutions that foster socialization, cultures are increasingly shaped by globalization. The machinery of globalization expands the range of international connections and makes individuals more aware of their "shrinking world." Chapter 3 highlighted the economic aspects of globalization. But globalization occurs in many arenas, some of which are noneconomic. This includes culture, although some of the most important values and systems of meaning relate to economics (such as beliefs about the superiority of the neoliberal, capitalist approach).

There is little denying globalization's impact on culture. When two cultures meet, one or both are bound to change. Globalization is an avenue for socialization with the Internet, Western films, and advertisements by multinational corporations tending to encourage consumerism, capitalism, and attachment to technology. Globalization also magnifies the importance of events outside a country. In a "globalizing" world, incidents such as the December 2004 Asian Tsunami influence more than just individuals who are directly affected. They can shape values on a global scale. Finally, globalization serves as a transmission belt for culture by encouraging increased migration across political borders. Migrants bring their values with them. Although the political culture of a particular group of immigrants may transform over time due to the influence of their new setting, so too may their beliefs have some bearing on that setting.

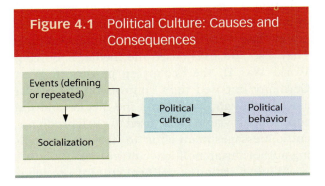

Figure 4.1 Political Culture: Causes and Consequences

Socialization, Experiences, and Events in the United Kingdom, Germany, France, and India

The United Kingdom, Germany, France, and India demonstrate the importance of social and governmental institutions, especially schools, as complements to the traditional socialization mechanisms of family and religion. Significant events in all four countries have also driven political culture toward its present form. These events include acts of violence, including those of relatively brief duration (terrorist bombings and riots) and more prolonged violent events (revolution, war, and ethno-religious strife).

The United Kingdom

Like other monarchies in Europe, the English Crown had attempted to foster traditional authority, based on the concept of a "divine right to rule." These efforts were only partially successful. English elites challenged the principle of an absolute monarchy based on divine power earlier than elsewhere in Europe (e.g., the Magna Carta in 1215). As a result, the number of people who comprised the political elite was larger in England than elsewhere.

Today, the socialization process in the United Kingdom is carried out through institutions such as the family, the media, and the educational system. The structure of the educational system especially contributes to the degree of elitism in British political culture. Which secondary school one attends carries much more weight in one's social standing and prospects for economic well-being in the United Kingdom than in a country like the United States. These elite private schools (actually called "public schools" in the United Kingdom) lead to entry in top universities and the best jobs after college graduation.[35] Universities themselves were reserved for the children of the upper class until less than a century ago. Fewer than 10 percent of British school children attend "public schools," while the rest attend what are called "state schools"—what in the United States would be called public schools.

As mentioned in the discussion of freedom versus security, the subway bombings in the United Kingdom in July 2005 were events dramatic enough to reshape political culture. As in the United States following 9/11, traditions about limits on government involvement in personal liberties and community affairs came face-to-face with calls for tightening restrictions upon groups and individuals suspected to be engaged in or supportive of terrorism. The British case demonstrates that short-lived single events such as terrorist attacks can push political culture noticeably in the immediate aftermath. It also provides evidence, however, that without repetition of such events, the previous core values may reemerge over time. In the end, the political culture may change, but not as dramatically as it appeared directly following the event.

Germany

Along with the family, the education system and the media have been the most important agents of socialization in Germany. The education system reinforces the hierarchical class structure from early on, with students deciding at age ten or eleven whether to pursue the university track or the vocational track. Most working-class children pursue vocational education rather than attend university. The totalitarian regimes of the Nazis and the GDR (post-World War II East Germany) relied on a mass-based party and its associated organizations, or front groups, throughout society in their efforts to reshape political culture. They also effectively used the media. Following World War II, the occupying powers in West Germany imposed tight controls on the media as well, though in this case the media (and the educational system) were used to push prodemocratic messages in an effort to weaken the existing authoritarian political culture.

While Germany's political culture—particularly its strong collectivist strand and hierarchical social relations—has its origins in the country's feudal past, major events in the twentieth century have also imprinted the cultural landscape. Germany's defeat in two world wars, the hardships of the Great Depression, the horrors of the Nazi period, the Communist regime in East Germany, and the reunification of the country in 1990 have shaped German political culture. The traumatic events of Nazi dictatorship and World War II left a particularly deep mark. In addition to their skepticism of nationalist appeals, most Germans now champion individual civil liberties and rule of law and support a bounded foreign policy aimed at peacekeeping missions instead of expansionist military excursions.

France

In France, both the state and the family play an important role in political socialization, though debates exist about which one should be its primary engine. Although opponents of the 1999 law granting recognition to same-sex couples argued that the family is the foundation of the French Republic, the only legal marriage in France is held at the local city hall, with the mayor or his or her designate asking the partners to pledge to raise their children as good citizens. The state directly engages in socialization through cultural devices like museums and television; powerful institutions like the military; key officials such as the prefects who are delegated from Paris to municipal governments (see Chapter 6), and the mayors who are often at the same time deputies in the National Assembly; and schools, which follow a curriculum crafted in Paris, where central authorities also give teachers their assignments.[36]

In addition, political parties, and their corresponding clubs and newspapers, engage in socialization activities.[37] Such party organizations—including labor unions—are an important part of local social life. More than that, the role of parties in advocating for or against the principles of the Revolution has solidified many aspects of political culture and shaped how the

French understand national memory and history. For example, the unfair court martial of Alfred Dreyfus, an officer of Jewish descent on the general staff, became a flash point in the 1890s that for more than a generation arrayed Republicans on one side and the forces of tradition around the military and the church on the other. Parties still use the name "Dreyfus" in debates today.

While the Revolution remains the defining event in the shaping of French political culture, contestation over the direction of politics and the political system's legitimacy continued into and throughout the twentieth century. When the partisans of tradition strengthened their position in the 1930s, leading to bloody riots, the popular and antiregime French Communist Party (PCF) joined a government of the Republican Left. The effects of the riots were not enough to maintain the alliance of Left-leaning leaders and their supporters. In the 1950s, for example, the PCF stayed out of ruling coalitions, joined by antiregime parties of the Right, making it difficult for Republican parties to form long-lasting governments.

India

The components of India's political culture rest upon both longstanding aspects of society and experiences at the time of, and subsequent to, independence. One is the caste system that has long characterized social relations; a second is the religious division between Hinduism and Islam; a third is the variety of ethnic groups in the country; and, a fourth is substantial regional variation. Each has contributed to the complexity of Indian political culture. Within this complexity, however, patterns of socialization are identifiable. The family remains a powerful vehicle for transmitting values, while the national educational system continues to press the "unity in diversity" theme on schoolchildren and college students alike.

Events have shaped aspects of India's political culture and political behavior in important ways too. The most dramatic event was the country's birth in 1947 and the horror of the Partition, which helped reinforce a certain level of cultural unity. The wars with Pakistan and China, along with the assassinations of Mahatma Gandhi, Indira Gandhi, and Rajiv Gandhi were shared experiences which had opposing impacts on facets of the political culture. On the one hand, they fostered a sense of unity among most Indians. On the other hand, anti-Muslim and anti-Sikh riots that accompanied some of these experiences worked in the opposite direction. The destruction of the Babri Mosque at Ayodhya in 1992 by a segment of the Hindu population challenged the "unity in diversity" aspect of India's political culture, but seemed in accord with the components of India's composite political culture discussed earlier in the chapter, that is, those involving the desire for power and belief in the importance of ends over means.

Socialization, Experiences, and Events in Mexico, Brazil, and Nigeria

The cases of Mexico, Brazil, and Nigeria highlight the effect of socialization efforts—governmental and societal—and of important events and shared experiences. In Mexico, the 1910 Revolution helped establish a connection between the government and the masses, at least until the end of the twentieth century. By 2000, the year in which the Institutional Revolutionary Party (PRI) ended its domination of the presidency, it was clear that many aspects of traditional Mexican political culture were breaking down. Unlike Mexico, Brazil never experienced the kind of foundational event that might have brought about a sense of shared values across social groups. Instead, events have affected different groups in different ways, contributing to the development of Brazil's diverse political culture. Likewise, Nigeria has had many experiences with the potential to affect its political culture. Some of these have indeed helped to foster unified values, while others have highlighted the deep divisions between different social groups in the country.

Mexico

As is typical of authoritarian political systems, the PRI tried to socialize the population not only to be loyal to the political system but also, to use Almond and Verba's terms (see the "In Theory and Practice" box on the United Kingdom earlier in the chapter), to accept their position as subjects rather than believe in the value of participation. Government control of the historical perspective presented in Mexican schools helped cultivate traditional political and social values. At least until the Vatican II proclamations, the Catholic Church in Mexico complemented these efforts. The Catholic Church and the country's education system remain powerful socializing institutions today, though one should not discount the importance of socialization within the family. Family bonds are generally stronger in Mexico than in its neighbor to the north.

A feeling of solidarity between Mexicans and their political system facilitated the long period of one-party rule in the twentieth century. The 1910 Revolution and the ideals articulated around that time helped establish this connection. The Mexican Revolution remains a dominant event in the shaping of Mexican culture and thus provides an example of the lingering effect that a single event can have on a political culture.

In the long run, however, the elections in 1997 (in which the PRI lost its majority in the national legislature) and the 2000 presidential election (when it lost the presidency) have the potential to be at least as defining. The elections signaled a shift in mass values and presented a new view of Mexican political culture—one based upon growing frustration with the high levels of corruption and inequality. By demonstrating to the Mexican people that they could peacefully change their political system, these elections also affirmed and encouraged such values. Indeed, survey data from 1997 and 2000 indicate a rather substantial shift in values like tolerance in a more prodemocratic direction.[38]

Brazil

Brazil's twentieth-century political history contained an assortment of fragile democracies, military coups, and unstable strongmen. Political party systems sometimes appeared and disappeared within a single generation. Ironically, given the Brazilian Republic's original goal of "order and progress," it achieved relatively little of either. Within this political turmoil, socialization fell to more traditional social forces, such as the family and religious institutions.

The most prominent event shaping contemporary Brazilian political culture, at least among older Brazilians, was the experience of military dictatorship from 1964 to 1985. Under the dictatorship, Brazil had a prolonged period of political stability accompanied by considerable economic growth. However, these achievements were made at the cost of repression and human rights abuses by the military junta. The result was a revalorization of democracy, particularly by the political Left, which had previously expressed skepticism that democracy could offer any hope of significant social change. In the process of bringing about a democratic transition, Brazilian society became mobilized to a degree never before experienced. New independent unions, social movements, and political parties formed to challenge the regime, culminating in a national campaign of *Diretas Ja*—direct elections now—which forced the military government to relinquish power and schedule a new constitutional assembly. While still fragile, Brazilian support for democracy is stronger today than it has been in the past.

Nevertheless, it is important to remember that nearly one-third of the Brazilian population—over 62 million—is under the age of eighteen.[39] They do not remember the military dictatorship. Their formative experiences include repeated episodes of economic crisis and

corruption scandals touching every presidency in post-transition Brazil. One president was even impeached and forced from office. Accordingly, trust in democratic institutions and politicians is quite low.

Nigeria

Consistent with the idea that Nigerians respect authority and accept vertical social relations, there is a strong belief that children should be obedient to their parents. As a result, socialization within the family is more likely to shape children's behavior than in many other countries. Once more, however, this varies from group to group. Ibo children tend to be encouraged to be more individualistic and independent than children of Hausa-Fulani families.

Socialization also takes place in Nigeria's government-controlled educational system and in the powerful social and political organizations that emerged during the anticolonial struggle. Often, these political organizations and government agencies socialize members and clients into the practice of corruption. Those who give and take bribes advance; those who do not are left out. Corruption is not part of traditional Nigerian political culture. It has been learned over the last two centuries and is one of mutual cultural features of an overarching Nigerian culture.

Some shared events and experiences counter the tendency for Nigeria's ethnic diversity to produce cultural heterogeneity. These include the colonial period, the Nigerian civil war (1967–1970), multiple periods of military rule, and Nigeria's attempts at democracy in the postcolonial period. Memories of colonial rule and the repressive military regimes that dominated much of Nigeria's postcolonial history have affected the population in all parts of the country.

Periods of military rule were fraught with dishonesty and uncertainty. Many came to believe that the elite use the rich resources of the country, including its significant petroleum reserves, to increase their personal fortunes, while the country as a whole grapples with rampant social and civil problems. The encounters with military rule have weakened the legitimacy of nondemocratic political systems. But they also have fed the desire for stability and security in the country, which can affect the legitimacy of Nigeria's democratic system as well.

Ongoing events that continue to affect Nigerian political culture include the latest chapter of democracy (since 1999) and repeated instances of Christian-Muslim violence. The current democratic regime has given Nigerians hope, but it has also reinforced the idea that corruption will be hard to eradicate. Clashes between Christians and Muslims continue to pose a challenge to forging an attachment to an overarching Nigerian identity.

Socialization, Experiences, and Events in the Russian Federation, China, and Iran

The long histories of Russia, China, and Iran have produced well-developed cultural traits, which have been encouraged by and supportive of their various nondemocratic political systems. Even in these cases, however, socialization and defining events over the last several decades have continued to have an impact on political culture in important ways. For Russians, the Soviet experience was one in which the population faced culture-altering events, such as the devastation of and ultimate victory in World War II, and the early post-Soviet period was even more traumatic. As it was in Soviet-era Russia, government-led socialization has been a cornerstone of Communist Party rule in China, although the country's extensive history and tradition dilute the impact of sudden shocks—even those as seemingly significant as the 1989 Tiananmen Square massacre—compared with many other countries. In Iran, the 1979 Revolution and subsequent government socialization efforts have left a deep imprint on political culture.

The Russian Federation

Of the ten TIC countries, events and government-led socialization have arguably had the greatest impact on political culture in Russia. The Soviets took advantage and reinforced existing Russian political culture as much or more than they set out to remake it. But they certainly did try to remake aspects of it. Under the Soviets, most aspects of one's daily life—schools, workplace, social organizations, media, and so forth—contributed to socialization. The Soviet leadership used its control of socializing institutions (with the notable exception of private institutions like the family) in an effort to develop support for the regime.

In the post-Soviet period, socialization has been more difficult to manipulate. This was especially true in the initial decade, prior to the ascendancy of Vladimir Putin. Under Putin, the state reasserted its authority over the flow of information. Media were consolidated and in some cases brought under state control. Schools, cultural events, and social organizations increasingly embraced Russian nationalism and appealed to the greatness of Putin. These efforts included distributing brochures about Putin's life to schoolchildren and prominently displaying his image on posters and his name on major city streets. Though these trends may reflect efforts to build a cult of personality, Russian scholar Boris Lanin claims they do not signal a complete return to the past: "There is simply more freedom of access to information now, especially thanks to means of communication, from the Internet to cell phones."[40]

The Russian people have also faced an excessive number of significant events with the potential to mold their political values. From 1985 to 2005 alone, Russia experienced:

- A new Communist political leader, quite different from the previous leaders

- A period of significant political, economic, and social reform
- A nearly complete collapse of the economy
- A coup against the Communist leader by those opposed to reform
- The collapse of the political system and territorial disintegration of the country
- The institution of a new political system with a non-Communist leader
- A violent conflict between branches of the new government that led to the use of military force against government officials
- A new constitution and democratic elections
- An internal conflict leading to military intervention against a region of the country
- Increasing instances of terrorism
- The resignation of the president
- The consolidation of power in the hands of the new president

It is not surprising that such experiences have reinforced certain elements of Russian political culture, including a desire for stability and order even at the expense of personal freedom.

Boris Yeltsin, left, reads a statement from atop a tank on August 19, 1991, as he urges the Russian people to resist a coup by hardliners against Soviet leader Mikhail Gorbachev.

(©AP Photo/File)

China

Prior to the Communist period, socialization was generally left to social institutions such as the family. With Communist rule came a much more aggressive role for government-led socialization, including its control of education and of the flow of information through the mass media. Consistent with Confucian and Communist ideals, Chinese schools emphasize effort over ability. At the same time, the many decades of Communist Party rule undermined the ethic of hard work—a legacy Russia also continues to face—since guaranteed employment and similar income levels give workers few incentives to work intensely. This failure to work hard has been openly discussed in government-run newspapers, and it is part of the reason for the government's open support of capitalist practices today. Other ongoing socialization effects may be less intentional, such as the extent to which the educational system perpetuates gender stereotypes. This process runs counter to the Communist government's ideological goals, which have been less patriarchal than those of traditional Confucian culture.

China has one of the longest recorded histories in the world. It has faced numerous challenges and significant events over that time, underlining the importance of order and security. With strong governments came order and prosperity, while the instability during periods of weak government was violent. The Chinese people associated limits on government with times of social chaos, and successive governments encouraged these beliefs.

China's long history somewhat limits an individual event's potential to influence political culture, and what effect it does have may be slower to materialize. The consequences of an event even as shocking as the June 1989 Tiananmen Square massacre may thus be long term rather than immediate. This tendency is compounded at the present time by the government's efforts to control the flow of political information and manipulate how an event is portrayed. At the same time, Chinese political culture is becoming increasingly heterogeneous as new values unleashed by marketization and China's exposure to values from countries such as the United States have begun to penetrate traditional and early Communist political culture.

Consistent with the idea that Chinese culture is somewhat resistant to sudden shocks, China scores very high on another cultural component

Geert Hofstede examines: long-term orientation. This is the extent to which society takes a long-term perspective to problems it faces, overcoming obstacles with time rather than forcibly attacking the problem.[41] China's score on this component of Hofstede's index is more than five times higher than that of the United Kingdom and nearly three times higher than the average of all countries he examines!

IN THEORY AND PRACTICE

China and Ronald Inglehart's Postmaterialism Theory

Many comparativists credit Ronald Inglehart with advancing the discussion of political culture through his development of **postmaterialism theory**. In works such as his 1990 book *Culture Shift*, Inglehart sets out to explain the emergence of postmaterialist values—beliefs that include the importance of freedom over order and protection of the natural environment—and differences in attachment to these beliefs within and between societies.[42] Inglehart proposes that underlying values are largely shaped by life experiences during the formative years of a person's teens and early twenties. Age cohorts who experience conditions of economic hardship in these years will be more concerned about security and order throughout the rest of their lives. Those whose formative years accompany economic prosperity, however, will be more likely to favor personal freedom and focus on noneconomic quality of life concerns such as the environment.

Inglehart's arguments extend the concept of political culture in two ways. First, while examining the extent to which countries differ on postmaterialist values, he also highlights differences within the population of a country. He demonstrates that different age cohorts in the population have values that are distinct from one another but remain largely stable over time. This challenges the idea that differences in core beliefs between young and old exist because people become more conservative as they grow older.

Inglehart also places culture in a much broader context than most existing works on political culture. He devotes significant effort to the development of a theory of the emergence of postmaterialist values, as well as a theory about the implications of this phenomenon. These implications include a global advance in postmaterialist beliefs, as economic development means more and more generations experience material comfort in their formative years, and the consequent changes in government policies that reflect this cultural shift. As a result, the overall story Inglehart tells integrates economic development, culture, and political change.

While Inglehart initially developed his postmaterialism theory around changes in values in economically developed countries of the West, the theory has interesting implications for China. Over the last three decades, China's economic growth has been impressive. For many young Chinese who went through their formative years during this time, economic hardship is not the concern it had been for their parents. If Inglehart is correct, these conditions will

Postmaterialism theory emphasizes causes and consequences of differences within a population between those who value freedom and quality of life positions such as environmental protection and those who value order and economic prosperity. It is associated with political scientist Ronald Inglehart.

challenge the traditional Chinese emphasis on order and stability at the expense of freedom. The student protests that took place at times in the 1980s—culminating with the Tiananmen Square uprising in 1989—may have been the first outward signs of this "culture shift." Thus, the Chinese government's encouragement of capitalist economic development is a double-edged sword. The government needs economic success to foster its performance legitimacy. But, if Inglehart is correct, such success will also foster an increased desire for freedom from government control.

Iran

Iran's political culture has been shaped by a long history of nondemocratic rule, including the two most important periods in recent decades: the monarchy under the shah and the theocratic government in power since the 1979 Islamic Revolution. But it is also shaped by the country's economic experiences since 1979 and the current government's strong socialization efforts.

Since the Islamic Revolution, the socialization role of religious organizations has taken on added significance. Likewise, the educational system has been used to foster support for the Revolution. Iranian textbooks highlight the shortcomings of the previous regime and portray the United States and the West in general in a negative light. Yet, as in most countries, it is the family that remains arguably the most important socializing institution. For example, when boys see, from an early age, how their fathers treat their mothers—and when the treatment of women in society reinforces what they see at home—they learn to place a corresponding value on gender equality.

Successful revolutions that lead to the overthrow of the political system and the establishment of a deeply different approach to societal organization are fairly rare. The 1979 Revolution was a success on both points, which is why it was such an important event. The shah's move toward secular modernization was halted, and Ayatollah Khomeini's vision of a theocratic political system with a tight control over society became the blueprint for the interactions between politics and society. Thus, as important as other events in Iranian history (both dramatic and repeated) are for its current political culture, the 1979 Revolution stands head and shoulders above them.

IN THEORY AND PRACTICE

Iran and Barber's "Jihad Versus McWorld" Framework

As discussed earlier, understanding the interplay between globalization and culture is one of the more important aspects of discussing political culture today. Many scholars have proposed theories about the causes and consequences of culture in an increasingly interconnected world. These include sociologist George Ritzer's "McDonaldization" theory[43] and Samuel Huntington's idea of the "clash of civilizations."[44] Perhaps the best example of a theory about the intersection of culture and globalization, however, is laid out in Benjamin Barber's book, *Jihad Versus McWorld*. As Barber provocatively states in the opening of the book, "The planet is falling precipitously apart and coming reluctantly together at the same time."[45]

Jihad Versus McWorld is Benjamin Barber's term for the tension between forces of particularism, which draw on ethnic and tribal identity and local attachments, and the forces of globalization.

Barber uses the term "Jihad" to capture the "dogmatic and violent particularism"[46] that is an extreme form of the blending of identity politics with the concept of self-determinism. "McWorld" is Barber's term for the forces of globalization that increasingly pull people around the world together.

In many ways, these two movements spin in opposite directions. Yet, one of Barber's key contributions is to demonstrate the extent to which tribalism and globalism *complement* one another. "Jihad" movements oppose Western culture but are willing to use the tools of that culture to further their agendas. Barber predicted such uses of technology nearly a decade before their use by al Qaeda and the insurgents fighting American forces in Iraq, stating that the "information revolution's instrumentalities are also Jihad's favored weapons."[47]

Iran provides an interesting example of the concept of the tensions between "Jihad" and "McWorld." On the one hand, much of the Iranian leaders' rhetoric is anti-Western (anti-American in particular), expressing fears that Western culture could infect Iran's Muslim society. On the other hand, Tehran's streets look more Western than many other Middle Eastern capitals. This is especially true of the young, who, like their counterparts in the latter years of the Soviet Union, have a respect for the West that contrasts with their government's official view. It is no accident that support for government reformers is based in this young, urban constituency.

The Iranian government has done an impressive job to date of isolating Iran from the cultural effects of globalization. But as the lower levels of hostility toward the West among the young indicate, they may do better by borrowing a page from what some call "glocalization"—working to mold globalization rather than trying to prevent it from penetrating into domestic society.[48] As Iran specialist Mahmood Sariolghalam has put it:

> In the end, Iranians cannot avoid settling for a system that will be founded on a combination of Iranian nationalism, Islamic faith, and globalization. This outcome might be a contradiction in terms, but any Eastern culture that desires to coexist in a contemporary global context that is dominated by the West will have to navigate these apparent contradictions and adapt itself to them.[49]

From Values and Systems of Meaning to Blueprints for Society: Political Ideologies

One of the central parts of political culture is the set of values about how (and how much) society ought to be governed. These values include the role of government in the economy and other aspects of government penetration into society. When these values are spelled out as part of a plan to improve society, they become political ideologies. Although Francis Fukuyama proclaimed that the collapse of Communism meant the end of ideological struggles, and thus "the end of history,"[50] most social scientists believe that, to paraphrase Mark Twain, the reports of the death of ideology as a political force have been greatly exaggerated.

A **political ideology** is a set of guiding principles about the proper design and functioning of politics and society. It is both normative and prescriptive, combining a sense of what ought to be with a blueprint for putting it in place. The statement "wealth should be more evenly distributed through a highly progressive system of taxation" is an ideological position.

One can use the concept of ideology to distinguish between regimes, such as the difference

A **political ideology** is a set of beliefs or guiding principles about the proper functioning of politics and society.

between Western-style democracy and Communist states. It can also be used to distinguish between groups within a certain political system, allowing one to say that the Democrats and Republicans in the United States have different ideologies. Political systems may have *official* ideologies; Communist systems were known for their clear sets of guiding principles. In other systems, including most democracies, the ideology may be less explicitly stated. That the state does not openly advocate an official ideology makes ideology no less important in such systems. In fact, one could argue that when people absorb ideologies through subtle socialization, the ideologies become more powerful than when they are imposed on people through overt government efforts.

Ideological Positions on Income Redistribution, Social Values, and Identity

Ideological concerns typically involve the role of government in society. The ability to penetrate society in order to extract resources is crucial for effective governing. But this does not mean that individuals agree on the proper extent to which government should redistribute income, intervene in social matters, or infringe on personal freedoms.

Ideologies related to the role of government in redistributing income can be loosely placed on a left to right spectrum. Figure 4.2 presents such a spectrum. In the spectrum's middle is the **moderate** ideological position. It includes positions which fall between those of the ideologies to its left and right. For example, moderates may support a system of taxation that is more progressive than that desired by the ideological Right, while rejecting more aggressive policies of economic regulation and income redistribution supported by the Left.

To the left of the moderate position is what is known in the United States as liberal approaches to politics. This is, unfortunately, not how this term is used in other parts of the world, including Europe, where "liberals" are often political moderates, advocating generally limited government while maintaining social welfare protections. Therefore, labeling the left of center position as **progressive** would be more appropriate for comparative politics. This position supports an active role for government in society and defends policies such as a strongly progressive taxation system that assists in the redistribution of income in society.

Social democratic ideologies traditionally have gone a step further, supporting the nationalization of major industries in the economy but stopping short of the overthrow of capitalism. Today, social democratic parties in Europe have generally abandoned calls for nationalization, centering their efforts on maintaining elements of the **welfare state**, a system of significant intervention in the economy and guarantees of economic and social assistance such as health

A **moderate** ideology on income redistribution is one that advocates positions that fall between progressive and conservative approaches.

A **progressive** ideology supports an active role for government in income redistribution through use of taxes and government programs.

Social democratic ideologies had traditionally supported nationalization of industry but today focus more on maintaining welfare state protections.

The **welfare state** is a system that guarantees economic and social assistance, such as health care and retirement benefits, from the government. The welfare system has been in decline in Europe since the late 1970s, partly because demographic patterns have made it increasingly difficult for governments to meet these obligations.

Figure 4.2   A Left-Right Ideological Spectrum Regarding Wealth Redistribution

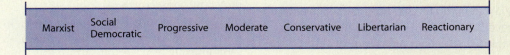

care and retirement benefits. Due to demographic patterns—aging populations in which more people require retirement benefits—and more recently to the collapse of Communist systems in Eastern Europe and the former Soviet Union, the welfare state has been under attack in Europe, particularly since the late 1970s.

Even further to the left would be **Marxist** ideologies. As Chapter 3 discussed in some detail, Marxist perspectives emphasize the importance of control over the means of production and the use of the political system by the economically powerful to maintain their dominant position at the expense of the working class. Marxist ideologies advocate gaining control of the government in the name of the working class, collective ownership of property, and other aggressive actions to reduce exploitation and economic inequality. With the collapse of most of the world's Marxist regimes since the 1980s, these ideologies took a more significant hit than their counterparts on the ideological left.

On the right of the spectrum is the **conservative** position. In the realm of economics, conservatives advocate a smaller government, supporting stronger property rights, less regulation of the economy, and a decreased emphasis on income redistribution. Further to the right are **libertarian** and **reactionary** approaches. Libertarians emphasize a minimal role for government in all aspects of people's lives. They strongly oppose government policies designed to remake society, including efforts at income and wealth redistribution. Reactionary ideologies advocate the return to a more traditional society, including the undoing of reforms meant to empower the lower classes.

Think and Discuss

The left-right ideological spectrum regarding wealth redistribution presented in this chapter lists the following ideological positions: Marxist, social democratic, progressive, moderate, conservative, libertarian, and reactionary. What portion of the American population do you believe falls into each of these categories? What does this tell you about American politics?

Ideologies do not focus exclusively on economics. Another major ideological division is social, often referred to in the United States as the "values question." On the topic of social values, the ideological Left advocates greater tolerance of unconventional lifestyles, while the Right favors more traditional values. On this ideological dimension, the Left is often highly opposed to government action, since such action often seeks to suppress nontraditional values. Meanwhile, in battles over social values, many on the Right *favor* government intervention. They see government as responsible for protecting traditional norms and social institutions such as marriage. Thus, a cultural conservative may have a very different idea about the role of government than an economic conservative. Libertarians tend to be more consistent in both realms, being highly suspicious of any government action taken in the name of the greater good.

Ideologies can also differ in relation to identity. The Left advocates tolerance of minority groups, multicultural education, and special privileges to groups that have faced discrimination in the past: women, homosexuals, and ethnic, racial, religious, and linguistic minorities. The Right emphasizes the value of an overarching identity to unite diverse peoples, considering affirmative action programs to be a form of discrimination; although it often supports other government initiatives, such as facilitating

Marxist ideologies support getting control of the government to benefit the working class and eliminate significant income differences in a particular society.

Conservative ideologies advocate minimal regulation of the economy and put little emphasis on income redistribution.

A **libertarian** ideology seeks even more limited government, in all facets of society, than that promoted by conservatives.

Reactionary ideologies advocate a return to traditional social arrangements, including those which economically privilege one group over another.

cultural unification by giving one language official status. The extreme Right's fascist or ethno-nationalist ideologies advocate the elimination of cultural diversity through forced assimilation, expulsion of minority identity groups, or genocide.

Ideologies based on narrow interpretations of religion have gained prominence in recent years. Though not the sole religious-based ideology, **Islamism** has received much attention in recent years. Islamism is, in general, an anti-West and antimodernization ideology. Advocating protection from the cultural influences of Western-led globalization and the use of Islamic Law in government rule, Islamists gained control of governments in Afghanistan—where they were subsequently forced from power—and, in a milder form, Iran. In its extreme form, Islamist ideology has been a potent tool for the mobilization of Islamic terrorists. Like other religious-based ideologies, however, Islamism also takes much less radical forms, including as a guiding principle for relatively moderate political parties who seek power through peaceful means.

> **Islamism** is an ideology advocating Islamic Law as the basis for government structure and policies and as a way to immunize Muslim countries from what are seen as the corrupting cultural influences of Western-led globalization.

Ideology in the United Kingdom, Germany, France, and India

Democracies push certain ideologies, both in an effort to unify the population and as a way of distinguishing between competing political parties. Indeed, the platforms of political parties refine and exhibit major ideological positions. The United Kingdom, Germany, France, and India are no exception, though ideology is less central in these countries than in many others. In the United Kingdom and Germany, broad agreement on economic and social welfare policy has limited ideological confrontation, while the major parties in India have accepted the idea of market-led economic growth. Even in France, where the ideological divide between parties had been pronounced during the twentieth century, the traditional political parties now agree on many overarching principles of politics and economics. Instead, it is the emergence of new groups, pushing for a different approach to democracy, which currently fuels ideological controversies in France.

The United Kingdom

Many of the best-known political and economic philosophers of the last several centuries have been British. The country was the home to John Locke, Adam Smith, David Hume, John Stuart Mill, and, some argue, the birthplace of modern nationalism. But the British tradition of evolutionary political change and the postwar settlement in the arena of economics created little space for sharp ideological divides. Extremist political parties have had little success, and even the more zealous leaders of the mainstream parties have not been able to implement visions for remaking society.

In the 1980s, Margaret Thatcher had some success openly injecting conservative ideology (and libertarian rhetoric) into British political dialogue. Ultimately, she had to compromise on a number of social and economic policies, and many of her efforts did not last beyond her term in office. Tony Blair's designation of a "New Labour" party, more centrist and less ideological, led him to become, for most of his term in office, one of the more popular and powerful prime ministers of the last century. While Blair's successor, Gordon Brown, has put the Labour Party more squarely on the political left, he has maintained many of Blair's more moderate approaches.

Topic in countries

Germany

Germany's **social market economy (SME)** ideology reconciles conservatives and progressives to a particular type of state intervention in the economy and society.[51] The SME predates World War II and was successfully resurrected in postwar West Germany. However, it has been slower to take root in the former East Germany, whose people lived for more than four decades following World War II under the Marxist ideology of central state ownership and planning.

Holding that the market is the best way to allocate resources and generate wealth but not to distribute such wealth, the state sets out the general guidelines of market activity. It leaves it to the major groups in the economy and society—such as employers associations, labor unions, and banks—to regulate their activities in line with these parameters. The SME also requires the state to protect and compensate losers in the market with generous welfare state programs. But while the state mandates these programs, they are administered by major social groups such as churches and trade unions.

France

Mainstream political parties during the Fifth Republic have been less divided by ideology than in earlier periods of French politics, and parties today are ideologically closer than in the Fifth Republic's early years. Labor became recognized as a legitimate interest by Right and Left governments during the Fifth Republic, for example—though not a full partner, as in Germany. Parties of the Right became more progressive under de Gaulle, emphasizing modernization, solidarity, and the social mission of the state through the provision of generous pensions, health care, housing, and unemployment benefits, and the promotion of an expert bureaucracy above private management of the economy.

On the Marxist Left, the PCF lost electoral support, from a high near 25 percent of the vote to about 5 percent today. As its support declined, the PCF forged closer ties with the Socialist Party, which led to François Mitterrand's successful co-optation of PCF politicians into coalition with the Socialist Party during the 1980s.

Working with the Socialists, the PCF became less ideologically radical than it once had been. For its part, the Socialist Party also moderated its positions over time, embracing progressive Catholics, dropping Marxism, and favoring greater economic reform. As parties of the moderate Left, the PCF and Socialists governed together most recently from 1997 until 2002.

At the same time that traditional political parties have become closer ideologically, a new ideology has deepened the divide between these parties and many French citizens. This emerging ideology combines Republican values like solidarity with greater democratization and participation in governance. Since the 1990s, and for the first time in France, community-based organizing has exploded outside the parameters of the established political parties. This process has had an impact on French political culture, deepening support in the country for protecting and providing services for women, immigrants and their children, gay men and lesbians, and the unemployed.

This trend has also brought the formation of innovative political parties and led some politicians in the traditional parties to make appeals directly to the emerging movements. The rappers in the band Zebda ran under the banner of a new political party, *Motiv-é-es* ("Motivated"), which called for greater democracy and gained more than 12 percent of the vote in the 2001 local election in Toulouse. That same year, a Socialist politician named Bertrand Delanoë capitalized on his outsider image as a gay man and his advocacy of local democratization to win the mayor's race in Paris.[52] More recently, a movement headed by a Socialist deputy has called for an overhaul of the French political system and the creation of a Sixth Republic.

India

The ideologies that have arisen in the Indian polity have often seemed incongruent with aspects of its fragmented political culture. This may be

The **social market economy (SME)** is the central ideological approach in Germany. It includes state-defined limits on the market and state-legislated welfare programs administered by social groups.

part of the reason for ideology's limited impact in India. The period following independence was marked by socialist ideas. Although the economy included some elements of capitalism, the state was to be the leader in economic development. According to Pavan Varma, "The socialist era, although not entirely unproductive, was antithetical to the genius of the Indian people."[53] During the same period, the Communist Party of India (CPI) and, after a split in 1964, the Communist Party of India (Marxist) (CPI[M]) were articulating an ideology that was even further from what Varma saw as "the genius of the Indian people."

Today, disputes between the major political parties do not center on grand economic ideologies. In 1991, the Congress Party formally shifted from pursuing state-led development to supporting market-based economic policy, though it did retain its commitment to secularism. In 1998, the Bharatiya Janata Party (BJP), with a similar view on the role of the state in the economy but with a communal orientation embodied in an ideology called *Hindutva*, defeated the Congress Party and dominated the Lok Sabha until 2004.

Ideology in Mexico, Brazil, and Nigeria

In Mexico, Brazil, and Nigeria, the long periods of nondemocracy centered more on pragmatic considerations than ideological commitment. The three countries' democratic periods have allowed ideological divisions to resurface. In Brazil, the theme of diversity carries over to discussions of ideology, with notable ideological differences between parties of the Left and Right. In Nigeria, ideological divides are more connected to cultural and identity divisions, such as the dispute over the implementation of Islamic Law (*Shari'a*) in Muslim-majority regions of the country.

Mexico

As the overseer of an authoritarian rather than a totalitarian political system, the Institutional Revolutionary Party (PRI) was less ideological than the ruling parties in the Communist systems of Eastern Europe and the Soviet Union. Authoritarian leaders are generally much more pragmatic than totalitarian ones (see Chapter 6). Their main goal is to preserve authoritarian rule rather than to remake society, and the PRI acted accordingly. It used the rhetoric of revolution when it was beneficial, but it reached out to all groups in society and sought to make them dependent on the PRI while discouraging them from being politically active. This is not the stuff of highly ideological systems. For quite a while, this pragmatic approach worked.

Business leaders, for example, were reluctant to pressure the government for change because the PRI had fairly effectively bought them off.

With democratization and the emergence of rival political parties with genuine opportunities to win elections, ideological disputes resurfaced. The extent to which Mexico should base economic development on free markets and free trade is a point of contention. This ideological divide between the major parties is certainly larger than in the United States though less pronounced than in other Latin American countries—including Brazil.

Brazil

The Brazilian political spectrum is fairly wide, certainly compared with countries such as the United States, where voters and parties are clustered in the center, but also compared with other Latin American countries. On a scale of 0 to 10, where 0 is "very Left" and 10 is "very Right," Brazilian citizens average a score of 5.1 according to the 2007 Latinobarometer.[54] However, this apparently moderate ranking conceals wide disparities. More than one-quarter (28 percent) of Brazilians consider themselves "Leftist," while almost one-third (31 percent) consider themselves "Rightist." Thus, around 60 percent of Brazilians place themselves *outside* the political center. In continental Latin America, only El Salvador, Nicaragua, and Venezuela have a higher percentage of noncentrists.

The first two have endured civil wars in the last twenty years, and the third is locked in an ongoing conflict that has produced two attempted coups.

This ideological diversity is reflected in the party system: Brazil has nearly four times as many political parties as Mexico, ranging from Communist parties on the left to conservative and religious parties on the right. As in the United States, evangelical politicians wield considerable influence. However, in contrast to the United States, these evangelical politicians often hold progressive economic positions along with socially conservative ones. A prominent example is Rosinha Garotinho, ex-governor of the state of Rio de Janeiro, who opposed gay unions but belonged to the Brazilian Socialist Party. Garotinho provides a helpful reminder that cultural and ideological patterns in other countries may look quite different from those in the United States.

Nigeria

Ideology has never been as central in Nigeria as in other countries. Politics tends to be personalized, with the characteristics of leaders being more important than the policy positions they hold. Under military rule, the government was happy if the general population showed no interest in politics. This pattern is not unique to Nigeria. As discussed in more detail in Chapter 6, most authoritarian regimes place much less emphasis on ideology and citizen involvement than either totalitarian or democratic systems do.

Again, this idea of limited interest in ideology is a generalization. Within the Nigerian federal system, some regional governments are more aggressive in pushing a social blueprint. This is most true in the Muslim north, where debates continue about the extent to which Islamic Law (*Shari'a*) should be imposed on society.

Ideology in the Russian Federation, China, and Iran

Russia, China, and Iran have shared a largely undemocratic approach to politics for much of their history, but ideology in them has varied significantly—both in comparison to one another and within each case over time. In Russia, both the Marxist ideology of the Soviet period and the ideological free-for-all of the 1990s have given way to Vladimir Putin's more pragmatic vision of doing whatever is necessary to create an internationally respected and economically prosperous Russia. In China, the Communist Party long ago abandoned a commitment to economic planning and state-controlled development, though it shares with leaders of Russia the use of nationalism as an alternative to the economic ideology of the past. In Iran, meanwhile, attempts to deepen the population's commitment to the ideological vision of the 1979 Revolution have become more prevalent in recent years.

The Russian Federation

Ideology was important in both tsarist and Soviet times. The government used control over communications in both periods to try to transmit its blueprint for society to the general population. Under the tsars, the most unified ideology occurred under Nicholas I, who propagated a three-headed ideology of Orthodoxy, autocracy, and *narodnost'*. These three components highlighted the basis of tsarist rule: the tsar as the head of the Orthodox Church (formalizing the concept of divine right to rule), the tsar as the unquestionable and absolute leader, and the tsar as the father-figure and unifier of the Russian nation. Although the tsars also struggled with the question of who belonged to the Russian nation, their efforts tended to emphasize ethnic Russian characteristics, including Orthodox Christianity, at the expense of a large number of ethnic minorities. This exclusion is one of the reasons that the Soviets felt compelled to create ethno-territorial homelands for minority groups in an effort to gain their loyalty.

Ideology was even more central during the Soviet period. Official Soviet newspapers, as well as other publications such as scholarly articles, were compelled to fit their presentation of facts into the framework of Soviet ideology.

Topic in countries

Scholars who studied the Soviet Union identified a number of components of official Soviet ideology including, among others, the monopoly of political power for the Communist Party, atheism, and the superiority of economic planning. Vladimir Shlapentokh, in his book on the Soviet Union as a "normal totalitarian society," distills the elements of Soviet ideology down to two: socialism and Russian nationalism.[55]

One of the Soviet period's many legacies for contemporary Russia is suspicion of official government ideology. Such suspicion is understandable. The population had to endure years of socialization about the correctness of Marxist-Leninist ideology. Even worse, around the time of and immediately following the collapse of Soviet Communism, the population learned just how bankrupt the official ideology was. Imagine realizing in your old age that much of what you had come to believe about your country, its economic system, and its political leaders had been a lie!

China

With the economic reforms of recent decades, ideology has declined in importance in China. As David Lampton, a political scientist specializing in Chinese politics, put it in 2001, the ideological emphasis of socialism's superiority to capitalism had already by then "been dead for 10 or 15 or more years in any significant way."[56]

To the extent that there is an official ideology today, it combines appeals to nationalism, arguments about the merits of capitalism, and a claim that the Communist Party is the best opportunity for continued economic development. Party membership remains huge—well over 50 million residents of China are official Party members—but those joining the Communist Party largely do so not because they share the vision of the Communist Revolution or the views of past leaders like Mao. Rather, it is one of the gateways to social and economic advancement. Thus, Communist Party members today behave more like rational actors and less like true-believer revolutionaries committed to an ideological blueprint for remaking society.

Iran

Iranians are no strangers to government-sponsored ideology. Under the shahs, the main ideology involved justification of monarchial rule. In the decades leading up to the 1979 Revolution, a new focus was added: modernization based on the model of Turkey (a secular political system and close relations with the United States).

The 1979 Islamic Revolution provided a new official vision. It advocated a theocratic state based on strict interpretation of Islamic Law. Thus, while ideology is nothing new to Iran, its central role in Iranian politics reached new heights in recent decades, a trend that became even more pronounced after the election of Iranian President Mahmoud Ahmadinejad in 2005.

COMPARATIVE EXERCISE

Toward an Understanding of Cultural Globalization

Many theoretical frameworks related to globalization and culture, such as Barber's "Jihad Versus McWorld," address how globalization can weaken domestic culture or spark cultural conflicts. Few of them, however, center on what might cause some countries to be more susceptible to cultural globalization than others. This chapter's comparative exercise examines this question by engaging in a cross-regional comparative study.

As discussed in Chapter 1, a cross-regional study combines certain features of a "most similar" comparative study with those of a "most different" study. Within selected regions, otherwise similar countries that vary on the dependent variable are first compared to one another. As in a most similar comparative project, the researcher tries to find variables for which a theoretical basis for a causal relationship with the dependent variable exists and that appear to correlate with the dependent variable. The researcher then compares results from this region to those of other regions. If the same variables appear to be important across the different regions, the researcher has a more convincing story than looking at similar countries from a single region.

Hypotheses, Measurement of the Dependent and Independent Variables, and Cases

Chapter 3 introduced the A.T. Kearney/Foreign Policy Globalization Index. The journal *Foreign Policy*, which publishes the general A.T. Kearney/Foreign Policy Globalization Index, also put out a Cultural Globalization Index in 2004. The data used were based on late 1990s observations, but they can still be helpful to get a sense of the extent to which cultural globalization varies from country to country. The index included scores and rankings from dozens of countries. The scores and rankings were constructed by looking at per capita import/export figures for newspapers, periodicals, and books in these countries. The higher the per capita "cultural trade" figures, the more the culture of a country is interconnected to other cultures around the world. Using the per capita figures, one can put countries into categories based on how globalized their cultures are. These ordinal rankings provide the measure for the dependent variable in the comparative exercise.

There are two independent variables that seem particularly relevant to examine. The first is the extent to which each country's economy as a whole is globalized. The *globalized economy hypothesis* is that countries which have highly globalized economies will also have highly globalized cultures. The measure for this variable is the percentage of the country's GDP that comes from imports and exports.

The other independent variable is the extent to which English is widely spoken in the coun-

try. English is, simply put, the language of globalized culture. At the start of the twenty-first century, an estimated 25 to 30 percent of the world's population had some working knowledge of English, between one-quarter and one-third of all books published annually were in English, an estimated 80 percent of the world's electronic information was stored in English, and around 80 percent of Internet homepages were in English.[57] Thus, the *English language hypothesis* is that countries with populations who have a strong command of the English language will have highly globalized cultures. This variable was measured through use of an informal "expert survey"—a technique which asks specialists on a given country how they would categorize the country.

This exercise compares countries in three regions—Europe, North America, and Asia—chosen because the Cultural Globalization Index data for countries in South America and Africa were far from complete. The European countries examined are Ireland, the United Kingdom, Germany, Poland, and Romania; in North America, Canada, the United States, and Mexico; in Asia, Singapore, Japan, Indonesia, and China. Despite being similar countries in many ways within their regions, they differ notably on the dependent variable (their level of cultural globalization).

Results

Table 4.2 presents a summary of the dependent variable and the two independent variables. Looking first at the European cases, the pattern of the English-speaking variable is much more consistent with the dependent variable than the economic globalization variable. The United Kingdom and Romania stand out as particularly telling cases. Among the North American countries, use of English again appears to have a stronger relationship with the dependent variable. This is true for Canada and particularly for the United States. Finally, in Asia, only Singapore

Table 4.2 Cultural Globalization, Economic Globalization, and English Language Use

Country	Region	Cultural Globalization Index[a] Ranking—Category[b]	(Imports + Exports) / GDP—Category[c]	English Language Knowledge—Category[d]
Ireland	Europe	Very High	Very High	Very High
UK	Europe	Very High	Moderate	Very High
Germany	Europe	High	Moderate	Moderate to High
Poland	Europe	Moderate	Moderate	Moderate
Romania	Europe	Low	High	Low to Moderate
Canada	North America	Very High	High	Very High
US	North America	High	Very Low	Very High
Mexico	North America	Moderate	Moderate	Low to Moderate
Singapore	Asia	Very High	Very High	High
Japan	Asia	Moderate	Very Low	Moderate
Indonesia	Asia	Very Low	High	Very Low
China	Asia	Very Low	Moderate	Very Low

[a]Source: Foreign Policy 2004 Globalization Index based on 1997 data.
[b]Very High = 1–10, High = 11–20, Moderate = 21–30, Low = 31–40, Very Low = 41–44
[c]Source: Nationmaster.com, based primarily on 2001 data.
[d]Source: Estimates by the author, based on discussions with experts on the various countries.

presents support for the idea of economic globalization as a factor in cultural globalization. The pattern between English language use and cultural globalization is much more consistent.

Thus, the analysis of the most similar comparisons in three different regions provides support for the theory that cultural globalization is strongest where English language use is at its highest. On the other hand, the relationship between cultural and economic globalization was surprisingly shaky. The cases provide little support for the economic globalization hypothesis.

Were this a more formal comparative politics research project, additional variables would have been considered. For example, although the economic globalization hypothesis was not supported, even a quick glance at Table 4.2 calls into question the exclusion of overall level of economic development as an independent variable. If one could make a theoretical case for the inclusion of that variable, the data would seem to support some kind of relationship between overall level of economic development and cultural globalization.

In addition, with a study like this, one must always be concerned about how the variables are measured. Looking only at imports and exports of books, periodicals, and newspapers may paint an incomplete picture of cultural globalization. Scholars such as George Ritzer would suggest that the presence of American companies like McDonald's can infect the local culture, even if the number of English-language books imported was quite low. It is certainly possible that with a more complex measure of cultural globalization, this comparative exercise would have provided stronger support for the claim that cultural and economic globalization are related. In addition, although "expert surveys" are not uncommon as a way of categorizing countries, finding more objective indicators of the portion of the population that has a functional knowledge of English would be an improvement. One possible source of such indicators is census data from each country. For now, and with these limitations in mind, the comparative study in this chapter appears to have confirmed the importance of the English language as a vehicle for exposure to globalized culture.

CONCLUSION

An appreciation of a particular country's political culture can be a powerful tool in understanding how that country can remain politically stable, even rigid, for long periods of time. Yet, as "sticky" as political culture is, it can be altered by important events, such as the September 11, 2001, terrorist attacks, or modified by long-term or repeated experiences such as the Great Depression. Such shifts bring with them a new cultural structure and a new set of implications for political institutions and the individuals who govern within them.

It is possible to criticize explanations of political outcomes that rely on political culture alone. One would certainly want to consider other explanatory factors, such as the economic structural factors examined in the previous chapter. Another potential criticism is the ecological fallacy—that collective concepts cannot explain individual behavior—discussed in Chapter 1. Additional critiques include that measuring political culture is problematic, above all when the collective concept of culture is specified through the aggregation of individual-level data. Indeed, the flip side of the ecological fallacy, often termed the **individualistic fallacy**, is based on the idea that collectives are not necessarily the sum of their individual parts. Summing individuals' values misses the group dynamics that can accompany the infusion of culture into the context of politics. Others argue against a focus on political culture because, they contend, the concept oversimplifies complex societies (relying on stereotyping as much as on empirically

valid characterizations), it cannot explain rapid political changes, and politics shapes culture rather than the other way around. All of these concerns are legitimate.

Yet the underlying values and systems of meaning in different countries around the world are important components of the comparative study of politics. Consider the example of understanding a nondemocratic political system, governed by a long-time dictator, which *appeared to* collapse very quickly. Suppose the following series of events led up to the political system's collapse:

■ Changing economic conditions and other repeated events led values to change slowly, under the surface, for a period of time.

■ These slow changes were not mirrored by changes in the political system.

■ Eventually, the difference between the cultural setting and the political reality evaporated legitimacy, opening the door for a political entrepreneur to challenge the existing system.

■ This opposition leader rallied mass opposition to the current leader and the political system itself, protests spread rapidly, and the leader resigned.

Political culture is a crucial element in this chain of events. Even if political culture is not sufficient to

The **individualistic fallacy** is the assumption that collective concepts like culture can be adequately measured by aggregating individual level data.

bring about such a major political change, it can fuel changes sparked by another factor.

Comparativists who emphasize the importance of political culture argue that underlying values and systems of meaning—particularly those about politics—shape political institutions and political decisions. Experiences may affect political culture, but political culture also gives meaning to many experiences. As such, political culture is a lens for viewing the world of politics. Perceived cultural uniqueness is also a central component of group identity, which itself can have important political consequences and is the topic of the next chapter.

Key Terms

Civic culture theory, p. 108
Collectivistic political cultures, p. 104
Confucianism, p. 119
Conservative, p. 134
Cultural heterogeneity, p. 103
Cultural homogeneity, p. 103

Culture, p. 102
Defining events, p. 122
Horizontal social relations, p. 103
Individualistic fallacy, p. 142
Individualistic political cultures, p. 104
Islamism, p. 135
Jihad Versus McWorld, p. 131
Libertarian, p. 134
Marxist, p. 134
Moderate, p. 133
Noblesse oblige, p. 106
Political ideology, p. 132
Postmaterialism theory, p. 130
Progressive, p. 133
Reactionary, p. 134
Repeated experiences, p. 122
Social democratic, p. 133
Socialization, p. 122
Social market economy (SME), p. 136
Subsidiarity, p. 109
Vertical social relations, p. 103
Welfare state, p. 133
Working class deference, p. 106

5
Identity Structure

One evening in the summer of 1996, an American professor conducting research in Tallinn, Estonia, was returning to his apartment. As he walked across the apartment building's courtyard, two Russian men, who were smoking cigarettes, yelled over to him, asking if he had any matches. The professor ignored them and continued toward his apartment. As he started up the stairs, the Russians (who by then had run across the courtyard) grabbed him and threw him against the wall. As words were exchanged, the professor realized that he was being mistaken for an Estonian. When he explained to the Russians that he was an American, they both apologized and even offered him a gift (a pen) as compensation. As one of the Russians put it, "We cannot let an Estonian ignore us like that when we speak Russian." ∎

Look for this icon 🌐 to point you to **Deepening Your Understanding** features on the companion website www.college.cengage.com/politicalscience/barrington, which provide greater depth for some key content.

The experiences of this American professor highlight the extent to which belonging to a particular identity group—or being mistaken for belonging to a particular identity group—can affect how an individual interacts with others. Identity group membership, whether real or imagined by others, is also relevant to politics. To understand political outcomes fully, one must consider the extent to which individuals and groups are bound together through identity.

Identity groups consist of individuals. At the same time, people's membership in particular identity groups largely determines how they perceive themselves as individuals. Put simply, humans have a need to *belong*, to be accepted as part of some collective "us." This may seem strange to students in the United States, where individualism is stressed over collectivism. But sociologists and social psychologists have long understood that an individual's identity is tightly wrapped up in his or her sense of belonging to various social groups. This desire to belong is both natural for members of a population and reinforced by the actions of political elites. The development and reinforcement of a sense of "us" also creates and reinforces a sense of "them." In general, people overemphasize the similarities they share with members of groups to which they belong and exaggerate the differences between them and those they perceive to be "others."

Because belonging is a powerful sentiment, political elites often target identity in their efforts to mobilize the population in support of their candidacy for office, their policy positions, or their opposition to leaders of some other group. Identity can also fuel mass protests, especially in response to particular events, without significant elite guidance. Protests by Muslims in the summer of 2006 over a Danish cartoon depicting Muhammad, for example, were elite-guided to an extent but also took on a life of their own. As Chapter 11 discusses, individuals take political stances and actions partly as a result of self-interested, rational calculations. Groups to which individuals belong, however, provide *collective* interests for them to consider, while also offering emotional counterweights to individual rational calculations.

Identity

Identity is the set of characteristics by which individuals or collectives understand themselves and are known to others. For individuals, these characteristics include the groups to which the individual belongs (family, clan, ethnic group, etc.) and the individual's personality traits. These give the individual a sense of who he or she is and allow others to recognize the individual both as a unique person and as a member of particular groups. Many characteristics, such as hair color, are not politically salient. Others, including race, ethnic identity, religion, gender, and sexual orientation, can be important in shaping individual political behavior.

The structure of the politically relevant group identities in a particular society can also play an important role in political outcomes. Much of this chapter focuses on concepts and theories related to collective identity rather than individual identity. The extent to which a population is divided into identity groups with emotionally powerful bonds and how much those groups complement other such groups can be critical to political stability. Such deep identity divisions also drive governments to adopt strategies to address identity diversity. These strategies can include policies designed to protect minority group cultures, to

> **Identity** is the set of characteristics—politically salient or otherwise—by which individuals or collectives of individuals are known to themselves and others. For individuals, these characteristics include the groups to which the individual belongs (family, clan, ethnic group, etc.), and for groups they include shared values and beliefs among group members.

enhance such minorities' socioeconomic standing in society, or to make certain forms of group identity less politically salient.

Shared values and beliefs help bind together major identity categories. In other words, identity often incorporates culture. Because members of an identity group do not get to know, or even meet, most of the other members of that group, they must "imagine" themselves as part of it.[1] Accepting that they have a shared culture is a crucial part of this process of imagining. As this chapter shows, however, some types of identity groups can more easily employ perceived cultural bonds than other groups.

In-Groups, Out-Groups, and Perceptions of Threat

The establishment of a group identity creates a **membership boundary**. Within this boundary, the group's members share an identity bond. The individuals of the group come to see themselves as a "we." Social scientists typically refer to the group to which such members belong as an **in-group**. But by defining who belongs, membership boundaries also define who does *not* belong, thus creating what is called an **out-group**. The belief that the members of the out-group are different from members of the in-group can be a powerful tool for creating the boundaries of the group. The "otherness" of the out-group may end up being more important to in-group unity than the perceived cultural or physical similarities of in-group members. Often, the out-group is believed to be culturally or intellectually inferior, although it is not unheard of for members of the in-group to have an inferiority complex in relation to the out-group. If members of an in-group view themselves as less educated or less wealthy than members of the out-group, they may envy the other group. They may also blame the other group for their circumstances, believing them to be the result of discrimination.

The sharpness of the membership boundary between an in-group and an out-group is both a cause and a result of relations between the two groups. Groups that have exchanged bloodshed in the past are more likely to clash in the future than if they had not experienced an initial conflict. This is partly because of memories of the previous conflict, which group leaders may invoke when discussing the "other." It is also because the conditions that led to the original conflict may still be in place.

To mobilize members, group leaders often emphasize the threat an external force poses to the survival of the group. This threat to the group from outside its ranks can come from a different group of the same identity type (e.g., a neighboring ethnic group), from the government of the group's state of residence, or from larger external forces such as globalization. As discussed in the previous chapter, a group may see globalization as posing a threat to its cultural survival. Rival identity groups or the government can pose a more direct and immediate threat—perhaps to the very lives of the group's members. Whether or not an outside threat is objectively real is irrelevant. Alleged out-group threats are an example of the view that perception is reality.

Think and Discuss

Why is identity so effective as a tool for political elites who are trying to mobilize members of the general public?

The divide between those who belong to a group and those who do not is known as the **membership boundary** of the group.

Social scientists use the term **in-group** to refer to a group (e.g., an ethnic group) to which a particular individual belongs.

Social scientists use the term **out-group** to refer to a group that is the same type of group as the in-group (e.g., another ethnic group) but one to which a particular individual does not belong.

Forms of Collective Identity

Because the various categories of identity create divisions in a particular society between "us" and "them" groups, they are typically referred to as **social cleavages**. This chapter discusses what most comparativists consider to be the most politically relevant social cleavages. Some groups not discussed here (e.g., age cohorts) are addressed in other parts of the book. In addition, while some comparativists consider language divisions to be a kind of identity division,[2] the evidence that language is itself a defining collective identity for most people is scant. Instead, language often serves as a crucial *marker* for ethnic identity.

National Identity

Chapter 2 discussed national identity and nationalism. National identity is arguably the most important group identity in the world today. When reinforced by existing state boundaries, a strong national identity can generate tensions with neighboring states. When national identity and state boundaries do not coincide, conflict is even more likely—either between two states or between a state and a portion of its population seeking to control territory.

Extensions of Kinship Bonds: Race, Ethnicity, Tribe, and Clan

A number of identity types extend the idea of kinship and "blood ties" to groups much larger than traditional familial groups. Four such group identities are highlighted here: race, ethnicity, tribe, and clan. These groups are not equally effective at bringing into play the idea that members are related to one another by blood, and the success of each varies by geography and culture. Yet, the ability for racial, ethnic, tribal, and clan leaders to invoke biological connections among members can produce an emotional spark unmatched by any other group identities, with the possible exception of religion.

Race   The first major kinship category is **race**. Race is one of the most complicated and contested forms of identity. In the natural sciences, the term has a fairly accepted meaning: races are subspecies (i.e., a division of a species of animal), which typically develop biological differences from one another due to geographic isolation. Applying the concept to humans, however, creates a number of difficulties. First, in an increasingly globalized world, it is difficult for large segments of the human population to remain geographically isolated. Second, even in earlier periods of history, when intermarriage among different peoples was much less common, groups often intermingled, making objective identification of racial boundaries unworkable. Finally, unlike divisions within species of animals, separation of humans across geographic distances does not result in significant differences in skills or intellect.

Applied to humans, race is defined as *a large human population considered distinct from other such groups on the basis of genetically transmitted physical differences*. The word "considered" in the definition is very important. Because each racial group is so large and has so much diversity within it, race is arguably the least objective, most socially constructed form of identity. Anthropologists and sociologists, for example, point out that someone considered "white" in one setting may be considered "black" in another setting. Again, the key is not whether the physical differences are real—most biologists

Social cleavages are the categories of identity that create "us/them" divisions in a particular society.

Race is an identity group made up of large segments of the human population whose members are considered distinct on the basis of genetically transmitted physical differences. Race is much less objectively supported in the case of humans than in the case of subspecies of other animals but has been socially established as an important identity category.

(and certainly most social scientists) do not believe that there are actually significant genetic differences between races of humans—but that people *believe* that they are real.

People believe racial differences exist for two reasons. First, certain physical differences that people associate with race do exist, at least if one is focusing on extreme variations in such differences. For example, skin color is a physical feature people closely associate with race. Ordering photographs of people's faces, many of which would look similar, on a black/white continuum can be difficult, yet most individuals would recognize a significant difference between pictures at each end of the continuum. Second, the historical construction of racial membership boundaries included powerful myths that these physical differences reflected important genetic differences. These myths generated stereotypes about intellectual potential, work ethic, and so on. Over time, differences in appearance became markers for racial boundaries, these boundaries were linked to racial stereotypes, and race became socially (and thus politically) relevant.

The artificially sharp divisions between races survive not only because of stereotypes passed on from one generation to the next but also because of government policies around the world that validate the idea of racial boundaries. In many countries, including the United States, race is an identity category on the national census. Government affirmative action programs designed to address past discrimination on the basis of race are also common, particularly in economically-advanced democracies. As well-intentioned and arguably effective as they may be, these programs often deepen the exact identity divisions that were blamed for the discrimination in the first place.

Ethnicity While race was arguably the most important group identity of the twentieth century, **ethnic identity**, also referred to as *ethnicity*, has almost certainly been the most important group identity of the last several decades. It has provided the emotional spark for the global reemergence of ethnic nationalism, given politicians a ready-made tool for mobilizing supporters, and been at the center of controversies over the right of minority groups to practice and protect their cultures. As Donald Horowitz, one of the most important scholars of ethnic conflict, writes:

> In societies where ethnicity suffuses organizational life, virtually all political events have ethnic consequences. . . . In divided societies, ethnic conflict is at the center of politics. Ethnic divisions pose challenges to the cohesion of states and sometimes to peaceful relations among states. Ethnic conflict strains the bonds that sustain civility and is often at the root of violence that results in looting, death, homelessness, and the flight of large numbers of people. In divided societies, ethnic affiliations are powerful, permeative, passionate, and pervasive.[3]

What is ethnic identity, and what makes it so powerful? Ethnic identity is the sense of belonging to an **ethnic group**, which itself is a large collective sharing a common history and culture and believed to be connected together through common descent. Ethnic groups use numerous markers to differentiate between in-group and out-group members. These markers include, but are not limited to, language, family names, dialect, dress, and religion. Ethnic identity is typically ascribed rather than chosen. It is difficult, and sometimes impossible, to penetrate an ethnic group even if one learns and adopts the group's culture and practices.

Ethnic identity (also known as *ethnicity*) is the sense of belonging to an ethnic group.

An **ethnic group** is a large collective sharing a common history and culture and believed to share a common descent. Unlike nations, ethnic groups may lack self-awareness and not have developed a belief in the right of their group to political control over a particular territory.

Ethnicity is a strong form of identity because it is able to connect tightly shared cultural understandings, beliefs in kinship bonds, and perceptions that an "other" poses a threat to the group's survival. These three features combine with a fourth, the existence of ethnically heterogeneous states, to make ethnicity a central social cleavage and a source of significant conflict around the world at present. It is worth discussing each of these four features in some detail.

Culture is as central to ethnic identity as it is to any of the group identities discussed in this chapter. Ethnic groups contain a common set of cultural features that help bind members together. These features help in-group members to recognize each other, although out-group members can also use them to identify these individuals as ethnically different. In this way, ethnic groups differ from racial groups, which tend to be much more culturally heterogeneous.

Ethnic identity bonds go beyond culture to include perceptions of shared kinship. Although members of racial groups also feel some degree of "blood ties," racial groups are often too large to maintain a strong sense of shared kinship. Thus, most scholars see the ethnic group as the largest social group that still evokes "family ties." As Donald Horowitz puts it, "the language of ethnicity is the language of kinship."[4] As a consequence, ethnic leaders can effectively portray the group as a large extended family. This "family" is united by a past of shared descent, a present of shared experiences and a deep loyalty to one another, and a future (including descendants not yet born) of shared fate.

The image of ethnic boundaries as a perimeter dividing contrasting "extended families" leads to a third important distinction about ethnicity. Although any identity group may believe that its survival is threatened, ethnic identity's

Did You Know? Seeming to understand the electoral ramifications of identity, Tony Sanchez, a candidate for governor of Texas, said in September 2001, "Issues are important, but they are not as important as the fact that this is an opportunity to vote for one of your own."[5]

understandings of common descent and blood ties give this perceived threat added emotional salience. Ethnic groups can come to see a threat posed by the "other" as jeopardizing not only their common values and beliefs but also the survival of their ethnic "extended family." In such instances, it is understandable how ethnic group members could support extreme actions against the source of the threat. Just as individuals will take actions in defense of their families that they would not take otherwise, members of an ethnic group may engage in terrible acts against out-group individuals to guarantee the ethnic group's survival.

Very few countries are anywhere close to being ethnically homogeneous. Most have at least one significant ethnic minority, and often there is more than one sizeable minority group. In some countries, including Nigeria, no ethnic group makes up a majority of the population. The existence of multiple ethnic groups within the territorial boundary of a state combines with the ethnicity's emotional potency to push it into the middle of politics. If politics is indeed about "who gets what," ethnic identity provides a ready-made answer.

Tribal and Clan Identity The smallest of the group identities associated with shared blood ties are tribes and clans. A **clan** is a kinship group made up of several families, related to each other either by a common ancestor or through marriage. Clans often have a recognized leader who mediates conflicts within the clan and to whom clan members owe loyalty. The term "clan" is derived from the Scottish word "clann" (meaning family). Clan ties were historically

A **clan** is an identity group made up of a number of families who are believed to be related through birth or marriage to a common ancestor.

important for the Scots, and they remain important today to those of Scottish descent around the world. For the most part, however, clan identity is much less important today among Europeans than it is in the Middle East, Central Asia, and Africa. Though informal compared with the institutions of the state, clan politics has at times been more influential than state politics in shaping the development paths of Central Asian states.[6] In Africa, Somalia provides an example of clan ties overwhelming the effort to construct a strong national identity based on a shared ethnic Somali identity.[7]

A **tribe** is larger than a clan, although it is also a collective whose members believe that they can trace their heritage to a single ancestor. Compared with ethnic groups, tribes tend to be more geographically contiguous and compact, as well as more culturally homogeneous. They may have a single recognized leader, although their political organization tends to be less structured than in clans. In some countries, both tribal and clan affiliations are important, and tribes typically include anywhere from a few to many clans.

The term "tribe" has fallen out of favor with political scientists. It carries a stigma, because it has often been used to refer to groups who are perceived to be economically and culturally "backward." The term is also used for groups of such varying size, from hundreds to millions of people, that in many cases either "ethnic group" or "clan" would be more appropriate. For other groups, however, "tribe" remains the most suitable label.

Religion

Throughout recorded history, religion and politics have been tightly bound together. With the exception of such theocracies as Iran and the Holy See, today's religious leaders are generally less directly involved in governing than religious leaders of the past. Yet religion remains an important part of individual identity and a significant

social division. At the mass level, those who practice religion ardently tend to be more socially and politically conservative than those who do not.

Religion is an organized system of beliefs and devotion regarding a supernatural force (God) or forces (multiple gods). Most major religions are monotheistic, believing in a single deity. An individual can practice a faith, but, like culture, religion requires a collective of such individuals or, in the words of political scientist Thomas Reese, "a community of believers."[8] Religion also requires some form of institutionalization, a regularized set of practices flowing from the exercise of the religious beliefs. Religion can have an emotionally-powerful cultural pull. After all, religion is based not only on beliefs but also on *faith*. Often, when faced with events or settings that are inconsistent with certain beliefs, individuals change their beliefs. This is much harder in the case of faith, since by definition it is something that one believes without empirical support and even in the face of incongruent observation.

Religion provides answers for questions otherwise unanswerable. Faith is the belief that these answers are not just reasonable but are the Truth. For many people, this deep belief makes religion the most important collective bond within their individual identity. It also makes the us/them divide between religious groups potentially sharp. In the case of religion, the members of the "other group" are not just different; they

---

A **tribe** is an identity group that is similar to a clan but larger. A tribe may be made up of a number of clans. Their leadership structure also tends to be less structured than clans, though this varies somewhat from case to case.

Religion is an organized system of beliefs and devotion regarding a spiritual force or forces. One of the most important components of religion is faith, deeply held belief about the existence of a deity (and other major tenets) without empirical proof in support of these beliefs.

do not accept the Truth. In many religions, the in-group portrays itself as a "chosen people," and out-group members are thus not chosen. These ideas that the other group has not been chosen and lacks understanding of the Truth can combine to generate intolerance, discrimination, or violence against members of the other group.

The most politically important religions globally include Christianity, Islam, Judaism, Hinduism, and Buddhism. Although found throughout the world, most of these religions dominate particular regions—for example, the hold of Islam on the Middle East, Christianity's prevalence in Latin America, and the preponderance of Hinduism in India—or are regionally concentrated such as Buddhism in Asia. Religious divisions between a majority of the population and minority groups are increasingly commonplace.

Confucianism is not treated as a religion in this chapter due to its lack of formal structure and organized worship, although the previous chapter contained a discussion of Confucianism as a centerpiece of East Asian political culture. If deemed a religion, Confucianism would be one of the world's five largest religions.

Christianity Historically and presently one of the world's most influential religions, Christianity has the largest number of adherents. Christians can be found in all regions of the world, making up an estimated 2.2 billion people or approximately one-third of the world's population. Christianity is less at the center of domestic politics in majority-Christian countries than in the past. At the same time, it remains a political force globally, due to its size and, in some of its branches at least, its defined hierarchical structure and moral code.

Like other large religions, Christianity has mainstream and fundamentalist believers, along with a number of members whose beliefs only weakly influence their behaviors. Some believers support the intertwining of politics and Christian doctrine, while others favor a sharper separation of the religious and governmental spheres. Also like other religions, Christianity is divided into a number of different groups, though it is possible to roughly place them into three broad categories: Roman Catholic, Protestant, and Eastern Orthodox. These three groups share important beliefs, summarized in statements such as the Nicene Creed and Apostles' Creed, but have divergent practices and some important contrasting positions on certain tenets of their faith. Of these major Christian groups, Protestantism has the greatest variety of beliefs and practices and, consequently, a large number of denominations.

Islam Islam is the world's second largest religion, with around 1.5 billion adherents. Muslims make up more than 20 percent of the world's population and the majority of the population in more than four dozen countries. As with other religions, only a portion of Muslims are extraordinarily devout. For devout believers, Islam provides a complete blueprint for life. Similar to Christians, however, not all devout Muslims favor its incorporation into the political system. Practicing Muslims observe a code, the Five Pillars, which summarizes the most central beliefs and practices, including prayer five times per day, fasting during Ramadan, and a pilgrimage to Mecca at least once during one's life. In some Muslim-majority countries, *Shari'a* (Islamic Law) has become a central foundation of government policy.

Like Christianity, Islam has significant internal divisions. The most notable is between Shi'ite and Sunni Muslims. (Some scholars also treat Sufism—a variant of Islam centered on the idea that one can find love and deeper knowledge through a mystical path that links the individual more directly with Allah—as a third key division within Islam.) Shortly after Muhammad's death, Shi'ites and Sunnis split over who should succeed him, with Shi'ites supporting Muhammad's cousin, Ali. The vast majority (around 85 to 90 percent) of Muslims are Sunnis, but many politically important groups—government officials in Iran, for example—are Shi'ites.

While many Sunnis are devout, a much smaller portion support the more radical variants of Sunni Islam such as Wahhabism and Deobandism. Centered in Saudi Arabia, Wahhabism is hostile to modernization and supports a return to traditional Islamic values and practices. Deobandi Islam, a form of Islam practiced by the Taliban of Afghanistan, has similar fundamentalist characteristics. In addition to its supporters in Afghanistan, it is popular with a segment of Pakistan's population.

Think and Discuss

How are Islam's Five Pillars—the belief that "There is no true God except Allah, and Muhammad is the Messenger of Allah," prayer five times per day, fasting during Ramadan, charity (alms-giving) to the poor, and a pilgrimage to Mecca at least one time during one's life—similar and different to the core "pillars" of Christianity?

Judaism Though Jews are much smaller in number than Christians and Muslims, Judaism has had a major impact on international politics. Some of the most internationally important conflicts of the past century involved the persecution of Jews in predominantly Christian countries and tensions between Jews and Muslims in the Middle East. The failure of countries surrounding Israel to accept the new state as legitimate sparked a series of wars between Israel and its Arab neighbors. These conflicts were exacerbated by the failure of the international community to constitute a Palestinian state—as the UN General Assembly had originally supported—alongside Israel. Though the groundwork was in place for a Palestinian state at the end of the first decade of the twenty-first century, its creation is unlikely to resolve tensions between Jews and Muslims (and Christians) in the Middle East in the near future.

Like Christianity and Islam, Judaism is monotheistic. Indeed, Christians, Muslims, and Jews share a common religious heritage. More than any other religion, however, Judaism carries with it a strong sense of identity based on common descent that makes Jewish identity as much an ethnic one as a religious one. Religion is often a marker of ethnic boundaries, but for Jews it is the central criterion of their identity. With the emergence of Zionism, a movement that developed in Europe in the 1800s advocating a Jewish state in the region around Jerusalem, Jewish identity became a national identity as well. After the Holocaust, the Zionist cause was accepted by the leading countries of the time, and the state of Israel emerged in 1948.

Hinduism Hinduism is the third largest religion, currently constituting around 15 percent of the world's population. Scholars believe it is more than three thousand years old. Hindus are primarily located in India and Nepal. Hinduism is less formally structured than either Christianity or Islam, and unlike many religions there is no single individual (Jesus, Muhammad, etc.) with whom the religion is closely associated.

Mahatma Gandhi emphasized the peaceful, nonviolent components of Hindu thought in his mobilization of the Indian population to the cause of India's independence from British control. His emphasis on a combination of noncooperation and nonviolence became one of Gandhi's most important and lasting legacies. More recently, however, Hinduism has become the central identity component of nationalist movements in India that advocate violent struggle against other religious groups in South Asia, particularly Muslims in Pakistan. As a result, the Hindu-Muslim divide has fed the conflict between India and Pakistan over the disputed territory of Kashmir.

Buddhism Like Hinduism, Buddhism originated in India. Unlike Hinduism, it spread far to the east of India: southeastward to Sri Lanka and through Vietnam; eastward into much of China, the Korean peninsula, and as far as Japan; and northeastward into Tibet and Mongolia. Around 400 million people practice Buddhism, including an increasing number of people in North America and Europe. Its political relevance comes from its emphasis on nonviolence and its encouragement of challenging authority, especially if that authority is perceived to have strayed from the path of wisdom, virtue, and discipline that Buddha emphasized.

Similar to Confucianism, some balk at labeling Buddhism a religion, since there is no focus on the worship of a creator. The religion is associated with a single individual (Siddahartha Gautama, who came to be known as Buddha). But Buddhists consider him to be a wise leader—the term Buddha means "enlightened one"—who came to his understandings through personal introspection rather than through intervention by God. As a result, the centerpiece of Buddhist beliefs is not faith but *self-reflective experience*. Its principles (including ideas about suffering being the result of obsession with achieving one's personal desires) are less rigid and detailed than the dogma of other major religions. It is also possible to practice it and still be a member of another religion, while most would consider it impossible to identify oneself simultaneously as Christian, Muslim, and Jewish. At the same time, the religion is more organized than Confucianism. There are formal structures (e.g., Buddhist monasteries), and adherents typically practice the religion at regular sessions, which emphasize meditation and involve a group leader.

Sex/Gender

When comparativists discuss identity divisions between men and women, they typically use the term gender. While "sex" is the appropriate term for biological differences between men and women (i.e., individuals as male or female), gender involves the perceived differences (masculine versus feminine) that help shape the identity groups of male and female. In other words, gender differences entail supposed physical and psychological traits, expected roles, and socially acceptable behaviors. Some of the physical

differences between men and women are readily apparent. More controversial, but gaining support among some biological scientists and psychologists, is the extent to which men and women process and react to information differently. Regardless of the extent to which such physical and psychological differences are real, their translation into social expectations about different types of behavior transforms them into gender differences. What a society considers masculine roles—and how rigid the boundaries are between masculine and feminine roles—can differ greatly from one country to another.

The term gender is also used to refer to differences in political behavior between men and women, as in the phrase "the gender gap." In the United States, women are generally less conservative than men.[9] This also appears to be the pattern in some Islamic countries, probably in part because conservative interpretations of Islam support subservient social roles for women. In many other countries, however, the gender gap takes the opposite form. In Eastern Europe and the former Soviet Union, women tend to be more conservative than men. In the post-Communist transition, women were hurt by social upheaval and economic reform much more than men, contributing to their suspicion of reform and preference for maintenance of the status quo.

Economic development and its accompanying social changes influence social and political attitudes among women, including their desire to participate in politics. As more women enter the workforce, politics becomes more crucial to their daily lives. As educational opportunities for women improve, they gain skills necessary for effective political participation. These trends fed the feminist movements of the 1970s and 1980s, which generated additional opportunities for

Gender refers to social understandings of traits, roles, and behavioral differences between men and women and to differences between them in political attitudes and behavior.

women and raised the consciousness of many women about gender relations.

Gender has also become a more prominent social divide because of globalization, which has brought a greater awareness of the treatment of women around the world. The increased reach and effectiveness of international organizations such as the United Nations, for example, has placed the status of women on the international political agenda, complementing domestic pressures for women's rights. In most countries, women are much better off than they were at the start of the twentieth century. (Remember, the Nineteenth Amendment to the United States Constitution, which guaranteed women the right to vote, was ratified only in 1920.)

Class

Political scientists consider class divisions to be one of the most important social cleavages. Class differences are a fact of life in nearly every country in the world. As discussed in Chapter 3, Karl Marx believed that understanding class divisions was essential to understanding politics. A key to Marx's predictions about the collapse of capitalism was members of the working class (the "proletariat") becoming aware of the extent to which the capitalist system exploited them and that other members of the working class shared this fate. This awareness, what Marx called "class consciousness," set the stage for the proletariat to overthrow capitalism and its allies in the political system.

Historically, class consciousness among the workers has played a role in uprisings, such as the Bolshevik has Revolution in Russia in 1917. Even more, however, such uprisings involved elites leading the action in the name of the working class, or took the form of peasant uprisings where the goal was not to overthrow the economic system but rather to seize land for their own use. Spontaneous uprisings among the lower classes with the goal of overthrowing the existing system have been few and far between. On the other hand, economic issues—working conditions, wages, number of hours worked per week,

unemployment, and so on—have been a source of political mobilization. They spurred the widespread development of trade unions in the twentieth century, and they continue to play a role in shaping electoral results, especially in Europe.

Intrastate Regional Identity

In many countries, political attitudes and deeply-held beliefs among members of the general population differ markedly depending on region, and much of the work in political science on mass attitudes in specific countries includes an analysis of regional variation. While differences in attitudes do not necessarily equate to differences in identity, people can develop a strong sense of attachment to the region in which they live.

For some people, this attachment develops into an important part of their identity. In the United States, for example, it is not unusual for individuals to incorporate their region of residence into their personal identity. Those who have lived in different states but in the same general region for a significant portion of their lives may see themselves as southerners or midwesterners. Those who live their entire lives in a single U.S. state are more likely to adopt a state identity over a regional one (seeing themselves as a Wisconsinite or a Floridian).

Those who live in outlying regions of a country often see residents of the central region as the "other," especially if the central region is also home to the capital city of the country. Political science studies indicate that those living in border regions commonly believe that those in the center—and certainly those in the capital—are privileged. They see the capital as not only the seat of political power but also as the area that receives the most attention from government officials. In Canada, center-periphery relations take an interesting twist. Many residents of the province of Quebec see the province of Ontario as the privileged center. Residents of Ontario consider Quebec to be the most privileged region. For residents of Canada's western provinces (and, to a lesser extent, residents of the Maritime provinces), *both* Ontario *and* Quebec make up the privileged center. The fact that nearly every Canadian prime minister has come from Ontario or Quebec only reinforces this perception.[10]

Although regional identities are less likely to be the primary identity for most people than other identity groups discussed in this section, identification with region of residence can reinforce other group identities. It is not unusual for an ethnic or religious group, for example, to be concentrated in a certain region of a country.

Transnational Regional Identity

The increasing interconnectedness among states in the international political system has begun to foster a form of transnational regional identity. This trend has been most obvious in Europe. The European Union is far ahead of any other regional organization in marshalling transnational integration among its member-states. It should not be surprising, therefore, that the EU considers the development of a strong attachment to European identity to be increasingly important.

How attached ordinary people are to such an identity, however, is another story. (Remember the comparative exercise in Chapter 2.) For the EU to succeed in its ultimate desire to create something akin to the United States in Europe, the populations of EU member-states will have to accept themselves, first and foremost, as European. In other words, European identity must become more than transnational. It must become an overarching, national identity. "Europeanness" is a long way from superceding the existing national and subnational identities in Europe, but the extent to which people see themselves as European in a meaningful way does vary across the countries of Europe and among individuals within EU member-states.

Identity Divisions in the United Kingdom, Germany, and France

Identity divisions have important effects on political outcomes in the United Kingdom, Germany, and France. The salience of particular identities, however, has shifted over time, with the original focus on class shifting to one on ethnicity and religion. Religious divisions have been transformed as well, as relations between Christians and Muslims have replaced the traditional rift between Protestants and Catholics (especially in the United Kingdom and Germany) as the key religious problem facing government leaders. As a result, the tension between long-time residents and immigrants, many of whom are Muslim, has also become a central political issue.

The United Kingdom

Identity is a focal point of British politics. Whether it is the extent to which the British see themselves as distinct from continental Europeans, the uneasy status quo between Catholics and Protestants in Northern Ireland, the growing sense of national identity among ethnic minorities like the Scots, or the renewed focus on the question of Islam in the United Kingdom, identity in one form or another dominates political discussions in the country. On the other hand, a significant identity division from the past, class, has become less salient over the last several decades.

During much of the twentieth century, class cleavages were the dominant British social divisions. The divisions were typically between the middle class (executives, managers, other white collar workers) and the working class (skilled and unskilled manual labor and the very poor). These class boundaries still roughly correspond to divisions in support for the two main political parties. The Conservative Party has generally had significantly greater support among the middle and lower middle class, while skilled and unskilled workers have supported the Labour Party. When one party has dominated the other for any significant amount of time, it has generally been due to defections of key economic constituents. This was the case, for example, in the Conservative Party's 1979 victory in parliamentary elections under Margaret Thatcher. Thatcher was able to

Topic in Countries

win over many workers by stressing lower taxes and limits on immigration.

As early as the 1960s and 1970s, ethnicity and religion moved to the fore in British politics. Ethnic identity divisions in the United Kingdom involve the main groups that have comprised British identity over the past couple centuries and new immigrant populations. The vast majority of the British are English, but the three "Celtic" groups—Scots, Irish, and Welsh—make up about one-sixth of the population. Until relatively recently, the main religious division in the United Kingdom was between Protestants and Roman Catholics, particularly in the region of Northern Ireland.

Over the last several decades, the issue of minority immigrant groups has become a focal point of British political discourse. Relations between immigrants and the rest of the population are better in the United Kingdom than in many countries, and intermarriage across ethnic and racial lines is significant in the large cities. Tensions remain though, particularly involving Muslim immigrants in the wake of the July 7, 2005, terrorist bombings. The waves of immigrants from former British colonies have brought not only new ethnic identities to the United Kingdom but religions such as Hinduism and Islam. There are now around 1,500,000 Muslims in the United Kingdom and another 500,000 Hindus.

Germany

The major identity divisions in contemporary Germany are class, ethnicity, and religion. Ethnicity was a deadly point of conflict in the twentieth century, culminating in the genocidal policies of the Nazi regime. Today, debates center on how far to accommodate ethnic and religious minorities. Regional identities also persist. Rather than being a source of violent conflict, however, tensions between different identity groups have, for the most part, been kept in check within the democratic politics of the Federal Republic.

Class has been a major cleavage in Germany since the industrial revolution in the nineteenth century. Up through the Great Depression, German society was marred by violent conflict between the communist Left and authoritarian parties of the Right supported by the middle classes and business elites. Class polarization was a major reason for the destruction of the Weimar democracy and the rise of Adolf Hitler. In the postwar period, the East German Communist regime officially oversaw a classless society, though differences in status and life chances remained—particularly between ordinary citizens and high-ranking members of the Communist Party (officially known as the Socialist Unity Party). In West Germany, widespread economic prosperity and generous welfare state policies did much to defuse class conflict. Still, the major parties of the Federal Republic continue to draw their core supporters from specific classes, with business elites supporting the Christian Democratic Party (CDU) and most workers supporting the Social Democratic Party (SPD). The smaller Free Democratic Party (FDP) tends to draw support from small business, the self-employed, and professionals.

Religious differences among the German population have been an important cleavage that has marked the country's development, with conflict between Protestants and Catholics being the major divide in the sixteenth and seventeenth centuries. Germany was the birthplace of the Protestant Reformation in the sixteenth century, and official state policy under Bismarck in the nineteenth century sanctioned persecution of the Catholic Church. In the postwar period, the advance of secularization—a trend evident across Europe—and the Christian Democratic Party's success as a catchall party bridging the religious divide have all but eliminated conflict between these two branches of Christianity. Today, the major religious divide in Germany is between the Christian majority and the Muslim minority.

Ethnic divisions have, at times, devastated German society and politics. The question of "who is a German?" took on a malignant form with the Nazi regime's declaration of the *Volk* community whose membership was limited to so-called Aryans, or those of German blood. This conception of national identity culminated in the murderous policies against Jews and other minorities under Hitler. Ethnicity remains a salient identity, partly because of the significant amount of immigration in the first decades of the Federal Republic. During the 1960s, Germany experienced a labor shortage, and the government responded by instituting a "guestworker" policy that attracted immigration from southern and Eastern Europe. Because many of these immigrants stayed permanently, Germany found itself with a significant minority population. Immigrants today comprise 7.3 million persons, or 8.8 percent of the population. At 1.8 million persons, Turks comprise the largest minority group.[11]

Regional affiliations have long been a feature of German society, with a strong sense of regional identity existing among residents of various *Länder*, especially Bavaria. Unification of Germany in 1990 did not bring with it a complete unity in outlook or living conditions. The experience of living under distinct regimes for forty years left deep economic, political, and psychological imprints on western and eastern Germans. This legacy has led many Germans to

Hundreds of thousands of fans of the German and Turkish national soccer teams turn out near Berlin's Brandenburg Gate to watch the 2008 European Football Championship semifinal match between Germany and Turkey on June 25, 2008. Public viewing areas with large screens were set up in a number of cities in Germany so fans could watch the game, which was played in Basel, Switzerland.

(©Sean Gallup/Getty Images)

comment on a "wall in their minds" that continues to divide the west and east of the country.

France

The French Republic is based on the concept of universalism, which recognizes each person as an equal individual interacting with the state free from the intervention of other social structures.[12] Differences—whether they are believed to be biological, cultural, or religious—have no political significance. As a result, identity-based movements in France raise the question of loyalty: Can one act politically as woman, Corsican, gay, Muslim, or Jewish and be loyal to the Republic? Even today, such movements are often reminded of what one revolutionary said about Jewish emancipation: to be citizens, "they must no longer form either a political body, or an order in the state."[13]

Historically, social class and religion have been the salient political identities, with the aristocracy and Catholics pitted against the middle class, against workers, and against Jewish and Protestant minorities. Regional identities have also been important. Alsatians claim to be the most French, and the Lyonnais note that their city was the ancient capital, while the Celtic Bretons initiated armed resistance to the Revolution and many Italian-speaking Corsicans still demand local autonomy.

Anti-Semitism has been a powerful force on the right and left. Under the Vichy government during World War II, many French officials cooperated with the Nazis in carrying out the Holocaust. For more than thirty years after the war, French officials from all parties ignored wartime complicity, even as some of those responsible were protected as they became high officials of the Republic.[14] Maurice Papon, who ordered the deportation of Jewish children to death camps, became the Paris prefect of police under Charles de Gaulle, and ultimately the budget minister. Though his role in the Holocaust was revealed in 1981, he was not tried until 1994.

With the nineteenth century conquest of present day Algeria, expansion across West Africa, and occupation of Indochina, colonial rule challenged the commitment to universalism, which required, in theory, all born under French authority to be citizens. Officials developed a political hierarchy that mirrored their racial prejudices, drawing from science to "prove" racial difference, justify the inequality of women, and discriminate against homosexuals. All residents of the French Republic were "potentially" equal, and it was the state's mission to bring "civilization." Colonial subjects were denied citizenship; like women at the time, they were not considered ready for its responsibilities.[15] For Arabs in Algeria, citizenship was nearly impossible, as the origins of their difference and their religion were considered primordial and dangerous.[16]

Today, contention over contemporary immigration remains a product of the relationships between France and the former colonies, and colonial racism and anti-Semitism continue to influence how the Republic addresses diversity. One example is the National Front, an extreme right-wing party founded in the 1970s by a former army intelligence officer and veterans of the Vichy government. Although some Republicans on both the left and right of the political spectrum believe the party's "French first" policy promotes intolerance, mainstream politicians have been unable to respond effectively to the National Front's xenophobic and homophobic rhetoric, often instead adopting the Front's perspective in an appeal to its supporters. It does not help that the makeup of France's National Assembly mirrors the National Front's "French first" vision. Of the National Assembly's 577 deputies, a mere 16 are of non-European origins; all but one of those represent districts outside European France, leaving almost no elected representation from minority communities within the hexagon.[17]

Identity Divisions in Mexico and Brazil

As in the European TIC cases, ethnicity has important effects on political outcomes in Mexico and Brazil. Much more than in the European cases, however, class remains a strong divide as well, with other collective identities like religion also playing consequential roles at times. In Mexico, the most important identity divisions are class, ethnicity, and religion. Regional divisions, while less prominent, have also been consequential. In Brazil, class and ethnicity have been consistently important, as befits a country of immigrants with high levels of economic inequality. However, religion, race, and to some extent gender, have become increasingly significant over the last few decades.

Mexico

Within Mexico, class is arguably the most important identity cleavage in terms of its political effects. A large portion of both the urban and rural Mexican population is poor. In the past, the one-party system prevented class divisions from driving political outcomes. In today's system, however, class lines increasingly coincide with political lines.

Varying estimates of Mexico's different ethnic groups complicate efforts to grasp ethnic identity's importance. As mentioned in Chapter 2, the vast majority of the Mexican population is *mestizo*, a group formed through mixing of European and native peoples over the past several centuries. Estimates of the percentage of the population that is *mestizo* vary greatly, from around 60 percent to well over 80 percent. A sizeable portion of the population is indigenous—often referred to as "Indian"—but the size of this group also depends on how it is defined. A little more than 10 percent of the population fits a strict definition: those who speak indigenous languages and maintain other openly indigenous cultural markers. However, as much as 30 percent of the Mexican population identifies itself as indigenous. The other sizeable ethnic group is European, that is, those who are descendants of Spanish and other colonists whose families did not intermix with the native population. They make up a little more than 8 percent of the population.

Tensions exist between the Indian and *mestizo* groups, though they are not as bad as similar minority-majority ethnic relations in other countries. This is partly because—with the exception of the rebellion in the Chiapas region that began in 1994—the Indian population has not been well organized politically. It is also because, similar to the Native American population in the United States, there are significant variations in culture among the more than fifty different indigenous groups, and strength of attachment to indigenous identity within this minority differs from person to person. As a result, this identity is less threatening to the rest of the population than it might be. Most Mexicans argue that the ethno-racial divide is not nearly as sharp as it is in countries such as the United States. At the same time, many Mexicans still associate European features with privilege, while those perceived to look indigenous (including dark-skinned *mestizos*) are subject to negative stereotyping and open discrimination.

Religion is more important to members of the general population in Mexico than in most of the TIC countries, and the vast majority of the population is Catholic. The extent to which religion divides the population in identity terms is relative to how deeply Catholic one is. Mexicans' depth of attachment to religious identity affects their attitudes about the Catholic Church's role in society, and thus its role in politics.

At times in Mexico's history, regional divisions have surfaced, and political leaders have successfully played the regional card during the period of Mexico's most significant political reform of the last two decades. The PAN (National Action Party), for example, has successfully seized on disenchantment in the north and west of the country. In addition, as is the case in many countries, people in many parts of the country resent the capital city, Mexico City, for its central role in national politics and its significant absorption of federal revenues. Such resentment has served as fertile ground for politicians seeking to mobilize supporters in peripheral regions.

Brazil

In the absence of a strong, overarching national identity, the types of social identity discussed in this chapter have been of great significance to Brazilians. The deepest and most intractable social cleavage in Brazil is class. From its origins as a slave-holding colony, Brazilian society has been marked by profound divisions between the wealthy few and the masses of poor. As Brazil developed economically, a substantial middle class emerged, mostly in the cities (agriculture is still dominated by large landowners). Nevertheless, Brazil remains one of the most unequal countries in the world, and inequality has grown over the last decade of neoliberal economic reform.

Unlike in the United Kingdom, this social cleavage is not consistently reflected in the party system. Since the formation of the Workers' Party (PT) in 1982, the PT has attempted, with some success, to speak for the working class and rural poor. However, many poor people continue to vote for whichever party offers them more immediate material benefits, an approach associated with "clientelism" (see Chapter 9 for a more detailed discussion of clientelism). In exchange for a housing project, or the extension of a sewer line, a well-heeled candidate can win the votes controlled by a local community leader. When the community leader delivers the votes, the candidate must deliver the goods. This system ensures that the short-term needs of the local poor population are met, but it avoids long-term legal changes, such as land reform, that might more substantially benefit the poor across the country.

Ethnicity is another obvious cleavage. Brazil is a country of immigrants from many parts of the world, including some 25 million of Italian heritage, 10 million of German descent, and 10 million Lebanese. The Brazilian city of

São Paulo has more ethnic Japanese than any city outside Japan.[18] However, discrimination against specific groups of immigrants is rare. Ethnic identity mostly finds peaceful expression in cultural communities, particularly towns or areas within a large city where immigrants of the same national origin live.

Brazil is the largest Catholic country in the world, with nearly three-quarters of its population declaring themselves Catholic on the latest national census. Because of the dominance of Catholicism, religion was not historically a salient social cleavage. However, religion has become increasingly politically significant in two distinct ways. First, a reform movement within the Catholic Church known as liberation theology had a profound effect on Brazil. It led to the formation of thousands of Ecclesial Base Communities (CEBs) that served as the nucleus around which many social movements later formed, including the main peasant movement (the Landless Movement, or MST) and countless urban popular movements which pushed for housing, health care, education, and other public services. The CEBs supported the independent labor movement, helped form the Workers' Party, and were at the forefront of the popular mobilizations that forced the military government to relinquish power in the 1980s. Though CEBs have become less politically active in recent years, there is no doubt that the Catholic Church played a major role in Brazilian democratization.

The second way in which religion has become politically significant in Brazil results from the rise of Protestant sects, mainly Pentecostals. Almost 15 percent of Brazilians belong to one of Brazil's many Pentecostal churches, most of them homegrown or split off from major U.S. denominations such as the Assembly of God. Pentecostalism is spreading throughout Latin America, but has been most successful in Brazil. Though Pentecostals focused initially on spiritual renewal, their increasing numbers have made them a political force to be reckoned with, especially since Pentecostalism appeals primarily to the poor who are otherwise hard for political parties to reach. Evangelicals have run their own candidates on various party tickets and actively supported them with the full authority of the church—Evangelicals vote for Evangelicals, as one campaign slogan said. In 1989, fearing a victory by the leftist PT, "national leaders of the largest Pentecostal denominations marshaled their spiritual and material resources,"[19] on behalf of the conservative presidential candidate Fernando Collor de Mello. In addition to financial support, pastors and congregational leaders told their flocks to vote for Collor. Even though such poor people might logically have seen in the PT a party more sympathetic to their needs than the wealthy Collor, "throughout the nation, believers heeded their pastors' advice and made a crucial contribution to Collor's electoral victory."[20]

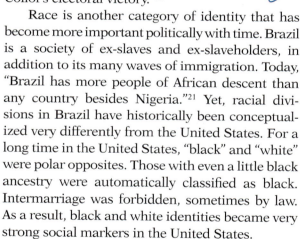

Race is another category of identity that has become more important politically with time. Brazil is a society of ex-slaves and ex-slaveholders, in addition to its many waves of immigration. Today, "Brazil has more people of African descent than any country besides Nigeria."[21] Yet, racial divisions in Brazil have historically been conceptualized very differently from the United States. For a long time in the United States, "black" and "white" were polar opposites. Those with even a little black ancestry were automatically classified as black. Intermarriage was forbidden, sometimes by law. As a result, black and white identities became very strong social markers in the United States.

In Brazil, people were not split by law or custom into two "races." Instead, individuals can be described by over a dozen racial terms identifying shades of skin color and facial features. Different observers might identify the same person in different ways, depending on their subjective impressions. Brothers and sisters with natural differences in skin tone may be classified with different racial terms. The Brazilian census did not even include a question about racial identity until 1940. Today, Brazilians can identify themselves on the census as white (54 percent), brown/mixed race (39 percent), black (6.2 percent), or other (1 percent).

Because of their mixed racial heritage, Brazilians often spoke of their society as a "racial democracy," in which little racial prejudice existed and intermarriage among people of different skin tones was common. At the same time, whiteness was seen as socially superior to blackness. Nineteenth century Brazilian intellectuals justified acceptance of intermarriage as promoting "whitening," in which extensive racial mixing would improve society by providing white genes to all members.

Many of these attitudes persist today. One (2001) study asked interviewers to classify subjects using racial terms, and then subjects classified themselves. Given the availability of other terms for various shades of color, relatively few Brazilians chose to identify themselves as "black." Moreover, interviewers' classifications were affected by the perceived social status of the subject. Among highly educated women who *self-identified* as black, for example, only 20 percent were classified as black by interviewers. Thus, "interviewers 'whitened' the classification of higher-educated persons."[22] Alternatively, as the Brazilian saying puts it, "money whitens." The connection between status and race is evident.

Did You Know? The famous "black" golfer Tiger Woods is half Thai, one-quarter African American, and part Native American.

Identity Divisions in the Russian Federation, China, and India

Russia, China, and India all face a multitude of identity divisions, including ethnicity, region, religion, and class. This identity mosaic has been in place in India throughout its history, and the case of India adds the complex identity category of caste to the mix. In China and Russia, class divisions and, to a lesser extent, religion, have emerged as identity factors over the last two decades.

The Russian Federation

Nearly all the major identity cleavages discussed in this chapter are important in the Russian Federation. Class divisions in Russia have become increasingly important since the collapse of the Communist system. During the Soviet period, class was not a central identity division, although Communist Party members—especially those at the top—certainly lived like members of the upper classes of non-Communist countries. Today, there is a visible rich class, particularly in the largest cities, who do not hold top political positions. The sizeable gap between the very poor and very rich has fed anger over post-Soviet economic and political reforms. The sense that most if not almost all of those who are rich got that way illegally has an important political impact. It allowed former President and current Prime Minister Vladimir Putin to crack down against several wealthy political opponents in the name of fighting corruption with little objection from the general population.

Religion is also an important basis of collective identity in Russia, particularly since the collapse of the Soviet Union. In the pre-Soviet era, the Russian Orthodox Church was strongly connected to the tsarist state. Although the Orthodox Church and the Soviet government had, to put it mildly, an uneasy relationship, the post-Soviet period has once more brought the Orthodox Church into the political mainstream. It found allies within the Russian government, which passed laws that privilege long-established religions such as Orthodox Christianity.

The second largest religious group is Muslims, making up as much as 15 percent of the population.[23] Birthrates among those who practice Islam are significantly higher than the rest of the Russian population. A number of high profile incidents across Russia, including the Beslan school tragedy in September 2004, have led ordinary Russians and even the government itself to rashly link the country's Muslim minorities to terrorism.

Identity **161**

The collapse of the USSR brought with it an ideological vacuum, leading many to turn to religion for answers. Religious cults flourish in such settings, and Russia is no exception. These religious movements effectively played on people's sense of purposelessness and disillusionment, resulting from the political, economic, and social upheavals of the previous two decades. Largely at the request of the Orthodox Church, the Russian government harassed nontraditional Russian religions, making it much more difficult for them to practice their faith openly and recruit new members.

As important as class and religion are, they remain less central to Russian politics than ethnicity. Ethnic cleavages had a significant effect on politics before the collapse of the Soviet Union and remain of great consequence today. Around 80 percent of Russia's population is ethnically Russian. The country's minorities tend to be concentrated in certain parts of the country, especially along Russia's long southern border. Ethnicity's current importance is one of the many enduring legacies of the Soviet period. Although officially a state based on Marxist principles, the Soviets emphasized ethnic identity by:

- Creating written languages for ethnic minorities who did not have them
- Establishing an ethno-federal system in which certain larger ethnic minorities gained their own "union republics" (see Chapter 6) within the USSR and other groups were given autonomous regions within some of these union republics
- Allowing, for the most part, leaders of the ethnic regions to come from the group for which the region was named
- Including ethnic identity in people's internal "passports"—identity documents that the government gave to Soviet citizens
- Engaging in political reforms that allowed ethnicity to become a central form of political mobilization in the years leading up to the country's collapse

China

Like Russia, China is a country with new class divisions, regionally concentrated ethnic minorities, and a renewed emphasis on religion following the abandonment of Marxist ideology. Class is a growing identity cleavage in many parts of the country. China's embrace of capitalism has brought significant wealth over the last several decades, but this wealth has been far from evenly distributed. A new, prosperous middle class has emerged alongside a small upper class. The majority of the population, however, remains poor by international standards. As in Russia, many of the poor resent the newly wealthy and perceive them as a symbol of widespread corruption.

China's emphasis on materialism, focus on economic development, and increasing interconnections with countries across the globe have produced a sense of loss in many Chinese. Like Russians, they face chaotic social problems in an ideological vacuum. In addition, a large number of Chinese feel that cultural connections (including China's historical commitment to collectivism) have diminished while corruption has flourished. In response, some Chinese have turned to religion, rediscovering traditional spiritual and cultural beliefs, such as Confucianism with its blueprint for an orderly society. An estimated 100 million practice Buddhism, and some have turned to Christianity. As in Russia, others have sought new religious outlets.

Although still officially a Marxist state, religion has emerged as a key political issue. The government has tried to control religion, not so much because of its ideological opposition to religion as because of its fear of religious groups' ability to mobilize the population against state policies and officials. The government officially recognizes a number of groups, but it has had difficulty preventing groups it does not officially recognize from practicing their religions.

One such group, **Falun Gong**, emerged in the early 1990s. Falun Gong's practices include meditation and physical exercise. Its members also believe an apocalypse is looming. The movement received a great deal of attention after thousands of Falun Gong members staged a protest in 1999 to force the government to recognize it officially as a religious group. Similar protests followed in 2000. The protests backfired, and the government targeted the organization's leaders and banned the group from engaging in public activities. Given the nature of the regime, this should not be surprising. The Communist government perceives as a threat any movement that both publicly protests government policy and demonstrates the capacity to mobilize a sizeable following. A precise count of Falun Gong's members is elusive, but analysts of China believe they number in the millions and quite possibly in the tens of millions.

While class and religious divisions pose difficulties for the Chinese government, ethnicity remains its greatest challenge. The government recognizes more than fifty different ethnic groups. The vast majority of the population is Han Chinese, a category that encompasses significant linguistic and cultural variation. (In many countries, the various linguistic groups that comprise the Han would be considered distinct ethnic groups.) Even before the Communist period, the government emphasized the unity of the Han, a policy the Communists have continued.

Ethnic minorities do not make up a large percentage of China's overall population, but with that population approaching one and a half billion, small percentages translate into large numbers. If these roughly 100 million members of China's ethnic minorities had their own country, for example, it would be one of the fifteen most populated countries in the world. China's minorities tend to be concentrated in border areas, often placing them in close proximity to members of their own group in neighboring countries. This makes it harder for the government to control the minority groups, and makes minority nationalist movements more viable.

Falun Gong is a religious movement in China with millions of members. It employs traditional meditation techniques and preaches that the end of the world is near. It faced government repression following protests seeking official recognition of it as a religious group.

IN THEORY AND PRACTICE

Primordialism, Constructivism, and Identity in China

The question of where identity comes from is the source of a major divide within the study of identity. The different positions can generally be grouped into two rival theoretical perspectives. The first approach, which social scientists label **primordialism**, holds that collective identity divisions are based on deep-rooted features (blood ties, physical appearance, etc.) that lead us/them national boundaries to form naturally and have divided people for thousands of years. While many scholars today criticize the primordial approach, it has had supporters within the scholarly community.[24] Recently, the strongest support for the primordial view of identity has come from the media and government officials. Reporters and pundits are fond of primordial explanations because their non-nuanced nature about a given identity conflict allows them to keep the story simple: "These groups hate each other today as

Primordialism maintains that identity divisions are based on deep-rooted features (blood ties, physical appearance, etc.) that have naturally divided people throughout history.

they always have." Government officials like primordialism because it releases them from responsibility to address identity conflicts in their own country or other countries around the world: "If they just hate each other, what can we do?"

The counter to primordialism is **constructivism**. This approach argues that identity is a social construction. While there are several strands of constructivism, cultural anthropologist John Comaroff argues they all share the idea that social identities "are products of human agency."[25] In other words, how people define each other as "us" or "them"—including what identity markers are emphasized—is not natural. It is the product of conscious effort by elites to label individual members of society and make those labels socially and politically important, and it can be quite fluid.

Between the primordial and constructivist extremes is a theoretical position that Ronald G. Suny, a specialist on ethnic and national identity in the former Soviet Union, has called the "**radical middle position**."[26] It is a middle ground position because it accepts some parts of primordialism and constructivism. It acknowledges that identities are socially constructed, but it also recognizes that elites engaged in such "construction projects" have a limited range of options. This perspective is "radical," because it deviates from the extreme constructivism that had come to dominate disciplines such as sociology at the end of the twentieth century.

Although research from psychology supports that humans have a natural tendency to divide themselves into groups and place importance on these groups, scholars seeking to understand identity have been hostile to a purely primordialist approach that emphasizes collective identities as natural and downplays the role of social construction of identity. China is the oldest civilization still in existence. As such, one might expect primordialism to explain Chinese identity divisions well. On the other hand, if primordialism fails to explain the political relevance of identity in the Chinese case, it would seriously call into question the general usefulness of the theory.

After taking power in China, the Communists sent researchers across the country to determine which groups should be officially recognized as ethnic minorities. Although more than 400 groups applied for such recognition, only 41 (later expanded to 55) were granted it. Most of those that did not receive recognition were lumped into the Han Chinese category.[27] In addition, the government worked to highlight unifying features of the Han and supported the widespread use of Standard Mandarin (the Beijing dialect of the Mandarin language). The process involved in the government's official sanctioning of some ethnic groups is more consistent with constructivism than with primordialism. On the other hand, that the attempts to culturally and linguistically homogenize the Han Chinese have been far from successful provides some support for primordialism. If anything, linguistic differences have deepened in recent years.[28]

As with many other cases of the emergence and maintenance of identity, Chinese elites have played a significant role in the construction of ethnic identities but have been unable to create identities in any way they choose. The Chinese case supports neither a pure constructivist nor a pure primordialist theoretical approach but instead seems best explained by the "radical middle" position between primordialism and constructivism.

Constructivism maintains that identity divisions are not natural. Rather, they are the product of elite efforts to define individuals as falling into different identity groups and to make such divisions politically relevant.

The **"radical middle position"** is a label for an approach that incorporates elements of constructivism and primordialism. While accepting that social and political elites play a central role in the creation and triggering of identity, the radical middle idea also highlights the way in which certain features used as identity markers appear to be more effective than others and emphasizes how historical events and existing circumstances constrain and provide opportunities for elites.

India

India's caste, religious, ethnic, and regional "memberships" have helped shape the country's politics. As noted in Chapter 4, each identity gives rise to elements of its own political culture and contributes in some fashion to the complexity of the composite Indian political culture. Indeed, the "diversity" in India's search for "unity in diversity" refers principally to the numerous identities that sometimes challenge, and sometimes reinforce, national identity. The intensity, scope, and longevity of these identities vary from group to group.

The greatest identity challenges came immediately before and after independence. Two were of particular importance. First, as the colonial era ended, India was faced with regional strains arising from the nature of British rule. Britain had not directly ruled almost half of India. In the months leading up to independence, more than 450 princely states were integrated into the Indian union, but that process did not mean the immediate abandonment of identities with those princes and those states. Furthermore, possessions of other colonial powers on the Indian subcontinent were not integrated at the time (e.g., the Portuguese possession of Goa), and some princely states refused to join India before independence (e.g., Hyderabad where the Nizam resisted integration). In the cases of Goa and Hyderabad, the Indian army brought the separate polities into the country. But, in these and other regions, the political transfer of territory did not mean the residents immediately ended their attachment to the former political units.

A more serious problem was that posed by political leaders speaking for those who identified themselves as Muslim. The Muslim League challenged the Indian national movement spearheaded by Gandhi, Nehru, and others associated with the Indian National Congress. Mohammed Ali Jinnah, the leader of the Muslim League, demanded a separate state for Muslims. The resulting Partition of India led to the movement of millions of Hindus from Pakistan to India, millions of Muslims from India to Pakistan, and the deaths of an estimated quarter of a million people. The partition also exacerbated the division within India between those who identified themselves as Hindu and Muslim.

Both regional and religious identities have continued to influence political outcomes in India. In 1956, almost a decade after the trauma of independence, India's federal units were reorganized primarily to conform with territories in which a common language was spoken. Nevertheless, virtually all federal units contained some people who spoke languages other than the dominant language. In the years since, India has faced one regional movement after another demanding either the creation of a new federal unit or secession from the country. In each case, the movements have claimed that the people concerned have a common identity and are disadvantaged by their inclusion in the existing federal unit.

In the years since independence, identity divisions have fostered riots and conflict at various times and in various places. Examples include conflicts in the 1980s involving Sikhs—a religious minority group concentrated in the Punjab region of northern India bordering Pakistan. Some Sikhs supported the creation of an independent state called Khalistan, which would have united the areas with a strong Sikh presence in both India and Pakistan. An Indian Army attack on militants in the Sikh Golden Temple in Amritsar led to Prime Minister Indira Gandhi's assassination by her Sikh bodyguards and, subsequently, riots in which many Sikhs were killed. Muslim and Hindu identity divisions deepened in 1992 when crowds of Hindus destroyed the Babri Mosque in Ayodhya and demanded that a Ram Temple be constructed on the site. A decade later, a fire on a train at the Godhra station in the western Indian territory of Gujarat killed a number of Hindus. Hindus in the area believed a gang of Muslims started the fire, prompting riots in which hundreds of Muslims were killed.

There are many other significant identities. India has long been characterized by a **caste** system which, in its simplest form, divides society into four groups, each of which has values and other attributes attached to it that distinguish it from the others. The caste system grew out of Hinduism, but manifestations of the hierarchy and cultural differences attached to it have affected Muslim and Christian communities in various parts of the country as well. The four main castes are the *Brahmin* (i.e., scholar-priests), *Kshatriya* (warriors), *Vaishya* (merchants), and *Sudra* (poor peasants and workers), while another group, *Dalits* (untouchables), are treated as beneath even the lowest caste category. In addition to these main divisions, there are numerous *jati*, or groups within these categories, in different parts of India. Although the caste system has been officially outlawed, it continues to be socially and politically important.

India possesses a great variety of peoples identified by ethnic markers. There are Punjabi, Bengali, Marathi, Tamil, Telugu, and numerous other peoples who speak different languages and who have political cultures derived from both similar and different historical experiences. The significance of such identities varies among individuals and relative to other identities. For example, some Tamils in the federal unit of Tamil Nadu support the Liberation Tigers of Tamil Eelam (LTTE, or "Tamil Tigers") in the group's battle with the Sri Lankan government, while others do not. Many Telugu-speaking people from the Telangana portion of Andhra Pradesh view Telugu-speaking people from other parts of the federal unit as "them," that is, not a part of their identity group.

Gender is also an issue in India's political struggles. Many women feel excluded. They cite the preference for male children and the killing of female fetuses, the demands for dowry, and the refusal of governments to pass legislation that would provide them with more reserved seats in the central legislative bodies.

A train is set on fire during violence in November 2006 by *Dalits* ("untouchables"), who were protesting vandalism of a statue of Bhimrao Ramji Ambedkar, an Indian political leader who played a central role in drafting the constitution and was a member of the untouchable category of the caste system.
(©AP Photo)

Caste is a hereditary identity category, primarily in Hindu society, which divides individuals based on social functions associated with each group. The caste system defines four main groups plus the *Dalit* (untouchable) category, as well as numerous subcategories within each of these groups.

Identity Divisions in Nigeria and Iran

Religion and ethnicity provide the most important identity divisions in Nigeria and Iran. In Nigeria, the religious divide is primarily between Muslims—who live mostly in the north of the country—and Christians. In Iran, it is between different groups of Muslims (such as the divide between the majority Shi'ite and the much smaller Sunni populations, as well as between the more fundamentalist believers and more secular ones). Particularly in Iran, gender is also an important identity issue, as women struggle to gain social and political equality.

Nigeria

Ethnicity and religion have been the most politically important identity cleavages in Nigeria prior to and since gaining its independence from the United Kingdom. Nigeria is one of the most ethnically heterogeneous countries in the world. Ethnic discrimination is common, including in hiring and the awarding of contracts. Though some of the country's smallest ethnic groups might be better described as tribes, Nigeria has hundreds of different ethnic groups. Members of the three largest groups, the Ibo (or Igbo), Hausa-Fulani, and Yoruba, have especially strong attachments to their ethnic identity. An examination of the tensions between these three groups is essential to understanding postindependence Nigerian politics.

The Ibo, Hausa-Fulani, and Yoruba comprise nearly two-thirds of the population. The Hausa-Fulani were originally two distinct ethnic groups that are today treated as a single group. A lack of accurate census figures makes it impossible to determine with precision each of the three group's portion of the population, but the Hausa-Fulani are the largest group. They are estimated to be around 30 percent of the population, with the Yoruba a little more than 20 percent and the Ibo a little less than 20 percent.

Over the last two decades, religion has increasingly become the topic of significant political debates in Nigeria. About half the population of Nigeria is Muslim, around 40 percent is Christian, and about 10 percent practices traditional indigenous religions or no religion. Hostilities between Muslims and Christians in Nigeria have revolved around the presence of foreign Christian missionaries—estimated to number more than one thousand[29]—and the adoption of *Shari'a* (Islamic Law) in Muslim regions of the country. Local political elites have intentionally exacerbated religious tensions in an effort to mobilize supporters. As a result, between 1990 and 2000 alone, around thirty significant religious clashes took place in the north of the country. These conflicts have continued, claiming thousands of lives in the first half of the next decade. Conflicts between Sunnis and the small number of Shi'ite Muslims have also occasionally turned violent, though they have affected far fewer people than Christian-Muslim conflicts.

Iran

While religion is a major identity division in Nigeria, it is the focal point of politics and social relations in Iran. Ethnicity is also important in Iran, with its sizeable ethnic minorities, some of whom are regionally concentrated. Unlike the other TIC countries, however, ethnicity is less politically relevant than religion. The divide between those with a strong attachment to traditional Islamic teaching and practice and those who desire a more secular society drives Iran's religiously dominated political discourse. Tensions related to gender have also become conspicuous. As the Iranian government has pursued more conservative policies regarding the status of women in recent years, many women who support political and social reform in the country have openly protested. The intersection of religion and gender is likely to remain a central issue in Iranian politics in the years ahead.

Iran is an "Islamic Republic," and government institutions and policy decisions reflect the dominant religion. Human rights groups and the U.S. government have frequently reported poor treatment of religious minorities, including Sunni Muslims, Jews, and Christians. Jews and Christians make up well under 1 percent of the population, but Sunni Muslims may be as much as 10 percent. Alongside the issue of religious minorities, and more politically important in the long run, is the identity division between those with a strong attachment to Shi'ite Islam and those Shi'ites who believe that religion should be less central to Iranian society and politics.

Because Iran is 99 percent Muslim, casual observers often fail to appreciate its degree of ethnic diversity. Persians make up only a slim majority of the population. The Azeris form as much as one-fourth of it. They are the majority ethnic group of Azerbaijan, a country neighboring Iran to the north.[30] Estimates of the number of Azeris in Iran vary, but there are perhaps twice as many Azeris in Iran as in Azerbaijan itself. Much smaller, but at least as politically troubling for the Iranian government, are ethnic Kurds who make up 8 percent of the population.

More than in the other TIC countries, gender is a potentially explosive identity division in Iran. In the aftermath of the 1979 Revolution, the Islamic government sought to turn back gains in legal status that women had won under the previous government. The repeal of the Family Protection Law, a provision that had improved the legal standing of women in marital and family matters, symbolized this effort.

After nearly two decades, women appeared to be making inroads in the political system with the election of the moderate president, Mohammad Khatami, in the late 1990s. Some women achieved top local government positions and a number of women supportive of social reform won election to the national parliament. Even before the end of Khatami's first term, however, the emphasis on greater gender equality seemed to be waning, and women became less optimistic about the potential for real reform under Khatami. The country's Guardian Council blocked various measures of the national legislature, the *Majles*, designed to improve women's social standing, including a 2000 law raising the legal age for a "woman" to marry from nine to fifteen and a 2003 measure supporting acceptance of a UN treaty on women's rights. The reestablishment of conservative control of the national legislature in February 2004 and Mahmoud Ahmadinejad's 2005 election as president solidified this trend.

> **Did You Know?**   Nearly every major capital city in the world, even Tel Aviv, has a Sunni mosque. Tehran does not. The absence of a Sunni mosque is a point of contention between Shi'ites and Sunnis in Iran. The U.S. State Department and various international organizations estimate that there may be as many as one million Sunnis living in and around Tehran.

IN THEORY AND PRACTICE

Feminist Theory and Iran

A number of theoretical perspectives related to identity highlight specific group identities. The most prominent of these is **feminist theory**, which focuses on the status of women in society and within the political process. It is based

Feminist theory examines the importance of gender (perceived trait differences between males and females), the actions of men and women in positions of power, and obstacles facing women in achieving economic, social, and political equality. It is associated with the normative call for greater equality between men and women.

on the assumption that the structure of society, which in many cases involves male domination of economic, social, and political institutions, is perpetuated by the society's positive view of masculine traits. Feminist comparativists are also concerned with how comparative politics studies feminist issues. In her 2002 book, *Theorizing Feminist Policy*, for example, political scientist Amy Mazur lays out a framework for studying government policies from a feminist perspective. She proposes several components to "feminist comparative policy" research, including a renewed focus on patriarchal state structures and the use of gender as an analysis category.[31]

Acceptance of feminist theory suffers somewhat from its prescriptive nature, in which empirical claims (e.g., pay disparities between men and women) and normative appeals (the need for greater equality between men and women) at times become closely intertwined. Rather than objectively testing the assumptions of the theory, empirical feminist research sometimes takes the form of finding anecdotal examples that support the theory's contentions.[32] Among political scientists, feminism also suffers from that which it highlights: the continued presence of males in many of the positions of power within the discipline. Although this is changing fairly rapidly in political science, the pace has been slower than in most other social sciences.

There are few countries in the world that better support feminism's central contentions than Iran. A large portion of society, and an even larger portion of government officials, see women as second-class citizens. For many westerners, the idea that girls can be forced to marry as young as age nine—often to men three or four times their age—defies understanding. The ongoing clash between traditional, ultra-conservative norms and desires for a more modern society is perhaps most evident in the question of the social and political status of women.

At least among the middle class, the Iranian gender gap in attitudes is much like it is in the United States, with women more likely than men to oppose conservative government officials. The conservative trend of the early 2000s troubled many Iranian women—especially the better educated in the capital of Tehran. They had seen Ahmadinejad firsthand as mayor of the city prior to his victory in the presidential election, and may have anticipated what would come next. Shortly after taking office, Ahmadinejad encouraged local officials and the national government to take steps to curtail women's rights. Proposed policies included segregated walkways and, in some cities at least, the creation of separate parks for men and women.

Even before Ahmadinejad's election, it had become clear that Iran's reestablishment of strongly conservative social views on gender roles was a dangerous tightrope act. On June 12, 2005, just days before the presidential election, thousands of women engaged in a sit-in at the University of Tehran to protest the government's increasingly hard line positions on gender and specific provisions in the Iranian Constitution that justified discrimination against women.

The government's attempt to turn back the clock on women's rights may strengthen gender as a form of collective identity. Whether this will lead a substantial number of women to radicalize and, putting their personal safety at risk, push back against the Iranian government is difficult to predict. The example of Afghanistan under the Taliban is not encouraging. Either way, insights from feminist theory can help explain what underlies the conditions facing Iranian women. Mazur's proposed framework for studying government policies from a feminist perspective seems especially relevant. It is hard to imagine understanding Iranian domestic politics without focusing on issues like the patriarchal state structures and using gender—the social and governmental views of "masculine" and "feminine" traits—as a category of analysis.

Cross-Cutting and Complementary Identity Divisions

When different forms of identity compete for an individual's loyalty, the conflicting loyalties cut into each other. The "competition" between the collective identities can weaken each identity's ability to serve as a tool for political mobilization. Thus, competition between identity divisions for an individual's loyalty tends to reduce societal conflicts. Such situations involve what are called **cross-cutting identity divisions** (also referred to as cross-cutting social cleavages).

For example, the religious beliefs of a certain group of individuals may include a strong commitment to nonviolence. At the same time, their ethnic group may be involved in a violent conflict with another ethnic group. In such instances, ethnic loyalty will often win out over religious beliefs. But it is unlikely that such individuals will abandon their religion. Instead, the religious beliefs may weaken the ethnic loyalty, perhaps leading the individuals only to tolerate, but not actively support, acts of violence against the other group.

Note that gender is almost always a cross-cutting division. It does line up with socioeconomic class, to an extent at least, in many countries around the world, but the most politically potent forms of identity—ethnicity, race, religion, and region—are always cross-cut by the gender divide. Ethnic or religious arguments tend to mobilize individuals more effectively than gender-based arguments. Though women may have a great deal in common with each other, they often feel that they have even more in common with other members of their race, ethnic group, or religion.

As effective as certain group identities can be in mobilizing individuals politically, identities become even more powerful when they reinforce one another. Class divisions, for example, are less politically relevant today than in the past. But when class boundaries coincide with other forms of identity (ethnic, regional, etc.), they can become highly salient. The other group boundaries are reinforced by the economic differences between "us" and "them." For the economically disadvantaged group (e.g., a predominantly working class and peasant ethnic group), economic challenges foster perceptions that the more advantaged group is discriminating against them.

Situations in which group identity boundaries coincide with one another are known as **complementary identity divisions** (as well as complementary social cleavages or accumulative social cleavages). Complementary divisions commonly involve ethnic minorities and majorities. Often, two ethnic groups speak different languages. They may also believe they are racially different from one another, may have different religions, and may live primarily in different regions of the country. The us/them boundaries of each form of identity—ethnic, racial, religious, and so on—correspond to and reinforce one another. The likelihood of conflict, including violent conflict, is much greater in cases of complementary identity divisions than in situations where cross-cutting divisions prevail.

Cross-cutting identity divisions (also known as cross-cutting cleavages) occur when people are torn between various collective identities important to their individual identity. In these cases, individuals have a weaker attachment and loyalty to any single group identity. The various identities can also pull such individuals in different directions over political issues.

Complementary identity divisions (also known as complementary social cleavages) are those which line up in a similar manner for large numbers of individuals. For example, if the members of an ethnic minority in a particular state also share a common religion, speak the same language, have similar physical features, and fall into the same economic class, ethnicity is complemented by these other divisions.

Complementary Group Identities in the United Kingdom, Germany, and France

In the United Kingdom, Germany, and France, complementary identity divisions are less prevalent and play a less central role in shaping political outcomes than in many of the other TIC cases. In all three, however, ethnic identity is reinforced by other identities. In the United Kingdom, ethnic and regional divisions line up, and immigration has created new complementary boundaries between ethnic and religious groups. In Germany, a similar pattern exists of coinciding lines between ethnicity and religion fostered by immigration since World War II. In France, the identity of immigrants and other minorities is complemented by the strong sense of these identity groups as bearers of "foreign" cultural values that threaten existing French principles that are considered universal.

The United Kingdom

Complementary cleavages are less prominent in the United Kingdom than in most of the other countries highlighted in this text, but they do exist and their reinforcing nature has consequences for British politics and social relations. Ethnicity and region complement each other somewhat, with English and Celtic ethnic groups concentrated in their respective regions of the country. This complementary cleavage between ethnicity and region has helped to fuel a nascent Scottish nationalism, along with a less successful nationalist movement in Wales, and it has contributed to the push to pursue the policy of "devolution," discussed in more detail in the next chapter.

Within Northern Ireland, religion and location of residence have complemented one another and helped fuel tensions between the two sides. One would think that ethnicity would not complement divisions between the groups within Northern Ireland, since both groups are Irish. But the Protestant population in the United Kingdom sees itself, first and foremost, as British, while Catholics maintain a stronger attachment to their Irish identity.

Like other European countries, complementary identity divisions also penetrate into politics via the issue of immigration. The newer immigrants have complementary boundaries involving ethnicity, religion, and even class. As early as the 1970s, these immigrants were political targets. Anger among the rest of the general population toward immigrants produced laws to slow immigration. The "7/7" train and bus bombings in 2005 deepened these identity divisions by bringing the presence of Muslims in the United Kingdom to the front of national consciousness.

Germany

As in the UK, complementary cleavages pose less of a political threat in Germany than in some of the other TIC countries. Religious and regional identities are correlated, with Catholics concentrated in the Rhineland and the south and Protestants in the north and east, but these divisions have faded as a source of conflict. Regional and class divisions also coincide somewhat. Following unification, severe unemployment in the east created a new class divide between generally more prosperous western Germans and their poorer eastern brethren.

Today, ethnicity and religion are the major complementary cleavages. Most ethnic Germans are of Christian background, while most of the Turkish minority identifies as Muslim. Class and ethnicity also correlate among the Turkish minority. Turks are more likely to be in occupations of lower socioeconomic status and to be less educated than native Germans.

France

Just as the first French Republicans demanded that Jews abandon any communal loyalties to become citizens, the question of loyalty to universal French principles over private identities remains a central part of politics in France. This focus on foreignness forces legal status to the center as the most important factor in identity, measured as either "French" or "foreign," to a greater extent than in many other countries. Each form of identity finds a complement in these legal categories, and identity politics organizes in ways that infer legal status through the attribution of foreignness.

This approach to identity is why French citizens of North or sub-Saharan African descent, for example, are nearly always described through the number of generations they are removed from immigration, no matter how well they have assimilated to French values and culture. There is a strong correlation between poverty and immigration status, compounded by prejudice in employment and housing against those whose names are not of European origins. This does not, however, apply to the children of immigrants from Europe, such as President Nicolas Sarkozy, whose father emigrated from Hungary.

The linkage between certain identity groups and the "foreign" label extends beyond ethnic minority immigrants. When feminists advocate for special policies targeting women, or gay men organize political events like the annual *marche des fiertés* (Pride Parade), politicians express concern that "American" values are coming to dominate French public life.

Complementary Group Identities in Mexico and Brazil

In both Mexico and Brazil, class divisions complement other identities, including regional, ethnic, racial, and gender. Members of indigenous groups in Mexico, for example, are dramatically poorer than members of the nonindigenous population. In Brazil, color and class have a strong correspondence.

Mexico

Region correlates with other collective identities in Mexico. The north and center of the country are much more urban and industrial than the south, which still relies heavily on agriculture. Northern economic development has fed a more individualistic capitalist spirit than is found in other parts of the country.

Region and class also complement indigenous ("Indian") identity. Class divisions and lower levels of education between the indigenous minority and the rest of the population reinforce this identity boundary, although the presence of a large number of poor in the ethnic majority weakens the potential for class to strongly complement the ethnic cleavage. The Indian population has tended to be concentrated in the south central and southeast of the country, with pockets in the northwest. An increasing portion of the indigenous population, however, now lives in Mexico City, joining others from the countryside who have moved to this massive urban area in hope of finding a better life. Due to the lingering stereotypes connected to skin color, finding such a life is especially difficult for the dark-skinned Indians in Mexico City.

Brazil

Most scholars now believe that Brazil's claim of "racial democracy" was a myth. Color is strongly correlated with economic and social status. Blacks have twice the unemployment rate of whites. They suffer disproportionately from poverty. When they do find work, they earn 57 percent less than white Brazilians in the same fields, and only 3 percent of students admitted to Brazilian universities each year are black or mixed race, even though close to half of the population identifies as black or mixed race.[33]

Women and children also suffer disproportionately from poverty, unemployment, and lack of opportunities for education. The usual cause is abandonment by a husband or partner.

If that woman is also black, her obstacles are even greater. The story of Benedita da Silva is therefore all the more extraordinary. Benedita (like soccer players, she goes by her first name) says of herself that she is a "triple minority"—poor, black, and female. She grew up in a poor shantytown in Rio de Janeiro. By the age of five she was working, helping her mother as a laundress. She married in her teens and had five children, only two of whom survived. Her story could have ended there like so many others. But

Benedita learned to read. She participated in an urban popular movement seeking better health care and services for her neighborhood, and then helped found the PT. Through her intelligence, charisma, and hard work, she rose within the party. After democratization, she became the first black woman elected to congress, and then the first female senator in Brazil of any race. She later served as governor of her state of Rio de Janeiro and as a member of the national cabinet under President Lula da Silva (no relation).

Complementary Group Identities in the Russian Federation, China, and India

Complementary identity divisions exist in Russia and China, though not as sharply as in some countries. In Russia, there is some correspondence between ethnic identity and region and, in parts of the country, between ethnic identity and religion, but intermarriage between Russians and ethnic minorities has undercut the extent to which ethnicity corresponds to other identities. In China, ethnicity, region, and religion correspond in some cases, most starkly in the case of the ethnic Uyghurs, a Muslim minority concentrated in the Xinjiang region. In India, the mix of disparate identities generates cross-cutting rather than complementary identity divisions for the most part, with instances of complementary divisions confined mostly to the local level.

The Russian Federation

Complementary identity divisions are not as strong in Russia as in some other countries, partly because of the frequency of interethnic marriage, particularly between ethnic Russians and members of non-Russian ethnic minorities. In addition, class divisions only recently solidified in a way that can complement ethnic identity. But coinciding divisions along ethnic, religious, and regional lines are still conspicuous, with race also playing a role in deepening the ethnic divide. Most ethnic Russians are Orthodox

Christians, while many ethnic minorities belong to other faiths. Russia's federal system—inherited from the Soviets—includes many regions named for ethnic minorities and considered the groups' homelands within Russia. These regions make up a majority of the Russian territory, though they contain less than 20 percent of its population. The effects of this "territorialization" of ethnicity are muted in many regions of Russia, however, by the presence of large numbers of ethnic Russians living in them.

By the first decade of the twenty-first century, Chechens, the group that the Russian region of Chechnya is named after, had become Russia's most discriminated against group. The Chechens provide an example of how ethnic identity can be tied to perceptions of race. Chechens and other Muslim minorities from the southern part of Russia are generally darker skinned than ethnic Russians from regions like Moscow or St. Petersburg. Many Russians consider these minorities to be "black," even though they look little like groups labeled black in other countries.

Other minorities, such as those from the far east of Russia, have strongly Asian features. In this case, however, race is as much cross-cutting as complementary to ethnicity. Intermarriage over the last two centuries has meant that many ethnic Russians, particularly outside of the northwest (European) part of the country, share such Asian features with the ethnic minorities.

Cleavage Structure Theory and the Russian Federation

Cleavage structure theory emphasizes identity complexity within a society. This approach uses the extent to which the population is divided into complementary instead of cross-cutting identity groups to explain political outcomes. Cleavage structure theory maintains that the role of identity as a political force is heightened when identity divisions complement one another. Majorities and minorities become "permanent." On the other hand, when identities "cross-cut" one another, identity is much less salient, and political elites have a harder time using group identities to mobilize people for political activities or in support of particular policies.

Arend Lijphart is one of a number of comparativists who have used cleavage structure theory to study democracy in societies with sharp social divisions.[34] According to Lijphart, cross-cutting divisions facilitate democracy. Since no permanent minorities exist, it is unlikely that any individual will always be on the losing side of votes using a majority rule mechanism. By contrast, identity traits of the candidates can drive electoral results far more than the candidates' policy positions in societies with sharp, complementary identity cleavages. As Donald Horowitz has so eloquently put it, in such settings an election becomes a census.[35]

Cleavage structure theory can help explain tensions between ethnic groups and even drives by one or more groups to secede from the state in which they reside. The Russian Federation faced both of these after 1991. If cleavage structure theory is correct, relations with the ethnic Russian population (and government) should be more strained for those groups with complementary divisions that make them highly distinct from ethnic Russians. One way to examine this possibility is to look at two groups, Chechens and Tatars, who share many features (e.g., both ethnic groups practice Islam) but differ in the extent to which

their identity divisions complement one another and create a sharp us/them division between the group and ethnic Russians. Political scientist Elizabeth Fromberg made precisely this comparison when seeking to understand why the Russian government negotiated a treaty on autonomy with Tatarstan but took military action against Chechnya. The resulting violence within Chechnya and by Chechens in other parts of Russia became one of the central issues of post-Soviet Russian politics. Fromberg does hint that an important part of the story of the different outcomes is the leaders involved and their calculations in deciding what actions to take—factors that are addressed in this book in Chapter 11—but argues that the central reason is the sharper, more complementary identity divisions between Chechens and Russians than between Tatars and Russians.[36]

The Chechens only came under Russian control in the middle 1800s, after a fierce decades-long fight against the expansion of the Russian Empire into their territory. They tended not to intermarry with Russians over the next century and a half, resisted assimilation, and thus maintained a strong sense of themselves as ethnically different from Russians. Chechens also made up the vast majority of Chechnya (70 percent) in the 1990s.

The Tatars and Russians have a longer relationship—from the 1500s to the present—that includes significant intermarriage. Tatars were open to assimilation, with many Tatars adopting the Russian language. Those who practiced religion tended to maintain their Islamic identity but were more

Cleavage structure theory explains political outcomes, including violence and democratic stability, by the extent to which identities are cross-cutting or complementary. Cross-cutting cleavages weaken identities; complementary divisions make them more salient.

secular than other Muslims.[37] Tatars and Russians were also more evenly split within Tatarstan in the first post-Soviet decade (48 percent and 43 percent, respectively).[38] In other words, regional divisions complemented the Chechen-Russian identity boundary to a greater extent than the boundary between Tatars and Russians. Take into consid-eration that Chechens also had a worse socioeco-nomic standing than the Tatars did (making them comparatively even less similar to the Russians),[39] and cleavage structure theory appears to provide a compelling story about relations between Russians and the Tatar and Chechen minorities within the Russian Federation.

Think and Disucss

In your opinion, which theory related to identity presented in this chapter's "In Theory and Practice" boxes is most convincing? Why?

China

The central complementary cleavage in China is between ethnicity and region. In the west of China, relatively small ethnic groups make up the majority of some regions' population. This is most obvious in the Xinjiang Uyghur Auton-omous Region, a huge area bordering India, Pakistan, Kyrgyzstan, Kazakhstan, Russia, and Mongolia. A large portion of its people is ethnic Uyghur, a Turkic-speaking group that is primar-ily Muslim. Nearly all Uyghurs in China live in Xinjiang. Like Chechnya in Russia, the combina-tion of Islam and acts of violence has prompted the central government to label Uyghur nation-alists as Muslim terrorists.

Although class does not strongly reinforce the ethno-regional divides, minorities believe that they are discriminated against economi-cally. Economic development has altered their way of life, partly due to increasing numbers of Han Chinese workers settling in the outly-ing regions, while the minorities feel they have gained little economically. Uyghurs in Xinjiang, for example, perceive the increasing presence of Han Chinese in their region as disrupting their culture and argue that Han control the best jobs and ultimately send this wealth out of the region.[40] Such perceptions about economic neglect or the concentration of economic ben-efits in the hands of the Han Chinese fuel desires for greater autonomy and even independence.

India

Although India's wide array of group identi-ties—the country has been called "the most socially heterogeneous nation-state of mod-ern times"[41]—guarantee that identity has an impact on political outcomes, this complexity also limits the extent to which identity bound-aries coincide. Generally speaking, Indians have multiple identities at all times, and while some of them reinforce each other, others often do not.

Religious, regional, caste, ethnic, and gen-der "entrepreneurs" in India have realized the importance of identity and have sought to politicize their particular identity category. To the extent they have been successful, it has often been more at the local or regional level, where instances of complementary cleavages are more common. At the level of the state as a whole, however, the organization of broad identity movements has been hampered by the failure of identity boundaries to coincide. As Ernst Haas puts it:

India has been saved by the fact that the divisions among its people, though numerous, are noninclusive; almost every individual belongs to more than one primary group and derives his or her identity from multiple sources. These multiple identities are not usually aggregated under a single master identity; they remain separate and separable. The result is an enormous network of cross-cutting social cleavages that inhibit the formation of super-ordinate claims to exclusive identities.[42]

Haas's use of the word "saved" highlights how important the existence of cross-cutting identity divisions has been for India's relative stability and successful experience with democracy.

Complementary Group Identities in Nigeria and Iran

Complementary identity divisions are an important factor that shapes politics in Nigeria and Iran. They have been more consequential for Nigerian politics, which has been ravaged by complementary identity divisions since independence. The main ethnic groups are regionally concentrated, with the religious divide between Muslims and Christians deepening the identity divisions further. In Iran, region and ethnicity correspond as well, causing the government to be concerned about the potential for ethnic Kurds and Azeris to develop nationalist aspirations.

Nigeria

Comparativists interested in the topic of identity, and particularly the way in which complementary social cleavages pose challenges to governments, have studied the Nigerian experience extensively. As a result, in addition to the general discussion in this section, Nigerian identity is the subject of this chapter's comparative exercise: a case study of events leading up to the outbreak of the Nigerian civil war in 1967.

Like Russia, Nigeria has struggled to develop a clear multiethnic national identity that cultivates mass attachment. Unlike Russia, however, the problem is not figuring out who belongs to the nation—Nigerians are citizens of Nigeria regardless of their ethnic background. Rather, Nigeria's challenge is how to get ordinary Nigerians to accept this identity and place it at the top of their collective identity loyalty hierarchy. These difficulties stem from deep

complementary cleavages, divisions that are more robust in Nigeria than in any of the other TIC countries.

Ethnicity and region are strongly complementary, a feature that has existed since long before independence. Members of the Hausa-Fulani are concentrated in the north; Ibo tend to live in the southeast; Yoruba generally live in the southwest. Religion reinforces these ethnic divides, since the Hausa-Fulani are generally Muslims, while large portions of the other two groups are Christians.

Iran

Complementary identity divisions are less notable in Iran than in Nigeria, but they are still important. In terms of the identity groups discussed in this chapter, the main complementary cleavage in Iran involves ethnicity and region. Kurds are concentrated in two regions, with one group in the northwest along the border with Iraq and the other in the north near the border with Azerbaijan. Likewise, the large Azeri minority tends to be concentrated in Iran's north. The regional concentration of these minority groups has been a concern for the Iranian government, which fears that the groups' ethnic identities may develop into ethnic nationalisms.

Although this chapter has not discussed age and type of locality as forms of identity, it is also important to note that attachment to religion in Iran does vary significantly by age and whether one lives in a large urban area. The strongest supporters of Khatami's efforts at social and political reforms were young, urban women.

Government Responses to Identity Diversity

Diversity within a population's identity groups directly affects political outcomes like elections, but it can also lead governments to adopt policies to address the political and social challenges it poses. The range of options that governments have is significant. This section focuses on racial and ethnic diversity and uses the example of a government controlled by the majority identity group and its policy alternatives in response to the presence of a sizeable minority group or groups.

The variety of government options when faced with an ethnically and/or racially diverse population can be laid out on a continuum, from least to most accommodating to the minority groups. The most severe action taken against the group would be an attempt to eliminate the individual members of the minority by killing them. When such an action is aimed at an entire group of people, it is known as **genocide**. Genocides of the last century include the Turks' attacks against Armenians during World War I, the Nazi efforts to eradicate Jews during World War II, the Hutu attempts to eliminate the Tutsi in Rwanda in 1994, and actions by the government of Sudan and government-supported militia against residents of the Sudanese region of Darfur.

One step removed from genocide is what is commonly known as **ethnic cleansing**. Ethnic cleansing campaigns can involve killings of minority group members, but the government's central goal is to remove the minority from its territory rather than to eliminate the group entirely. Military or paramilitary units may be used to drive a minority across the border into another country. Ethnic cleansing is, unfortunately, common in situations of ethnic conflict involving majority and minority groups. NATO justified its efforts against the Serbs in 1999 as designed to prevent ethnic cleansing of Albanians in the Serbian territory of Kosovo.

The next step along the continuum is **assimilation**. A government policy of forced assimilation compels minority groups to abandon existing cultural characteristics and take on those of the majority group. Rather than attacking the individuals who comprise the minority group in an effort to eliminate the group or force it from the state's territory, assimilation attacks the minority group's *identity*. Once the group's unique cultural features have been eliminated, disappearance of the group's identity is not far behind. Examples of assimilation efforts include forcing aboriginal children in Canada to live in boarding schools in the early part of the twentieth century. This intentional separation from their parents was designed to sever aboriginal children from any aboriginal cultural influences.

Less extreme than assimilation is a policy of **integration**. Unlike the already-mentioned alternatives, integration does not seek to eliminate the minority group or its culture. Rather, the minority recognizes and accepts that the majority group will be culturally privileged in exchange for the majority recognizing the minority's right to practice its culture. The majority's language may be the medium of instruction in schools or used in government meetings, and its religious symbols may be prominently displayed publicly. Such integration "bargains" were a centerpiece of postindependence Malaysian politics and, more recently, at the forefront of relations

Genocide is the attempt to eliminate an entire group of people by killing them.

Ethnic cleansing involves efforts to remove an entire ethnic group from its territory. This may involve killing a portion of the group, but forcing them to flee accomplishes the goal as well.

Assimilation is a government response to identity diversity which forces a minority group to abandon its cultural characteristics and take on those of the majority group.

Integration is a government policy for dealing with identity diversity that allows minority groups to continue to practice their culture in exchange for accepting that the majority group's culture will be the dominant one.

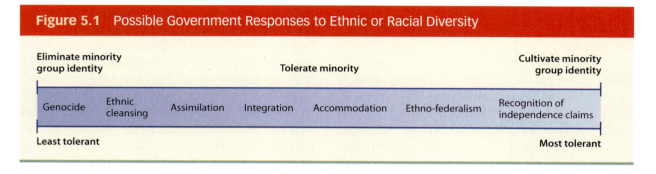

Figure 5.1 Possible Government Responses to Ethnic or Racial Diversity

Eliminate minority group identity | Tolerate minority | Cultivate minority group identity

Genocide | Ethnic cleansing | Assimilation | Integration | Accommodation | Ethno-federalism | Recognition of independence claims

Least tolerant | Most tolerant

between the Estonian and Latvian governments and their Russian-speaking minorities.[43]

The next approach is best labeled **accommodation**. Accommodation involves greater cultural freedom for the minority, including a degree of cultural autonomy, as well as extensive rights or privileges reserved for members of the minority ethnic group. Cultural autonomy provisions include the right of minority group children to attend schools in which instructors speak the minority group's language. Group privileges may include programs generally labeled "affirmative action" policies in the United States. These policies give certain preferences to members of minority groups—special treatment in hiring, quotas for certain government positions, and so on—and are often designed to address past discrimination against the minority.

Continuing along the spectrum is **ethno-federalism**. The idea behind an ethno-federal approach is to give a minority more than just a degree of cultural autonomy. Rather, the minority receives territorial autonomy with a high degree of control over a particular region. Like other forms of federalism, ethno-federal systems do not give complete power to the group to control the region in any way it sees fit, but specific powers are designated to the regional government that the central government of the country cannot take away. Ethno-federal arrangements exist in a number of countries around the world, including Belgium, Canada, and Russia.

Those who support such an approach argue that it is a way to prevent full-fledged ethnic nationalism leading to territorial secession.

This approach, however, has not had a great track record of placating minorities or of holding the state together. Chapter 2 put forward the two questions that nationalists have to answer in their pursuit of mass support for their cause: who belongs to the nation and what territory should the nation control. By linking territory to ethnic identity, and by drawing the homeland of an ethnic minority on the map, ethno-federal approaches answer both questions. It is possible that ethno-federalism will appease a disgruntled ethnic minority. It is also possible, however, that once the minority gets a taste of territorial control, it will desire to take the next step to complete independence. If such a pursuit emerges, ethno-federalism has done the nationalists' job for them by defining the (minority) nation's membership and territorial boundaries.

If the minority pursues secession and the creation of its own, internationally recognized independent state, the majority must decide whether to accept the territorial partition of the state it presently controls. The most accommodating approach that the majority-controlled government can take is to recognize minority claims for territorial independence. Such acceptance is

Accommodation is a government response to identity diversity that involves a degree of cultural autonomy and extensive rights or privileges for members of a minority group.

Ethno-federalism is a government response to identity diversity in which a minority receives territorial autonomy in exchange for not pursuing complete independence.

relatively rare, especially without either a successful armed struggle by the minority or the intervention of the international community. Peaceful divorces sometimes occur, such as the relatively harmonious dismemberment of the Soviet Union in late 1991 and the dismantling of Czechoslovakia into the Czech Republic and Slovakia in 1993. But the violent break-up of Yugoslavia, the on and off violence between Ethiopia and Eritrea, or the intervention of the international community to secure independence for East Timor following violence there are more typical examples.

Approaches to Ethnic and Religious Diversity in the United Kingdom, Germany, and France

Across their histories, government responses to diversity in the United Kingdom, Germany, and France have differed sharply. For the most part, the governments' approaches have evolved in a more accommodating direction. This is most evident in the case of Germany following the horrors of Hitler's genocidal policies during the Nazi period. However, the treatment of minority immigrant groups—particularly Muslim minorities—remains an area of controversy in all three states. This is a theme across Europe, where the continent's Christian (and largely secular) majority struggles to come to terms with the religious practices, and notable religious differences, of Muslim residents.

The United Kingdom

In the past, the British government pursued assimilation, ethnic cleansing, and even quasi-genocidal actions against minorities. As time went on, assimilation, including the encouragement of English settlement in Scotland, gave way to integration and accommodation. Today, the British government encourages ethnic minority identity, although there is still a strong desire for ethnic and racial minorities to see themselves, first and foremost, as British.

This concern for loyalty and attachment to British identity took a more assimilationist turn following the "7/7" events of 2005. Much like in the United States after September 11, 2001, Muslims felt the need to prove their loyalty to the country and attachment to British national identity. Some minority group leaders even proposed adopting an American-style system of hyphenated group names (Indian-British, Pakistani-British, etc.).[44] They believed this would highlight the common British bond across the United Kingdom's various ethnic groups, but others feared it would weaken national British identity by drawing even more attention to subnational collective identities. Though the national government seemed open to the idea initially, the ensuing controversy stalled the proposal.

Germany

Government policies toward diverse identities have spanned the continuum from genocide to efforts at accommodation. During the twentieth century, Germany's citizenship law revolved around the view that German national identity was based on ethnicity. This made it difficult for immigrants and their offspring born on German soil to integrate into German society. The Nazi regime took this ethnic conception of German national identity to its extreme, defining the *Volk* in racial terms and engaging in the genocidal policies of the Holocaust.

After 1949, the Federal Republic sought to atone for Nazi atrocities by pursuing a generous policy toward immigrants seeking asylum from persecution in their home countries. The influx of asylum seekers in the 1990s sparked violent responses from native Germans, particularly in the east where unemployment was rampant. Unemployed youth were attracted to extreme-right groups, which blamed immigrants for Germany's economic malaise. The violence prompted the government to tighten up its asylum laws.[45] At the same time, citizenship policies remained highly restrictive, making it difficult for immigrants to integrate into German society.

The question of integrating Muslim minorities took on a new importance after September 11, 2001, although Germany so far has been spared from major terrorist attacks by militant Islamists. A new citizenship law in place since 2000 extends citizenship to immigrant children born on German soil and provides for an easier naturalization process. Intended to help integrate the German-born offspring of earlier waves of Turkish guest workers, it has led to an increase in the number of naturalized citizens.[46] Overall, however, the new citizenship policy's effects have been limited. Only a small portion of the immigrant population has naturalized, and Turks continue to face social exclusion on a number of fronts, as seen in high-school dropout rates, low socioeconomic status, residential segregation, and low rates of intermarriage with ethnic Germans.[47] Addressing these issues of integration requires labor market and education policies, not just changes to requirements for receiving citizenship.

German law accommodates the religious practices of the Catholic, Lutheran, and Judaic faiths. The German Constitution grants these religious bodies official status as public corporations and with it, a share of income tax revenues to finance the welfare state activities they provide on behalf of the state. However, German law has not yet extended that official status to Islam.[48]

The major political parties continue to debate the appropriate government policy toward minorities. Many in the CDU argue that Germany is not a nation of immigrants and minorities should assimilate into German society. The SPD and Greens, by contrast, tend to promote multicultural policies. However, an immigration law enacted by the SPD-Green government in 2004 accepted the idea that cultural assimilation should be encouraged, as the law required immigrants to take German language lessons.[49]

France

The mission of the French Republic is to create a stable and modern society out of diversity, though the principle of universalism denies the political relevance of difference. Public housing policies discourage rigid racial or ethnic ghettos in poor communities. French census statistics do not count race or ethnicity, only legal status or origins of the foreign born. When the National Assembly passed a bill permitting the collection of statistics that included an individual's race or ethnic identity, the French Constitutional Court (the *Conseil Constitutionnel*) struck down the provision as in violation of the statement in Article 1 of the French Constitution that France "ensures the equality of all citizens before the law, without distinction of origin, race, or religion."[50]

However, discrimination based on foreign origins is widespread, and public officials often associate problems like poverty—and the riots outside Paris in 2005—with immigration, even though most unemployed youth were born in France and have assimilated to French culture. While education is free and access to higher education is based on merit, resources are not distributed equally to all schools. The government funds private schools for Jewish and Catholic families, but no such schools for Muslims. Only one of the *grandes écoles*—Sciences-Po—has an affirmative action plan based on economic status.

Three recent issues illustrate the tensions within universalism challenged by diversity: *Parité*, *PaCS*, and *laïcité*. Women, not granted the vote until 1944, remain underrepresented in politics. Consequently, in the 1990s a group of feminists put forward a proposal to require the promotion of women candidates to elective office, known as *Parité* ("Parity"). This movement differed from earlier French feminism, which had taken the position, consistent with French universalism, that by nature and law women were entirely equal to men.[51] Instead, the *Parité* movement seemed inspired by American feminist thought, which is generally supportive of quotas and other affirmative action approaches to address imbalances. Indeed, the proposal's opponents expressed fear that it would foster both "fragmentation" and "Americanization."[52] Ultimately, the government promoted a compromise that has increased representation modestly.

The *Pacte Civil de Solidarité* was proposed to provide official recognition for same-gender partners, and it experienced a similar fate. French Republicans expressed outrage that a law would be considered whose sole beneficiaries would be an identity group. Unlike Americans, they said, French lawmakers could not support a special legal status available only to some French citizens.[53] But gay men and lesbians were advocating for full marriage rights, while lawmakers sought to limit access to that Republican institution of marriage. Another compromise, *PaCS* provided rights and protections but, unlike marriage, it is open to homosexual and heterosexual couples.

In the last decade, French lawmakers of both genders have also expressed concern that Muslim girls were covering their heads in public schools. President Chirac established a special commission in 2003, the second time the issue was considered by the government since 1989. Did the scarves these young women wore represent a violation of the principle of *laïcité*, which guarantees the right to be free from religious interference? In reality, the French have long viewed the headscarf as a symbol of a primordial Islamism incompatible with Western culture, and they tried to abolish it in colonial Algeria.[54] During the debate over the law, members of the National Assembly from both the Left and Right characterized the headscarf as a symbol of a separatist Muslim community, of primordial origins, where men dominate women and refuse to accept Western values. In the end, the law banned headscarves from public schools, as well as Jewish yarmulkes and any crucifix large enough to be considered ostentatious.

Approaches to Ethnic and Religious Diversity in Mexico and Brazil

Like in many countries, the approach to ethnic diversity in Mexico and Brazil has varied, with a greater emphasis on more tolerant approaches over time. In Mexico, this has meant moving from an emphasis on assimilation to one more accepting of the accommodation of identity differences. In Brazil, the past nonrecognition of race as an identity category has given way to identity programs designed to make up for previous and ongoing discrimination.

Mexico
The main "diversity" question in Mexico regards the indigenous population and its culture. In the past, Mexico pursued assimilation, showing little concern for its Indian population. Areas where the population did not assimilate were left to fend for themselves economically and educationally. Mexican government statistics

that label a smaller portion of the population indigenous than many scholars believe is the case are a remnant of this approach.

Mexico's blossoming democracy seems to have bolstered moves toward accommodation, and the erection of statues of Aztec leaders across Mexico in recent years is one sign of the government's efforts to rediscover the native past. Although former President Vicente Fox was unable to follow through on his promises in response to the uprising in Chiapas, he was more open to addressing indigenous group concerns than past leaders. Chiapas elevated the plight of the Indians within the national consciousness and sparked a deeper attachment to indigenous identity. Following the uprising, various Indian groups formed the National Indigenous Congress (CNI). CNI became active politically, though it could not stop passage of an indigenous rights law that most indigenous groups felt set back their cause rather than improving it.

Topic in countries

Brazil

Because the Brazilian government did not recognize race as a salient social division until very recently, past government policy could best be described as one of integration. No active efforts were made to force minority groups to conform to a national standard of behavior, language, or religious affiliation, as in assimilation. On the other hand, by not acknowledging racial divisions, the government failed to address the very real racial discrimination and economic challenges faced by the descendants of slaves.

Brazil is only now beginning to recognize the problem. Strange though it might seem to Americans, the first affirmative action quotas in Brazil (saving places at university for students of color) were adopted as late as 2003, amid huge controversy. The current government of President Lula da Silva has moved more in the direction of accommodation, seeking to address programs specifically to black Brazilians. However, the dominant focus of his administration continues to be poverty. Brazilian governments tend to classify their social policies in terms of class rather than race, even if the two categories substantially overlap.

Approaches to Ethnic and Religious Diversity in the Russian Federation, China, and India

As highlighted in Chapter 2, Russia, China, and India have all struggled to develop a national identity that unites their many subnational identity groups. In Russia in particular, national identity is more nuanced and puzzling than in most other countries. As a result, the country's policies aimed at addressing ethnic diversity have at times appeared to lack direction. Compared with Russia, China has viewed the idea of cultivating, or even accommodating, ethnic and religious diversity with considerable suspicion. With independence, India took steps to address its caste system and created affirmative action programs for other traditionally underprivileged groups. At the same time, India has sometimes taken harsh measures against groups, particularly when the government perceives that the groups' desire for greater control over their own affairs threatens the country's territorial integrity and fragile national unity.

The Russian Federation

Government officials deciding how to address Russia's ethnic and religious diversity face the problem of multiple ideas of what it means to be "Russian." This question has been the focus of intellectuals and government officials in Russia for centuries. The Russian language has two words for "Russians"—*russkie* and *rossiiane*—the former referring to ethnic Russians and the latter referring to the citizens of the Russian Federation. If one includes Russians outside the Russian Federation or groups like "Russian-speakers," the number of words grows even more. Along with these different meanings of Russian are different conceptions of the Russian state, particularly whether Russia is the homeland of ethnic Russians (including those outside its borders) or whether, like the United States, it is the country of a broadly inclusive civic nation.

In the past, an ethnic conception of national identity existed alongside an openness to ethnic assimilation. Jews became Russians by converting to Orthodox Christianity; others learned to speak Russian, adopted Russian customs, and changed their last names to make them sound Russian. The tsarist government often encouraged such behavior, and even engaged in forced assimilation at times by, among other things, banning non-Russian languages from being spoken publicly in parts of the empire. The Soviets also encouraged non-Russians to learn Russian, while accommodating minority cultures to a large degree.

Since the Soviet Union's breakup, the Russian government has pursued a mixed bag of diversity-related policies. The Russian ethnofederal system has been maintained, and the former Constitution includes the right to use languages other than Russian. Yet other policies favor ethnic Russians. Police often target ethnic minorities, especially those living in large cities outside their "home" republic (such as Chechens in Moscow).

This mixed approach is perhaps not surprising, given the ongoing struggles to define Russian identity itself. In one of the more telling examples of this struggle, mentioned briefly in Chapter 4, Russian President Boris Yeltsin established a commission to study and report on the "Russian National Idea" shortly after he won reelection in 1996. The commission sought to find a set of guiding principles to unite the Russian population, something along the lines of the U.S. concept of the "American Dream." After a year, the commission produced a report, "Russia in Search of an Idea," which emphasized the value of thinking about what united Russians but produced no definitive Russian national idea. Russia seems no closer today to an answer to the questions of its national identity and its *raison d'être* as a state than it was in the 1800s.

China

Historically, the Chinese government has been suspicious of ethnic minority groups. The Chinese have often perceived such groups as not only different but also inferior. Assimilation was consequently less of a priority for the Imperial Chinese than for the Russian tsars, since by definition it would have meant diluting the cultural supremacy of the Han Chinese.

The Communists have not translated these attitudes into a policy of complete neglect of their minorities. Rather, they have engaged in a balancing act between integration and accommodation on the one hand and repression of ethnic minorities on the other. For example, the government has linked ethnic identity and territory by designating five regions and dozens of smaller areas as autonomous territories.[55] By emphasizing the unique cultures that make the minorities "others," the government reinforces the image of Han Chinese as a single, unified ethnic group. At the same time, the government has shown concern over the potential for ethnic identity to turn into ethnic separatism, especially in the oil-rich western provinces.

The Xinjiang region provides examples of how the Chinese government approaches diversity when it feels an ethnic minority group's heightened identity has spawned nationalist ambitions. The government has strongly encouraged Han Chinese to settle the Xinjiang region in an effort to weaken autonomy of ethnic Uyghurs. While less than 10 percent of the population of the area at the time of the Communist revolution in the late 1940s, the Han Chinese have swelled to between 40 percent and 50 percent of the region's population today. The increasing presence of Han Chinese (including ethnic Han from the military and police) has only served to deepen the ethnic divide.

The Communist government has restricted open expressions of Islamic faith in Xinjiang. It has prohibited traditional Muslim dress, the teaching of Islam to children, and even public prayer during Ramadan. Chinese police routinely harass Muslim clerics. These policies have made the practice of Islam less visible but increased its standing as a centerpiece of Uyghur identity.

The government has targeted those it believes to be leaders of the separatist movement, arresting thousands and executing perhaps hundreds. Some of these actions have garnered international attention, including the high profile arrest of Uyghur businesswoman Rebiya Kadeer in 1999 on charges of "revealing state secrets."[56] Kadeer was released in 2005, on the eve of U.S. Secretary of State Condoleezza Rice's visit to China.

India

The Indian Government has responded in multiple ways to the politicization of various identities. Affirmative action has been a response to the exclusion of those who identify with, or who are identified as, a lower caste or tribe. Some "seats" in educational institutions and jobs with the government are reserved for "Scheduled Castes" (SC), "Scheduled Tribes" (ST), and "Other Backward Classes" (OBCs). Women were provided reserved seats in local government. Efforts have been made to reserve seats for Muslims too. As the proportions of places being reserved for these groups have grown, some Brahmins have demanded reservation lest there be no opportunities left for them, and the courts have stepped in to place limits on the portion of seats and jobs that can be reserved for specific groups.

A variety of tools have been used to deal with the demands of regional groups. At times, the Indian government has imposed President's Rule (where the central government replaces the government of a federal unit). At other times, the central government and/or the government of the particular federal unit have provided financial and other forms of aid; have added new federal units; have created governments in separatist regions and given them limited powers; have given a variety of special privileges, such as limiting government employees to indigenous people; have imprisoned regional leaders; have co-opted separatist leaders; and have used the army to suppress such movements.

Similarly, the central government has used a wide range of tools to deal with other non-national identities. From 2002–2007, the president of India was Dr. A.P.J. Abdul Kalam, a Muslim; in 2007, the person selected to be president was a woman, Pratibha Devisingh Patil. The symbolism of these selections fostered greater national identity on the part of Muslims and women in the country.

Approaches to Ethnic and Religious Diversity in Nigeria and Iran

Nigeria and Iran challenge the general global trend toward more tolerant approaches to identity diversity. Nigeria initially pursued an ethno-federal approach, though it abandoned that arrangement after it became clear that reinforcing ethnic identity with internal territorial divisions was a recipe for the collapse of the newly independent state. At the same time, it has rejected any idea of assimilating the various ethnic groups into a single identity, leaning more in the direction of accommodation under an India-style theme of "unity in diversity." In Iran, the government has often chosen to repress minority identities rather than accommodate them. These actions are more visible against religious minorities than ethnic ones, but even ethnic minorities have faced pressure to conform socially and support the regime politically.

Nigeria

The Nigerian government has shifted its identity diversity approach since independence, and contradictory approaches have sometimes overlapped. The government undid the ethno-federal approach after the Nigerian civil war of the late 1960s and actively tried to develop attachment to an overarching Nigerian identity—moving in a less tolerant direction on the spectrum of policy options discussed earlier in the chapter. On the other hand, the lack of any one ethnic group making up the vast majority of the population made assimilation impossible, and the government (civilian and military alike) feared minorities' perceptions that it did not respect their cultural practices. As captured by President Olusegun Obasanjo's farewell address in May 2007, the government stressed harmony and unity rather than uniformity.

Because of its prominence as a form of collective identity, religion has been at the center of Nigerian government action. At times, the government has taken actions to make religion less visible, including its lightly enforced ban on published religious advertisements and control over religious programming on television and radio. At other times, the government has appeared to support religious expression—lifting its restrictions on religious programming and accepting the injection of religion into regional and local politics. Although the Nigerian Constitution prohibits lower levels of government from establishing official religions in their regions, Muslim parts of the country are allowed to implement *Shari'a* through local laws and a *Shari'a*-based court system. Regional governments in Nigeria's north noticeably increased their use of *Shari'a* following the reestablishment of democracy in 1999.

Government policy on religion highlights the way in which the existence of a federal system, even when no longer tied to ethnicity, can add to policy variation. Some regional governments have banned open-air religious services away from places of worship in an attempt to limit religious violence.[57] Meanwhile, in the north of the country, *Shari'a*-based provisions adopted by many regional governments regulate which acts are defined as crimes and endorse punishments that include amputation, flogging, and execution by stoning. In the province of Kano, schoolgirls were required to wear headscarves whether they were Muslims or not.[58] The *Shari'a* question highlights one of the difficulties that governments of ethnically and religiously diverse countries face: accommodating the culture of a minority may require tolerating practices that appear highly intolerant.

Iran

The government's response to ethnic and religious diversity has included significant discrimination, principally against minority religions. Unlike many countries in the world, Iran's Constitution specifies an official religion, Shi'ite Islam. The government officially recognizes certain religious minorities; Jews, Christians, and Zoroastrians (a Kurdish religion) have a small number of reserved seats in the *Majles* (Iran's national assembly). Yet discrimination against these groups and others is common. The election of President Mahmoud Ahmadinejad and his subsequent anti-Israel statements, including his suggestion in late 2005 that European governments should offer to move Israel to Europe, did not bode well for Jews in Iran. Iran's religious police monitor Christian churches, though probably less to intimidate the Christian believers than to prevent Muslims from entering the churches and potentially converting to Christianity.

Ethnic minorities arguably face less government discrimination than religious minorities, although the government carefully monitors groups that are large and concentrated enough to develop nationalist movements. The Azeris and Kurds are two such groups. Both have at least limited contacts with members of their ethnic cohort in neighboring countries. The international community has increasingly taken note of the fate of the Kurds over the last two decades, and a violent crackdown against Kurdish activists in the west of Iran in 2005 drew international criticism.[59]

Think and Discuss

What factors lead a government to take more tolerant or less tolerant actions against ethnic, racial, or religious minorities? What strategies has the American government used in response to ethnic, racial, and religious diversity?

COMPARATIVE EXERCISE

Identity, Territory, and Civil War in Nigeria

Internal regional boundaries can complement or cross-cut existing social divisions. The Nigerian case provides an opportunity to examine the relationship between internal identity structures and internal political boundaries, since it is both the scene of deep social divisions and a federal system. This chapter's comparative exercise takes a case study approach, examining the sequences of events in Nigeria from the time of independence leading up to the outbreak of civil war in 1967. Examining Nigeria's path to civil war, this case study centers on the question: Was the outbreak of the Nigerian civil war (the dependent variable) caused by complementary identity divisions that were made worse by the design of the country's political institutions?

Overview of the Nigerian Case

In the preindependence period, the British reinforced the centrality of ethnic identity by designing a federal system that linked regional divisions in the country to its three main ethnic groups. In addition, as in other British colonies, Nigeria had a taste of democratic practices even before independence. The British hoped the experience of elections prior to independence would facilitate the consolidation of postindependence democracy. Unfortunately, these elections led to the formation of regional parties appealing to particular ethnic groups. The British oversaw elections in 1951 and 1959. In both cases, ethnicity was the defining aspect of the campaign.

Independence for Nigeria brought the First Republic, a democratic federal system with the three large regional divisions inherited from the British. A fourth, the midwestern region, was added in 1963. The regions continued to correspond to areas of concentration of the main ethnic groups, so this change did little to weaken the ethnically concentrated political parties in the north, west, and east. Encouraged by this federal arrangement, the major political parties during the First Republic continued to base their support largely on only one ethnic group. The regions thus effectively turned into one-party systems, leaving only the federal government as a setting for "genuine political competition."[60] The Northern People's Congress (NPC) party, the main party of the ruling coalition of the federal government, was largely supported by the Hausa-Fulani. The other main parties accused the NPC of using the federal government to benefit the north and its ethnic base there.

Elections in 1964 once more highlighted the main political parties' ethnic and regional support, with the NPC securing a majority of seats in parliament. Things worsened over the next two years, as the divide between Ibo and Hausa-Fulani elites deepened. The years 1966 and 1967 were chaotic. The country's First Republic ended early in 1966 with an Ibo-led military coup. This resulted in the assassination of the country's prime minister and the leaders of the western and northern regions. Ibo leaders announced an end to the federal system. This triggered fears in the north, leading to another coup in July of that year. Yakubu Gowon, a Christian from Nigeria's north, became leader of the country.

In 1967, Gowon proposed to change the federal system by increasing the number of regions to twelve. The Ibo refused to join the new system. Their pursuit of independence for the eastern region, Biafra, marked the beginning of the Nigerian civil war. Upward of a million people lost their lives in the resulting ethno-nationalist conflict.

Discussion

There is obviously more to the story of the outbreak of the Nigerian civil war than this brief overview can highlight. A genuine comparative politics research project investigating the years leading up to the civil war could produce a book-length discussion and would also include in-depth investigations into the roles of individual leaders and their decisions.[61]

That said, the modest description of events leading up to the civil war supports three contentions about identity and internal political boundaries. First, the Nigerian events are consistent with cleavage structure theory's assertion (see the "In Theory and Practice" box on Russia) that complementary social cleavages are politically destabilizing. Second, the Nigerian experience shows how ethno-federalism can increase the political importance of ethnicity, encourage ethnic nationalism, and help spark violence. Because nationalism unites identity and territory, internal political boundary designs that also involve both identity and territory risk fanning nationalist sentiments. Finally, although it was not part of the central research question, the examination of the Nigerian case highlights how certain democratic practices such as elections can contribute to the complementary nature of these social divisions. As this book moves from social and economic structures to political structures—including federalism and electoral arrangements—in the chapters ahead, it will be helpful to keep in mind these findings from the Nigerian case about the interactions between identity and political institutions.

CONCLUSION

Identity matters in politics. This makes sense, considering identity's role in shaping how individuals view themselves and those around them. This chapter discussed those collective identities that, along with national identity, have the greatest effect on politics: ethnicity, race, religion, region, gender, and class. These are just some of what individual identity involves. The age cohort to which one belongs, one's sexual orientation, one's occupation, one's level of education, and many other traits combine with personal beliefs to form an individual's identity. Comparativists can, and often do, study the political implications of these other identity-related features.

The TIC countries provide many lessons about identity and politics. Ethnicity is an important identity division in each of the ten. Russia and China highlight how religion can emerge more forcefully as a part of people's identity in times of chaotic social transformation and ideological upheaval. Particular events can "reenergize" us/them boundaries, as in the United Kingdom after the "7/7" bombings or Russia after the Beslan school tragedy. The cases also show that governments in different countries can take disparate actions in response to identity diversity, different governments in the same country can develop alternative approaches over time, and sometimes one country can have contrasting policies at the same time.

Perhaps most of all, the cases indicate that when identity divisions complement one another, "identity politics" is not only the norm but also a powerful feature of any country's domestic politics. Deep complementary divisions pose policy challenges for a government. It also appears that in societies with deep complementary cleavages, the design of the political system—specifically, its ability to cut across deep social divisions—becomes a crucial factor in political stability and preventing widespread violence.

As with other approaches highlighted in this book, focusing on identity to understand political outcomes can be criticized. These criticisms include that identity is too complex and individually variable to be a useful explanation of a person's political choices and that emphasizing feelings such as "belonging" allows one to explain any action as the result of identity. As a student of comparative politics, it is important that you are aware of these criticisms. Yet, as with critiques of other approaches, criticisms of identity-based understandings of political outcomes should not lead to a knee-jerk rejection of the approach. Indeed, the inherent sense of belonging that collective identity stimulates in individuals is what makes identity so politically powerful. "Identity politics" is, accordingly, omnipresent. A sense of shared identity provides opportunities to mobilize masses to act on the basis of that identity, such as encouraging people to turn out and vote for a candidate who is "one of us."

But identity is not only a tool that elites use to secure political office. An important theme of this chapter is that identity is an underlying structural factor that constrains political leaders as much as it provides opportunities to them. In addition, while identities are socially constructed—largely through the action of intellectual and political leaders—the "radical middle position" between primordialism and constructivism asserts that such elites cannot craft and use identity in any way they see fit. Past incidents, current circumstances, and existing identity boundaries all affect how elites can create or mold collective identities and use them for political ends.

To conclude, three important reminders are in order. First, *all* societies are divided by collective identities. There is no perfectly homogeneous society, in which everyone belongs to the same identity groups. Within every sizeable population, there is a "we" and a "they."

Second, individuals can be likewise divided by the multiple components of their personal identities. An individual can be, simultaneously, American, of Irish ancestry, Christian, white, English-speaking, Midwest resident, female, middle class, and any number of other categories which that individual prioritizes when defining herself. Just as cross-cutting cleavages may internally divide large groups, so too may individuals

have numerous, and often conflicting, politically relevant elements to their identities.

Finally, identity plays an important role in politics, but, like other structural factors, it does not completely dictate how people will behave politically. Identity is only one piece of the puzzle of understanding political outcomes. The following several chapters take a step toward completing this puzzle by moving away from economic and social structures and toward the foundation of the political process. This next step begins in Chapter 6, with a discussion of governmental institutions as structures, which, like economic and social structures, provide political leaders with a combination of constraints and opportunities.

Key Terms

Accommodation, p. 178
Assimilation, p. 177
Caste, p. 166
Clan, p. 149
Cleavage structure theory, p. 174
Complementary identity divisions, p. 170
Constructivism, p. 164
Cross-cutting identity divisions, p. 170
Ethnic group, p. 148
Ethnic cleansing, p. 177
Ethnic identity, p. 148
Ethno-federalism, p. 178
Falun Gong, p. 163
Feminist theory, p. 168
Gender, p. 153
Genocide, p. 177
Identity, p. 145
In-group, p. 146
Integration, p. 177
Membership boundary, p. 146
Out-group, p. 146
Primordialism, p. 163
Race, p. 147
"Radical middle position", p. 164
Religion, p. 150
Social cleavages, p. 147
Tribe, p. 150

Learning Objectives

After reading this chapter, you should be able to:

- Define key concepts such as political institution, democracy, authoritarianism, totalitarianism, and federal versus unitary systems.
- Explain the role of a constitution.
- Discuss the general type of political system and important constitutional issues in the ten Topic in Countries cases.
- Grasp the "veto points" theoretical perspective examined in this chapter's comparative exercise.

6
Political Systems and Their Rules

During the Soviet period, Russians sometimes told the following joke among friends:

A man walks into a dining hall, looks at the menu, and orders the beef dinner. The woman behind the counter replies, "We don't have any." The man looks at the menu again and orders the chicken. The woman behind the counter replies, "We don't have any." The man looks at the menu a third time and orders the borscht.[1] The woman behind the counter shakes her head and says, "We don't have any." The man slams down the menu and says, "Is this the menu or our constitution?"

This joke captures the frustration that many Soviet citizens felt about the difference between what was written in their constitution and the actual practice of the Soviet government. It also raises an important point for the comparative study of politics: political

Look for this icon 🌐 to point you to **Deepening Your Understanding** features on the companion website www.college.cengage.com/politicalscience/ barrington, which provide greater depth for some key content.

institutions matter, but the way they work in practice may differ significantly from the official "rules of the game." The comparative study of politics has long centered on the role of governmental institutions, a subject "central to political science since its inception."[2] Such institutions frame the actions of political leaders, constraining them and creating opportunities for them at the same time. These institutions emerge and change at different points in time, sometimes complementing one another and other times coming into conflict. Even the various components of a single political institution, such as a national legislature, may have different goals, different norms, and different formal rules.

Political institutions are, therefore, both complex and important. If the state is the arena of the "game" of politics, then the state's institutions are the "teams." Each team's playbook (the design of the institution and its internal rules and norms) shapes its actions. These actions, along with how the teams interact within the overall rules of the game (the constitution), determine the game's outcome.

This chapter highlights general concepts related to political systems, political institutions, and the rules that govern them. This discussion includes the major types of political regimes—democracy, totalitarianism, and authoritarianism—as well as the arrangements between different levels of government. It also involves a number of theories that attempt to explain how institutions are formed, how they change or persist over time, and what difference their design makes in determining political outcomes. ∎

Political Institutions

Political systems are made up of political institutions. Social scientists define the term **institution** in different ways. Most political scientists envision institutions as "purposive organizations" (created for a particular purpose) and the formal rules that structure them. Other social scientists, particularly sociologists, may conceptualize institutions as informal norms, social understandings, or longtime customs (e.g., the "institution of marriage"). What both of these views share is the understanding that an institution involves rules that govern individual behavior. Thus, institutions are sets of rules, taking the form of purposive organizations or informal norms, which shape individual behavior.

Political institutions refer to governing organizations—or other organized groups seeking to shape political outcomes, such as interest groups and political parties. Unless otherwise

stated in this chapter, however, the term political institution will refer to governing bodies and the rules that structure the behavior of individuals within them. These political institutions are quite unique compared with other social institutions. Political institutions are distinctive because their rules "reach outward," seeking to control the actions of people who do not participate in the institutions themselves.[3] Most *social* institutions have rules designed to govern the behavior of their participants, but *political* institutions create rules for society as a whole. In addition, as discussed in Chapter 2, one of the key features of political institutions is their

An **institution** is a set of formal or informal rules, often taking the form of a purposive organization, which shape individual behavior.

Political institutions are governing organizations or other associations seeking to shape political outcomes and the rules governing behavior of individuals working within them.

sovereignty. The rules political institutions produce take precedence over any conflicting rules from social institutions.

Regime Types

Scholars studying politics, from ancient philosophers on, have long been concerned about how political institutions come together to form types of political systems or "regimes." The events of World War II and the Cold War pushed comparativists to concentrate even more on nondemocratic political systems and compare them to the democratic systems of Western Europe and North America. Scholars were particularly interested in a relatively new type of political regime: totalitarianism. This was one of three general regime types that political scientists had identified at the time, democracy and authoritarianism being the other two. In more recent decades, the variants within each of these three types have drawn greater attention, and scholars have begun to categorize some real world political systems as hybrids of these main types (i.e., "semiauthoritarianism," "semidemocracy"). The broad descriptions of the three main regime types in this section are ideal types. As such, these major regime types provide a measuring stick with which to compare political systems, even though the pure form of the regime type may never be realized in practice.

Democracy

There are many ways to think about **democracy**. A vague statement like "government of, by, and for the people" might be quickly dismissed as unhelpful. Yet it points to an important difference between democracy and nondemocratic systems: citizens participate in the governing process in a democracy, and their participation can actually influence the kinds of policies the political system produces. This participation is generally indirect, as in the selection of

"representatives" to serve in government on behalf of the general population.

Selection of Government Officials Through Free and Fair Elections The first defining characteristic of modern democracy is mass involvement in the selection of representatives through elections. Chapter 9 presents other ways in which elites and masses are linked in democracies besides electoral competition, but elections remain the central vehicle for mass involvement and an essential force for holding government officials accountable for their actions. Elections are a necessary feature of democracy, but their presence is far from sufficient to label a system democratic. After all, totalitarian systems and even many authoritarian ones hold regular elections.

What distinguishes electoral practices in democracies from those of nondemocratic systems is that the nondemocratic systems exclude large portions of the population from participating (e.g., South Africa during apartheid) or do not provide voters with a real choice between candidates. Political scientist Robert Dahl labels the portion of the adult population that is eligible to vote as a system's "inclusiveness"; he calls the extent to which they have a real choice between candidates as the system's level of "contestation."[4] Representative democracies are political systems that have high levels of both inclusiveness and contestation.

A related, and probably more common, way to think about elections in a democracy is the extent to which they are *free and fair*. In "free" elections:

- Individuals have the ability to vote.
- Their votes are made in secret.
- Candidates have the ability to run for office.
- Candidates have the ability to campaign for office by providing information to voters.

Democracy is a regime type that involves the selection of government officials through free and fair elections, a balance between the principle of majority rule and the protection of minority interests, and constitutional limitations on government actions.

"Fair" elections require:

- Voters to have access to impartial coverage of the campaign in the media
- Voters to have reasonable access to polling places
- The vote of each eligible voter—and only of eligible voters—to be counted
- The vote of each eligible voter to be counted equally
- The losing candidate to acknowledge and accept the results (including, if necessary, a peaceful transfer of power from one set of ruling elites to another)
- The electoral process to be administered and monitored by an impartial body of electoral specialists

All these things must occur without significant restrictions, governmental interference, or other attempts at intimidation. The elections must also be meaningful, selecting the office holders for the political system's positions of real power. Free and fair elections for positions that amount to little more than window dressing are hardly a criterion of democracy.

Think and Discuss

Look at the list of criteria associated with free and fair elections in this chapter. How do American elections measure up based on these criteria?

The Balance of Majority Rule and Minority Protection A second feature of democracy is that it balances the principle of majority rule with the protection of minority interests. Dahl calls this provision "Madisonian democracy," named for James Madison's preoccupation with balancing majority and minority power in the design of the American political system.[5] For the most part, democratic representatives are chosen based on the idea that those who receive the most votes should win. Likewise, laws are, generally, produced from democratic governments when a majority of the elected officials support the provision.

But there are also often protections against what might be called mob rule or, for Madison, "majority tyranny." The intensity of the masses is taken into account in some electoral systems, and the activity of interest groups certainly reflects their members' intensity (as well as their other resources, such as money). There may also be constitutional provisions to check the majority's ability to dictate policy. In the United States, majority tyranny is limited by the large number of requirements along the way to a bill becoming a law. These steps can lead what Dahl calls a "tentative majority" to break apart in the face of an intense minority.

Limitations on Government Action A third feature of democracy, and another way that majorities can be limited, is the constitutional prohibition of certain government actions. These so-called negative rights—freedoms that government cannot take away from the people—include such things as freedoms of speech, religious practice, and assembly. A democracy requires that people be free to criticize governmental action. This is part of the free flow of information necessary for voters to hold government officials accountable. This also means the media must be free to investigate and criticize without fear of reprisal. The degree of freedom the media enjoy is a strong indicator of the level of democracy in a particular political system.

Variants of Democracy The institutional differences between one democracy and another can be significant. In a unitary democratic system, the central government has complete autonomy over all lower levels of government, and those lower levels have no powers reserved for them; in a federal democratic state, lower levels of government retain designated powers that the central government cannot take away. These two options are discussed in more detail later in this chapter.

Democratic systems can also be presidential, where the executive and legislative branches are separated (both in their selection by voters and in the exercise of their powers), or they can be parliamentary, where the legislative and executive branches are fused and the chief executive serves only with the consent of the legislature. These two approaches are a central topic of Chapter 7.

Democratic systems can have politically powerful judicial branches with the power to overturn legislative initiatives as unconstitutional. Alternatively, their judiciaries can be restricted to resolving disputes about the violation of laws already on the books, having no authority to evaluate whether new laws comply with the constitution. Such judicial arrangements are a focus of Chapter 8.

Democracies may vary in how they bring interest groups into the political process. In a *pluralist* system, such as the United States, multiple interest groups compete for the attention of representatives through lobbying (and campaign contributions). In a *corporatist* system, the government selects key organizations to represent major social groups, and their representatives sit at the table with the government officials crafting policy affecting their groups (see Chapter 9).

Democracies can elect their legislative representatives through the use of *first past the post* (FPTP) district systems—in which the candidate with the most votes in the district wins a seat in the government—or through *proportional representation* (PR) systems, in which political parties receive seats in a legislative body in proportion to how well they do in the elections, or through a hybrid of these approaches. Electoral arrangements and their consequences are major themes in Chapter 10.

These various institutional arrangements can be combined in different ways. Scholars have given labels to particular institutional combinations. One valuable distinction, described in greatest detail by political scientist Arend Lijphart, is that between **majoritarian democracy** and **consensus democracy** (see the "Applying Concepts" box on majoritarian versus consensus democracy on page 194). Lijphart distinguishes between these two forms of democracy by examining ten criteria that fall into two main categories: an executives–political parties dimension and a federal-unitary dimension. According to Lijphart, the consensus combination leads to more cooperation and compromise rather than the politics of conflict found in the majoritarian approach. The British political system is very close in practice to the majoritarian ideal type, and Germany's democratic system approximates the consensus democracy ideal. The American political system, on the other hand, mixes features of the majoritarian and consensus approaches.

Lijphart claims that the conventional wisdom among scholars is that there is a trade-off: consensus democracy provides better representation and protection of minority views, but majoritarian democracy leads to more effective government. Lijphart's work challenges this view, arguing that consensus democracy is equally effective in maintaining order and managing the economy but better in its representation. As a result, Lijphart advocates consensus democracy as superior to the majoritarian approach.[6]

Did You Know? Australia and Belgium are two countries that have compulsory voting. Citizens who fail to vote can be fined or jailed. While some might consider the practice undemocratic, it contributes to very high voter turnout rates (roughly 95 percent turnout in Australia).

Majoritarian democracy combines strong executives, few checks on the power of the majority to pass laws and amend the constitution, and conflictual politics between two major political parties.

Consensus democracy unites proportional representation elections and a multiparty system with the diffusion of power across branches and levels of government.

APPLYING CONCEPTS

"Majoritarian Versus Consensus Democracy"

Arend Lijphart distinguishes between majoritarian and consensus democracy by looking at a number of criteria. The ideal type *majoritarian* democracy combines:

- A first past the post (FPTP) plurality electoral system
- A powerful executive
- Control of the chief executive and cabinet by a single party rather than through a coalition of political parties
- A pluralist approach to interest groups in which groups compete against each other
- A unitary and centralized government
- A unicameral legislature
- A flexible constitution that can be changed by a simple majority
- No judicial review of legislation
- A central bank under the control of the executive

Consensus democracies, on the other hand, bring together:

- A proportional representation (PR) electoral mechanism
- A multi-party system
- Coalition governments
- A balance of power between the legislature and the executive
- A "corporatist" system of interest group representation (see Chapter 9)
- A federal and decentralized government
- A division of power between two equally strong legislative houses
- Rigid constitutions that are difficult to amend
- Judicial review of legislation
- An independent central bank

Robert Dahl describes four sets of democracies, based on the combination of electoral arrangements and presidential versus parliamentary approaches. The **European model of democracy**—basically Lijphart's consensus democracy—combines parliamentary and proportional representation (PR) arrangements. The **Westminster model of democracy**—basically Lijphart's majoritarian system—joins a parliamentary approach with first past the post (FPTP) district voting. This kind of system is in place in the United Kingdom and many former British colonies, including Canada. The **American model of democracy** brings together presidentialism with FPTP district voting for legislative elections. Finally, the **Latin American model of democracy** is the combination of a presidential system with a PR electoral system for the legislature.[7]

Even Dahl's categories are imprecise; there are a number of exceptions in Europe and Latin America. Dahl and Lijphart's efforts to create middle-range categories (below the level of democracy in general but above the level of an individual country), however, are valuable. They allow more effective comparison of one democracy to another. They also serve as a helpful reminder that the American version of democracy is far from the only democratic option. It is, in fact, quite unique among democracies, with features such as political party primaries—giving voters the right to choose who runs under a particular party label in the general election instead of letting the parties themselves decide this—that seem downright odd to those unaccustomed to them.

The **European model of democracy** is a term used by Robert Dahl to discuss democratic systems that combine parliamentary and PR arrangements.

The **Westminster model of democracy** combines a parliamentary approach with a first past the post (plurality) electoral system. This is the system in the United Kingdom and many former British colonies.

The **American model of democracy** is Dahl's term for a democratic system that combines a presidential system with FPTP district voting for legislative elections.

The **Latin American model of democracy** is Dahl's term for political systems which combine presidentialism with a proportional representation electoral system.

Totalitarianism

The second major regime type is **totalitarianism**. Though far different from democracy, it also differs greatly from the ideal authoritarian system. This type of political system was a central preoccupation of scholars following World War II, since the two real world examples that came closest to the totalitarian ideal were the Nazi German system under Hitler and the Communist system of the Soviet Union under Stalin.

Features of Totalitarianism Two of the most important works on totalitarianism in political science are Hannah Arendt's *The Origins of Totalitarianism* and Carl Friedrich and Zbigniew Brzezinski's *Totalitarian Dictatorship and Autocracy*.[8] One of the most important things Arendt contributed to the discussion of totalitarianism is the idea that a totalitarian system seeks the "atomization" of society, except when performing party-sponsored functions. By atomization, Arendt meant the breaking down of society into its component parts (individuals) who become unable or unwilling to join together with other individuals to form autonomous groups. Controlling the way in which individuals relate to one another by atomizing society is a crucial step in the efforts of the totalitarian government to radically alter social and/or economic relations in the country.

This does not mean that people in a totalitarian system are apolitical. Like democracy, totalitarianism is a system that emphasizes mass mobilization. In other words, it seeks the active participation of the masses in support of its goals. While democracy allows significantly more autonomy for citizens about how (and whether) they will participate in politics, totalitarianism completely shapes the form of that participation.

Friedrich and Brzezinski are best known for outlining six basic features of a totalitarian system. The first feature is an *official ideology*. Totalitarian ideology includes a blueprint for restructuring society and justification for the monopoly of political power. It also emphasizes the place of the

state in world historical development; the struggle with other states or systems of government; the past, present, and future greatness of the state; and the state's people (or at least much of its population) as a "superior" race.

The second characteristic is the existence of a *single political party* that has a monopoly on political power in the system. This party is part of the rulers' effort at total control of society. Previous political organizations, even volunteer organizations, are either destroyed or brought under the control of the party. This party is usually headed by a single person—certainly this has been the practice among the systems closest to the totalitarian ideal in practice—but such a leader is not a necessary feature of totalitarianism.

The third feature is the reliance on *terror* to maintain order in society. Totalitarian systems also seek to build legitimacy, but it is their willingness to terrorize the population—making people afraid even to talk with family members about problems with the political system—that makes them unique. An essential part of totalitarian terror is the presence of a secret police force. Because they seek to remake society, totalitarian governments are ruthless in dealing with political and cultural opponents. The secret police force is their main tool in this repression.

The fourth feature is complete *control of communications*. One could argue that it is impossible in practice to control all communications in society. But manipulating the flow of information (e.g., through complete control of the official media) is important for justifying the actions of the government, building support for its social blueprint, and enhancing the system's legitimacy.

Totalitarianism is a regime type defined by an effort to remake society and "atomize" the population. It includes an official ideology; a single mass political party, usually with a single leader, that has a monopoly of political power; a secret police force and the use of terror against the population; a monopoly over means of communication; a monopoly over weapons in society; and a command economy.

The fifth feature is the *control over the means of force* in society. This is, arguably, less important as a defining feature of totalitarianism than the previous four, since other types of regimes—including many democracies—attempt this as well. For Friedrich and Brzezinski, however, it is an important part of totalitarian systems' complete control over society.

The final trait of totalitarianism identified by Friedrich and Brzezinski is a *command economy*. Command economies are those in which decisions about what products to produce and how much the products cost to buy are controlled by government officials. This control over the economy allows the government to direct economic resources in a manner consistent with its efforts to remake society. Such control also aids in dominating all aspects of people's lives and means the workplace can become a tool for socialization.

Variants of Totalitarianism: Fascism and Communism Within totalitarianism are two central variants, fascism and communism. **Fascism** is a form of totalitarianism that emphasizes racial, religious, or ethnic superiority and engages in militarism. The dominant state is justified as crucial to develop fully the capacity of the superior race or ethnic group, maintain a pure culture, or fight those—internal or external—enemies who threaten the dominance of the superior group. **Communism** is a variant of totalitarianism that emphasizes collective ownership of the means of production in an effort to end the exploitation of the working class inherent in capitalism. In communism, the dominant state is justified as crucial to the elimination of the capitalist class and the protection of the communist system from external (anticommunist) threats.

Authoritarianism

The final major regime type is **authoritarianism**. The two real-world political systems most

Nazi troops stand in formation while top Nazi officials make their entrance during a Nazi Party rally in 1935.

(© Heinrich Hoffmann/George Eastman House/Getty Images)

identified as approaching the authoritarian ideal are Spain under Francisco Franco (1939–1975) and Chile under Augusto Pinochet Ugarte

Fascism is a variant of totalitarianism based on militarism and an emphasis on remaking society along racial, religious, or ethnic lines.

Communism is a variant of totalitarianism in which the state seeks to remake society in the name of the working class through, among other things, state ownership of the means of production.

Authoritarianism is a regime type defined by its rule by a single leader or small group of leaders, limited political participation, existent but limited autonomy of society from state control, the lack of an overarching ideology, and limited control over the economy.

(1973–1988). As an ideal type, authoritarianism shares some features with totalitarianism but has many distinct features as well.

Features of Authoritarianism The first feature of authoritarianism is the presence of a *dominant leader or small group of leaders*. This leader may rule through a political party (what political scientist Juan Linz calls "party dictatorships") or the leader may shun political parties altogether. In general, there is much less emphasis on political parties in authoritarian systems than in either of the other two major regime types.

This is partly because of the next feature of authoritarian systems: *limited political participation*. Authoritarian leaders, in fact, prefer a depoliticized population. The less people think about politics and the more they go about their normal lives without worrying about trying to change the political system the better for an authoritarian leader. Ideally, an authoritarian leader only has to mobilize the population in rare instances, such as to demonstrate support of a particular policy among the general public.

This does not imply that authoritarian systems seek to atomize the population in the way totalitarian systems do. A third feature of authoritarian systems is a degree of *autonomy of society from state control*. People cannot do whatever they want, but there is not a desire to control all possible activities of individuals. Voluntary associations and other groups may be allowed to form. If such a group becomes a threat to the system or the leader—by working on political issues or otherwise accumulating a significant amount of power—it is either co-opted or eliminated. Likewise, not all communication is controlled by the state in authoritarian

systems. Censorship still exists in the media, but this often takes the form of citizen self-censorship (since it is clear that reporters will be arrested if they write something unflattering about the leader) rather than the government having a direct control over all media content.

The fourth feature of authoritarianism is the general *lack of an ideology*. Authoritarian systems may focus their activities on a particular goal, but this goal is usually something like restoring order to a chaotic situation, eliminating government corruption, or improving the country's economic performance. This goal is not a blueprint for remaking society.

Finally, there is often *limited control over the economy*. Authoritarian political systems commonly exist side-by-side with free market economies. The economy may be regulated, and those who might be able to translate their economic power into political power are watched. But there is not complete control and state economic planning as in a totalitarian system.

Variants of Authoritarianism Variants of authoritarianism include military, party, and bureaucratic. Political scientist Juan Linz has emphasized the first two of these variants; Guillermo O'Donnell has stressed the third.[9] **Military authoritarianism** is common in many parts of the world, including Latin America and Africa. Linz argues that militaries are often privileged in authoritarian systems, but in a military authoritarian system the rulers

Did You Know? Ernest Hemingway's 1940 novel *For Whom the Bell Tolls* is a fictional account of the events of the Spanish Civil War (1936–1939), which brought Francisco Franco to power. Many reviews at the time and since consider the book to be Hemingway's best and one of the greatest novels about war of all time. While fictional, the novel includes many details about the conflict, including the USSR's support of the Republicans and Italy's support of the Fascists. The book also inspired a 1984 song of the same name by the rock group Metallica.

Military authoritarianism is a form of authoritarian government in which the leaders of the government are also military leaders. It has been most common in Latin America and Africa.

themselves are members of the military. **Party authoritarianism** exists when political life in an authoritarian system is organized and run through a single political party. Although the dominant party is more important than parties are in most authoritarian cases, this form of authoritarianism lacks some of the features (e.g., command control of the economy) that would allow one to label it totalitarian. Mexico, prior to its recent democratization, provides an example of a party authoritarian system. The Institutional Revolutionary Party (PRI) dominated politics for much of the twentieth century. **Bureaucratic authoritarianism**, according to O'Donnell, is found in societies with high levels of modernization. This modernization requires the political leaders, who may be members of the military, civilians, or both, to rely on experts ("technocrats") to assist them in creating and administering government policy.

Semiauthoritarianism/Semidemocracy

A final regime type is worth discussion even though it is, in many ways, simply a hybrid of two others. Increasingly, scholars have discussed the prevalence of **semiauthoritarianism** or **semidemocracy**. The difference between the two hybrid types is largely a matter of degree. Both labels refer to systems in which the components of democracy are openly incorporated into an otherwise authoritarian system. For example, in a semidemocracy, elections exist but are limited, the judiciary is not fully independent, and the media are only partially free.

In the past, such systems were often seen as a stopping point on the way either to a full-fledged authoritarian system or a fully democratic one. Today, scholars recognize that semiauthoritarian systems are much more stable than they had appeared to be in the past. Authoritarian leaders have learned how to allow degrees of both contestation and inclusiveness without directly putting their hold on power at risk.

At the same time, the "color revolutions" of the first decade of the twenty-first century demonstrate the dangers of allowing citizens to believe they have a real say in the selection of government officials. These uprisings, which all occurred during the first half of the decade and involved hundreds of thousands of protesters, toppled leaders in Serbia, Georgia, Ukraine, and Kyrgyzstan. A leader of a semiauthoritarian system may still believe it is necessary to steal an election to maintain power. The "color revolutions," however, highlight that stealing an election is risky. The general population may not always sit idly by and watch such events unfold.

Party authoritarianism involves the control of an authoritarian system by a single political party. The PRI's control of Mexico for much of the 1900s is an example.

Bureaucratic authoritarianism occurs in countries where the economy is modernized enough to require authoritarian leaders to work closely with a large bureaucracy that has expertise on policy matters.

Semiauthoritarianism and **semidemocracy** are systems in which elements of democracy are integrated into an otherwise authoritarian system. The two labels are essentially synonymous, with the distinction between them involving slight differences in how democratically the system functions.

Regime Type in the United Kingdom, Germany, France, and India

The current political systems in the United Kingdom, Germany, France, and India are all consolidated liberal democracies. Yet, they differ in many significant ways. The British, German, and Indian political systems place great power in the hands of the prime minister (called the chancellor in Germany), while the French system places significant powers in the president's hands. They also differ in the overall extent to which they approach Lijphart's majoritarian and consensus democracy ideal types, with the United Kingdom closely approximating the majoritarian system, the German system embodying the consensus variant, and France and India falling in between.

The United Kingdom

An irony of the British political system is that it is both a model of democracy for many countries and a system that some believe borders on dictatorship in practice. Its standing as a democratic model comes from its own early development of parliamentary democracy—the British parliament is known as the "mother of parliaments"—as well as its work with formerly British colonies to design their postindependence political systems. The portrayal of the United Kingdom as a quasi-dictatorship comes from its majoritarian qualities.

The British political system is the real world expression of the "Westminster model" of democracy. It is so close to the pure form of Lijphart's majoritarian democracy that the labels "majoritarian democracy" and "Westminster democracy" are essentially synonymous. Lijphart indeed uses them interchangeably in one of his best known books.[10] Though some of its majoritarian features are being altered by constitutional reforms under the Labour Party, these reforms have been much more limited in reality than the rhetoric (by government officials and scholars alike) would indicate.

The United Kingdom remains one of the most majoritarian democratic systems in the world. It has even been dubbed an "elective dictatorship," because a majority party controlling the House of Commons, and thus the position of the prime minister, has the ability to pass its legislation at will.

Why, then, is the British system considered democratic? First, it is important to keep in mind that majoritarian democracy is still democracy. Leaders are selected by the general population through free and fair elections, minority interests are somewhat protected, and the power of government is limited—both constitutionally and, particularly important for the British case, culturally. Members of the prime minister's party can check the power of the prime minister by pressuring the party leadership to rethink a proposal. This happened in 2004, for example, with a controversial bill to ban hunting with dogs. The presence of a formal and visible opposition and the ability of members of parliament to openly question the prime minister and cabinet officials during "Question Time" also keeps the prime minister's government in line by showcasing a viable alternative to its control.[11]

Germany

Over the last century, Germans have experienced semiauthoritarianism, both types of totalitarian regimes—the fascist variant under the Nazis and the communist variant in East Germany following World War II—and democracy. A democratic regime took root in West Germany after 1949 and has since been extended to the east following unification in 1990. Germany today exemplifies Lijphart's consensus democracy.

The Second Reich (1871–1918) was a semiauthoritarian system. The system had the veneer of parliamentary institutions, but the real power lay with the emperor and his appointed chancellor.[12] The Weimar Republic that followed was an unstable democracy that was fatally undermined by a polarized society unwilling to support it. It also

Topic in Countries

suffered from a constitutional design that granted the president emergency decree powers at the expense of the prime minister and parliament and from an electoral system that encouraged severe party fragmentation and unstable governments.[13]

The fascist variant of totalitarianism came during the rule of the National Socialist (Nazi) Party from 1933 to 1945. National Socialist ideology preached the superiority of an ethnically (and racially) defined nation; the regime glorified and pursued militarism; and the population was mobilized through the Nazi Party and its affiliated societal groups, and subordinated through terrorism and propaganda. After the division of Germany in 1949, the Soviet Union constituted the German Democratic Republic (East Germany) as a communist totalitarian regime. Under the Communists, the East German economy was centrally planned and the population was controlled through a secret police and manipulation of the flow of information.

The democratic regime established in the Federal Republic (West Germany) in 1949 provides the basis for Germany's current democracy. This system deliberately dispersed state power as an antidote to the centralized state under the Nazi dictatorship. Germany specialist Peter Katzenstein has termed this dispersal of state power as a condition of "semisovereignty" that is realized through coalition governments, federalism, and a corporatist form of interest group consultation.[14] The combination of coalition governments, federalism, and the representation of interests under corporatism lead comparativists to view Germany as the model of a consensual democratic political system. The system requires a high degree of negotiation and compromise among key actors involved in making and implementing policy. One reason for this is Germany's electoral system, which combines FPTP and PR elements. This electoral arrangement creates a multiparty system consisting of two large parties and several smaller parties, in which coalition governments are the rule.

Compromise is also necessary because German federalism accords the territorial units below the level of the federal government—the *Länder*—substantial powers. They are represented in the upper house (*Bundesrat*) of the parliament, they share certain powers with the federal government, and they play a significant role in administering and implementing federal legislation.

Another way the German system encourages cooperation is the federal government's reliance on interest groups to implement laws on its behalf. This obviates the need for a large federal bureaucracy. Instead, as discussed in Chapter 4, the government accords these groups substantial autonomy to manage their respective sector of the economy or domain of public policy and consults these groups regularly when formulating policy.[15]

France

The cover of one of the most influential texts on the French state, *L'État en France de 1789 à nos jours* by Pierre Rosanvallon, is illustrated with a locomotive labeled ETAT ("STATE"). Moving forward through history, the locomotive as a metaphor for the state suggests continuity and power within a regularized constitutional framework. Such a suggestion is somewhat ironic, given that France has had five republics, three kingdoms, and two empires, as well as the Vichy State—all since the Revolution of 1789. In other ways, however, the metaphor is quite appropriate. Despite the many constitutional changes, the French state has evolved through a growing agreement over a proper constitutional order. This agreement appeared first in norms and practice, much like the British Constitution. Later, this agreement became manifest through written documents and laws, such as the Constitution of the Fifth Republic, adopted in 1958.

The Fifth Republic combines aspects of majoritarian and consensus democratic systems and integrates various procedures and arrangements from nearly all of the country's previous constitutions. A constitution that provides for strong executive and legislative functions and a judicial bureaucracy—and a bicameral parliament with senators selected by a special electoral college—appears to favor some degree of consensus. Indeed, a number of agencies serve an advisory role in the legislative process, quasi-judicial bodies review proposed laws and administrative actions, and there is a broad consensus on many of the basic principles of governance and policy. However, consensus in the highly partisan French system is a product of the powerful influence and authority of an elite class in the bureaucracy, political parties, and elected office, the members of which share important norms and habits.[16]

As is common in majoritarian systems, French democracy is anchored by the possibility of an alternation in government at the next election, where the opposition might defeat the governing party. Between 1981 and 2002, for example, no government was reelected, and even the victory of the outgoing majority in the 2007 election might reflect newly inaugurated President Nicolas Sarkozy's break with the previous government more than his position as leader of the same party. Some might consider the increasing strength of the prime minister vis-à-vis the president under Chirac a sign of "regime change," but the extent of such a change in "habits" but not institutions remains speculative at the present time.[17]

When the party of the French president controls a majority in the National Assembly and the Senate, he or she can exercise broad powers over legislation and administration—appointing a prime minister who administers the laws and directs legislation, acting as representative of the nation to protect the constitution and arbitrate disputes, and serving as leader of his or her party to implement a policy agenda. When the party in opposition to the president holds a majority in the National Assembly, what the French call "cohabitation," the president can take advantage of intraparty rivalries, as François Mitterrand did when he was president, though his power to delay legislation is limited, and he cannot dismiss a government by his own hand without calling new elections. In addition, the president can submit a proposal for referendum, sending a law directly to the people for a vote and bypassing the government and the legislature.

India

The state of India has been a parliamentary democracy since independence, with the exception of the 1974–1976 period of "the Emergency," when Indira Gandhi seized power. There are regular elections, people can organize and protest, the press is largely free, and governments change. As a result, India's political system is regularly labeled "the world's largest democracy."

Yet, the system continues to change—sometimes in ways that undermine the democracy label and sometimes in ways that reaffirm it. Formerly, the system was dominated by a single party and seemed to be controlled by a relatively small group of politicians. Today, no party can obtain a majority and representation extends to formerly marginalized groups. In the past, the Indian parliament was conducted with great decorum, while today it faces increasing disruption. The political system has also faced enormous challenges, including terrible poverty in the midst of great wealth, riots and protests, assassinations and suicides, a huge backlog of court cases, and corruption. That India remains "the world's largest democracy" is a remarkable accomplishment.

Regime Type in Mexico, Brazil, and Nigeria

Mexico, Brazil, and Nigeria all have political systems, though the long-term survival of democracy in these cases, particularly Nigeria, is far less certain than for the Western European TICs and India discussed in the previous section. Mexico, Brazil, and Nigeria also share American-style arrangements that place many powers in the president's hands, but also spread out power to other national political bodies and levels of government. They have all had a significant period of authoritarian rule in their recent histories, with the shadow of recent military rule hanging over both Brazil and Nigeria. Other challenges to long-term democratic stability, such as corruption, plague all three countries as well.

Mexico

Long considered a party-authoritarian system, Mexico is today considered a moderately successful democracy. Mexico's current political system is the result of liberalization in the 1980s and 1990s, which turned an authoritarian system under the control of the Institutional Revolutionary Party (PRI) into a semiauthoritarian system and, ultimately, a fledgling democracy heralded by the 2000 presidential election and victory of a non-PRI candidate, Vicente Fox. Today, Mexico is considered an unconsolidated democracy. Government corruption remains a problem, above all in the judiciary and police.

Fitting its status as both a North American and a Latin American country, Mexico's regime falls in between Dahl's American and Latin American models of democracy. Both models include a presidential component with checks and balances between the executive and legislative branches, but their electoral systems differ. The American model employs a first past the post (FPTP) district system, while the Latin American model uses proportional representation (PR). Mexico's legislative electoral arrangements combine FPTP/district and PR approaches, with three-fifths of the seats coming from district races and the others determined through PR. The result is three large political parties and several smaller ones, with the largest parties holding the vast majority of the seats in both houses of the Mexican national legislature.

IN THEORY AND PRACTICE

Political Change in Mexico and Easton's Systems Theory

In its early decades (from the late 1800s into the 1930s), political science paid great attention to institutions. This work centered heavily on descriptions of formal institutions—typically a country's constitution, which was seen as the foundation of the political structure, as well as the institutional expression of political culture.[18] These efforts, what some now call **old institutionalism**, tended to be rather descriptive, as well as normative. When political science turned in the direction of behavioralism in the 1950s and 1960s, detailed descriptions of formal institutions were replaced by a focus on the broader process of translating political inputs into political outputs. When political scientists considered the political system, its particular design was less important

Old institutionalism is a label for the traditional approach of political science to the study of political institutions, common from the late 1800s into the middle 1900s. This approach was highly descriptive and often normative, generally failing to generate explanations for the causes and consequences of differing institutional arrangements.

than the pressure and backing it received and the policies it produced.

This tendency to gloss over the characteristics of the institutions within the political system was most apparent in the work of David Easton, who treated the institutional arrangements within the political system as a "black box," with no detailed discussion of institutional arrangements or the actions of political leaders working within the system. Instead, Easton concentrated on the way that demands and supports that enter a political system are then translated into policy outcomes; the process includes a feedback loop, as outputs spark new demands and supports (see Figure 6.1). Easton's approach came to be known as **systems theory**, although in reality it was much more of a model than a theory.

Although Easton's approach to modeling political institutions as a black box that turns inputs into outputs is simple, even simplistic, it does provide a framework for understanding important political outcomes. Easton stresses three forms of supports that flow into the system: supports for the government, for the regime, and

for the "political community," the latter referring to the extent of attachment to an overarching national identity.

In the last few decades of PRI rule in Mexico, all three sets of supports were strained. The population viewed the government as increasingly corrupt and ineffective and the system as stifling representation of their interests. The commitment to a unified Mexican national identity was also shaky. At the same time, demands on the system (Easton's other type of input) were increasing.

The government tried to address increasing demands and shore up flagging support through policy initiatives and by allowing non-PRI candidates to win more and more local and regional elections. But these outputs were not enough to alter the configuration of inputs. Thus, *even without knowing what was going on inside the black box of the political system*, Easton's framework allows one to make some sense of the significant political reforms in Mexico. With supports decreasing, demands increasing, and outputs failing to feed back in a way that changed this pattern, the government was pressured to accept significant political liberalization.

Figure 6.1 Easton's Model of the Political System

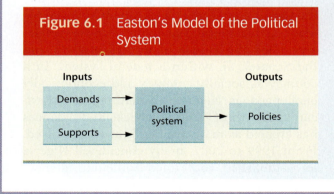

Systems theory is the name given to the efforts by David Easton to model the political process as a set of inputs (demands and supports) that feed into the political system and outputs (policies) that flow from it. The outputs lead to new demands and supports. The system itself was treated as a "black box," with little attention given to institutional design.

Brazil

Like many of its South American neighbors, Brazil experienced alternating periods of democracy and military authoritarian governments throughout much of the twentieth century. However, Brazil has maintained a stable democratic government since 1985. Although some serious

problems remain in Brazilian democracy, such as corruption, Brazil ranked higher in 2008 on Freedom House's ratings of the extent of democracy than all of the other TIC cases except the United Kingdom, Germany, and France.[19]

Brazil's current political system is the product of a protracted period of liberalization, which began at the initiative of the military government more than ten years before the first nonmilitary president was elected in 1985. At first, the military's goal was simply to ease public dissatisfaction by permitting a little more freedom to speak and to organize. Within this limited space, popular movements and independent unions began to emerge.

The military allowed elections for the legislature, but banned most leftist politicians and organized the rest into two legal parties—an "opposition" party known as the MDB (Movement for Brazilian Democracy) and a promilitary party known as Arena (Alliance for National Renovation). In reality, neither party opposed the military junta; they were known in Brazilian circles as the parties of "Yes" and "Yes, Sir!" Nevertheless, Brazilians saw the less-servile MDB as an opportunity to express their opposition to the military government.

As popular support for the MDB grew, the military searched for ways to maintain control. Hoping to divide the opposition vote, it legalized additional political parties in the late 1970s. The effort failed. Most of the political opposition joined together in a broad national movement calling for direct elections of the national executive in 1985. When the military candidate lost the election, a new constitutional convention was called.

The slow pace of Brazil's transition and the still powerful position of the military and its conservative allies during the constitutional convention meant that Brazil's new political system included important safeguards for elites. The Latin American model of strong presidentialism with a legislature elected by proportional representation was followed in Brazil—at least with respect to the lower house of the national legislature, the Chamber of Deputies. Like deputies in the lower house, the president serves a four-year term. Members of the upper house (the Senate), however, serve eight-year terms. The federal territorial units (*estados*) elect three senators each, using a plurality system where seats go to the three candidates who receive the most votes. The length of senatorial terms, the constitutional powers granted the Senate, and the fact that rural conservative *estados* outnumber industrial and centrist *estados* have given powerful regional elites the ability to block many reform measures, such as land reform, that would damage conservative interests.

Nigeria

The previous three chapters highlighted the socioeconomic traits that make Nigeria a prototypical developing country: an underdeveloped economy, dependence on natural resource exports, a political culture unattached to democratic practices, and an ethnically and religiously diverse population. Likewise, its political structures represent well the characteristics of developing countries. Nigeria possesses a politically unstable postcolonial history, personalized politics, and a pattern of military intervention in the political system.

The combination of majoritarian and consensus features makes it look quite a lot like the United States, with a president, a vice president, a bicameral legislature (whose houses are called the House of Representatives and the Senate), all within a federal system. In a country as socially complex and economically challenged as Nigeria, emulating the American approach of multiple checks and balances has created as many problems as it has solved. From 1999 to 2007, many considered Nigeria an established (but unconsolidated) democracy. Since the 2007 elections, observers have been increasingly reluctant to label the country a democracy.

Politics in Nigeria is highly personalized. Who holds a particular position can be more important than the official powers of that position. Until that changes, and until corruption is greatly diminished, democracy will have a difficult time consolidating itself as the only regime type Nigerian elites and masses consider legitimate.

Nigeria also faces the challenge of its recent past. The history of postcolonial Nigeria has been one of alternating short periods of unstable democracy and long periods of military authoritarianism. An understanding of the current Nigerian regime is thus impossible without understanding the influence of the military (a topic addressed in more detail in Chapter 8). It is difficult to consolidate democracy in a country with a tradition of military intervention in politics. The executive and legislature cannot focus only on each other; they must always be looking over their shoulders.

Regime Type in the Russian Federation, China, and Iran

The Russian Federation, China, and Iran all fall far from the democratic ideal. Russia had a brief experience with democracy in the 1990s, but moved steadily toward authoritarianism under the former president and current prime minister, Vladimir Putin. China's political leaders continue to keep democracy at bay, although the formal positions of power in the government correlate much more with actual political power today than in decades past. The Iranian system has sent mixed signals to those hoping for greater political freedom, leaning toward limited political reforms, followed by a retrenchment of authoritarian politics and renewed hints of the possibility of liberalization. Even during the periods when reformers were most visible, however, the government looked little like a liberal democracy.

The Russian Federation
Russia is an example of the way that leftover institutions from a previous political system can foster political turmoil. Soviet-era institutions persisted into the early post-Soviet period, leading to a major confrontation in 1993 that ultimately involved the use of military force against the Russian parliament. The new system that emerged from this conflict concentrated power in the president's hands. Following a period of minimal abuse of these powers under Boris Yeltsin, his successor, Vladimir Putin, used them to turn Russia in an authoritarian direction.

When Putin became president of Russia at the end of 1999, it marked the end of the "Yeltsin era." Under Boris Yeltsin, Russians had witnessed two economic collapses (at the beginning of the 1990s and one later in the decade); an attempted coup against Yeltsin, leading to the use of the military against members of the Russian parliament; the inability of the Russian military to gain control of the region of Chechnya; and a presidential election in 1996 that contained numerous irregularities. At the same time, Russia was ruled through democratic institutions for the longest period in its history.

It is hard to dispute that Russia has become less democratic since 2000. It increasingly resembles an authoritarian system, with government opponents failing to win seats in parliament, prosecuted for criminal activities, or both. With Putin's political allies in full control of the legislative branch following elections in 2003, the Russian political system became one with even fewer checks and balances in practice than it had on paper. By the end of Putin's term in 2008, Russia had earned the semidemocratic, or even semiauthoritarian, label.

China
China's institutions have frustrated students of comparative politics for decades. The dual hierarchy of state and party administrators can be confusing, particularly since nearly all top government officials are also high-ranking members of the Chinese Communist Party (CCP).

At least as important, the lack of correspondence between official government position and actual power for the first several decades of CCP rule was unmatched among world powers. Mao Zedong was CCP Chairman, but he ruled more through his personal legitimacy as leader of the Revolution than through his institutional powers. When Deng Xiaoping emerged as the leader after Mao's death, he held neither the position of government premier nor General Secretary of the CCP—the leadership position that replaced the position of Chairman after Mao's death. Perhaps indicating where much of the real power lies in China, the most important official position that Deng held was Chairman of the CCP Central Military Commission and its government counterpart, the state Central Military Commission. When Deng was replaced by Jiang Zemin as the country's most visible leader, it also signaled the growing importance of official positions of power. This trend has continued to the present.

Shortly after Mao Zedong died in the fall of 1976, his wife and three others, collectively known as the "Gang of Four," were arrested. This event signaled China's move away from the ideologically driven system Mao had cultivated. Within two years, Deng Xiaoping had solidified his hold over the Communist Party, making it possible for him to introduce his package of significant economic reforms.

Prior to Deng's encouragement of such reforms, most scholars had labeled China a Communist, totalitarian system. Since the 1980s, China has begun to look more and more like a party authoritarian system. The government is much less involved in the economy than it had been in the past, and it intrudes less into people's lives, as long as they do not speak out against it. The government has even allowed capitalists (e.g., private sector business owners) to join the Communist Party for the last several years.

Today, China's party authoritarianism lacks the clear ideology that it had when it more closely resembled a totalitarian system. Nationalism underpins the government's claims to legitimacy much more than Marxist ideology. The government's goals include continuation of the rapid economic development in the decades since economic reforms, enhancement of China's reputation as a global economic and military power, and maintenance of its domestic political power. Unlike the Soviet Union, China has successfully reformed its economy without losing control of the political system. How long the party authoritarian system can withstand pressures for further political reform, however, is a central question facing Chinese political leaders.

IN THEORY AND PRACTICE

China and Skocpol's *States and Social Revolutions*

While most political scientists were turning away from a focus on state institutions in the 1960s and 1970s, scholars such as Theda Skocpol set the stage for the reemergence of a focus on state institutions in political science. Skocpol's 1979 book *States and Social Revolutions* was a landmark moment for comparative politics, a trumpet blast calling for comparative politics to "bring the state back in"—a phrase she and others later coined.

Skocpol set out to move beyond comparativists who focused solely on socioeconomic structure. To Skocpol, the state was not just something to think of as a dependent variable, driven by underlying economic structures. It was also an independent variable—or at least an important factor in its own right if not fully independent from other structures—affecting political outcomes like revolutions.

China is one of the three main countries that Theda Skocpol examines in detail in *States and Social Revolutions*. Skocpol takes a "most different" approach to her study of revolutions, arguing that three very different states—France, Russia, and China—had similar experiences leading to major revolutions. Skocpol emphasizes the way that international pressures and domestic opposition combined with the current institutional arrangement of the state to cause the state to respond ineffectively to the challenges it faced.

In China, the Manchu Dynasty leaders were increasingly forced to rely on local leaders for military support. This led local landlords to demand greater autonomy, creating a vicious circle of increasing local control. When the central government finally tried to reestablish control, local landlords rose up and overthrew the Imperial government. This ushered in the nationalist period, which ended with the Communist seizure of power in 1949.

Skocpol's explanation of the collapse of the imperial system has relevance for Chinese politics today. More and more, Chinese local and regional leaders have pressured the central government to expand the authority of lower levels of government. Skocpol's study shows how relying on local officials can undercut the ability of the central government to maintain control. Even if Chinese leaders have not read Skocpol (and a number of them probably have!), they do know their own history. Thus, while one could expect further decentralization in China, one should also expect it to go slowly. CCP leaders have ushered in a number of reforms over the last few decades, but they have no desire to oversee the collapse of their political system.

Iran

Iran's political system is comparatively unusual, but it reflects the influence of Islam in the practice of day-to-day politics. Like society broadly, the political structure has been shaped to a great extent by the 1979 Islamic Revolution. For much of the period following the Islamic Revolution, discussing Iran's political system meant discussing the role of its religious clerics. This system of infusing religious ideology and religious leaders into the political system is a crucial feature of Iranian politics. As covered in Chapter 2, comparativists label such an approach a "theocracy." For a time in the late 1990s and early 2000s, Iran began more and more to resemble a representative democracy. This led many scholars in the United States to begin openly discussing the beginning of genuine democratization in Iran.

Events in 2004 and 2005 called into question such optimistic notes. Although the Iranian legislature included a large number of reformers between 2000 and 2004, the religious clerics who control which candidates are allowed to run for national office blocked most reformers from the ballot in 2004. Combined with the term of moderate-reformist president Mohammed Khatami coming to an end in 2005, this signaled a conservative turn.

By the middle of 2006, at the same time tensions with the United States were escalating, Iran seemed as far from an emerging democracy as it had at nearly any point since the 1979 Revolution. At the end of that year, however, elections to the Assembly of Experts—the body in Iran that selects the Supreme Leader and advises him on various issues—pointed to renewed dissatisfaction with the hardliners controlling the Iranian government. While many reformers were prevented from running in the March 14, 2008, elections to the national legislature, the *Majles*, the success of those who were on the ballot hinted at continued problems for conservatives like President Mahmoud Ahmadinejad, with the next presidential election planned for mid 2009.

IN THEORY AND PRACTICE

Iran and Rational Choice New Institutionalism

Even before Skocpol's call for a fresh look at state institutions, others had begun to look to organizational theory to better understand institutions and their consequences. This ushered in what came to be called **new institutionalism**. This term applies to various theoretically based studies that examine institutions as structures marking a political system's historical changes, shaping individual choices, or reflecting society's underlying values and identities.

For new institutionalists, political institutions are not a "black box." They are the central factor that determines political outcomes. New institutionalists believe that political institutions do not simply aggregate interests but reshape them.[20] In short, "institutions matter."[21] Writing in 1996, Peter Hall and Rosemary Taylor provided a helpful overview of the various theories identified with the new institutionalism movement. Hall and Taylor's article points to three sets of new institutionalism theories: "rational choice," "sociological," and "historical." While **sociological new institutionalism** sees institutions as social constructions flowing from the underlying culture of the society in which the institutions develop, **historical new institutionalism** acknowledges that political institutions are the product of social forces, rational calculations, and the political institutional arrangements that existed in previous periods.

Rational choice new institutionalism, on the other hand, takes institutions to be exclusively the product of rational calculations. It thus shares many elements with rational choice theory, a theoretical perspective discussed in detail in Chapter 11. These include the belief that "individuals and their strategic calculations ought to be the central concern of social science"[22] and the assumption that individuals are calculating and self-interested, seeking to maximize the likelihood that they will achieve their preferred outcomes. The rational choice form of new institutionalism also holds that institutions constrain rational individuals by narrowing the field of possible choices or by altering calculations about the costs and benefits of a particular strategy. Individuals facing such constraints may seek to change the institution in response. As a result, institutions are designed and updated by individuals in an ongoing effort to maximize the benefits and minimize the costs of working within a given institutional framework.

Because Iranian leaders are often portrayed in the West as religious "fanatics" incapable of rational thought, can rational choice new institutionalism possibly help explain the function of Iranian politics? Applying this approach to Iran would certainly make one think hard about the portrayal of Iranian leaders like President Mahmoud Ahmadinejad. The result might be an acknowledgment that political leaders, Western and Middle Eastern alike, tend to be both rational actors and true believers. As they

New institutionalism theories emphasize the role of political institutions in political outcomes. Rather than seeing the political system as a black box, or as a reflection of socioeconomic structures, new institutionalism theories stress the importance of differences in institutional arrangements and the extent to which the political system is an actor in politics with a certain degree of autonomy from society.

Sociological new institutionalism includes a broader conceptualization of institutions to include informal norms. It sees institutions as reflecting society's underlying culture rather than as the product of rational choices in the pursuit of increased efficiency.

Historical new institutionalism is a theoretical approach that emphasizes political institutions as a central determinant of the choices that government officials make, examines institutional change over time, and stresses how different institutions can have contradictory agendas leading to conflict and inefficient policy outcomes.

Rational choice new institutionalism argues that institutions are the product of rational calculations on the part of individuals and limit the options of rational individuals seeking to make efficient and effective policy. Although institutions narrow the field of possible choices, they are also designed and updated by individuals in an ongoing effort to increase institutional efficiency.

design institutions, they do so both because they believe in certain ideals and because they seek to maximize their goals. As they make decisions within those institutions, they continue to pursue these goals, but their beliefs shape what they perceive to be appropriate at the same time that the institutional rules constrain their options.

The design of Iran's theocracy is no exception. It reflects the religious leaders' commitment to the governance of Iran through their interpretation of Islamic Law, but it also points to their efforts to prevent reformist pressures, such as those that emerged during the 1990s and early 2000s, from weakening their hold on power. Specific institutional arrangements, such as the position of the Supreme Leader and the role of the Council of Guardians, were carefully crafted in an effort to maximize the goals of the Islamic leaders of the 1979 Revolution. These institutions do not always produce the most efficient and effective policies for the country, but they are politically—or, perhaps more to the point, "theocratically"—efficient. They combine to make Iran a theocracy, but they also help maintain it as such.

The Constitution: A Regime's Rules for Making Rules

During the early decades of political science, scholars paid a great deal of attention to formal institutions. As a result, constitutions were a favorite topic. Political science has since gained a greater appreciation for the importance of informal institutions and the rules that political institutions themselves create about their day-to-day activities that cannot be found in the constitution. That said, constitutions remain an important topic, often serving as the starting point for comparativists seeking to understand the workings of a particular political system.

A **constitution** acts as the official "rules of the game" for a particular political system. If followed, the constitution prevents laws from being passed arbitrarily. Constitutions include a list of positions of governmental authority, the specific powers of these positions, and other rules for making new rules (i.e., the process for creating laws or passing constitutional amendments). By laying out the official powers of the various governmental institutions, a constitution also places restraints on government officials. In the U.S. Constitution, for example, certain powers are given only to the legislative branch. The president has no authority to exercise these particular powers. A president who tried would be subject to impeachment and removal from office.

Many formal rules and limits on governmental power are ignored by leaders, particularly in authoritarian and totalitarian systems. Yet, without doubt, a constitution is much more effective if it is followed. If its rules are adhered to, a constitution adds legitimacy to the system, conferring what Max Weber called rational authority (see Chapter 1). Citizens may not like a specific law, but they accept it as legitimate because they believe that the process through which laws were made is itself legitimate. Following the consistent process for passing laws is also an important part of the condition known as **rule of law**. Rule of law involves the belief (and practice) by the government that it has to follow laws even as it is making new ones. The concept extends beyond lawmaking, also referring to society's lack of tolerance of corruption and its acceptance of the idea that agreements such as signed contracts are binding.

A **constitution** includes the description of official major government bodies and positions, the powers these positions have, and the process for making new laws.

Rule of law is a condition in which laws are passed according to the constitution, government officials are not above the law, and society respects contracts as legally binding.

The term **constitutionalism** refers to the idea that constitutions are designed to limit the power of government, that government officials must follow the laws of the land, and that upholding these limitations and following these laws is a key source of legitimacy. The concept of constitutionalism also includes the idea that, as the "rules for making new rules," provisions in a constitution are above ordinary law. Ordinary laws must conform to constitutional provisions. These constitutional stipulations can be changed, but in most democracies this requires an elaborate process, well beyond the majority support of the national legislature. Constitutionalism is at the heart of the American political system, as well as other democracies.

To limit governments effectively, the limits must be clearly understood. As a result, most constitutions are written down in a single document, and most are quite long and detailed. Largely because it is one of the oldest written constitutions in existence, the U.S. Constitution is comparatively very short and quite vague about many aspects of day-to-day governing. As time went on, officials writing new constitutions used their own and other countries' experiences to generate more and more constitutional provisions.

The vagueness of the U.S. Constitution is part of the story of its success. The ability for interpretation of its wording to evolve over time has enhanced its durability. On the other hand, this has also led to major disputes. As the large number of 5-to-4 Supreme Court decisions over the last two decades attests, interpreting the U.S. Constitution is not a simple matter.

Think and Discuss

Is the U.S. Constitution really as vague as the discussion above suggests? Provide specific examples from the U.S. Constitution to support your position.

> **Constitutionalism** is a label for the belief that constitutions should limit government power, that government officials must obey the country's laws, and that a government's legitimacy comes from obeying these limitations and laws.

The Constitution in the United Kingdom, Germany, France, and India

Though they are all stable democracies, the constitutional approaches to democratic rule in the United Kingdom, France, Germany, and India vary greatly. The British Constitution contains unwritten elements. The German Constitution, based on the legal blueprint for the Federal Republic (West Germany) after World War II, balances individual rights and collective interests. The current French Constitution, in place since 1958, was the vision of General de Gaulle and provides for a strong president. The Indian Constitution has been heavily amended since its adoption in 1950, but these amendments have not undone the significant power of the central government.

The United Kingdom

The Constitution is one of the most confusing features of the British political system. Like other aspects of British politics, the Constitution is the result of protracted evolution.[23] Unlike nearly every other democracy in the world, the United Kingdom's Constitution is not written down in a single document. Instead, the Constitution is a collection of government acts, legal opinions, and generally accepted norms and customs. Written components include old documents such as the Magna Carta and newer acts of parliament designed to remake the political system.

How can a system function without a single document containing the political rules of the game? The British Constitution works partly because of British political culture's emphasis on the importance of tradition, respect for authority, and sense of obligation by elites to act responsibly. It is easy to think that written down rules are superior to understood norms, but the latter can actually be more powerful—and certainly harder to get around. Thus, the combination of constitutional flexibility and cultural responsibility fosters political stability in the United Kingdom even though a partly unwritten constitution might produce chaos elsewhere.

When the Labour Party, led by Tony Blair, won the 1997 parliamentary elections, it marked the end of nearly two decades of Conservative Party control. Though perhaps not predominant in the minds of the voters, one of the central positions of the Labour Party platform was a substantial overhaul of the British Constitution to make the system more effective and accountable. In short, their vision was of a less majoritarian and more consensus-based political system. Ironically, because of the majoritarian nature of British democracy, there was no check on the government's ability to change the fundamental rules of the game of British politics. It required only the commitment of the Labour Party to follow through on its promises.

According to British political scientist Matthew Flinders, constitutional reform can be cosmetic, moderate, or fundamental.[24] Labour's rhetoric called for many fundamental changes, and some have called what Labour has done a "quiet revolution."[25] In truth, the reforms to date have tended to be moderate or even cosmetic. Parliament did consider many constitutional reform bills, there were successes on "devolution" (discussed later in this chapter), and government was able to institute some reforms of the House of Lords (including a dramatic reduction in numbers of hereditary peers). Other substantial reforms stalled, however, due to weariness about the amount of time being devoted to the subject compared with other issues more salient to the general public.[26] Even the efforts to more fundamentally alter the House of Lords hit roadblocks in 2004 and 2005. Looking at Lijphart's criteria, Flinders claims that the combination of reforms that have occurred and those that have stalled has in many ways made the system more majoritarian.[27]

Germany

The Constitution of the Federal Republic, often referred to as the Basic Law, marked a conscious break with the lawlessness of Germany's Nazi past and established the German system as a democracy under the rule of law.[28] Thus, the constitution spells out a number of individual rights and freedoms, including a right to privacy and a right to choose one's occupation, as well as a right to political asylum. Likewise, it acknowledges the important role of political parties to form the will of the people and the obligation of the state to "protect the natural sources of life," and declares the Federal Republic a "democratic and social federal state."[29]

This latter clause represents a synthesis between two principles, one where the state respects individual rights and equality and another that recognizes the legitimacy of organized interests. The emphasis on legitimate organized interests allows the state to regulate the economy in a social direction but at the same time discourages detailed government intervention or state planning.[30] This balance between broad social welfare protection and limits on government action, laid out in the German Constitution, is a hallmark of Germany's Consensual approach to democratic governance.

France

The Constitution of the Fifth Republic has its origins in the war over the independence of colonial Algeria and the opposition of former General de Gaulle, leader of the Free French forces during World War II, to the institutions of the Fourth Republic.[31] In May 1958, the French army in Algeria launched a successful invasion of Corsica, a French island just south of the Riviera, and planned an assault on Paris to oust a government whose war policies they viewed as incompetent. They called for de Gaulle's return to power. Under pressure from the military, in the streets, and within parliament, the political establishment called on de Gaulle, and parliament invested him with the authority to draft a new constitution and rule by decree. Such power in the hands of the government was itself a violation of the constitution, but there was a broad consensus within almost all parties that de Gaulle could bring about the changes needed to resolve the crisis.

De Gaulle's Constitution, approved in October 1958, bears the general's unmistakable stamp. It establishes a quasi-monarchical president, but it first embraces the fundamental principles of the Revolution, including the Rights of Man and the Citizen adopted in 1789, popular sovereignty, and *laïcité* (secularism), as well as the chief symbols of the French Republic such as the tricolor "bleu, blanc, rouge" flag and the national anthem, "*La Marseillaise*." His constitution drew its inspiration from French history, reaching back to nearly every regime in the various arrangements and provisions of government.[32] De Gaulle also provided for exceptional powers to the president in his "reserved domain," primarily focusing on defense and foreign policy, and prohibited members of the government, including the prime minister, from serving in either the National Assembly or Senate.

India

After several years of debate, a constituent assembly adopted the Indian Constitution in 1950. Its many provisions are spelled out in such great detail that it is widely believed to be the longest written constitution of any country in the world. The Constitution's Preamble declares India to be a "Sovereign Socialist Secular Democratic Republic."[33] The word "socialist" describes the goal of the framers of the Constitution, although many of India's policies have moved the country away from socialism. The other words, "sovereign," "secular," "democratic," and "republic," are appropriate descriptors of the political system today.

Two features of the Indian Constitution are worthy of note. First, it provides for considerable centralization of power. The powers given to the central legislative bodies, for example, include those to amend the constitution and break up the federal units. Second, the detailed nature of the Indian Constitution has meant that legislators have had to amend it frequently to accomplish their goals. By 2007, there were ninety-four amendments.

Topic in Countries

The Constitution in Mexico, Brazil, and Nigeria

While their political systems resemble the American one in many ways, the constitutional developments of Mexico, Brazil, and Nigeria look little like those of the United States. Brazil and Nigeria have had numerous constitutions since gaining independence, their current constitutions were adopted relatively recently, and both constitutions are much longer than their American counterpart. By comparison, Mexico's Constitution more closely resembles its northern neighbor's, but it is still less than a century old, has been heavily amended, and includes interesting provisions such as prohibiting national political leaders from seeking reelection.

Mexico

Mexico's Constitution is comparatively old. Officially known as the Political Constitution of the United Mexican States, it was originally written in 1917 and has been heavily amended since then. One of its lasting features is that it prohibits presidents or representatives in the national legislature from running for reelection. Similar to its American counterpart, the Mexican Constitution provides for a number of checks and balances in a federal, presidential system with a bicameral national legislature. In the past, when the Institutional Revolutionary Party (PRI) dominated the presidency and the legislature, these checks and balances were less relevant. Vicente Fox learned quickly that the Mexican presidency, which had appeared so powerful under the PRI, is not nearly so powerful when the president's party does not control the legislative branch. During his term in office, Fox was at the mercy of powers granted to the legislature in the Mexican Constitution.

Mexico's combination of presidentialism and a multiparty system is a recipe for gridlock.

Although analysts of and participants in Mexican politics have discussed numerous dramatic political reforms, including replacing the presidential system with a parliamentary one,[34] the current gridlock-conducive system seems destined to remain in place. Reforming any system to increase the concentration of political power can be difficult. Those who believe the reforms might threaten their political power will use their existing powers to block the reforms. In addition, changing the system to allow the president to more easily force through such reforms sets the stage for a possible reemergence of authoritarianism centered around a strong president.

Brazil

The 1988 Brazilian Constitution (its seventh since independence) was a compromise between groups with very different visions of Brazilian society and how it should be governed. The result, as stated by former President Fernando Henrique Cardoso, was "a completely unrealistic wish list. It guaranteed outlandish 'rights' that Brazil simply could not afford, creating laws and expectations that would haunt the country's politicians for years thereafter."[35]

Among other provisions, its 245 articles guarantee federal employees job security for life after only two years of service. Generous health care, pension plans, environmental protection, family leave, and free education are constitutionally defined as obligations of the state. Article 227 grants children constitutional rights to "life, health, nourishment, education, leisure, professional training, culture, dignity, respect, freedom . . . as well as [protection from] all forms of negligence, discrimination, exploitation, violence, cruelty, and oppression." Article 229 even defines the duty of parents as, "to assist, raise and educate their underage children and . . . the duty of children of age to help and assist their parents in old age, need or sickness."[36] As laudable as these goals might be, constitutional

scholars have worried that the sheer impossibility of enforcing such rights might undermine Brazil's efforts to establish the rule of law: some provisions of the Constitution simply had to be ignored, and if these could be ignored with impunity, other more enforceable rights might also be ignored.

The constitution also enshrined privileges for the outgoing military government that guaranteed it a continuing say in how Brazil would be run. As a result, although the army is under the authority of the president, there is no civilian Ministry of Defense to oversee military budgets and behavior, active-duty officers serve in the cabinet, and the military runs the aviation and aeronautics industries, as well as others critical to national defense.

Nigeria

Including constitutions written by the British during colonial rule, the Nigerian Constitution, developed to coincide with the reestablishment of democracy in 1999, was Nigeria's seventh in roughly five decades. The constitution was not a dramatic change from that governing the political system during the last serious attempt at democracy in the late 1970s and early 1980s, although the number of regions in Nigeria's federal system was increased to thirty-six.

The Nigerian Constitution is long and detailed. It has 320 articles, most of them several paragraphs in length. It includes a section on the obligations of the government, many of which relate to fostering unity in the country. Throughout the constitution, provisions exist to cross-cut social divisions in the country with particular political arrangements. These include the requirement that a successful candidate for the presidency obtain 25 percent or more of the vote in two-thirds of the thirty-six regions. Perhaps somewhat ominously, the "Miscellaneous Provisions" section includes the circumstances under which the president can declare a state of emergency.

The Constitution in the Russian Federation, China, and Iran

The constitutions of Russia, China, and Iran demonstrate how even in nondemocracies, leaders worry about the official "rules of the game." At the same time, all three highlight how one must be careful not to assume a constitution faithfully outlines the *actual* allocation of, and limits on, political power. Rule of law remains shaky in all three countries.

The Russian Federation

In the fall of 1993, President Boris Yeltsin decreed that the Russian parliament must disband and eventually ordered military units to attack the parliament building to remove members of the parliament who refused. In December 2003, Russian voters approved a new constitution and selected members of a new lower house of parliament, the *Duma*. The new constitution eliminated the position of vice president but included a dual executive system with a prime minister as well as a powerful president.

In late 2005, President Putin announced that he would not seek a third term when his current term ended in 2008. At the same time, however, he indicated that he could not let Russia degenerate into political chaos. Thus, while he could have chosen to step down quietly, as Yeltsin did, he could have also decided to extend his stay in office by amending the constitution to allow a third term. He could have also simply ignored the constitution, declaring the need to suspend presidential elections to prevent political chaos. Instead, he did none of these things and shifted to the position of prime minister after his hand-picked successor, Dmitry Medvedev, became president.

In the past, Putin had appeared to show less concern for the rule of law than many in the West—if not many in Russia—would have liked him to show. Yet his decision to maintain power by following the letter of the Russian Constitution, albeit creatively, points to his unwillingness to completely ignore the system's overarching

rules. Events in the coming years will shed light on whether Putin's respect for the constitution in 2008 reflected a deeper commitment to the rule of law than many observers assumed, or whether he simply did not feel he could get away with thumbing his nose at the constitution at the time.

China

The Chinese Constitution demonstrates well that long detailed constitutions do not necessarily translate into a democratic political system. The most recent version of the Chinese Constitution, ratified in 1982 and amended twice since, is one of the longer constitutions in the world. It contains 138 articles, which follow a long preamble. Unlike most preambles which provide a short overview of the principles underlying the arrangements of the political system, the preamble to the Chinese Constitution provides the Communist Party's take on the history of Chinese civilization and foreign relations. With official government positions mattering more than they did prior to the death of Deng Xiaoping, the institutional powers laid out in the Chinese Constitution have also become more important. The constitution lays out a dual executive system, with a president considered to be the head of state and a premier (prime minister) who oversees the day-to-day governing of the country.

Like other constitutions, however, the Chinese version is only as effective as the government's willingness to obey it. Rule of law is far from established in China, and the judicial system remains a hostage of the political dominance of the Communist Party. There are signs that the Communist government is open to improvements in this area, partly because foreign businesses have made clear to the government that corruption and the general lack of respect for contracts threatens China's further economic development. The 2008 Olympics in Beijing also provided an incentive for the Chinese government to appear more democratic, though it remains too early to determine whether China's hosting of the Olympics will have a lasting impact on its political system.

Iran

Following the ouster of the shah, the mullahs (religious clerics) who emerged as the country's new leaders put in place a new constitution in December 1979. In 1989, a revised constitution removed the position of prime minister. Despite such changes, the Iranian Constitution continues to reflect the 1979 Islamic Revolution and helps validate its designation as a theocracy.

Among the provisions of the constitution are the establishment of Shi'a Islam as the country's official religion and the creation of a position known as the Supreme Leader. The Supreme Leader is part of the Iranian executive branch but is more powerful than the other chief executive, the Iranian president. The Supreme Leader is the ultimate arbiter of political questions in Iran. He is allowed to use his interpretation of passages in the Koran and other Islamic documents to rule on any issue under consideration in the political system. The Supreme Leader works with other theocratic bodies in the political system, including the Expediency Council and the Guardian Council, institutions whose powers are outlined in the next chapter.

Levels of Government

One of the important aspects of a political system laid out in most constitutions is the relationship between the central government and lower levels of government in the country. The question of levels of government requires a discussion of three topics: unitary versus federal systems, local government, and devolution.

Though people normally think of the central government when discussing features of a state, governments exist at many levels. In the United States, city councils and village boards exist alongside the governments of the fifty American states and the federal government. International governmental organizations such as the United Nations may also produce policy decisions that they intend states in the international community to follow. The European Union has absorbed a portion of its member states' sovereignty.

In considering levels of government, comparativists examine the various functions of central and lower-level governments and the relationship between these two levels. Since the responsibilities of local government in a particular country depend on the relationship between the central and lower levels, it is helpful to discuss this relationship prior to discussing particular local government functions.

Unitary Versus Federal Arrangements

In any country, the relationship between the levels of government generally falls into one of two categories: **unitary system** or **federal system**. The difference between a unitary relationship and a federal one centers on the answer to the question of whether there are territorial units within a state that have *specific powers that the central government cannot take away*. If there are such units, the system is a federal one. In a federal system, these lower-level government powers may be **reserved powers** for the lower

A **unitary system** is one in which the central government has authority over all lower levels of government, and those lower levels have no powers reserved for them.

A **federal system** provides lower levels of government with designated powers that the central government cannot take away.

Reserved powers are those designated to a particular level of government that another level of government cannot take away. In federal systems, these powers are granted to levels of government below that of the central government.

levels alone. This is the approach of the American federal system. The federal and lower levels of government may also possess certain **shared powers**. This is more typical of the German federal system. Either way, certain powers exist that the central government cannot take away from the lower levels. In a unitary system, the central government has complete authority over lower levels of government; any powers held by the lower levels can be taken away by the central government.

One way to think about this is that sovereignty is shared in a federal system between the central government and regional governments within the state. This idea of shared sovereignty raises the question of the European Union. Is the EU a federation? For the moment, it is not a federal or unitary state, since it is comprised of multiple states. At present, it comes closer to the definition of a **confederation**—an affiliation between two or more states in which the state governments control the central government. As time goes on, however, the EU may come to resemble a federal state. Its efforts over the last two decades at integration of European countries have involved not only expansion of the organization to include new member-states but also a deepening of the interconnectedness of existing member-states.

What are the advantages of a federal system? Giving powers to lower levels of government makes governing a very large country easier. It is no accident that the physically largest countries in the world tend to have federal arrangements, while few very small countries have adopted this approach. In addition, a federal system better accommodates regional differences in policy preferences and can help guard against the concentration of political power. Finally, as discussed in the previous chapter, these territorial units within the boundaries of the state can help overcome deep social divisions if the territorial divisions cut across the social divisions rather than complement them.

Disadvantages include a lack of uniformity in policy across the country. This can be a problem for residents of the country who travel from one part to another. It may not be as simple as different traffic rules. In the United States, state governments control the creation of most electoral rules—even for federal elections. How one registers to vote in Wisconsin, for example, may be quite different from how one registers in Texas. In addition, though interest groups are prevalent at the federal level in the United States, their power may be more exaggerated at lower levels of government. Finally, if the territorial lines within the country correspond to deep social divisions, the federal system reinforces those divisions. Whether this makes violent conflict and attempts to break apart the state more or less likely is a subject of debate, addressed in greater detail later in the chapter.

Local Government

All states, whether federal or unitary, include local government. Though central governments

---

Shared powers are those held by both the central government and lower levels of government. In a federal system, these shared powers cannot be taken over entirely by the central government.

A **confederation** is an affiliation between two or more states not involving a strong central government. The states involved maintain the vast majority of their sovereignty, though they do surrender some of it to the agreements that establish the confederal arrangement.

receive the bulk of the attention in comparative politics, much day-to-day governing takes place at the local level. Think about the extent to which local government decisions affected what you did today. Bus fares, placement of stop signs and crosswalks, assignment of policing duties, and many other things that may have had an impact on you today were likely decided at the local level. One of two central tasks of local government is to provide local services such as schools, roads, water, and sewer.

Local government's second task is to implement and enforce decisions of higher levels of government. These decisions can take the form of unfunded mandates, where the local government did not make the policy but is expected to cover the costs of implementing it. There may also be a sizeable commitment of funds from higher levels of government to assist local officials in these activities. Though enforcement of laws and administration of government programs is often more effective at the local level, the central government often has an easier time raising money for such supervision.

Local governments have powers to make such decisions because it is practical for them to do so. There are only so many issues a central or provincial government can, or should, try to tackle. Whether to place a stop sign on the corner of First Street and Russell Street in a village of 1,500 people is not one of them. Making decisions at the local level can also give those decisions more legitimacy. Although residents' participation in local government meetings is often shockingly rare, at least in the United States, there is a sense that the local officials know best and have the best interests of the community in mind. Such comments are rarely made about higher levels of government.

Because there are certain advantages to local governance, even unitary systems allow local governments to make a number of policy decisions and to enforce many others the central government has made. Thus, a unitary system does not imply feeble local governments. What local governments in a unitary system do lack is sovereignty, certainly compared with the ability to control its own affairs that the central government in that unitary system possesses.

"Devolving" Government Powers from Central Governments to Lower Levels

Devolution involves the transfer of power from a central government to lower governments, usually at the regional (i.e., provincial) level. This process does not necessarily turn the system into a federal one, though that can be the ultimate result if the devolved powers become enshrined as rightfully belonging to the lower level governments. The reason that devolution does not automatically lead to federation brings back the topic of sovereignty. In devolution, the central government does not surrender its ultimate sovereignty to the lower level of government. The powers are not reserved to the lower level, and thus they may be taken back at any time. In practice, however, once power is given to a unit of government, taking it back becomes difficult. Even if a central government has maintained the right to take back devolved powers, it may decide that it is politically impossible to do so.

Devolution is the process of transferring power from a central government to lower governments. It does not necessarily turn the system into a federal one.

Levels of Government in the United Kingdom, Germany, France, and India

The United Kingdom, Germany, France, and India provide examples of the range of possible federal and unitary arrangements. The United Kingdom and France both have unitary systems, although devolution of central government authority to the regions has been notable in the United Kingdom, particularly for the regions of Scotland and Northern Ireland. France, on the other hand, is a more traditional unitary system, where the government has shown little desire to increase the powers of local governments. Germany and India are both federal systems. Befitting its consensus-style democracy, Germany's federal system is based more on shared powers than reserved powers, and the federal government relies on the regional governments to enforce national policies and administer federal programs. By contrast, India is a federal system in which the central government yields significant power.

The United Kingdom

Despite the existence of the United Kingdom's four main regions, and the quite distinct identities of the societies within them, the British state has long been considered a unitary one. The central government has been able to dictate to lower levels on all matters. The issue of how much control the regions should have over daily political decisions has been a source of tension, however, and for more than a decade the British government has been actively involved in the process of devolution. Arguably the only area in which Labour Party constitutional reforms can be called fundamental is the shift in the division of powers between levels of government.

The early years of the process included a number of important parliamentary acts, such as the Referendums Act (1997), which allowed residents of Scotland and Wales to vote on the question of increased regional powers; the Scotland

Act (1998), which established an elected Scottish parliament; the Government of Wales Act (1998), which did the same thing for Wales; and the Northern Ireland Act (1998), which authorized a referendum and regional government based on the April 1998 Good Friday agreement.

As many expected, the process of enhancing self-governance in Northern Ireland faced a rocky road. Prior to 1972, Protestants in Northern Ireland controlled a quite powerful regional government. These powers included overseeing policing in the region, which led to oppression of Catholics supporting the union of Northern Ireland and the country of Ireland to its south. Protests in the late 1960s and early 1970s, including the reestablishment of the Irish Republican Army (IRA) in 1971, brought erratic responses from the central government. At times, the British Army worked to protect Catholics; often, it worked with the regional government to repress them. The British government eliminated the Northern Ireland parliament in 1972, instituted a Protestant-Catholic regional executive in 1974, and then quickly abandoned those efforts after Protestant workers staged a series of crippling strikes. London's direct rule continued until the 1998 Good Friday agreement laid the groundwork for reestablishing some degree of local rule in Northern Ireland. Despite the deep divisions and the failure of earlier efforts to increase regional control, the implementation of devolution provisions in Northern Ireland gained momentum in the decade following the Good Friday agreement.

Though events in Northern Ireland garner more attention in the United States, devolution in Scotland has been more pronounced and the regional government has a comparatively large amount of power. The 1998 Scotland Act authorized the formation of a Scottish Parliament. Under the terms of the act, the 129 members of the Scottish Parliament (MSPs) can pass laws covering a range of issues affecting Scotland.

The parliament even has limited authority to levy taxes, a power yet to be given to either the Northern Irish or Welsh regional government.

In one of the first "crises" for the Scottish regional government, its new parliament building was completed three years late and at ten times its original cost.[37] Those opposed to devolution probably took some glee in watching the Scots learn that not all aspects of governing oneself are pleasant. In other ways, however, Scotland has showed the promise of devolution by being out in front of social and political reforms. While the Labour Party's consideration of proportional representation elections for parliament stalled, elections in Scotland have moved away from the first past the post (FPTP) approach used in British national elections. The Scottish Parliament has also taken steps to ban smoking in public places, and its proposed legislation went well beyond what had been discussed at the national level.[38]

Devolution for Wales and England is another story. The National Assembly of Wales is, in terms of official powers, weaker than both the Scottish and the Northern Irish assemblies. It has begun to act more independently over the last decade, although this has often taken the form of its Labour Party acting more like the old Labour Party—that is, rather to the left of the "New Labour" Party that former Prime Minister Tony Blair cultivated. The attempt to bring devolution to England has faced the most serious hurdles. Perhaps because the English are used to controlling the national government or because the proposed multiple regional assemblies in the English region lacked real legislative authority, few in England have been passionate about having their own regional assemblies. A referendum in 2004 to create an elected regional assembly in the northeast of England was soundly defeated, drawing less than 50 percent turnout and dealing a fatal blow to devolution across the region of England.[39]

The United Kingdom's devolution policy has opened the door to regions having greater control over their own affairs, but it has not yet transformed the system into a federal one. The issues on which the Scottish Parliament can pass legislation, for example, are known as "devolved matters." It is important to note that they are not reserved powers, as in a federal system. Instead, the 1998 Scotland Act used the term "reserved matters" to refer to issues left to the central government—that is, subjects about which the Scottish Parliament *cannot* pass legislation. Reserved matters include foreign affairs, defense, national security, and employment. This terminology highlights the distinction between devolution and federalism. While a federal system would establish reserved powers for a region within the British state, devolution gives the regional government no guarantee that they will retain these powers. Though one can reasonably expect powers at the regional level to be maintained or even strengthened in the future, there is no assurance of this unless the constitution is amended again to incorporate the principle of reserved powers for the regions of the United Kingdom. Thus, the British devolution process provides an important example of a unitary system with strengthened powers for lower levels of government without fully transforming into a federal system.

Germany

German federalism has been termed "cooperative federalism" or "interlocking politics," labels that emphasize interdependence and cooperation rather than exclusive powers for different levels of government.[40] Under this type of federalism, the national government enacts legislation but relies on the governments of the 16 *Länder* to implement federal laws. The two levels of government also engage in joint tasks in a number of policy areas. State and local governments receive a specified share of federal tax revenues, while fiscal equalization procedures redistribute revenues from richer to poorer states. However, the *Länder* have primary jurisdiction in specific policy domains such as education, environment, media, cultural affairs, and law enforcement.[41]

The governments of *Länder* have also vetoed about 60 percent of federal legislation through their representation in the *Bundesrat*, far higher than the 10 percent figure that the constitution's framers envisioned.[42] Critics have charged that the veto power of the *Länder* has encouraged legislative gridlock. In an effort to speed up the legislative process, the federal government and the *Länder* agreed to constitutional reform of federalism in 2006. That agreement constricted the reach of the *Bundesrat*'s veto, but in exchange, the federal government accorded the *Länder* enhanced control over policies concerning education, environment, and regulation of business opening hours.[43]

France

The French system is based on the individual's relationship to the national government, and local institutions and authorities have consequently always been treated as suspect.[44] Within its unitary framework, France is divided into twenty-six regions. These regions are broken up into a total of one hundred *départements* (departments), roughly equivalent to counties in countries like the United Kingdom. Within the departments are 342 *arrondissements* (districts) and a total of more than 36,000 communes—localities that vary dramatically in size and population across the country. The French Constitution recognizes self-governing local territorial councils to represent communes and regions and even grants authority to make regulations and to raise revenues, but the language is vague and the national government actually determines the delegation of powers. In other words, as in other unitary systems, the powers of lower units of government exist at the pleasure of the national government.

The French national and local governments are linked through the use of **prefects**. Each of France's departments has one prefect, who is a representative of the national government and under the authority of the minister of the interior. The prefect oversees the administration of the department, but always on behalf of the interior ministry. The national and local governments are also linked through the possibility—realized in practice quite frequently—for members of the Senate and the National Assembly, as well as government ministers, to serve as mayors or members of local councils. Mayors themselves are not directly elected, serving at the will of a majority of the municipal council and so without independent executive authority.

This system produces little support for decentralization. Governments of the Right and Left publicly have placed a greater priority on the question of local authority and the economic development of provincial France, but the prefects and the national elected officials who serve in local office have little desire to see their authority in the hands of more independent officials.[45] Others argue that the national government has been reluctant to turn to local authorities, even in the arena of economic reform, fearing empowering new actors who could mobilize against the center.[46]

Nowhere have the tensions over local governance been more pronounced than in Corsica, the island birthplace of Napoleon Bonaparte. Corsicans are of Italian origin and fought an insurrection against French rule in the eighteenth century. At the same time that he successfully pushed for greater uniformity in local adminis-

Prefects are representatives of the national government, with one for each of France's one hundred departments. The prefects are under the authority of France's interior ministry.

tration, then Prime Minister Lionel Jospin negotiated an agreement with Corsican nationalists in 2000 that would have increased the powers of the island's elected assembly. Jospin had hoped that the agreement would bring an end to bombings and violence in Corsica.[47] Instead, the proposal became one of Jospin's most startling failures. It brought about the resignation of his minister of the interior and was ultimately defeated by Corsicans themselves in a July 2003 referendum.

India

The Indian political system is federal in form, with twenty-eight "federal units" below the level of the federal government, each with its own legislature. Yet it differs from federal systems in the United States and elsewhere, as the central government in India possesses considerably greater power relative to the lower units of government than in most other federal systems.

As is typical of federal systems, India has three levels of government. First, at the center are the two houses of parliament, the *Lok Sabha* (the House of the People) and the *Rajya Sabha* (the Council of States). Symbolizing the interdependence of the executive and legislative branches in a parliamentary democracy, the Indian Constitution defines the president as a part of the parliament, and the president appoints a prime minister capable of controlling a majority of the seats in the *Lok Sabha*.[48]

Second, at the level of the federal territorial units, the principal legislative body is the *Vidhan Sabha* (the Legislative Assembly). It is the regional equivalent of the *Lok Sabha*, with its members directly elected by the people from constituencies of approximately equal size for a period of up to five years. Six of the twenty-eight federal units (Uttar Pradesh, Bihar, Karnataka, Maharashtra, Jammu and Kashmir, and, most recently, Andhra Pradesh) have a second legislative body called the

Vidhan Parishad (the Legislative Council). This council is the regional equivalent of the *Rajya Sabha*, though the selection process and its powers are somewhat different. Its members are selected through a process involving direct and indirect elections and nominations.[49] Furthermore, their role is essentially advisory; they have even less power to block decisions of the *Vidhan Sabha* than the *Rajya Sabha* has to block decisions of the *Lok Sabha* at the federal level.

Third, the forms and powers of local government vary more from place to place than they do for governments at the regional level. The constitution had assigned the task of instituting village government to the federal territorial units. This meant that the development of local governing bodies was uneven. Disputes over the powers they should be given and how they should be funded contributed to their slow development virtually everywhere. In 1992, the Seventy-third Amendment Act was passed with the objective of fostering the development of local governments and standardizing their form around a basic unit called the *gram panchayat*. Nevertheless, the effort to create democratic and active local governments in rural areas has had varying success and remains one of the challenges facing the Indian political system.

Similarly, problems with municipal government led to the passage of the Seventy-fourth Amendment Act (1993), which sought to improve urban governance. Rapidly growing cities have placed severe challenges on municipal governments, which often lack the resources and power to carry out policies to meet these challenges. Although local governing institutions have greater capacities to deal with constituents than they had in the past, the complexities of the problems before them have increased even more.[50]

Levels of Government in Mexico, Brazil, and Nigeria

Given the relatively large size of their territory and population, it is not surprising that Mexico, Brazil, and Nigeria are all federal systems. In Mexico, the long dominance of the Institutional Revolutionary Party (PRI) meant that its federal system had functioned more like a unitary system in practice, but this pattern disappeared with the end of the PRI's domination over the Mexican political system. Brazil's federal arrangements have meant significant power for regional leaders, which has helped perpetuate the country's significant levels of economic inequality. Nigeria's federal system has been altered several times—mostly by adding states—after the initial ethno-federal approach helped undercut the postindependence democracy.

Mexico

Mexico is a federal system, with thirty-one regional territories and one federal district, Mexico City. Like the United States, the regional territories are called states. (In an effort to avoid confusion over the use of the term state, this section refers to the regional territories by the equivalent Spanish word, *estados*.) A governor and legislature run the government of each of the *estados*, and localities within each of them have mayors and municipal councils. There are more than two thousand municipalities (*municipios*) in Mexico.

Estados have authority to pass laws and levy taxes, though they remain dependent on the federal government for much of their revenue. The *estados* also supply local governments with a large amount of revenue. In the past, this was one of many factors that contributed to corruption in Mexican politics. The Mexican Constitution reserves certain powers to the federal government and prohibits the federal government and the *estados* from engaging in certain acts. According to Article 124 of the Mexican Constitution, powers not discussed in the Constitution fall to the *estados*.

There have been two noticeable differences between the American and Mexican federal systems since the adoption of the Mexican Constitution in 1917. The more important of the two, the dominance of the PRI at all levels of government, is also one that has changed dramatically over the last several decades. At the height of its power, the PRI controlled the federal government, the *estados* governments, and even most municipal governments in Mexico. This was significant since it meant that the officially federal system was more like a unitary one in practice. The first signs of cracks in PRI control appeared at the level of the *municipios* and then the *estados*. By the 1990s, it was not unusual for the PRI to lose elections at these levels, though it did not surrender power at the federal level until 2000.

The second difference is that all the legislatures of the *estados* are unicameral (made up of only one house). Only one American state, Nebraska, has a unicameral legislature. The preponderance of unicameral legislatures in Mexico may sound trivial, but it played a role in helping concentrate the PRI's power. Though having to govern in a federal system makes total control of all levels more difficult, the PRI only needed to control the governorship and one legislative house in each of the *estados* to dominate regional politics.

Brazil

Brazil is a federal system, with authority granted to lower levels of government to a great extent. Brazil is divided into twenty-six regional territories that form the level of government below that of the federal government, along with a federal district that is home to Brazil's capital, Brasília. (Like Mexico, the discussion of Brazil in this textbook uses the term *estados*, which is also the word for "states" in Portugese, when referring to these twenty-six regional territories.)

The Brazilian Constitution confers upon *estados* all powers not expressly reserved for the federal government. The *estados* establish their own constitutions; can tax, spend, and regulate freely; have their own flags and anthems; and share with the federal government the power to legislate on important items such as social security, education, and the environment. They can create their own "metropolitan districts," a level of administration in between the *estado* and municipal governments to facilitate management of large cities and neighboring communities.

At the same time, municipal governments have substantial financial and legal autonomy from the higher levels of government. The period of Portuguese colonialism combined with the extraordinarily difficult topography of Brazil to leave a legacy of "relatively greater municipal autonomy . . . [that] still distinguishes the Brazilian local government system from its counterparts elsewhere in Latin America."[51] The 1988 Constitution further bolstered the position of municipal governments. The local government share of total government spending rose from 11 percent in 1980 to 18 percent in 1990, higher than in any other Latin American nation except Colombia.[52] By way of comparison, Mexican municipalities control only 3 percent of total government spending.[53] In many ways, these provisions have been among the most democratic achievements of post-1988 Brazil. Municipalities have become laboratories for experiments in participatory democracy.

There have been some problems. For one, the Brazilian Constitution is notoriously unclear about the division of responsibilities between the levels of government. As Andrew Nickson notes, "The outcome of this complex legal arrangement is that there is almost no service uniformly offered by all municipalities, and very few in which the state may not be an alternate provider or regulator."[54] Thus, the governor of São Paulo (one of the most diverse and economically important of Brazil's *estados*) shares responsibility with the mayor of the city of São Paulo for the provision of many public services, including public transportation, education, and health care. This arrangement leads to much confusion and creates incentives for govern-

ments to try to avoid responsibility by shifting it to other levels.

In the highly economically unequal country of Brazil, this type of strong federalism has also tended to preserve the privileges of some of Brazil's most wealthy and powerful elites. As Chapter 2 discussed, many of the *estados* cover considerable territory but are sparsely populated. Large landowners historically have dominated the more rural areas of the country's interior. By giving governors broad powers, the system allows these landowners to control what amounts to small kingdoms. They have a huge influence over local politics and protect their property rights against "outside" (i.e., national) influences.

Strong federalism has thus limited the federal government's ability to tap into local resources in order to finance programs to help the poor or to redistribute wealth and land. Compromises—such as those protecting military autonomy—may have been necessary to secure the consent of the military and conservative interests during democratization. By permitting elites to veto reforms of vital interest to Brazil's poor majority, however, the choice to give broad powers to lower levels of government has lessened the Brazilian federal government's effectiveness and, ultimately, the regime's legitimacy.

Nigeria

It is no accident that the current Nigerian Constitution contains a number of detailed passages regarding national unity and overcoming social divisions. Since the civil war of the 1960s, subsequent governments, democratic and authoritarian alike, have had this goal in mind when considering changes to the political system. The comparative exercise in Chapter 5 laid out the way that interior political boundaries associated with Nigeria's federal system initially reinforced existing social divisions by looking at the period from 1960 to 1967. The Nigerian ethno-federal approach led directly to the civil war in Nigeria that broke out in 1967 and eventually claimed as many as one million lives. The government learned from the civil war and abandoned the ethno-federal approach in favor of one in which the territorial boundaries within the country provide a cross-cutting cleavage. The Nigerian experience can, therefore, inform the debate among scholars about the role of federal arrangements in weakening secessionist desires and preventing ethno-national conflict.

To do so requires an examination of two periods following the civil war, 1979–1984 and 1992–1994. These two periods were similar to the years 1960–1967 in many ways. Each period includes the span of one of the country's democratic "Republics" and the first full year of the military regime that replaced it. Other variables—level of development, demographic features of the population, and so on—were relatively constant across these years. Thus, possible factors that some associate with ethnic violence (e.g., regime transition) cannot explain differences in ethnic violence. And there were differences. Unlike the 1960–1967 period, the result of the regime transitions was not widespread ethnic violence.

The 1979–1984 period began with Olusegun Obasanjo as leader of the military government. Obasanjo had come to power after the previous military leader, Murtala Muhammad, was killed in an unsuccessful coup in 1976. Muhammad had promised to return the country to democracy, a promise that Obasanjo fulfilled. Elections were held in the middle of 1979.

Nigeria's Second Republic was a presidential system, replacing the parliamentary approach of the early independence period. Another major change was a reform to the federal system designed to address the problem of ethnic divisions. The federal approach persisted, but the number of states was increased to nineteen. This and other provisions in the electoral laws of the country reduced the incentives for ethnically-based parties. Though some violence existed in the Second Republic, political tensions were due much less to ethnic divisions than to widespread corruption. The general public correctly saw elections in 1983 as fraudulent. The coup that ended the Second Republic in 1983 was welcomed by the general population. Over the next year, the military government took a number of measures designed to attack corruption in the country.

The period of 1992–1994 included the awkwardly named Third Republic—the aborted attempt at reinstating democracy in 1992 and 1993. Voters democratically elected regional governments and local councils during this time, but in the end the military never surrendered rule over the federal government. The transition toward the Third Republic began in the middle 1980s when Ibrahim Babangida came to power through yet another coup. He declared his intention to return the country to democratic rule. The military government also again increased the number of regions in the federal system (to thirty).

Presidential elections were held in June 1993, but when Babangida did not like the results, he promptly declared the election invalid. The Third Republic ended before it got started. Babangida's hand-picked successor was overthrown in a coup that brought General Sani Abacha to power. Abacha ruled with a firm hand until his death in 1998, which paved the way for Nigeria's Fourth Republic in 1999. The Third Republic and its aftermath brought some violence, including significant government repression. Once again, however, the regime had not collapsed because of ethnic violence, and the violence was dramatically less than had been the case in the 1960s. Without the ethno-federal system to reinforce ethnic divisions, political tensions in Nigeria had more to do with economic policy and corruption than with ethnic appeals.

Think and Discuss

Table 6.1 summarizes the comparative exercise in Chapter 5 and the discussion of Nigerian federalism in this chapter. What kind of comparative method approach is this? How convincing is it? What else, besides the presence or absence of an ethno-federal approach, might explain the variation in the dependent variable?

| Table 6.1 | Ethnic Violence in Nigeria | | |
Case	D.V.: Significant Violence?	I.V. #1: Regime Change/Coup?	I.V. #2: Ethno-Federal System?
1960–1967	YES	YES	YES
1979–1984	NO	YES	NO
1992–1994	NO	YES	NO

Levels of Government in the Russian Federation, China, and Iran

Russia, China, and Iran demonstrate the difficulties that the federal versus unitary distinction can pose. Russia remains a federal system, though one in which the central government continues to consolidate power at the expense of the regional governments. China has a unitary system, yet regional authorities continue to gain power at the expense of the central government. Iran is also a unitary state, but one in which local authorities had been granted noteworthy levels of autonomy, only to have the national government signal a move back in the direction of centralized control.

The Russian Federation

Russia's current federal system is one of its continuing legacies from the Soviet period. The Russian Soviet Federative Socialist Republic (RSFSR) of the Soviet Union was the USSR's only union republic officially labeled a federation. Other republics contained autonomous regions but none to the extent of the RSFSR. When Russia emerged from the collapse of the USSR as an independent state, it inherited these regions, some of which had more official autonomy than others, and some of which were named for particular ethnic minorities.

Today, there are 83 regions in Russia with various standing. The regions include 21 republics, 46 "oblasts," 1 "autonomous oblast," 9 "krais," and 4 autonomous "okrugs." Moscow and St. Petersburg are also treated as distinct regions,

deemed "cities of federal significance." Each of the republics—nominally the "homelands" of a non-Russian minority such as the Tatars and Bashkirs—has the right to its own constitution. Oblasts and krais are more like traditional provinces of a federal system. Autonomous okrugs are ethnic subdivisions of oblasts or krais that have claimed, and been granted, special status.

As president, Boris Yeltsin relied on the regions' support in his struggles with other parts of the federal government. This resulted in demands for greater regional autonomy, both following the events of October 1993 and after Yeltsin won reelection in 1996. These leaders cut deals with the federal government on taxes, and some signed their own foreign trade agreements. The regional governments also routinely ignored Yeltsin's decrees, and numerous regions adopted laws contrary to both federal law and the Russian Constitution.

Yeltsin began to challenge the regions late in his presidency, and Putin spent much of his presidency looking for ways to strengthen the hand of the federal government. In 2000, Putin established seven "federal districts," adding a new layer to the federal system. Each federal district brought together a dozen or so regions, providing an additional link between the central government and the 83 regions. In September 2004, Putin pushed through a provision to eliminate direct election of regional governors. Instead, Moscow would now appoint them. In addition, the Russian government has encouraged the ongoing contraction of the number of regions. Mergers of regions took place in 2005, 2007, and 2008, bringing the total down from 89 to the present number of 83. Additional mergers, reducing further the number of regions, remain a distinct possibility in the years ahead.

Though some regional leaders have complained about these tactics, they have been unable to do much to stop them. Thus, Russia stands in stark contrast to the United Kingdom's devolution policy, which increased regional power but maintained the United Kingdom's status as a unitary system. The Russian central government has taken back powers from the regions yet maintained a federal structure.

China

Like Russia, China has a large number of regions, which take different forms. Of the 31 regions, 4 are municipalities, 5 are autonomous regions for ethnic minorities, and the remainder are provinces. Unlike Russia, however, China is a unitary state. A number of comparative politics and economics scholars have noted a conspicuous shift in the balance of power between the central government and China's regions over the last two decades. Again unlike Russia, this shift has been one of increasing regional powers at the expense of the central government. This has been particularly evident in recent economic policy, and it has coincided with the ongoing implementation of market economic reforms and the declining adherence to official ideology. Some economists have labeled this trend Chinese "fiscal federalism" or "federalism, Chinese style."[55]

Clearly, changes have occurred. But is China devolving powers to the regions? Is it becoming a federal system? The answer to the first question is a tentative yes. China has increased the powers of regional and local governments dramatically. But these changes have focused on economics. No longer an archetypal unitary state, China remains quite centralized politically. It has not devolved power to its regions like the United Kingdom has.

The second question is easier to answer. China is not yet a federal state. An act called the "Law-Making Law of the People's Republic of China," adopted in March 2000 following seven years of work, *appeared* to set the stage for federalism by laying out the central government's exclusive legislating powers.[56] Yet the law left the central government in the position to control activities at the regional level if necessary. While opening the door for legislating by local governments in areas not explicitly presented as central government matters, it provided that the central government can override such actions with contrary legislation.

Thus, China remains a unitary system for now. Changes like the Law on Law-Making signal a shift away from central control. But greater powers for lower levels of government alone do not signal the transition to a federal system. Only when such powers are granted, and protected, constitutionally could one discuss federalism in China.

Iran

Iran is a unitary system. The country is divided into thirty provinces, which are further divided into smaller units (analogous to American counties and municipalities). As in the past, provincial leaders—known today as governors–general—are quite powerful. They are appointed by the central government's interior minister. Befitting Iran's status as a theocracy, religious representatives of the central government also have significant power within the provinces.

Beginning in the late 1990s, the national government increased the authority of local governments. This policy included finally following through on local elections, which had been promised in the 1979 Constitution. When elections took place in 1999, they brought reformers to power in a large number of cities. Several hundred women were elected at the local level, forming the majority of the councils in some localities.[57] Local governments increasingly served as sounding boards for disgruntled citizens who felt unable to express their concerns directly to the national government.

Some label the process of increasing local government responsibility and accountability in Iran as "controlled decentralization." Like China, the strengthening of local rule does not approach the extent of devolution efforts in the United Kingdom. In addition, the trends at the national level in 2004 and 2005, where the stance of pro-reform leaders were dramatically weakened, did not bode well for increasing liberalization and responsibility at the local level in Iran. Certain scholars of Iranian politics believe that, in an effort to deflect criticism from itself, the central government will blame local governments for economic or other performance problems.[58] This would assist those in the central government who support turning back the policies of the previous decade that expanded local powers.

COMPARATIVE EXERCISE

Major Policy Change and Veto Points in the United Kingdom and China

One of the most important theoretical perspectives developed about political institutions is the theory of **veto points**, identified most closely with political scientist George Tsebelis. Veto points are individuals or collective bodies (e.g., legislative chambers) that must agree to a policy change before it is adopted; their failure to accept a proposed policy change amounts to a veto of the proposal.[59] Tsebelis argues that systems with a large number of veto points are likely to have much policy stability, since one of the "veto players" is likely to prevent major policy change.[60]

Parliamentary systems generally have fewer veto points than presidential systems (see Chapter 7), and unicameral (single-chamber) legislatures have fewer veto points than bicameral ones. But Tsebelis contends the makeup of the executive and legislative branches is not the entire story. One must also understand the party system and ideological divisions between the main parties. If a president is from the same party as the party controlling the legislature, there could be fewer veto points than in a parliamentary system ruled by a coalition of small parties (what he calls "partisan veto players") with divergent ideological views.

This comparative exercise examines Tsebelis's veto points theory. There are many examples from the TIC countries one could use to assess the role of veto points in influencing policy outcomes. Local elites in Brazil, for example, have used veto points to thwart land reform efforts, while former Iranian President Mohammed Khatami faced roadblocks in his efforts to reform the Iranian political system because of veto points working against him. This comparative exercise centers on major changes that occurred in two of the TIC countries: the significant weakening of the "welfare state" provisions in the United Kingdom under Margaret Thatcher and the marketization program of the Chinese government under Deng Xiaoping.

A Most Different Comparison

These two examples provide the basis for a "most different" comparative approach. At the time of the policy shifts in question, the United Kingdom was a highly prosperous capitalist democracy while China was a developing country under Communist Party rule. The cultures and histories of the two countries differ greatly as well.

Veto points are individuals or collective political bodies whose failure to accept a policy change results in the policy not being adopted.

Yet both countries instituted reforms that undid an underlying component of their political and/or economic systems. Under Thatcher, the British began unraveling social welfare provisions that had served as the backbone of government economic policy throughout the post–World War II era. By embracing capitalism, the Chinese reforms directly challenged a primary ideological claim to legitimacy. Thus, across these two very different cases, realization of the dependent variable—successful implementation of a major, regime-altering policy change—is present.

Hypothesis and Results

What can explain the consistency of the dependent variable across these two quite different cases? The work of George Tsebelis provides a possible explanation. Tsebelis's veto points theory suggests the following hypothesis: *Neither of the two countries in which the significant change occurred had a large number of veto points in practice.* Does an examination of the cases support this hypothesis or reject it?

In the case of Thatcher's Britain, the prime minister was able to put into place policies that decreased the government's role in the economy and decreased government social welfare programs, which she thought fostered dependency on the government. Though the "welfare state retrenchment" had begun under the Labour Party government preceding her, Thatcher's government turned their modest reforms into a full-scale policy shift.[61] Because of the form of Britain's parliamentary system, there were few checks on Thatcher's ability to pursue these changes. The House of Commons was controlled by the Conservative Party, which Thatcher led. The House of Lords could get in the way and slow the reform process down, but the members of the House of Lords were also mostly Conservatives.

After Mao Zedong's death, China altered dramatically its approach to economic policy. Open hostility to market capitalism was replaced by a mixed economic system, which maintained most state-run enterprises but also allowed—especially in certain large cities—a large privately run sector to develop. The typical rules of the game related to institutions were not in play in China under Deng Xiaoping. Though less the case than it had been under Mao, personal prestige was still more important than institutional position under Deng. In addition, China was a one-party system; partisan veto points were not present. The legislative branch also did not provide the kind of veto point it can in other systems. In China, the legislature has rarely stood up to dictates from the country's executive leadership, a pattern that was evident as Deng pushed forward with his dramatic reforms.

Thus, an examination of the process of these major reform efforts in the United Kingdom and China provides an interesting test of the veto point hypothesis. Table 6.2 summarizes these findings. Despite their general differences, both countries instituted significant institutional change. This pattern in the dependent variable cannot be explained by the type of political system; it differed across the two cases. The veto points variable, however, follows the pattern of the dependent variable. Had either of the systems had a large number of veto points, the veto points hypothesis would have been rejected. Instead, the evidence supports the hypothesis.

What this analysis cannot explain is *why* the actors chose to pursue the policies they did. As is often the case with structural arguments, political institutions provide opportunities but do not fully explain the motives of the leaders or the timing of their decisions. In this case, the small number of veto points afforded the opportunity for significant policy change. Understanding the actual driving forces behind these changes, however, requires a deeper understanding of other factors. These include socioeconomic structural conditions, as well as the backgrounds, character, and interests of such individuals as Margaret Thatcher and Deng Xiaoping.

Table 6.2   Major Reform and Institutions in the United Kingdom and China

Case	Dep. Var.: Significant Reform?	Indep. Var. #1: Political System	Indep. Var. #2: Veto Points
UK 1979–1990	**YES** (Thatcher "revolution")	**Parliamentary democracy**	**FEW**
China 1979–1989	**YES** (Marketization)	**Communist,** with power based more on personal prestige than official government position	**FEW**

In addition, the dependent variable's measurement and the analysis of the independent variables in this exercise were overly simplified. It is dangerous to use a particular event to capture a general concept like Tsebelis's "policy stability." If one were to examine these cases in a bona fide, detailed comparative study, many more policy outcomes than one per country would be considered. This would lead to a policy stability index, based on a large amount of data about the adoption or rejection of policy proposals, which would serve as the dependent variable.

Finally, this exercise examined only two cases and considered only the type of political system and whether there were few or many veto points. One would also want to consider more cases and additional independent variables than there was room to consider here, hopefully ruling out a large number of them that do not fit with the pattern of the dependent variable. Other most different studies of cases where major policy change has been blocked—such as Brazil and Iran—would also help establish how general Tsebelis's theory is. Still, this limited comparative study does provide some support for Tsebelis's theory. By showing how the veto points perspective can help explain a similar outcome in two very different cases, it points to the applicability of Tsebelis's theory in divergent settings.

CONCLUSION

This chapter introduced concepts and theories related to the political structural approach to comparative politics. This approach pays close attention to the institutional arrangements in a particular political system. It allows comparativists to categorize the political system in broad terms (democracy, totalitarianism, or authoritarianism), consider subcategories within these broad categories (majoritarian versus consensus democracy), and formulate causal arguments that place institutional arrangements at the center of understandings of political outcomes.

Like examinations of socioeconomic structures, approaches that focus solely on political institutions and their rules can be criticized. Such criticisms include that institutionalists too often focus on describing the rules of the game and too rarely consider the socioeconomic reasons that the institutions look the way they do. As political scientist Adam Przeworski provocatively asks, "if different institutions are possible only under different conditions, how can we tell whether what matters are institutions or the conditions?"[62] It is indeed important to consider the origins of institutions, and most "new institutionalists," regardless of the variant of new institutionalism they utilize, build a discussion of the emergence of evolution of government institutions into their discussions about their political effects.

In addition, even if certain criticisms of examining political institutions to understanding political outcomes make sense, one must be careful not to overreact. The structure of the political system—the arrangement of political institutions and the rules that govern decision making within them—matters because it provides the most direct setting in which political decisions occur. In other words, it is the closest structural component to the process of political decision making. As Adam Przeworski also declares, political institutions can "prevent people from doing what they would have otherwise done or induce them to do what they otherwise would not have done."[63] This chapter's overview of the constitutions, institutional arrangements, and their effects on politics in the Topic in Countries cases supports Przeworski's contention. In Brazil, for example, the large number of veto points has allowed wealthy local elites to protect their holdings. Even if the vast majority of the Brazilian population desires dramatic land reform, it is unlikely to happen without changes first to the country's political arrangements.

The TIC cases also demonstrate that political institutions are not the entire story. The United Kingdom's combination of a partially unwritten constitution and increasing powers to lower levels of government in a unitary system is distinct. It works, fairly well at least, in the British case. Similar institutional approaches in other cases—cases with differing socioeconomic structures and distinct leaders—would likely produce very different outcomes.

Students of comparative politics should not ignore the socioeconomic structural forces discussed in the previous three chapters. But the arrangement of political institutions is an important factor that shapes the kinds of major

political outcomes in which comparativists are interested. The next two chapters move beyond the general discussion of political institutions to examine particular arrangements involving governing institutions and variations in them from one country to another.

Key Terms

American model of democracy, p. 194
Authoritarianism, p. 196
Bureaucratic authoritarianism, p. 198
Communism, p. 196
Confederation, p. 216
Consensus democracy, p. 193
Constitution, p. 209
Constitutionalism, p. 210
Democracy, p. 191
Devolution, p. 217
European model of democracy, p. 194
Fascism, p. 196
Federal system, p. 215
Historical new institutionalism, p. 208
Institution, p. 190
Latin American model of democracy, p. 194
Majoritarian democracy, p. 193
Military authoritarianism, p. 197
New institutionalism, p. 208
Old institutionalism, p. 202
Party authoritarianism, p. 198
Political institutions, p. 190
Prefects, p. 220
Rational choice new institutionalism, p. 208
Reserved powers, p. 215
Rule of law, p. 209
Semiauthoritarianism, p. 198
Semidemocracy, p. 198
Shared powers, p. 216
Sociological new institutionalism, p. 208
Systems theory, p. 203
Totalitarianism, p. 195
Unitary system, p. 215
Veto points, p. 227
Westminster model of democracy, p. 194

Learning Objectives

After reading this chapter, you should be able to:

■ Identify the main tasks of a legislative branch.

■ Identify the main tasks of a political executive.

■ Discuss the main features, advantages, and disadvantages of a parliamentary system, a presidential system, and a semipresidential system.

■ Describe the executive and legislative arrangements in the ten TIC cases.

■ Summarize the lessons from this chapter's comparative exercise.

7

Legislatures and Executives

On July 21, 2007, Pratibha Patil became India's first female president. Selected by the Indian parliament, some viewed her election as a milestone, particularly for a country where women continue to face significant discrimination. While Patil's selection was indeed historic, and while it demonstrated India's commitment to use the presidency as a vehicle for advancing politically underrepresented identity groups, the position of president in India comes with relatively little real power. The president is, officially, India's head of state, but the concrete executive powers in the country fall to the prime minister. Without understanding the difference between a parliamentary system and a presidential one, and without knowing that India has a president but functions largely as a parliamentary system, it would be easy to overstate the political importance of Patil's ascension to the position of Indian president. Patil's selection as president, though symbolically important, shaped political outcomes much less than the rule of Indira Gandhi, India's (female) prime minister during 1966–1977 and 1980–1984. ■

Look for this icon to point you to **Deepening Your Understanding** features on the companion website www.college.cengage.com/politicalscience/ barrington, which provide greater depth for some key content.

The previous chapter addressed some of the basic differences between political systems, including the fundamentals of federal versus unitary systems and the consequences of choosing the federal option instead of the unitary one. This chapter addresses another essential choice about a country's political structure: the government's legislative and executive functions. As societies and political systems became more complex throughout history, it became almost impossible to concentrate all decision-making power in the hands of a single leader. Even Joseph Stalin, who may have made more daily governing decisions than any political leader in the twentieth century, had under him an array of decision-making and -enforcing institutions.

Nearly all political systems, democratic and nondemocratic alike, contain a legislative institution—the part of the government officially in charge of legislating (making laws). General hostility toward a political system is often aimed at this institution. The early history of legislatures was one of increasing power over time, as they battled monarchs for input into governing decisions. In more recent times, the trend has been in the other direction, with executives once again becoming the initiator of policies and legislatures increasingly ceding power to them.[1] Yet, in many democracies, these legislatures remain the heart and soul of lawmaking and maintain significant control over the policymaking process.

Governments also must execute (implement) the laws that are adopted. There are two general approaches to the challenge of creating and implementing government policy. One, familiar to students in the United States, is to separate the executive functions from the legislative functions, creating two distinct branches of government. The second approach is to fuse these responsibilities by linking the executive and legislature tightly together. These two approaches are labeled, respectively, presidential and parliamentary. There is also a growing tendency to create hybrid, "semipresidential" systems with features of both. Before discussing some of the specific duties of legislatures and executives, it is helpful to discuss these broad approaches to fusing or separating the legislative and executive branches.

Parliamentary, Presidential, and Semipresidential Systems

Parliamentary and presidential alternatives to democratic rule differ primarily on whether the executive and the legislature are separated or fused. This section of the chapter underscores the basic differences between these two categories of democratic government. It also highlights the increasingly common semipresidential approach.

Parliamentary Systems

A **parliamentary system** is a conventional approach to democracy, particularly in Europe and Asia. The head of the government and the political system's chief executive is usually called the **prime minister,** but the position may also be referred to as premier (as in the case of China) or chancellor (in Germany). In a parliamentary system, there is a strong connection between the chief executive and the legislature—a fusion of the branches of government that is absent in presidential systems. Fusing the executive and legislative branches engenders

In **parliamentary systems**, the chief executive is directly responsible to the legislature. As a result, leaders and their governments (cabinet officials and other top ministers) can be removed from office by the parliament, and elections can be held at irregular intervals.

The **prime minister** is the label normally given to the chief executive of the government in a parliamentary system. The prime minister coordinates the cabinet's work and takes the lead in pursuing policy changes in parliament.

several key attributes, which help distinguish parliamentary systems from presidential and semipresidential ones.

Selection of the Chief Executive and Formation of the Government

The hallmark of the fusion of the executive and legislative branches in parliamentary systems is the choice of the chief executive. Constituents do not directly elect the prime minister. Rather, the head of state (a monarch or weak president) usually holds the *official* power to select the prime minister. In practice, this is a formality. The head of state selects the prime minister of the political system based on the results of parliamentary elections.

The new prime minister then forms and heads "the government" (the cabinet and other important ministry heads), overseeing the actions of these officials and coordinating their efforts to formulate new policies. In parliamentary systems such as the United Kingdom and Germany, the chief executive is a sitting member of parliament, an **MP**, as are other government ministers. Although strange to those used to a separation of power between branches and legal restrictions preventing simultaneous service in multiple branches of government, this arrangement is completely compatible with the parliamentary democracy approach.

The prime minister is usually the leader of the party with the most seats in parliament. If no party has a majority of seats, two or more political parties will typically form a **coalition**. A coalition is a group of parties that agree to work together to pass legislation and occupy cabinet positions. A head of state with the power to name the prime minister will generally not do so without a coalition agreement in place. The prime minister is almost always the leader of the ruling coalition's biggest party, but when a coalition is made up of several parties of roughly similar size, the prime minister could come from one of the smaller ones.

The formation of coalitions can involve some of the most intense political bargaining imaginable. The prizes in this bargaining are policy positions and **portfolios**, positions in the government associated with particular ministries. An individual may even be included in the government without heading a ministry or other government department. Such a person is called a **minister without portfolio**. Since those putting together a coalition seek to control a majority of seats in the legislature, small parties can become kingmakers, putting a coalition "over the top." In the process, such parties may be rewarded with government portfolios and policy victories that far exceed what the number of their seats in parliament would otherwise warrant.

The most common coalition is called a **minimum necessary winning coalition**. The party forming the coalition seeks only as many other parties as is necessary to control a bare majority of the parliament's seats. If a parliament has one hundred seats, the minimum necessary winning coalition is one that controls at least fifty-one seats. Such a coalition requires strong **party discipline**, with members of a party following the directions of party leaders about how to vote on parliamentary bills. In the example of the fifty-one-seat ruling coalition, the defection of only

MP is the acronym for member of parliament.

A **coalition** is a group of political parties that agree to share cabinet seats and other important positions in government ministries and work together to pass legislation in a parliament.

A **portfolio** is a position in the government associated with a particular ministry.

It is possible for an individual to be considered a member of the government without heading a ministry. This person is called a **minister without portfolio**.

A **minimum necessary winning coalition** involves only the parties required to gain control of a majority of the seats in the parliament.

The level of **party discipline** in a parliamentary system refers to the extent to which MPs follow the directions of their party leaders on how to vote on a particular bill. A minimum necessary winning coalition requires strong party discipline to survive.

one member of the coalition would cause the defeat of a government-sponsored bill.

A **grand coalition** involves two or more of the largest parties and gives the coalition control over a large majority of seats. Grand coalitions are rare. In most cases, the multi-party system's largest parties do not get along. They are often left-of-center and right-of-center parties that disagree with each other about issues as basic as government's role in society. Their leaders may also personally dislike each other, making it difficult for one to accept the other as prime minister. If a grand coalition is formed, these issue and personality disputes often make it less stable than a smaller coalition. As a result, grand coalitions mostly occur only when government unity is seen as necessary to address serious economic, social, and political problems.

On rare occasions, the head of state may also accept the formation of a **minority government**. In such a case, the main party or coalition does not include enough MPs to control a majority of seats. Each vote requires the government to put together a coalition specific to that decision. In most cases, this is a recipe for instability and gridlock. It can work, however, if the prime minister is very popular, or if a smaller party has chosen not to be a part of the coalition but has much in common with the coalition's main party. It can also be seen as a temporary measure, forestalling the new elections that most members of parliament fear.

Separation of Head of Government and Head of State

In parliamentary systems, the head of state is normally separated from the head of government, and the head of state is the much weaker of the two. The head of state (a weak president or monarch) has little role in actual governing. Instead, as ceremonial executive

Did You Know? In perhaps the ultimate example of a figurehead leader, the head of state of Canada is the queen of England. As a result, technically, the queen of England enacts all the laws of Canada, and the prime minister of Canada is selected by the Governor General (the official representative of the queen). In reality, there is little interaction between the monarch and the Canadian government. Some Canadian politicians have called for a move to break these formal ties, and there is strong support in Canada to do so once the queen dies or steps down.

leader, the head of state provides continuity. Though government leadership may change, the head of state provides a symbol of stability for the masses. The general population may also see the head of state as "above politics," giving them something in the political system to support when normal politics gets particularly distasteful (often around election time!).

Irregular Intervals Between Elections and Votes of Confidence

MPs have a stipulated term in office, but this term is the *maximum* amount of time before new elections must be held. Prior to that deadline, the chief executive could change hands and/or the leader could call early parliamentary elections. This again may strike many Americans, used to congressional elections every two years and presidential elections every four, as odd. Remember, the government is accountable to the legislature in a parliamentary system. It can only remain in power with the support of a majority of the members of parliament.

In some parliamentary systems, the failure of even one government-supported bill to pass warrants new elections. In most systems, it is only a warning sign to the government about its lack of support. In such cases, the prime minister might call on the minister most responsible for

---

A **grand coalition** involves two or more large parties and gives the coalition control over a large majority of seats.

A **minority government** exists when the chief executive in a parliamentary system comes from a party or coalition that does not control a majority of the seats in the parliament. It occurs rarely, and is often seen as a temporary measure meant to forestall new elections.

the policy's crafting to resign. The prime minister may also choose to resign, leading the head of state to "dissolve" the parliament and order new elections or a new government's formation from the existing parliament. Thus, it is possible for the prime minister to change without a change in the parliament's makeup. The parliament's ruling party may choose a new leader—such as when John Major replaced Margaret Thatcher as British prime minister without new elections—or different political parties in the parliament may assemble a new ruling coalition.

In addition to signaling displeasure by defeating a bill, parliament can also force the prime minister's hand. One such measure is called a **vote of confidence**. The government itself picks a particular vote that it considers to be a confidence vote, and states that it will resign and call for new elections if it loses the vote. Many systems allow a second option, called a **vote of no confidence** or **vote of censure**. The opposition sponsors this motion, and it usually forces the government to resign if it passes. Again, the head of state is likely to call for new elections in such a situation, although rules about whether this must occur differ from system to system.

Failed votes of confidence or successful votes of no confidence that lead to new elections are relatively rare. Members of a party in the ruling coalition fear new elections, since their party may lose seats and, consequently, may not be involved in the next ruling coalition. When a failed vote of confidence triggers new elections, an MP could also lose his or her own seat and be out of a job altogether. MPs, therefore, are hesitant to support challenges to governments in which their party is a coalition member and are very reluctant to do so if their party controls a majority of parliament seats.

In most parliamentary systems, prime ministers can also call for early elections in an effort to improve their position in parliament. This is often done formally by the government resigning, leaving the head of state with little choice but to dissolve parliament. Why would a prime minister

force early elections, especially if the prime minister's party already holds a majority of seats? If the prime minister's party has become more popular since the previous elections, it makes sense to capitalize on that popularity. Why wait until the next scheduled election and risk becoming less popular in the meantime? The new elections also "reset the clock" on the parliament's term, guaranteeing the prime minister a longer tenure in office. This was the thinking in September of 2008 when Canadian Prime Minister Stephen Harper moved to hold early elections to bolster the position of his Conservative Party.

Prime ministers in charge of coalition governments are much less likely to pursue this course than those who head parties with a majority of seats. Unless the prime minister is very confident that new elections will result in the prime minister's party winning a majority of seats, the danger of not being able to assemble a ruling coalition after the election outweighs the potential gains. Other parties in the coalition government may not do as well in the election, or—perhaps angered by the early elections—they might defect to another party to form a coalition after the election. If it were not a part of the subsequent ruling coalition, the prime minister's party could end up with more seats but much less power.

Think and Discuss

Is the lack of fixed terms in parliamentary systems a good thing or a bad thing? Why?

A **vote of confidence** is a vote called for by the sitting government in a parliamentary system. Typically, if this vote *fails*, the government is forced to resign and new parliamentary elections may be held.

A **vote of no confidence** has a similar effect to a vote of confidence, but the opposition sponsors it, and it results in the formation of a new government or the holding of new parliamentary elections if it *passes*.

In some systems, a vote of no confidence is called a **vote of censure**.

The "Opposition" Because they fuse the executive and legislative branches of government, parliamentary systems formalize the idea of an "opposition" to the government more than presidential systems do. Broadly, all the MPs not from a party in the governing coalition comprise the opposition. Some parliamentary systems take this a step further, allowing the main opposition party or parties to form a **shadow government**. A shadow government is a set of MPs who would replace the current government ministers if the opposition party or parties were to win the next election. Because there is no need to pass legislation—and thus no need to create a genuine coalition—the members of the shadow government generally come from the largest opposition party only.

Advantages of Parliamentary Systems *Advantage #1: Efficiency in passing legislation*. With minimal veto points and a lack of checks and balances, things get done more easily in a parliamentary system. There is less chance for gridlock, unless significant divisions develop within a ruling coalition. The path to passing a law can still be lengthy, but it is more clear-cut than in a presidential system. If a prime minister wants a law passed and that prime minister's party controls a majority of the parliament, the law is most likely going to pass. Even strong disagreements between members of a ruling coalition will usually result in the formation of a new government rather than an endless stalemate.

Advantage #2: Clearer accountability for voters. The fusion of executive and legislative branches means voters can more easily reward or punish those in office in a parliamentary system. If voters dislike the ruling party's policies, they can cast their ballots for a different party. As a result, government should be more representative than it is in presidential systems since it is held accountable more easily than in presidential systems.

In reality, voters in parliamentary systems do not always have it so easy. Often, the government in a parliamentary system is the result of a coalition of several political parties. Voters seeking to punish the government could decide to vote for one of the opposition parties instead. But are policy failures really the fault of all of the coalition partners, or just one or two of the parties? Voters who want to reward the government face a similarly difficult decision. Should the prime minister's party be repaid with a vote, or should one of the smaller parties who helped hold the coalition together be rewarded for its actions?

Disadvantages of Parliamentary Systems *Disadvantage #1: Instability*. Particularly if coalitions are needed to produce a majority, parliamentary governments can be highly unstable. Even majority party situations require strong party discipline to prevent government collapse. As a result, the prime minister and other leading government officials may be in office only a year before losing power, making it quite difficult for a prime minister and cabinet to pursue their legislative agenda. In these cases, as in Italy for decades after World War II, much of the decision-making power shifts to the more stable portion of the executive branch, the bureaucracy.

Disadvantage #2: Concentration of power and hasty decisions. The concentration of power in parliamentary systems can indeed lead to efficient policymaking, but it can also lead to hasty decisions. In a unicameral parliament controlled by a majority party, there is no check on the prime minister. Members of the prime minister's party face strong pressures to go along with government decisions. Repeated readings of the bill, which are supposed to result in thoughtful

---

A **shadow government** is a group of MPs who would replace the current government if the opposition party or parties were to win the next election. It is generally made up of the top MPs from the largest opposition party.

consideration and amendments, end up being formalities. For every American who complains about how difficult it is for a bill to become a law in the United States, there is a resident of a country with a parliamentary system wishing it was not so easy!

Parliamentary Systems in the United Kingdom, Germany, and India

While they look different in some ways, the political systems of the United Kingdom, Germany, and India are all considered parliamentary ones. Each has a prime minister (in Germany known as the chancellor) with significant political power. Each also has a separate head of state (the queen in the United Kingdom, the president in Germany and India) with little real power over day-to-day politics.

The United Kingdom

The United Kingdom captures well many of the key ideas about a parliamentary system. In fact, it is often considered *the* parliamentary system, a model for others around the world. As discussed in Chapter 6, countries that use parliamentary systems similar to the United Kingdom's are said to have "Westminster parliamentary" systems. This term comes from the Palace of Westminster, where the British parliament meets in session.

The United Kingdom's parliamentary system features a monarchy, which has evolved over time from the chief executive position into a weak head of state. These days, the chief executive is the prime minister, the leader of the main party in the lower house of the legislature, the House of Commons. Thanks to an electoral system that has encouraged a small number of major parties, it is also a more stable parliamentary system than most.

Germany

The parliamentary system of the Federal Republic disperses central government power and limits executive authority. This design was a deliberate response to the excesses of the Nazi regime's centralized dictatorship. Moreover, to avoid the defects of the interwar Weimar Republic, the current system situates primary authority for governing firmly with the chancellor (prime minister), giving the president largely ceremonial duties.

Two features of the German political system—coalition governments and federalism—often require chancellors to compromise or face legislative deadlock and policy immobility. Coalition governments, made necessary when no party has a majority of the seats, require cooperation between political parties at the national level. As discussed in the previous chapter, German-style federalism requires cooperation between the different levels of government.

India

Like Germany, India has a parliamentary and federal system of government. At the center, the legislature is bicameral, consisting of the *Lok Sabha* (House of the People) and the *Rajya Sabha* (Council of States). In twenty-two of the twenty-eight federal units, it is unicameral, consisting of the *Vidhan Sabha* (Legislative Assembly), while in six of the federal units there is a second house, the *Vidhan Parishad* (Legislative Council).

The head of the Indian government is the prime minister. (The equivalent position in the federal units is the "chief minister.") The prime minister comes from the main party of the *Lok Sabha*. As mentioned at the opening of the chapter, the Indian head of state is the president. As in other parliamentary systems, the president in India has quite limited powers.

Figure 7.1 Presidential Versus Parliamentary Systems: Who Selects Whom

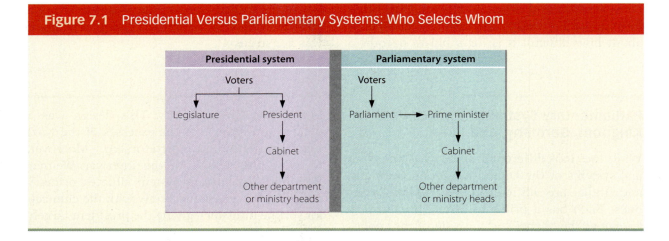

Presidential Systems

Many countries of the Americas and Africa feature a **presidential system**. Given the image in many people's minds of an all-powerful president, it is ironic that democratic presidential systems first emerged as a way of diffusing political power to avoid tyrannical rule. Three basic features of presidential systems achieve this diffusion: the general electorate selecting the chief executive, the chief executive and legislature having fixed terms, and a separation of powers between the executive and the legislature that results in two independent branches of government.

Did You Know? Since its inception, Israel's parliament, the *Knesset*, has had a large number of small political parties holding seats in the body, complicating the selection of a prime minister. As a result, reforms to the Israeli political system in 1996 gave Israeli voters the power to directly elect the prime minister, an experiment that lasted until 2001. The fact that voters elected the prime minister did not, however, make the system presidential. In true parliamentary form, the *Knesset* could still vote the prime minister out of office, even during the period of direct elections of the prime minister.

have none—the vice president may also be elected through a popular vote at the same time.

In practice, the selection of the president does not always rest solely with the general population. The American electoral process places the ultimate vote for the president in the hands of the members of the Electoral College. These individuals become electors on the basis of popular votes for the president within each state. Thus, the distinguishing feature of presidential systems is not that the masses *directly* choose the president; rather, it is that the selection of the chief executive does not depend on the outcome of legislative elections.

Direct Election of the Chief Executive A defining feature of presidential systems is how voters select the chief executive. As Figure 7.1 indicates, this vote is separate from the selection of members of the legislature, though these two votes may be cast at the same time as part of a general election. If the system includes a vice president—some systems actually have more than one vice president; some

Fixed Terms for the Executive and Legislature Presidential systems are noteworthy for their fixed terms of office. Voters who select a president in

A **presidential system** is one in which the general population votes for the chief executive, there are fixed terms for the chief executive and the legislature, and a separation of powers exists between the executive and legislative branches.

a system with four-year presidential terms know they can expect another presidential election in four years. In addition, legislatures cannot remove presidents—other than through impeachment— and executives generally cannot force early legislative elections. For good or bad, the president and the legislature are stuck with one another until their terms expire.

Separation of Powers and Checks and Balances

Because American students grow up learning about the virtues of checks and balances,[2] many assume all presidential systems take the extreme approach to them found in the American system. This assumption is incorrect. All presidential systems separate legislative and executive powers, and many of them include provisions for the override of presidential vetoes or require the legislature's consent when the president selects cabinet members. But presidents are often quite powerful, with at least as much independent power as the legislature, including broad powers to issue decrees that have the force of law and ways to (legally) get around what appears at first glance to be a rather substantial check on their power.

Even in presidential systems without an elaborate system of checks and balances, one ultimate check is common: the power of the legislature to remove the president through impeachment. For at least three reasons, however, impeachment is generally neither simple nor common. First, voters select the president (and, as a consequence, the other top officials of the executive branch) for a term in office fixed by law. The legislature thus faces the burden of justifying not only that the chief executive needs to be replaced earlier than scheduled but also that the legislature, and not the voters, should make this decision.

Second, because the executive and legislative branches are separated in a presidential system, impeachment is a major event. Unlike votes of confidence, which in a parliamentary system are customary ways of removing a government, nothing about impeachment is normal. Mention of it can trigger talk of a "constitutional crisis."

Finally, the impeachment process usually involves a lengthy investigation and legislative hearings prior to a vote to remove. Even after all this—and much to the relief of such leaders as Bill Clinton who have gone through it—the process may not result in a successful vote to remove the president from office. In such an instance, the impeachment process can damage beyond repair relations between the legislature and the president, and the general population may believe that members of the legislature engaged in a vindictive act that wasted time and money.

Fusion of the Head of State and Head of Government

In parliamentary systems, the head of state is normally separated from the head of government. This is largely moot in practice, since the head of state is often a figurehead position. In presidential systems, the president is usually both chief executive of the government and representative of the state to the outside world.

The Potential for Divided Government

Another distinguishing feature of presidential systems is the strong possibility of **divided government**. A government is divided when the president's political party is different from the party that controls the legislature. In such a scenario, the checks and balances can result in gridlock: the inability to pass legislation when each party blocks the actions of the other. In a system with fewer checks and balances, the result can be a "war of laws," in which acts of the legislature are countered by decrees from the president.

Advantages of Presidential Systems

Advantage #1: A check on the "majority rule" aspect of legislatures. All presidential systems include a role for the president in the legislative process, allowing the president to help control legislatures. Since legislatures make most of their decisions on the

---

Divided government exists when the president's political party is different from the political party that controls the legislative branch.

basis of majority rule, the president may be one of the only checks on a majority in a legislature that seeks to pass imprudent legislation. The president is, to use the term from the previous chapter, a "veto point" in the legislative process. This is most obvious in cases of divided government. But even when the president and members of a legislative majority are from the same party, presidents often take very seriously their role as a wall against the rapid charge of a particular piece of legislation. This also stabilizes a system over time, as presidential systems are less likely than parliamentary ones to hurriedly undo policies of the government officials who were previously in power.

Advantage #2: A national mandate. A president is typically the only nationally elected government official. In parliamentary systems, voters only indirectly select the prime minister on the basis of legislative elections. The presidents can therefore claim national mandates in a way that is difficult for many prime ministers to match. This mandate comes in handy when the legislature is controlled by a party other than the president's but also in times of national crisis.

Disadvantages of Presidential Systems *Disadvantage #1: The difficulty of removing an unpopular president.* Thanks to the president's fixed term, there are few options for a country with a sitting president who has become very unpopular. The president may decide to resign, particularly if a constitutional crisis is looming. The legislature may also try to impeach the president, but, as discussed earlier, this is unlikely. Most often, the country is stuck with the unpopular president until the next election.

To be fair, parliamentary systems in which a majority party controls the parliament can face a similar problem. Not forced to call new elections, the majority party may decide to ride out the storm until the next election. Even in these cases, however, relief is easier than in a presidential system. The majority party can decide to change party leaders and, as a result, change

prime ministers. Presidents cannot be replaced by their parties without a new election.

Disadvantage #2: The propensity for gridlock. One person's thoughtful deliberation and prevention of hasty policy decisions is another person's gridlock. When the president's political party does not hold a majority of the legislature's seats, it can be very difficult to pass legislation. As Jimmy Carter found out during his four years as president of the United States, even having a legislature controlled by your own party is no guarantee that your policies will pass quickly, or resemble the original initiatives once they do. Those who dislike large government programs see this as a benefit. But when gridlock results in a government shutdown over budget disputes—or the failure to respond in a timely fashion to a looming economic or military crisis—presidential systems can spiral out of control. The resulting chaos can lead to attempts to fix the source of the problem. This is generally achieved either through concentrating more power in the hands of the president, or through the overthrow of the entire system in favor of an authoritarian one.

Disadvantage #3: Creeping authoritarianism. Many presidential systems increasingly concentrate power in the hands of the president over time, a process known as **creeping authoritarianism**. Even when there is no crisis to trigger "authoritarianization," presidents tend to enjoy their power. They may become frustrated with the checks and balances built into the system, and find ways to overcome them—including through amendments to the country's constitution. As presidential power increases, political opponents may face repression, elections may be rigged, and civil rights may be taken away from the general population.

Creeping authoritarianism is the gradual transition from a presidential democracy into an authoritarian system. Over time, power becomes increasingly concentrated in the hands of the president. This leads the legislature to become little more than a rubber stamp, encourages the president to repress political opponents, and can result in sham elections and/or the loss of civil rights for the general population.

Surprisingly, legislatures may go along with these steps, even supporting constitutional sanctioning of excessive presidential power. This is most likely when the president's political party has a majority of seats in the legislature, but it can also happen when a president becomes very popular. Students (and policymakers) in the West like to think that the general population dislikes political tyranny, but across time and in different settings the masses have had a soft spot for charismatic and powerful chief executives. A president can project charisma in a way a 500–seat parliament cannot.

The Russian political system worries many observers of Russian politics for this very reason. Technically a semipresidential system, the Russian system places a great deal of power in the hands of the president. Boris Yeltsin, Russian president from the collapse of the Soviet Union until 1999, displayed authoritarian tendencies at times. His successor, Vladimir Putin, turned these tendencies into creeping authoritarianism before becoming prime minister in 2008.

The Presidential Systems of Mexico, Brazil, Nigeria, and Iran

Of the ten Topic in Countries (TIC) cases, four of them are presidential systems, giving the role of the chief executive to a position, the president, separated from the legislative branch. The Mexican, Brazilian, and Nigerian presidential systems resemble the American one in many ways. They all have a president who, when the president's party controls a majority of the seats in the legislature, can be quite powerful in setting the political agenda. The Iranian system is more complicated. Because it lacks a prime minister, it is typically labeled as a presidential system. However, as discussed in detail later in the chapter, its executive arrangements are complicated, and the power of the president is checked not only by the legislative branch but also by other, unelected executive positions designed to protect the system's theocratic character.

Mexico

As a presidential system, Mexico fuses the head of government and head of state into one position. Prior to the political liberalization of the 1980s and 1990s, the president ruled over Mexican politics with few checks on his power. The period of liberalization that culminated with Vicente Fox's victory in the 2000 presidential election, however, changed the rules of the game. The system was still presidential, but the president could no longer easily overcome the resistance of a political opposition.

Fox was the first Mexican president in seven decades not from the Institutional Revolutionary Party (PRI). He also became the first president during that period who was elected without his party controlling a majority of the seats in the national legislature. This feature, combined with Mexico's embrace of democracy, makes it impossible for the president to dictate to the legislature in the way that presidents could in the preceding era of PRI dominance. Fox and his successor, Felipe Calderón, have both struggled to govern in a presidential system whose previously hollow checks on presidential power have, over the last decade, proven highly effective.

Brazil

When the military surrendered power in 1985 after two decades of rule, many who had opposed the military supported the creation of a parliamentary system. Instead, the 1988 Brazilian Constitution continued the presidential approach of the Second Republic (1946–1964). As noted in Chapter 6, the current Brazilian system is the result of a compromise between those who sought broader participation and decentralized democracy and those who wished to preserve political order, and their own privileges. The result is a political system that frequently experiences deadlock between a powerful presidency and a fragmented legislature.

Thus, Brazil's political system resembles Mexico's in many ways, even sharing the same names for the two houses of the national legislature: the Chamber of Deputies and the Senate. Yet, the Brazilian system gives its president both advantages and disadvantages versus his Mexican counterpart. On paper, the president in Brazil is more powerful than in Mexico. Brazil has many more political parties in the legislature than Mexico, however, making it even more difficult for the president to put together a coalition in the legislature to pass important policy initiatives.

IN THEORY AND PRACTICE

Brazil and Theories about Presidential Systems

The differences between presidential and parliamentary systems constitute a central theme of this chapter. The consequences of adopting a parliamentary approach versus a presidential one have been at the center of numerous comparative politics debates over the last several decades. One of the most cited exchanges on this topic appears in a 1990 issue of the *Journal of Democracy*.[3] The debate captures two contrasting views about parliamentary and presidential systems in new democracies. This box addresses the first of these views, as articulated by Juan Linz. The second, Donald Horowitz's response to Linz, is the topic of the "In Theory and Practice" box on Nigeria on page 243.

Linz's argument, what one can label a **theory of parliamentary superiority**, is largely drawn from his observations of countries such as Brazil, with strong presidents and divided legislatures. In such situations, dramatic confrontations between presidents and legislatures have often provided the context for military coups in Latin America. Even when conflicts do not result in breakdown, deadlock may force presidents faced with uncooperative legislatures to go outside the process of democratic debate and legislate by decree.

Linz also argues that presidential systems are too rigid and too "zero-sum"—where a gain by one side is always balanced with a loss by the other side—to produce healthy democracies. It is extremely difficult to get rid of an incompetent president who has lost the confidence of the public, but easy for a parliamentary government to go back to the people with little more than a no-confidence vote of the parliament. Finally, the powers of the president represent an intoxicating prize that may tempt rivals to break the rules, cheat, lie, or commit fraud rather than risk losing the presidential office.

These are legitimate concerns. In Brazil, acceptance of illegal campaign contributions played a part in President Fernando Collor de Mello's downfall in 1992. Moreover, no posttransition president has enjoyed anything close to a majority of his own party in the legislature. The result, as predicted, has often been presidential rule by decree. Alternatively, presidents have governed by bribing opposition congressmen to support their initiatives, an approach that encourages corruption and diminishes the legitimacy of democratic government. Less dramatically, but more crucially, voters cannot expect their chosen president to be able to pass the policies he promises to enact. In a

Juan Linz's **theory of parliamentary superiority** attacks presidential systems for encouraging political conflicts without providing the means to resolve them.

parliamentary system, either the parliament cooperates with the prime minister or the government falls. This powerful incentive for cooperation is missing in presidential systems.

Nevertheless, Brazilians have repeatedly chosen presidentialism over parliamentary government. Brazil actually tried parliamentary government twice, once during the monarchy, and once during a brief period from 1961–1963. Neither experiment was a success. The first parliamentary government ended with the empire, the second with a referendum to restore presidentialism. Still, in 1993 a new proposal was floated to change the system to parliamentary government. Provoked

by the collapse of Collor's government, some people argued that putting so much power in the hands of one person was dangerous. However, the ability of the Congress to remove Collor through institutional means convinced most people that presidentialism could work. Once again, parliamentarism was defeated in a public referendum. In each case, Brazilians chose stability over efficiency. As Chapter 10 spells out, Brazilian parties are weak. In such a context, parliamentarism may produce only unstable governments. Presidentialism, Brazilians believed, offered the stability of fixed terms with the ability to remove a criminal from office.

Nigeria

The history of postcolonial Nigeria has been one of alternating short periods of unstable democracy and long periods of (only somewhat more stable) military authoritarianism. As such, an understanding of the roles of the president and legislature is impossible without understanding the influence of the military. It is difficult to consolidate democracy in a country with a tradition of military intervention in politics (see Chapter 8). The executive and legislature cannot focus only on each other; they must always be looking over their shoulders.

Nigeria actually had been a parliamentary system, with the British monarch as the official head of state, upon its independence from

Britain in 1960. By the time the military intervened for the first time (1966), the country had broken official ties with the United Kingdom. Drawing inspiration more from the United States than its former colonial ruler, the country turned to a presidential system when democracy was attempted for the second time (1979–1983). It has maintained this approach for the aborted Third Republic (1993) and the current Fourth Republic (1999–present). The first elected president of the Fourth Republic, Olusegun Obasanjo, was a former military leader. After serving two terms he stepped down, paving the way for his chosen successor, Umaru Yar'Adua, to be elected in a disputed vote in 2007.

IN THEORY AND PRACTICE

Nigeria and Theories About Presidential Systems

The In Theory and Practice box on Brazil introduced Juan Linz's arguments for the superiority of parliamentary systems. In response to Linz, Donald Horowitz argues that presidential systems can be more beneficial to new democracies than parliamentary ones. His **theory of presidential system design** criticizes Linz's characterization

of presidential systems. Pointing out that Linz's emphasis on Latin American cases such as Brazil

Donald Horowitz's **theory of presidential system design** points to ways that certain presidential system features can enhance political stability compared with certain parliamentary approaches.

ignores problems with parliamentary systems in Africa and Asia, Horowitz challenges Linz's association of presidentialism with winner-take-all electoral rules and the lack of coalitions in the legislature. He states that such features are the norm in certain parliamentary systems as well and points out particular approaches to selecting the president that can foster stability rather than limit it. Horowitz argues that choosing the president through a system that requires widespread support for the ultimate winner across different ethnic groups, for example, makes presidential elections a source of unity rather than division in ethnically divided societies.[4]

Nigeria is a particularly instructive case in which to examine the Linz-Horowitz debate. Following independence, Nigeria was initially a parliamentary democracy; from the Second Republic on, it employed the presidential model. Nigeria also applies to many of the points that Horowitz raises about crafting a presidential system to address the flaws Linz highlights. For example, Nigeria established rules requiring successful presidential candidates to demonstrate considerable electoral support in more than one region of the country (see Chapter 10).

Horowitz's arguments help explain why Nigerians adopted the presidential system that they did, and Nigeria certainly demonstrates how such rules can be applied in practice. At the same time, it is hard to call Nigeria a shining example of presidential system stability. The Second Republic collapsed after only a few years, and the Third Republic never got off the ground. While the Fourth Republic survived the transition of presidential power from Olusegun Obasanjo to Umaru Yar'Adua, the year preceding Yar'Adua's election was one of great turmoil, and many inside and outside of Nigeria questioned the fairness of the elections. Thus, Horowitz's theory helps us understand certain choices made in Nigeria. In the end, however, Nigeria's flawed experiences with both the parliamentary and presidential approaches highlight that neither Linz's nor Horowitz's theory provides the full story of democratic success in countries like Nigeria.

Iran

For much of the period following the 1979 Revolution, discussing Iran's legislature and president took a backseat to focusing on its religious clerics. Iran's theocratic features drove political developments more than the president's and legislature's institutional powers. Discussions of Iranian politics in the West focused on the position of the Supreme Leader, which for the decade following the Revolution was Ayatollah Ruhollah Khomeini.

For a time in the late 1990s and early 2000s, however, Iran began to look a little more like a representative democracy. This led some political analysts of Iran to discuss the potential for genuine democratization in the country, perhaps led by a popular president supportive of political reform. Casual observers of the country put great stock—far too much stock—in the ability of the president to foster political reform. Beginning in 2004, a series of events called into question such optimistic notes. Once again, observers used the president, who after 2005 was Mahmoud Ahmadinejad, to symbolize the direction of the country.

While focusing hope for change or condemnation for repression on the president of Iran is understandable, it is also a flawed practice. The Iranian political system remains one in which political power is dispersed in a more complex way than most casual observers of Iran understand. In many ways, it resembles a presidential system more than a parliamentary one, but the presidency is less powerful than other, unelected institutions in the Iranian government. This includes the Supreme Leader, currently Ayatollah Ali Hoseini-Khamenei, who quietly remains a more influential figure than Ahmadinejad, even as Ahmadinejad garners headlines in the West.

Semipresidential Systems

Sometimes, the political system combines the basic characteristics of both a parliamentary and a presidential system. This **semipresidential system** is the approach in several European countries—particularly among the post-Communist states, but also in France, Austria, Portugal, and Finland. The system has a prime minister who is responsible to the parliament—and often a member of it—as well as a directly elected president. The president is separated from the legislative branch and, of principal interest for this discussion, is *more than just a figurehead*. In a semipresidential system, the president is responsible for many, but not all, of the tasks of the chief executive in a presidential system. In some cases, all government ministers report to the prime minister. In others, some ministers report to the prime minister while others report to the president. Because both executive officials have important powers, comparativists also commonly call this a "dual executive" system.

To be a semipresidential system requires more than the presence of both a president and prime minister. Many parliamentary systems have figurehead presidents. Like parliamentary systems, semipresidential systems generally separate the positions of head of state (the president) and head of government (the prime minister). But as head of state, the president is never just a figurehead in this dual executive format. Both the president and prime minister have noteworthy powers.

Advantages of the Semipresidential System

Advantage #1: Providing cover for the president. A semipresidential system can shield the president from criticism. Unpopular policies can be blamed on the prime minister. To the extent that a popular, stable president is a positive—and countries with semipresidential systems, such as post-Soviet Russia and France after 1958, have often desperately needed stability—the president's ability to deflect criticism onto a prime minister can be helpful.

Advantage #2: The ability to remove unpopular prime ministers with the stability of fixed terms. In most semipresidential systems, the parliament has the power to remove an unpopular prime minister. At the same time, semipresidential systems also have fixed terms for the president, which help to stabilize the system. Theoretically, this offers the best of both worlds: responsiveness to the will of an unhappy electorate without the revolving door effect of some parliamentary systems.

Advantage #3: Additional checks and balances. Given their creativity in formulating a system with such diffuse power, it is surprising that the American founders did not think of the semipresidential system. It adds yet another veto point. Though the president can dismiss the prime minister in most semipresidential systems, this does not necessarily mean the prime minister will blindly do the president's bidding. At a minimum, semipresidential systems take the direct control of important segments of the bureaucracy away from the president, limiting the tendency for presidents to concentrate more power in their own hands over time.

Disadvantages of the Semipresidential System

Disadvantage #1: Confusion about accountability. Parliamentary systems give voters a relatively clear sense of who is responsible for policy successes and failures; presidential systems make this more difficult, particularly when there is divided government. Semipresidential systems add another layer of complexity for voters.

Consider a situation in which a president and a prime minister belong to different political parties, the prime minister's party controls

---

A **semipresidential system** combines the basic features of a parliamentary and a presidential system. It has both a directly elected president with significant powers and a prime minister who is responsible to the parliament, and often to the president as well.

the parliament, the country's economy is performing poorly, and parliamentary elections are approaching. Voters might decide that the prime minister, as head of government, and the prime minister's party are responsible for the poor performance and vote for another party. Then again, the president also has a role in economic decisions. To justly hold accountable the majority party, voters would have to first weigh the relative role in economic matters of the president, the prime minister, and the prime minister's party. Clearly such situations pose challenges for voters. The challenge is even greater in practice, since the countries in which semipresidential systems are most common—for example, the post-Communist states of the former Soviet Union—also tend to be those in which voters are least experienced with democratic elections.

Disadvantage #2: Confusion and inefficiency in the legislative process. A basic distinction between parliamentary and presidential systems is the extent to which the executive is responsible to the legislature. In presidential systems, the executive is accountable to voters, while in a parliamentary system the legislature can dismiss the chief executive. In semipresidential systems, the capacity for votes of confidence make the prime minister responsible to parliament, but the president may also have the power to dismiss the prime minister. The prime minister faces difficulties formulating policy that pleases all those who need to be pleased. As a result, bickering between the president and the parliament can lead to incoherent policy and to the prime minister becoming a sacrificial lamb. It is not surprising that semipresidential systems often go through few presidents but many prime ministers.

The Semipresidential Systems of France, the Russian Federation, and China

While they are very different in the extent to which they are democratic, France, Russia, and China all employ a semipresidential political system that combines features of the presidential and parliamentary approaches. They all, for example, have both a president and a prime minister with substantial political powers. In all three, the president has also been a more visible symbol of the regime than the prime minister, although with Vladimir Putin moving from the position of president to that of prime minister in Russia, it remains to be seen how much of the presidency's power he takes with him.

France

Like Nigeria, France provides an example of different approaches to designing a democratic political system at different points in time. The French Third and Fourth Republics demonstrate both the adaptability and the dangers of parliamentary systems. While *governments* changed frequently, the *regime* of the Third Republic showed great stability. It was modern France's most durable constitutional order, in force from the 1870s until the Nazi blitzkrieg of 1940. France specialist Stanley Hoffmann described the Third Republic as a "republican synthesis" or consensus on the state, but also a "stalemate society" that constrained social and economic change.[5] The Fourth Republic was quite different. Despite political volatility, decolonization, and the war in Algeria (at the time a department of France), the Fourth Republic included significant reforms of the administration of economic and social life that helped bring about the "30 Glorious Years" of industrial development and social transformation at levels previously unseen in France.

In comparison, the Fifth Republic was crafted to provide continuity and stability in governance, ensure the capacity and resolve needed to modernize as well as meet crises, and minimize the importance of partisan bickering. The Fifth Republic was initiated literally at the barrel of a gun, with the military poised to overthrow the government, and was the vision of retired general and former Free French leader Charles de Gaulle.

Tailored to de Gaulle's personality and his conception of the country's political crisis, the result was an idiosyncratic system of hybrids and compromises intended to secure a top-down transformation of society. The complex mix of powers across the institutions—allowing the president to oust the prime minister and individual ministers despite having no official power to fire them—left even the noted scholars of the day unable to agree on how to measure the Fifth Republic.[6] The French people, however, were less tentative about the new system. Despite all the compromises and idiosyncrasies, more than 80 percent of French voters approved the Fifth Republic in a national referendum.

Did You Know? Prior to the establishment in 1958 of its current semipresidential system, France was among the world's least stable parliamentary systems based on the duration in power of a particular government. During the Third and Fourth Republics—1870 to 1940 and 1946 to 1958—French governments lasted on average only around eight months.

The Russian Federation After his election as president of the Russian republic of the Soviet Union (the RSFSR) in 1991, Boris Yeltsin had to work with a number of sources of power within the political structure. A new legislative body, the Congress of People's Deputies (CPD), was the Russian republic's version of the same body created by Gorbachev at the Soviet level. A smaller bicameral legislative body, the RSFSR Supreme Soviet, met more often and held greater power than the Russian CPD. There was also a government, headed by a prime minister, responsible to the legislature. Add in a constitutional court and a vice president—not to mention the Soviet government

Did You Know? For the first six months after the collapse of the Soviet Union, Boris Yeltsin was both president and prime minister of Russia. Eventually, he surrendered the prime minister position to Yegor Gaidar. This did little to solve the ongoing political disputes in the country, however, as Russia spiraled toward the October 1993 crisis that led Yeltsin to order the use of military force against the parliament.

under the increasingly shaky control of Mikhael Gorbachev—and Yeltsin found himself in a complicated and challenging setting.

The Soviet Union collapsed at the end of 1991. The RSFSR government became the government of the Russian Federation. Though Yeltsin was quite popular, the country faced a number of problems, including a horrible economy. The legislature gave Yeltsin strong powers to address the problems, including the ability to issue decrees related to the economy. As 1992 went on, relations between the parliament and the president began to break down. By 1993, hostilities were openly apparent. Yeltsin faced opposition from his own vice president, and increasingly from the country's constitutional court. In early October 1993, the dispute boiled over. Under Yeltsin's orders, troops surrounded the parliament building and took it by force.

In December 1993, a national vote ratified the new constitution and selected members of a new parliament. The new constitution established a semipresidential system, with a strong president and comparatively weak prime minister. The vice presidency was eliminated. These changes led to significant stability in the position of the president. Because the president could easily dismiss the prime minister, however, there was a great deal of turnover of prime ministers. From early 1998 to late 1999 alone, Russia had five different prime ministers.

This trend continued under Vladimir Putin, until he stepped down at the end of his second term as president—as he was constitutionally required to do—to serve instead as prime

Figure 7.2   The Structure of the Russian Government

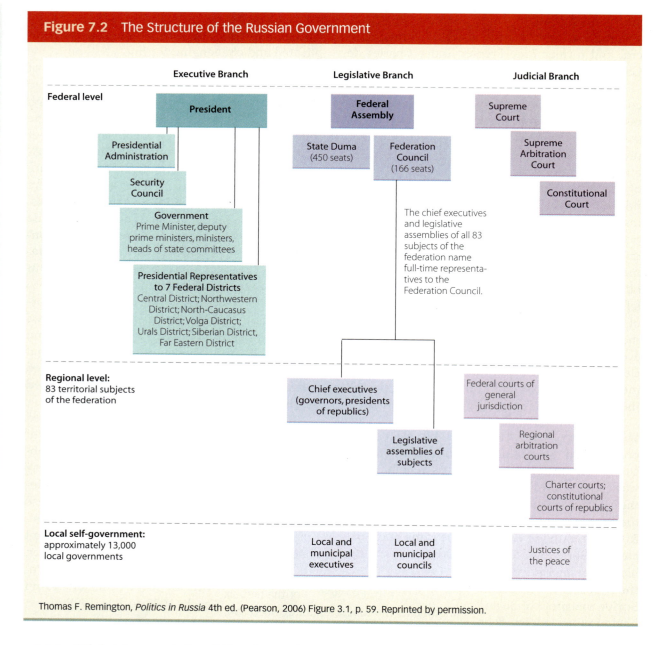

Thomas F. Remington, *Politics in Russia* 4th ed. (Pearson, 2006) Figure 3.1, p. 59. Reprinted by permission.

minister. While it is too early for a full understanding of the implications of Putin's choice, it is likely that Russia will remain a semipresidential system. The president may lose some power to the prime minister over the years, but it seems unlikely that Russia will quickly turn into a parliamentary system with a figurehead president, who represents the state but has little say over its day-to-day governing.

China

Trying to understand China's political institutions can be frustrating. China is a semipresidential system, with both a president and prime minister (known as the "premier"). There is also a dual hierarchy of state and party administrators, with nearly all top government officials as high-ranking members of the Chinese Communist Party (CCP).

In addition, for much of China's Communist period, official government position corresponded little to actual political power. Mao Zedong was chairman of the CCP, but he ruled more through his personal legitimacy as leader of the revolution than through his institutional powers. When Deng Xiaoping eventually emerged as the leader after Mao's death, he held neither the position of premier of the government nor general secretary of the CCP, the party leadership position that replaced the position of chairman after Mao's death. Perhaps indicating where much of the power in China lay at the time, the most important official position Deng held was chairman of the CCP Central Military Commission and its government counterpart, the state Central Military Commission.

Following Mao's death, the official positions in the state institutions began to correspond more closely to the individuals with actual political power. This process has accelerated in recent years. Deng's replacement as leader of the country, Jiang Zemin, took over his positions as leader of the military, while also holding the position of president of the country and general secretary of the CCP. In a move that highlighted the growing importance of official government positions, China's current president, Hu Jintao, was vice president under Jiang.

With the increased importance of official governmental positions, students and scholars of Chinese politics must pay closer attention to which individual holds which political office. This does not mean, however, that one can look at those positions alone. Knowing the leaders' personalities and connections remains crucial to understanding Chinese politics.

Legislatures

Legislatures are multimember bodies that play a central role—in some cases only officially—in the creation of political policy. The term comes from their legislating role. In democracies, their members are elected by the general public. As such, the legislature's members are often called representatives. Most nondemocracies also have legislatures. In nondemocratic states, legislatures often *appear* to play an essential role in the development of national laws. In these cases, legislatures add some legitimacy by giving the impression of a constitutional power structure that represents the interests of the general public. In truth, legislatures in most nondemocracies serve only to "rubber stamp" judgments of the executive.

Tasks of Legislatures

Legislatures' official responsibilities, and their de facto power, vary greatly from country to country. Even within democracies, the functions of legislatures differ significantly depending on whether the system is a parliamentary or presidential one. Still, all legislatures have certain tasks or responsibilities regardless of the political system. These include legislating; authorizing taxes; approving government spending; providing services to constituents or the general population; selection, approval, and dismissal of officials; and general oversight of the executive.

Legislating   The primary function of a legislature is to make laws. In presidential systems like the United States, this function is shared with

Legislatures are multimember government institutions. Though their role as lawmaker may be shared with other institutions, lawmaking is formally the core responsibility of legislatures. In some cases, legislatures may simply rubber stamp decisions made by the executive. In other cases, they play a crucial role in the development of government policy. They also authorize government expenditures, intervene on behalf of constituents, approve and dismiss government officials, and oversee executive branch activities.

the executive branch; the chief executive must approve of legislative initiatives before they become law. Presidents cannot force their policy preferences on the legislature, while the legislature cannot—except in cases of an override of a presidential veto—make laws without the support of the president.

In a parliamentary system, the situation is different. A bill's passage requires only the legislature's approval. A bill may have to go through multiple readings, and many parliaments have quite elaborate committee structures, but it is ultimately up to the legislature to determine the bill's fate. In addition, much of the work is done behind the scenes by the government ministries most connected to the policy issue of the bill, even before the bill is submitted. By the time the prime minister's government presents a bill to parliament—and the vast majority of bills in parliamentary systems are submitted by the sitting government—most of the potentially controversial issues have already been resolved.

Authorizing Government Spending The executive branch is in charge of administering government policy, but doing so costs money and legislatures often have significant control over the raising and spending of government funds. Legislatures craft and approve tax policies, they authorize the government to spend money on specific programs, and they pass an overall budget. Thus, while making laws is the heart and soul of a legislature, its taxing and spending decisions are the guts. The best government program ever conceived has little chance of success if there is no money to fund it.

In democracies, the budget can be a source of tension between the legislature and the chief executive. Policies passed into law often need a separate authorization in order to obtain funding; this can lead to heated debates. The legislature's fiscal role is a key part of the checks and balances system in the United States, with the House of Representatives taking the lead on taxing and spending. Temporary government shutdowns

(e.g., in the United States during the Clinton Administration) can result. In other countries, tensions have been worse; a constitutional crisis over the budget in Australia in the mid-1970s resulted in the removal of the prime minister.

Once more, legislatures in nondemocracies have little real power in this area. They may *officially* authorize spending, and can even play a role in working out some of the details of revenue generation and distribution. But on important budget decisions, legislatures again become rubber stamps—doing the leader's bidding on budgetary matters.

Constituency Service/Omsbuds Activities Legislators also provide service through their intervention on behalf of members of the general population. In countries with a district system, where members of the legislature are elected to represent particular districts, this task is generally known as **constituency service**. In countries with a proportional representation electoral system, these actions are often called **omsbuds activities**. Though generally unfamiliar to Americans, this term is common in Europe and other parts of the world. The term comes from the Swedish word *omsbudsman*, referring to the individual who provides the assistance. Omsbuds activities often involve members of the government advocating on behalf of an individual with government bureaucrats.

The amount of time a given representative devotes to service activities varies from country to country and from legislator to legislator. Because systems with electoral districts make clear who voters' representatives are, representatives in such systems are expected to make constituency service a central part of their jobs.

> In a system with legislative districts, legislators' activities on behalf of particular residents in their districts are known as **constituency service.**
>
> In systems where legislators do not represent particular districts, these undertakings are called **omsbuds activities.**

Thus, service activities are more common in systems that choose representatives from electoral districts than in systems using proportional representation approaches. Within a given district system, those representatives whose reelection prospects are less definite may also worry more about constituency service. Successful constituency service activities build goodwill with residents of the district, and they can be effective stories on the campaign trail.

Selection, Approval, and Removal of Government Officials

Legislators often play an important role in selecting, approving, or removing other government officials. This can include key ministerial appointments in the cabinet of the chief executive or judicial nominees. Some parliamentary systems also feature a weak president, who is directly selected by parliament.

In parliamentary systems, the legislature removes executive branch officials through actions such as a vote of no confidence, discussed earlier. In presidential systems, the legislature can remove the chief executive through a process called impeachment. Similar moves may be made against other members of the executive branch or legislators accused of improper conduct in office, but this process is generally much less onerous than impeachment of a president.

Oversight of the Executive

Legislatures often oversee and investigate the activities of the executive branch. This oversight capacity takes both a regular and an extraordinary form. Government officials report to committees or to the legislature as a whole at regular intervals, but they may also be required to testify at special hearings. These special hearings often take place before regular legislative committees, but the legislature may also authorize ad hoc commissions to direct an investigation, such as the 9/11 Commission in the United States, which investigated the events leading up to the terrorist attacks on the United States in 2001.

APPLYING CONCEPTS

What Does It Mean to Be a "Representative"?

Though members of a legislative body are often referred to as representatives, what representation should mean in practice has been a source of debate throughout history. There are two basic ideas: representative as *mirror of public opinion* and representative as *trustee of the public good*. Under the "mirror" notion, representatives should ascertain the views of the general population about a particular issue and reflect those views with their votes. The "trustee" vision, on the other hand, sees representatives as leaders whose job is to determine what is in the population's best interest and support those positions, even if the population disagrees with them. How can one represent a group of people without reflecting their opinions? Representative government not only reflects the will of the people, but it also assumes that the citizenry may not be adequately informed about most political issues to make reasonable judgments.

Edmund Burke, a political figure during the late 1700s in Britain, made a strong statement supportive of the idea of representatives as trustees. Giving a speech in 1774 to the residents of Bristol, the district that had just elected him to the House of Commons, Burke told his constituents not to expect him to reflect their opinions. He admitted he knew little about the district, but he also argued that this made no difference. According to Burke, a representative's first and only task is to serve the public interest of the entire country.

Regular reports and testimony are generally less newsworthy than extraordinary investigations, although the questioning of government ministers in the British House of Commons during Question Time is typically testy and can be one of the more enjoyable political events to watch.

Other Aspects of Legislatures

In addition to the various duties of legislatures, those who study the importance of legislatures and their design point to a number of other factors that are important to take into account. These include the number of members in the legislature, the length of the members' terms, whether the legislature is unicameral or bicameral, and the role of committees in the legislature's activities. The answers to these questions vary from case to case, and the particular combination of traits can have an impact on the legislature's effectiveness, the kinds of policies it produces, and its relations with the executive branch.

How Many Members? The size of national legislatures varies greatly around the world. Some legislatures have as few as a dozen members. Others, such as the Chinese legislature, have thousands. As a general rule, the larger the population in a country, the larger its legislature. This makes sense, since countries with more people often face more complex political choices. A larger number of members allows better representation of local interests in large and heavily populated countries, as well as a degree of specialization within the legislature. A legislative body with too few members in such a setting would overburden its members.

There is a point, however, at which a legislature becomes too big. It is hard to imagine genuine debate, a useful exchange of ideas, or efficient lawmaking in a legislative body with more than one thousand members. As a result, legislatures of that size, including in China, may not meet on a regular basis, relying instead on standing committees authorized to pass legislation on their behalf.

How Long Do Members Serve? The length of time that members serve varies from legislature to legislature and depends on the official length of a single term in office and legislators' prospects for reelection. In presidential systems, the term of office is fixed. U.S. House of Representatives members, for example, serve two-year terms. A more common term length around the world is four years. In parliamentary systems, terms can vary from election to election, due to the provisions for the calling of early elections, generally absent in presidential systems.

Even a short single term can lead to a long time in office if a member is continually reelected. "Career politicians," those who serve in political office for much of their adult lives, are not unusual in the United States. Sitting U.S. Senator Robert Byrd of West Virginia, for example, was first elected to the Senate in 1958 (and reelected most recently in 2006), while Senators Daniel Inouye from Hawaii and Ted Kennedy from Massachusetts were originally elected in 1962. Although there is more turnover in the U.S. House of Representatives and the Senate than many people think—the average House member serves about six terms, while the average senator serves only around two terms—American politicians remain in office longer than their counterparts in many other countries. This is largely due to the use of electoral districts rather than proportional representation voting (see Chapter 10), the creation of "safe seats" (congressional districts with boundaries drawn to insure that the incumbent will win reelection), and the importance of money in the American electoral process, which benefits incumbents.

Is the Legislature Unicameral or Bicameral? Most legislatures are made up of one or two houses (also known as "chambers"). A legislature consisting of just one house is known as **unicameral**. A system with two houses, such as the United States, has a **bicameral** legislature. Internationally, unicameral legislatures are not

Unicameral legislatures have only one house (chamber).

Bicameral legislatures have two houses. In a bicameral system, the two houses (or chambers) are usually referred to as the lower and upper houses, and the powers between the two houses may be relatively equal or, more commonly, weighted in favor of the lower house.

unusual. They make a great deal of sense in countries less concerned than the United States with separation of powers, those more eager for efficient lawmaking, or in unitary systems, discussed in Chapter 6, where there is no need to have members of the government represent different regions at the national level.

The two houses of a bicameral system are labeled the upper house and lower house. The relative power between the two houses of the legislature in these systems varies. In some cases, the houses are almost equal in power. More often, the lower house is the more powerful and the first to consider legislation. In these cases, the upper house may provide a check on the power of the lower house, but it rarely initiates government action. In extreme cases, the upper house is more like a rubber stamp. At best, it can delay legislation but cannot stop it.

Upper houses also vary in how members are selected. Even in democracies, the general population may not directly elect members of the upper house. In federal democratic systems, like that established in Germany, they may be appointed by the legislatures of the various regional governments. This was also the method for selecting members of the U.S. Senate prior to the Seventeenth Amendment ratified in 1913, which established the direct election of senators. In other cases, such as Canada, the prime minister appoints upper house members in proportion to the population of the regions of the country.

The previous chapter introduced the idea of "veto points" in a political system. Bicameral legislatures have one more veto point than unicameral legislatures—and even more if committees are powerful. As a result, bicameral systems generally produce policy more slowly, sometimes falling victim to gridlock. The additional veto point also offers a check on the ambitions of a majority party in a way a single-chamber legislature does not. A majority party may represent the will of the majority at one moment, but not necessarily the interests of the country in the long run. Bicameral systems are also more compatible with elements of federalism and can better represent local or regional interests at the national level.

How Powerful Are Legislative Committees?

A **committee** is a group of members in a legislative body that works on a particular set of topics. Most legislative bodies use them to help craft bills prior to a final vote. They may also play an important role in the oversight process, with certain committees monitoring the activities of particular executive ministries, agencies, or departments. Committees allow members of a legislature to develop and use expertise in certain issue areas, but powerful committees can also slow down the process of formulating and implementing new policies.

Most committee activities take place in a permanent group that meets on a regular basis, called a **standing committee**. Such committees often mirror the agencies, departments, or ministries of the executive. A committee that regularly addresses environmental issues would craft a bill on environmental protection. In addition, a legislature may create an **ad hoc committee** (or commission) to deal with specific important problems that do not easily fit into the existing permanent committee structure.

The power of committees varies. The committees in the U.S. Congress are among the most powerful in the world. Some parliamentary systems, particularly in northern Europe, also place a large amount of power in the hands of committees. Although the prime minister and the cabinet come up with the ideas behind most legislative acts, the committees in these countries hammer out many of the details and may even alter the policy proposals dramatically during the course of their deliberations.

A **committee** is a group of members of a legislature that works on particular topics.

A **standing committee** is one which meets on a regular basis.

An **ad hoc committee** deals with special circumstances that do not fit neatly into the existing committee structure.

The Legislature in the United Kingdom, Germany, and India

Because the United Kingdom, Germany, and India are parliamentary systems, the legislatures at times appear to be rubber stamps for the will of the prime minister. Yet, the design and activities of the legislatures remain crucial to understanding important political outcomes in these countries. All three of the legislatures have the final say in crafting political policy, and even when the prime minister's party controls a majority of parliament's seats in the United Kingdom, the prime minister does not always get his or her way. In Germany and India, parliament creates challenges for the executive branch, whether it be the role of the upper house in Germany in representing the country's regions or the tendency for spirited debate to slow down the policy process in India.

The United Kingdom

The emergence of **parliamentary supremacy** is among the most important developments in British history. Under parliamentary supremacy, no other domestic body of political power— neither the monarch in the past nor the judicial system today—can block an act of parliament. As a result, parliamentary statutes are also, by definition, constitutional. All that keeps parliament in line domestically is a quite powerful cultural norm that individuals in positions of political power have a responsibility to act in the interest of the general public.

Parliament is the center of British political power, and the House of Commons is the center of parliamentary power—so much so that the term parliament is often used to refer to the House of Commons alone rather than to the full bicameral legislature. Although parliament was established in the middle of the thirteenth century, the House of Commons did not gain its fully dominant position until 1911, when the Parliament Act stripped the House of Lords of veto power, replacing it with the power only to delay the passage of legislation.

In the House of Commons, members sit on long benches facing the middle of the room. Because members of the government are also sitting Members of Parliament (MPs), these individuals have front row seats near the prime minister during parliamentary debates and are known as **frontbenchers**. MPs without seats in the government (or the shadow government) are **backbenchers**. The opposition party's MPs sit on benches across the room from the ruling party. As a result, the opposition party leader, an officially recognized position in Westminster systems, sits directly across from the prime minister. The opposition members who make up the shadow cabinet sit across from their frontbencher counterparts in the ruling government.

The British take the concept of a parliamentary shadow government, introduced earlier in the chapter, seriously in other ways as well. Twenty days of each parliamentary session are designated "opposition days." On these days, the opposition parties choose the subjects to be debated on the floor. Although these debates do not generally produce policy changes, they

---

Parliamentary supremacy is a feature of the Westminster system in which no other branch of government can block an act supported by parliament.

In the United Kingdom, **frontbenchers** are members of the government who sit in the front row near the prime minister during parliamentary debates.

MPs who do not hold seats in the government (or shadow government) are called **backbenchers**.

Westminster, home to the British parliament
(©Jupiter Images)

do allow the public to see those in the opposition party who would hold positions of power if that party were to win the next parliamentary election.

These shadow positions also allow future party leaders to rise through the ranks of the opposition party. Before becoming prime minister, for example, Tony Blair held the Labour Party's "shadow" minister positions for treasury, energy, and employment, and became shadow home secretary in 1994. He then ascended to the position of shadow prime minister, where he led a successful campaign to remake the image of the Labour Party. The result was three consecutive electoral victories for Labour (1997, 2001, and 2005) under Blair's leadership.

Because the prime minister usually enjoys a sizeable majority in parliament, defeats on the floor of the legislature are uncommon. Amendments submitted without the support of the government rarely pass. Backbenchers occasionally break ranks with their party leadership, but almost never in cases where it could mean the defeat of the motion under consideration. As a result, the House of Commons has few legislative surprises. Successful motions of no confidence are particularly rare; the last one to pass (by one vote) took place in March 1979. This led to the May 1979 elections that returned the Conservatives, under Margaret Thatcher, to power.

Members of parliament also respect their constituency service obligations. Many of these activities concern the health care system, which is free to the general population but which can involve lengthy waits prior to receiving care. Accordingly, many of the questions that MPs pose to cabinet ministers or the prime minister during Question Time relate to health care and often begin with a short story about a constituent whose efforts to receive adequate and timely care were obstructed.

The upper house of parliament, the House of Lords, has nearly 750 members, hundreds fewer than it had in 1999. Traditionally membership in the House of Lords was based on nobility. The British government also appointed members to serve alongside the nobility. These "life peers"—Lords members who serve for life—received their positions as reward for their service to the country (Margaret Thatcher was named a life peer, for example, in 1992).

In 1999, the government reformed the House of Lords to abolish most hereditary lords. Tony Blair appointed a commission to make recommendations for turning the House of Lords into a more typical upper chamber of a bicameral legislature. During the transition period, the life peers, numbering around 600, were retained. Only 92 of the more than 700 hereditary lords maintained their seats. The other members of the House of Lords, numbering a little more than 50, are bishops and archbishops of the Church of England and "law lords"—28 judges who serve as a court of final appeal for civil and criminal cases. The evolution of the House of Lords will be one of the more interesting processes for followers of British politics to watch over the next several years.

IN THEORY AND PRACTICE

The United Kingdom and Party Government Theory

Political scientists have long tried to explain and predict patterns in legislative behavior, developing a number of theories, including George Tsebelis's theory of the importance of veto points discussed in the previous chapter, to help understand legislative outcomes. One such argument, known as **party government theory**, is associated with political scientists Gary Cox and Matthew McCubbins.[7] Their approach challenges the assumption in other studies that party unity is based largely on individual party members' preferences. Rather, Cox and McCubbins argue that the key factor in legislative voting patterns is the extent to which the majority party leadership controls which bills are voted on. Although Cox and McCubbins focus mostly on the U.S. Congress, where the majority party leadership controls the daily legislative agenda, the power to manage the legislative agenda is typically greater in parliamentary systems, especially where there is a single majority party rather than a ruling coalition.

As a result, party government theory can be helpful in understanding legislative outcomes in the United Kingdom. In the House of Commons, practices like Question Time and "opposition days" provide a chance for debate on subjects that the government might prefer not to be discussed openly in parliament. The ability for voters to glimpse what the opposition parties would do in power does not translate into opposition party bills actually being considered for adoption. Instead, the government retains tight control over which bills get the required number of readings to stand as serious legislation. Thus, party government theory would predict quite stable voting patterns by MPs in a given session of parliament, and indeed that is the case.

> **Party government theory** suggests that the extent to which the rules of an institution allow the majority party to control the institution's actions drives the political outcomes emanating from the institution.

Think and Discuss

Many political science theories about legislatures and executives draw heavily from the American experience. Although comparativists also regularly use them, why might such theories be difficult to apply outside the United States?

Germany

The German parliament is bicameral. The lower house, the *Bundestag*, is directly elected every four years. Party discipline is a feature of the *Bundestag*, which means that the governing coalition can normally expect that the legislature will enact its program. On rare occasions, the chancellor has lost his or her majority in the *Bundestag*, and early elections have followed. Such episodes are rare, not only because an early election poses risks to sitting *Bundestag* deputies, but also because Germany's "constructive vote of no confidence" makes such revolts harder to realize. Under this provision, the opposition must agree in advance on a successor to the chancellor for the vote of no confidence to count. The designers of the Federal Republic's political system included this safeguard to foreclose the possibility of unstable governments that had plagued the Weimar Republic.

But the expression of federalism through the upper chamber, the *Bundesrat*, can pose even greater challenges to the chancellor's rule. The *Bundesrat*'s sixty-nine members are not directly elected by the people but appointed by the *Land* governments and must vote according to their instructions. (*Länder* that are more populous have up to six *Bundesrat* delegates each; smaller ones have as few as three delegates.) Since *Land* elections occur in rolling fashion and on a schedule that diverges from *Bundestag* elections, the chancellor faces the very real possibility of opposition parties holding a majority of the *Bundesrat*'s seats.

Also, the *Bundesrat* has formidable jurisdiction in the federal legislative process. Like the British House of Lords, the *Bundesrat* has delay powers, known as a **suspensive veto**, which the *Bundestag* can override. However, on matters that directly affect the interests of the *Länder*, the *Bundesrat* wields an absolute veto; without its assent, the legislation dies. The German Constitution's framers expected this would affect only 10 percent of federal legislation, but judicial decisions widened it to encompass about 60 percent of federal laws.[8] A constitutional reform worked out by the federal and *Land* governments is expected to circumscribe sharply this veto power.[9]

Even when the chancellor's party enjoys majorities in both chambers, there is no guarantee of legislative passage. This is because *Bundesrat* delegates may put *Land* interests ahead of party loyalty and extract compromises in exchange for their support of legislation. If such concessions are not forthcoming, the chancellor's program may face a *Bundesrat* veto.

India

The Indian parliament is bicameral, with the lower house, the *Lok Sabha*, being the paramount legislative body. The upper house is the *Rajya Sabha*. One of the features of both bodies is that protests, common outside parliament, have moved into parliament and taken up increasing amounts of time. According to the *Lok Sabha*'s records, during the first two sessions of the Fourteenth *Lok Sabha* (June 2–10, 2004 and July 5–August 26, 2004), 38 percent of the time the *Lok Sabha* sought to conduct business was lost to such disruptions.[10] As a result, budgets are sometimes adopted without any debate. There is a growing frustration among Indians with the inability of parliament to conduct business as it used to.

Normally there are three *Lok Sabha* sessions each year, the Budget session (February–May), the Monsoon session (July–September), and the Winter session (November–December).[11] The speaker, elected by the members of the *Lok Sabha*, presides over the house. The speaker may not be from the dominant party in the coalition government. There is a committee system by which considerable work on bills and other matters is undertaken. The *Lok Sabha* has the sole power to pass monetary bills. If there is a conflict over other bills, a joint session of the *Lok Sabha* and the upper house, the *Rajya Sabha*, is held. Since the former has twice as many seats as the latter, it is the *Lok Sabha*'s position which normally is dominant.

The *Lok Sabha* is directly elected from districts of similar size in population. Of the 545 members, 530 are elected from the federal units, 13 come from union territories, and 2—selected by the president—represent the Anglo-Indian community. Members serve for a maximum of five years, although a vote of no confidence may mean early elections.

The *Rajya Sabha* consists of 240 members, 228 elected by the legislatures of the federal units and union territories and 12 nominated by the president. They serve six-year terms with one-third elected every year. It meets continuously and is not disbanded if the government collapses and new *Lok Sabha* elections are held. The vice president formally presides over sessions, though most of the time the *Rajya Sabha*'s deputy chairman performs that function.

A **suspensive veto** is a power, often given to the upper house of a bicameral legislature, to delay enactment of legislation but not prevent it. The British House of Lords and the German *Bundesrat* both have suspensive veto authority.

The Legislature in Mexico, Brazil, Nigeria, and Iran

Because Mexico, Brazil, Nigeria, and Iran are presidential systems, one of the important themes from examinations of their national legislatures is the relationship between the legislature and the president. Prior to its recent democratization, such "relations" in Mexico involved the president dominating the legislative agenda. This is no longer the case. In Brazil, the situation is more complicated. The legislature has a difficult time working with the president but an equally difficult time controlling his activities. In Nigeria, the legislature's ability to check and balance the power of the president exists more on paper than in reality, while in Iran even a legislature that sees eye-to-eye with the president is constrained by other important political institutions.

Mexico

Mexico's legislature, the Congress, is bicameral. The upper house, the Senate, is similar to its American counterpart. It has 128 members: 4 each from Mexico's 31 states and 4 more from the Federal District of Mexico City, elected through a system that blends elements of first past the post (FPTP) single member districts and proportional representation (PR). Senators serve six-year terms. Unlike the United States, all the senators are elected at the same time, and these elections coincide with the presidential vote. The PRI dominated the Senate until 2000, when opposition parties won 68 seats. This contrasts starkly with the period from the late 1920s to the late 1980s, during which only one non-PRI candidate won a Senate seat.

The lower house is called the Chamber of Deputies. It has 500 members. Historically elected through single-member districts, PR features were added over the last few decades of the twentieth century to increase the number of non-PRI members. At present, 300 members come from the winners of district races and 200 seats are distributed through proportional representation. Chamber of Deputies members serve three-year terms. The PRI, which had dominated the Chamber of Deputies for most of the twentieth century, lost its majority in 1997.

Like the president, members of Congress cannot be reelected. However, they can, and a good number do, sit out a term and then run again. The rule preventing members of Congress from serving in consecutive terms means that they are much less experienced on average than representatives and senators in the United States. Some members of Congress in Mexico have been pushing to change the rule and allow members in both bodies to serve in consecutive terms.

The two houses' powers are similar to those of their American equivalents. Most bills must pass both houses, and it is possible to override a presidential veto. The lower house has greater discretion over budgetary matters, while the upper house has a stronger say in matters related to foreign policy. Like the president, the Mexican Congress has the power to issue decrees. While generally limited in scope, decrees cannot be vetoed by the president. Compared with the United States, there is less oversight of the executive and fewer powers to challenge the executive's control of governmental appointments. This is partly due to the prohibition against consecutive terms. This leads members of both houses, sometimes early in their terms, to begin to look for positions they might hold when their term ends. Since the late 1990s, however, the Congress has emerged as a much more significant part of the political system than in previous decades. With the PRI no longer in control of both the executive and legislative branches, legislators have discovered their branch's considerable constitutional powers.

Congress has more powers to check the actions of the president than it has traditionally displayed. Until the 1990s, Mexican presidents dominated the activities of the legislative branch.[12] Presidents initiated well over 75 percent of all bills considered, and the PRI-controlled

Congress never rejected a president-supported bill. This speaks to the institutional power of the president in Mexico, but even more to the PRI's domination over the political system. Because the PRI controlled both the presidency and a majority of seats in the legislature, the president operated much like a prime minister in a parliamentary system where one party controls the parliament.

With an increasing number of opposition party members in the two chambers in the 1980s and early 1990s, the Mexican Congress began to display hostility toward the president. With the 1997 and 2000 elections, congressional deference to the desires of the executive came to an end. In 2001, for example, Vicente Fox and the Congress came to blows over a tax reform proposal. The Mexican government has long depended on oil revenues for much of its government spending. Fox sought to improve tax collection capabilities of the federal government and proposed higher taxes on a variety of items, including medicine. Congress aggressively opposed the plan, and even members of Fox's own party ultimately withdrew their support. A new plan emerged, taxing luxury products and corporations instead. This was a strong sign that Mexican politics had not only changed at the ballot box but also within the halls of government.

The 2001 rift led some observers, such as political scientist Stephen Haber, to label the Mexican system as mired in gridlock.[13] The situation appeared to improve at times over the rest of Fox's term, only to flare up in more disappointments. In 2002, the Senate took advantage of a constitutional provision requiring its ascent for presidential trips abroad to block a planned trip by Fox to the United States and Canada. In 2004, members of Congress openly criticized Fox's wife, Marta, as rumors spread she may have ambitions to be president. In 2006, Fox was unable to give his final State of the Nation address before Congress, after legislators upset by the results of that year's presidential election

(see Chapter 10) stormed the stage. Fox submitted the speech in writing, went back to the presidential residence, and addressed the country on television.[14]

Brazil

Like the United States, Brazil has a bicameral legislature, comprised of a Federal Senate (the upper house) and a Chamber of Deputies (the lower house). Deputies serve four-year terms which coincide with the presidential term. Senators serve eight-year terms, with at least one-third of the Senate up for reelection every presidential election year (in alternate presidential election years, two-thirds will stand for reelection).

The 1988 Constitution also gave the legislature potentially important powers to check the president. In addition to the usual legislative powers, the approval of Congress is required to confirm treaties, declarations of war and peace, and declarations of a state of siege. Congress must authorize all presidential initiatives having to do with nuclear power, all radio or television concessions, and all grants of public land over a certain size. Senate approval is necessary to confirm Supreme Court justices, the attorney general, and presidents of the Central Bank. The Senate must also approve presidential proposals to increase the national debt. Presidential vetoes can be overridden with a mere majority of the legislature as opposed to the two-thirds majority required in the United States.

The Constitution also grants the Brazilian Congress power to oversee the actions of the executive and the judiciary. Members of either house may summon an official in the executive branch to appear in Congress and answer questions. The Congress can impeach the president (and did, in the case of Fernando Collor de Mello in 1992). More frequently, the Congress appoints special "parliamentary investigative commissions" (CPIs). Creation of a CPI requires support from at least one-third of a house of Congress. A CPI has full subpoena and investigative powers to ensure the disclosure of personal financial and telephone records, as well as the appearance of material witnesses before Congress. CPIs are used frequently for political purposes (to embarrass opponents), but also have produced significant accountability of executive branch officials, including the evidence used to impeach President Collor.

In granting these powers to the legislature, Brazilians who favored broader power sharing hoped to check the military's preference for a strong executive. In practice, neither group has been fully satisfied. The legislature has been unable in many cases to effectively check the president, but has also failed to act *with* the president effectively to promote a coherent policy platform. The principal reasons have to do with the way that the electoral system selects legislators (see Chapter 10), which results in a highly fragmented legislature.[15]

Nigeria

Nigeria's legislature is bicameral. The upper house is the Senate. The 109 members serve four-year terms. Unlike the United States, the entire Senate is elected at the same time; there is no staggering of terms for its members. There are 3 senators each from the 36 states and 1 from the Federal Capital Territory of Abuja (the capital was moved from Lagos to Abuja in 1991). The lower house is called the House of Representatives. It has 360 members, again elected to four-year terms at the same time as the Senate.

Elections to both houses last took place in April 2007. President Umaru Yar'Adua's People's Democratic Party (PDP) won large majorities in both houses. The previous president, Olusegun Obasanjo, had enjoyed large majorities in both houses as well. As a result, the potential for checks and balances in Nigeria's Fourth Republic has not been realized. Opposition politicians had criticized many of Obasanjo's actions in office, such as allowing the army to put down protests with levels of violence more fitting Nigeria's authoritarian periods, along with not preventing corruption (considered among the worst in the

world). But, unlike Mexico, the opposition has been able to do little more than complain.

Iran

Iran's legislature is unicameral. This body, the *Majles*, has 290 members elected to four-year terms. The vast majority of these (285) are chosen in electoral districts, while the remaining 5 are reserved for members of the country's religious minorities. One of Iran's governmental bodies, the Guardian Council, must approve candidates running for seats in the *Majles* (the Guardian Council is discussed in detail later in the chapter). As a result of this screening of candidates for the *Majles*, it is less moderate than it would be if all potential candidates were allowed to run. Conservatives have tended to control its ranks, with the exception of the years 2000 to 2004. As a result, the *Majles* blocked many efforts at reforming the political system.

From 2000 to 2004, however, a pro-reform *Majles*, working in convention with President Mohammed Khatami, pursued a number of social and political reforms. In 2004, the Guardian Council used its powers to screen applicants to prevent another four years of reformist legislative initiatives. The Guardian Council blocked the candidacy of over 2,000 individuals it deemed unacceptable, including 80 who were serving at the time in the *Majles*. This represented half of all the candidates running. As a result, the population did not have the opportunity to make a genuine choice, and the legitimacy of the *Majles* was damaged. Turnout was low, thanks in part to calls by reformers to boycott the vote. Conservatives swept back into control of a majority of the seats of the *Majles*.

The pattern was similar in 2008. Once again, the Guardian Council ruled out a large number of pro-reform candidates, leaving reformers to contest fewer than half of the seats. The result was a conservative majority, which looked poised to continue to frustrate those in Iran (and in the West) hoping for liberalization of the country's theocratic regime.

The Legislature in France, the Russian Federation, and China

The legislatures in all three of the semipresidential TIC cases—France, Russia, and China—are relatively weak. The French president and prime minister control much of the legislative agenda. Like legislatures in other democracies, however, the French National Assembly and the Senate sometimes use their powers of oversight of the executive to cause problems for the chief executives, particularly the president. In Russia, the bicameral legislature in the 1990s had at times enjoyed causing problems for the president and prime minister as well. For the last decade, however, the legislative branch of the Russian political system has increasingly acted as a rubber stamp of the chief executives' desires. Likewise, China's national legislature provides few checks on executive power and many rubber stamps of executive initiatives.

France

The French Parliament is weaker than most national legislatures. Divided between the directly elected National Assembly and a Senate selected by an electoral college, parliament is charged with approval of the budget and the passage of laws that can be initiated in either house or by the government. The Constitution of the Fifth Republic specifically limits the number of days parliament can sit, and the Assembly sets its own agenda only one day each month, resulting in a limited and directed workload. With six-year terms, the 326 senators are the longest serving state officials in France (the president's term was reduced from seven to five years in 2002). The Senate cannot be dissolved. The 577-deputy National Assembly can sit no longer than five years, but early elections can also be called.

Although not as strong as some legislatures, the French parliament is far from a powerless rubber stamp. Both houses can institute inquiries into government actions. Even though the prime minister and other ministers cannot serve as members of either house, they must personally submit themselves to questioning by parliament. Ultimate authority for passage of legislation rests with the National Assembly. It is technically able to overcome the Senate's or president's opposition to a new proposal if necessary. In practice, the National Assembly has never voted a proposal into law over the specific objections of the government.[16] The parliament can vote to remove a government through a censure resolution. Again, that is an extremely unlikely recourse in practice as the prime minister has always been selected from the party with the majority of seats in the National Assembly.

The parliament will sometimes take initiative, especially when the Senate—typically more conservative than the National Assembly—faces off against a president or government of the Left. In the early 1990s, for example, AIDS activists appealed to the parliament to vote an indictment against former Socialist Prime Minister Laurent Fabius for delaying a blood test that would have prevented the transmission of the disease through treatments routinely used by hemophiliacs. Both houses investigated, but the Socialists in the National Assembly issued a report that whitewashed the former government. For its part, the Senate voted to invoke a special legal procedure only used for criminal accusations against ministers, and the Socialist majority blocked the proposal.

A new center-right majority elected in 1993, however, forced Mitterrand to accept a constitutional amendment establishing a new independent court, the Court of Justice of the Republic. Fabius, former minister Georgina Dufoix, and former secretary of state Edmond Hervé were tried by the new court on charges of involuntary homicide in 1999. Although the two ministers were acquitted and Hervé was convicted without penalty, the action demonstrates the extent to which the French parliament can hold executive branch officials accountable for wrongdoing in certain situations.

The Russian Federation

Russia's parliament, the Federal Assembly, is a bicameral body. The lower house, the *Duma*, has been the more consistent of the two, both in its powers and in the process of selecting its members. The *Duma* has 450 members. Until 2007, half of the *Duma*'s members came from single-member districts and half came from proportional representation (PR). Since 2007, members of the *Duma* are selected entirely through PR, a move supported by then-President Vladimir Putin to make it easier for his United Russia party to control the *Duma*. The *Duma* also confirms the president's choice for prime minister, as well as other ministers, except for certain ministries related to security and the military.

The upper house, the Federation Council, has been much more of a moving target since 1993. It has 166 members, 2 from each of Russia's 83 regions. From 1993 to 1995, these members were elected by the general population. From 1995 to 2000, the chief executive and head of the legislature of each of the regions also served as the representatives to the Federation Council. This made it difficult for the body to meet on a regular basis. In 2000, Putin pushed through another change. The two members are now permanent representatives selected by the regional governments. Thus, although the Federation Council shares with the U.S. Senate the concept of representing the regions within the country, it has gone from a method of selecting members the U.S. Senate now uses to the method it originally used.

The Federation Council plays a much weaker role than the *Duma* in the formulation of policy. Its consent is not even needed for bills other than those concerning defense and economic policy. Even on bills that it rejects, the *Duma* can override this "veto" by a two-thirds vote. This does not mean the body has no teeth at all. It confirms border changes to the country or its regions, judicial appointments, and presidential decisions to declare a state of emergency. It can also authorize impeachment proceedings against the president.

It appears that the two houses of the Federal Assembly are unwilling to head off Russia's creeping authoritarianism. As Vladimir Putin showed, the Russian president's significant institutional powers allow him to rule with a firm fist, especially if supported by a sympathetic legislature. If, however, a party in opposition to the president could somehow gain a majority of the seats in parliament, it is *possible* that a situation similar to that of Mexico could emerge. The system's semipresidential nature and its more than meager checks and balances *could* emerge more forcefully down the road. For this to happen, however, Russia would have to turn back its creeping authoritarianism and, as Mexico did, begin a sincere process of democratization.

China

China's national legislature is known as the National People's Congress (NPC). The Chinese Constitution defines the NPC as "the highest organ of state power." Traditionally, the People's Congress served simply to sanction the executive's policies. This has begun to change, however, as Communist leaders place more real power in the hands of state institutions. In addition to its role in approving the government's economic plans, budgets, and other major policies, the NPC selects China's president and vice president, confirms the president's selection of a premier, and approves other major governmental appointments. It confirmed President Hu Jintao and Premier Wen Jiabao in 2003 and again in 2008.

The NPC meets once a year. Provincial-level people's congresses and those serving in the military elect its nearly 3,000 members to five-year terms. Because the NPC is not in regular session throughout the year—and because its size would make it unwieldy for day-to-day legislating—much of the legislative work is ceded to the NPC's Standing Committee. The 1987 decision to give the Standing Committee the power to enact laws was designed to improve efficiency in legislating. The Standing Committee consists of 175 members of the NPC. In recent years, members have often been specialists either in law or in particular topics the Standing Committee is likely to address. Though the entire NPC must still adopt some laws, the Standing Committee now handles a large portion of legislation.

The Executive

Though it is conceivable for a political system to lack a national legislature, no modern political system lacks an executive. Ordinarily, a single individual, known as the chief executive, heads the executive. These days, chief executives typically carry the title of president or prime minister. In the past, titles such as king, queen, tsar, or emperor were more common.

Domestic Politics Tasks of Executives

The executive administers government policy through a substantial sized segment of the government, known as the bureaucracy. The executive also coordinates the development of new government policy. Finally, it represents the state in foreign affairs.

Implementing Policies and Supervising the Bureaucracy The executive implements and administers government policy. Effectively carrying out government policies is too big a job, even in a small country, for the chief executive and top ministers alone. As a result, the bureaucracy—a large body of unelected government officials working in government ministries and agencies—runs many of the day-to-day affairs of the state.

Ministers and agency heads directly oversee the various bureaucratic departments. The chief executive usually appoints and removes ministers—often with legislative approval; sometimes another executive such as the head of state performs this task. Chief executives in the British and German political systems are responsible for around one hundred such appointments. Along with the chief executive, the most important ministers form the **cabinet**. Cabinets can vary significantly in size, from half a dozen to two dozen or more members.

While the ministers and agency heads are often political appointees, the middle and lower levels of the bureaucracy are staffed by civil servants. Theoretically, civil servants objectively serve whomever controls the executive branch. Particular bureaucrats may thus maintain their positions across a number of chief executives, providing a degree of stability and expertise within their policy area. (Chapter 8 deals with the structure and activities of bureaucracies in more detail.)

Coordinating Policy Development and Budgets Even in democratic systems with a strong legislature separated from the executive branch, the executive plays a large role in budgeting and other policymaking. Cabinet members work with their agencies to formulate recommendations. Using events such as press

> A **cabinet** consists of the chief executive and most important ministers. It meets on a regular basis to formulate policy and advise the chief executive on particular decisions.

conferences or national addresses, presidents and prime ministers mobilize public support of their policy positions.

Though legislatures have ultimate control of the government purse strings in most democracies, the executive generally presents the budget for legislatures to consider. Voters are likely to hold the chief executive responsible for national economic performance. Thus, taxing and spending proposals garner much of executives' attention. Bill Clinton's 1992 internal campaign slogan—It's the economy, stupid!—typifies the president's preoccupation with economic matters in the United States.

In nondemocracies and most parliamentary democracies, the executive is even more active in policy development. In a parliamentary democracy, the legislature may have a great deal of input on policies, or it may serve as almost a rubber stamp similar to its nondemocratic counterparts. This is especially true when a single party controls a majority of seats in parliament. The executive formulates *and* ensures passage of most policy provisions, making the chief executive the "chief legislator" as well.[17] Therefore, while no legislature fully controls the lawmaking process, in certain situations the executive may possess such power.

Foreign Policy Tasks of Executives

The chief executive represents and leads the state in matters of foreign affairs, engaging in diplomatic efforts, treaty negotiations, and decisions about the use of military force. It is reasonable to concentrate power over negotiations and crisis management. Imagine a five hundred–member legislature trying to negotiate with another five hundred–member legislature to head off a looming international crisis! The executive also often takes the lead on more mundane, day-to-day foreign policy tasks, though again the legislature may maintain its oversight role.

Depending on the system, the official head of state may be a weak, figurehead leader. In these cases, the head of state is the official representative of the state in international matters, but the head of the *government* actually coordinates foreign policy and takes part in international negotiations. In other systems, including presidential ones such as the United States, the executive wears both hats.

The decision to use military force is one of the most important a chief executive can make. The U.S. Congress has the power to sanction military action abroad, both by its constitutional power to declare war and its ability to regulate military expenditures through the War Powers Act. But even in the United States, there is a tendency to defer to the executive in decisions of war and peace. In many countries, the chief executive also commands the military. In countries without a tradition of civilian control of the military, including numerous nondemocratic systems and some unconsolidated democracies, the executive can have a difficult time keeping the military in check. In such cases, a leader must rely on close relations with top military officers, hoping that they remain loyal.

Think and Discuss

What is the most important power common to political executives? Why is it so important?

The Executive in the United Kingdom, Germany, and India

The United Kingdom, Germany, and India all officially have two chief executives, one serving as the head of the government and the other as the head of state. In all three, however, the head of state position is largely ceremonial. In the United Kingdom, this had not always been the case. The monarch once wielded significant power, but became increasingly irrelevant over time. The German and Indian presidents are also largely ceremonial positions. Both have many powers on paper, but fewer real powers in practice.

The United Kingdom

The history of British political institutions centers on the relationship between the monarch and other competing sources of power. The monarchy has been an ever-present symbol of the English and British state. Only during the period from 1649 to 1660, when the British civil war brought Oliver Cromwell to power, did the monarchy disappear. But its presence has not coincided with the kind of absolute power enjoyed by monarchs in other countries. Since the signing of the Magna Carta in 1215, limitations on the monarch's power have been a centerpiece of British politics.

Today the monarch is little more than a ceremonial figurehead. The queen, currently Elizabeth II, has a long list of official duties and powers, but none of these are genuine in practice. She can call for early parliamentary elections, but she does this only at the request of the prime minister. She must give her approval to all acts of parliament, but the monarch has not vetoed a piece of legislation since the early 1700s. She can meet on a regular basis with government officials and can even offer advice; the government, however, has no obligation to listen. The queen also gives an annual speech before parliament, much like the State of the Union address given by the president in the United States. There is one important difference between the two speeches, however: the queen delivers a speech written for her by the sitting prime minister and government, while the U.S. president gets to use his or her own speech writers.

So why have a monarchy at all? Many people in the United Kingdom, particularly with the scandals that engulfed the royal family in the late twentieth century, have asked themselves that very question. It is quite possible that the official role for the monarchy will eventually disappear, but one should not count on it. That the monarchy has survived at all is a testament to several features of British institutional development. Changes tend to be evolutionary rather than revolutionary. Parts of the past system survive, even during periods of significant reform. The British place a high level of importance on symbolism in the conduct of politics. As chaotic and discourteous as debates in the House of Commons may appear to American students, the conduct of political business frequently takes on a highly formal character. The queen's annual address is one of the world's great political ceremonies, making the announcement of the entrance of the U.S. president onto the floor of the House of Representatives before the State of the Union address look trivial by comparison.

The prime minister is the chief executive of the political system. Like all executives, the success of British prime ministers is driven by a combination of institutional opportunities and constraints—the size of the majority in parliament, for example—and a prime minister's leadership style. This position is one of significant power, particularly if the prime minister's party controls a sizeable majority of the seats in the House of Commons. Because of the fusion between the executive and the legislature in the Westminster system, the legislature scrutinizes the workings of the government much less than in most presidential systems. The prime minister can replace members of the cabinet and can even elevate a particular ministry to cabinet-level status without the consent of parliament.

This does not mean the prime minister runs roughshod over the cabinet. Cabinet members meet regularly with the prime minister and play a central role in creating government policy. As a result, the British political system is sometimes referred to as a "cabinet government" and the prime minister as "first among equals" in the cabinet. Debate within cabinet meetings can get heated, but once a collective decision is reached, members are expected to support it unconditionally. Cabinet members speaking out publicly against a policy introduced into the House of Commons are likely to find themselves out of the cabinet and back in their positions as regular MPs.

Germany

Germany's parliamentary system provides for a chancellor and a president, but real power rests with the chancellor. The president has formal power to appoint the chancellor, judges, and civil servants and to sign laws passed by parliament, though in all these capacities he is expected to respect the outcome of elections and the will of the chancellor and parliament. The office of the president, then, is largely ceremonial and the occupant is expected to be "above politics." Unlike the Weimar Republic, the president is neither directly elected nor can he issue decrees, though he may declare an emergency that would allow the government to do so. The president is selected every five years by an assembly consisting of all deputies of the lower house of the parliament (*Bundestag*) and delegates from the *Länder*.[18]

Executive authority rests with the chancellor. The chancellor appoints the cabinet and has the responsibility to set the policy direction of the government. Consequently, the Chancellor's Office, in addition to government ministries, provides an important source of policy expertise. Consistent with parliamentary government, bills originate with the executive branch rather than with the legislature. The German chancellor does face constraints on his or her exercise of this authority, however, particularly compared with the British prime minister. Unlike the latter, who normally enjoys the advantages of a legislative majority in the House of Commons, single party government, and a unitary system, the German chancellor faces coalition governments and federalism, both of which require negotiation and compromise to avoid deadlock.

Typical of parliamentary systems, the chancellor is normally the leader of the larger party that forms the government following *Bundestag* elections. Germany's mixed electoral system—with half of the seats allocated on a single member district/simple plurality basis and the other half on a proportional representation basis—helps generate a multiparty system, which in turn, makes coalition governments the norm. Most of the time, governments are of the minimum necessary winning coalition type, with either the Christian Democrats (CDU) or the Social Democrats (SPD) in coalition with a single smaller party.

The 2005 *Bundestag* elections, however, made coalition-building much more complicated. The two major parties were nearly even in terms of seats. But, the erosion of electoral support for both the CDU and SPD, along with the entry of the small Left Party into parliament, made a minimum necessary winning coalition formed from only two parties numerically impossible.[19] As a result, the CDU or SPD either had to seek the support of at least two smaller parties to form a government, or the two major parties had to agree to form a grand coalition between themselves.

Following several weeks of uncertainty and negotiations among the political parties, they chose the latter, producing only the second grand coalition between the CDU and SPD in the history of the Federal Republic. This current grand coalition has been in power since 2005, with the CDU's Angela Merkel serving as chancellor.

In spite of some difficult negotiations between the coalition partners, the current coalition has defied the expectations of many skeptics, who had predicted a brief tenure in office marked by policy stalemate. Such predictions were based in part on the experiences of the first grand coalition, from 1966–1969, formed in response to West Germany's first post–World War II economic recession.

India

The Indian prime minister is the head of government and normally, but not always, a member of the *Lok Sabha*. The chief executive overseeing domestic policy, the prime minister selects and heads the Council of Ministers and oversees the bureaucracy. Typical of parliamentary systems but unlike some systems with both a prime minister and president, the prime minister is also responsible for foreign policy.

Like most parliamentary systems, the Indian prime minister is usually the head of the party with the largest number of seats in the lower house of parliament. In 2004, however, the leader of the Congress Party, Sonia Gandhi, decided not to take the position. Italian by birth, some politicians perceived her background to have the potential for creating political problems. Consequently, she deferred to Manmohan Singh to be the prime minister. Singh, the first Sikh to become prime minister (see Chapter 5), developed a reputation with members of various political parties as an honest and capable politician.[20]

The president exercises executive powers on the advice of the prime minister and the cabinet. In general, the president possesses many formal powers but few real powers, although the extent of presidential power is contingent upon situational factors. The inability of a single party to control the *Lok Sabha* during most of the last twenty years and the instability associated with coalitional government have given the president somewhat greater discretion. When the *Lok Sabha* is evenly divided among potential coalitions or when the president

dissolves parliament, for example, the president has some discretion even over the appointment of the prime minister.

The president signs laws, may address both houses, and is the commander in chief of the army. The president can also veto legislation, but a simple majority can override the veto in a revote. In extraordinary circumstances when parliament is not in session, the president may issue decrees on the advice of the prime minister, but they must be put before the parliament within six weeks of the start of its subsequent session. Also on the advice of the prime minister, the president may declare "President's Rule" over a federal unit whose government is viewed as unable to function—a power that, at times, has been used for political ends—and is able to declare a state of emergency. (President Fakhruddin Ali Ahmed issued such a degree in 1975.) If not approved by parliament within two months, the state of emergency decree lapses. The expectation that the president would follow the advice of the prime minister was not a part of the 1950 Constitution, but the Forty-second Amendment to the Constitution, which went into effect in 1976, specified that the president should act in accord with the direction provided by the Council of Ministers.

The president is elected for a term of five years by an electoral college that consists of all the legislators at the center and federal unit levels. The votes at the federal unit level are adjusted so that they represent approximately equal populations, and the proportions are applied to the votes of parliamentarians from each federal territorial unit—a complex system meant to produce national representation. As discussed at the beginning of the chapter, the first woman to be elected president, Pratibha Patil, was chosen in 2007. The vice president serves for a similar period and is elected by a joint meeting of the *Lok Sabha* and *Rajya Sabha*. The vice president is the ex-officio chairman of the *Rajya Sabha* and takes over the president's functions when he or she is unable to continue in the position.

The Executive in Mexico, Brazil, Nigeria, and Iran

The four presidential systems among the TIC cases, Mexico, Brazil, Nigeria, and Iran, highlight how a president can be constrained (or aided) as much by the partisan or ideological makeup of the legislature as by the official powers of the executive and legislative branches. In Mexico, what looked like a system with a powerful president increasingly resembled a recipe for gridlock. In Brazil, the president's power is enhanced by a divided legislature that is unable to organize effectively to thwart the president's agenda—along with significant official powers including, in the past, the ability to bypass legislative approval on important policies. In Nigeria, the presidential system that replaced Nigeria's initial parliamentary design gives the president great power, especially when his party controls a majority of the seats in the legislature. Even the authoritarian system of Iran, where the president is checked by unelected components of the executive, shows how a president and legislature working in tandem can pressure for political change and how a president with a hostile legislature can get little done.

Mexico

The president in Mexico has substantial powers. During the long period of Institutional Revolutionary Party (PRI) dominance, the system was often called a "six-year monarchy." In other words, the Mexican president had great power, but the president had to turn this power over to someone else after six years. During its dominance of the political system, the PRI thought little of this concentration of power. Since PRI candidates always won presidential elections (if necessary by fraudulent electoral practices), a strong president was seen as an efficient way of managing the political system, a system that amounted to authoritarianism centered around a single party. By the time the PRI lost majority control of Congress in 1997, the system of dictatorial presidential rule had begun to evaporate. With Vicente Fox's election in 2000, it disappeared entirely. As Mexican politics specialist Denise Dresser puts it, "The imperial presidency has ended and the informal presidency has begun. Instead of imposing from above, the president now has to engage in bargaining and deal brokering in order to generate support from below."[21]

This is not to imply the Mexican presidency has become a feeble institution. Mexican presidents have more power to issue decrees—policy directives with the force of law that have a fixed expiration date—and appoint government officials than their American counterparts. The president tightly regulates foreign investment in the country, and the position even comes with the ability to oversee the content of school textbooks. The president also oversees a large patronage system in Mexico, providing additional capacity to influence political outcomes. The secretaries of government departments that make up the cabinet handle much of the day-to-day administrative duties. Though the cabinet rarely meets as an entire group, the president works closely with individual cabinet members. Cabinet members have a fair amount of discretion, but they must tread lightly or risk alienating the president and being replaced.

Did You Know? In November 2004, President Vicente Fox's use of the veto ended up in the Mexican Supreme Court. Labeling the 2004 budget a transparent attempt to gut the bureaucracy by forcing thirty thousand federal jobs to be cut, Fox vetoed it.[22] The leadership of the Chamber of Deputies, the house with the authority to pass the budget, claimed that the budget amounted to a decree that could not be vetoed. The Supreme Court ultimately ruled that the president could veto the budget, but that Congress could override the veto with a two-thirds vote.

Mexican voters select a president for a single, six-year term (referred to as the *sexenio*). The president cannot be reelected, and there is no vice president. Fox's election in 2000 was a rather surprising development in a number of ways: He was not a PRI candidate, he received the most votes, and he was actually declared the winner.

Until relatively recently, a sitting PRI president had significant say over the person the party would nominate as successor. Though chosen in secret, the PRI nominee came from the president's cabinet and was part of a "pre-candidate" list announced publicly about two months before the party convention nominated the candidate. Finally, in 1999 the PRI instituted an open primary system, which led to the selection of Francisco Labastida—the man who would become the first PRI candidate to lose a presidential election.

Brazil

The powers and selection of the Brazilian chief executive display similarities and differences with other presidential systems. Like the United States (but unlike Mexico), the president serves a four-year term and may serve up to two terms in office. Like the French president (but unlike in Mexico), the president of Brazil is directly elected by an absolute majority of the vote. If no candidate receives a majority of the vote on the first ballot (which is the usual outcome), then a second ballot is held one month later between the first- and second-place finishers.

During the month between the first and second ballots, the top two candidates try to line up the support of the less fortunate presidential candidates and their political factions in a process of coalition-building. They may exchange promises of future cabinet positions, government posts, or legislative committee assignments. These deals are intended not only to secure the endorsement of the loser for the second round, but also to facili-tate subsequent legislative decision making in the Congress. The size of each party's future congressional bench is already known (legislators do not face a two-round election), so candidates take into account the future value of each party's support in the Congress, as well as the immediate benefit in terms of second round presidential votes. The month between the first and second ballots is perhaps the most important—and least public—period in a Brazilian presidential election.

Once inaugurated, the Brazilian president controls the apparatus of the state, including the exclusive right to appoint and dismiss cabinet ministers, to fill and abolish federal government positions, and to decree a state of siege. He presides over the National Defense Council, is supreme commander of the Armed Forces, and has the right to allow foreign troops to pass through Brazilian national territory.

In addition to benefiting from the lack of a majority party in Congress, the president also has broad legislative powers that go well beyond what a U.S. president enjoys. He can directly introduce bills into the legislature, has the constitutional responsibility to introduce budget proposals, can veto bills (either wholly or in part), and can issue provisional measures with the force of law (Article 62). Originally, the power to issue provisional measures was unchecked by restrictions on how long a "provisional" measure could last. However, legislators began to feel that presidents used this power indiscriminately to avoid taking important measures to the Congress for legislative approval. For example, Brazil's controversial currency reform plan, the Real Plan, was issued as a "provisional measure" over eighty times with the same text. Thus, this article was amended in 2001 to give the Congress the right—though not the duty—to force the president to bring a specific measure to the legislature for debate.

Nigeria

Nigeria's latest attempt at democratic rule followed the reign of General Sani Abacha from November 1993 to his death in May 1998. The military leader that replaced Abacha, General Abdulsalam Abubakar, made good on a promise for genuine elections. A complete break between the military and the ruling institutions, however, was not in the cards. General Olusegun Obasanjo, a former military ruler from the 1970s, came out of retirement to win the presidential election.

Not all observers saw Obasanjo's victory as a negative. After all, Obasanjo had surrendered power under the transition that culminated in the Second Republic. Since he took office, however, there were concerns about Obasanjo's populism and authoritarian tendencies. He won reelection in April of 2003 in what, by Nigerian standards, was a relatively free and fair electoral process. In June 2007, he stepped down following the election of Umaru Yar'Adua the preceding month.

Outside observers and Yar'Adua's opponents criticized the 2007 election as a step backward from democracy. In 2008, the Presidential Election Petitions Tribunal met to review the allegations by Yar'Adua's two main opponents that the election was unfair. The five-judge panel ruled in favor of Yar'Adua, rejecting the call for a new election. While much of the criticism of the 2007 presidential election was justified, the election was also a milestone—representing the first time since independence that an elected Nigerian president had peacefully handed over power to his successor.

Similar to the United States, the Nigerian president is limited to two terms. The president can veto legislation but can also have this veto overridden. Other checks exist as well, though the dominance of Yar'Adua's People's Democratic Party (PDP) over the two houses of the legislature limits their importance.

There are important differences between the Nigerian and American systems, however, which reflect Nigeria's goal of reaching out to all segments of a diverse population. The president must win a plurality of the vote (and this must be at least 25 percent) in two-thirds of the country's 36 internal regions. The president oversees governmental affairs with the help of a large cabinet of ministers, with members from all 36 regions of the country. Finally, the vice president must come from a region other than that of the president.

Iran

Following the 1979 Islamic Revolution, the new leaders of Iran put in place a new constitution. The constitution created a system with a dual chief executive, but one very different from those discussed previously in this chapter. Instead of a president and prime minister, the Iranian system included a president and a position known as the Supreme Leader. This individual is also considered to be a *faqih*, or "spiritual guide."

As the title indicates, the position of Supreme Leader carries with it tremendous power to shape legislative, executive, and even judicial outcomes in Iran. The first Supreme Leader was Ayatollah Ruhollah Khomeini. An ayatollah is a leading cleric—the word means "sign of God"—and Khomeini was recognized for his leadership in the effort to oust the shah, Iran's authoritarian leader prior to the 1979 Revolution. Khomeini died in 1989 and was replaced by Ayatollah Ali Hoseini-Khamenei, who is the current Supreme Leader.

The Supreme Leader works closely with three bodies that straddle the line between executive and legislature. The first is the Council of Guardians of the Constitution, or Guardian Council for short. The Guardian Council has twelve members, six of whom are specialists on Islamic law appointed by the Supreme Leader. Another six are selected by the national legislature, the *Majles*, from a group nominated by the High Council of Justice—Iran's version of a supreme court. The Guardian Council examines proposals from the *Majles*, to determine whether they are consistent with the principles of *Shari'a* (Islamic law). If the Guardian Council does not accept an act of the *Majles*, it is returned in order to be corrected. The Guardian Council also has veto power over candidates running for seats in the *Majles*.

The Expediency Council, whose members are appointed by the Supreme Leader, attends to clashes between the Guardian Council and the *Majles*. Such disputes can include the Guardian Council returning a proposal but the *Majles* refusing to accept the Guardian Council's position. The Expediency Council was the brainchild of Ayatollah Khomeini, who grew concerned about the odd occasion when the Guardian Council blocked legislative measures that he supported. Declaring that commandments of the government may need to take precedence over *Shari'a* in certain situations, Khomeini pushed for inclusion of the Expediency Council in the amended 1989 Constitution. After reformers gained control of the *Majles* following the 2000 elections, the Expediency Council became a more central part of the Iranian political system, adding another check on the reformers by the more conservative elements of the executive. The Expediency Council is currently headed by former Iranian president, Akbar Hashemi-Rafsanjani.

The eighty-six-member Assembly of Experts selects the Supreme Leader and advises him on various issues. It is therefore somewhat analogous to the Vatican's College of Cardinals, except that the Iranian people elect the Assembly of Experts in an election held every eight years. Candidates must be clerics, and, once more, the Guardian Council can block certain individuals from running. The most recent election took place in November 2006.

Although the Supreme Leader is the more powerful of the two chief executives, the Constitution gives the president significant powers. Being directly elected also gives the president a degree of legitimacy that the clerics in many other institutions in the Iranian government struggle to achieve. The president oversees day-to-day government affairs and relies on a cabinet to formulate policy proposals, much as the other chief executives we have discussed. Certain cabinet officials, however, are closely monitored by the religious leaders, including those working on defense and foreign policy and those overseeing cultural and social programs.

Iran's current president is Mahmoud Ahmadinejad, who won a runoff against Rafsanjani in 2005. He faces reelection in 2009. In many ways, Ahmadinejad is the converse of his predecessor, Mohammed Khatami. Khatami was a moderate reformer who won a convincing victory in 1997—getting almost 70 percent of the vote—against a conservative candidate supported by the religious establishment. Khatami's victory was a warning to the clerics that many in the general population were ready for a more moderate approach to politics. He won reelection in convincing fashion in 2001, with 78 percent of the vote.

Ahmadinejad, on the other hand, is a conservative who defeated a prominent and more moderate opponent. A large portion of pro-reform voters refused to participate in the election, aiding his victory. At the same time, Ahmadinejad's electoral success was a sign both to reformers and to more pro–business moderate-conservatives, such as Rafsanjani, that a sizeable portion of Iranians was ready to accept a more hard line government.

IN THEORY AND PRACTICE

Iran and the Theory of "Going Public"

Theories addressing a president's ability to set the legislative agenda draw on the concept of the "bully pulpit," the ability of a president to make direct appeals to the citizenry. One such theory, posed by Samuel Kernell, is the **theory of "going public."**[23] In it, Kernell highlights the president's use of the media to promote particular policies.[24] Kernell's premise is based on the United States, but his argument can inform comparative politics studies as well. As electronic media around the world become more common, chief executives are turning ever more to radio, television, and the Internet to bolster support for their policies.

But does Kernell's theory apply to nondemocratic, developing countries like Iran? Because of the existence of the Supreme Leader and bodies, such as the Guardian Council, Iran's president is more constrained than most. The Iranian president not only has to worry about getting legislation on the agenda, but he also has to worry that the Guardian Council may block an initiative even if it makes it out of the legislature.

Although the Iranian president does not have the institutional powers of other presidents, he does have the "bully pulpit." Iran's former president, Mohammed Khatami, was well known for taking his message directly to the Iranian people. Though his vision of extensive reforms was ultimately unrealized, reforms under Khatami went further than many in the West expected. Were it not for his ability to "go public" and generate public enthusiasm for his ideas, it is unlikely that political and social reforms would have been discussed so openly in Iran during Khatami's years in office.

The **theory of "going public"** highlights the way that the American president can promote specific policies by using the media to change public opinion.

The Executive in France, the Russian Federation, and China

The French, Russian, and Chinese semipresidential systems concentrate significant power, both officially and in practice, in the hands of the executive. For France, the Fifth Republic's powerful president has provided the stability that Charles de Gaulle envisioned. Likewise, the presidency in the Russian system, a system designed by former President Boris Yeltsin and his supporters, has been the much more stable half of Russia's dual executive. In China, holding the presidency (especially if simultaneously serving as the General Secretary of the Chinese Communist Party as well) has become associated with being the country's recognized leader, something that was not true under such past leaders as Mao Zedong and Deng Xiaoping.

France

Charles de Gaulle became the first president of the Fifth Republic; he was elected not by the people but by an electoral college. He immediately imposed his vision of executive power on the political system, bringing together a broad coalition of right- and left-leaning politicians and expert "technocrats" who were above partisan politics. Following approval of a referendum establishing direct elections for the presidency, de Gaulle was reelected in 1965. As the only official chosen by a direct vote of all French citizens, de Gaulle was, in his vision at least, the "man of the nation. . . . The only one to hold and delegate the authority of the state."[25]

The key to de Gaulle's constitutional device, however, is not the dual executive itself, but how he was able to use this devise to consolidate power in the two offices of the executive.

In addition to its two heads, the French executive branch has a more muscular body than most, including the American presidency. The Fifth Republic Constitution grants the executive, through the prime minister, extensive power over the legislative and administrative agenda—for example, the ability to set the agenda for almost all the meetings of the National Assembly. At the same time, it shields the government from parliament by prohibiting members of parliament from serving in government ministries. The government can issue decrees and regulations in a range of areas without action of parliament and can be authorized by a legislative vote to issue decrees in new areas. The executive can even adopt new policies that are tantamount to law, taking effect if parliament does not vote to reject the proposals.

In this dual executive system, the president's officially designated powers are few in number but significant in practice. For example, the French president does not have the power to veto legislation. If the president opposes a law, his only recourse is to submit it to the Constitutional Council for review (see Chapter 8) or send it back to parliament for another vote. Yet the president's influence prior to votes on legislation—in concert with the authority to dissolve the National Assembly and force new elections—makes official veto power less necessary than in a presidential system such as the United States.

The president's relationship with the prime minister and other government ministers is also an important part of the story. The president appoints the prime minister, presides over the Council of Ministers, and appoints other ministers upon recommendation of the prime minister. The president also shares responsibility with the prime minister and other ministers for cosigning a variety of appointments or decrees (special laws and regulations). The president cannot dismiss the government unless the prime minister submits a letter of resignation. However, the president's ability to dissolve the National Assembly and force new elections can place significant pressure on the prime minister to resign if the two chief executives come in conflict with one another.

Through an extensive personal network, cohesive and pragmatic high civil service, and party loyalty in parliament and the ministries, the president can fast track legislative reform with little parliamentary oversight. At such times, the Council of Ministers is truly the president's government—certainly in much more real terms than the British cabinet is the queen's government. Simply put, a president with a majority in the National Assembly sets the French policy agenda.

Generally, de Gaulle's Constitution works as intended. Even François Mitterrand, the Socialist who opposed de Gaulle's investiture in 1958, adapted to the system when he was elected president in 1981, dissolving the National Assembly and winning an absolute majority in the subsequent election. When Mitterrand faced a parliament elected in 1986 with a majority hostile to his presidency, many feared that the dual executive could not survive "cohabitation." As de Gaulle might have done in the same situation, Mitterrand insisted on the president's specified prerogatives and powers. He represented France to the world. He designated the prime minister and government, not the new majority, even if he had to select them from the majority. He even refused to sign a number of decrees or proposals in the area of economic liberalization, forcing the new government to submit all these proposals for parliamentary review and approval. Though he could not block a law, he could delay it, hopefully until after the next election.

By contrast, the new left-wing majority elected under the center-right President Jacques Chirac in 1997 was unified and strong enough to force the president's hand. Consequently, Chirac was the only lame duck in the history of the Fifth Republic. Hoping to avoid any of the pitfalls Chirac faced, in 2007 the newly elected president, Nicolas Sarkozy, called together a diverse government from his own party (on the political right), centrists, and even the Socialist opposition on the left. Sarkozy's goal was to set an agenda that would be above party bickering.

The Russian Federation

In Russia's semipresidential system, there has been little attempt to balance the powers of the two chief executives. Prime ministers who have run afoul of the president could begin looking for a new line of work. This is not to say the prime minister is insignificant. The prime minister oversees a large number of government ministries and formulates many specific policy proposals. The president determines the government's overall approach, but the prime minister is the one who implements most government policies. The prime minister also becomes acting president if the president resigns. Presidential elections must then be held within three months.

These powers include the ability to choose the prime minister. Unlike parliamentary systems with a weak president, the power to select the head

of the government is not just a formality. The president can also remove individual ministers at any time. The president makes cabinet appointments, including as high up as the deputy prime minister, without parliament's consent and can introduce bills in the assembly.[26] The president can veto bills passed by parliament, issue edicts (decrees) that have the force of law, and authorize a national referendum. During the 1990s, the veto was a widely used tool. In her study of Russian vetoes, political scientist Andrea Chandler points out that between 1993 and 1999 Boris Yeltsin vetoed more than 220 bills—around one-fourth of all bills passed by the *Duma* and half as many bills as American presidents had vetoed in the one hundred years prior.[27] After Chandler published her study, President Vladimir Putin gained a working majority in the *Duma*, and vetoes became much less common.

Additionally, the president directly controls the so-called "power ministries": Defense, Interior, Foreign Affairs, the Foreign Intelligence Service, the Federal Agency for Government Communication and Information, the Federal Border Service and the Federal Security Service—the current manifestation of the Soviet KGB. The president also oversees the Security Council. This body is made up of the president, prime minister, representatives to the seven federal districts, the heads of the "power ministries," a permanent secretary of the council, and other officials the president wants to include. Putin tended to stack its top positions with former intelligence and military officials, and he used it in his effort to strengthen the power of the central government versus the regions.[28]

There are some limitations on the president's power. Presidential decrees cannot contravene the constitution, and the legislature can overturn them through the passage of a contrary statute. A two-thirds vote by both houses of the assembly can also override presidential vetoes of legislation. The president needs the approval of the lower house, the *Duma*, for the nomination of a prime minister. If the *Duma* rejects a

View of the Kremlin from the Moscow River
(©Jose Fuste Raga/Corbis)

nomination three times, however, the president can dissolve the *Duma* and order new legislative elections. The president can be forced to remove a sitting prime minister if the *Duma* passes two votes of no confidence in the prime minister within three months. If this happens, however, the president can also again dissolve the *Duma* and call for new elections. Finally, the president is officially limited to two terms, a provision Putin publicly stated he would abide by, and did abide by, surprising some observers of Russian politics and many Russian citizens as well.

Whether Putin's move into the prime minister's chair brings changes to the relative powers of the two chief executive positions remains to be seen. It is unlikely, however, that President Dmitry Medvedev dominates over the "power ministries" in the way that Yeltsin and, especially Putin, did. Following a military conflict in late 2008 between Russia and one of its southern neighbors, Georgia, analysts interpreted events such as the Russian government's decision to leave a large number of troops on the territory of Georgia as an example of Putin's increasing assertiveness in foreign policy rather than Medvedev's.[29]

China

Assessing the extent to which China's two chief executive positions, president and premier, balance each other out can be difficult. China's president, Hu Jintao, is recognized as the country's leader. Yet this is at least in part because he holds a number of other posts, including his position as General Secretary of the Chinese Communist Party (CCP). Since Jiang Zemin and now Hu Jintao have chosen to pair their position as CCP General Secretary with the state presidency, however, it is a sign that the presidency is far from a figurehead position. The president serves a five-year term, as does the vice president, who is currently Zeng Qinghong. Both Hu Jintao and Zeng Qinghong were elected (by the National People's Congress) in March 2003 and again in March 2008. The president nominates the premier and plays a particularly important role in crafting Chinese foreign policy.

The premier is the chief executive of the Chinese government responsible for day-to-day governing. The current premier (since March 2003) is Wen Jiabao. The premier oversees the activities of the forty-five-member State Council, a cabinet-like structure that manages the large Chinese bureaucracy. The premier is assisted by four vice premiers. The premier and State Council are charged with administering specific government policies, particularly those on the domestic side related to economic performance. These policies are influenced greatly, however, by the CCP leadership's broad recommendations.

A final executive body is worth noting. Consistent with the highly autonomous nature of the Chinese military (see Chapter 8), the state Central Military Commission is a group of state officials in charge of directing the armed forces. It mirrors a similarly named body in the CCP. While the CCP Central Military Commission sets general military policy, the state Central Military Commission is charged with overseeing the military budget, as well as appointments to top military positions. In the past, the president or party General Secretary served as commander in chief, but now this position is given to the chairman of the state Central Military Commission. When Hu Jintao took over Jiang Zemin's other positions, he did not immediately become the chairman of the state and party Central Military Commissions. He instead held the vice-chairman position. Jiang Zemin has since surrendered his position as chairman of these bodies, marking Hu's control of most of the top positions in current Chinese politics.

Think and Discuss

Which of the countries examined in the TIC sections have the most interesting relations between the executive and legislative branches? Why?

Exercise

COMPARATIVE EXERCISE

Creeping Authoritarianism and Democratic Restoration in Peru

This chapter's discussion of creeping authoritarianism linked it to presidential systems. But while some presidential systems succumb to creeping authoritarianism, others do not. What contributes to the likelihood of creeping authoritarianism? This comparative exercise examines this question through a case study. During the 1990s, Peru changed from a presidential democracy to an authoritarian regime. As a result, a better understanding of the Peruvian case may provide insight into the causes of, and possible tools for preventing, a gradual accumulation of presidential power that ultimately leads to the breakdown of a democratic presidential system.

Overview of the Peruvian Case

President Alberto Fujimori, an academic-turned-politician, was elected president of Peru in 1990. Peru's economy at the time was a mess, with inflation around 8,000 percent, a $20 billion foreign debt, and large portions of the population living in poverty. Many government officials, including the judiciary, were corrupt, thanks in large part to the important role of illegal drug distribution in the Peruvian economy. To make matters even worse, the country was in the midst of a civil war, with the government fighting against the terrorist activities of the Shining Path—a Maoist revolutionary group seeking to bring peasant-based communism to the country.

Resolving such a situation demands a stable and efficient government, but Peru's legislature opposed many of Fujimori's efforts at economic and political reform. Tensions between the executive and legislative branches mounted. In April 1992, Fujimori suspended the constitution, beginning a spiral toward authoritarianism. New legislative elections took place, and a revised constitution strengthened the president. With military support, and through a strong internal intelligence service, Fujimori accumulated power as the decade wore on.

Creeping authoritarianism under Fujimori was epitomized by his decision to seek a third term as president in 2000, despite a constitutional provision limiting the president to two terms. Amid allegations of massive vote fraud, Fujimori declared victory. His main challenger, Alejandro Toledo, led popular protests over the elections that drew tens of thousands of participants. Fujimori might have survived were it not for the release of a videotape in which a politician was shown being bribed to support Fujimori's party. New protests led Fujimori to offer his resignation. The Congress actually rejected his resignation, but only so it could declare him "morally unfit" for office and remove him from power. Fujimori fled Peru for Japan.

New presidential and legislative elections took place in April 2001 with Toledo winning a narrow victory over a former president of Peru, Alan García Perez. Though democracy was restored, the Toledo Administration faced a rocky road. Corruption allegations persisted, strikes continued to cripple the economy, and the Shining Path remained a violent irritant to the government. In response, Toledo appointed a prime minister from another political party and offered to open his financial records but also declared a state of emergency in part of the country.

The subsequent presidential election in June 2006 brought García to power. He defeated a populist, retired military officer, Ollanta Humala Tasso, in a run-off. García's support was especially strong around the capital of Lima, while Humala won in the poorer and less populated regions of the country. The peaceful transfer of power into García's hands provides hope for consolidation of the democracy, but the country remains regionally and economically divided.

Many who supported García appeared to do so for "lesser of two evils" reasons, and a deep confidence in democracy has yet to materialize. How successfully García can bridge Peru's socioeconomic divides is crucial to the survival of Peru's restored democracy.

Discussion

What are the lessons from the Peruvian experience about creeping authoritarianism? First, it can grow out of a crisis situation that the president and legislature fail to address effectively. Second, it requires the support of the armed forces. Third, presidents seeking to accumulate and hang onto power may face mass uprisings if they act *too much* like corrupt dictators. After Fujimori decided to run for a third term, stole the election, and got caught on tape bribing officials, the population had had enough. This third lesson from Peru is supported by additional evidence over the last decade from the post-Communist countries of Serbia, Georgia, Ukraine, and Kyrgyzstan, where street protests overturned fraudulent election results.

Looking at a single case has its limitations. It is not obvious that the lessons from Peru can be applied to other countries, nor is it clear when the population will have enough of a leader who steals elections. The lessons from Peru would need to be examined in other cases, such as Serbia and Ukraine, before general causal statements could be supported. It would also be important to examine cases of presidential democratic systems that did not give way to creeping authoritarianism. If the variables identified as potential causes of creeping authoritarianism did not lead to it in those cases, these variables may not be as important as first thought. It would then be necessary to look deeper into the cases.

CONCLUSION

Legislatures and executives are key components of a country's political structure. The division of powers between the legislature and executive is among the political system's most important traits. Some comparative politics scholars contend that legislatures have lost the battle for political supremacy with executives. After all, legislatures in nondemocracies regularly do the bidding of the executive without comment. In parliamentary systems, the fall of the government places the members of the legislature in jeopardy; the members' party might lose its position as part of the ruling coalition; and the MPs might lose their seats if the collapse of the government results in new elections. Even in many presidential systems, there are incentives for legislatures to defer to the executive.

As countries like Mexico demonstrate, however, one should not write the epitaph for legislatures so quickly. Powers on paper that had looked unimportant in the past can become important if the chief executive's party does not control a majority of legislative seats. In such cases, executives must work with the legislature or face crippling gridlock.

Executives and legislatures come into being and operate under a set of rules which, at least in most democracies, are followed. But they are also composed of individuals who have ideas, interests, and wills of their own. Just like a football game, the rules limit the actions of the participants, but they do not dictate the form of the plays. As a result, a fuller understanding of political outcomes requires one to examine not only how legislative and executive structures tend to operate but also to be familiar with the individuals that serve in those institutions.

It also requires examining the broader structural context, including other political institutions, elected or otherwise. The next chapter covers the parts of government that, even in a democracy, are run by unelected officials. These institutions—the judiciary, the bureaucracy, and the military—are often as important to a country's daily governing as either its chief executive or national legislature.

Key Terms

Ad hoc committee, p. 253
Backbenchers, p. 254
Bicameral, p. 252
Cabinet, p. 263
Coalition, p. 233
Committee, p. 253
Constituency service, p. 250
Creeping authoritarianism, p. 240
Divided government, p. 239
Frontbenchers, p. 254

Grand coalition, p. 234
Legislatures, p. 249
Minimum necessary winning coalition, p. 233
Minister without portfolio, p. 233
Minority government, p. 234
MP, p. 233
Omsbuds activities, p. 250
Parliamentary supremacy, p. 254
Parliamentary system, p. 232
Party discipline, p. 233
Party government theory, p. 256
Portfolio, p. 233
Presidential system, p. 238
Prime minister, p. 232
Semipresidential system, p. 245
Shadow government, p. 236
Standing committee, p. 253
Suspensive veto, p. 257
Theory of "going public," p. 272
Theory of parliamentary superiority, p. 242
Theory of presidential system design, p. 243
Unicameral, p. 252
Vote of censure, p. 235
Vote of confidence, p. 235
Vote of no confidence, p. 235

Learning Objectives

After reading this chapter, you should be able to:

■ Discuss the tasks of the judiciary, bureaucracy, and military.

■ Describe how each of these unelected governmental components can shape policy decisions in democracies.

■ Discuss the advantages and disadvantages of judicial review.

■ Discuss the strengths and weaknesses of a strong bureaucracy.

■ Describe theories associated with the judiciary, bureaucracy, and military discussed in the chapter's "In Theory and Practice" boxes.

8

The Unelected Components of Government: Judiciaries, Bureaucracies, and Militaries

In July 2007, Sanjeev Sabhlok, a former officer in the Indian Administrative Service (IAS), wrote an opinion piece that appeared in the *Times of India*.[1] That same month, the seventh book of J. K. Rowling's wildly popular Harry Potter series, *Harry Potter and the Deathly Hallows*, was released.[2] At first glance, these two events would appear to have little in common, but both Sabhlok's editorial and Rowling's fictional story cast light on a broadly held perception of government bureaucracy: that it is inefficient and filled with individuals who lack integrity and basic competence. Sabhlok's call for reform of the Indian bureaucracy was palpable and based on his own real-world experiences. Rowling's attacks on bureaucrats were more subtle—coming mostly in discussions of the "Ministry of Magic"—and took place in the context of a fictional story. Yet, in his study

Look for this icon to point you to **Deepening Your Understanding** features on the companion website www.college.cengage.com/politicalscience/barrington, which provide greater depth for some key content.

of the Harry Potter series' portrayal of bureaucrats, law professor Benjamin Barton argued that "Rowling's scathing portrait of government" was highly effective.[3] The unelected nature of bureaucracies undoubtedly contributes to their reputation as unaccountable and self-serving. ∎

The previous chapter spotlighted the parts of a central government—the legislature and the chief executive—whose members are often directly elected in a democracy. This chapter turns to the major political institutions whose officials are almost always unelected: the judiciary, the bureaucracy, and the military. All three of these institutions are involved in the policy process. This involvement ranges from carrying out policy to making numerous decisions on a daily basis that have the effect of law. How much the individuals who serve in these institutions actively create policy varies significantly from country to country. This chapter examines some of the factors that determine their level of involvement.

Like executives and legislatures, these three components of government are important in both democratic and nondemocratic systems alike. Although the judicial branch is typically controlled by the executive branch in nondemocratic systems, judges are still needed to rule in civil and criminal cases. Bureaucrats in nondemocratic systems need to worry about the extent to which their day-to-day decision making might alienate the chief executive, but nondemocracies still rely on bureaucratic expertise. In all types of political systems, the military plays a crucial role in the defense of the country.

The Judiciary

The judiciary is commonly considered the third branch of government. It stabilizes the political system by solving disputes involving the country's laws. Courts often have to solve disagreements between citizens, but they can also settle conflicts between companies and governmental institutions, between different levels of government, or between institutions at the same level of government (e.g., disputes between the legislature and the president).

Although comparative political works addressing the role of the courts in different settings started to appear in the 1950s, only in the last decade or so has the topic of "judicial politics" drawn significant attention from comparativists.[4] Today, comparativists interested in the courts seek to understand what influences a specific judicial decision (i.e., the rulings of members of a court as a dependent variable) and examine the role of the courts more generally in shaping political outcomes (i.e., the institution of the court as an independent variable).

Compared with the legislature or chief executive, the judiciary is supposed to be "above politics"—that is, *not* primarily driven by political concerns. One of the most important concepts related to the judiciary, then, is **judicial independence**, the idea that the cases the judicial branch examines and the decisions it makes are not the result of pressure from the legislature or the executive. Lifetime (or long, single-term) judicial appointments enhance independence. When other officials can determine the cases that the court hears or can easily punish judges for their decisions, judicial independence is weak. Such punishments of judges include removing them from office in democracies and throwing them in jail (or worse) in nondemocracies.

Judicial independence refers to the extent to which the judiciary is free from influence from the other branches of government. It is a crucial feature that distinguishes judiciaries from one country to another.

Lawyers participate in an anti-government rally in Karachi, Pakistan, in April of 2007, protesting the decreasing independence of the judiciary during the leadership of President Pervez Musharraf. Musharraf's removal of Supreme Court Chief Justice Iftikhar Mohammed Chaudhry the preceding month triggered a wave of demonstrations. Musharraf ultimately resigned as president of Pakistan in August of 2008.
(©AP Photo/Shakil Adil)

The flip side of judicial independence is the extent to which other political actors accept judicial decisions. Courts do not have their own police forces to enforce their decisions, and they cannot levy taxes to fund the policy shifts their rulings sometimes require. Yet, at least in most of the world's democracies, other branches and lower levels of government accept and enforce judicial rulings. Political leaders recognize that failure to enforce judicial decisions with which they disagree would threaten the integrity of the entire political system.

An important distinction involving judicial rulings is the difference between **civil law** and **common law**. Of the two approaches, civil law is far more prevalent globally. Theoretically at least, in civil law systems judges interpret the law only. Their ability to exercise individual judgment is limited. The judges rely on an existing legal code and supplementary laws passed since the code's adoption. In common law systems, judges' case rulings have the effect of law. These rulings are known as **case law**. Common law systems, such as the American one, restrict a judge's flexibility through the principle of **stare decisis**—the idea that lower courts must adhere to higher court rulings and that previous court rulings on a topic provide a precedent, which is (largely) binding on future decisions for courts at the same level of authority. Precedent is less important in a civil law system, since each judge is expected to apply the existing legal code to the particular case under review and not use the case to rewrite the legal principle in question.

Tasks of the Judiciary

The main official task of the judiciary is to "adjudicate," settling disputes relating to existing laws. Courts are also responsible for sanctioning certain social activities, such as divorces, name changes, and inheritance distributions. In some countries, the judicial branch is much more powerful. It can overturn laws by declaring them unconstitutional or prescribe policy remedies to address problems brought before it.

Determining Violation of Law and Appropriate Punishment

The fundamental role of courts is to adjudicate laws by deciding the guilt or innocence of individuals charged with a crime. In some countries, judges are empowered to make these decisions entirely on their own, while in other countries, juries may be used to assess a defendant's guilt. Judges generally have the power to decide on appropriate

A **civil law** system is one based on a strong adherence to existing statutes. Judges have little discretion to interpret the law.

A **common law** system, on the other hand, allows judges more room to interpret the law, and their decisions set precedent for lower courts and future court rulings.

In common law systems, judicial decisions have the force of law, a concept known as **case law**.

The idea of binding precedent is known as **stare decisis**.

Table 8.1 Number of Lawyers: Total and Per 10,000 Residents in Selected European Countries

Selected Post-Communist Countries	No. of Lawyers	No. per 10,000 Residents
Armenia	473	1.5
Russian Federation	58,872	4.1
Estonia	917	6.8
Poland	26,403	6.9
Czech Republic	7,334	7.2
Selected Western European Countries		
France	40,847	6.8
Germany	116,305	14.1
Ireland	7,848	20.0
Italy	128,903	22.5
Spain	108,502	25.9

Source: "European Judicial Systems 2002," Publication of the European Commission for the Efficiency of Justice, Council of Europe, Strasbourg, December 10, 2004, Table 44.

punishments for those found guilty, though juries may also advise judges or even decide between punishment options, such as in capital punishment decisions in the United States.

Review of the Constitutionality of Existing Law and Policy

Judicial independence is especially important in the exercise of **judicial review**, the courts' authority to determine whether new laws or policies violate the constitution (**constitutional judicial review**) or contradict existing laws (**statutory judicial review**). A ruling that a particular law or policy is unconstitutional often leads the legislature to revise the law in light of the court ruling. This revised law will, hopefully, achieve the policy goals of the original law but be acceptable to the court. In the case of a statutory review decision, the possibility for the legislature to solve a problem by simply passing a new law is even greater.

Think and Discuss

Look at Table 8.1 above. What might the different numbers of lawyers per 10,000 people tell us about the judicial system of these various countries?

Interpretation of Vague Laws Passed by the Other Branches of Government

In a sense, all judicial decisions involve interpretation. No law is so clear or so obvious that everyone agrees about its intent and meaning, but some laws are much less clear than others. Legislatures and chief executives faced with a controversial and deeply divisive issue often delegate authority over the matter to other parts of the government, including courts. One way to do this is to write intentionally vague laws that force the courts to fill in the blanks. This allows a legislator or chief executive to shift blame for an unpopular policy decision onto the judiciary.

Judicial review is the power of the judiciary to rule on whether laws and government policies are consistent with the constitution or existing laws.

Constitutional judicial review refers to the power to declare that a law violates the constitution.

Statutory judicial review is the power to judge whether government policies are consistent with government statutes.

Creation of New Government Policy in Response to a Pressing Social Problem Another task some judiciaries have goes beyond filling in blanks in vague laws. Sometimes in the context of a ruling on constitutionality, and sometimes as part of the resolution of some other kind of dispute, a court may choose to prescribe particular policy goals or even detailed policy provisions. In such cases, the court leaves its role as an adjudicator and enters the realm of the legislator or bureaucrat. Those who dislike these actions deride them as "legislating from the bench." When judges dictate policy guidelines to other branches of government, their activities are often called **judicial activism**. An "activist court" is one that uses decisions before it to make sweeping policy changes.

In the United States, a classic example of judicial activism is the Supreme Court's 1954 *Brown* v. *Board of Education* decision. The court could have chosen to limit its ruling only to the school district in question; it instead ruled that racial segregation in American schools was unconstitutional. Some associate activist courts with left-of-center policy prescriptions. But no judges are immune from the temptation to legislate from bench. Though it may sound like an oxymoron, conservative judicial activism is an increasingly recognized practice.[5]

Settlement of Civil Disputes and Disputes Between Units of Government In addition to ruling on criminal cases, judiciaries often resolve arguments—known as civil disputes—between individuals, between an individual and a company, or between companies. Civil (noncriminal) disputes fall into a category known as **tort law**. A tort is a wrong or harm against an individual. In many countries, individuals can sue companies or other individuals that they believe harmed them through negligence or other inappropriate behavior.

Courts also sometimes resolve disagreements between units of government. These may involve two levels of government in a federal system or two components of the government at the same level. In Pakistan, for example, the Supreme Court rules on disputes between the federal and provincial governments or between two or more provincial governments.

Legal Sanctioning of Particular Acts The judicial system can also provide an official, legally binding decision to address other contentious matters—for example, child custody battles stemming from divorce—and sanction specified actions that are not in dispute. Such actions include name changes, adoptions, divorces, and the distribution of property following an individual's death. For example, although private and government agencies may be involved in the process of matching children up for adoption with new adoptive parents, a court decision may be required to finalize the adoption, giving it legal endorsement and authorization.

Think and Discuss

What is the single most important task of the judiciary? What makes this task so important?

Organization of the Judicial Branch

In any political system, the court system forms a complex hierarchy. Courts at the same level of this hierarchy exist in different parts of the country, and courts at different levels of it can

Judicial activism is a label used to describe a court ruling that implements new political policies rather than narrowly interpreting the legal question under review.

Tort law refers to disputes involving "torts" (harms done to an individual), including injury and nuisance. Such disputes are often resolved in the courts following the filing of a lawsuit by the harmed party.

be located in the same city. In a federal system, there are likely to be local, provincial ("state" in the United States), and federal courts—each with different constitutional responsibilities. In many countries, a single court sits at the top of this hierarchy. In the United States, this position is held by the Supreme Court, which is both the final court of appeal in the American political system and the ultimate authority on whether a particular state or federal law violates the U.S. Constitution. Other such examples include Australia's High Court, Finland's Supreme Court, and Paraguay's Supreme Court of Justice.

In other countries, these two tasks (highest appellate court and constitutional arbiter) are divided between two courts. The court that hears final appeals is sometimes known as the Supreme Court, while the other court is generally known as the Constitutional Court. Countries as different as Benin, Gabon, Lithuania, South Africa, South Korea, and Thailand have both a Supreme Court and Constitutional Court.

Advantages and Disadvantages of Strong Judiciaries

As with any institutional arrangement, there are both advantages and disadvantages to establishing a strong judicial branch with important policymaking powers. This section presents two such advantages and two disadvantages.

Advantage #1: A Check on "Majority Tyranny"

One of the important questions about democracy is how to balance majority rule and the protection of those in the minority. A politically independent court system can serve as a veto point (see Chapter 6) in a political system, checking the ability of the majority to easily impose its will on the minority. As legal scholar Jeremy Waldron relates, "Courts give reasons for their decisions, whereas legislatures do not, and this is a sign that courts, unlike legislatures, take seriously the issues of rights that they address."[6] While

in the past many other new democracies took minority protection less seriously than majority rule, this chapter's Comparative Exercise spotlights the large number of democratizing countries in recent decades that have implemented significant judicial review powers.

Advantage #2: A Key Component of the "Rule of Law" in Politics and Economics

Political systems in which the judiciary is subservient to the executive and legislative branches often struggle with developing and fostering the "rule of law," a concept discussed in Chapter 6. Corruption takes the place of transparent, legally based government action. The concept of rule of law extends to social and economic relations as well. For a country to develop economically, it is very important that agreements such as contracts are actually binding on those who enter into them. This is especially true if the government and businesses hope to attract investment from individuals and companies outside the country. When the judiciary is beholden to the executive, and when the executive itself is corrupt, rule of law is the last thing that drives legal decisions related to business practices.

Disadvantage #1: Power in the Hands of Unelected Officials

An important potential disadvantage of a powerful judicial branch is that government officials who have not been elected have significant discretion over government policy. If legislators and executives are constitutionally reckless in their policymaking, giving strong powers to unelected judges might indeed help alleviate the problem. But, in democracies at least, most elected officials have incentives to make good faith efforts to make policy consistent with the rules of the country's constitution. Such policies improve their prospects for being reelected (since blatantly violating the constitution would open the door for voters to hold them accountable for such actions at election time) and protect the democratic system from which they derive their political power.

Disadvantage #2: The Potential to Advance a Political Agenda Rather Than Ruling Impartially

A strong judiciary with constitutional and statutory review powers is built on the assumption that judges can objectively consider the issues before them. This is a substantial assumption. There is a danger that judges overseeing a powerful court will instead let their personal political outlooks drive their judicial decisions. Of course, it is difficult to tell whether judges are overturning a law because they personally disagree with it or because they legitimately believe it violates the constitution. One's own views tend to color interpretations of judicial rulings. People rarely level accusations of unfounded judicial activism at court decisions with which they agree.

The Judiciary in the United Kingdom, Germany, and France

Although the United Kingdom, Germany, and France are all mature democracies, their approaches to integrating the judicial branch into their democratic political systems appear quite different from one another. There is no tradition of judicial review in the United Kingdom, largely because of the notion of parliamentary sovereignty discussed in the previous chapter. Historically, the British judiciary has been fused to the legislative branch, although potentially important changes have begun to be implemented. In Germany, on the other hand, the country's courts, including the Federal Constitutional Court, are separated from the legislative and executive branches and have considerable power. The French judiciary as well is not fused with the other branches, but it clearly is the weaker and more subordinate branch. French courts were designed this way in the Fifth Republic to avoid judicial meddling and ensure the people's sovereignty through their elected representatives.

The United Kingdom

The United Kingdom uses a common law approach, and its extensive and complex judicial branch tries civil and criminal cases. Like its fused executive and legislative branches, a portion of the judiciary has historically been fused with the legislature as well. In the past, the highest British appeals court was the Appellate Committee of the House of Lords. Twelve "Lords of Appeal in Ordinary" (more commonly called the "Law Lords") decided on legal matters, with their decisions binding on all lower courts. Their jurisdiction over civil cases extended to the United Kingdom as a whole but only for England, Wales, and Northern Ireland in criminal cases.

As part of the overhaul of the British political system under the government of Tony Blair, the Constitutional Reform Bill became law in March 2005. This law has altered the tradition of a fused legislature and judiciary by, among other things, creating a new United Kingdom Supreme Court, which will convene for the first time in 2009. Consistent with the British political system's theme of evolutionary change, the Law Lords will become the first justices of the Supreme Court and surrender their seats in the House of Lords.

The other interesting feature of the judiciary is the relative absence of judicial review authority. An act of parliament is, by definition, constitutional. This does not mean that the Law Lords never weigh in on parliamentary acts, and one would expect their intervention to continue to increase rather than decrease in the years ahead. One reason for this is the amplified role of European judicial bodies in the wake of continuing European integration. In addition to the European Court of Justice and the European Court of Human Rights "now regularly reviewing British legislation for compatibility with international obligations,"[7] the Law Lords have increasingly used European standards to evaluate acts of the British parliament. In December 2004, for example, the Lords' Appellate

Committee declared that the Anti-terrorism, Crime and Security Act, an act passed by the British government in 2001, violated the European Convention on Human Rights, of which the United Kingdom is a signatory. Although the Law Lords' ruling did not invalidate the law, it placed great pressure on Prime Minister Tony Blair's government to address the concerns in the ruling and led the government to replace the law the following year.

As comparative law specialist Tom Ginsburg points out, the idea that commitments to the European Union mean acts of parliament are no longer completely sovereign has opened the door for broader intervention by domestic judges. As Ginsburg puts it, if parliament does not possess complete sovereignty, then the traditional objection to judicial intervention by the British "is much less potent."[8] In the years ahead, it will be interesting to see whether the new British Supreme Court will attempt to establish more forcefully a role for itself as a check on parliament.

Germany

The Federal Republic of Germany was founded on the principle of a *Rechtsstaat*, or a state based on the rule of law.[9] This principle stands in stark contrast to the lawlessness of the Nazi regime and its politicization of the judiciary through the appointment of Nazi Party members throughout the judiciary and civil service. The post–World War II Constitution delineates basic rights of individual citizens and societal groups and provides for an independent judiciary.

The Federal Constitutional Court, Germany's equivalent of the U.S. Supreme Court, exhibits substantial authority and independence from the executive. The court possesses judicial review over other branches of government and has the authority to act as the final arbiter of disputes between state and federal levels of government. Justices on the court can only be removed by the federal president on the recommendation of the court itself. In response to the

country's tumultuous past, the court is charged with protecting the constitutional and political order against antidemocratic forces. The court used this authority to ban far-Left and far-Right parties that it deemed were a threat to democracy in the 1950s and 1960s.[10]

The organization of the judicial system reflects the influences of Germany's own brand of federalism. Eight of the sixteen justices to the Federal Constitutional Court are appointed by the upper house of parliament, the *Bundesrat*, the other eight by the lower house, the *Bundestag*. This arrangement gives voice to both the governments of the *Länder* and the political parties.[11] In contrast to the structure of the judiciary in the federal system of the United States, there are no separate federal and *Land* courts in the German federal system, with the exception of the Federal Constitutional Court. The remaining courts in Germany are established by the *Länder*.

Germany also has an extensive system of specialized administrative courts that adjudicate labor and social welfare disputes.[12] Moreover, Germany has a longstanding public law tradition that legally designates societal organizations as corporatist bodies with important public policy responsibilities. Examples include the Catholic and Lutheran churches, which receive public funding to provide welfare state services on behalf of the state through nursing homes, hospitals, and day care centers. In addition, doctors and insurers are organized as

Justices of the German Federal Constitutional Court stand in a courtroom in Karlsruhe, Germany, on August 9, 2005.

(©AP Photo/Michael Probst)

public law bodies, whose task is to administer the national health insurance system and implement health care legislation on behalf of the state.[13]

France

For a country to have a former prime minister defending himself in court against charges of involuntary homicide is noteworthy. As discussed in the last chapter, that was the fate of Laurent Fabius, tried in 1999 for policy choices he made related to HIV prevention in the 1980s. Though cases like that against Fabius make it tempting to represent the 1990s as a period of judicial penetration into French politics, it is important to distinguish court cases against government officials from judicial activism. Despite a series of trials against former officials related to financial irregularities, corruption, and even crimes against humanity during the Holocaust, French courts typically take a backseat to the executive and legislative branches.

The limited nature of judicial power in the Fifth Republic contrasts with a long history of the use of the judiciary for political ends. Courts have served repeatedly as an arena for the contestation of political differences, with state authorities even turning to the courts to prosecute their political opponents. These include the celebrated writer Emile Zola, who was convicted of criminal libel in 1898 for denouncing the court martial of Alfred Dreyfus as a miscarriage of justice, and more than a dozen government ministers tried before France's highest court since the French Revolution,[14] including one who had advocated for a negotiated settlement to end World War I.[15] The Vichy government, which governed France during World War II from July 1940 to August 1944, attempted to try former Prime Minister Léon Blum for failing to prepare France for the Nazi invasion. The post–World War II government established special jurisdictions for prosecuting Vichy-era officials. According to one famous French lawyer, who defended Algerians during the insurrection against French rule, "Such trials reveal that society is a state of civil war."[16]

What links France's judiciary today to its counterparts in past regimes is its reliance on civil law, where judges resolve each case individually, according to statute and inspired neither by common law nor *stare decisis* and judicial interpretation. France is the earliest and arguably most influential model for the civil law approach. From time to time, however, the French courts have found informal ways to acknowledge precedent and consider the rulings of other judges.[17] More recently, European court requirements that rulings be enforced as constitutionally binding have compelled them to do so more openly.[18]

A judicial career in France is bureaucratic in nature, governed by training and seniority. The judiciary itself is divided into three distinct arenas of law: civil or private law, criminal law, and administrative law. Criminal cases are not adversarial in the Anglo-American sense, but inquisitorial, where the judge can engage the witnesses and the defendants, and victims of crimes are represented in criminal courts as civil parties, with their own attorneys. In fact, French courts have a relatively weak "presumption of innocence," and much of the proceeding addresses punishment rather than guilt. At the pinnacle of the civil and criminal courts is the *Cour de Cassation*, which, unlike the U.S. Supreme Court, must review and decide on every case filed, serving to delay judgments more than adjudicate conflicts.[19]

Cases arising under administrative law—those dealing with actions of the state and her representatives in the civil service—are adjudicated in district administrative courts, with appeals culminating in the *Conseil d'État*. The Constitutional Council is not constituted as a court, and members, who are not judges, can only rule on a proposal before it becomes law if it is submitted by the president, other high officials, or a group of sixty deputies or senators. The *Cour de Justice de la République* includes members of the parliament as judges of cases involving former ministers, and the *Haute Cour de Justice* hears impeachment cases against the president.

The Judiciary in Mexico, Brazil, Nigeria, and India

The judiciaries of Mexico, Brazil, Nigeria, and India have many differences but share in struggling to be fully autonomous, appropriately staffed and funded, and free from corruption. The fundamental changes that have altered the Mexican political system over the past three decades have had less of an impact on the judiciary, bureaucracy, and military than they have had on the presidency and national legislature. The judiciary is still coming into its own as an autonomous institution. Like other aspects of Brazilian politics, the complexity and diversity of its courts make understanding them difficult. Taken as a whole, they have a fair amount of autonomy and the public has gained confidence in them, yet they remain heavily overworked and underfunded. In Nigeria, the judiciary is still recovering from corruption and neglect under military rule. The judiciary in India has been active in challenging the actions of legislatures. As with other topics, however, diversity and change in India make generalizations about any of its unelected governmental institutions tenuous.

Mexico

Mexico has a civil law tradition and a history of judicial subservience to other branches of government. The writers of the Mexican Constitution intended the judicial branch to serve as a check on the legislature and executive, but in practice it was controlled by the executive in general and the president in particular. The Senate tended to rubber stamp the president's judicial selections during the era of PRI dominance. Showing the lack of judicial independence, the justices of the Mexican Supreme Court would typically resign following a presidential election—allowing the new president to hand pick new judges—even though they were able to serve for life according to the constitution.

The judicial branch became more independent in the 1990s, largely as a result of a set of judicial reforms under President Ernesto Zedillo in 1994. These changes were adopted in part because PRI leaders suspected that they might lose control of the federal government. In particular, they feared the loss of the presidency would allow their opponents to use a weak judicial branch to support reprisals against them. Thus, the reforms that included judicial review powers became the PRI's "insurance policy."[20] Mexico does not yet have a fully independent judiciary. The practice of judicial review is relatively new, and a culture of judicial independence is still evolving. However, Mexico's judiciary has come a long way from the body that automatically authorized executive decisions in the past.

The Mexican judicial system also reflects the country's federal arrangements. The *estados* have their own judiciaries, with powers to rule on the basis of laws passed in that *estados*. The structures of the *estados* courts are not uniform, however, and the reform process affected *estados* judicial systems in different ways.[21] Corruption in law enforcement institutions, including the courts, remains a larger problem in some of the *estados* than in others.

Brazil

The Brazilian judicial system is complex. In addition to *estado* and municipal courts that deal with ordinary criminal and civil matters, Brazil has a federal court system, regional courts of appeal, a Federal Supreme Court with authority to rule on the constitutionality of federal or *estado* laws and actions, and a separate court (the Superior Justice Tribunal) that functions as the top court of appeal for nonconstitutional issues. There are also parallel court systems for issues involving interpretation of labor law, electoral law, and a separate system of military courts.

Of these courts, the most powerful is the Supreme Federal Court. The court is composed of eleven justices, appointed by the president and approved by the Senate. The court may declare an action or law unconstitutional and is responsible for hearing cases involving top public officials (such as the president or members of Congress) charged with criminal acts; these cases do not go to ordinary courts for trial. The Supreme Federal Court has, therefore, significant ability to check the legislature or the executive, as well as the governments of the various *estados*.

It is also relatively autonomous, in part because of the life terms granted to justices.[22] Although a new independent tribunal was created in 2004 to monitor the behavior of all judges (who used to monitor themselves), this tribunal has yet to demonstrate real clout; the fact that its members serve for only two years and are limited to two terms suggests that it may lack the ability and the expertise to serve as a serious investigative tool for the other branches.

Nevertheless, the Brazilian judiciary is underfunded and overwhelmed. Brazil has roughly one judge for every 23,000 Brazilians, as opposed to one judge for every 9,000 people in the United States and one judge for every 3,500 people in Germany.[23] Brazil also inherited from the Portuguese a civil law system. Higher court decisions were not binding on lower courts until 2004; even now, the court must declare a "summary judgment" to make a specific decision binding. Thus, if many people are affected by the same government action, every one of them might have to file an individual case before the Supreme Federal Court in order to get relief. Needless to say, this increases the number of cases compared with a system in which *stare decisis* is the default approach to court rulings.

Ironically, increased public confidence in the judiciary exacerbated its heavy workload and hurt its efficiency. As confidence in the courts grew, litigation increased. In 1989, 6,622

Did You Know? The United States is exceptional in its widespread use of juries for a broad range of civil and criminal cases. In Brazil, for example, a single judge will decide most cases brought to court. Normally, only cases involving crimes against people are expected to go to juries.

lawsuits were filed in the Supreme Federal Court.[24] In 2003, the court received 109,965 cases.[25] This proliferation of cases before the Supreme Federal Court was a central reason for the 2004 constitutional reform that enabled the court to make its decisions binding on lower courts. At the same time, the lingering problems in the judiciary have limited the extent of increased public confidence in the legal system. Surveys of Brazilian business managers conducted by organizations such as the World Bank have found that a large portion lack confidence in the court system's ability to resolve their disputes in a timely fashion.[26]

Nigeria

Consistent with its federal system, Nigeria's judiciary has both federal courts and regional courts. The Supreme Court is the country's highest court, responsible for handling appeals from the Federal Court of Appeals, which itself hears appeals from lower federal courts and regional courts, including the country's various *Shari'a* (Islamic Law) courts. It also handles disputes between regions or between a region and the federal government.

During the long period of military rule, the court system was not just controlled; it was also neglected.[27] The military preferred its own courts to those associated with the civilian political system. This neglect, including poor pay for judges, contributed to corruption taking root in the judicial branch. To its credit, the federal government has taken steps to address the problem, including working with international organizations such as the United Nations to study the Nigerian system and make recommendations for judicial reform. In 2001, the UN and Nigeria launched the Strengthening Judicial Integrity and Capacity project as part of the UN Office on Drugs and Crime's Global Program Against Corruption (GPAC).

Another major concern is the controversy over the actions of *Shari'a* courts in many of the northern Nigerian regions. Following laws in these regions, which themselves are based on Islamic Law, these courts have ordered amputations, floggings, and even death by stoning. The stoning sentences were each overturned by *Shari'a* appeals courts. These decisions, made largely on procedural grounds, avoided an appeal to the federal level. Whether these appeals court decisions reflect a waning desire to implement *Shari'a* in the north is unclear. Many analysts believe that a federal court, perhaps even the Supreme Court, may ultimately have to decide if *Shari'a* sentences are constitutional.

India

The judiciary has played a significant role in the governance of India. Using its powers of judicial review, it has been a check on Indian legislators. By encouraging a certain type of litigation, described later in this section, it has provided a tool for greater civic involvement in governance.

As is the case with judiciaries in other countries, India's judiciary is structured hierarchically. The Supreme Court, headed by a chief justice, is situated at the top of this hierarchy. High Courts, responsible for individual federal territorial units or groups of federal units, come next. Below that are three or four levels of civil and criminal courts in rural and metropolitan areas. Although the range of consultation on the appointment of justices has varied over time, the chief justice and other Supreme Court justices are appointed by the president on the advice of the prime minister and cabinet. The president appoints High Court judges, after consultation with the chief justice of India, the chief justice of the High Court, and the governor(s) of the federal territorial unit(s) that fall under the court's jurisdiction. Governors appoint judges in their territories, after consultation with the responsible High Court and the Public Services Commissions.

The most significant source of tension between the courts and the legislatures surrounds the authority to declare laws unconstitutional. Initially, the Supreme Court recognized the right of the *Lok Sabha* and *Rajya Sabha* to amend the constitution at will. In 1967, it decided in the *Golak Nath* case that the Fundamental Rights laid out in the constitution were supreme, and the legislature could not make laws that violated them. Responding to the court's action, the parliamentary bodies passed the Twenty-first Amendment in 1971, which gave the *Lok Sabha* and *Rajya Sabha* the power to amend any part of the Constitution. In 1973, the amendment was challenged in the *Keshavananda Bharti* case, and the Supreme Court held that Parliament could not exercise its amendment powers to alter the "basic structure" of the Constitution—a precedent that continues to guide the Court's review of legislation.[28] A former attorney general of India, Soli Sorabjee, identified five fundamental features that characterize the "basic structure," stating, "The first is secularism; second, democracy; third, rule of law; fourth, federalism; and the fifth is an independent judiciary with the power of judicial review."[29]

A second source of tension comes from the Supreme Court's encouragement of Public Interest Litigation (PIL). Because exact parameters for what constitutes PIL are not laid out in Indian law, the idea allows for significant judicial interpretation. Essentially, any litigation with the stated purpose of protecting the "public interest" could qualify. This includes cases designed to force government officials to enforce laws or protect the citizenry from dangers such as pollution and terrorism. Rather than restricting such cases to claims by the particular victims of alleged violations of public interest protection, PIL cases can be filed by anyone. In the last two decades, much of the PIL has challenged decisions made by the legislature and executive.

In recent years, judiciary-legislature tensions have generated numerous disputes over whether one was interfering with the responsibilities assigned to the other. An example is a case in September and October 2007 in which the Supreme

Court ordered the chief minister of Tamil Nadu to call off a *bandh* (a shutdown of business and government activities as a demonstration of protest against something) scheduled for the next day. He responded by pledging not to participate and declared that he would fast rather than participate in the *bandh*. Nevertheless, bus drivers and many others did not go to work, producing a *bandh*-like situation. The opposition went back to the court and said the court's order was not carried out. One Supreme Court judge, B.N. Agrawal, said that if what he had heard was true, the prime minister should advise the president to introduce President's Rule in Tamil Nadu. The remarks prompted strong complaints, asserting that such a statement crossed the boundary between the powers of the judiciary and those of the executive and legislature.[30]

The struggle with India's executive and legislative branches is not the only challenge the judiciary faces. It has an immense backlog of cases and is grossly understaffed. At the end of 2005, there were 29,210,015 cases pending, with the backlog increasing by about 200,000 cases in the High Court and 2 million cases in other courts each year. To make matters worse, by April 2006, there were 2,886 vacancies for judges across the country.[31]

The Judiciary in the Russian Federation, China, and Iran

In Russia, China, and Iran, the judicial branch has little autonomy from the legislative branch and, even more, the executive branch. In Russia, the judiciary has been hindered by a desperate shortage of judges and lawyers, the lack of appropriate pay for judicial officials, and an ongoing reluctance to embrace the concept of rule of law. In China, some of the reform efforts over the last several decades have targeted the judiciary. Such efforts have been hampered on a number of fronts, not the least of which is the extent to which serious reform of the political institutions in China threatens the Chinese Communist Party's (CCP's) hold on political power. As a result, the judicial system remains under heavy CCP control. Likewise, the extent to which Iran's judiciary can function autonomously and professionally is constrained both by the country's theocratic system and its prevalent corruption.

The Russian Federation

A common theme in Russia's development as a fledgling democracy following the Soviet collapse was the need to establish the rule of law. This not only meant that government officials should follow the country's constitution and laws; it also meant that the legal system needed an overhaul. Russian judges—typically holdovers from the Soviet legal system—were underpaid, not used to real autonomy, and not used to making decisions outside of political considerations.

Rule of law and a more professional judiciary were slower to develop than other institutional practices of democracy. The Constitutional Court became a respected body in the years following the new Russian Constitution in December 1993, aided by Yeltsin's acceptance of its ruling in April of that year about the validity of the national referendum on support for the president, the parliament, and Yeltsin's reforms. Like other aspects of Russian politics, however, the court felt its autonomy increasingly threatened by the reforms of the Putin era. Although it has maintained a degree of independence, the decision of the *Duma* in 2007 to move the court from Moscow to St. Petersburg—over the opposition of the Constitutional Court justices—was symbolic of the court facing increasing pressure from the executive and legislative branches. Even the backers of the law passed in the *Duma* to authorize the move did not argue that it would help the performance of the court. Instead, they argued that the move to St. Petersburg "will upgrade the political status of Russia's second-largest city and Putin's hometown."[32]

In comparison to the Constitutional Court, other components of the judiciary have struggled even more. The replacement of old judges—and the acceptance of a culture of professionalism among those who remained—has been a slow process. Judges were notoriously corrupt in the 1990s, often basing their rulings on whichever side paid the most in bribes. Russia lacked a sufficient number of qualified judges, but the shortage of prosecutors and defense attorneys was even more acute. Some estimates place the number of independent lawyers in Russia as low as 25,000. Contrary to the view of U.S. law by many Americans, justice in Russia would benefit from more lawyers, not fewer.

IN THEORY AND PRACTICE

Russia and the Theory of Inverse Judicial Power

A central question about the judiciary is why some courts are aggressive policymakers and others defer to the executive or legislature. The **inverse judicial power theory** argues that the courts' power is inversely related to the power and unity of the other branches. Courts are more likely to be activist when the other branches lack coherence. Political scientist John Ferejohn argues that judicial activism is most likely when the "legislature is too fragmented to react,"[33] and Cornell Clayton adds that in times of legislative weakness, the power to legislate can "relocate itself to other institutions, such as the courts."[34] Clayton calls this theoretical perspective a "separation of powers" approach, since it highlights constraints on the judiciary in terms of the other branches rather than the constitutional powers of the judiciary itself.[35]

In the past, comparativists often focused more on the unqualified, official power of the judiciary than on its relative power versus the other branches of government. More recently, comparative work on judicial behavior has challenged this tendency. Studies in 2002 by Shannon Ishiyama Smithey and John Ishiyama and in 2003 by Erik Herron and Kirk Randazzo pointed to the need to examine contextual factors such as the strength of the judiciary versus the executive in order to understand post-Communist judicial activism and judicial review.[36]

The theory of inverse judicial power holds that judiciaries become more independent and able to influence political policies in a country when the institutions of the legislative and executive branches are weak. This theory can help us understand the challenges facing the Russian judiciary at present. In 2002, halfway through President Putin's first term, a report on Russia by the International Commission of Jurists stated, "One of the principal problems confronting the judiciary is the undue influence of the executive on composition of the courts."[37] It is hard to imagine how the judiciary could have become more autonomous since then. Indeed increased threats to judicial independence have emerged alongside the increasing hold of Putin's United Russia party over both the executive and legislative branches in the Russian Federation.

The **inverse judicial power theory** explains judicial activism as a function of the relative power of the courts versus other branches of government. When the legislative branch is divided and weak, for example, the duties of legislating can transfer more easily to the courts.

China

In some ways, the Chinese judiciary functions like those of other authoritarian countries—trying individuals accused of crimes but saying little about laws passed by the government. However, the excesses of the Great Proletarian Cultural Revolution (Mao's final effort at dramatic reform from 1966 to 1976, in which tens of thousands were executed) planted a seed about the need to reconsider China's legal system following Mao's death. Change was slow, but the 1999 Chinese Supreme Court announcement of a five-year plan to reform the judicial system seemed to point to an understanding of the need for significant change. Some in the government understand the importance of a properly functioning legal system for economic performance and efforts to deal with increasing social tensions; others are concerned about the political consequences of weakening the control of the judiciary by the China Communist Party (CCP).[38]

Thus, one of the central questions remains the extent to which the Chinese judiciary will be allowed to function independently from the CCP and state leadership. The National People's Congress can remove Supreme Court officials, and local people's congresses can remove local judges. In addition, as in Russia, judges are scarce, poorly paid, and often corrupt. The court system has also become overwhelmed by an explosion in civil cases. Nearly 4.5 million civil cases were filed in 2004 alone.[39]

Most of these civil cases did not involve government officials or institutions. Despite the 1989 adoption of an "administrative litigation law" to allow such lawsuits, many Chinese are still unaware of how to bring an administrative lawsuit, expect interference from the CCP and other government officials during the trial, or fear retaliation from the government after the trial.[40] The Supreme Court claims that most of the components of its five-year reform plan have been adopted, but most analysts believe that China is a long way from the "fair, open, highly effective, honest, and well-functioning" judicial system the court had promised.[41] For the government, the

dangers of taking the concept of rule of law seriously simply outweigh the benefits.

Iran

The Iranian judiciary is an important part of the theocratic regime. It provides the government with some legitimacy, yet its rulings tend to support the government's more conservative elements. The courts have been used to ban moderate publications and arrest those who publish pro-reform messages on Iranian websites. The courts do not have judicial review authority—that power is reserved for the Guardian Council, and to an extent the Expediency Council and Supreme Leader. The judiciary is also not independent from the Supreme Leader, who is given constitutional authority (Article 57) to oversee the judicial branch. The Supreme Leader makes his views on many issues well known, sometimes via "briefings" to members of the judiciary, and the selection of top judicial positions is tightly controlled.[42] Thus, while the Iranian Constitution talks about judicial independence, its preamble also states clearly that the judiciary is to enforce "ideological conformity" and prevent "deviations within the Islamic nation."

Such prevention of deviation can take extreme form. Iran has one of the highest execution rates in the world, and it has been known to execute minors.[43] Judicial decisions have been particularly harsh against women. In one well-documented case, Atefeh Sahaleh Rajabi, a sixteen-year-old from the city of Neka, was hanged in public in August 2004. She was denied access to a lawyer during her trial, and was reported to be suffering from mental illness. The judge, Hadji Rezai, used apparently forged documents to claim that she was twenty-two. In addition, the judge actually put the noose around the girl's neck, saying he sentenced her to death in part for her "sharp tongue" in court. Unlike in the case of many of the *Shari'a*-based death sentences in Nigeria that have been overturned by religious courts, the Iranian Supreme Court upheld her sentence. The young man accused of having sex with her received one hundred lashes and was set free.[44]

The Bureaucracy

Legislatures make laws, but it is up to the executive branch to oversee their implementation. This job falls largely to a particular part of the executive branch known as the **bureaucracy**. The bureaucracy is divided vertically, into the various departments, agencies, or ministries of a government, and horizontally, into layers based on responsibilities, tasks, and authority. Departments, agencies, and ministries are responsible for implementing policy in particular issue areas: for example, agriculture, labor, and the environment. Though technically part of the executive branch, the bureaucracy's power and autonomy from the legislative branch—and even from those at the top of the executive branch—has earned it the label of the **fourth branch of government**.

Tasks of the Bureaucracy

As governments have taken on greater responsibilities in increasingly complex societies, bureaucracies have developed primarily to implement government policy. As governments continue to grow in size and scope, the responsibilities of the bureaucracy have grown as well. Although a central task of the legislative branch is to oversee actions of the bureaucracy, the size of most bureaucracies today makes this difficult. In addition, as discussed in the previous chapter, many legislatures are happy to delegate responsibilities to the executive branch. As a result, in addition to executing laws developed by the legislature and top officials of the executive branch, bureaucracies play an increasingly important role in policy creation. As political scientist Stephen Brooks puts it, "The bureaucracy enters the policy process both early and late."[45]

Implementation of Laws and Policies Officially, the central task of bureaucracies is to execute laws and policies created by the legislature and chief executive. Laws and programs do not administer themselves, and it is hard to imagine how a government could do what it is expected to do—raise taxes, spend money, defend the country, and so on—without a large work force to implement policies. At upper levels of the bureaucracy, implementation includes broad planning about how to administer policies. At the lower levels, it includes routine administrative duties, such as performing inspections of particular businesses or processing checks from individuals and corporations paying taxes.

Agenda-Setting and Advising on Policy Specifics Bureaucrats also play a significant role in policy creation. Sometimes, high-ranking members of the bureaucracy use their connections with legislators and the chief executive to stress certain broad approaches. Members of particular bureaucratic departments may emphasize the importance of their policy area (e.g., transportation safety) within a broader policy concern (e.g., homeland security). They hope their efforts play a role in *setting the policy agenda*. As Chapter 13 discusses, agenda setting is a primary step in the policy process. It provides the overarching framework for the policies the political process generates.

At other times, bureaucrats *provide detailed information* to legislators or others in the executive branch as a developing policy is being drafted or an existing policy is being revised. Legislatures and chief executives rely on officials in assorted bureaucratic departments for advice about issues within those departments' policy areas. As discussed in the previous chapter, legislative committees may call officials from the executive branch to testify. This is part of the legislature's

---

The **bureaucracy** is the large part of the executive branch dedicated to the implementation of government policy.

The bureaucracy's significant powers have earned it the label of the **fourth branch of government**.

oversight function, but it can also help the legislature formulate policy. In the United States, it is common for members of the bureaucracy to testify before congressional committees or subcommittees about a particular bill.

Middle-level bureaucrats may give similar advice—broad or detailed, in person or through reports—to superiors in their department. These senior officials then craft policy recommendations that are submitted to the legislature for consideration. The position of officials directly below the level of minister, department secretary, or agency director can wield significant influence over policy by *filtering suggestions* from below before passing them on to the minister, secretary, or director. Likewise, the minister plays a similar role in filtering policy suggestions before passing them along to the chief executive or the legislature.

Interpretation of Existing but Vague Laws

Part of how legislatures delegate to the executive branch is to pass vague laws. The lack of clarity in a particular law, intentional or unintentional, allows the bureaucrats to add in specific details. Such practice is common, even in the case of policies that apply to the functions of the bureaucratic department. Political scientists John Ferejohn and Charles Shipan argue that this happens more often than one might think. They claim that most statutes are "constraints" as opposed to "detailed directives" and that "relatively few governmental decisions are directly mandated by legislative acts."[46] The legislature and chief executive may want certain laws to be vague in the interest of efficiency, leaving the details up to those who know the most about the issue. They may also favor vague laws for political reasons, since a vague law allows them to avoid taking a detailed stance on controversial issues.

Policy Creation
Depending on the nature of the issue, bureaucracies sometimes have significant powers to create new government policies from scratch. When specific rules governing an issue do not exist the bureaucracy may be called on— or decide on its own—to fill the void with new rules and regulations that have the force of law. The bureaucracy establishes the parameters of new government action, which become prevailing and official policy unless they are preempted by a legislative or judicial response.[47] Such instances move bureaucrats well beyond their roles as implementers, agenda-setters, advisors, and interpreters. They become unelected legislators.

Think and Discuss

What is the bureaucracy's single most important task? What makes this task so important?

Organization of Bureaucracies

Bureaucracies are made up of various permanent bodies—ministries, departments, agencies, bureaus, and so on—that, taken altogether, comprise the majority of the executive branch. Officials at the top of each governmental section link the chief executive to the bureaucracy. The chief executive typically appoints these top officials, and therefore they generally serve in their positions only as long as that chief executive is in power. For personal reasons or because of poor performance, they may leave in the middle of the chief executive's term in office.

The American federal bureaucracy has four types of government agencies: cabinet departments, regulatory agencies, government corporations, and independent executive agencies. The **cabinet departments** are those most closely linked to the chief executive. With the exception of the

Cabinet departments are the bureaucratic sections in the United States most closely tied to the president.

Justice Department, headed by the attorney general, a **secretary** heads each of the fifteen departments of the president's cabinet. The most recent cabinet department addition, Homeland Security, arose in 2002 in response to the September 11, 2001, terrorist attacks. There are four times as many independent agencies as departments. These include the Environmental Protection Agency (EPA) and the Federal Reserve. In many other countries, cabinet departments are known as **ministries**, and they are headed by **ministers**.

Middle- and lower-level bureaucrats are generally not political appointees. Instead, they are part of a national **civil service** and are known as **civil servants**. They are expected to serve in an objective manner regardless of who heads the executive branch. Unlike political appointees, civil servants ordinarily retain their positions through changes in the chief executive. Consistent with the idea of protecting civil servants from the politics of the governmental process, some countries have specific laws and regulations making it difficult for a civil servant to be fired. In the United States, for example, civil servants serve for a "probationary period," after which they can appeal a dismissal to a government body such as the Merit Systems Protection Board.[48]

In most democracies, civil servants earn their positions through the **merit system**. In theory, a merit system allows individuals to enter and advance through the bureaucracy due to general competence (e.g., knowledge of the law), expertise in a particular policy field, and/or their performance on the job. The opposite of a merit system is known as a **spoils system**. In a spoils system, even middle-level officials are political appointees, who earn their positions through their connections to government leaders or in return for favors done for such officials.

In merit systems, bureaucrats develop their knowledge and expertise through educational training (often at the post-undergraduate level),

additional training once in the civil service, and experience from working for a particular agency over a period of time. Bureaucracies can differ significantly in their approach to the question of training and qualifications. U.S. Government departments generally take a **specialist approach**, where they hire individuals to fill a specific role. In such cases, individuals are likely to remain in one department for their entire government career. Other countries employ a **generalist approach**, in which individuals are hired for their general knowledge or legal expertise. The portion of members of the bureaucracy with a law degree is higher in many European countries than it is in the United States. In generalist systems, bureaucrats are

Each U.S. cabinet department is headed by a **secretary**, who is a member of the cabinet.

In many other countries, the cabinet-level departments are known as **ministries** and are headed by **ministers**.

The **civil service** is made up of middle- and lower-level bureaucrats, known as **civil servants**, who are hired for their professional or technical expertise. They may remain in their positions for long periods of time, even when the head of their department changes.

A **merit system** is one in which members of the bureaucracy earn their initial positions and promotions on the basis of their qualifications and performance.

A **spoils system** is one in which bureaucrats get their initial jobs and promotions on the basis of their connections to top government positions or favors done for such officials.

In the **specialist approach** to recruitment into the bureaucracy, workers are hired to fill a specific role in a particular government department and typically stay in that department for most or all of their government careers.

In the **generalist approach**, individuals are hired for their general knowledge or expertise, typically including advanced legal training.

likely to move from one department to another over their careers.

Advantages and Disadvantages of Large and Powerful Bureaucracies

The way that many people criticize bureaucracies, in the United States at least, it might be hard to think of any advantages to large and powerful bureaucracies. Yet most Americans appreciate many of the government programs that the bureaucracy administers and generally have favorable impressions of the specific civil servants with whom they have had contact.

Advantage #1: Stability

One advantage of a large and powerful bureaucracy is a degree of governmental stability. In the United States, civil servants may hold positions across several presidential administrations. In other countries, bureaucratic stability is even more important. In parliamentary systems going through a period of unstable governments—that is, the prime minister and cabinet being replaced every few months—mid- and lower-level civil servants keep the government running. In such cases, bureaucrats also take on greater policymaking responsibilities than they already possess.

Advantage #2: Expertise

Combined with a system of hiring based on merit, bureaucratic stability allows individuals to develop a high degree of expertise in their policy area, particularly in systems where officials often spend their entire careers in the same department. Sociologist Max Weber's vision of bureaucracy was one of a hierarchy of government officials, selected for their competence, promoted for their performance, who make impartial and sensible decisions based on established rules. For Weber, the expansion of size and scope of bureaucracies was a rational response to increasing social and economic complexity.

Advantage #3: Impartial and Fair Application of Rules

Weber also saw bureaucracies as a way to move beyond the arbitrary creation and enforcement of rules. In European monarchies prior to the Industrial Revolution and the spread of democracy, government officials routinely used their positions to grant favors to those they knew or those with particular economic or social clout. For Weber, the ability to apply general rules to specific cases—and thus reduce the likelihood of favoritism—was a defining feature of bureaucracy, leading to principled and reasonable government deeds.[49] Of course, bureaucracies are more likely to be fair and impartial in practice when they are closely watched by others in the government charged with overseeing their activities. Thus, oversight of the bureaucracy is not only about insuring that bureaucrats do not overstep their policymaking bounds. It is also about helping establish that their decisions about individual situations are consistent and evenhanded.

Disadvantage #1: Inefficiency Through Overexpansion and Wasteful Spending

While Max Weber saw bureaucratic expansion as a rational response to increasing social complexity, others believe that bureaucrats desire to expand the bureaucracy's size and scope in order to benefit themselves. Increases in staff and budget put more resources under department leaders' control, make these officials more important, and further their prospects for career advancement. This internal incentive to expand can lead departments to manipulate information about their issue areas to justify expansion. In addition, though governments occasionally recognize and publicly praise efficient and effective agencies, departments that use resources efficiently run the risk of having their budgets cut in response. After all, if an agency is not using all its budgeted funds, why give it as much money next year as it received this year?

While it seems like bureaucracies do not always do things as efficiently as private firms might, observing and measuring such inefficiency can be difficult. Unlike a small, local business working on a single project, government agencies face multiple goals and tasks at the same time. Singling out their economically inefficient handling of a particular small project, therefore, ignores what might have been an honest and equitable approach to the project, as well as their better handling of other projects.[50] Uncovering anecdotes about a particular agency's program using tax dollars inefficiently is easy. Finding an alternative that spends tax dollars efficiently but still achieves the program's goals is often much more difficult.

Disadvantage #2: Power in the Hands of Unelected Officials One might tolerate inefficiency if bureaucracies were responsive and consistent in the creation and enforcement of their policies. As the discussion of India and the Harry Potter series at this chapter's opening highlights, however, robust bureaucracies often cause concern in democracies, because of potential partiality and a lack of responsiveness. Bureaucrats are not responsible to voters—the term bureaucracy, in fact, comes from a French word, *bureaucratie*, referring to rule by unelected government officials (or, more precisely, rule by offices).

How one can best address this concern is unclear. Placing too many restraints on bureaucrats' decisions, in an effort to make them more accountable, limits one of their key strengths: their expertise on the issue at hand. In addition, there is a tension between the two goals of responsiveness and impartiality. Applying rules without taking into account the context of the individual situation in question—what some decry as a "rules are rules" mentality—can make a government agency more impartial but also more distant and less responsive.[51]

Disadvantage #3: Resistance to Reform and Creative Solutions What one person sees as stability and fairness, another person could label rigidity and narrow-mindedness. Bureaucracies tend to be rigid organizations that resist reform, the introduction of untested innovations, and creative responses to current problems. Reform challenges those currently in positions of power, that is, the individuals with the authority to approve reform proposals and oversee their implementation. As a result, a government department generally only embraces those reforms that increase its scope and power and only welcomes those innovations that do not involve performing new tasks. Bureaucracies typically do not look for, and in fact may actively run away from, creative solutions that involve bending rules, enduring unsuccessful outcomes, or establishing new precedent. Those presenting inventive requests to such departments face the frustrating response: "If I did it for you, I would have to do it for everyone."[52]

In his well-known book on bureaucracy, James Q. Wilson suggests that bureaucracies' inflexibility should not be surprising. After all, bureaucracies are, in many ways, "supposed to resist" innovation; as with any kind of institution, bureaucracies were created to replace "uncertain expectations and haphazard activities" with stability, routine, and equal treatment of similar cases.[53] As a result, bureaucracies tend to rely on preestablished rules, referred to as standard operating procedures (SOPs). SOPs lay out ahead of time how an agency should handle a particular type of problem when it arises. They are based on logic and past experiences and thus seem both more efficient and less risky than trying to come up with new solutions on the spot. Chapter 11 covers SOPs further in its discussion of individuals and political decision making.

The Bureaucracy in the United Kingdom, Germany, and France

The bureaucracies in the United Kingdom, Germany, and France have historically been both large and powerful. Despite forces supporting a reduction of their political clout, they remain an important piece of the puzzle of political outcomes in all three countries. Like the changes that have occurred in the judicial branch, the British bureaucracy has also been overhauled. During the 1980s and 1990s, the country became an exemplar of reform aimed at privatization and greater bureaucratic efficiency. Likewise, while Germany's bureaucracy historically played a significant role in its economic development, its bureaucracy today is much less centralized. The central government broadly guides the actions of civil servants at the regional level, who make up the vast majority of the country's bureaucratic personnel. Even France, which has the largest and arguably most powerful civil service in Europe, has faced pressure to alter the pattern of bureaucratic growth and the elitist system of civil servant selection.

The United Kingdom

At the height of the "postwar settlement" in Europe, during which the political Left accepted capitalist economics in exchange for the political Right accepting large welfare state programs, the British bureaucracy reached its peak size. Nearly three-quarters of a million people were employed in the British civil service. With Margaret Thatcher's reform efforts in the 1980s, the size of the bureaucracy declined dramatically to fewer than 500,000.

A centerpiece of Thatcher's reforms, and what allowed the reduction in bureaucracy, was the privatization of a large number of formerly government-run programs and businesses. Privatization efforts targeted a variety of government entities, from utilities to public housing projects. Thatcher's commitment to reducing the size and scope of government shaped her term in office, but it also lasted beyond her tenure. Even British Rail, something dear to the heart of many Britons, was privatized in 1993 after Thatcher left office.

While shrinking the bureaucracy, Thatcher also listened to bureaucrats' desire for greater autonomy and performance rewards. Bureaucrats were given more autonomy, but they were also held more responsible for the results of their activities. The government introduced performance targets and other measures designed to fight inefficient spending and the constant pursuit of budget increases. These reforms maintained the British bureaucracy's strong culture of impartiality and subordination to the elected officials above them, but they also gave bureaucrats an increased ability to exercise discretion over government policy details.[54]

IN THEORY AND PRACTICE

Bureaucratic Autonomy Theory and the United Kingdom

Bureaucratic autonomy theory addresses how bureaucracies develop autonomy over time. It holds that bureaucrats take steps to maximize their department's independence, including emphasizing its objective, civil service components, developing formalized decision-making rules, and controlling information that might be

Bureaucratic autonomy theory contends that bureaucrats emphasize their professional, civil service expertise and control information in order to make oversight of their activities more difficult and maximize their independence from political control.

used in oversight of its activities.[55] According to this approach, bureaucrats are most vulnerable to control by principals when they are first hired or just after a new department's creation. They have not had time to develop expertise and a track record of performance, and rules designed to limit their autonomy may still be effective. Once they become established and their expertise becomes recognized, however, officials are more difficult to control. As "experienced bureaucrats," they become hard to replace.[56]

Even before Margaret Thatcher's reforms encouraged greater bureaucratic autonomy in exchange for improved performance, the British bureaucracy was already quite autonomous. This was due in part to the existence of the **permanent secretary** position in the British system. This position is the highest ranking official below the minister. Held by a senior member of the civil service of that ministry, a permanent secretary generally retains the position even if the minister is replaced. Together, the permanent secretary and subordinate deputy secretaries and undersecretar-

ies form what is known as the Higher Civil Service of the British government.[57]

According to bureaucratic autonomy theory, British bureaucrats should defend their independence in part by controlling information. Permanent secretaries often filter information from their subordinates, but they have also employed a quite different technique: burying the minister or prime minister with paper in an effort to prevent the minister from commenting on specific recommendations. Together, these techniques have given permanent secretaries the ability to influence the details of government policy, as well as the de facto ability to delay or even kill policy initiatives that they feel are not in the interest of the country.[58]

> Just below the position of minister in the United Kingdom, the **permanent secretary** is a senior member of the British civil service who usually continues in this position even if the minister changes.

Germany

The bureaucracy has played a significant role in German political and economic development. Germany became a nation-state and an industrial power in the late nineteenth century under the aegis of the Prussian administration, which sought to catch up with the more advanced industrial nation-states of Britain and the United States.[59] Sociologist Max Weber's archetype of a modern and efficient bureaucracy, discussed earlier in the chapter, was modeled on the Prussian administration.

The bureaucracy in the Federal Republic is far more decentralized than its predecessors under the imperial and Nazi regimes. At the federal level, the administration is small, especially when compared with other European countries. The federal bureaucracy accounts for only about 10 percent of all civil servants

in Germany.[60] This compactness reflects the fact that the primary task of *federal* civil servants is to formulate policy by drafting government bills and administrative regulations. Consistent with the German conception of federalism based on "interlocking politics" (see Chapter 6), implementation of federal law rests primarily with the *Länder*.[61] In addition, despite its hierarchical structure, the top levels of the bureaucracy have little leverage over the actions of the lower levels.[62]

France

The astounding growth of the bureaucracy is one of the central features of contemporary France. State employment grew from 800,000 in 1945 to more than 2.5 million in 2003. Even the top level of elite civil servants numbers more than 8,000 people.[63] The growth of the French bureaucracy continued even after most other European countries began to reduce the number of public employees. This reflects an approach to public life that places at the center of the state's mission the rational development of policy for the common good. The French government spends more than 400 billion euros every year on social programs (including pensions, health, and unemployment), as well as the extensive public infrastructure in scientific research, education, and transportation (including high speed trains, commuter rail, and airlines).

While other states function through powerful bureaucracies, bureaucratic training and experience translate into both political position and leadership in industry in France more than in any other democratic country.[64] The elite civil service is meritocratic in theory, with admission through competitive exams to the *grandes écoles* school system, though in reality the elite share similar social backgrounds. Some of these schools date from before the Revolution, like the *École Nationale des Ponts et Chaussées* (Bridges and Roads), an engineering school. The top schools founded later, such as *Sciences-Po* and the *École Nationale d'Administration* (ENA), train in more general knowledge.

Though the French state has long been noted for the central role of these top civil servants, since the Fourth Republic and the strong intervention of the state in the economy, elite training has become of even greater importance. Top graduates are recruited into the pinnacle of the state, the *grands corps* that focus on administration and finance or the technology sectors. Bringing to their careers a "moral ambition" based on the national interest, their lifetime positions enable them to take temporary or permanent leave to enter the highest levels of politics and business, creating what scholar Michael Loriaux calls a "political economy where the boundary between public and private is extraordinarily porous."[65] ENA graduates, for example, have dominated ministerial appointments, served as prime ministers from the Right and Left, been CEOs of state-run and private companies, chaired the major political parties, and been elected to parliament and local government; one even served as president. The CEO of Nissan in Japan, now owned by the French company Renault, is a graduate of the *École Polytechnique*.

Today, the civil service faces two challenges. First, policymaking has increasingly migrated to the European Union. Although many officials remain attached to a uniquely French state, others have taken EU administrative posts.[66] Second, a discontented electorate, frustrated with an aloof and unaccountable class of politicians, has challenged the old ENA-dominated system. This growing revolt partially explains the victory of lawyer Nicholas Sarkozy over ENA graduate Ségolène Royal in the 2007 presidential election. Sarkozy's first government was overwhelmingly dominated by lawyers and those trained in business schools or outside France.

Symbolic of the French bureaucracy's reputation for inefficiency, documents stack up on a desk at a Social Security (*sécurité sociale*) office in Paris.

(©Bernard Bisson/Sygma/Corbis)

The Bureaucracy in Mexico, Brazil, Nigeria, and India

The bureaucracies of Mexico, Brazil, Nigeria, and India share a certain level of competence and professionalism, though this level is far below what many citizens in these countries would prefer. Corruption and inefficiency remain a problem in all four. Compared with the significant reforms of the electoral process and the changes in executive-legislative relations in Mexico over the last decade, the Mexican bureaucracy has resisted efforts at significant reform. Brazil has been an established democracy for longer than Mexico, but its bureaucracy shares with Mexico's a resistance to greater transparency and responsiveness. The Nigerian bureaucracy is the most corrupt of the four, with prevalent favoritism along ethnic, regional, and family lines. In India, the bureaucracy has both sustained governance when political instability has arisen and contributed to popular frustration with government by its slowness to act and its susceptibility to the influences of power and money.

Mexico

The bureaucracy played an important role in the PRI's dominance of Mexican politics. The president appointed a large number of bureaucrats, tending to hand top bureaucratic positions over to the most loyal members of the PRI or those most owed political favors. Those whom the president appointed in turn appointed a number of officials below them in their department, again taking into account how the appointments benefited themselves and the PRI. Even those who served for long periods of time in the bureaucracy tended to bounce around within it, going where their political connections led them. Thus, the Mexican bureaucracy was more political machine than merit-based civil service.

As with the judiciary, however, changes began to take place during the liberalization of the 1980s and 1990s. President Carlos Salinas de Gortari stressed professionalism in key departments (energy, treasury, etc.) even before President Zedillo and, even more so, Vicente Fox worked to shake up the system of PRI-connected officials. The nature of the bureaucracy was one of the many elements of the Mexican system that Fox sought to change when he became president in 2000. He led by example, appointing people to his cabinet who were not close friends and proposing a Transparency Commission to investigate allegations of corruption involving government officials. At the beginning of Fox's term, one of his economic advisors estimated that up to 10 percent of the 2.5 million government employees received a paycheck but did no work for the government at all.[67]

As his term came to an end in 2006, many considered Fox's efforts to deal with the bureaucracy a failure. He had said that those in the government who lacked a professional, team-oriented attitude would be fired. Instead, the bureaucracy's culture remained largely unaltered, and its slow response time and corruption continued to harm economic development. In 2006, it took nearly two months to open a new business in Mexico, compared to less than a week in Canada and the United States.[68] Some estimates placed the total value of bribes to Mexican government officials at more than $11 billion, or 12 percent of Mexico's gross domestic product.

Brazil

Many of the same problems facing the judiciary in Brazil are replicated in the Brazilian bureaucracy. Compared with many developing countries, Brazil's bureaucracy ranks fairly high in terms of professionalism and competence. However, it continues to face widespread perceptions that it is too cumbersome and deeply affected by corruption. According to the Corruption Perception Index, which measures perceptions of public corruption around the world, Brazil receives a score of 3.5 out of 10, where 10 represents a completely "clean" government; Brazil comes in

72nd in the world (out of 180 countries) in this corruption rating.[69]

The Brazilian bureaucracy can also be very inefficient. According to one study, starting a business in Brazil is much harder than in Mexico, taking an average of more than four months.[70] Surveys over the last decade point to a higher percentage of senior business managers in Brazil believing that interpretations of regulations are inconsistent and unpredictable than in any of the other TIC cases.[71] Most ordinary Brazilians feel the same way—a key reason for the popularity of the *jeito* (see Chapter 4).

Nigeria

Perhaps more than any other aspect of Nigerian politics, the bureaucracy reflects the underlying problems and challenges facing Nigeria. As two Nigerian scholars argued in 2004, corruption in the Nigerian bureaucracy mirrors corruption in Nigerian society; the result is that "corruption is a permanent integral feature of bureaucracy" in the country.[72]

Favoritism in the bureaucracy tends to correspond to ethnic and regional lines or family ties. Favoritism along ethnic lines is both a feature of corruption and part of the government's efforts at fostering ethnic diversity in its ranks. Because the north of the country makes up a sizeable part of the population but is underrepresented among those training for government jobs, individuals from the north tend to be privileged in filling many positions—a policy that does not sit well with those in the south seeking government jobs. The emphasis on local and family connections also poses challenges to developing a merit-based bureaucracy. Even disciplining ineffective or corrupt officials becomes a challenge when an elder from the individual's home area intervenes.[73]

India

During the colonial period, the Indian Civil Service (ICS) was referred to as the "steel frame" that held India together. Its successor, the Indian Administrative Service (IAS), continues the tradition of careful selection of leading civil servants. Although it has lost some of its prestige over the years, the top echelon of administrators in India constitutes a very select group. It is estimated that there are more than 19 million public sector employees, though only five to six thousand are found in the IAS.[74] Of those who apply for such positions, only about 0.01 percent are selected. Around half of the positions are reserved for underrepresented groups, contributing to a shift in the social makeup away from a cadre dominated by urban, Westernized, and upper-class men.[75] The Union Public Service Commission (UPSC), appointed by the president on the advice of the prime minister, is the body responsible for recruiting, disciplining, and looking after this elite cadre.

About 70 percent of the IAS officers are assigned to serve the governments of the federal territorial units. To foster a sense of national identity, half of those in a given federal territorial unit are supposed to come from another of the territorial units. However, since languages used in the various federal territorial units differ greatly, and the IAS officers are unlikely to be able to use many of them effectively, adherence to this distribution rule has become difficult. This has led to the observation "that the services are increasingly becoming 'all-India' in name only."[76]

Numerous additional problems affect these IAS officers and bureaucrats serving under them. The transition from the colonial goal of "order" to the goal of state-led "development" strained the bureaucracy. These strains have increased in recent years, as India's pursuit of economic development in a liberalized economy continues to generate new demands. In addition, civil servants are paid little, so the lure of entering the private sector is strong and has resulted in the loss of highly qualified personnel. Indian politics specialist Bimal Jalan has referred to this trend as an "atrophy . . . of the Indian civil services," with the remaining officials displaying a combination of "non-accountability, corruption and ineptitude."[77]

The Bureaucracy in the Russian Federation, China, and Iran

The bureaucracies of Russia, China, and Iran reflect both past political practices and contemporary political dictates. During the first decade or so of the post-Soviet period, much of the bureaucracy was still staffed by Soviet-era bureaucrats. Though this had begun to change by 2000, bureaucratic corruption appeared to worsen in the decade that followed, as former Soviet officials were replaced by those who owed their loyalty to Vladimir Putin and his increasingly authoritarian approach to Russian politics. While the Chinese government has pursued market reforms of the economy to improve economic performance, reform of the Chinese bureaucracy, which remains large and less than efficient, is representative of the dissonance between the private and public sectors in China. In Iran, the problem of corruption is similarly apparent. Blurring the lines between the public and private sector, various organizations work closely with the Iranian bureaucracy in particular economic endeavors, leading to personal gain for the business class, the bureaucrats, and many of Iran's top religious officials.

The Russian Federation

For years following the breakup of the USSR, the vast majority of Russian civil servants were leftovers from the Soviet system. During the Soviet period, Communist leaders controlled appointments to the state bureaucracy. They did this in part through the **nomenklatura system**: a long list of names containing competent and, more important, loyal and politically connected individuals. The official *nomenklatura* contained as many as 1.5 million names of such individuals (sometimes called the *nomenklaturshchiki*) at the end of the Soviet period. Around one million bureaucrats in the Russian government were inherited from its ranks.[78] This list represented the fusing of the merit and spoils systems in practice in the Soviet Union. Although it was disbanded at the end of the Soviet period, its legacy remains.

The nature of the Russian bureaucracy as a holdover of Soviet *nomenklaturshchiki* has begun to change, as many of these bureaucrats have retired. However, the culture of the bureaucracy has remained a problem. During the late Soviet period, many bureaucrats were threatened by Gorbachev's reforms, which they correctly viewed as an attack on the more conservative, middle level of the bureaucracy. An "us versus them" attitude developed between bureaucrats and top government officials, a mentality that was only reinforced by statements of Boris Yeltsin and Vladimir Putin in the early post-Soviet period. Putin had promised significant cuts to the bureaucracy in the early 2000s, but his actions fell short of his rhetoric. The number of bureaucrats swelled rather than contracted during Putin's tenure in office, as he used positions in the bureaucracy to reward those who displayed political loyalty.

In addition, while the 1990s saw at least some movement toward a more merit-based and honest bureaucracy, the move away from democracy under Vladimir Putin reopened the door to corruption and a spoils system. In April 2005, Mikhail Khodorkovsky, a billionaire arrested and tried by the Russian government on charges of embezzlement and tax evasion, lashed out against what he called the "criminal bureaucracy" in Russia.[79] Few ordinary Russians had sympathy for Khodorkovsky, although many of them shared his view of the bureaucracy. A 2006 World Bank report on corruption highlighted

> The **nomenklatura system** was the method of controlling bureaucratic appointments during the Soviet period by selecting individuals from a preexisting list of names (the *nomenklatura*). These individuals, sometimes called the *nomenklaturshchiki*, gained their position on the list through a combination of merit and political connections.

Russia as one of the few post-Communist countries in which corruption, including payments to government officials, worsened from 2002 to 2005.[80]

China

Both because China's legislative branch has little real power, and because the Chinese system has required such a large bureaucracy, bureaucrats in China have more day-to-day power than their counterparts in many other countries. At the same time, they have also been at the mercy of Communist leadership decisions about major reforms. From Mao Zedong's Great Leap Forward to Deng Xiaoping's overhaul of the economic system, Chinese officials have not always been able to count on the stability that most bureaucrats prefer.

Although the country has continued on the path of Deng's reforms, his successors, Jiang Zemin and Hu Jintao, have emphasized stability and technical expertise to an even greater extent than Deng had. Unlike Mao and Deng, both Jiang and Hu were **technocrats**—government officials who rose through the ranks of the bureaucracy as experts in their field rather than because of their ideological fervor. Throughout the Communist period, technocrats have been in conflict with **reds**—those known for their fervent commitment to Communist ideology—about the proper path of Chinese economic development. The red versus technocrat (also referred to as the "red versus expert") debate was a source of tension in the Soviet Union as well.

Finally, even with its significant economic reforms, China has maintained one feature borrowed from Soviet communism: the *nomenklatura* system. Some estimates put the number of names on the Chinese government *nomenklatura* list as high as 10 million. This is many more than in the USSR at the time of its collapse, though similar in terms of portion of the population.

Iran

Iran has a long history, dating back centuries, of a large and important bureaucracy. The current Iranian government strives to control the bureaucracy in order to use it for political purposes. Just as with the judiciary, part of the way in which top government officials in Iran hold sway over the bureaucracy is through the selection of individuals committed to the ideology of the rulers. Emphasizing ideological loyalty, however, can have its costs. Bureaucrats are also expected to be experts in their fields, and finding a combination of expertise and ideological commitment can be difficult. Similar to the "red versus technocrat" debate in China, the Iranian bureaucracy has the potential for a "mullah versus technocrat" debate, particularly at the middle and lower levels. (A *mullah* is an Islamic religious teacher, but the word is also used for the more conservative Muslim clerics who hold important positions in the government.)

For now, two things appear to be keeping the Iranian bureaucracy from fracturing into such a conflict. First, an interesting alliance has developed between the business class in Iran—known as the *bazaari* class—and the religious establishment. The nexus for this relationship are the *bonyads*, which are, officially, charitable organizations. These groups blur the line between state and society, as they are technically autonomous but work closely with the bureaucracy and other government officials and control huge portions of the economy. Some estimates suggest the *bonyads* control up to 40 percent of the country's economy.

Technocrats are bureaucrats who emphasize technical expertise and often have significant scientific knowledge.

Reds are those more committed to Communist ideology. The two sides have often been in conflict about Chinese economic development.

The worth of one *bonyad* alone, the Mostazafan va Janbazan foundation, has been calculated to be upwards of $12 billion.[81] The *bonyads* bring together wealthy businessmen, who see the value in working with the mullahs, and the religious officials, who benefit from the wealth of *bonyads*. Second, the mullahs and technocrats avoid concentration because both groups benefit from bureaucratic corruption. The corruption involving the *bazaari* class and the religious establishment in economic and social matters provides the potential for bureaucratic positions to generate significant personal gain.

Corruption also facilitates the bureaucracy's slow response to ordinary citizen requests and emergencies alike. The earthquake that struck the city of Bam, killing over 30,000 people in early 2004, highlighted the inefficiencies of the Iranian bureaucracy. A year later, much of the debris had still not been removed, partly because of the enforcement of rules requiring the owners of houses to give permission before they are cleared.[82]

The Military

In some ways, the military is much like any other part of the bureaucracy. It is hierarchical, it follows standard operating procedures, and it helps craft and implement policies in its areas of interest and expertise. In other ways, the military is quite different from other bureaucratic agencies. It is, potentially at least, the most imposing component of the state. Its significant control over the means of force gives it the ability to overthrow the existing government if military leaders turn against the government and if lower levels of the military follow the direction of those at the top. It is also harder to generalize about the military and its role in the policy process than in the case of other bureaucratic departments. Of the various unelected government components, the military varies the most in how active its members are in determining policy. This variation exists across countries, but it can also exist within the same country at different points in time.

Some countries have a strong tradition of **civilian control of the military**. This means that the military does not control government decision making—even about matters affecting it, such as military spending. In the United States, military decisions are ultimately in the hands of nonmilitary leaders, including the president as commander in chief and the secretary of defense, who by law must be a civilian. In most countries that practice civilian control, the military still enjoys a degree of autonomy. Political leaders typically yield to military officers in matters of day-to-day operations and specific decisions in the conduct of military exercises, though civilian commanders in chief are sometimes tempted to micromanage military operations.

Tasks of the Military Under Civilian Control

Militaries under civilian control have two essential tasks: defending the country and

Civilian control of the military refers to a situation in which the military is subordinate to nonmilitary government officials. These nonmilitary officials make fundamental decisions regarding foreign and security policy, although they often delegate to military officers the authority to make decisions regarding the day-to-day operation of the military and its conduct of military undertakings.

developing into a "professional" fighting force. Historically, militaries have also been charged with controlling the territory of an empire. This is less common today, although militaries may emphasize developing a capability to participate in military actions abroad to deal with regional or international crises. Militaries may also be expected to maintain order internally, but systems with civilian control of the military typically prefer to leave this task up to the country's police.

Defending the Country The primary purpose of a military is to provide security by deterring attack by an external force. Most states try to maintain a certain level of military strength and preparedness compared with neighboring states or other potential rivals. Increased military spending by one state can trigger corresponding increases in spending by a rival, leading to an "arms race" between the two. Civilian leaders make such decisions, but like other forms of bureaucracy, the military can influence these decisions by manipulating information about its needs and the rival's capabilities.

Developing into a "Professional" Fighting Force Another task of militaries not in control of the government is to "professionalize" their ranks, becoming more focused, specialized, and better able to address military matters such as national security. In a professionalized military, both the officer corps and lower ranks are well trained, often through the use of academies requiring years of education. In this way, the military becomes a specialized civil service, with those holding positions in the various levels of the military hierarchy earning their positions for reasons of merit.

Controlling the Empire Governments have also used civilian-controlled militaries for expansion into new territory or control of existing colonies. Until the middle of the twentieth century, European states used their military strength to support colonial expansion far from Europe and to subjugate these colonies. Other states, such as tsarist Russia, built empires by seizing neighboring territory. Such empires consisted of a core area connected to a conquered periphery, with the periphery typically more culturally diverse and less developed economically than the core. Such expansive use of the military typically requires much more military spending than militaries focused on defensive security. It can also lead to **militarism**, the preoccupation with a strong military force and an emphasis on the likely need to use it aggressively. In such situations, military leaders are likely to become more central to policymaking, eventually threatening the practice of civilian control.

Think and Discuss

What is the single most important task of the military? What makes this task so important?

Military Rule and Praetorianism

In some cases, military officers intervene to overthrow the existing government and become the rulers of the political system, an act known as a **coup d'état**. Residents of mature democracies

Militarism is a setting in which the state focuses on having a strong military force and emphasizes the need to be prepared to use it aggressively.

A **coup d'état** (or "coup" for short) is the act of overthrowing an existing government. Coups often take place at the hands of the military, when an officer or small group of officers overthrows a civilian government or an existing military government.

often associate military coups with a selfish power grab by a military officer. Most military coups are indeed led by a single officer or small group of officers, but they are not always selfish power grabs nor are they always unpopular among the general population. In times of a faltering economy or political chaos, citizens may be quite happy, at least in the short term, to exchange political rights for resurrection of the economy or restoration of order.

The military may seize power for a number of reasons, including a government's poor performance, a faltering economy, or corrupt political leaders and bureaucrats. Mass unrest may be widespread, with strikes, protests, and violence. When military leaders point to such problems as a justification for their seizure of power, they imply that they will remain in power only until the problems are resolved. In other words, the masses, civilian politicians, and the military leaders themselves often see military government as a temporary fix.

Military rule can take many forms. Some military governments install a democratic-looking assembly, with the military leadership handpicking its members. Others center on a single popular leader, who typically holds the position of president. Still others are run by a **junta**, a group made up of the heads of the assorted components of the armed forces. Even in this case, power may become concentrated in the hands of one military leader over time. *Juntas* were common in military governments in Latin America during the twentieth century.

In recent decades, military rule has become less common and military coups against new democracies have been less successful. Why are militaries less interested or able to intervene in politics? Norms about civilian control appear to have penetrated into a number of militaries which had not previously held such values. Military leaders may have also learned that running

a country and trying to solve economic and social problems can be difficult and draining on military resources. Finally, the establishment of civilian control of the military has been a popular response to cases where military governments have committed human rights abuses.[83]

Even when the military does not have complete control of a government, it may have a great deal of say over its own affairs, including sizeable control over defense spending decisions. The military's role in decision making may be indirect and obscured, as military leaders work with (or put pressure on) the official rulers behind the scenes. In countries where civilian control is weak and ineffective, militaries can even become heavily involved in policymaking outside the arena of military spending and security policy without openly seizing control of the government.

Comparativists use the term **praetorianism** to describe a political system in which the military is an active and regular participant in politics, either openly or covertly.[84] In one of his early works, political scientist Samuel Huntington asserts that praetorianism is likely when the military is cohesive and independent of civilian control while civilian political institutions are weak and ineffective. In praetorian systems, even when the military does not directly control the political system, the threat of military intervention is constantly on the minds of civilian leaders.

A **junta** is a collective, comprised of the heads of the various segments of the armed forces, which oversees policy decisions in some military governments. In recent history, this approach has been most common in Latin America.

Praetorianism is a label used to describe a political system where the military is an active participant in politics. The military may take over and run the government or it may remain active behind the scenes.

Advantages and Disadvantages of a Strong Political Role for the Military

For those used to civilian control, military involvement in politics may have obvious disadvantages. But a politically active military can be beneficial as well. A military government may play up these advantages to justify its seizure, and maintenance, of political power.

Advantage #1: Making Tough Policy Decisions

Military governments normally do not need to worry about how much people like what they are doing. While all governments prefer to be popular, military governments generally do not give citizens the chance to vote them out of office. This allows the military to make unpopular decisions that may be necessary for a country's long-term stability and improved prosperity. Government leaders who have to worry about being reelected, on the other hand, are often reluctant to make tough policy choices. In such cases, problems can slowly get worse as the government implements only small policy changes when more serious reforms are needed.

Advantage #2: Restoring Order and Battling Corruption

The military's ability to make tough policy choices enables it to tackle corruption and instability more forcefully than democratic governments often can. Although military leaders may use their power for personal gain, some military governments have waged successful fights against corruption. In South Korea, for example, the military government of General Park Chung Hee made significant strides against corruption during the 1960s—before becoming increasingly repressive in the 1970s, leading to the general's assassination in 1979.

Disadvantage #1: Unwillingness to Surrender Power

Military leaders often seize control of the political system with good intentions: ending social chaos, fostering economic development, or attacking embedded corruption. Even after they have achieved their stated goals, however, they are often reluctant to abandon control of the political system. The appeal of the power to run a country can drive such leaders to do whatever is necessary to maintain control. In other cases, military leaders may legitimately believe that the country will be worse off if they relinquish power. Although some might view the military government's completion of its "mission" as ending the need for military rule, military leaders may come to believe that military rule is a superior form of government or that they personally are superior leaders—particularly in countries with a history of poor performance by elected leaders.

Disadvantage #2: A Permanent Presence in Politics

Even when military leaders surrender power and help establish a democratic system, their presence in politics does not magically evaporate. Once a military has intervened in politics, it is likely to intervene again in the future. Establishing a commitment to civilian control of the military ordinarily takes time. Military officers and ordinary soldiers may believe they have a right or even a duty not to "surrender" themselves to civilian control and to intervene in politics again if necessary. Even civilian leaders may support continued military involvement in politics, allowing the military great autonomy to set defense policy and provide input on internal stability in the country. Thus, for comparativists who study military involvement in politics, it is nothing special to find a country where the military has repeatedly overthrown the sitting government and maintained a significant role in politics between its periods of direct rule.

The Military in the United Kingdom, Germany, and France

The United Kingdom, Germany, and France provide quite different examples—even today, but especially historically—of the military's role in politics. The United Kingdom remains an archetype of civilian control of the military, developing a professional military force in large part because of its large overseas empire up until a half century ago. Germany's military is subservient to its civilian leaders today, but a tradition of militarism, from the Prussians through the Nazis, required an aggressive effort at civilian control which significantly limited Germany's military activities until relatively recently. France's military, the largest of the three TIC cases, remains a fixture of French foreign policy. At the same time, it is much less directly involved in French domestic politics than it has been at earlier points in history.

The United Kingdom

Though by no means the largest, the British military is one of the world's most powerful. It is also a model example of a professionalized military strongly accepting of civilian control. The prime minister and Ministry of Defence determine military policy. Although participation in the Iraq War became controversial among the general British population, the idea that political leaders make such decisions is not controversial among the members of the military itself.

This is somewhat ironic given the country's history. The military only began to encourage professionalism in the early eighteenth century. Prior to that, British military forces had involved militias. While this was adequate for

defense of the country, it was impractical for the running of an empire overseas. Slowly, the British military became a professional force to be feared, both for its discipline and, eventually, its technical expertise. At the same time, a culture of professionalism developed that was reinforced by the combination of domestic political stability and a largely external focus (the two world wars, the Cold War, the Iraq War, etc.).

The major exception to this generalization was the use of the military to maintain control over Northern Ireland. British troops were sent to Northern Ireland in 1969 in an effort to contain the growing violence, but their presence did little to weaken the resolve of Catholics opposed to British control. Serving in this capacity was difficult on military morale. It will be interesting to see whether serving in the increasingly unpopular military campaign in Iraq could have a similar effect on morale. Already by late 2005, British politicians were comparing morale among the troops in Iraq with the level of morale among those who served in Northern Ireland.[85]

Germany

The military played a dominant role in German society and politics in the country's modern history. The Prussian military's values of order, hierarchy, and obedience permeated broader German society in the nineteenth century.[86] An aggressive foreign policy culminating in World War I reflected German generals' influence in politics. Following Germany's defeat in World War II, the armed forces were finally discredited, and their numbers and mission became subsequently circumscribed. Under the Federal Republic, the armed forces came under firm civilian control, with the defense minister in command during peacetime and the chancellor serving as the commander in chief during periods of war.[87]

From the days of Germany's efforts against Napoleon, all young men in Germany have faced compulsory military service. The practice continues today, although conscientious objectors can perform alternative service instead. Since World War II, most Germans have not desired a large military. Indeed, from rearmament during the 1950s to the decision to send troops to Afghanistan in 2003, any notable increase in German military activity has been controversial. The Green Party's acceptance of peacekeeping missions in the 1990s—breaking its longstanding commitment to pacifism—was a wrenching decision for its members. At the same time, the fact that German troops have participated in UN peacekeeping missions since the 1990s and served as part of the coalition forces in Afghanistan indicates that Germany has become a mature, "normal" nation-state, able to assert its national interests without stoking fears of resurgent militarism among its neighbors.

France

The French military is the largest in Europe. Independent from the command structure of the American-led NATO forces and maintaining an independent stock of nuclear weapons, it is a bulwark of the French state and its ambitions as a regional and global power. Despite the colonial empire's demise in the 1950s and military failures in Vietnam and Algeria, the French military has consistently extended French influence and power into the former colonies of Africa and the territories in the South Pacific.

The military's relationship with the Republic has been complex. The First Republic came to an end at the hands of Napoleon, who in a military coup d'état sent his troops into the Council of 500 to expel its membership when they would not elect him to head a new government. General Patrice MacMahon, who was named a marshall in 1859 and crushed the Paris Commune in 1871, was a powerful president in the first years of the Third Republic. MacMahon defended the interests of a monarchist majority when they could not agree on who should be king. In the 1880s, the supporters of General Georges Boulanger threatened a coup, but he ultimately refused to take the risk. A decade later, the Dreyfus case pitted the forces of tradition against the Republicans, who viewed Dreyfus's conviction as the result of an anti-Semitic conspiracy in the Army General Staff. In the twentieth century, Marshal Pétain went from being praised as the victor of Verdun in World War I, to head of the Vichy government during World War II, to standing trial following the war for collaborating with the Nazis. General de Gaulle, architect of the Fifth Republic, came to power in 1958, after the intervention of the military.

Despite these experiences, the French military is not an ideal representation of praetorianism. Its political involvement has been sporadic rather than ongoing, and today it shapes politics much less than it is used by government leaders for political ends. At the same time, some observers in the past have pointed to a lingering militarism captured by the French penchant for the strongman on a white horse. As recently as the 2007 presidential campaign, President Sarkozy, who was raised just outside Paris, was featured in one television commercial riding one of the famous white horses from the Carmargue region in southern France.

The Military in Mexico, Brazil, Nigeria, and India

Although Mexico, Brazil, Nigeria, and India are similar in many ways, they have had quite different experiences with their militaries. Both Mexico and India have had little history of military involvement in politics. Because Mexico already had strong civilian control of the military during the period of dominance by the Institutional Revolutionary Party (PRI), relations between the military and the civilian government have remained largely unchanged during Mexico's democratization. In India, the military has largely stayed out of politics, except when used by the government to put down political uprisings.

On the other hand, the military has been a visible feature of politics in Brazil and Nigeria. In Brazil, the penetration of the military into the political system has been a difficult pattern to break. Even today, nearly a quarter century since the establishment of democracy, the country strains to assert civilian oversight. To an even greater extent than Brazil, the Nigerian military, while not in power at the moment, is never far removed from politics. President Olusegun Obasanjo took steps following his election to weaken the autonomy of the military, but the long history of military rule lurks in the background of everyday Nigerian politics.

Mexico

With the possible exception of postcolonial Africa, no region of the world has been associated with military intervention in politics more than Latin America. Until recently, military rule was common in many Latin American states, particularly from the 1940s to 1980s. In a few of these countries (including Guatemala, Haiti, Honduras, Paraguay, Peru, and especially Argentina), the military governed more than once during this period. Mexico challenged this pattern. It did not have a military government during the middle part of the twentieth century. Mexico's "revolutionary" history in the nineteenth century and early twentieth

century was followed by more institutionalized politics during much of the twentieth century.

This was reflected in the role of the military in politics. In periods of revolution and social upheaval, the military was a significant political actor. With the emergence of the PRI, the military took a backseat to the dominant political party and the position of the Mexican president. This trend has continued during the transition from authoritarianism to consolidated democracy that continues today.

Brazil

One of the biggest challenges for Brazil's democracy has been reining in the military and forging civilian control. The 1988 Constitution enshrined privileges for the outgoing military government, guaranteeing it a continuing say in how Brazil would be run. Although the Brazilian army is under the authority of the president, there is no civilian Ministry of Defense to oversee military budgets and behavior. Active-duty officers serve in the cabinet. The military runs the aviation and aeronautics industries, as well as others critical to national defense.

In addition, the military has retained formal control over the Military Police, the branch of police responsible for public order. Unlike most police forces, Brazilian police are divided into the Military Police, who arrest people and patrol the streets, and the Civil Police, who investigate crimes. Both of these forces are officially at the disposal of governors (*not* mayors or municipalities), but few would claim that the Military Police are fully responsible to civilians.

One of the most serious human rights issues in democratic Brazil has been a very high rate of killings by police. A large number of alleged criminals, as well as bystanders, die each year in shootings that critics call irresponsible and abusive, with little effective punishment of officers involved. In three of Brazil's *estados*, police were responsible for over 15 percent of all homicides from 1994–2001.[88] Police in the densely populated *estados* of Rio de Janeiro and São Paulo killed nearly ten thousand people in the five-year period between 1999 and 2004, in situations described officially as "resistance followed by death."[89] In some locations, the rate at which police officers kill their fellow citizens has actually risen since the transition to democracy. These abuses continue to undermine both the rule of law and popular trust in the Brazilian government.

Slowly, civilians have begun to assume more oversight of the military. Military budgets have been slashed to just 2.6 percent of GDP; top military commanders have been added to the list of people who may be tried for criminal offenses by the Supreme Federal Tribunal; and military officers—including the Military Police—may be charged in regular criminal courts (rather than the military courts) if prosecutors judge their crimes to be unrelated to their military functions. Human rights watch groups have increased their pressure on politicians to reclassify some acts of police killings as ordinary murders, and the overall rate of killings by the police has declined modestly since the mid-1990s. Nevertheless, the military remains a powerful actor within Brazilian society, incompletely subject to civilian oversight.

Nigeria

The Nigeria military has arguably had a greater presence in politics than the military of any of the other TIC cases. In the first forty years of Nigeria's independence, only around a decade combined was spent under civilian rule. This changed with the election of Olusegun Obasanjo, himself a former military leader of the country, as president in 1999. Despite some rocky times—members of parliament called for him to resign or face impeachment in 2002, for example—Obasanjo's consecutive terms marked the longest period of civilian rule since independence. Among Obasanjo's first policies as president was to retire dozens of top generals who played a major role in the previous military government.

Still, in a country such as Nigeria with such a tradition of military rule, any civilian government is tenuous. Prior to Obasanjo's return, scholars debated whether the military leadership would actually "return to the barracks" and allow the country to try democracy again, while also questioning whether civilian rule could last for any sizeable amount of time even if they did.[90] Military leaders feared the loss of prestige and control over military policy that would accompany democratization, as well as the potential for democracy to reopen ethnic and religious tensions in the country. They also benefited from controlling the government purse strings. At the same time, the Nigerian military has valued its image as an institution of reform, willing to hand over power to a democratically elected civilian government once order has been restored and corruption addressed.[91]

IN THEORY AND PRACTICE

New Professionalism Theory and the Military in Nigeria

Some political scientists argue that the extent to which militaries intervene in politics is inversely related to their level of professionalism. The more a military resembles a professional force concerned with defense of national security, the less likely it is for such a military to get involved in political matters. Others have countered that professional militaries may actually be more committed to issues such as economic development and the expulsion of corruption from politics than the governments they replace. As a result, "professionalized" militaries may be more likely to intervene in domestic politics to address domestic governmental failures.

Writing in the 1970s, comparativist Alfred Stepan attempted to solve this tension. His approach, what came to be known as the **new professionalism theory**, highlights the importance of the military's perception of its mission. Stepan proposed that professionalism draws militaries away from politics only when the main threat to society and the political system comes from outside the country. On the other hand, when the military perceives a significant *internal* threat (economic crisis, violent protests, etc.), professionalism leads military officers to support intervention into politics to improve government performance or restore order.[92]

On the surface, Nigeria seems to support the predictions of Stepan's new professionalism theory. Nigeria's significantly greater power than its neighbors, combined with its considerable social, economic, and political turmoil, has meant the mission of Nigeria's military has had a strong domestic focus. One might question how professionalized the Nigerian military has been in recent decades, but its commitment to improving the economy and its belief that only it can fix the country's problems have seemed genuine.

At the same time, Nigeria provides an interesting potential amendment to the new professionalism theory, demonstrating how the study of a single case in some detail can sometimes lead to revisions in an existing theoretical perspective. The military has intervened in Nigerian politics not only when it observes economic tribulations but also when it feels that the civilian government has become too corrupt to fix the problem.

Yet, instead of the military curing corruption, the corruption has simply infected the military. Leaders in the 1980s and 1990s such as Ibrahim Babangida and Sani Abacha were among the most corrupt political leaders in the world. Abacha oversaw glaring violations of human rights, while possibly pilfering as much as $5 billion from the government during his five years in power.

One must always be concerned about the extent to which a military such as Nigeria's, with a long history of governing the country, will accept the concept of civilian rule. Even as it becomes more professionalized, its focus on internal missions might lead it back into the political arena. But the Nigerian case points out that one must also consider the extent to which officers who value a more professionalized military may see military rule in the past as spreading the disease of corruption into the highest levels of the military. A recognition that past interventions have made it a less professional military might provide a counterbalance to a focus on an internal mission and the sense that it alone can solve Nigeria's numerous social, economic, and political problems.

Alfred Stepan's **new professionalism theory** maintains that whether a professionalized military will intervene in politics depends on what it sees as its mission. Threats from outside the country lead a professionalized military to stay out of politics, while internal threats draw the military into politics, sometimes including a coup against the existing regime.

Think and Discuss

Which of the theories discussed in this chapter seems most convincing and why?

India

The Indian Armed Forces contain more than 1.3 million troops, with paramilitary forces adding another 1.1 million.[93] They possess nuclear weapons and the ability to deliver them. With these features, the military could wield significant political power. However, unlike the military in many developing countries, the armed forces have remained essentially apolitical. Rather than directing the political system, they have, on numerous occasions, responded to the direction of elected political leaders. They regained control of Hyderabad in 1948 after its leader announced his intention to join Pakistan. They fought the Portuguese for control of Goa, Daman, and Diu in 1961. They fought wars with Pakistan in 1947–1948, 1965, 1971, and, in the Kargil intrusion, in 1998. They fought China in 1962, went to Sri Lanka as a peacekeeping force in 1987, and blocked an attempted coup in the Maldives in 1988.

In other ways, the Indian Armed Forces resemble those in many developing countries. They have been used to restore order within the country, including controlling riots and struggling against secessionists in the Punjab and the northeast. As Ramesh Thakur noted more than a decade ago, "The line between police, paramilitary and military forces has been increasingly blurred with changing threats to the nation's internal and external security."[94] There have also been corruption scandals in the procurement of weapons, although the culprits have generally been civilian leaders rather than members of the military.

The Military in the Russian Federation, China, and Iran

The militaries of the Russian Federation, China, and Iran have all been used by their governments to help maintain control of their countries, yet the extent to which the governments fully control their militaries differ. In Russia, the military has struggled to overcome numerous problems, including its loss of status as one of the two most powerful militaries in the world and its use within the borders of Russia (twice) to attempt to put down a separatist uprising in the region of Chechnya. At the same time, the post-Soviet Russian government has largely continued the tradition of civilian control of the military established during the Soviet period. While the Chinese judiciary and bureaucracy remain tools of the Communist regime, the military has become increasingly independent from the government, a trend that bodes well neither for CCP control of the political system nor for the political system's liberalization. The leaders of Iran's theocratic system have tried to contain the military and use it to serve their purposes. They have been only partially successful.

The Russian Federation

The Russian government inherited from its Soviet counterpart a weakened military, but one with a long history of submitting to civilian control. Its mission was clearly externally focused. Not only had the Cold War provided a strong external enemy, the United States, but Soviet ideology stressed internal harmony. The twin ideas of subordination to civilian rule and the lack of a need for the military to solve internal problems were transmitted into the culture of the military through Communist Party penetration and oversight.[95]

Late in the Soviet period, military force was used several times in attempts to solve internal problems. On April 9, 1989, troops were sent in to disperse protestors in Tbilisi, the capital of the Soviet republic of Georgia. In January 1990, Interior Ministry, KGB forces, and regular military troops were used in the republic of Azerbaijan. In January 1991, similar steps were taken in Lithuania—by then openly hostile to Soviet rule—leading to the deaths of seventeen individuals who defended republic government buildings. Some officers openly criticized the government's use of the regular army against Soviet citizens in such cases.

In August 1991, the military was mobilized to maintain order during the attempted coup against Soviet leader Mikhail Gorbachev. Unlike the previous events, in which the military was following the orders of civilian leaders, this time the defense minister, Marshall Dmitry Yazov, was a key participant in the planning and execution of the coup. Other military leaders, however, opposed the coup and worked to prevent certain orders from being carried out. The division in the military was one of the central causes of the collapse of the coup (and ultimately of the Soviet Union).

The central events in the intersection of military and political matters in post-Soviet Russia concerned the republic of Chechnya, a region of Russia that sought independence from the country. The Russian military intervened twice in Chechnya, the first time from 1994 to 1996 and the second beginning in 1999. Though the second intervention was much more successful than the first, Chechnya has remained a problem for Russia. The permanent stationing of troops during the 2000s led to a number of casualties, even after the military had largely gained control of the region.

The other politically charged issue related to the military is the problem of hazing, particularly of new recruits. Yet another difficulty inherited from the Soviet period, the tradition of beating young conscripts—known as *dedovshchina*, or the "rule of grandfathers" in Russian—continued after the Soviet collapse. Several high profile cases in 2005 and 2006 forced the Russian defense minister, Sergei Ivanov, to vow to crack down on the practice. In one incident that garnered national attention, a young soldier named Andrei Sychyov was beaten so badly by older soldiers that his legs and genitals had to be amputated. According to government statistics, the combination of hazing, crime, and suicide led to more than one thousand noncombat deaths in the Russian military in 2005 alone.[96]

China

Partly because the Communists came to power after a lengthy civil war, the People's Liberation Army (PLA) has played a central role in Chinese politics since 1949. CCP leaders such as Mao Zedong and Deng Xiaoping believed that the military should be under the control of the CCP, but the party and military were more intertwined in China than in the Soviet Union. Top CCP officials also held top positions in the State and Party Central Military Commission (CMC). Some consider this part of a successful effort by the CCP to co-opt and subordinate the military, but it has also put the military into the center of Chinese politics.

Unlike the failed Soviet coup against Mikhail Gorbachev in the Soviet Union (in which military units from around Moscow were used to gain control of Moscow), the Chinese government used military units based far from the capital of Beijing in its crackdown against protestors in Tiananmen Square in 1989. But the use of the Chinese military to put down this uprising still had a great effect on the military and its relationship with the government. Some in the government questioned the military's loyalty in the aftermath of Tiananmen Square, and surveillance of the army by the Communist leadership increased in the years following 1989. At the same time, the government became more dependent on the military and less able to control it following the event.[97] In 1990, the military budget was increased by more than 15 percent.

Iran

Since the Islamic Revolution in 1979, the Iranian government has worked hard to maintain control over its military. Many officers who had been loyal to the shah were executed, other purges took place during the 1980s, and the war with Iraq helped to weaken and demoralize the military further.[98] In short, Iran was experiencing the opposite situation from what Samuel Huntington described as one leading to praetorianism. Rather than a strong military and weak civilian government, Iran has had a weak and fractured military alongside strong civilian political institutions. This pattern has become even more pronounced since the solidification of conservative control over the elected positions of the national legislature and the presidency in 2004 and 2005.

While it has taken advantage of the internal divisions within the Iranian military, the theocratic government of Iran has also worked to indoctrinate the military. Part of this effort has involved establishing and increasing the importance of the **Islamic Revolution Guard Corps** (**IRGC or "Revolutionary Guards"**). The IRGC began as a fairly informal militia, recruited from groups who were among the strongest supporters of the 1979 Revolution. Its numbers swelled in the decades following the revolution, and it eventually became treated as a regular, professional military. The government established a separate IRGC academy, gave the IRGC tasks commonly reserved for regular forces such as border patrol, and allowed it to enforce dress codes and other practices related to Islamic Law.[99]

Despite these efforts, the military has not always supported the Iranian regime. Though no military coup has taken place since the Islamic Revolution, statements by retired military officers in support of free and fair elections and executions of members of the Revolutionary Guards following charges of espionage led some scholars to weigh the possibility of the military's more direct involvement in Iranian politics.[100] Even without a coup, dissatisfaction in the military could provide fuel to uprisings at the mass level. If orders are given for police or Revolutionary Guard units to disperse protesters through violent means, for example, it is not impossible to imagine the military turning against these other units of force to defend the protesting masses.

> Iran has both a regular military and additional units known as the **Islamic Revolution Guard Corps** (or **IRGC**). Also known as the "**Revolutionary Guards**," these soldiers are increasingly important in the maintenance of internal order in the country.

COMPARATIVE EXERCISE

Judicial Review Authority in New Democracies

The majority of the comparative exercises in this textbook involve examining hypothesized causal relationships. Not all research questions, however, focus on causal questions. As discussed in Chapter 1, particularly in the initial stages of research on a certain topic, researchers must first establish that basic patterns exist before they try to explain them. Such research questions center on "who, what, when, where, or how" rather than "why" questions.

This chapter's comparative exercise involves such an approach. Its research question is: *To what extent does judicial review authority vary in newer democracies (those countries that democratized from the 1970s to the 2000s)?* If such variation can be established, subsequent research would focus on possible explanations for the observed patterns.

Overview of the Data on Judicial Review Authority

Alongside the most recent wave of democratization, there has been a global trend in the direction of judicial review. As Tom Ginsburg argues, the association between the parliamentary sovereignty concept and political oppression in Africa and Asia has discredited the idea that parliaments need not be checked by the judiciary. As a result, parliamentary sovereignty is "a waning idea" and in many countries has "faded away."[101]

However, to point to a general trend toward greater judicial authority does not indicate how countries vary within this trend. Indeed, while American judicial review developed through a landmark case (*Marbury v. Madison*), in other countries the process of reviewing laws for constitutional violations is written into the constitution—often in a specific and detailed manner. Likewise, some systems use the same courts to review the constitutionality of laws

Exercise

that are used to hear criminal cases and appeals, but others give that power to a so-called Constitutional Court.

In Ginsburg's 2003 book *Judicial Review in New Democracies*, he sets out both to establish that such variation exists and to explain the different patterns in a number of new democracies. He identifies, for example, six categories of judicial review and places each of the more than seventy third wave democracies (see Chapter 12 for a discussion of the third wave of democratization) into one of these categories.

These include Constitutional Review, in which a special body (a Constitutional Court) rules on questions of constitutionality, and Judicial Review, where the power to rule on constitutional questions is held by existing courts. A third category is a hybrid of the first two, while two additional categories are versions of the first two but where the power of constitutional review is limited. The sixth is a hybrid of the two limited types.

Table 8.2 displays these results. The vast majority of the cases fall into the Constitutional

Table 8.2   Type of Constitutional Review in Third Wave Democracies

CR	JR	JR/CR	LCR	LJR	LCR/LJR
Albania	Argentina	Brazil	Benin	Honduras	Chile
Armenia	Bangladesh	**Bulgaria**	Burkina-Faso	Jordan	Zambia
Bosnia-Herzegovina	Bolivia	Ecuador	Ethiopia	Nicaragua	
Central African	Cape Verde	Guatemala	Gabon	Paraguay	
Republic	Dominican	Mozambique	**Latvia**		
Columbia	Republic	Peru	Morocco		
Croatia	El Salvador	Sao Tome &	**Romania**		
Czech Republic	**Estonia**	Principe	**Russia**		
Georgia	Fiji	South Africa	Senegal		
Greece	Ghana		**Slovakia**		
Hungary	Guinea-Bissau		Spain		
Indonesia	Guyana				
Korea	Lesotho				
Kyrgyz Republic	Malawi				
Lithuania	Namibia				
Macedonia	Nepal				
Madagascar	Panama				
Mali	Philippines				
Moldova	Seychelles				
Mongolia	Sierra Leone				
Poland	Suriname				
Slovenia	Tanzania				
Taiwan	Uruguay				
Thailand					
Ukraine					

CR = Constitutional Review by a Special Body
JR = Review by Courts
L = Scope of Review or Access Limited
Country Name in Bold = Post-Soviet or Eastern European Post-Communist State
Source: Adapted from Tom Ginsburg, *Judicial Review in New Democracies: Constitutional Courts in Asian Cases* (Cambridge: Cambridge University Press, 2003), Table 1.1.

Review or Judicial Review categories, consistent with Ginsburg's contention that recent cases of political liberalization have moved away from the idea of parliamentary sovereignty and toward a stronger role for courts in the legislative process. When one thinks about the types of countries that fall into each of the categories, one pattern clearly emerges. The countries that emerged from the collapse of the Soviet Union and the other Eastern European Communist states are primarily found in the Constitutional Review category and, to a lesser extent, in the Limited Constitutional Review grouping. In all, 90 percent of them are found in the Constitutional Review and Limited Constitutional Review categories. Only two of the post-Communist states are found in any of the categories that involve judicial review by regular courts.

Discussion

An examination of constitutional review practices in more recent democracies highlights the tendency toward strong constitutional review or judicial review powers for the judiciary. Within

this broad trend, the pattern involving the Eastern European and Eurasian post-Communist states is striking. It is hard to imagine that, by chance, the post-Communist states would cluster so strongly in favor of constitutional review but against the use of existing courts.

As a result, this effort to categorize new democracies not only identifies variation across the cases that begs an explanation, but it also points to a place to start: the puzzle of post-Communist states leaning so heavily on special bodies for constitutional review. Ginsburg proposes some possible explanations, including that the existing judiciary in democratizing post-Communist states had been trained and promoted by the Communist regime, the public's view of the regular courts as corrupt, and the resulting potential for constitutional review to be tainted by the use of existing courts.[102] However, Ginsburg's research centered on cases from Asia, leaving many more to examine. Although his book presents an interesting and persuasive story about this subset of cases, perhaps its most important contribution is bringing to light a pattern in need of explanation and a puzzle for future comparativists to solve.

CONCLUSION

This chapter provided an overview of three unelected government institutions. All three have the potential to play important roles in policy creation—judges by "legislating from the bench," bureaucrats by agenda framing in their policy area or crafting specific policy provisions, and the military by pressuring government officials or even forcing them from power. All three of them also have advantages and disadvantages associated with their involvement in politics. Unelected officials can make tough

decisions, protect minority interests, and utilize their expertise, but they can also impose their personal views and resist efforts to limit their influence.

Think and Discuss

Do the advantages of powerful unelected officials outweigh the disadvantages?

The discussion of these unelected components in the Topic in Countries cases also highlighted how the relationship between these institutions and the legislature and chief executive can change over time. In Germany today, for example, the power, autonomy, and accountability of Germany's unelected branches are firmly embedded in its wider democratic institutions. This is quite different, however, from past practice. Germany's independent and powerful judiciary, less centralized bureaucracy, and civilian-controlled military represent a substantial change in the nature of these institutions compared with the imperial and Nazi dictatorships.

Finally, the cases show how these three institutions play important roles within but also pose challenges to democratic rule. Unelected officials are particularly vulnerable to the temptations of corruption, though these temptations can be limited through efforts such as increasing the number of judges and paying them reasonable salaries. Other changes are broader and even more difficult to bring about, such as fostering a strong attachment to the principle of rule of law. Interestingly, the question of independence versus control differs across the three types of institutions. Corruption appears less likely for a judiciary when it is independent from executive branch control. In the case of the bureaucracy and the military, however, greater executive and legislative oversight appears to be an important part of the solution. Thus, in a country such as Brazil where all three unelected components of the state enjoy significant formal powers and autonomy from the elected branches, these powers are not always exercised efficiently or appropriately, resulting in problems for democratic consolidation.

Key Terms

Bureaucracy, p. 294
Bureaucratic autonomy theory, p. 299
Cabinet departments, p. 295
Case law, p. 281
Civil law, p. 281
Civil servants, p. 296
Civil service, p. 296
Civilian control of the military, p. 306
Common law, p. 281
Constitutional judicial review, p. 282
Coup d'état, p. 307
Fourth branch of government, p. 294
Generalist approach, p. 296
Islamic Revolution Guard Corps (IRGC), p. 317
Inverse judicial power theory, p. 292
Judicial activism, p. 283
Judicial independence, p. 280
Judicial review, p. 282
Junta, p. 308
Merit system, p. 296
Militarism, p. 307
Ministers, p. 296
Ministries, p. 296
New professionalism theory, p. 314
***Nomenklatura* system,** p. 304
Permanent secretary, p. 300
Praetorianism, p. 308
Reds, p. 305
Revolutionary Guards, p. 317
Secretary, p. 296
Specialist approach, p. 296
Spoils system, p. 296
Stare decisis, p. 281
Statutory judicial review, p. 282
Technocrats, p. 305
Tort law, p. 283

9

Political Participation, Clientelism, and Interest Groups

Learning Objectives

After reading this chapter, you should be able to:

- Discuss the difference between elites and masses and describe different ways that the idea of an elite is conceptualized in comparative politics.

- Describe different forms of mass participation and give examples.

- Discuss the difference between programmatic and clientelist linkage.

- Describe the difference between an interest group and a social movement.

- Characterize alternative arrangements for incorporating interest groups into the policymaking process.

I n 1500, an expedition led by Pedro Álvares Cabral discovered the territory of what would become the Portuguese colony of Brazil. The man serving as the clerk of the expedition, Pêro Vaz de Caminha, wrote a letter to King Manuel of Portugal, in which he informed the king of the discovery. He also took advantage of the opportunity to attach a request to the good news—asking the king to find a job for his nephew. Given that this exchange of favors is a part of the story of Brazil's birth, it is perhaps not surprising that, even today, crafting governmental policies based on shared ideological viewpoints often takes a backseat to personal connections within members of the Brazilian political elite and between members of the elite and ordinary citizens. ■

Look for this icon to point you to **Deepening Your Understanding** features on the companion website www.college.cengage.com/politicalscience/barrington, which provide greater depth for some key content.

A basic attribute of government is that a relatively small number of individuals are selected—or select themselves—to make policy decisions for the rest of the population. In most countries, political structures exist to link this small group of leaders to members of the general public. The extent to which the populace takes advantage of these structures varies from country to country and among individuals within the same country. Seeking to understand these patterns is a core undertaking of comparative politics.

The fourth section of the book focuses more closely on individuals and their role in the political process than the previous sections did. This chapter is the first to employ this focus. It considers the differences between political "elites" and "masses," various ways in which the general public can participate in politics, and certain institutional approaches (such as interest groups) that link elites and masses.

Comparative politics often focuses on elections and political parties as the hallmarks of democratic mass participation and elite-mass linkage. Elections and parties are indeed important, and the next chapter examines them in detail. But in between the frenzied episodes of democratic electoral politics are long periods of everyday politics. As comparativists Phillipe Schmitter and Terry Karl put it:

> During the intervals between elections, citizens can seek to influence public policy through a wide variety of other intermediaries: interest associations, social movements, locality groupings, clientelist arrangements, and so forth. Modern democracy, in other words, offers a variety of competitive processes and channels for the expression of interests and values—associational as well as partisan, functional as well as territorial, collective as well as individual. All are integral to its practice.[1]

And thus all are worthy of study.

Who Are the "Elites"?

A **political elite** is a group of individuals who are far more involved in day-to-day political decisions than ordinary citizens. Those who hold official government positions, those who can influence such leaders because of their social or financial standing, and those who can shape public opinion related to government policy are all part of the political elite. Obviously, not everyone in this elite group is equally powerful, but all can affect political outcomes far more than ordinary citizens. The percentage of the population that falls into the political elite varies from country to country. In many countries—including the United States—it is well less than 1 percent.

As with many political science concepts, defining the term *political elite* is easier than identifying those who fall into it in practice, especially in cases of individuals who do not hold official governmental positions. How might one figure out if people without official positions are actually part of the political elite? One possibility is to look at decision-making processes and see which people appear to be wielding influence. This is what Robert Dahl did in his landmark book *Who Governs?*—a study of local decision making in New Haven, Connecticut.

The debate over whether there is a single elite or several competing elites further complicates the issue. Sociologist C. Wright Mills, influenced greatly by Max Weber, argued that the elite are relatively unified. Mills stressed the idea of a **power elite**; a single elite made up of economic,

A **political elite** is a group of individuals who are far more involved in daily politics than ordinary citizens. They hold political office, influence office holders through their social or economic positions, or influence public opinion.

Power elite is a term used by C. Wright Mills to describe the political elite. While made up of different elements—political, military, and economic leaders—this elite group works in unison to control the government and produces policies that serve its interests.

(©Harley Schwadron)

opting for those who fit with its values and goals. In this case, family members of the current elite often become the elite of the future. Such favoritism shown to relatives in the granting of official positions is known as **nepotism**. Nepotism is common in developing countries, particularly those in which clan or tribal identity is politically salient.

Think and Discuss

Is it good or bad for a democratic political system to have a strong political elite?

political, and military leaders. He contended that these three groups work together, acting in unison to rule the political system. Mills did not argue that the members of the power elite participate in a great conspiracy, but rather their similar social backgrounds lead them to have similar goals and values. On the other hand, in *Who Governs?*, Dahl argues that if one looks at who benefits from governmental decisions, groups of elites compete against each other for policy victories and no single group is always the policy winner.

Another question to consider is how similar the elite is to the masses in terms of socioeconomic status and political orientation. If the members of the elite are very different socially, some worry that members of the elite cannot adequately represent the masses. It is, after all, hard to represent people to whom you cannot relate. Others feel that this is not an issue if elites have incentives, such as reelection, to diligently represent the mass public.

A third question concerns whether membership in the elite is open or closed. If it is open, there are mechanisms for new people to work their way into the elite on their own. The previous chapter, for example, discussed the use of merit systems in selecting bureaucratic officials. These systems allow those without family connections or other personal advantages to earn their way into government positions. If the elite is closed, however, the elite itself chooses its new members,

"The Masses" and Their Political Participation

In contrast to the political elite, the **masses** are not involved in day-to-day governing. They do not hold official positions, and they generally know less about and have less interest in politics than the elite. Unless large numbers of them act together (such as by voting or participating in a social movement), they also lack the social, economic, or political resources to play a major role in policymaking. But they are still political participants. **Political participation** refers to the set of activities intended to influence the selection of officials and their policies. If politics is about who gets what, individuals participate in politics in the hopes of getting what they want.

Mass political participation is a part of all variants of democracy, where, at minimum, the general population is supposed to take part in selecting key government officials. Totalitarian

Nepotism is favoritism given to relatives in the granting of positions or distribution of resources.

The **masses** are those not in the political elite. They normally know less about, have less interest in, and participate less in politics than members of the elite.

Political participation is the process of engaging in activities that are intended to influence the selection of officials and the policies that they create.

Figure 9.1 Examples of Unconventional and Conventional Political Participation

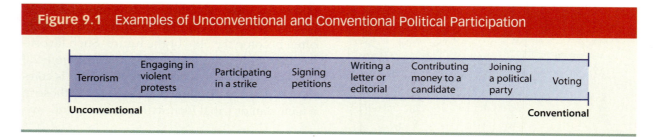

systems also emphasize mass political mobilization, but in a much more controlled manner than democracies. Only "ideal type" authoritarian systems do not feature involvement of the masses as a cornerstone of politics; in those systems, masses are subjects rather than citizens. In practice, however, even authoritarian systems seek to make the public feel as though it is participating in the selection of government officials and playing a role in the creation of government policy. In short, all systems either want masses to participate or want them to think they can participate.

Conventional Versus Unconventional Participation

Political participation can be divided into two categories, conventional and unconventional participation. **Conventional participation** is the set of activities that political elites sanction and that existing political institutions are able to channel effectively. This means that what a government leader would consider conventional participation in one political system might not be the same activities that a leader of another system would deem conventional. Leaders of nondemocratic political systems, for example, are likely to be suspicious of any kind of political participation other than those activities that the state has created and tightly controls. Within democracies, most political scientists agree on the kinds of activities that they consider conventional participation. Such activities include voting and belonging to political parties or other social groups.

Unconventional participation is participation in activities of which political elites do not approve, often because such participation is politically destabilizing. Such behavior includes strikes, boycotts, violence, and terrorism. Categorizing less extreme forms of protest, such as signing petitions, can be difficult. Some scholars include them in their list of unconventional participatory activities,[2] while others do not. It can, therefore, help to think of unconventional and conventional participation as end points of a range of political activities (as in Figure 9.1).

Those who engage in unconventional activities often feel alienated by the political system and believe that participation through normal political channels is pointless. Protest allows them to bypass these channels, providing what political scientist Russell Dalton calls a "direct-action technique of confronting political elites, instead of participating within a framework defined by elites."[3] While such alienation does not justify more extreme types of unconventional participation, it is important to understand how alienation and a lack of legitimacy can lead some to see unconventional participation as a reasonable response to their social and political situation.

Conventional participation is political participation that existing political institutions can effectively channel, that does not advocate or promote political or social instability, and thus of which the political elite approves.

Unconventional participation is the set of politically destabilizing activities not approved by the political elite. These activities include strikes, boycotts, and terrorism.

Nonparticipation

In addition to conventional and unconventional participation, a large number of individuals choose not to participate in the political system at all. Even in democracies, a portion of the population does not participate on a regular basis. These individuals often feel alienated from politics, have little understanding of political events, and have no interest in trying to understand them better. This is the portion of the general population that Gabriel Almond and Sidney Verba labeled "parochials" in their book *The Civic Culture*, discussed in Chapter 4. In many countries, nonparticipants are overwhelming young, poor, less educated, and members of ethnic minorities.

Those who do not participate share a sense of frustration with those who turn to unconventional participation, but there are key differences between the two groups. Those who engage in unconventional participation have more knowledge of and interest in politics, and often find themselves mobilized by leaders of a particular political movement. This chapter's "In Theory and Practice" boxes discuss other propositions about people's political participation.

Comparing Mass Participation in Different Countries

The portion of people among the masses who participate more than others and overall participation levels (e.g., turnout rates in elections) vary from state to state. States can also differ in how effectively they can channel mass participation in ways that do not threaten political stability. For those with strong and effective political institutions, increases in mass participation can help the system by providing information about the desires of the general population. Such participation also improves the legitimacy of the political system.

On the other hand, undisciplined mass participation can be destabilizing. In the late 1960s, Samuel Huntington published an

APPLYING CONCEPTS

The Staging of Unconventional Participation

It is important to distinguish between unconventional participation involving "grassroots" actions that the political elite does not condone and what *appears* to be unconventional activities that are actually encouraged or even staged by the government. Officials may encourage protests to provide an excuse for a military coup or for the government to crack down on opposition groups. An authoritarian leader may also covertly organize marches in favor of the government to create the impression of legitimacy. Even when these protests shut down large parts of a capital city, the leader may view them as being a net benefit. Thus, those who study social movements and protest activities must do more than count numbers of protesters. They must also get a sense of how the protesters came together and why they chose to participate.

In 2008, the leader of Zimbabwe, Robert Mugabe, faced allegations of electoral fraud. An accusation of manipulating mass participation was nothing new to Mugabe, long seen by many observers as one of the world's most brutal dictators. On rare occasions, mass protests against his rule had occurred, such as a February 2006 march by a small number of women demanding "bread and roses" (representing their desire for food and dignity). More typically, however, what appeared to be unconventional political participation involved activities that the Mugabe government has staged and/or actively supported.

Such participation has included repeated attacks on white farmers by Mugabe supporters over the last decade. Mugabe initially denied involvement in the attacks—which ultimately resulted in more than 90 percent of white farmers losing their land—claiming they came from genuine mass frustration with legacies of colonial rule. Soon, however, Mugabe openly supported the actions, coordinated redistribution of the land, and handed over the best farmland to government officials, members of the military, and other key supporters. The result has been a dramatic decline in agricultural production and conditions bordering on famine.

important work on economic development and its political effects, *Political Order in Changing Societies*, which framed political stability as a function of the political system's ability to channel mass participation.[4] Huntington stressed the way that economic and social development can lead the general population to demand a greater say in their government. He argued that the inability to adequately address demands for increasing participation is destabilizing and can lead the political system to collapse.

Think and Discuss

Why do some authoritarian leaders try to create the illusion of unguided mass political participation in their political systems? To what extent do such efforts run the risk of fostering desires for genuine participation?

Participation in the United Kingdom, Germany, France, and India

Political participation in the United Kingdom, Germany, France, and India is often conventional, yet all four have seen instances of unconventional participation over the last several decades. As consolidated democracies, the stability of the political systems of the four countries is rarely threatened by these incidents of unconventional participation. At the same time, the growth of violence related to the situation of immigrants has concerned leaders in the three European cases, while in India the government has been unable to put an end to the many instances of unconventional participation by radical Communist groups.

The United Kingdom

The actions of the British mass public, as well as the United Kingdom's political elite, are shaped by the cultural principles of *noblesse oblige* and working class deference, discussed in Chapter 4. The public tends to accept the system's legitimacy. Part of the reason for this is the extent to which British political leaders take their responsibility for the population's welfare seriously.

In general, voting rates in the United Kingdom are higher than in some other mature democracies, but lower than many other European countries. Turnout has varied—driven partly by differences in mass perceptions of the competitiveness of the elections and the level of dissatisfaction with the ruling party—but there has also been a general downward trend since the early 1990s. After World War II, turnout rates had been above 70 percent of registered voters for parliamentary elections, and often near or above 80 percent. In 2001, turnout dropped below 60 percent and rebounded only slightly, to 61.4 percent, in 2005.[5] Similar to other mature democracies, including the United States, conventional participation rates are much lower for younger citizens than older ones.

With the exception of the violence in Northern Ireland, the United Kingdom has had comparatively few instances of unconventional political participation over the past few decades. However, fitting with working class deference, a large percentage of the population chooses not to participate in British politics. Russell Dalton's examination of mass participation in the United Kingdom, the United States, West Germany, and France found that, other than voting, the British public participates at comparatively low levels.[6]

Germany

Germans vote in high numbers. In the Federal Republic, turnout averaged about 87 percent from the 1950s through the 1980s and nearly 80 percent in the 1990s.[7] Compared with voting, participation in other types of political activity has been lower. West Germans withdrew from organized activities in the years immediately after 1945, a natural reaction to coerced participation under the Nazi regime, but their participation in voluntary group activities rebounded in due course. In 2002, nearly 60 percent of Germans in the western part of the country participated in some type of organized group activity, which is on par with or even better than other Western democracies. A similar story of citizens' withdrawal from organized groups appears to have occurred in the east since reunification but without the subsequent increase in participation that occurred in West Germany. As a result, participation in all types of groups remains lower among easterners than westerners.[8]

Although most political activity in the post–World War II period has been conventional, periods of unconventional politics marked politics in both West and East Germany. Like other Western European countries and the United States, portions of the mass population in West Germany became radicalized in the late 1960s and the 1970s. The resulting demonstrations were often peaceful, though some generated violent clashes with police. Postwar West Germany also experienced more extreme behavior. On the radical left, the Red Army Faction carried out assassinations of business elites in the 1970s and 1980s. Anti-immigrant neo-Nazi parties and movements on the extreme right have found fertile soil in areas with high unemployment since the 1990s.[9] Both types of extremist movements have very small memberships, but their presence and message have given unease to mainstream parties, political elites, and ordinary citizens.

The German Democratic Republic (East Germany) outlawed independent political groups and harassed, jailed, or expelled dissidents to prevent broader opposition movements from emerging, but unconventional political activity occasionally flared up. In 1953, for example, workers in major East German cities struck against the regime and its harsh policies. Soviet tanks quickly crushed the revolt. Then, in the twilight months of the regime in 1989, an umbrella group of dissident activists called

New Forum emerged. New Forum sought an East Germany that was democratic—though not American-style capitalist—but independent of West Germany. The group's appeal was limited, and most East German voters ultimately opted for unification with the Federal Republic.[10]

France

From the French Revolution itself through the violent student-led protests of May 1968 and continuing today with large-scale demonstrations organized by farmers and students, France is no stranger to unconventional participation. The French labor movement, for example, follows the "Latin confrontational model," in which unions protest government policies as much as they take part in direct wage negotiations, with specific claims articulated as a defense of the common good.[11] Such massive public protests include those against pension reform in 2003, which failed to block the measure, and successful opposition initiated in part by students to a 2006 proposal to limit job security for first-time employees.[12] Mobilization within the private sector is generally much less successful than that among public sector employees, and most strikes that take place as part of the collective bargaining process involve government workers. The strikes are widely supported, as many in the general population view them either through the lens of solidarity and the common good or as playing a key role in setting the standard for wages and benefits in the private sector. Less organized unconventional acts, such as the 2005 riots spurred by high levels of unemployment among young people living in public housing estates, have also left their mark on French politics.

Of course, not all mass participation in France is unconventional. Survey results indicate that the French public thinks about and discusses politics more than many other general populations. The French also vote at a relatively high rate, with turnout for parliamentary elections above 80 percent at times from the

1950s through the 1970s. By the 1980s, turn-out dropped below 70 percent, and it was only 60.3 percent in 2002. It is important to note, however, that a similar drop-off did not occur in presidential elections, in which turnout has averaged above 80 percent during the Fifth Republic and was exactly 84 percent in 2007.

India

As might be expected in a democratic country with a diverse population of over a billion people, portions of the masses in India are very actively engaged in a variety of political and social venues, using an assortment of methods to achieve an array of goals both through direct action and through influencing political leaders. Both the unconventional and violent and the conventional and nonviolent approaches to mass political participation are found in India today. This variety of approaches is consistent with India's struggle for independence from British control. For example, Gandhi is widely known for having enlisted the masses in major nonviolent protests against the British and supporting the interests of major sections of the population. Yet, others, such as Bhagat Singh, thought that violence was necessary if the masses were to end British rule.

The general population of India participates though conventional channels, though at lower rates than the European countries discussed in this section. Turnout for parliamentary elections has averaged slightly under 60 percent but has been quite stable. From 1952 through 2004, it was never lower than 55 percent and never higher than 65 percent. Both the low numbers and the relative stability in them are due in large part to the long-time dominance of the Indian National Congress (INC) Party in these elections.

Examples of unconventional participation in India are numerous. Many political organizations engage in confrontational politics to publicize their interests. There is no country in the world where so many disruptions of normal life occur in efforts to get political leaders to act—or

Phoolan Devi, a candidate for parliament, speaks at a political rally in Mirzapur, India, in April of 1996. Devi became a hero in India among low-caste Hindu women after serving eleven years in prison for the murder of a group of upper-caste men who had raped her.

(©AP Photo/Saurabh Das)

not to act. The words used in the English press for many of them are borrowed from Hindi and other indigenous languages. There are *bandhs* (where all businesses and other normal activities are blocked), *gheraos* (where leaders are surrounded and kept where they are for long periods of time), fasts, *yatras* (processions that may move through a large part of the countryside advocating some sort of action), *hartals* (where a general strike occurs), rail and road *rokos* (where trains and cars are not allowed to move), as well as many other forms.[13] Each sends a message involving a demand for action on an issue of interest to the participants.

Other unconventional acts have been less peaceful. Along with various secessionist movements discussed later in the chapter, groups that forcibly take land from landlords have operated outside the formal political system for decades. In the late 1960s, the Naxalite movement (a violent Communist movement linked to Maoist thought) was born in West Bengal. Despite massive efforts of the government to stamp it out, Naxalites, or similar groups, have spread to almost half of India's federal units.

The movement, which had fragmented, has been reuniting in recent years. In 2004 the CPI (ML) People's War Group joined the Maoist Communist Centre, India (MCC-I) to form the CPI-Maoists. The fact that such militant movements continue to operate is indicative of both the absence of real political representation of many very poor rural inhabitants and the continuing role of violence as a form of unconventional participation in India.

Participation in Mexico, Brazil, and Nigeria

Living in relatively young democracies, the populations of Mexico, Brazil, and Nigeria are to an extent still getting used to the ability to participate in conventional ways that can have meaningful results. Of the three, the voting rates in Brazil (the eldest of the three democracies) have been both the highest and most consistent over the past two decades. The three countries have shared prevalent instances of violent, unconventional participation in recent years, often from groups who believe that they have been abandoned by the political system.

Mexico

The move away from authoritarianism in the late twentieth and early twenty-first centuries has affected mass participation in Mexico. The highest turnout in the legislative elections was during the period of liberalization yet before many consider Mexico to have established its democracy. Participation in legislative elections has also varied greatly. In 1994, turnout peaked at around 78 percent. In 1997, it dropped under 58 percent, then rose above 63 percent in 2000, hit a low of 41.7 percent in 2003, and rebounded to 58.9 percent in 2006. Similar to lower rates of voting in U.S. midterm elections, Mexican turnout for legislative elections tends to be higher in a year that there is also a presidential election. Presidential election rates have trended consistently downward, with a high of 78.5 percent in 1994, a drop to 64 percent in 2000, and a further slide to 59 percent in 2006.

Unconventional activities like the Chiapas uprising have also become more visible in recent decades. Compared with other Latin American countries, however, the Mexican population is less likely to engage in unconventional political activities. In the 1999–2001 wave of the World Values Survey, fewer than 4 percent of Mexican respondents stated that they had attended a political demonstration, a figure that was lower, in some cases much lower, than respondents in countries such as Argentina, Brazil, Chile, Colombia, Peru, Uruguay, and Venezuela.[14]

Brazil

Partly as a result of the ineffective linkage between masses and elites in Brazil, popular participation frequently involves unconventional action, including, at one extreme, "self-help" activities seeking to avoid state contact and, at the other, mass protests directed at the state. Brazilians are nearly twice as likely as Mexicans to say they would attend a demonstration or occupy a building; indeed, they are first or second in Latin America in their willingness to engage in most types of unconventional political action.[15]

Like France, unconventional participation has been prevalent in the arena of organized labor. Consistent with his rhetoric, Brazil's President Luiz Inácio Lula da Silva got his start as a militant union organizer. One example of such activities' effectiveness is the Unified Workers' Central (CUT), a union that became nationally known for its defiant rejection of military rule. Its confrontational approaches forced wage concessions and salary increases from their employers. The CUT's success in winning material improvements for their workers led to more militant methods by other unions, even those that did not share its radical ideological perspectives.

Nigeria

Nigeria's democratic leaders have sought to direct mass participation into conventional outlets like voting. To an extent, they have been successful. Although turnout for the 1999 presidential elections was only slightly over 52 percent, it increased to 69 percent in 2003 before falling to an estimated 57.5 percent in 2007.[16] Ethnic conflict is also less severe than in the early postindependence period. On the other hand, increasing instances of electoral fraud since 1999 threaten to create significant disillusionment among the general population and depress future rates of conventional political participation.

In addition, violent unconventional political participation remains a problem. In the Niger Delta region of Nigeria, for example, groups have engaged in unconventional activities while also seeking international support over the issues of oil drilling, resulting negative environmental effects, and limited redistribution of the oil wealth to local residents. Some protests have been relatively nonviolent, such as occupations of ChevronTexaco facilities by unarmed female villagers in 2002 and 2003. More recently, other groups in the Niger Delta engaged in more violent protests, threatening "all out war" with the Nigerian government and attacking international oil company personnel and facilities.[17] These actions have periodically forced other oil companies, such as Shell, to halt operations.

Participation in the Russian Federation, China, and Iran

The governments of the Russian Federation, China, and Iran closely monitor mass participation and seek to direct it in ways supportive of the regime. Although these three systems are far from models of free and fair elections, citizens find other ways to participate. These include conventional participatory activities, such as presenting grievances to government officials, and unconventional activities, from nonviolent protests to violent clashes with the police or military. In both Russia and China, terrorist actions, as well as activities that the governments of each label terrorist actions, have gained the attention of the government and external observers.

The Russian Federation

In the early post-Soviet period, scholars studying mass political participation in Russia believed that the country had the potential to develop a pattern of participation "familiar in the established democracies but alien under the old

Soviet system."[18] While such optimism appeared warranted in the early 1990s, by the end of that decade patterns of participation had begun to change. Surveys from the late 1990s indicated that participation in conventional political activities was lower in Russia than in any of the twelve other post-Communist countries examined.[19] By the end of former President Putin's second term, the frenzy of the initial period of political transition from 1990 through 1993 had been replaced by a system in which the government, while popular, was increasingly seen as a distant elite, the belief that ordinary citizens could affect political outcomes was in decline, and nonparticipation was becoming a way of life for many Russians. Putin and his political allies had to work hard to convince people to turn out to vote for his successor, Dmitry Medvedev, in 2008.

As a result, turnout for presidential elections, which was near 69 percent in 1996 and 2000, dropped to 64.4 percent in 2004. Although it officially increased to 69.7 percent in 2008, many observers questioned this figure. There were numerous reports of voting irregularities across the country and managers pressuring their workers to turn out. In the region of Ingushetia, for example, the official turnout rate for the previous December's parliamentary elections was 98 percent, and the president of the region, former KGB agent and Putin ally Murat Zyazikov, predicted a similarly "massive" turnout for the 2008 presidential vote.[20] While Ingushetia's *official* turnout ended up being over 92 percent, independent observers estimated that the region's turnout was as low as 3.5 percent.[21]

Alongside increasing incidents of fraudulent claims about conventional participation rates, others have turned to unconventional participation methods. Even in the early post-Soviet period, survey results indicated that Russians were comparatively open to unconventional participation.[22] Actual participation in one or more of what comparativists Ronald Inglehart and Gabriela Catterberg call "elite-challenging actions," however, was lower in the post-Soviet period than before and during the collapse of the Soviet system.[23] While most Russians eschew unconventional tactics, terrorist attacks by supporters of independence for the region of Chechnya garnered headlines over the last decade. These included the Moscow theater hostage crisis in 2002 in which more than one hundred people died and the school hostage crisis in the city of Beslan in 2004 that ended in the deaths of more than three hundred children and adults.

China

Because China's Communist Party still attempts to control the political system tightly, conventional participation in China is less important than it is in many of the other TIC cases. The population has often seen participating in officially sanctioned activities as more of a duty (or simply in one's personal self-interest) than as a right. However, it would be a mistake to assume the Chinese avoid conventional participation. First, as discussed in more detail in

the next chapter, China allows relatively open elections at the village level. Whether this will spread to higher levels of government remains to be seen, but through these village elections at least some Chinese have had a taste of participating in elections where the outcome is not predetermined. Second, citizens often take steps to report lower-level government officials whom they believe are unresponsive, ineffective, or corrupt. These actions include letter writing or in-person appeals to higher-level authorities, as well as efforts to use local media outlets—and increasingly the Internet—to put pressure on the individual official in question.

Unconventional participation has also had a notable impact on Chinese politics. Often, protests are small and concerned with local issues, but they are not infrequent. Government estimates put the number of what Chinese officials call "mass group incidents" in the tens of thousands annually at the beginning of the twenty-first century.[24] Other incidents are of a larger scale. The June 1989 Tiananmen Square uprising is the best example of unconventional participation since Mao's death, and the government's harsh response to the demonstration limited similar actions for years afterward.

More recently, another large protest began in March 2008 in the region of Tibet. Clashes turned violent between police and protesters seeking greater cultural autonomy—for some, complete independence—for Tibetans and an end to the settlement of ethnic Chinese into the region. Initially confined to Tibet, the protests eventually spread into neighboring regions as well. Though to a lesser extent than the damage the Tiananmen Square crackdown did to China's international reputation on the issue of human rights, the repression of the Tibet protesters further weakened China's international position, on the eve of the 2008 Beijing Summer Olympics. However, China cares more about what those inside its borders say and think than those outside, and the government effectively used the media to portray the Tibetan protests as riots aimed at ethnic Chinese and with the potential to destabilize China's economy.

Iran

Supporters of the Iranian Islamic Revolution saw the shah as too secular, too isolated, and too authoritarian. Accordingly, the 1979 Revolution was about reinvigorating the practice of Islam in the country *and* increasing mass representation in the government. When revolutions have multiple and discordant goals, it is not unusual for one goal to be sacrificed for another. In Iran, the goal of making Iranian society less secular and more Islamic quickly took precedence over the goal of making Iranian politics more democratic. People do participate (the 2005 presidential election garnered almost 60 percent turnout), but the power of unelected bodies like the Guardian Council and their ability to limit the extent of contestation in national elections mean that many Iranian citizens choose to withdraw from politics.

Mass protests occasionally materialize in Iran, such as the sizeable prodemocracy demonstrations that took place in 1999, 2002, and 2003 and important protests in support of women's rights in 2005 and 2006. Despite the growing frustrations of many ordinary citizens, however, the nature of the political system has made such actions infrequent. Not only does unconventional political behavior carry potentially significant costs, but also the system is designed to make most Iranians believe that unconventional participation is unlikely to achieve its goals. Consequently, the Iranian masses are most likely to engage in conventional participation or to choose not to participate at all. Nonparticipation has been especially common among younger urban residents of Iran.

Connecting Elites to Masses: Programmatic or Clientelist Linkage?

Masses are tied more closely to elites in democracies than in authoritarian or totalitarian systems. Yet elites and masses in all systems are somewhat interdependent. The masses depend on the elite to govern and to distribute resources, but ordinary citizens must also submit to elite rule for it to survive. In a democracy, the population must consent to the members of the elite with official positions in order for them to maintain political power.

Broadly speaking, there are two main approaches to linking elites and masses: **programmatic representation** and **clientelism**.[25] Programmatic linkage is often associated with political parties and elections, while clientelism is generally seen as unrelated to political groupings such as parties. In fact, both forms of elite-mass linkage sometimes involve parties and sometimes do not. The key difference between them is whether elites are linked to masses through stated policy positions or through personal connections.

Programmatic Linkage

One approach to linking elites and masses common in democracies involves politicians representing a large portion of the population through the stands they take on government policies. This method of elite-mass linkage is often referred to

> **Programmatic representation** involves linking the masses to the political elite through institutions such as political parties that stress particular political programs.
>
> **Clientelism** is an approach to linking elites and masses based on patron-client relationships. Individuals in the general public have political patrons, whom they turn to for assistance in times of need and to whom political or financial favors are owed in return.

as programmatic representation. To decide who they want to represent them, the people assess the programs spelled out in political party platforms and the performance of individual political leaders. In other words, individuals seeking public office represent segments of the general population through "programmatic appeals and policy achievements."[26] In such systems, numerous people represent individual members of the general public and/or serve as an outlet for their frustrations with the political system. Americans, for example, can express opinions to and seek help from the president, members of Congress, state legislators, local government leaders, and bureaucrats at the various levels of government.

Clientelism

Masses are not always linked to elites as part of a large group. They can also be connected as individuals in a patron-client relationship. In systems based on patron-client relationships, known as clientelism, everyone except those at the very top has a patron who, in principle, looks out for the client's interests. The client receives certain benefits, which are either material goods held privately by the patron or public goods under the control of the patron as a governmental official.[27] In exchange, the client owes the patron support—at election time or in other ways. Clientelism is most common in nondemocratic systems, though some democracies have elements of clientelism as well. Japan, Italy, and Mexico, for example, have maintained a degree of clientelism in an otherwise democratic system.

Clientelism is most pervasive when an individual is unable to receive the services a patron provides from a different political official or from a broader governmental or social institution. Consequently, the extent to which a political system operates through clientelist arrangements depends on the structure of the political system, on social relations more broadly, and on

features of the country's population. Those in rural areas or with little education, for example, are more likely to become clients than educated city dwellers. As comparativist Herbert Kitschelt puts it, "Vote-rich but resource-poor constituencies receive selective material incentives before and after elections in exchange for surrendering their vote."[28] They lack the skills or opportunities to receive benefits outside the clientelist framework. But, as Kitschelt points out, there can also be wealthy clients. In such cases, "resource-rich but vote-poor constituencies provide politicians with money in exchange for material favors."[29]

The previous chapter discussed the extent to which corruption among unelected officials is a problem in a variety of countries. Clientelism can foster such corruption, which is one of the reasons political scientists tend to view clientelism as something that "contaminates" political life.[30] Clientelist systems need not, by definition, involve high levels of corruption. Patrons with a commitment to public service may use their positions for their clients' benefit rather than their own. In practice, however, clientelism and corruption seem to go hand in hand. Although political officials are not the only ones in society with the ability to provide things people want, their public position gives them significant advantages in this regard. Governments implement programs targeting particular groups or locales and make rules governing social and economic behavior. In doing so, they spend money and employ a large number of bureaucrats to oversee policy implementation. Having control over how these resources are distributed can give senior political officials significant influence.

Elite-Mass Linkage, Information, and Representation

Whether a linkage is more programmatic or more clientelist in nature, the public can use it to send messages to elites about their policy preferences. In patron-client systems, the flow of information from bottom to top of the patron-client hierarchy can be quite good. People know how to get in touch with their patron. In programmatic systems, the political elite gets information from the public either from opinion polls or from the **attentive public**, those among the masses who follow political events, belong to organizations, send letters, call their political leaders, or otherwise make their feelings known. The attentive public is generally quite different in its life experiences and its political attitudes than the rest of the mass public. Thus, clientelist systems can, arguably, provide a better gauge of public opinion and the desires of the masses than often occurs in programmatic systems. Unfortunately, they do not provide as strong incentives for the elite to respond to these mass desires.

> The **attentive public** is the part of the general population that is not part of the political elite but is more involved in politics than the rest of the masses. They tend to belong to politically germane organizations and engage in high-effort participation such as letter writing and protests.

Programmatic Versus Clientelistic Linkage in the United Kingdom, Germany, France, and India

Like many other long-established democracies, personal connections and clientelist relationships had been central to the political systems of the United Kingdom, Germany, and France long ago, but programmatic appeals have become more important today. Of the three, France retains the most clientelist system, though even in that case elite-mass linkage is based on a mix of programmatic connections and patron-client ties. The pattern of programmatic appeals replacing clientelism also emerged in India. The Indian case highlights the importance of not necessarily associating corruption, which is still a problem in India, with an extensive system of clientelist interactions between citizens and political elites.

The United Kingdom

In the days of feudal lords, a clientelist system dominated the lives of ordinary people. What people received came from their lords, and unquestioned loyalty was expected in return. Even as the British political system began to incorporate elements of modern democracy, clientelism remained an essential way in which British masses and elites were linked.

Today, programmatic linkage has largely replaced clientelism. Political parties and specific political leaders stake out ideological positions and seek the support of the electorate based on their performance in office and stated policy goals. Activities such as Prime Minister's Question Time help citizens get a sense of political leaders' ideologies and positions on specific policies. In addition, the strength of British political parties, including their ability to dictate which of their candidates runs in a particular electoral district, makes it difficult for prominent politicians to engage in clientelism at the expense of the interests of the party.

Germany

Clientelistic relationships dominated feudal society in Germany during medieval times. Programmatic parties with clearly articulated, class-based, ideological programs emerged in German politics from the latter half of the nineteenth century until World War II. They continue to provide a major link between political elites and masses today. Following World War II, however, the two major parties of the Federal Republic—the Christian Democrats (CDU) and the Social Democrats—muted the class content of their programs and became more similar in their messages in order to attract as many

Topic in countries

voters as possible. In short, they became "catch-all" parties to appeal across class, religious, and regional lines in order to win elections.[31]

To the east in the German Democratic Republic, the Communist Party initially employed Marxist ideology as the basis of its programmatic appeal to the masses. Like other Communist parties, however, the regime relied on "privilege and clientelism" in its later decades to create an elite whose loyalty derived from the perquisites of party membership, such as travel to the West and access to scarce consumer goods.[32]

France

As touched upon in previous chapters, the French Republic is organized through a centralized state empowering a trained and meritocratic elite. French Republican values emphasize a common good, national representative government, and the application of reason in the pursuit of modernization and social stability. Often the various tendencies in French politics produce practical as well as ideological conflicts. In such instances, the "Jacobin" imperative of centralization and modernization—named for the revolutionary group that placed all power in a "Committee of Public Safety" during the 1790s—tends to take precedence over representative institutions.

The combination of the elite nature of French politics, tight networks among the highest civil servants, and their control of leading political and economic positions lends itself to a complicated mix of programmatic and clientelistic political organizing. As the members of the elite are trained to make rational decisions in the common good, their grip on social power has tended to emphasize programmatic and policy-based appeals from parties and governments alike. This naturally plays well in the context of a political culture driven by ideological conflict, as displayed on evening television, dominated by issue-oriented talk shows featuring a panel of experts and a passive audience.

But the elites are embedded in social networks, and their very aloofness—they are often called "mandarins" to emphasize how separate they are from society—reinforces their trust in each other at the expense of society. This has produced a variety of party- and state-based systems of patronage, especially at the local level where national leaders exert a great deal of influence. Consequently, France experienced a whole series of corruption scandals since the 1980s, including the *Affaire Elf* that revealed a complicated network of elite and party corruption prior to and during the privatization of the giant state-owned oil company, Elf. Another patronage scandal involved the suicide of former Socialist Party Prime Minister Pierre Bérégovoy in 1993. Other examples include the construction, housing, and party finance scandals that plagued former president Jacques Chirac during his long tenure (1977–1995) as Mayor of Paris.

India

Programmatic approaches to elite-mass linkage have been conspicuous in politics since independence. Unlike some of the other democratic TIC cases, however, such efforts have not always been based on nationwide appeals. Particularly in recent years, regional programmatic appeals have grown in number and effectiveness.

At the start of independence, the dominant Indian Congress Party (INC) appealed for support by offering a program of a social democratic nature, that is, involving both the development of a hegemonic public sector and the allowance of some private enterprise. The Communist Party of India sought followers by advocating the advancement of workers and peasants. Still other parties championed alternative national and local issues. Over the years, domestic and international problems and pressures reduced the appeal of the INC program and led to a substantial rise in the number of parties with a variety of alternative policy objectives. In response, by the early 1990s, the INC formally began advocating a liberalized economy. By the late 1990s, its primary challenger was the Bharatiya

Janata Party (BJP), a party whose appeal was its call for building of a society based upon Hinduism. Regional parties continued to multiply pushing programs designed to benefit regional interests.

Clientelism may not be as significant in India as it is in other parts of the world, but deference to power is a widespread feature of the country's various cultures. Clientelist linkages have accompanied the appeals of parties and party leaders to their programs. Parties promise social group leaders special benefits in exchange for the votes of the group's members. As a lure for support, they also use reservation of jobs and seats in educational institutions. A so-called "creamy layer" of privileged individuals within the Scheduled Caste/Scheduled Tribe category developed, indicative of the small group of beneficiaries linked by clientelism.

Programmatic Versus Clientelistic Linkage in Mexico, Brazil, and Nigeria

Mexico, Brazil, and Nigeria share a long history of clientelist approaches to elite-mass linkage and a continuation of these practices even during the current period of democracy. Democracy has brought some increased importance to programmatic appeals, but elites and masses continue to be linked through clientelism to a greater extent than through programmatic alternatives.

Mexico

Mexico is retreating, albeit slowly, from the clientelism that existed during the period of dominance by the Institutional Revolutionary Party (PRI). The PRI controlled the federal government for much of the twentieth century in part through its extensive use of clientelist arrangements. On top of the many other obstacles facing opposition parties during the period of PRI dominance, the political system's roots in clientelism put opponents of the PRI at a particular disadvantage. Non-PRI candidates had to fight for electoral support with neither the institutional organization nor the access to state resources required to turn clientelism into a national political strategy.

Clientelism was especially crucial to linking PRI elites to the poor and rural population. Programmatic appeals meant less to these groups than direct, and immediate, economic benefits. These benefits were distributed through the *cacique* (a Spanish term for the local party boss), who in return expected political support for himself and for the PRI in regional or national political activities, such as presidential elections.

Mexico's democratization has increased the importance of programmatic linkage. As political scientist Jonathan Fox puts it, the Mexican transition provided an opportunity to examine the transition from "clients to citizens," in which "poor people gain access to whatever material resources the state has to offer without having to forfeit their right to articulate their interests autonomously."[33] Indeed, the decline of the PRI's stranglehold on Mexican politics has allowed clients to become citizens—but only to an extent. Particularly in local and *estado* politics, strong patron-client connections remain in place. While the PRI's grip on the federal government has declined dramatically, it continues to use local clientelist methods in large parts of the country. In other areas, the PRI has lost its control of local politics through clientelism only to see another major party, typically the PAN or PRD, adopt its former tactics. The result, claim researchers such as comparativist Tina Hilgers, is that "the unwritten rules of clientelism" continue on as "a solidly established—albeit informal—institution" in Mexican politics.[34]

Brazil

One of the key reasons for the high levels of unconventional behavior is Brazil's failure to develop a strong political party system. With the noteworthy exception of the Brazilian Workers' Party (PT), Brazilian political parties lack a clear programmatic profile or institutionalized linkages to interest groups, unions, and social movements. Most linkages, therefore, are highly personalistic and clientelistic between individual politicians and their local client groups. In some cases, these relationships last for many years. In others, groups bargain with different politicians every electoral cycle to see who will offer the most for their votes.

The combination of prevalent clientelism and largely nonexistent efforts at programmatic linkage has had important political consequences. Specifically, it makes it very difficult for Brazil's legislature to create and enact clear policy agendas. Instead, most politicians spend their time in office trying to grab enough "pork" (i.e., state resources) to keep their clients happy up to and during the next electoral cycle. In order to enact any significant new policies, government leaders, including the president, have to play along with the game of "pork"-funded clientelism.[35]

Although clientelism is strong in Brazil, its long-term stability is not guaranteed. In contrast to France and Mexico, where clientelism is stronger at the local level than the national level, some Brazilian local governments have adopted initiatives that challenge clientelist practices. One such initiative is known as "participatory budgeting" (PB). PB is a system that allows citizens to take part in meetings where they select among various general policy directions, vote on specific policy initiatives, and elect "PB delegates," who represent them in additional meetings with other such delegates, representatives of local organizations, and government officials.[36]

Not all local governments have been open to the PB approach. It is not accidental that PB institutional reforms developed under the local leadership of the PT, the party that has the strongest programmatic identity and the strongest ties to social organizations. Yet, mostly due to pressure from such social organizations, PB often survives alternation in power to more conservative parties, which might not have chosen to create these practices but do allow them to continue.

The PB process alone will not undo the country's existing clientelist arrangements, even at the local level. Studies of these experiences suggest that, especially in the early stages, groups affiliated with the party in government have dominated the PB processes. Along with Brazil's blossoming civil society, however, participatory decision-making institutions such as PB represent an emerging challenge to dominance of Brazilian clientelism over the development of government policy and the distribution of state resources.[37] Research on the attitudes of the PB delegates indicates that they believe support from other PB delegates and from representatives of civil society organizations is more important than support from government officials.[38]

Nigeria

Clientelism has contributed to the corruption that has plagued Nigerian politics since independence. Clientelism provided a structural support for authoritarian military leaders such as Ibrahim Babangida, but leaders such as Babangida also worked to deepen clientelist ties. Oil revenues greased the clientelist system, providing significant resources for patrons to provide to their clients—while skimming a significant portion off the top for themselves. Like other aspects of Nigerian politics, tribal and family connections play an important role in clientelist practices, and clientelism remains especially prevalent in smaller towns and in the countryside.

Even during periods of democratic rule, parties have been organized more along clientelist lines than as programmatic mechanisms for linking elites and masses.[39] As in other countries where clientelism is widespread, the political parties act mostly as umbrellas for the collection of local and regional political machines. Despite former President Olusegun Obasanjo's promises of significant reform and efforts to attack corruption—promises continued by his successor—Nigerian politics remain more about who you know than about what they stand for.

Programmatic Versus Clientelistic Linkage in the Russian Federation, China, and Iran

Clientelism and the general importance of personal connections is a dominant theme in Russian, Chinese, and Iranian politics. In Russia, programmatic approaches failed to take hold in the early post-Soviet period. In China, elites and masses are increasingly distant politically and primarily linked through clientelism. Both Russia and China also have their own version of patronage-based linkage systems, *blat* and *guanxi,* respectively, which link masses and elites as well as members of the general population with each other. In Iran, clientelism drives many political outcomes, though subtle programmatic appeals related to political and social reform can affect electoral results.

The Russian Federation

Although former President Boris Yeltsin's government was not always consistent in its support of promarket economic policies, post-Soviet Russian politicians provided a rather stark contrast between those in favor of moving away from the country's Soviet past and those supporting a turn back in that direction. Thus, Russian politics in the first decade of the post-Soviet period *should* have been based largely on programmatic linkage. The collapse of the Soviet system, however, discredited a focus on ideology. With few exceptions, political parties were fragile and often issued vague policy platforms. It was particularly difficult for voters to develop a firm attachment to parties in favor of market economic reforms. Instead, Russian politics was highly personalized. Parties formed around popular individuals and personality triumphed over policy substance.

Clientelism is a longstanding Russian tradition. During the Soviet period, clientelism was less about connecting the elite to the masses than about connecting the different layers of the elite to each other. Within the Communist Party,

the key to moving up was to know someone at a higher level in the party. With the Soviet collapse in 1991, personal political ties remained a central factor in Russian politics. Organized crime, with its own brand of clientelism, became a central part of Russian life in the early post-Soviet period and bled into the halls of government. President Putin cracked down on corruption, but rarely targeted his own political associates. Instead, he used the existence of corrupt clientelist practices as an excuse to target political opponents, while quietly supporting such practices by his political allies.

In addition to traditional clientelism, pre-Soviet, Soviet, and post-Soviet Russian society has been organized through a system based on *blat* (the Russian word for "connections"). Although the *blat* system did not extend down to ordinary people to the same extent that it functioned at the elite level, ordinary citizens were not excluded from it. Even those without membership in the Communist Party knew people with the ability to provide them access to a particular good or service—or at least knew someone who knew someone with such an ability. The person who received such a benefit through his or her connections (in Russian, *po blatu*) was not necessarily expected to return the favor immediately or through monetary payment. Rather, *blat* was a system of interactions, in which favors were eventually repaid, in one form or another, over time.

A system that draws on personal connections, reciprocal interactions, and compensation through barter makes sense in conditions, such as those under Communist rule, of perpetual shortage.[40] It is less obvious that the *blat* system should remain a necessary feature of post-Soviet Russian society. Since the end of the Soviet period, those with an urgent need for a particular good or service have increasingly had to pay strangers to obtain it—legally or otherwise—rather than turning to old acquaintances with access. Granted, those with connections benefited greatly at times in the post-Soviet period, something that was most evident during the privatization of formerly state-owned enterprises. But the *blat* system has become less central to Russian political and social life than it had been in the latter stages of the Soviet period, even if it has not entirely disappeared.

China

In one-party systems, the party typically uses an official ideology in its effort to link itself to the masses. Thus, there is a form of programmatic linkage. Rather than using ideological and policy positions to woo voters, the party works to convince the general population that its vision is correct. In China the importance of ideology has been on the decline since the death of Mao Zedong. Once the CCP allowed capitalists (i.e., business owners) to be members, it was hard to see how the party based itself on Communist ideology. Some programmatic elements remain, but rather than Communist ideology the CCP emphasizes economic development and nationalism.

Clientelism and personal connections have a lot to do with how people interact with government officials and how government officials interact with each other. Clientelist arrangements have always been a part of politics under the rule of the CCP, especially at the local level.[41] Even with the introduction of the post-Mao economic reforms, clientelist connections never went away. In fact, as corruption has become an increasingly serious problem in Chinese politics, clientelism has become even more evident. In a setting where the government directly controls much less of the country's wealth than it used to, government officials are still able to use their positions of authority to improve their personal social and economic standing.

Like the *blat* system in Russia, ordinary Chinese have often relied on their personal connections to get things they need. Known as the *guanxi* system, the use of personal networks in China has subtle differences from its Russian counterpart. Many Russians view engaging in *blat* transactions as pleasurable, while Chinese

view the performance of services through *guanxi* as a social responsibility; at the same time, the loss of *blat* is more serious, often perceived as a matter of life and death.[42]

Guanxi also shares many features with *blat*. Both imply repeated exchanges between individuals who are familiar with each other, and both combine trust and cooperation with power and domination.[43] Also like the Russian system of *blat*, *guanxi* has declined slightly in its use and importance with the development of a market economy. Connections remain important, but in both countries corruption can often involve large sums of money and increasingly includes payments to strangers.

Iran

Clientelism in Iran predated the Islamic Revolution. It survived the disruptions that the revolution unleashed, and it has become a particularly noticeable feature of Iranian politics in the nearly two decades since Ayatollah Khomeini's death in 1989. According to sociologist Kazem Alamdari, Khomeini's death marked the end of populism and the blossoming of clientelism.[44]

Clientelism has formed around rival government power bases, such as former President Akbar Hashemi Rafsanjani, and it corresponds to a "combination of the patrimonial and the saintly, in which both traditional and religious relations between superior and subordinates have been revived."[45] Heavy regulation of the economy and a powerful bureaucracy have reinforced clientelism, hurting Iran's chances to use its oil wealth to benefit the general population.

At the same time, programmatic appeals have a certain importance. Those vocally supportive of an overhaul of Iran's theocracy are unlikely to be allowed to run for political office (and may find themselves in jail!). However, Iranian voters have become quite sophisticated at picking up on subtle differences in what candidates in *Majles* or presidential elections say about social relations, gender, the economy, and global interconnections.

Social Movements

When a sizeable portion of the population participates in activities related to a general socioeconomic or political issue, their activities are known as a **social movement**. Members of social movements share general concerns related to politics, economics, and society. They work to promote or resist broad socioeconomic or political changes through informal networks that organize activities such as public protests.

Traditionally, social movements formed around economic issues, such as workers' movements seeking better working conditions, higher wages, and a shorter work week. After World War II, these traditional social movement issues began to take a backseat to other quality-of-life issues (women's rights, environmentalism, etc.). The set of activities addressing these topics came to be known as **new social movements**. Such movements have tended to be even less coordinated than in the case of the traditional economic-based movements of the past, and organizations working on the issues have been generally shorter lived. New social movements became a central focus of comparativists in Western Europe in the late twentieth century, but their research drew heavily upon the work of American comparative politics scholars such as Ronald Inglehart and his ideas about a postmaterialist culture shift (see Chapter 4).

The membership of social movements is less clear than that of specific organizations. Individuals and groups combine to pursue their shared goals in a social movement, and this membership is often fragile and constantly varying. In his classic 1978 work on social movements, *From Mobilization to Revolution*, Charles Tilly characterized social participants as falling into four categories. "Zealots" are those so devoted to the movement that they will participate despite the costs. "Run-of-the-mill" participants are sympathetic to the cause, but they participate on and off and only when they expect to get more

from the activities than their participation costs them. "Misers" support the general goals of the movement, but are only willing to participate if they expect a significantly greater return than the costs of participating. Finally, "opportunists" have no real attachment to the cause but participate in the movement's activities for purely personal gain.[46] More recently, Friedhelm Neidhart and Dieter Rucht have also distinguished among different types of members and supporters of a social movement, though in a slightly different manner from Tilly. In declining order of participation and sense of attachment to the movement, they label these individuals core activists, participants, contributors, and sympathizers; they claim that the latter two groups are not real members but rather are part of the movement's "supportive environment."[47]

Interest Groups

Interest groups are similar to social movements, but an interest group is both more organized and more focused than a social movement. Interest groups are specific organizations with a fairly well-defined membership. These members share concerns about a particular issue and work toward the adoption of policies consistent with their positions. Interest groups seek to shape policies without pursuing governmental

---

Social movements are informal networks sharing a common viewpoint, working to promote or resist certain political, economic, or social changes, and engaging in activities such as mass protests.

New social movements are large movements that emerged following World War II to address non-economic issues, such as women's rights and the environment. They represent what Ronald Inglehart has called a postmaterialist culture shift in economically developed countries.

Interest groups are organizations whose members share concerns about an issue. They seek to shape government policies on this issue without seeking governmental office.

office. Thus, while one could speak of the environmental movement as a social movement, a group such as the Sierra Club is an interest group; the broad set of activities in support of human rights is a social movement, whereas Amnesty International is an interest group.

While some political analysts portray interest groups in a negative light, they provide the ruling elite with information about the wishes of major segments of the population. They serve as "messengers" between political leaders and the population at large, providing political leaders with some sense about how the general public feels about certain issues and how intense their feelings are. Yet it is wrong to assume that they represent the opinions and desires of the population as a whole. Just as members of the attentive public tend to be the ones to contact politicians directly, they also tend to be the ones to participate in interest group activities or the financial support of such activities.

The characteristics and approach of interest groups vary significantly across countries and within them. In general, however, the effectiveness of an interest group depends on its organization, the size of its membership, and the number of other resources—especially money—that it has at its disposal. Almost by definition, large, well-organized, and wealthy interest groups will be important players in politics.

Types of Interest Groups

A vast number of different interest groups operate around the world. Political scientists tend to focus on three main types: economic groups, advocacy groups, and local issue groups. **Economic groups** are interest groups that form for financial or occupational reasons and represent particular sectors of the economy. These include major labor unions, business groups such as the chamber of commerce, and interest groups representing farmers. The importance of unions varies from country to country, though unions' membership and influence have gener-

ally declined over the last several decades in economically developed countries. In almost every country, however, farmers continue to have more political clout than their percentage of the population would indicate. They produce an important good, which is a form of resource for the group, and they can punish the government by withholding their products if they do not like what the government is doing.

Advocacy groups center on a particular issue or "cause" that they believe is an important political or social issue for the country as a whole. Examples in the United States include groups such as the National Rifle Association (NRA) and environmental groups such as Greenpeace and the Sierra Club. Because members often see little financial benefit from achieving their goals, advocacy groups are often less well organized than economic groups. The NRA is an exception. It is one of the best organized and most powerful American interest groups.

Local issue groups are interest groups that form because of concerns with "backyard" issues, for example, the proposed location of a new landfill in a particular town. The topics that such groups focus on are known as **NIMBY** ("not in my backyard!") **issues**. They generally do not expand to become players on the national political scene. They also tend to be fairly short lived, dissipating once the issue has been addressed.

Economic groups are interest groups that form around shared economic interests and represent particular sectors of the economy. They include labor unions and business groups.

Advocacy groups are interest groups that form around a particular issue or "cause" they believe in and seek to influence government policy at the national level. In the United States, they include groups such as the Sierra Club and the NRA.

Local issue groups are groups that form to address a specific, short-term issue in a community.

Specific, short-term issues in a community are known as **NIMBY**—or "not in my backyard!"—**issues**.

This does not mean such groups are ineffective. Local issue groups are often successful because they are passionate about the topic and close to the action, and local governments cannot afford to ignore even a relatively small number of vocal residents.

The Organization of Interest Groups: Pluralism, Corporatism, and State Control

In addition to different types of interest groups, the way that interest groups are organized in relation to the state varies between countries. In some, interest groups are largely autonomous from state institutions; they interact with the state through efforts to convince political officials to adopt particular policies. In other cases, major interest groups are brought more directly into the political process. They are given a seat at the table as partners alongside government officials. Finally, in still other states, state institutions control interest groups. They function as extensions of the state, providing another way that the masses are linked to the state.

Pluralism The first arrangement, and the one most familiar to Americans, is **pluralism**. In a pluralist system, interest groups are autonomous from the state. They lobby the government to take their positions on policy, but are not officially involved in the decision-making process. Instead, the interest groups compete with one another for the attention of government officials.

In addition, because interest groups in pluralist systems generally form on their own without state assistance or the state sanctioning a group as the "official" interest group for a particular issue, pluralist systems have a large number of interest groups, spreading out interest groups' political power.[48] Even within a single issue area such as environmentalism, there may be a number of competing groups. The political system is designed to receive information from this large and diverse set of interest groups, though in practice not all groups have equal influence.

Corporatism Within democratic political systems, the central alternative to pluralism is **corporatism**. Although its name might lead one to believe it involves the domination of corporations, its defining feature is the way in which certain interest groups are more closely connected to the state than occurs in pluralism. In a corporatist system, the state recognizes one or two groups in important sectors (business, labor, farming, etc.) as official interest groups. These groups are known as **peak organizations**. Such interest groups are often "umbrella organizations"—groups that themselves are made up of a number of smaller groups—and may represent significant portions of the general population.

In corporatism, interest groups do not simply lobby the government. They actually participate in debating the merits of, and writing, proposed policies. Peak organizations affected by the policy in question partake in crafting it. Significant debate may take place, but the emphasis is on finding a cooperative solution to the policy problem that the main interest groups can all support. When a bill finally comes up for a vote on the floor of the national legislature, the main organizations in the major social sectors have already had their say and, theoretically, support the bill.

Pluralism is an interest groups approach in which groups form autonomously, lobby government officials, and compete with other groups engaged in similar activities.

Corporatism is an alternative approach to organizing interest groups where the state officially recognizes certain large interest groups as the official representatives of large segments of society and brings the leaders of those groups to the table as policy is being created.

Large interest groups given official status in corporatism are known as **peak organizations**.

There are two variants of corporatism related to the power of the groups compared with the state. **State corporatism** is a system in which the state brings certain interest groups into the process. The interest groups are "junior partners" in the policymaking process, and their range of activities may be quite limited. The other form is **societal corporatism**, where the major interest groups emerge fairly autonomously, tend to drive the policymaking process, and are thus the "senior partners" in that process. The state is brought in to arbitrate disputes among the major groups and legitimate their decisions rather than the other way around. In other words, in societal corporatism the dominant interest groups force themselves into the policymaking process, while in state corporatism the state sets the rules of the game. It invites interest groups into discussions about government policy, and even creates them if they do not already exist or cannot be easily co-opted by government leaders.[49]

Societal corporatism is considered more democratic than state corporatism, which is often associated with authoritarian governance. Indeed, societal corporatism has been more common in northern European democracies, while state corporatism has flourished at times in authoritarian systems in Latin America and Asia. Because societal corporatism is seen as the less traditional approach, emerging only in the middle part of the twentieth century, some use the label **neo-corporatism** to refer to this variant of corporatism.

A cornerstone of both types of corporatism is the state's endorsement of certain "official" groups. As comparativist Philippe Schmitter puts it, peak organizations are "recognized or licensed (if not created) by the state and granted a deliberate representational monopoly."[50] In such systems, certain groups are left out of the policymaking process. Not surprisingly, those left out may turn to more unconventional forms of participation.

Traditionally, the major official groups in European corporatist systems represented business, labor unions, farmers, and sometimes established religion. "New social movement" groups, such as environmentalists, were excluded from debates over policy, even for policies about which they cared deeply. Their displeasure produced two results. First, some groups transformed into political parties as a way of forcing themselves into the political process. This is an important part of the story behind the emergence of Green parties in Europe. Second, their protests about the nature of the corporatist system led to reforms, making the system more open to these new social forces.

State-Controlled Groups The final form of interest group–state relations is the **state control system**. This approach is most common in totalitarian or strong authoritarian systems. The state-control approach goes a step beyond state corporatism. Official interest groups are present, but they are creations of the state and under its complete control. The groups have no autonomy, and they exist to serve the interests of the state.[51] The state uses the groups to enforce its decisions and provide some legitimacy. This does not mean that the relationship is completely a one-way street. Government officials may also look to the groups for information as they make policy decisions. Thus, while the interest groups are largely an arm of the state, they are also a

---

State corporatism is a variant of corporatism where the state recognizes and even creates the main interest groups, where the interest groups have little autonomy, and where the interest groups are "junior partners" during policymaking.

In **societal corporatism**, the main interest groups form independently of state action, force the state to accept them in the policymaking process, and have greater autonomy from state control.

The label **neo-corporatism** is often used to refer to societal corporatism.

In a **state control system**, the state creates and controls the main interest groups. The groups thus have no autonomy from the state.

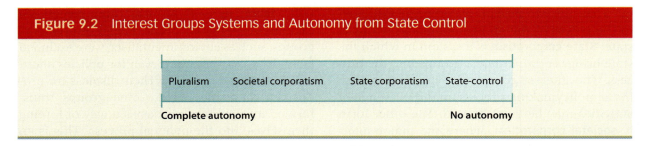

Figure 9.2 Interest Groups Systems and Autonomy from State Control

way for the state to link itself to the masses and gather information about mass attitudes and policy preferences.

It is possible to put the four arrangements just discussed on a spectrum based on the degree of autonomy from the state that the interest groups hold. Figure 9.2 presents such a spectrum. Pluralism is associated with complete autonomy from the government, while the state control system features no autonomy at all.

Advantages and Disadvantages of Pluralism

Pluralism and corporatism are distinct, and in many ways contrary, alternatives to interest group organization. As a result, the advantages of one tend to correspond to the disadvantages of the other and vice versa. This section therefore only focuses on the advantages and disadvantages of pluralism.

Advantage #1: A Marketplace of Ideas One of the strongest claims in favor of pluralism is based on the idea that, in the end, conflict involving competition between rival interest groups produces better policy. Unlike corporatist policymaking, where the state creates a virtual monopoly for certain interest groups, pluralism forces groups to make the strongest possible argument in favor of their position. Even groups with roughly similar ideas compete against one another for the adoption of their version of the policy in question. In theory at least, the result of such competition is that the

policy which emerges is based on the best, most reasoned argument about the issue.

Advantage #2: Even Minor Groups Can Be Heard Corporatism relies on "peak organizations" to represent society. Pluralism allows any group to try to influence the policy process. In a pluralist system, small groups are not automatically excluded even though they do not represent privileged sectors of society, such as labor and business. Of course, this does not guarantee that small groups will have the levels of access and influence that large groups do. The characteristics of a group, such as membership size and financial resources, can affect the extent to which its pleas are heard. However, pluralism does give even small groups the opportunity to *try to be heard* by those in positions of political power.

Disadvantage #1: Inefficiency Through Competition Between Similar Groups The flip side of the image of pluralism as a marketplace of ideas is the view that it encourages inefficient competition among similar interest groups. Two environmental groups with slightly different views of a proposed bill, for example, may work against one another to maximize the chance that their specific position is adopted. A united front would lead to a more efficient use of resources.

One could respond that nothing prevents such groups from working together. Indeed, such cooperation does sometimes occur, particularly when there is a great deal at stake in the outcome. But because the groups are autonomous from the state, they rely on the support of their members to survive. A group that works too closely with—or, worse, appears to be dependent on—a group with similar policy concerns can lead members to defect to that other group. Pluralism thus encourages groups to work for policy successes independently of those with related policy preferences.

Disadvantage #2: Money Talks

The competitive lobbying that is the centerpiece of pluralism involves providing information to officials. The information that an interest group provides, of course, does not necessarily present a complete or balanced picture. Rather, a group is likely to present information that supports its position.

This would not be a problem if all sides in a debate had equal resources with which to get their message out and had equal access to government officials. Particularly in the United States, equality of both resources and access is far from the norm. Those with more, especially with more money, can better get their message across through direct lobbying efforts and through indirect lobbying—using information campaigns to encourage the masses to put pressure on their political officials, leading the officials to support the position of the interest group. Groups with more money can also contribute more to political candidates. While it is difficult to prove that campaign contributions in the United States have a direct effect on policy positions, there is solid evidence that such campaign contributions do improve a group's access to political officials once they take office.

Civil Society

Related to the idea of interest groups and autonomy from the state is the concept of **civil society**. Political scientists use the term civil society in a number of ways. Most commonly,

it refers to the array of voluntary social organizations not controlled by the state. Examples in the United States include local service organizations (the Rotary Club), local fraternal societies (the Lions Club), groups catering to personal hobbies and interests (chess clubs), and groups with more political relevance (such as national interest groups like the NRA and AARP).

In an ideal-type totalitarian system, there is no civil society. In authoritarian systems, the nonpolitical segments of civil society may be abundant, but groups that begin to look politically threatening are either co-opted into or crushed by the state. In democratic systems where interest groups are organized through pluralism, the politically salient portion of civil society is generally strong. In democratic corporatist systems, the politically relevant component of civil society is usually a bit weaker, since the state plays a role in privileging certain groups over others.

A problem with the concept of civil society is the question of how autonomous from the state a group should be to be considered part of civil society. We might exclude peak organizations in state corporatist systems from civil society, but what about nongovernmental organizations at the local level that receive significant funding from the state? As happens with other questions, some of the arguments between comparativists about civil society boil down to different conceptualizations and different approaches to measuring the concept.

Think and Discuss

In what ways can civil society organizations be a force for instability and intolerance?

Civil society is generally used to refer to the set of groups that are both autonomous from the state and that people join voluntarily.

Interest Groups and Social Movements in the United Kingdom, Germany, France, and India

The United Kingdom, Germany, France, and India show the extent to which approaches to interest group organization can vary within democracies. Relations between the state and interest groups are based on societal corporatism in Germany. The French approach of "concertation" contains corporatist-like elements but is far less structured than typical corporatist arrangements. In the United Kingdom, the trend has been away from corporatism and toward pluralism, while India has also begun to embrace a more pluralist approach involving interest group competition.

Social movements in the four countries have also played a visible role in politics. In both the United Kingdom and Germany, environmentalism, the peace movement, women's groups, and broad mobilization on both sides of the immigration issue have been part of the landscape of domestic politics. A new revolution in French politics has transformed labor and produced an explosion of civil society organizations and new social movements. In India, the desire for greater regional autonomy has been a major issue driving social movement development, along with the environment and concerns over the treatment of *Dalits* ("untouchables") in the caste system.

The United Kingdom

While less dramatic than its change from a clientelist to programmatic system, British interest group participation has changed over time as well. In the past, Britain was much more corporatist than it is today, with several "peak organizations." Among Margaret Thatcher's reforms was an effort to reduce the direct impact of groups by reducing the number of government boards where interest groups were directly involved in crafting policy. This especially weakened the power of unions. As with many of Thatcher's

other reforms, her attack on corporatism survived the years of Labour Party control of the British government under Tony Blair.

The result of the decline of corporatism is a greater emphasis on lobbying, and a greater role for small groups. Unlike the United States, there is little lobbying around the final vote on a bill. Instead, interest group efforts focus on the initial draft of a proposed policy and the period of time between readings of the bill in the House of Commons. Groups can have a strong impact on details in bills but typically cannot stop a bill from passing. The strength of British interest groups is aided by the district voting system. Groups can point out to the MP how much their members in the MP's district support a particular policy. As discussed in Chapter 7, an MP in the government's party faces a hard time voting no on a government-sponsored bill, but an active MP can help amend a bill as it makes its way through parliament.

The fairly low levels of overall participation in the United Kingdom do not indicate a lack of social movements or interest group membership. The United Kingdom has a substantial civil society.[52] Among the various types of social movements, peace, environmental, women's, and immigration-related movements have been the most prominent. The peace movement, a force during the Vietnam War and as an anti-nuclear weapons forum during the Cold War, reemerged during the Iraq War. Even after Prime Minister Tony Blair, who had been one of the strongest allies of the United States on the issue both before and after the invasion of Iraq, stepped down in favor of Gordon Brown, the anti–Iraq War movement worked to mobilize citizens in London against maintaining a significant presence in Iraq. In October 2007, thousands of protesters successfully marched on the British parliament building. Police had threatened to prohibit them from marching along their chosen path, relying on legislation from the nineteenth century designed to protect the MPs and members of the House of

Lords from radical mobs, but at the last minute worked out a compromise with leaders of the antiwar movement.[53]

Like the environmental movement in countries like the United States, environmentalism in the United Kingdom involves a number of formal organizations and informal groups. Some (e.g., Greenpeace–United Kingdom) are local branches of international nongovernmental organizations, while others are unique to the United Kingdom. More radical environment activists support and engage in unconventional actions—preventing road construction projects, for example—but the more established environmental interest groups tend to prefer working through official channels.

The women's movement has been less visible. In fact, in recent years some British scholars have questioned the current standing of a women's movement that was so conspicuous in the United Kingdom in the 1970s. While some stress that it has simply taken a new form, others ask whether the movement exists at all.[54] The women's movement was not helped by the fact that one of the strongest faces of women's penetration into the British political system, Margaret Thatcher, opposed more aggressive government responses to address socioeconomic and political gender imbalances.[55]

Finally, the immigration issue has sparked social movements on both sides. Prior to the 1980s, anti-immigrant groups had drawn support from both the Left (with concerns about working class and union employments) and the Right (with concerns about cultural effects and a perceived link to increased instances of criminal activity). When Margaret Thatcher made immigration a central part of the Conservative Party platform, anti-immigrant groups became increasingly associated with forces of the political Right. Of course, not all on the right oppose increased immigration, since many see escalating immigration as a benefit to British businesses. As in other Western European countries, the process of European integration has fostered growing concerns on the part of some citizens that the United Kingdom is increasingly unable to guarantee that long-time residents will find jobs, to protect its culture, or to ensure its national security.

Germany

Societal corporatism has been the principal structure of relations between interest groups and the state in the Federal Republic. Peak associations representing major economic interests such as labor, business, and the professions negotiate policies with the state. As in countries like France, this sometimes occurs in formal round-table forums (or concertation), but oftentimes is even more informal. Unlike France, societal corporatism extends beyond the realm of policy formulation to encompass policy *implementation* as well. These peak associations, as well as those representing the main religious denominations in the area of social welfare, implement policies and administer their particular domain of industrial relations or the welfare state on behalf of the government. In doing so, they enjoy substantial autonomy from state interference as long as they fulfill their public obligations to implement the law.[56] This system of societal corporatism was transplanted to eastern Germany following unification and supplanted the Communist Party—controlled organizations of civil society.

Among western Germans after World War II and eastern Germans after 1990, the aversion to group participation in the years immediately following the end of totalitarian rule reflected the weakness of civil society due to the suppression of voluntary associations by the previous dictatorial regimes. State control of German society was a hallmark of its experiences with both the fascist and Communist variants of totalitarianism. The Nazi Party and, later, the Communist Party in the GDR created party—controlled front groups that organized all aspects of political, social, and economic life, from youth groups, to business and professional associations, and labor organizations. Both regimes banned independent organizations. In the GDR, other parties existed as officially sanctioned "bloc" or "satellite" parties but were not truly independent.[57]

Civil society reemerged in the Federal Republic over time, aided by the societal corporatist system of interest group representation. From the 1960s to the present, social movements representing university students, antinuclear forces, pacifism, feminism, and environmentalism organized to effect political change. These "citizens' initiatives" (or *Bürgerinitiativen*) sometimes engaged in a range of unconventional activities. As discussed earlier in the chapter, their activities were often nonviolent but did sometimes lead to physical skirmishes with police. The Green Party emerged from these social movements in the late 1970s.[58] Corporatist institutions and organizations were transferred from the west of the country to the east following unification. Membership in trade unions and employers' associations in the east quickly dropped off, however, as employers and workers sought to bypass collective wage agreements and strike company-level deals to save jobs and enterprises.[59]

France

As we might expect from elite dominance in government and business, the incorporation of interests—particularly labor interests—into the common good has been problematic in France. Because French Republicans distrusted any form of "mediation" or organization that stood between the state and the citizen, the activities of labor unions were legally restricted prior to 1884, as were nonprofit associations until 1901. The Fifth Republic attempted to include corporatist peak negotiations through concertation—direct consultation with key interests organized in peak associations less binding than corporatist negotiations—as well as more pluralist sector-by-sector and enterprise-based decision making. While generally less successful in representing labor interests, such approaches did produce the Auroux Laws, adopted in 1982 by the Socialist-Communist coalition government, which included a variety of factory-level structures with elected worker representation to negotiate and oversee wages and working conditions.

The French labor movement lacks both a cohesive national identity and a single peak organization, instead dividing along ideological and partisan lines. Some labor organizations are primarily social movements that confront the state, while others act as social partners with the state.[60] When measured in terms of membership, the French labor movement is also one of the weakest in Europe, with less than 10 percent of the workforce. This compares with nearly all workers in Sweden, 50 percent in the United Kingdom, and even 16 percent in the United States. Today, there are five primary unions: the oldest is the *Confédération Générale du Travail* (General Confederation of Labor—CGT), founded in 1895 and formally tied to the Communist Party until 2003; the largest is *Confédération Française Démocratique du Travail* (CFDT), a social democratic movement aligned with the Socialist Party; *Force Ouvrière* (FO), the third largest, split from the CGT during the Cold War; the antineoliberal *G10 Solidaires* confederation is the newest; and the *Confédération Française des Travailleurs Chrétiens* (CFTC) was founded in 1919. There are also unions for specific sectors of public employees, students, and other social groups.

By contrast, employers are represented in unified national peak organizations. The *Mouvement des entreprises de France* (MEDEF) was founded in its original form under the direction of the state in the immediate aftermath of World War II. MEDEF represents 750,000 business leaders. Also at the end of the war, small- and medium-sized businesses came together through the *Confédération Générale des Petites et Moyennes Entreprises*. However, the heterogeneity of MEDEF in particular has caused increasing stress as the state has ceded authority to private enterprise.[61]

The *Conseil Economique et Social* brings together labor, business, the state, and a variety of other social actors to review and report on pending legislation. Consistent with the lack of a peak labor organization, the state negotiates directly with the most powerful unions representing the 2.5 million civil servants on a sector-by-sector basis. The state also brings labor and business together through the quasi-judicial *Conseils de Prud'hommes*, or Workers Tribunals. With an elected governing council shared equally by business and labor, these tribunals are a kind of binding arbitration to resolve workplace conflicts.

The difficulties organized labor faces correspond to broader tendencies, with elites in France hesitant to embrace an engaged and active civil society. The expansion of French civil society and the corresponding development of the first alternative social movements emerged from the events of May 1968, which began with disruptive and often violent student-organized demonstrations in central Paris.[62] These new social movements—including feminist, environmentalist, lesbian/gay, immigrants' rights, human rights, health care, and even faith-based issue organizing—were unanticipated and overwhelming for politicians and scholars alike, as they reflected the emergence of a new type of disillusionment with the state's monopoly on authority, advocating instead greater citizen participation.[63]

In other ways, the birth of new social movements in France does not appear all that new. The term "new" does not reflect the long history of human rights or feminist organizing in modern France.[64] The "children of Sodom," for example, petitioned the Revolutionary government to decriminalize same-gender sexual relations in 1790, and France was the first country to abolition such laws under Napoleon.[65] Indeed, many of these "new" organizations follow the typical pattern of issue articulation in French culture and mirror the party and ideological institutions that dominate French politics. The *Confédération Paysanne*, for instance, is an organization representing French farmers, but it is organized along ideological and institutional lines typical of a French labor union and promotes the preservation of small scale and sustainable agriculture in part to preserve rural communities.[66] *S.O.S.-Racisme* has an almost clientelistic relationship to the Socialist Party, and a number of immigrant and gay rights organizations work very closely with the alternative Left around the declining Communist Party and the growing League of Revolutionary Struggle and the Workers Struggle.

India

Over time, interest group representation in India transitioned from one in the early period following independence, in which the Indian National Congress (INC) Party developed its own student associations, peasant groups, and trade unions (characterized as "state-dominated pluralism"), to the development of a form of "authoritarian corporatism" during the Emergency (1975–1977), to a form of "competitive pluralism" in subsequent years.[67] Today, there are numerous interest groups, many of which have affiliations with political parties, in most sectors of the economy. For example, student groups have been active in all parts of the country on many different issues. These groups have been a source of future party leaders and compete with each other for prominence.

Most of the country's workers are not unionized. Estimates of union membership range between 10 and 15 million members. Each of the main unions is affiliated with a political party: the Indian National Trade Union Congress (INTUC) with the INC, the Bharatiya Sangh (BMS) with the Bharatiya Janata Party (BJP), the Centre of Indian Trade Unions (CITU) with the Communist Party of India (CPI[M]), and the All-India Trade Union Congress (AITUC) with the Communist Party of India (CPI).

The farmers' movements that developed among peasants in the 1950s and 1960s, as well as those that developed with the "Green Revolution" in the 1970s and 1980s, faced numerous problems. According to comparativists Robert Hardgrave and Stanley Kochanek, "The strength and solidarity of the farmers' movement totally collapsed following the introduction of economic reforms in 1991."[68] Subsequently, political parties became the principal narrators of the farmers' interests.

Other groups include those advocating the interests of Scheduled Castes, Scheduled Tribes, and Other Backward Classes groups. Hindu-nationalist-oriented groups associated with the Rashtriya Swayamsevak Sangh (RSS) have tended to share interests with the BJP. There are women's advocacy groups, civil liberties groups, environmental groups, and many others—including thousands of NGOs, many funded from abroad, representing a wide range of interests.

Social movements have developed in India over the years, including those seeking to block dam building, to stop deforestation, and to stop privatization of public companies. Separatist movements demanding either secession from India or a separate federal unit have developed with varying intensity for decades. Ever since federal unit boundaries were established with the implementation of the States Reorganization Commission's report in 1956, demands for changes, sometimes peaceful and sometimes violent, have occurred. From the 1960s through the 1980s, the federal unit of Assam in the northeast was split into several federal units in an effort to quell uprisings. Movements to create separate federal units for the Bodo and others in the same area persist today. On the opposite side of the country, in the 1980s there was a militant effort to create "Khalistan" with the secession of the federal unit of Punjab. In 2000, three new federal units were created in response to generally peaceful movements, that is, Uttaranchal (now Uttara-chand) out of Uttar Pradesh, Jharkhand out of Bihar, and Chhattisgarh out of Madhya Pradesh.

Interest Groups and Social Movements in Mexico, Brazil, and Nigeria

With the democratizations in Mexico, Brazil, and Nigeria, interest groups and social movements have gained renewed importance. Along with Mexico's slow retreat from clientelism, the old corporatist system dominated by the Institutional Revolutionary Party (PRI) has become notably weaker over the last decade. Brazil's corporatist system, on the other hand, has largely survived democratization, partly because it had been tied to the state rather than to a single political party as in Mexico. Not all interest groups, however, have agreed to play by Brazil's corporatist rules, choosing confrontation over cooperation. With the return of democracy to Nigeria, as imperfect as it may be, interest groups, which had existed to an extent even during military rule, have become increasingly important. In all three countries, democracy has helped foster an increasingly conspicuous civil society.

Mexico

Like other aspects of Mexican politics, the nature of social movements and the structure of interest group representation are changing. Comparativists long considered Mexico a corporatist country, but one that differed both from an ideal state corporatist system and an ideal societal corporatist one. While connected to the state, Mexican interest groups were more tightly connected to the PRI itself, which set up and largely controlled them. As a result, some called Mexico a case of **party corporatism**,[69] like many Communist countries in Europe and Asia in the twentieth century.

As with many of Mexico's other political reforms, the changes in interest group connections with the government have been controversial among those who benefited from the old arrangements. Because their claim to influence in the state depends both on incorporation in the PRI and on PRI control of the state, official unions strongly resisted policies that threatened the PRI

Party corporatism refers to the variant of corporatism in Mexico during the PRI's dominance of the Mexican political system. The approach was similar to state corporatism, but the interest groups were connected to state institutions through their close relationship with the PRI.

and their connections to it.[70] Likewise, many of the old guard members of the PRI resisted weakening connections with labor unions that they had so effectively mobilized in the past to support the party's dominance.

Genuine social movements in Mexico were difficult during the era of PRI dominance. However, they did exist. University students pushed for a more democratic political system in the late 1960s, a social movement that the government, not yet ready for liberalization, decided to crush. The result was the deaths of around three hundred protesters. Peasant uprisings, involving seizures of land loosely coordinated by leftist organizations in Mexico, took place in the early to mid-1970s.[71] The rebellion in the state of Chiapas in the mid-1990s was the definition of a social movement based on unconventional participation.

IN THEORY AND PRACTICE

Disturbance Theory and Mexico

Political scientists have spent a great deal of time theorizing about who participates in interest groups and social movements and how

The leader of the Zapatista National Liberation Army (EZLN), Subcomandante Insurgente Marcos gives the victory sign to supporters as he marches from the U.S. Embassy to the main Zocalo plaza in Mexico City, on May 1, 2006. Marcos joined calls to boycott U.S. goods in what was dubbed "A Day Without Gringos," an action timed to coincide with a call for immigrants to boycott work, school, and shopping in the United States.

(©AP Photo/Moises Castillo)

such groups form and mobilize members. One of the first scholars to address this question was David Truman, in a 1951 book called *The Governmental Process*.[72] Truman argued that interest groups form as a response to social and economic change, particularly when such development creates a "disturbance" in society. As a result, his ideas came to be known as **disturbance theory**.

Though it does not completely explain the uprising in Chiapas in the mid-1990s, disturbance theory does provide some insight. The implementation of the North American Free Trade Agreement (NAFTA) clearly fueled the Chiapas explosion. On January 1, 1994, coinciding with NAFTA's implementation, the Zapatista Army of National Liberation (EZLN) seized four towns. NAFTA embodied what EZLN leaders saw as Mexico's failure to address problems facing the country's peasants—problems exacerbated by globalization. Thus, while not the original source of the "disturbance" around which EZLN mobilized, NAFTA's implementation was a trigger for the violent uprising.

Disturbance theory is a term for the theory, developed by David Truman, that interest groups form from economic and social changes which create "disturbances" in society. Such disturbances lead those who share concerns about the problem to form groups to solve it.

Yet, there is more to the story than the social and economic problems NAFTA symbolized. The EZLN is led by a charismatic individual, Subcomandante Insurgente Marcos. Marcos had been working to politicize Chiapas's population since 1983, and his fiery rhetoric was instrumental in the movement's international notoriety and local successes. Thus, Chiapas points out how key members of a social movement can at times play a key role in translating the existence of a socioeconomic disturbance into the actions of that social movement.

Brazil

Brazil's system of labor representation has historically been highly corporatist. Unlike in the Mexican case, however, unions and other class-based organizations were not tied to the state through a political party. Instead, Brazil developed a state corporatist approach, in which the system of peak unions resulted from top down, state direction. Although formal state support systems discouraging pluralistic competition are not in place for other types of organizations, many have adopted the format of peak organizations in order to be heard more clearly at the national level. The systems that developed in the *estados* mirrored that at the national level.

Some of the traditional labor unions, such as the General Workers' Central (CGT), continue to operate much as the corporatist system intended, as more or less passive supporters of the state. Others, however, such as the Unified Workers' Central (CUT), have developed along much more confrontational lines. The unions that today belong to the CUT were once traditional co-opted labor unions such as the CGT, but internal rebellions led by the powerful metalworkers' unions in the São Paulo region of Brazil began to challenge the military regime in the late 1970s.

While a model for the use of unconventional tactics in Brazil, the CUT is far from an antisystem organization. It was the CUT that originally founded the Workers' Party (PT) and continues to dominate its leadership. In addition, the CUT happily takes advantage of some of the privileges of state corporatism, especially its monopoly of representation and the state's collection of union dues. This has allowed CUT unions to stand up for their employee unions against the state better than if they had resorted to unconventional activities alone.

Along with Mexico and Chile, Brazil has one of the most vibrant civil societies in Latin America. According to the World Values Survey, Brazil would be classified as having a "strong" civil society, weaker than the United States or the United Kingdom, but stronger than Italy, France, Japan, or Spain.[73] Yet the individual civil society organizations, though numerous, have not been effectively linked to political elites.

Most of Brazil's social movements developed more autonomously from the state than labor unions, and in some cases have been quite confrontational. Particularly since the 1970s, nongovernmental organizations within the country have worked to raise awareness of many pressing national problems and mobilize the population to support actions to address them. These include movements on the environment, homelessness, and AIDS.

One of the most interesting Brazilian social movements is the *Movimento dos Trabalhadores*

Sem Terra (MST) or "Landless Movement." The MST has worked to pressure the government to address the significant inequality in land ownership in Brazil, particularly in some of the larger and more rural *estados*. Its activities that have gained the most attention, however, are those designed to bypass the political process entirely, such as the forceful seizure of land and the establishment of agricultural cooperatives beginning in the mid-1980s. The combination of its size—the MST is considered the largest social movement in Latin America—and its unconventional political participation led many leaders of the federal and *estados* governments to condemn its activities. With the election of President Luiz Inacio Lula da Silva, some in the MST thought it had secured a strong ally. Over time, however, MST leaders (along with the broader Brazilian population) began to question Lula's support for genuine land reform.

Nigeria

During periods of military rule, the government repressed social movements, specific interest groups, and the leaders of both if they posed a threat to its rule. As a result, individual interest groups are not as visible in Nigeria as in more established democracies. Like other groups in Nigerian society, interest groups tend to be organized through tribal-based clientelism, though some broader groups exist that are designed to represent segments of the population in regions of the country or even the country as a whole. Some of the strongest are economic organizations, both more traditional groups representing business and labor and those connecting members of particular professions. At times, unions have been strong and independent; at other times, repressed. The Nigerian Labor Congress is the country's largest union organization. It has organized successful unconventional activities, including general strikes, to pressure the government.

Even during periods of military rule, some social movements and groups were allowed to function, sometimes by finding sympathetic officials in the military government who desired a transition back to democracy. Since the reestablishment of democracy in 1999, social movements have become even more visible, including ethnic minority movements, women's movements, and youth movements. The youth movements are divided between peaceful collaborations and "ethnic militias."[74] Groups in the Niger Delta also demonstrate the intermixing of peaceful and violent activities. The Ogoni minority in Nigeria's south, for example, created a specific organization, the Movement for the Survival of the Ogoni People, to "market" their concerns to international nongovernmental organizations, putting the issue of the Niger Delta onto the international agenda for the first time.[75] As discussed earlier in the chapter, collective activities in the Niger Delta also sometimes include kidnappings and sabotage.

Thus, while interest groups and social movements are still underdeveloped, the presence of civil society in Nigeria is a reality. But, once again, Nigeria demonstrates that one should not assume all civil society organizations or social movement activities are "civil." Some of the more organized associations are designed to unite people along ethnic and religious lines—playing a role in reinforcing the already deep social divisions in the country—while others have increasingly turned to violence in their unconventional political activities.

Interest Groups and Social Movements in the Russian Federation, China, and Iran

Despite facing co-optation and outright repression, interest groups and social movements continue to exist in Russia, China, and Iran. Their autonomy from the state and their impact on political outcomes in these countries, however, is more limited than in most of the other TIC cases. In Russia, social movements and autonomous interest groups, which exploded onto the scene during the late Soviet and early post-Soviet periods, have increasingly become targets of the government under Vladimir Putin. In China, interest groups are brought into politics through a corporatist approach. In Iran, some groups that are seen as regime supportive actually have some control over their own affairs, although the development of new interest groups and social movements remains a challenge. Those likely to be perceived as potentially threatening to the theocratic system find it hard to recruit members.

The Russian Federation

Independent interest groups emerged during the early post-Soviet period, but Russia never developed a highly pluralist arrangement. Officially sanctioned labor unions worked with the government on a variety of policies, particularly during the early post-Soviet years.[76] The business community also developed close ties with the government, with the line between the government and private companies (as well as organized criminal groups) at times difficult to discern. Private businesses first benefited from the privatization of state property and then watched as the government began to increase its presence in the economy as an owner of large businesses. As Andrei Illarionov, a former close economic advisor to President Putin, explained in 2006, in Russia:

> State-owned companies have become the assault weapons of the corporate state. Having mastered the main principle of state-corporatism—"privatize profit, nationalize loss"—they have turned to massive intervention in the private sector. . . . Any request from the state—whether it's a donation to a "necessary" project or the sale of the company itself to the "correct" buyers—is fulfilled. Declining is not an option.[77]

Consequently, although state corporatism may be the best descriptor at the present Russian interest group system, the renewal of a state control system is not difficult to imagine.

In the late Soviet period, social movements became widespread. Mikhail Gorbachev's policies allowed a genuine civil society to emerge. People followed and talked about political events, and they participated in a large number of conventional and unconventional political activities. Environmentalists, for example, protested past and present Soviet policies, and their collaboration with nationalist movements in a number of union republics played a role in the USSR's ultimate collapse.

Following that collapse, however, Russian social movements faced a number of challenges. Many in the general Russian population were politically burnt out, the economy was a mess throughout the 1990s, and the creeping authoritarianism of the Putin period made autonomous activity and unconventional participation potentially more costly than it had been under Boris Yeltsin. As a result, local and national political elites increasingly manipulated social movements for their own ends.[78]

China

As with other one-party systems, the Chinese Communist Party has been highly suspicious of autonomous organizations. This is especially true of interest groups concerned about government policy. Consequently, the CCP-led government has co-opted, created, and directly or indirectly controlled many such organizations. As China specialist Bruce Dickson puts it, "In

China, the state has created a dense web of economic and social organizations in order to channel state interest articulation, regularize the flow of information between the state and key groups in society, replace direct state controls over the economy and society with at least partial social regulation, and screen out unwanted groups."[79]

In other words, far from one of absolute state control common to one-party systems, the system appears more corporatist. Interest groups in China are used and closely watched by the state, but they are no longer completely controlled by it. This approach has worked, to date, to limit the size and organizational capacity of individual protests, if not their overall numbers. By continuing to curtail civil society

groups that might organize larger protests, the Chinese government has prevented pockets of discontent from turning into effective social movements.

Yet, as economic and social interests gain more power and become more autonomous from the state, interest groups may seek to co-opt government officials rather than the other way around. Dickson points out that some scholars see China losing control of interest groups to such an extent that societal corporatism will come to replace state corporatist arrangements.[80] China is not there yet—government officials still keep close watch on politically relevant interest groups—but it will be interesting to watch how interest groups relate to the state in the future.

IN THEORY AND PRACTICE

The Military Industrial Complex in China

For political scientists who study interest groups, an important set of arguments concern the concept of "subgovernments." These arguments, which one could collectively call **subgovernment theory**, explain how a subset of the overall government generally has authority to make decisions regarding a particular issue. Theories about subgovernments often discuss them as **iron triangles**. The term "triangle" captures the way in which a subgovernment's components are connected, while "iron" refers to how a subgovernment prevents other entities from penetrating the triangle.

As Figure 9.3 shows, an iron triangle is made up of a government agency working on a certain issue, those responsible for producing legislation on the issue and overseeing the agency (e.g., Congress in the United States), and interest groups who work on the issue. As discussed in the previous chapter, the agency's tasks may include both regulating these interest groups and making significant policy decisions. Government agencies in the United States help perpetuate iron triangles

by including pet projects of key members of Congress in their budget requests.[81]

One of the best-known examples of an iron triangle is the **military industrial complex (MIC)**,

Subgovernment theory emphasizes the extent to which interest groups concerned about a particular issue work tightly with interested legislators and bureaucrats. The resulting "subgovernment" shuts out other government officials and members of the general public from key decisions on that issue.

Iron triangles involve three groups with similar interests on a particular topic: government agencies, those responsible for overseeing the agencies, and interest groups pushing for particular policies related to work of the agency. Because these groups control large amounts of information, policies and government spending may reflect their shared interests.

An often cited example of an iron triangle in the United States is the **military industrial complex (MIC)**, in which the military and/or Department of Defense, Congress, and defense contractors control and manipulate information to justify increased defense spending.

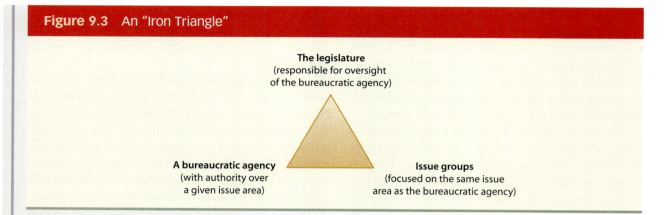

Figure 9.3   An "Iron Triangle"

The legislature
(responsible for oversight
of the bureaucratic agency)

A bureaucratic agency
(with authority over
a given issue area)

Issue groups
(focused on the same issue
area as the bureaucratic agency)

a term made famous by U.S. President Dwight Eisenhower in his farewell address. In the United States, the MIC involves Congress, defense contractors, and the military and related executive branch entities such as the Department of Defense. These three components have the potential to control information about military capabilities and needs and have a shared interest in maximizing defense spending. The military wants spending increases to improve effectiveness and better protect soldiers. Members of Congress view defense spending increases as a chance to get money for their districts. Contractors like more defense spending because it increases profits.

The Chinese Communist Party both closely monitors the activities of the Chinese military and allows it a certain degree of autonomy. Can subgovernment theory help explain this? Is there an MIC in China? Observers of China often use the MIC label, but until the late 1990s it was difficult to fit China into an iron triangle framework, because the military controlled all three corners of the triangle.

Following the launch of economic reforms, the government began to discuss the need to privatize weapons production. In 1998, Chinese leader Jiang Zemin announced an end to the practice of military control of weapons production. As a result, civilian enterprises, both state-owned and privately controlled, have largely taken over arms production under careful government regulation.[82] This has made the MIC in China more typical in that the military has become a consumer of weapons, with production shifting to weapons manufacturing industries, and the process overseen and financed by the government.

The effect of these changes is still unclear. The flow of weapons within and from China has become more transparent. To what extent the other goals of the government—improvements in efficiency of production and quality of the weapons, for example—are being met is less certain. Quality appears to have improved, but military spending has also jumped significantly since the late 1990s. With military production employing around 3 million workers in the early part of this decade,[83] one should not expect reforms to take hold quickly. Thus, while the MIC is beginning to look more like those of other countries, the previous approach to weapons production continues to influence the effectiveness, and cost, of Chinese defense spending.

Think and Discuss

To what extent does the logic behind the concept of a military industrial complex make sense? What might prevent the three groups from working together to increase defense spending?

Iran

In a system like Iran's, it would be unusual to find a large civil society, with a wide array of social movements and interest groups functioning independently of the state. Some interest groups, however, are granted a large amount of autonomy. Those that perform regime-supportive functions are allowed to keep a good deal of the wealth they generate and/or receive significant financial support from the government. As discussed in the previous chapter, the *bonyads*, interest groups uniting wealthy businessmen and religious officials, work closely with the government. These groups control a significant portion of the Iranian economy.

Thus, the structure of interactions between the state and interest groups in Iran is difficult to categorize. A narrow range of groups that the state believes aids its cause function in a quasi-pluralistic manner. Other groups are more closely tied to the state in a form of state corporatism.

Some are wholly the creation of and tightly controlled by the state, while still other potential groups are repressed and prevented from engaging in political activities.

Like narrower interest groups, some broad social movements exist outside government control, particularly the movement for increased rights for women. At the same time, as discussed in the "In Theory and Practice" box in this section, it is dangerous to engage in unconventional participation in Iran. In addition, as spelled out in Chapters 6–8, Iran's political institutions are designed to insulate the government from popular pressure. While the president and *Majles* may feel some need to respond to popular demands, the existence of institutions such as the Supreme Leader and the Guardian Council reflect the idea that the clerics in the Iranian government know better than ordinary citizens what is in the best interests of the country.

IN THEORY AND PRACTICE

The Collective Action Problem and Iran

Many political scientists who work on political behavior related to interest groups and social movements focus on how rational individuals would behave based on the circumstances in which they find themselves. Chapter 11 discusses the role of rationality in political outcomes in greater detail. Here, it is necessary to consider the difficulty of getting rational individuals to engage in collective activities, such as participating in interest groups. While scholars like Truman believe interest groups form naturally (see the "In Theory and Practice" box on Mexico on pages 351–352), others have questioned whether sacrificing time and money to work on a particular cause is rational for any individual. This was the topic of a classic work on interest groups and one of the most influential social science works in the second half of the twentieth century: Mancur Olson's 1965 book, *The Logic of Collective Action*.

Olson sought to understand why individuals would join a group when membership in the group imposes costs—membership dues, time commitments, and so on—if the benefits generated by the group were broadly available to nonmembers as well. With costs targeted to individual members but benefits spread out to all people whether they belong to the group or not, individuals have strong incentives not to join the organization. The problem posed by these incentives to "free ride" is known as the **collective action problem** (also sometimes called the "free rider

The term **collective action problem** refers to the difficulty of getting a rational person to participate in a collective activity if the costs of participating are targeted to those who participate but benefits generated are available to the general public.

problem"). Olson's work helped make the collective action problem a central social science concept. The implications of targeting or spreading out costs and benefits of collective actions help one to understand the tactics of membership in groups, such as one of the most important interest groups in the United States, the American Association of Retired Persons (AARP).

In comparative politics, Olson's ideas help one to understand the difficulties of organizing political activity in many countries. Iranian interest groups are fewer in number and function less openly than their counterparts in more democratic systems. Those that do prosper often generate sizeable revenues from their activities, and group members are allowed to keep a large amount of this wealth for themselves. In such circumstances, the collective action problem is less severe than it is for most interest groups. Rather than collective benefits, these groups' activities produce concentrated benefits, which more than outweigh the costs of participating in the group's activities.

For groups that would challenge the Iranian system, however, the collective action problem is more severe than normal. These groups seek benefits spread across the general population, but the costs of participating in social movement and interest group activities are concentrated on the participants themselves. In Iran, such costs are not just about money and time. Individuals who challenge the state and its conservative social order risk arrest or even death. Unless President Ahmadinejad is successful in challenging the wealth-concentrating nature of the current Iranian system, one would expect interest groups that play the game of clientelism and corruption to continue to thrive while those who seek social and economic reform continue to struggle.

COMPARATIVE EXERCISE

Understanding Protest Activity in Romania

Many of the comparative exercises so far in this book have centered on a small number of cases. This reflects the widespread occurrence of single case studies, or "small N" analyses in comparative politics. However, even when they are interested in understanding a particular country, many comparativists engage in "large N" research: quantitative analyses of a sizeable number of cases—localities, social groups, individuals, and so on—within that country. A common form of such research involves the examination of surveys of a country's population, with the individual respondent serving as the unit of analysis. This chapter's comparative exercise summarizes the use of such data in an existing comparative politics research project.

The Usefulness of Survey Data

Surveys are a useful tool for those interested in conventional and unconventional political participation and elite-mass linkage. They can provide evidence about what factors seem related to political participation when it may be impossible to observe the actual participation as it occurs. By taking a sample of the population and asking the participants to discuss their level and types of political participation, researchers can get a good sense of how to explain such participation.

Of course, to engage in such research, one must assume that respondents are answering truthfully. With certain types of participation, that may be a shaky assumption. In the case of voting (one of the key topics of the next chapter), self-reported turnout rates tend to be higher than actual turnout rates. People like to say they voted even when they did not.

The World Values Survey (WVS) project is one of the largest mass survey studies ever conducted. Overseen by political scientist Ronald Inglehart, data from the WVS have been collected in a large number of countries over the last several decades. One of the topics in this survey is political participation. Examining data from these surveys, Inglehart and Gabriela Catterberg point out that unconventional participation increased in Western European countries from the mid-1970s to 2000 and that the populations of countries with high levels of GNP per capita engage in more such activities than those of poorer countries.[84]

Socioeconomic Status and Mass Participation

What might explain these patterns? A great deal of research on participation has supported the view that the better educated and wealthier people are more likely to participate in political activities. This argument, **socioeconomic status theory**, was driven initially by scholars studying American political behavior. Sidney Verba and Norman Nie's 1972 book, *Participation in America*, for example, stressed socioeconomic status (SES) measured as an aggregation of income, education, and type of occupation.[85] While developed to explain patterns in the United States, socioeconomic status theory can be, and has been, applied to other countries.

Inglehart and Catterberg's findings at the country level are consistent with the general thrust of socioeconomic status theory. However, as highlighted in Chapter 1, one must be very careful about assuming that aggregate findings hold at the individual level (the "ecological fallacy"). Therefore, a better test of the socioeconomic status theory would be to use the WVS data from a certain country to examine the extent to which higher SES individuals are more likely to engage in unconventional participation.

A Study of Attitudes in Romania

A number of existing studies have employed WVS data to examine variation in political participation. Eric M. Uslander conducted one such study, which analyzed WVS data from Romania.[86] In addition to examining level of education—one of the key SES components—the study sought to determine the effects of a large number of attitudes, including interpersonal trust and trust in government institutions, and behaviors like participating in civic organizations, belonging to political organizations, and regularly discussing politics with others.

In light of the body of research supporting socioeconomic status theory, it is surprising that Uslaner's analysis did not support his hypothesis that education has a statistically significant effect on unconventional behavior. The education variable was not significant at the .05 level of statistical significance, the most commonly used level when deciding whether a hypothesis is supported or can be rejected. Hypotheses about a number of the attitudes and behaviors that Uslander examined as independent variables, however, were supported (see Table 9.1).

Socioeconomic status theory argues that differences in rates of political participation among the general population can be explained by differences in socioeconomic status: income, education, and occupation type.

Table 9.1 Analysis of Factors Related to Protest Participation in Romania

Independent Variables	Statistically Significant (at $p \leq .05$)?
Behavioral Variables	
Member of political organizations	NO
Discuss politics with others	YES (positive relationship)
Frequency TV/radio news	YES (positive relationship)
Participate in civic organizations	YES (positive relationship)
Attitudinal Variables	
Political efficacy	NO
Working for party is effective	NO
Generalized trust	NO
Trust in parliament	NO
Centrist political ideology	NO
Get ahead by hard work	NO
Tolerate meetings of extremists	YES (negative relationship)
Courts treat all equally	YES (negative relationship)
Demographic Variables	
Education	NO
Age	YES (negative relationship)
Union member	YES (positive relationship)

N = 511

Source: Eric M. Uslaner, "Bowling Almost Alone: Political Participation in a New Democracy," Table 4.

Do the results from Uslander's study call socioeconomic status theory into question? To an extent, yes, at least in Romania. However, two caveats are in order. First, Uslander did not look at income, another commonly examined SES component. It is possible that inclusion of that variable in his model would have provided support for socioeconomic status theory.

Second, it is important to remember that a large N statistical analysis that does not support claims of a *direct effect* of a certain variable is not the same thing as a finding that this variable has no effect whatsoever. This book's introductory chapter highlighted how political scientists are interested in understanding causal relationships between variables, and such relationships can be both direct *and* indirect. In addition to basic variables like education level, Uslander included twelve attitudes and behaviors as independent variables in his statistical model. Without reexamining the WVS data Uslander used in his study, it is impossible to say for certain, but it is likely that education had an effect on these attitudes and behaviors. Other studies have found a relationship between education and attitudes and behaviors such as tolerance of extremism, faith in the judicial system, discussing politics with others, and participating in civic organizations—all of which were variables that Uslander found to have a significant direct effect on protest behavior. Thus, education may have important *indirect effects* on protest participation in Romania, its effects working through factors that Uslander treated as independent variables.

CONCLUSION

This chapter explored the concepts of elites and masses, alternative forms of mass participation, and ways that political elites are linked to the general population in different countries. These forms of participation and linkage range from the public and malicious (such as terrorism), to the quiet and difficult to observe (such as backroom interest group lobbying).

In the 1950s, C. Wright Mills portrayed the United States as having a society with an "increasingly unified . . . elite of power," a middle level comprised of a "drifting set of stalemated, balancing forces," and a bottom that is "politically fragmented" and "increasingly powerless."[87] One could argue that this portrayal fits developing countries such as Nigeria and Iran better than a country like the United States. Even in these countries, however, at least some of these "powerless" members of the "bottom" of society seek to influence the political system by means of both conventional and unconventional participation, through the formation of interest groups, and by working with international organizations to further their cause.

By examining forms of participation and elite-mass linkage, this chapter also marked the beginning of a progression in the book toward the idea that that one should take into account individuals and their decisions as causal factors affecting political outcomes. This focus continues across the next two chapters, on parties and elections (Chapter 10) and on leadership and individual decision making (Chapter 11).

Key Terms

Advocacy groups, p. 341
Attentive public, p. 334
Civil society, p. 345
Clientelism, p. 332
Collective action problem, p. 357
Conventional participation, p. 324
Corporatism, p. 342
Disturbance theory, p. 351
Economic groups, p. 341
Interest groups, p. 340
Iron triangles, p. 355
Local issue groups, p. 341
Masses, p. 323
Military industrial complex (MIC), p. 355
Neo-corporatism, p. 343
Nepotism, p. 323
New social movements, p. 340
NIMBY issues, p. 341
Party corporatism, p. 350
Peak organizations, p. 342
Pluralism, p. 342
Political elite, p. 322
Political participation, p. 323
Power elite, p. 322
Programmatic representation, p. 332
Social movements, p. 340
Societal corporatism, p. 343
Socioeconomic status theory, p. 359
State control system, p. 343
State corporatism, p. 343
Subgovernment theory, p. 355
Unconventional participation, p. 324

10

Political Parties and Electoral Systems

Learning Objectives

After reading this chapter, you should be able to:

■ Describe how political parties differ from interest groups.

■ Differentiate among the different types of party systems.

■ Characterize the alternative electoral arrangements used in democratic elections, and explain the relationship between electoral systems and party systems.

■ Describe the party systems and key electoral outcomes in the United Kingdom, Germany, France, Mexico, Brazil, Russia, China, India, Nigeria, and Iran.

In February 2008, Ali Eshraghi was informed that he would not be allowed to run for a seat in the *Majles*, Iran's national legislature. He had registered to run, but his candidacy was rejected by an Interior Ministry committee. The committee's ruling was the first step of a three-stage process of vetting potential *Majles* candidates. In some ways, Eshraghi's fate was not unique. He was one of more than two thousand candidates whom the committee rejected. What made his story exceptional, however, was his family ties. Eshraghi was the grandson of Ayatollah Ruhollah Khomeini, Iran's Supreme Leader from the 1979 Revolution until his death in 1989.

Eshraghi publicly questioned the decision and criticized investigations during the vetting process, in which neighbors were interviewed about his personal life, "including if he shaved, smoked and what kind of car he drove."[1] The outrage over his situation

Look for this icon 🌐 to point you to **Deepening Your Understanding** features on the companion website www.college.cengage.com/politicalscience/barrington, which provide greater depth for some key content.

forced a reversal, and Eshraghi was allowed on the ballot. He ended up withdrawing from the race before the election, however, after stories about his personal life began circulating on Iranian websites. Although the decision was overturned, the initial rejection of Eshraghi's candidacy shows the degree to which the leaders of Iran's theocracy fear anyone who may support political and social reform. It also shows how, even in a political system such as the one in Iran, elections matter. ■

The previous chapter introduced the concept of elite-mass linkage by focusing on topics such as conventional and unconventional participation, clientelism, and interest groups. While a portion of Chapter 9's discussion of mass participation centered on voting, this chapter looks in much more detail at the process of selecting candidates for political office and the grouping of those candidates within political parties. As a result, this chapter turns to the structures that link masses and elites with which even casual observers of politics are somewhat familiar: political parties, party systems, elections, and the various alternative electoral arrangements.

Political Parties and Party Systems

Political parties are the most politically relevant groups in most political systems. They are a central link between the elites and masses, especially in democratic systems. Strong political parties facilitate the programmatic linkage approach discussed in the previous chapter. Parties can also, however, be a part of clientelism, as members of the party give clients favors in exchange for support in the following election. As a result of their importance, a great deal of work has been devoted to understanding political parties and party systems.

Political parties are organizations that seek political office, typically through participation in elections. Those competing for and holding office openly share the label of their political party. Political scientist Anthony Downs summarized these ideas in his definition of a political party: a

group of people "seeking to control the governing apparatus by gaining office in a duly constituted election."[2] This pursuit of political office is a key difference between parties and interest groups.

In addition, while interest groups tend to focus on a single issue, political parties must make their positions known on a large number of issues. In political science, the phrase that captures this is the need for parties to "articulate and aggregate interests." In his famous work on political parties, the French scholar Maurice Duverger pointed out that such articulation not only helps link parties to their followers but also binds together the smaller units of a national party (branches, local organizations, etc.). As Duverger puts it, a party "is not a community but a collection of communities."[3] While interest groups also make their preferences known (i.e., they do articulate their interests), they generally do not aggregate large numbers of issues beneath an overarching platform.

The Value of Political Parties

Political parties receive a great deal of criticism, and they have generally declined in strength around the world over the last several decades.[4] But it is important to keep in mind the important functions they play—especially in democratic systems. In the early 1940s, at a time when Germany's Nazi Party had brought the major powers into a

> **Political parties** are organizations that articulate their stance on a large number of policy positions and run candidates for political office.

world war, E. E. Schattschneider wrote a famous book titled *Party Government*, in which he linked political parties and democracy. Schattschneider claimed that political parties created democracy, and "modern democracy is unthinkable save in terms of the political parties."[5]

Parties propose new policies and state what they plan to do in office. Parties need not be programmatic; many early parties were highly clientelist.[6] Today, many parties around the world continue to center around the personality and popularity of their party leaders more than they emphasize their policy positions. But the existence of parties that stress ideologically-based policy preferences certainly makes programmatic linkage easier.

Parties also simplify the decision-making process for voters by bringing together politicians who share similar views. A party label carries with it a rough summary of that party's candidates' ideological leanings. Because parties make their general views known, voters need not learn the specific policy positions of every candidate. In the United States, for example, a voter choosing between a Democrat and a Republican may do so without extensive knowledge about the two candidates.

Finally, parties are also important for accountability. If voters know a certain party is in charge and those voters do not like how things are going in the country, they can punish the party in power by voting for another party. Without party labels, it is harder to hold political leaders accountable. In presidential systems, voters can punish a sitting president fairly easily by voting for someone else. Determining the culpability of individual legislators, however, requires a more nuanced understanding of voting records and political power struggles than most voters possess.

Party Identification

Because of the importance of political parties, comparativists also study **party identification**, the attachment individuals have to specific political parties. Voters with strong party identification typically support candidates from the same party in election after election. Weak party identification has positive and negative effects on a political system. The less people identify with parties, the more fluid the system is and the larger the swings in the makeup of the government from election to election. Weak party identification also tends to make politics more personalized, where the candidate's image becomes more important than what the candidate's party stands for in the policy arena. However, weak party identification can also indicate voters who are more moderate, who are paying attention to policies rather than blindly following a party label, and who thus hold parties and candidates more accountable from election to election.

Party Systems

The collection of the main parties in a country makes up that country's **party system**. When looking at party systems, scholars focus on the number of major parties and how polarized they are (how far apart they are on major issues). Comparativists normally put a particular country's party system into one of five categories: one-party, one-party dominant, two-party, two-and-a-half party, and multiparty. The nature of a country's party system relates to outcomes like political stability. Usually, political systems with more parties and with parties that are more polarized are less stable than systems with fewer parties that are more similar to one another on key issues.

The discussion of party systems assumes that parties are important in all countries. However, in some countries, particularly authoritarian systems or very small countries, political parties play a small role or no role at all in elections and

Party identification is an individual's attachment to a particular political party.

A **party system** is the number of prominent political parties in a given country.

the organization of policymaking in the national legislature. The "no party" system approach is far from the norm around the world, but it is in place in one of the Topic in Countries cases, Iran.

One-Party Systems In totalitarian and some authoritarian systems, a single party coordinates government activities and mobilizes mass support. Such cases are examples of a **one-party system** (or single-party system). One-party systems have no competitiveness; if elections are held, only candidates from the one party are on the ballot. Voters are not free to remove their support from the ruling party and give it to another.

Comparativist Giovanni Sartori emphasizes that, beyond sharing the core feature of a single party, one-party systems vary greatly in practice. As he writes, they are "more or less oppressive, more or less pervasive, more or less intolerant, more or less extractive."[7] He distinguishes among three types: totalitarian, where the party is ideological, coercive, and destructive of autonomous groups; pragmatic, where the party has much less ideological focus, coercive capacity, and desire to destroy autonomous groups; and authoritarian, which falls in between these other two. One might prefer to lump his pragmatic and authoritarian categories together, but his point is valuable. In assorted one-party systems, the party does not necessarily function in the same way, and political leaders do not necessarily have the same kinds of goals. Even the same one-party system can evolve over time, from one type to another. For example, China was for several decades after the Communist Revolution closer to Sartori's totalitarian variant. It is now much more like his authoritarian category of one-party systems.

One-Party Dominant Systems It is also possible for one party to dominate for long periods of time without completely controlling all aspects of politics. Other political parties are not banned and smaller parties may even receive a sizeable percentage of the vote combined, but only the main party is expected to win elections and control the government. Comparativists label this as a **one-party dominant system**. Sartori called such a party "hegemonic"; other parties in the system are "secondary" or "second class."[8] One-party dominant systems can paper over sharp differences within the main party. Factions within that party take the place of parties competing with each other openly. Since the conflicts in such a case are generally behind closed doors, this helps foster political stability. The masses are less likely to be drawn into political conflicts than in a system with more equally powerful parties.

Extended dominance of a single party can raise questions about the democratic nature of the political system. The dominance of the Institutional Revolutionary Party (PRI) in Mexico for much of the twentieth century was partly due to its popularity but also because of its undemocratic manipulation of the political system in general and of elections in particular. Thus, the presence of one dominant party in a country requires careful study of the political system, the party, and its tactics to determine if the party dominates because it governs effectively and is popular or because its tight control of the political system limits the choices of voters.

One-party dominant systems can emerge following a country's independence and/or establishment of democracy when the individuals associated with bringing the country its independence or its democracy form a political party. This was the case in India, when the Congress

---

Also known as a single-party system, a **one-party system** is one in which a single political party generates support for the government. The system lacks competitiveness; voters have no option to support a party in opposition to the government.

In a **one-party dominant system**, one large party controls the political system, but small parties exist and may even compete in elections.

Party (INC) dominated following independence. It can also happen when an otherwise one-party system allows small, nonthreatening parties to exist, as in Poland during the period of Communist Party rule.

Two-Party Systems   In a **two-party system**, two large parties compete with one another for control of the government. One or the other will gain a majority of the seats in the legislature, making coalition governments unnecessary. Other very small parties may exist, but their success does not translate into a notable number of seats in the national legislature nor does their degree of electoral success influence which of the two main parties ultimately controls that legislature.

The United States is the classic example of a two-party system. Small ("third") parties, such as the Greens or Libertarian Party, compete for political office. Only on rare occasions, however, does such a party take a seat even in state government not to mention at the national level. At times, a strong independent candidate will swing the result of a presidential election (as Ross Perot and Ralph Nader arguably did in the United States in 1992 and 2000, respectively). But, as the next section discusses in more detail, the electoral system for congressional elections—combined with a similar state-by-state system for presidential elections and the lack of strong regional parties—encourages the perpetuation of a party system where the two main parties receive nearly all the votes in national legislative elections.

Two-and-a-Half Party Systems   The **two-and-a-half party system** concept was introduced to political science by Jean Blondel in a 1968 article about party systems in Western democracies.[9] As awkward as it is, the term two-and-a-half party system stuck, largely because it captured an important feature of these systems: Though a "third party" exists and has influence, its vote totals and seats in the national legislature are significantly lower than those of the two

main parties. Blondel differentiated between two- and two-and-a-half party systems based on the percentage of the national vote that the two main parties receive and the size of the third party compared with the first two over time. Blondel considered the United States a two-party system because the Republicans and Democrats earned around 99 percent of the national vote combined from 1945 to 1966.[10] Blondel regarded West Germany as a two-and-a-half party system, however, because during that period its third party was much smaller than the two largest, but these two largest parties won only around 80 percent of the vote combined.

In two-and-a-half party systems, one of the two largest parties usually gains a majority of the seats in the national legislature. Thus, even though it receives a sizeable percentage of the national vote, the third party in a two-and-a-half party system usually does not gain a large enough number of seats to force the creation of a coalition government. Its electoral fortunes still matter from election to election, however, since whichever of the two main parties loses votes to the third party will determine which of the two large parties controls the government. In addition, when other small parties begin to secure seats, the presence of this third party can prevent a majority government. If this happens for a number of subsequent elections, it would mark the transformation of the party system from a two-and-a-half party system to a multiparty one. This chapter's Comparative Exercise section discusses this possibility in the case of Canada.

A **two-party system** is one in which two parties compete for majority control of the government. Small parties exist but play no role in electoral outcomes at the national level.

In a **two-and-a-half party system**, two large parties exist alongside a third party that receives a smaller but notable share of the national vote. This third party earns significantly fewer seats in the national legislature than the two large parties.

Multiparty Systems The final type of party system is the **multiparty system**. This term is used when a political system has a larger number of key parties than the two-and-a-half party system. Although there may be two parties that are larger than the others, these parties are far from dominant. None of the largest parties generally gain a majority of the seats in the national legislature; coalitions are the norm. Generally every decade or so, each of the two largest parties has the opportunity to serve as the main party in a ruling coalition government.

In his famous work on parties and party systems, Duverger reminded his readers that multiparty systems should not be confused with systems in which there is little party identification among the general public.[11] Party identification in multiparty systems can be relatively stable over time, particularly in cases where the main parties reflect deep social divisions. Because the number of relevant parties is greater in a multiparty system, however, even small changes in their electoral fortunes can transform the makeup of the legislature. Consider, for example, a party that earned 40 of 100 seats and formed a coalition with a smaller party that had 12 seats of its own. In the next election, if the large party lost only 3 seats, it would be unable to form the same coalition to control a majority of the legislative seats, even if the smaller party ended up with the same number of seats.

Figure 10.1 summarizes the differences among party systems on two dimensions: the importance of small parties and the dominance by the largest party in the political system. As one moves from a one-party system to a multiparty type, small parties become increasingly important. In contrast, a single party's ability to dominate the political system wanes.

Advantages and Disadvantages of a Large Number of Major Political Parties

It is interesting to consider the advantages of a system with many key parties compared with the American-style two-party system. To do so, one need only focus on the multiparty approach. Its strengths tend to be the weaknesses of a system with only two major parties, while the disadvantages of a multiparty system correspond to the two-party system's advantages.

Advantage #1: Better Representation of the Masses
The greater the number of political parties, the better the options for voters. Particularly in countries with well-educated populations, voters often have a good sense of where they themselves stand on a host of issues. Assuming the parties make their policy views known, the existence of more parties translates into a greater opportunity for voters to find a party that matches their particular combination of views. If a voter is

A **multiparty system** is one with several important political parties, none of which generally gains a majority of the seats in the national legislature.

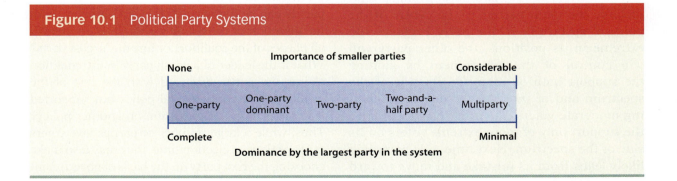

Figure 10.1 Political Party Systems

Importance of smaller parties

None   Considerable

One-party | One-party dominant | Two-party | Two-and-a-half party | Multiparty

Complete   Minimal

Dominance by the largest party in the system

economically liberal but socially conservative, for example, a multiparty system is more likely than a two-party system to offer that voter a party with corresponding positions.

Advantage #2: Better Representation of Minority Interests

Along with providing voters better options, multiparty systems better reflect societal divisions. Smaller groups need not join together with larger ones to have any chance to gain seats in a legislature. Thus, increasing the number of major parties increases the likelihood that minority groups will be represented in the national government.

Disadvantage #1: Political Instability Due to Fragile Coalitions

The more parties with seats in the national legislature, the less likely that one party holds a majority of the seats. In other words, multiparty systems create the need for coalitions. As one continues to increase the number of parties in the legislature, such coalitions also require more parties to gain the necessary minimum number of seats to pass legislation. In such situations, coalitions become increasingly unstable. Having only a few defections among legislators in a ruling coalition can be enough to kill a particular policy proposal. Disputes among ruling parties can be fierce, as each party sees itself as key to sustaining the coalition. The result is instability and, in parliamentary systems, the strong possibility of early elections.

Disadvantage #2: Undue Influence of Small and Extreme Parties

Two-party systems tend to force the main parties to the center of the political spectrum. If one party becomes too extreme in its positions, the other party will win control of the government by gaining the support both of voters on its side of the spectrum and of those in the center. Alienating moderate voters, the other party will have the support only of more extreme voters on its side of the spectrum. Next time, this party will likely learn from its mistake and move toward the center as well.

In a multiparty system, there is less need to win the support of moderate voters in order to be influential. As a result, multiparty systems do not encourage parties to moderate their policy positions and provide little incentive for people from different groups to find common political ground. In many countries, ethnicity has replaced economic issues as the central mobilizing force in politics. This is especially true where there are many parties. Not only might every ethnic group develop its own ethnic party, but also a large ethnic group might develop multiple parties that continually "outbid" each other in an attempt to be seen as the ethnic group's true political guardians. In multiparty systems, these kinds of small and extreme parties often hold seats in the national legislature.

When such parties occupy seats in the legislature, they have the potential to become key players in the coalition process discussed under disadvantage #1. A larger party might need a small, extreme party to put together a coalition government. In the bargaining that ensues, the small party can gain concessions on issues of importance to it. In the case of parliamentary systems, the small party may also ask for a cabinet position related to its central concerns.

Disadvantage #3: Difficulty in Holding Political Parties Accountable

A final disadvantage is the challenge a large number of parties poses for voters seeking to reward or punish leaders for performance in office. Following from the first two disadvantages, coalitions with a large number of parties can be the norm. If they are unhappy with the direction of the country, should voters punish all parties of the coalition, or just the largest party? What if the leader of a small party in the coalition claims the party disagreed with the rest of the coalition on a controversial policy but supported it in order to get a concession on another policy? Thus, while a large number of parties give voters more options at election time, they may also make choosing the best party on the basis of government performance a difficult proposition.

Political Parties in Iran, China, the Russian Federation, and Nigeria

In addition to sharing a history of undemocratic political systems, Iran, China, Russia, and Nigeria currently have either one main political party or no main parties at all. In Iran, a system that had been heading in the direction of a one-party dominant system became instead a "no party" system. China is a classic one-party system, while Russia and Nigeria both currently have one dominant party but also other parties that receive a noticeable portion of the vote.

Iran

Following the 1979 Revolution, two of the most important Iranian political parties were the People's Mojahedin Organization of Iran (PMOI) and the Islamic Republican Party (IRP). PMOI advocated a blend of socialist ideas and Islamic character. PMOI became a key member of the National Council of Resistance of Iran (NCR), an umbrella organization that formed in 1981 to oppose the turn away from democracy following the Revolution. NCR was forced to leave Iran—the organization is based in Paris at the present time—while PMOI was based in Iraq from 1986 until the American invasion in 2003. The party's organization in Iraq was disbanded by American forces and the new Iraqi government, though it maintains its affiliation with the NCR.

Though Ayatollah Khomeini never belonged to the IRP, he supported it during and after the Revolution. IRP leaders played a major role in drafting the post-revolution constitution. They also intimidated the other smaller political parties through threats and, at times, violence. By the end of 1980, only the PMOI remained a serious challenge. The two parties turned on each other, with violent clashes, bombings of party offices, and assassinations of leading party officials. In the end, the IRP emerged on top, and remaining PMOI leaders fled the country.

Iran was poised to become a one-party dominant or even one-party system in the early 1980s. In 1986, however, the IRP became divided, apparently over both economic policy and how uncompromising the government should be with the West. In response, the party's leaders—including the then-Iranian president and current Supreme Leader of the country, Ali Khamenei, and the man who would be president following Khamenei, Akbar-Hashemi Rafsanjani—asked Ayatollah Khomeini to support the disbanding of the IRP. He agreed, and Iran's political system was transformed into one in which political parties played little role.

The Iranian Constitution permits political parties and other organizations. However, it states that the parties cannot violate principles of "freedom, sovereignty, and national unity" or question the Islamic foundations of the state.[12] The government has used this statement to justify banning established political parties that threatened its vision of a theocratic Iranian state. During the rule of President Khatami, the idea of a wider range of political parties became more accepted. Khatami encouraged the formation of new political groups, and an effort was made to recognize and officially register these new organizations. As a result, a large number of political groups formed, but few of them became politically significant, and scholars have labeled them not "real political parties,"[13] "nascent political parties,"[14] or political "bands."[15] Thus, electoral alliances form before elections—a conservative alliance, Islamic Iran Developers' Council (*Etelaf-e Abadgaran-e Iran-e Eslami*), for example, did very well in the 2004 elections to the national legislature, the *Majles*—but they do not always act in unison following them.

The candidates who openly advocate democratization or a secular government are banned by the Guardian Council. Those that the Guardian Council allows to run generally fall into three groups. Hardliners, such as current Iranian President Mahmoud Ahmadinejad, support an extreme theocratic state and question the vast wealth of the business sector in the country. Pragmatic conservatives, including former President Rafsanjani, support the regime as it is currently constituted, including its relationship with the business class. Moderates, such as former President Khatami, favor an increase in political and social freedoms within the broad framework of an Islamic state.

China

Every other TIC country discussion in this chapter contains a discussion of multiple political parties. In China, the Chinese Communist Party (CCP) is the only party allowed to function openly. China is, consequently, a classic example of a one-party system. Though far from the ideal type of a totalitarian system, the Chinese Communists have learned from the fate of the USSR, have understood the dangers of allowing political opposition, and have maintained a monopoly of political power for themselves.

The leadership of the CCP was officially in the hands of the chairman until the position was abolished in 1982. Mao was party chairman from 1949 until his death in 1976. He was also general secretary of the CCP during this time. In the Soviet Union, the general secretary position became synonymous with the leader of the country. Because

Figure 10.2   The Structure of the Chinese Communist Party

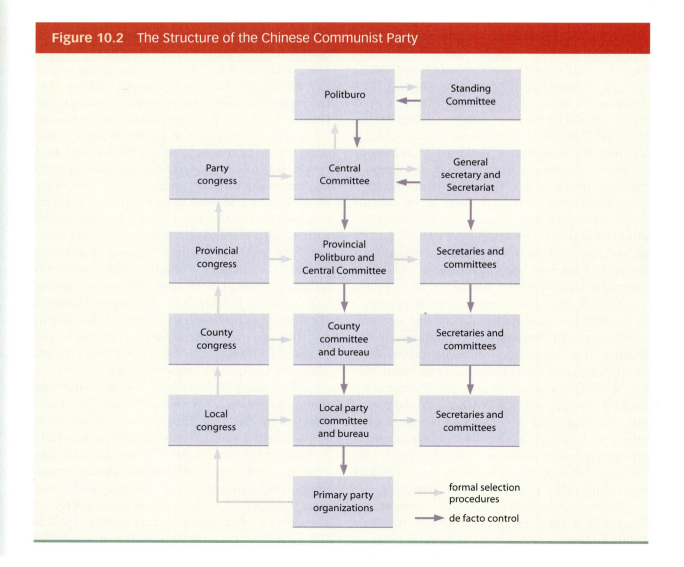

official position was still less important than personal prestige in China during Deng Xiaoping's tenure, he was not general secretary but was still recognized as China's real leader.

Most major policy decisions are made in the top collective body in the party, the Politburo. The Politburo has between twenty and thirty members and sets both party and national government policy. While open debate is not something the CCP encourages, the discussions in the Politburo behind closed doors can be very lively. The Politburo also has a smaller standing committee that makes decisions when the entire body is not meeting. Below the Politburo is the Central Committee, which is the part of the party that officially selects the Politburo members. As in the case of the Soviet Union, more often than not it rubber stamps decisions of the Politburo and the leader of the country—including who should be added or taken off the Politburo—more than it pushes the Politburo on policy or genuinely shapes its membership. Today, the Central Committee has more than three hundred members. Below the Central Committee, but technically the highest organ of the CCP, is the party congress. The party congress meets every few years. The congress officially picks the Central Committee (though in reality it is picked for them), and it ratifies major policy changes the CCP is proposing.

These different organizations have versions at the local level as well. As with the national level, there is significant overlap in membership between the local party organs and the local government offices. The smallest unit is the Primary Party Unit (or cell), but there are also local party meetings and a local politburo. Officials at the local level play a role in overseeing the implementation of national policy and keeping an eye on members of the state hierarchy. They can also play a role in delaying the implementation of new policies with which they disagree.

In the past, an important function of the party, particularly at the local level, was to organize activities designed to socialize the population. As Marxist ideology became less and less important to the party's approach to politics, the efforts put into this socialization function also declined. If the declaration by leader Hu Jintao in 2005 can be believed, however, the party does consider a more active role in overseeing the activities of large- and medium-sized businesses to play an important role in reining in corruption.[16] Whether this will limit corruption, or simply lead to a Russian-style involvement in the economy, where renewed state ownership of businesses emerges within an otherwise capitalist framework, is something to watch in the years ahead.

The Russian Federation

During its first post-Soviet decade, the Russian party system was difficult to grasp. Some parties did relatively well in one election before virtually disappearing in the next one. Only two parties consistently cleared the 5 percent threshold in parliamentary elections, and party identification was extremely fragile. This began to change with President Putin's emergence on the political scene at the end of 1999. By the time Putin had won reelection in 2004, Russia appeared headed for a one-party dominant system controlled by the pro-Putin United Russia Party.

Russian political parties during the post-Soviet period can be placed into four groups. The first "group" is actually a single party, the Communist Party of Russia, which has remained a visible player in Russian politics since the Soviet collapse. Prior to the period of creeping authoritarianism under Putin, it was the most popular party in the country. It won the largest percentage of the party vote in the 1995 and 1999 parliamentary elections. Its supporters are largely older and rural voters, those most threatened by the economic changes in the country since the Soviet period.

The second group is comprised of nationalist parties, emphasizing a strong state and a strong international reputation. The classic example of this group is Vladimir Zhirinovsky's Liberal Democratic Party (LDP). Zhirinovsky's party was created with the blessing of the Yeltsin government, partly to provide an alternative to the Communist Party for those displeased with economic reform.

The nationalists also included the Fatherland–All Russia (OVR) Party, affiliated with the popular mayor of Moscow, Yuri Luzhkov, in the late 1990s. Luzhkov later defected to Putin's United Russia Party, and the nationalist parties have been less important since Putin's consolidation of power after the 2000 presidential election.

The third group is made up of pro-Western, pro-reform parties. In the early 1990s, the main reform parties were Russia's Choice (headed by a former prime minister, Yegor Gaidar) and Yabloko (led by the economist Grigory Yavlinsky). Many observers of Russian politics expected these parties to do well in elections after the Soviet collapse, but their performance fell short of expectations. Yabloko maintained its presence as a small but important party until the early 2000s, but the successor party to Russia's Choice, Russia's Democratic Choice, failed to clear the 5 percent threshold in the 1995 parliamentary elections. At the end of the 1990s, it reemerged as the Union of Right Forces, which cleared the threshold in the 1999 elections but not in 2003.

The final group is made up of progovernment parties. In the early 1990s, these overlapped somewhat with the reform parties. President Yeltsin refused to form—or even really endorse—any party in 1993, though most believed he hoped that Russia's Choice would win the elections. In the middle of the 1990s, the main progovernment party was Our Home Is Russia, a party supportive of political reform but mostly concerned with improving the prospects of the Yeltsin administration and the prime minister at that time, Viktor Chenomyrdin.

By the end of the 1990s, the progovernment "party" was a hastily thrown together group known as the Unity Bloc. Openly, but unofficially, supported by then–Prime Minister Putin, the bloc was formed to challenge the other major parties in the 1999 parliamentary elections and pave the way for Putin's presidential victory in 2000. By 2003, this progovernment party had taken the name United Russia. The party did well in the 2003 parliamentary elections and has facilitated Putin's control over Russian politics ever since.

By the middle of 2007, United Russia was poised to become the central party of Russia's emerging one-party dominant system. The final stages in that process took place in late 2007 and early 2008. In December 2007, United Russia dominated elections to the *Duma*, Russia's lower house of parliament. In March 2008, United Russia-supported Dmitry Medvedev won the presidential election and became Putin's successor.

Nigeria

Of all the consequences of military intervention in Nigerian politics, one of the most important has been its effect on political parties. At least since the Civil War, military leaders have been deeply suspicious of political parties. Rather than seeing them as a crucial vehicle for linking elites and masses, parties were perceived to be undisciplined, divisive, and instruments of corruption.[17] In 1991, when a transition to democracy in the country was supposedly underway, the government banned numerous existing political parties, creating instead two official parties. This attempt at a forced two-party system demonstrated both a lack of appreciation for more subtle ways to influence the development of party systems and the view that large, **catch-all parties** were superior to smaller parties representing narrower interests. Political scientist Otto Kirchheimer has described a catch-all party as one that softens its ideology and moderates its policy stances to appeal to more than one group in the electorate. The aim is to draw in a broad swathe of voters, especially moderate voters.[18]

In its next attempt at fostering a stable democratic transition, the military government initially recognized nine political parties. In line with its efforts to prevent ethnically concentrated parties, the government required that parties open membership to all individuals, regardless of ethnicity or religion, carry a name free of any particular

Catch-all parties are those that adopt a range of ideologically moderate policies designed to capture broad segments of the population, particularly those from the middle of the political spectrum.

ethnic or regional affiliation, and have "functional branches" in at least twenty-four of Nigeria's federal units.[19] Ultimately, the government ruled that only three political parties met the criteria for official registration. Two of these three parties, People's Democratic Party (PDP) and the All People's Party (APP), were created to a large extent from scratch. The third party, the Alliance for Democracy (AD), had its roots in an earlier political party associated with the Yoruba ethnic group. The PDP was the most important party in the first decade following the reestablishment of democracy in 1999. The APP reemerged in 2003 as the All Nigerian People's Party (ANPP).

During the first several years of the Fourth Republic, the number of political parties exploded. While the PDP, ANPP, and AD remained the three most prominent parties, around thirty Nigerian groups met the definition of political parties by 2003. This prompted the president of the country, Olusegun Obasanjo, to call for steps to reduce the number of parties. If he had feared fragmentation that would prevent effective cooperation between the executive and legislative branches, these fears turned out to be unfounded. Despite more than fifty active parties by 2008, the PDP has had no problem establishing itself as the country's majority party.

Indeed, after the 2007 presidential and legislative elections, the PDP was in firm control of both the executive and legislative branches of the Nigerian government. The ANPP was the largest opposition party but was relegated to the status of a minor party in what was increasingly looking like an emerging one-party dominant system. The AD tried to bolster its prospects by merging with other small parties to form the Action Congress (AC) in September 2006. It did little to help combat the trend toward PDP dominance. This trend, and the many concerns that the opposition parties and outside observers expressed about the 2007 elections, has caused some to argue that, similar to Russia, Nigeria is well down the path leading away from democracy.[20]

Political Parties in the United Kingdom

When Maurice Duverger wrote his study of parties and party systems, scholars had not yet differentiated between two- and two-and-a-half party systems. As a result, he labeled the British party system as a two-party system, but one with unique features compared with the U.S. system.[21] Writing a decade later in the late 1960s, Jean Blondel still considered the United Kingdom a two-party case, based on voting patterns from the mid-1940s to mid-1960s that led one of its two main political parties to control a majority of seats in parliament.[22]

In recent years, however, the United Kingdom's party system has become even more different from the classic American-style two-party variant. For example, the British system now has a solid third party, which regularly secures a sizeable percentage of the national vote but, because of the FPTP electoral system, few seats in the parliament. Thus, most comparativists now describe the United Kingdom as a two-and-a-half party system, the only such system among the ten TIC cases.

British parties serve the function of articulating and aggregating interests well. Party platforms are important and generally offer clear choices. Some of this has to do with the strength of British parties compared with a country such as the United States. MP's have more difficulty voting against their party than do members of the U.S. Congress. The United Kingdom has no primary system. The party determines in what district a candidate will run, and an MP who repeatedly votes against the party is unlikely to hold a seat in parliament after the next election.

The two largest political parties in the United Kingdom are the Labour Party and the Conservative Party. The Labour Party, often calling itself

New Labour since the mid-1990s, is the party of Prime Minister Gordon Brown. It held a majority of the seats in the House of Commons directly after World War II and for much of the 1960s and 1970s, and has once again held a majority since 1997 under Brown and his predecessor, Tony Blair. The Conservative Party, also referred to as the "Tories," controlled the government for much of the 1950s and in the 1980s and early 1990s. During that time, many voters saw Labour as quite far to the left of center. Blair succeeded in his efforts to move Labour toward the center, capturing many working-class voters that had supported Margaret Thatcher and the Conservatives in the 1980s.

The third major party in the United Kingdom today is the Liberal Democrats. It formed when the Liberal Party and the Social Democratic Party (SDP) combined in 1988. The Liberal Party had existed since the 1800s. Its "liberal" label came from its support of economic liberalism, meaning free trade and government nonintervention in the economy. In other words, it was a right-of-center party. The SDP, on the other hand, was a left-of-center party, established in 1981. As one might expect given the backgrounds of the two parties that created it, the Liberal Democratic Party's policy positions have not always been easily cast as left or right of center. Over the last decade, however, it appears to have moved to the left of the Labour Party on a large number of issues including the environment.

Political Parties in Germany, France, India, Mexico, and Brazil

The remaining five TIC cases are all multiparty systems. In none of them is one of the major parties likely to control a majority of seats in the national legislature, although France has had three periods during the Fifth Republic in which a single party controlled a majority of the seats in the National Assembly. A multiparty system was historically not the case in India and Mexico. Both countries had one-party dominant systems, under the Indian National Congress (INC) and the Institutional Revolutionary Party (PRI), respectively, which became multiparty systems as other parties increased their share of the vote.

Germany

German parties transmit their policy stances to voters through their platforms, which they issue in advance of elections. The differences between the two major parties have been less distinct than one might expect from programmatic parties. The two major parties are the Christian Democratic Union (CDU) on the center-right and the Social Democratic Party (SPD) on the center-left. The CDU also affiliates with its sister party in Bavaria, the Christian Social Union (CSU), which is the more socially conservative of the two. Like the Democratic and Republican parties in the United States, the CDU and SPD are known as catch-all parties par excellence. The CDU's support, for example, cuts across class and religious lines. While appealing to many voters in the business and middle classes, it has also attracted the support of Catholic trade unionists. The CDU controlled the chancellorship from 1949–1969, 1982–1998, and since 2005 as part of Germany's most recent CDU-SPD grand coalition (see Chapter 7).

The SPD was initially a party rooted in the working class and committed to socialism. But its stance alienated many voters, and in 1959 it accepted capitalism and the welfare state in order to broaden its electoral appeal. The strategic shift led to the SPD's participation, with the CDU, in the Federal Republic's first grand coalition from 1966 to 1969. Subsequently, the SPD became the lead party in a ruling coalition with the Free Democratic Party (FDP). Under the leadership of Willy Brandt and, later, Helmut Schmidt, the SDP-FDP coalition controlled the Bundestag until 1982, when the FDP joined a coalition government with the CDU headed by Helmut Kohl. Although the SPD was out of the government for the next sixteen years, its catch-all nature allowed it to maintain strong support among trade unionists while also appealing to the middle classes, setting the stage for its return to power in 1998.

A number of smaller parties fill out Germany's multiparty system. The FDP attracts profession-als and the self-employed with its message of limited government and the free market. It has been the kingmaker in coalition governments for much of the post–World War II period. The Green Party first entered the *Bundestag* in 1983 on a program of environmentalism, feminism, democracy, and peace. It counts the younger, university-educated strata (particularly teach-ers) among its supporters. Though it had been

in coalition governments in the *Länder*, the Greens were not a coalition partner at the national level until 1998, when Chancellor Gerhard Schröder of the SPD formed a coali-tion government with the Greens that lasted until 2005.

Following German unification in 1990, the former Communist Party (SED) of East Germany transformed itself into the Party of Democratic Socialism (PDS), and won some *Bundestag* seats from the reunited country's new eastern *Länder*. Its support, however, was confined to the boundaries of the former East Germany, and its voters were mainly former SED members and those disillu-sioned by the mass unemployment in the wake of unification. Since 2006, the PDS has been super-seded by the Left Party, which is comprised of dissident left-wing Social Democrats who bolted from the SPD and who joined forces with the PDS to contest the 2005 election. The two groups for-mally merged as a single party in 2006.

IN THEORY AND PRACTICE

Realignment Theory and Germany

Realignment theory concerns how certain elections shake up political systems, altering ("realigning") long-term levels of support for major political parties.[23] Realignment theory emerged when a number of scholars, including V. O. Key and E. E. Schattschneider, noticed that American elections followed a regular pattern of continuity followed by occasional significant change. The elections in which the outcome radi-cally alters the political landscape of a country for decades are known as **critical elections**. Looking at American political history, critical elections appear to take place roughly once every three decades. In other countries, such a pattern is less identifiable. Still, most democratic systems have seen one or more elections that represented a realignment of the electorate.

Some scholars believe that Germany may be undergoing a realignment of its party system,

albeit one that is more complex and protracted than the "ideal" shift at the heart of realignment theory. The entry of the Greens into the *Bundestag* in 1983 signaled the arrival of a party promoting a postmaterialist agenda that did not fit easily into the traditional left-right divide. The coali-tion government between the Greens and the SPD in 1998 demonstrated that there were now two small parties—the Greens and FDP—that could serve as coalition partners with either of the two larger parties.

Based on the study of American elections, **realignment theory** contends that the fortunes of major political parties remain stable for long periods followed by a dramatic change.

Elections that mark the beginning of a realignment are known as **critical elections**.

The party system fragmented further with the 2005 election. That election produced a "hung parliament" with no clear-cut winner. Both the SPD and CDU lost support to the smaller parties. Neither of the two larger parties could muster a majority coalition government with just one of the smaller parties alone; in fact, there were several coalition possibilities involving three parties. After weeks of tough negotiations, the CDU and SPD settled for a grand coalition.

The two main parties' predicament was driven by the appearance of a new party. Some left-wing SPD members, disappointed with Schröder's market-oriented policies, quit the party and formed an electoral alliance with the PDS in the east. Together, they won more than 8 percent of the vote in the 2005 election and fifty-four seats in the *Bundestag*. The groups formalized their electoral alliance in a merger as the Left Party in 2006. Unlike the PDS, the Left Party enjoys electoral support in both west and east, as *Land* elections in 2008 demonstrated.

Hence, this new party has placed the SPD in a difficult bind. By participating in the grand coalition, the SPD has alienated its traditional left-wing and labor union supporters, who began to vote for the Left Party in *Land* elections. In response, the SPD's leader, Kurt Beck, took an increasingly radical stance on labor market and welfare state policies and even contemplated forming a coalition government with the Left Party in the *Land* of Hessen. This shift, however, strained its relations with the CDU coalition partner and made it more difficult to govern. Even worse, opinion polls indicated that centrist voters were beginning to desert the SPD to the benefit of the CDU. With a *Bundestag* election looming in 2009, the SPD changed tack by dumping Beck in September 2008 and installing a more centrist leadership team.[24] Given this fragmentation of the party system, German politics appear to be headed into a more uncertain period in the near future.

France

The ideological categories that political scientists and others use today to label parties in countries such as the United States were invented in France at the time of the French Revolution. In the first assemblies, the more radical advocates of the Revolution sat to the left of the speaker, and the more conservative deputies sat on his right. Since then, those advocating greater change have been called Leftists, and those who defend the status quo have been known as Rightists. Until the late nineteenth century, formal politics was organized around unofficial parliamentary groups. Organization and persuasion were the work of newspapers and "clubs," such as the *Société d'Instruction Républicaine*, intended to educate rather than turn out voters to the polls.[25] France's contemporary parties and electoral politics, however, are more recent and complex phenomena.

Since the Third Republic, French party ideologies have fallen into four broad categories. Republicans divide between a reformist current on the left and conservative (and sometimes Christian

Democratic) one on the right. Far left revolutionary parties seek social and political transformation, while the far right parties of order seek a return to tradition and authority.[26] Though these broad currents are stable over time, the parties within them have changed. This combination of durable currents and fluctuating parties leads political scientists to describe France as a "multiparty bipolar system," with a large number of parties organized around two dominant political forces, one on the right and the other on the left.[27] The larger parties at the center of each pole approach programmatic, ideological formations, but they remain divided among "notables" and their political families organized around policy and personality conflicts.

The Right has dominated the Fifth Republic. Today, the leading party is the Union for a Popular Majority (UMP), the party of President Nicolas Sarkozy founded in 2002. The UMP can trace its origins to the parties that supported de Gaulle under the Fourth and Fifth Republics. Originally, Gaullism included a strong social or left wing, represented by de Gaulle's close ally Jacques

Chaban-Delmas, who ran for president as the official candidate of the Gaullist party in 1974. At that time, Jacques Chirac split with the Gaullists, establishing the Rally for the Republic two years later, and using it as a national platform for a more conservative form of Gaullism through the end of his first presidency. Though Chirac had encouraged Sarkozy's career, a personal feud grew between the two men, and only reluctantly did Chirac hand over the UMP to Sarkozy.

Programmatically, President Sarkozy has extended the base of the party to the right. He took votes from the far right by outmaneuvering the extremist National Front on citizenship and immigration law, and he handed a ministry to a prominent pro-life politician who leads the opposition to same-sex marriage. In other ways, Sarkozy has taken the UMP to the left. He promoted a more moderate leadership (including Prime Minister François Fillon), increased racial and gender diversity in the government, and gave the position of foreign affairs minister to Bernard Kouchner, a Socialist who founded Doctors Without Borders in 1971.

Also in the governing coalition are a small group of deputies who are former members of the Union for French Democracy (UDF), a Christian democratic party organized to support Valerie Giscard d'Estaing, president of France from 1974–1981. In 2007, the leader of the UDF split with the Gaullists over Sarkozy's candidacy, mulled over a coalition with the Socialists, and ultimately transformed his party into the center-left MoDem or Democratic Movement.

The Socialist Party dominates the Left, tracing its origins to the SFIO, which literally translates as the French Section of the Workers' International. During 1960, the SFIO collapsed when the Left split between those supporting de Gaulle and pursuing a common strategy with the Communist Party. A variety of currents and notables, including progressive Catholics and later Gaullists exiled by Chirac's maneuvers, came together in the new Socialist Party under the leadership of François Mitterrand and accepted a common program with the Communist Party.

The Socialists won the presidency and an absolute majority in the National Assembly in 1981, though as sometimes happens in France they brought the Communists into a coalition government to add to their majority. In 1984, the Socialists abandoned a unified programmatic appeal and struggled with internal divisions over economic reform, social policy, and democratization. The 1997 elections and subsequent "plural Left" coalition government under Lionel Jospin are an important exception, as the coalition was founded on a common policy agenda uniting the Communist Party, the environmentalist Green Party, and the Republican and Citizen Movement, which had previously split from the Socialists. Current notables, called the "elephants" during the 2007 elections, include former Prime Minister Laurent Fabius, now an anti-neoliberal Leftist, and the more centrist allies of Jospin, such as Dominique Strauss-Kahn (who became head of the International Monetary Fund in 2007).

IN THEORY AND PRACTICE

The Cleavage Structure Theory of Party Systems and Political Parties in France

In seeking to explain party system development, Seymour Martin Lipset and Stein Rokkan emphasize underlying socioeconomic differences—economic distinctions such as class, and divisions between some nation-builders at the geographic and political "core" and those who represented the religious or ethnolinguistic "periphery."[28] Lipset and Rokkan's approach is an extension of cleavage structure theory discussed in Chapter 5, and their theory can thus be suitably labeled the **cleavage structure theory of party systems**.

This theory is historical, in that Lipset and Rokkan look to significant crises in the past. The resulting cleavages affect subsequent political competition and conflict. In their causal argument, parties are the dependent product of competition between actors firmly rooted in other social institutions. The Lipset and Rokkan argument can be applied to the emergence of ethnic parties. Indeed, in his book *Ethnic Groups in Conflict*, Donald Horowitz supports Lipset and Rokkan by demonstrating that, in countries with sharp ethnic divisions, the main parties reflect these divisions.[29]

When applied to European cases, however, the cleavage structure theory of party systems has pointed to the importance of economic class and the church. A key part of Lipset and Rokkan's analysis concerns the nineteenth-century rise of working-class parties across Europe to challenge both traditional landed and church authorities, as well as the new urban elite. Peter Katzenstein, in *Small States in World Markets*, deepens such historically rooted cleavage theories to understand the influence of working-class parties in shaping the social welfare state.[30]

For Lipset and Rokkan, it is important that parties and party systems "froze" in the 1920s. Indeed, many scholars look to the interwar period, sometimes called "the twenty-year crisis," as one primary source of contemporary political systems. In France, the conflicts and competitions between various social actors in the nineteenth century ultimately produced a relatively stable party system. But heightened conflicts and new working-class mobilization after World War I presented new challenges, with the emergence of fascism across Europe encouraging the rebirth of a conservative or traditional mass movement on the right, and the Russian Revolution causing a split between Socialist and Communist working-class parties on the left. Such intense class conflict became a feature of the French party system, often overlapping with a cleavage between secularists and the church. After World War II, the antagonisms between progressive Catholics and Communists began to dampen as they had worked together in the Resistance, and a new party brought together segments of the Left and Right in support of General de Gaulle and, ultimately, his Fifth Republic.

Today, the French party system, with its class- and church-based cleavages, looks remarkably similar to that of the 1920s. The parties that were strongest then have largely disappeared, but with only a few exceptions at the extremes, the social cleavages of the 1920s continue to provide the bases of support for the main parties within the general population. This continuing divide is particularly interesting—and especially strong evidence for Lipset and Rokkan's theory—since there is arguably a greater consensus over the institutions and values of the Republic among the political elite than ever before in French history.

> The **cleavage structure theory of party systems** contends that a country's party system is less a function of its electoral rules than of its underlying socioeconomic divisions. A country with two complementary social cleavages is likely to have a two-party system.

India

India has six national parties, identified as such by the Indian Election Commission because they have achieved a set minimum level of support across federal units. Other types of parties are categorized by the Commission as "state parties," that is, those that get a set minimum number of votes in a federal unit and "officially recognized parties," that is, those that don't meet the minimum number. Many independent candidates run for office as well. The most prominent national parties include the Indian National Congress (INC, also known as the Congress Party or, simply, Congress), Bharatiya Janata Party (BJP), and the Communist parties, that is, the Communist Party of India (Marxist) (CPI[M]) and the Communist Party of India (CPI).[31]

The INC, founded in 1885, was the dominant party in the country until the end of the Emergency in 1977 when it lost the national election for the first time. Since then, it has remained a key, but not consistently a dominant, player in the struggle for national power and for regional power in many parts of the country. Its character has changed over time in at least two respects: from one where regional leaders held extensive power to one where power was centralized into the hands of the party president, and from one advocating social democratic policies to one fostering a liberalized economy. It is a secular party, though from time to time its leaders have used communal sentiments to foster its objectives. Like the CDU and SPD in Germany, the INC in India has been labeled a "catch-all" party, with a range of policies designed to draw votes from the diverse communities that constitute the Indian population. Except in 1977, no other party has managed to garner enough seats in the *Lok Sabha* to rule in ways other than through a coalition.

Nepotism within political parties, where sons, daughters, and wives of prominent politicians "inherit" leading positions, has been common. The most well known is that of the Nehru family and its control of the INC. Nehru's daughter, Indira Gandhi, and her son, Rajiv Gandhi, were both prime ministers. Rajiv Gandhi's wife became the leader of the INC, and their son, Rahul Gandhi, a general secretary of the party.

Today, the INC's main national rival is the BJP. The BJP espouses a religious/cultural ideology known as *Hindutva*, which equates Hinduism with Indian nationalism. It was founded in 1980 as the successor to the Bharatiya Jana

Sangh, which had been founded in 1951 as the political wing of the Rashtriya Swayamsevak Sangh (RSS). The RSS had been founded in 1925 and spawned a variety of organizations with similar ideologies known collectively as the Sangh Parivar. These included the Shiv Sena (1966), which is a political party propagating a Marathi nationalism as well as *Hindutva*; the Vishwa Hindu Parishad (VHP) (1967); and the VHP's youth wing, the Bajrang Dal (1984). Some of the actions of these organizations, such as the destruction of the Babri mosque in Ayodhya, are viewed by many as particularistic and divisive. But, when the BJP came to power at the center in 1998 as the leader of the coalition called the National Democratic Alliance, it behaved much like the INC had—attributed by some to the fact that it was constrained by secular parties in its coalition.

There are two major Communist parties, the CPI and the CPI(M), which broke away from the former in 1964. The latter is the most significant and has controlled the federal unit of West Bengal for decades, has alternated in power in the state of Kerala since 1957, and has governed in Tripura. Their secular nature leads them to support Congress and oppose the BJP. In the fourteenth *Lok Sabha* (which began in 2004), their support for the INC-led coalition was decisive and that gave them exceptional power over what the coalition could, or could not, do.

Regional parties have grown substantially in number, power, and importance. They control the Legislative Assemblies of many states. By their nature, none of them is likely to become a dominant national party. However, their support has become essential to the INC and the BJP in the construction of ruling coalitions at the center.

Mexico

Writing in the mid-1970s, Giovanni Sartori viewed Mexico as a one-party dominant system with the PRI serving as a "clear-cut case of

[a] hegemonic party that permits second class parties as long as, and to the extent that, they remain as they are."[32] Clearly, the smaller parties in Mexico did not accept this bargain and, increasingly in the decades after Sartori wrote, neither did the leaders of the PRI. While a one-party dominant system for much of the twentieth century, today the Mexican party system is in flux. Whether it is heading toward a two-and-a-half party system or a multiparty system remains an open question. Mexico's electoral arrangements make a multiparty system more likely than in other presidential systems, and—unlike two-and-a-half party systems—the three largest parties all have significant representation in the national legislature, yet with no party gaining majority status.

The PRI had controlled Mexican politics by appealing to a large number of groups. Its oxymoronic name shows its attempt to appeal to a broad constituency, as does the name selected for its current electoral alliance with the Green Party: The Alliance for Mexico. At the peak of its success, the party emphasized three "sectors": labor, peasant, military, and "popular" (middle class). To be a member of the party, one had to belong to an official organization in one of these three sectors. Its link to these major segments of society, and its clientelist dealings with individuals at the local level, helped it mobilize significant support at election time. If that was not enough, the PRI-led government manipulated election returns to guarantee continued PRI control.

As discussed in Chapter 6, the PRI's surrender of control over the political system was a slow process, overseen by party leaders such as President Carlos Salinas in the late 1980s and early 1990s and Ernesto Zedillo for the rest of that decade. Its descent included the assassinations of a presidential candidate and other party officials, the loss of control of a number of state and local governments, the loss of the presidency in 2000, and an especially poor showing in the 2006 elections that dropped it

to the third most important party in Mexican federal politics.

The 2006 national election indicated that, far from dominating federal politics as it had in the past, the PRI was in danger of being relegated to third-party status. But parties that control a country during a long period of authoritarian rule have advantages. Their name recognition, organizational head start, and clientelist connections at the local level (see Chapter 9) can be significant assets in open electoral competition. In addition, compared with its two main rivals, the PRI is a more national party—needing to rely less on strength in particular regions for its electoral success. Thus, the PRI is unlikely to disappear completely from the political scene. It remains a force in local politics, and despite the 2006 results, one should not count it out in future federal elections, including presidential ones.

Since 2000 the National Action Party (PAN) has quickly become the leading party in Mexico at the federal level. Its candidates have won the last two presidential contests, and it controls the largest portion of seats in both houses of the Congress. Viewed as both probusiness and pro-Catholic, the party has strong support in the industrial north. The party began its ascent as a national political force by winning races for governor in certain states in the north and west. While the party held fewer than eighteen mayoral offices in the mid-1980s, a decade later it controlled around 250. But it was Vicente Fox's victory in the 2000 presidential election that signaled both the broad appeal of the PAN and its potential to replace the PRI as the leading party in the country.[33]

The other major party in Mexico is the Party of the Democratic Revolution (PRD). The PRD-led Alliance for the Welfare of All nearly won the presidency in 2006 and made significant gains in the national legislative elections. It offers a left-of-center alternative to the PAN's right-of-center policy positions and has a strong base of support in the south and east of the country.

IN THEORY AND PRACTICE

Party Organization Theory and Mexico

In 1984, Joseph Schlesinger proposed a way to understand how parties are organized and, more broadly, how they behave in democratic political systems.[34] Schlesinger's **party organization theory** is based on the idea that such an understanding requires considering three key features of political parties: that they are "market-based," that their policies provide collective benefits, and that their work is performed in large part by unpaid volunteers.

Schlesinger contended that, like businesses, parties are "market-based organizations" that trade certain goods for a desired resource.[35] While businesses engage in economic exchange, elections involve political exchange. Voters help parties gain office, and parties try to adopt policies those voters favor. Schlesinger points out, however, that these policies are collective benefits, generating a collective action problem (see Chapter 9). Finding people to take on the costs of party work is difficult if they receive the policy benefit whether they do this work or not. Parties are partially able to overcome this problem because the most important people in the party do directly and personally benefit from its success—they become the office holders. As a result, they accept the organizational costs and act as the party's "entrepreneurs."[36] These entrepreneurs play a central role in party organization.

Others gain less directly, and lower level party members, especially unpaid volunteers, are typically less dedicated to working for the party over the long term. Relying heavily on volunteers makes parties very different from businesses or government agencies but similar to interest groups. Thus, parties are like businesses in their market-based exchanges, like interest groups and government agencies in that they produce collective goods, and like interest groups in their reliance on workers who are compensated indirectly. Schlesinger argues that this unique combination of features makes political parties function through "organized trial and error."[37]

At first glance, the creation of the Party of Democratic Revolution (PRD) in Mexico appears to provide a good example of Schlesinger's emphasis on "entrepreneurs." A number of left-leaning former PRI officials founded the party, including Cuauhtémoc Cárdenas Solórzano. Cárdenas was the son of a former PRI leader and president of the country. Trying to follow in his father's footsteps, he sought the PRI's nomination for president in 1988. When he did not receive it, he formed an electoral alliance of leftist parties to compete against the PRI candidate, Carlos Salinas. Many contend that Cárdenas rightfully won the election—claims supported by survey data and a mysterious shutdown of the computerized vote counting system on election night—but Salinas was named the winner.

The experience led Cárdenas to form the PRD. He competed again in the 1994 and 2000 elections. He finished third in 2000, partly because some PRD members defected to support the candidacy of Vicente Fox. The PRD also worked to distance itself from the idea that it was only a vehicle for Cárdenas's pursuit of the presidency, an effort that appeared to be paying off by 2006. While the party has moved beyond Cárdenas, it is clear that without his personal interest in becoming president and his resulting efforts to take on the PRI, the PRD would not exist today.

At the same time, there is more to the story of Cárdenas's entrepreneurial efforts than pure personal ambition. Cárdenas and his allies in the PRI to the left of Salinas were neither seeking political power for its own sake nor acting on a perceived birthright for Cárdenas to be president. Indeed, Cárdenas never expected to come as close

Party organization theory is associated with Joseph Schlesinger, who argued that understanding parties requires considering the ways in which they are similar to and different from businesses, interest groups, and government agencies.

to winning the presidency in 1988 as he did. In addition, by challenging Salinas, Cárdenas lost his chance of serving in a comfortable public servant position, he received constant death threats, some of his closest friends were murdered, and he spent much of his inheritance on exhausting political campaigning. Thus, the example of Cárdenas and PRD shows the importance of political party entrepreneurs, but it also challenges the view that such entrepreneurs accept the costs of party formation only because they expect the personal benefits to more than outweigh these costs. In Cárdenas's case, fundamental policy differences with Salinas, especially over the proper extent of market reforms in the economy, were deemed important enough by him to push him into entrepreneurial, party-forming activity that, at times, appeared to be as fruitless as it was costly.

Brazil

Since 1990, the first national elections following the transition to democracy, no political party has succeeded in winning more than 20 percent of the vote or 22 percent of the seats in the Chamber of Deputies. The average number of parties represented in the Chamber since 1988 is nineteen; there have never been fewer than eighteen

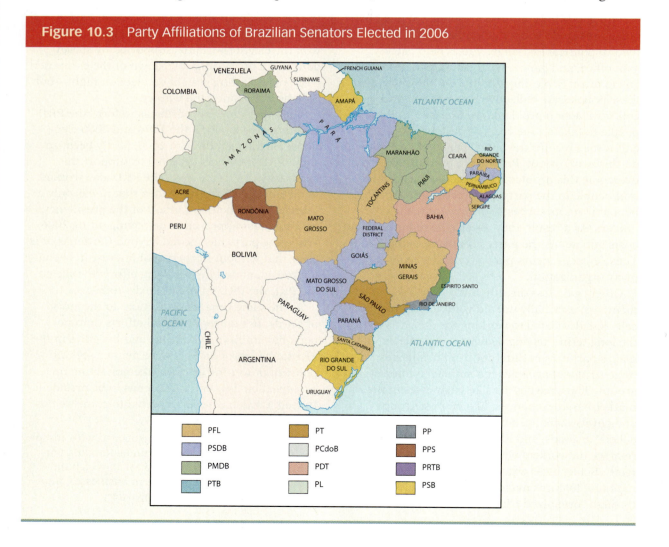

Figure 10.3 Party Affiliations of Brazilian Senators Elected in 2006

parties represented. The ideological spectrum is correspondingly wide: Parties have ranged from far right monarchist parties to far left Communist and Trotskyite parties.

Moreover, the parties that participate in the system are themselves unstable—disappearing, splitting, merging, and forming new parties with some frequency. And politicians frequently change their party affiliations before, during, and after elections. In this sense, the Brazilian party system after transition has looked much like the Russian party system during the 1990s, with voters straining to identify party programs and most parties less relevant politically than individual politicians.

Nevertheless, four major parties have stood out over time. Two of these parties have been among the top vote-getters since the first 1990 legislative election: the Brazilian Democratic Movement Party (PMDB) and the Liberal Front Party (PFL). The PMDB is a successor of the Movement for Brazilian Democracy (MDB), which competed in rigged elections during the military dictatorship itself. As its name suggests, the MDB attempted to resist the military government from within the system, and it retains a centrist political stance. Because the only thing that united its original members was moderate opposition to the military regime, it has a fairly vague ideology (critics say it has none).

The PFL is a successor of the other, more promilitary party permitted under the military dictatorship, the Alliance for National Renovation (ARENA). However, the PFL drew from some of the more liberal elements of the military coalition, who supported conservative values but felt it was time for a democratic transition. It remains a right-of-center political party, though it changed its name to *Democratas* (Democrats) in 2007.

The other two major parties have placed among the top four vote getters in each of the last three legislative elections, and both have won the presidency twice. The Workers' Party (PT), which currently holds the presidency, is the older and more leftist party, founded by labor union organizers and social movement leaders in 1980. Of all Brazil's parties, the PT is the most ideologically coherent, most strongly connected to civil society organizations, most disciplined, and most committed to social change. Its politicians are much less likely to switch parties midstream, as a history of party activism is considered important for winning party candidacies. The Brazilian Social Democratic Party (PSDB) occupies a middle ground between the PT and the PMDB. Originally part of the PMDB, its founders split from that party in order to create a party with a more coherent, center-left ideological platform. The PSDB's most important leader, well-known sociologist Fernando Henrique Cardoso, was president of Brazil from 1994–2002.

Elections and Electoral Systems

An **election** is a form of conventional mass participation in which individuals express a preference for candidates or political parties seeking political office. It is the primary way that members of a national legislature are selected around the world. In a large number of countries, the chief executive of the government is also directly elected. While many people in the United States grumble about the conduct of American political campaigns, elections are a particularly important form of democratic participation. Democratic elections give ordinary citizens a direct say in the shape of their government and the policies it produces. As Adam Przeworski so succinctly puts it, "democracy is a system in which parties lose elections."[38] In other words, unlike elections in nondemocratic systems where the results are

> An **election** is a form of conventional mass participation in which the population selects among various individual candidates or political parties seeking political office.

predetermined, in democratic systems a ruling party or sitting president can actually be removed from power through an election.

Types of Electoral Systems

Elections are considered the backbone of democracy, but there is little agreement about the best set of rules for translating votes into legislative seats. Electoral arrangements can generally be divided into two categories: proportional representation (PR) and first past the post (FPTP). In PR systems, the percentage of votes each party receives nationally roughly corresponds to its percentage of seats in the legislature. FPTP systems pick representatives individually, with the candidate who wins the most votes in a certain region of the country securing the seat, regardless of how that candidate's party performed elsewhere. There are many variants of these two main types and a number of countries incorporate hybrid systems which bring PR and FPTP together. Germany, for example, combines PR and FPTP voting, giving each voter two votes, with one vote counting toward each type of electoral arrangement.

Proportional Representation (PR) In a pure **proportional representation (PR)** system, the percentage of the vote a certain party gets becomes the percentage of the seats that the party secures in the legislature. For example, if the legislature has one hundred seats, and Party X gets 25 percent of the national vote, it would receive twenty-five of the one hundred seats for its members. Prior to the election in PR systems, a party typically produces a list of candidates who would hold the seats it wins. In the case of Party X, one would go down its list and find the first twenty-five names. These individuals would become members of the legislature; number twenty-six on the list would not. The leader of the party (and the potential prime minister if the system is also a parliamentary one) would be the first person on the list.

The pure form of PR encourages a large number of small parties. Using the one hundred–person

legislature example again, if a politician believes that he or she could form a party and get even 1 percent of the vote, this individual would secure a seat in the legislature. Consequently, a pure PR system could lead to dozens of similarly sized parties, unstable coalition governments, and chaotic legislating. In practice, such extreme problems do not occur, partly because most PR-based electoral systems do not rely on a pure PR approach. Instead, the rules of how votes translate into seats are amended to discourage a large number of small political parties.

One of the central ways that PR systems deviate from their pure form is through the use of a **threshold**. A threshold is the minimum percentage of the vote that a party must receive in order to secure even one seat in the legislature. Israel has had one of the lowest thresholds of any country (1 percent into the 1990s; 2 percent today), but the most common threshold around the world is 5 percent. A 5 percent threshold means that a party which receives even 4.99 percent of the vote would earn no seats. With a 5 percent threshold, it makes little sense for a politician to form a party that is likely to get only 1 percent of the vote. The threshold rule thus encourages small parties to combine forces with other small parties to guarantee that the threshold is cleared. This reduces the overall number of parties to a more manageable number, improving stability and the ability to generate policy effectively.

Large parties also benefit from the threshold when smaller parties fail to clear it. The votes for

A **proportional representation (PR)** system is an electoral system in which voters cast their votes for political parties and the percentage of the vote that each party receives translates into the percentage of seats that the party receives in the legislature.

A **threshold** is a rule that forces parties to receive a certain percentage of the vote in a PR system before they receive seats in the legislature. The most common threshold is 5 percent, meaning parties that receive under 5 percent of the vote would receive no seats.

the parties that do not clear the threshold become void. As a result, the percentage of the seats for the parties that do cross the threshold is greater than their percentage of the vote. A party that receives 40 percent of the vote in the election, for example, could end up with a majority of the seats if a number of small parties do not reach the 5 percent barrier.

First Past the Post (FPTP) The other basic form of electoral system is the **first past the post (FPTP)** system. In FPTP, voters typically do not vote for political parties. Rather, they cast a vote for an individual political candidate, who is running for a seat linked to a relatively small electoral district. Whichever candidate receives the support of the voters in that district earns the seat from that district. This form of election is familiar to most Americans; it is what the United States uses to select members of the House of Representatives, and it is model for most state and local government elections as well.

FPTP systems typically use a plurality rule rather than a majority rule. This means that the individual selected from the electoral district is the one who receives the most votes, even if that person does not receive a majority (over 50 percent) of the votes. As a result, FPTP systems are sometimes called "plurality systems." Finally, FPTP systems usually involve only one person being selected from the electoral district. As a result, they are also referred to as **single-member district (SMD)** systems (or even just "district systems"). You might even see combinations of these terms such as SMD-plurality systems. Whatever the label, the basic idea is the same: voters select from among individual candidates running in a district, and the seat from that district is handed out on the basis of which candidate receives the most votes.

Just as the pure PR system can produce a large number of small parties, a pure FPTP system can result in a large number of candidates and the winner earning the seat in office with a small percentage of the vote. For example, even if only five

candidates were running for office in a pure FPTP system, it is possible for a candidate to win with just over 20 percent of the vote. This is a concern, since an extreme candidate with a loyal base of followers could secure a seat from that district even though the vast majority of the voters would not want that candidate in office.

In practice, such an occurrence is rare, partly because multiple candidates from the same political party are generally not allowed to run in the same district. The party selects which candidate from the party runs in the district, or voters select the candidate from that party through a **primary election**. A primary—common in the United States, but relatively rare in other parts of the world—is an election where candidates from one political party vie for the right to represent the party in the final ("general") election. In other parts of the world, the American reliance on primaries seems strange. After all, the primary allows voters, not a political party, to decide which candidate runs under that political party's label in the general election.

Variations and Hybrid Systems There are a number of other variations on PR and FPTP systems, and some countries combine the two approaches. A few of the variants are particularly

A **first past the post (FPTP)** system is one in which voters select a particular candidate for each office on the ballot, and the candidate receiving a plurality of the vote is the winner.

Because voters generally choose only one representative per electoral district, first past the post systems are sometimes called **single-member district (SMD)** systems.

A **primary election** is one where multiple candidates from the same political party compete against each other for the right to represent the party in a general election for a particular political office. Primaries are relatively rare outside the United States, since voters, not political parties, decide who runs under the party label in the general election.

worthy of mention. One approach is the **multi-member district (MMD)** system. In MMD systems, several candidates are selected from a single district. These districts are larger than they would be in an SMD system but smaller than the country as a whole. Sometimes, the districts all select the same number of candidates; for example, five candidates earn office from each district. In other cases, the districts vary across the country in the number of seats they fill.

Different approaches are available for choosing the representatives from districts in an MMD system. Particularly in districts with a large number of seats, a PR approach could also be used; a party might secure more than one seat from the same district depending on its performance. A FPTP approach could be used, with representatives from a three-seat district being the three highest vote recipients. The FPTP approach could be combined with a threshold requirement. In this case, voters may get to vote for as many candidates as there are seats from the district, but to win one of the seats, a candidate must secure above a certain percentage of the vote. Although the MMD approach generally provides different groups in a particular area of the country, including minority groups, a better chance to be represented by the candidate of their choice, the threshold requirement forces candidates to have broad support in the district to be elected.

Other systems provide alternatives to the plurality rule. One option is the use of a **runoff**. In a runoff, the two candidates who receive the most votes in the first round of voting compete again. The candidate who gets a majority of the vote in this second round is elected. As a result, a runoff system is also known as a **majority** (or **majoritarian**) **system**, since a majority of the voters must support a candidate before he or she can hold political office. In majoritarian systems, extreme candidates rarely win elections, since voters have a chance to vote against those candidates in the second round. The runoff approach is not only used in legislative elections. Runoffs are common in presidential elections around the world as well.

In the **preference system**, voters are allowed to rank each candidate seeking office in an electoral district. In a common form of preference voting, the first step involves counting the first place votes from all ballots. If no candidate receives a majority of the votes, the candidate who finished last is removed, and the second place vote totals are added to the first place votes. If there is still no candidate with a majority, the process is repeated with the third place votes and so on until a majority of votes has been secured. Such a system benefits candidates who are everyone's second choice but few people's first choice.

Preference approaches can be used to choose a single candidate from an electoral district, or they can be combined with MMD systems to determine which group of candidates earns seats from that multi-member district. Rather than a majority of the votes, candidates have to earn a certain predetermined portion of the total votes cast to be elected. The combination of a preference arrangement and multi-member districts is typically known as a **single transferable vote (STV) system**. While some scholars label STV systems as a form of PR, the resulting distribution of seats is generally far less proportional than a traditional PR system based on a national party vote.[39] Ireland uses STV in its national legislative elections.

A **multi-member district (MMD)** system is a variant of the FPTP approach in which more than one candidate is selected from a particular electoral district.

A **runoff** is an election in which the two candidates who receive the most votes in the first round compete in a second round.

A runoff system is also known as a **majority** (or **majoritarian**) **system**, since a candidate needs a majority of the vote in the second round to win.

A **preference system** allows voters to rank candidates in a single-member or multi-member district race. These rankings are taken into account until the seat or seats are filled.

A **single transferable vote (STV) system** combines preference voting with multi-member districts.

A final technique, the **hybrid electoral system**, combines FPTP and PR approaches by dividing the total seats of the legislature into two groups. One group of seats is determined by the outcome of FPTP district voting. The remaining seats are distributed based on the results of the PR vote. In such hybrid systems, voters are given two votes—one for a party and one for a candidate in a district. In the PR vote, voters do not have to support the party of the candidate they chose in the FPTP district vote. This approach benefits voters who like a particular party in general but feel a strong attachment to a candidate of another party. Until recently, Russia used a hybrid system, and the hybrid approach remains in use in Germany.

Advantages and Disadvantages of PR Electoral Systems

In many countries, electoral reform is an ongoing process. Many reforms around the world have had the goal of making FPTP systems look more like PR systems. Do the relative merits of the two main approaches justify this trend? This section focuses on the advantages and disadvantages of PR systems, which—because PR and FPTP take such opposite approaches—correspond respectively to the disadvantages and advantages of FPTP systems.

Advantage #1: Minority Interests Are Represented Even with a threshold in place, PR systems allow small parties to win seats. This gives these small parties a platform to voice their concerns. It can also make them important political players. Since PR systems allow more parties to hold seats in the legislature, it is rare for a party to secure a majority of the seats. As a result, coalition governments are common, and small parties can receive important cabinet positions and policy victories in exchange for putting the coalition over the top in its quest to control a majority of the seats in the legislature.

Advantage #2: Women Are More Likely to Be Elected to Office FPTP systems tend to generate fewer female representatives in national legislatures. One could argue that a number of other causal factors may be in play here, including the possibility that countries that are more culturally patriarchal also happen to have FPTP electoral systems. However, the evidence that PR plays a role in female participation is hard to dispute. In every country in which women hold at least 25 percent of legislative seats, PR is used in the selection of the members of the legislature.[40] In addition, in countries such as Russia and Germany that have used hybrid electoral arrangements, more women have held PR-linked seats than FPTP-districts seats.

Advantage #3: An Emphasis on Ideas over Personalities PR systems lead voters to select among political parties rather than individual candidates, making the policy positions of the parties arguably more important in FPTP systems. It becomes impossible for a candidate to run as an independent in a PR system. Of course, party leaders are often well-known individuals, and it is certainly possible for voters in PR systems to select a party based on how they view the party leader. PR does not, therefore, *eliminate* the importance of individuals and their personalities. At least compared with FPTP systems, however, PR systems do make personalities less central than ideas and policy positions.

Disadvantage #1: Too Many Small Parties with Disproportionate Importance Thresholds make it more difficult for small parties to win seats, but even in systems with a 5 percent threshold, it is not unusual for one or more parties that received less than 10 percent of the vote to hold

A **hybrid electoral system** combines PR and FPTP methods. Voters select both a party and a candidate, and the legislature is divided into PR and district seats.

seats. Such parties can become kingmakers of coalition governments and therefore wield much more influence than their electoral support justifies. While FPTP systems can shut small parties out of the legislature, PR systems can give them a disproportionate amount of power.

Disadvantage #2: PR Facilitates Extremist Parties
While PR electoral systems give small parties in the center of the political spectrum a chance to be heard in the halls of the legislature, they provide similar opportunities to small extremist parties. Depending on how high the threshold is set, a far-left or far-right party may only have the support of a few percent of the population and still earn seats in the legislature. One could argue

this should not be a major concern for those considering the relative merits of the PR approach, since such parties are usually not brought into coalition governments. At the same time, any seats at all can allow members of extremist parties to disrupt legislative proceedings or find other ways to broadcast their policy positions from the "stage" of the national legislature.

Think and Discuss

Does a PR system's advantage in better representing minorities outweigh its disadvantage of small parties potentially hijacking the process of creating and maintaining a ruling coalition? Why?

Topic in countries

Elections in the Proportional Representation Systems of Brazil and Russia

Electoral systems employing proportional mechanisms are common around the world, particularly in many European countries. Yet, among the ten TIC cases, only Brazil and Russia use a PR approach in selecting representatives to their legislatures' lower houses. In Brazil's case, the PR approach is different from those in many countries, as voters can select a party but also have the option to rank candidates on that party's list. Russia's system is a more pure PR one, but Russia came to this approach relatively recently. In the first portion of the post-Soviet period, Russia used a hybrid system, combining PR and FPTP district votes to select members of the lower house of parliament, the *Duma*.

Brazil

At the national level, Brazil actually uses three different electoral systems. Members of the Chamber of Deputies, the lower house of Congress, are selected through a variant of PR. Because comparativists often consider

the electoral system for a national assembly's lower house to be most important in determining the country's party system and legislative-executive relations, Brazil is often labeled as a "PR country." Senators in Brazil, however, are elected through FPTP. The president is chosen through a majority (runoff) system. If no presidential candidate receives a majority of the vote in the first round, a runoff is held one month later in which only the top two candidates participate.

The Chamber of Deputies is elected via a system of **open list proportional representation**. This is a variation on the more typical pattern described earlier in the chapter, in which parties choose the candidates to be nominated and rank them on a list, with candidates at the top of the list taking their seats first. In an open list system, voters choose the party they prefer, but also—within

In an **open list proportional representation** electoral system, a voter casts a vote for a particular party but also plays a role in the decision of which candidates receive the seats earned by that party. In Brazil, voters cast only one vote, for either a party or a candidate.

that party—the specific candidate they prefer. In the case of Brazil, voters can cast a simple party vote, approving any candidate from that party, or they may choose a specific candidate. Most voters in Brazil choose a candidate. The percentage of seats a party receives is determined by the sum of the votes received by all of its candidates, and the ranking of the candidates is determined by how many votes they individually receive. The candidates who actually take office are the most popular candidates within their own party; the party vote only determines how many of them will be seated. Thus, candidates compete against candidates from their own political party, not just against other parties.

As a result, parties tend to be highly internally divided. Even within party benches in the legislature it is often difficult for party leaders to commit the support of their *entire* delegation in the kind of log-rolling often done in other multiparty systems. Although fewer parties win seats in the Senate, the Senate tends to reflect regional interests rather than the interests of the national parties to which senators belong. Thus, senators may not cooperate with deputies from the same political party in the lower house. Moreover, since proportional representation results in a larger number of parties in the legislature, it is nearly impossible for the president to win a legislative majority of his own party.

Under these conditions, putting together even a minimal legislative majority can be very tough. Some presidents have resorted to the powers of the office to act without a congressional majority, by issuing provisional decrees. Another technique is the liberal use of bribes and favoritism in handing out government offices to individual legislators who agree to cooperate with presidential initiatives. Even the government of President Lula da Silva, whose party had long criticized such practices as rank corruption, got caught distributing fat monthly 'bonuses' to opposition congressmen in return for their votes in favor of government legislation. These perverse results of the electoral system hamper the consolidation of Brazilian democracy.

The Russian Federation

The Russian Federation has had many important elections since its emergence from the collapse of the USSR. In addition to a national referendum in April 1993 and ratification of the new constitution in December of that year, parliamentary elections were held in 1993, 1995, 1999, 2003, and 2007. Presidential elections were held in 1996, 2000, 2004, and 2008. Several central themes emerged across the course of these elections. Promarket and pro-Western political parties performed terribly in the parliamentary elections of the 1990s. On the other hand, the Unity/United Russia Party, associated with Vladimir Putin, performed well after 2000. Furthermore, it has become increasingly questionable whether Russian elections were free and fair.

In Russia's first parliamentary elections, held in December 1993 to coincide with the vote on the new constitution, voters selecting members of the *Duma* had two votes: one for a candidate in a district and one for a party. Half of the *Duma*'s 450 seats came from the district vote using FPTP rules, and the other 225 were based on the party vote using PR. Pro-reform parties did worse than expected. They saw each other as their main rivals and attacked each other rather than working together. Russia's Choice ended up with around the same number of seats as Zhirinovsky's Liberal Democratic Party (LDP). The LDP actually won the PR vote handily, securing around 24 percent compared with 15 percent for Russia's Choice and 13 percent for the Communists. Independents won a large number of district races, reflecting the personal nature of Russian politics.

In 1995, voters again selected members of the *Duma* through the hybrid electoral arrangement, this time for four-year terms. More parties ran in 1995 (forty-three, compared with only thirteen parties or blocs of parties in 1993), but only seven earned seats in the *Duma*. In addition, of the roughly 2,800 candidates who ran in the 225 district races, more than 1,000 ran as independents. The Communist Party did best in the elections, and its portion of the party vote increased from 1993 (to 24 percent in 1995). Yet, it earned only around 150 of the *Duma*'s 450 seats, far short of a majority. The percentage of the vote for the LDP dropped significantly, as the Communists replaced the LDP as the party of those seeking to protest Yeltsin's policies.

In the final elections before Yelstin stepped down as president, the Communists continued their strong showing. They again won around 24 percent of the party vote. The surprise was the upstart Unity Bloc, informally affiliated with then–Prime Minister Putin. Unity won 23 percent of the PR vote. OVR also did well, earning 13 percent of the vote in part due to extremely favorable coverage from Moscow-based television stations.

In 2003, United Russia won the election, earning 37.6 percent of the vote. This gave it 120 seats from the PR vote alone. In combination with another 102 seats from district races and sympathetic independent candidates, the party controlled over 300 seats in the *Duma*. This marked the first time since the collapse of the USSR that a single party could count on the support of a majority of the members of the *Duma*. Two parties that had done well before, the Communists and the LDP, continued their presence in the *Duma*, earning about 12.5 percent and 11.5 percent of the party vote, respectively. Yabloko, however, failed to clear the 5 percent threshold for the first time, along with the Union of Right Forces. Thus, by 2003, the pro-reform parties had been eclipsed.

The process of consolidation of the party system reached a high point in 2007. With the country having switched to a PR-only electoral system, Russian voters no longer chose individual candidates from electoral districts. Instead, they cast a single vote for a political party. While eleven parties were on the ballot, only four received enough votes to qualify to receive seats in the 450-seat *Duma*. Of the four, United Russia dominated the elections, receiving over 64 percent of the vote and 315 seats. Two of the other parties that cleared the threshold, the LDP and A Just Russia, received a sizeable number of seats—40 and 38, respectively—but both were widely viewed as pro-Putin parties. As in 2003, the only serious opposition party was the Communist Party of Russia, which received less than 12 percent of the votes and only 57 seats. Shortly after the elections, United Russia and other pro-Putin

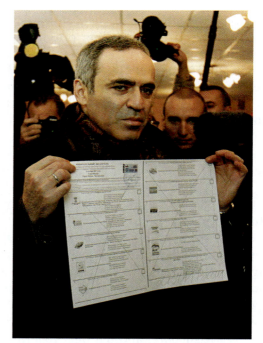

The leader of "The Other Russia" opposition movement, former world chess champion Garry Kasparov, holds up his ballot for Russia's parliamentary elections in December 2007. Kasparov had crossed out the official choices and written in the name of his political party.

(©Maxim Marmur/AFP/Getty Images)

parties pledged their support to Putin's hand-picked successor, Dmitry Medvedev, to replace Putin as president in 2008.

The trend in parliamentary elections of an emerging one-party dominant system after 2000 corresponds to the outcome of the presidential contests as well. In 1996, President Yeltsin won reelection in a runoff against the head of the Communist Party, Gennadi Zyuganov. Both candidates had won around one-third of the vote in the first round (Yeltsin, 35 percent; Zyuganov, 32 percent). Yeltsin was able to win the second round partly by co-opting General Alexander Lebed, who had received 15 percent of the vote in the first round, to take a position in the Yeltsin government. He also benefited from extremely biased coverage in the media and a terribly run campaign by the Communists. Yeltsin received 54 percent of the vote in the second round.

In 2000, acting-President Putin, who had become president when Yeltsin unexpectedly resigned on New Year's Eve of 1999, sought election for his first full term. Putin's strategy was to look busy running the government and control how he was presented in the media as much as possible. He failed to participate in any of the presidential debates but published a book, *In the First Person*, just before the vote. Putin won 53 percent of the vote in the first round making a runoff vote unnecessary. Communist Party leader Zyuganov received 30 percent of the vote, showing the still solid core of Communist supporters in the country. While Putin's other opponents did well only in select regions of the country, Putin did well nearly everywhere. Amid some concerns about fraud in the election, he won every region that Yeltsin had in 1996 plus more than thirty others.

In 2004, Putin was reelected, capturing 69 percent of the vote in the first round. Once more, there were claims of electoral irregularities, but the real story was how the Putin campaign controlled information prior to the vote. The Russian electronic media became Putin campaign outlets, and most of the candidates campaigned as if part of a predetermined process.

In March 2008, Dmitry Medvedev ran as Putin's chosen successor and won handily. Putin had actively supported Medvedev's candidacy, and Medvedev had strongly hinted that Putin would be in line to be the country's prime minister. When Putin announced he would accept such an appointment, the new face of Russian politics had taken shape.

For Russia to be a democracy, its elections must be free and fair. Based on the criteria discussed in Chapter 6, Russian elections have been largely, but not entirely, free. The role of money is a concern, and certainly not all candidates have had the ability to get their messages out to an equal degree.[41] But, in broad terms, individuals vote in secret, and candidates can run for office and have the ability to campaign by providing information to voters. However, on the question of fairness, Russian elections have fallen short and look to be getting worse rather than better, part of the pattern of "creeping authoritarianism" discussed in other portions of this book. Russian media coverage of campaigns has favored incumbent government candidates throughout the post-Soviet period. Vladimir Putin's tightening of control over the media since 2000 has only made media favoritism toward progovernment candidates even more pronounced.

While electoral results at the federal level have raised questions about the democratic nature of the country, elections at the regional level have displayed a less clear-cut pattern. In some regions, electoral competition was significant during the 1990s; in others, it was impossible to call the elections democratic.[42] After 2000, the regional elections began to reflect patterns at the federal level. United Russia dominated the regional elections in 2005.

Topic in countries

Elections in the First Past the Post Systems of the United Kingdom, France, India, and Nigeria

Four of the TIC cases, the United Kingdom, France, India, and Nigeria, use FPTP arrangements in their legislative elections. Two of these, the United Kingdom and India, are parliamentary systems, in which the results of these legislative elections determine the selection of the chief executive. In the United Kingdom, this approach has tended to generate majority parties in parliament, while in India coalition governments have become common. The other two cases, France and Nigeria, hold separate elections for a president alongside their selection of legislative representatives.

The United Kingdom

Because the United Kingdom is a parliamentary system, voters do not directly select the prime minister. Like other parliamentary systems, the prime minister is the leader of the party that secures a majority of the seats in the parliament. Unlike many parliamentary systems, however, voters select individual candidates in districts through FPTP arrangements rather than by casting votes for a political party. Interestingly, the United Kingdom almost adopted a single transferable vote (STV) system after World War I. This system is used in Northern Ireland in local elections and in elections held in Northern Ireland to select representatives to the European Parliament.

The United Kingdom's FPTP system causes problems for smaller parties such as the Liberal Democrats and tends to create an artificial majority for the largest party. In 1992, for example, the Liberal Democrats received around 18 percent of the vote across the country as a whole but won only 20 seats (about 3 percent) in the House of Commons. On the other hand, in the "landslide" victory that brought Tony Blair and the Labour Party to power in 1997, Labour won only 43.2 percent of all votes cast but earned 418 seats, a sizeable majority of the 646-seat House of Commons.

The FPTP rules have helped prevent minority governments and maintain the United Kingdom's two-and-a-half party system. Yet, going into the May 5, 2005, elections for the British House of Commons, it was unclear which of the two main parties would win, and some even believed a coalition government might be necessary. Instead, the British FPTP electoral system once again translated a popular vote minority into legislative majority. While maintaining its majority party status, Labour controlled fewer seats than it had since 1997. Blair also maintained his position as prime minister, but stating, "I have listened and I have learned," he clearly recognized he was not as popular as he had been.[43] In 2006, he announced plans to step down as prime minister.

In 2005, Labour won only 35.2 percent of the vote nationally, a full 8 percent less than in 1997. The Liberal Democratic Party won 22 percent of the vote and, more important, nearly 10 percent of the seats in the House of Commons. These successes led party leader Charles Kennedy to hail the 2005 elections as signaling the Liberal Democrats as a "real alternative" to Labour and the Conservatives in the future.[44] Given the sharp regional divisions in the United Kingdom, the two main parties combined earning only around 75 percent of the national vote, and the Liberal Democrats' vote totals within 10 percent of the second largest party, it is possible to imagine a shake-up in British electoral politics in the future, even one that may require a coalition government to control parliament. If coalition governments were to become a regular feature of British politics, the party system would lose its two-and-a-half party label in favor of a multiparty designation.

Part of the story of the weakened position of both Labour and the Conservatives is that, since Communism's collapse, class and economic ideological divisions have become less central to electoral politics in countries such as the United Kingdom. In their place, regional and other identity divisions have become more important. Chapter 5 highlighted the United Kingdom's regional divisions, roughly corresponding to its four main ethnic groups—English, Scots, Welsh, and Northern Irish.

Given recent trends and examples from countries such as Canada (see this chapter's Comparative Exercise), one might expect nationalist parties or the Liberal Democrats to become stronger in Scotland and Wales. If Labour were to lose its stranglehold on seats from Scotland (where it won 40 of the 59 seats in 2005) and Wales (29 of 40 seats), it would make maintaining control of the House of Commons much more difficult. Because the vast majority of UK citizens live in England, however, the regional and urban/rural cleavages within England may be even more important. Particularly if immigration continues to be controversial, ethnic divisions within England are likely to have increasing implications for British electoral outcomes.

France

The French electoral process, for both the national legislature and the presidency, is majoritarian, with two rounds of balloting. For legislative elections, parties field candidates in single-member districts in a modified FPTP format. Candidates who win the most votes cast, provided the number corresponds to at least 25 percent of the number of registered voters, are elected outright in the first round. When no candidate meets these criteria, legislative candidates with vote totals of at least 12.5 percent of registered voters advance to the second round. In presidential elections, the two top candidates advance to a second round if no candidate receives a majority of the first-round vote. This complicated system is an innovation of the Fifth Republic, designed to allow for both programmatic and charismatic party appeals. Typically, intense negotiations emerge when three candidates qualify for the second round.

The system does not always work in presidential elections as promised. Jacques Chaban-Delmas, as the official Gaullist candidate, failed to reach the second round of voting in 1974, and the system twice resulted in the exclusion of the Left from the second round. In 2002, with no grand coalition formed on the Left or Right, voters scattered their ballots among sixteen candidates. With massive abstentions, no one, not even sitting President Jacques Chirac, received more than 20 percent of the vote. Combined, candidates from parties on the far right garnered more than 20 percent, while those to the left of the Socialist Party earned more than 23 percent, including nearly 10 percent for two Trotskyite parties. As a result, Socialist candidate Lionel Jospin was knocked out, and, in the second round, Chirac faced the extremist founder of the National Front, Jean-Marie Le Pen, even though Le Pen had not gained significantly from previous elections.[45] Spurred on by massive demonstrations of high school students against Le Pen (and perhaps embarrassed by them), voters on the left, holding their noses, sent Chirac his second term over the man infamous for denying the Holocaust and physically assaulting a female opponent.[46]

Compared with the disarray of 2002, the 2007 legislative and presidential elections were noteworthy for their normalcy. They also involved important innovations. First, both major parties fielded their candidates via internal presidential "primaries." The Socialists adopted the internal primary to increase transparency, while the UMP did so to ensure Sarkozy's candidacy over Chirac's objections. Second, the Socialists nominated the first woman, an unmarried mother, over the opposition of the leading party "elephants." Finally, for the first time since 1981, the voters refused to hand a victory to candidates of the opposition. "Coming home" after 2002, voters on the left gave the Socialist candidate a strong first round showing. In the end, however, voters returned the UMP to power in both presidential and parliamentary balloting.

India

Elections to the *Lok Sabha* are mammoth undertakings. They require the delineation of 543 constituencies, the issuance to registered voters of hundreds of millions of photo ID cards, and the establishment of approximately 800,000 polling stations. About 5 million polling personnel and security forces are involved in running a general election. In recent *Lok Sabha* elections, the turnout has been about 60 percent, meaning nearly 400 million voters go to the polls.[47]

The Election Commission supervises the process. The Commission consists of a chief election commissioner and two other election commissioners, all three of whom are appointed by the president. They appoint a chief electoral officer at the federal unit level from among the senior civil servants. Once the election is scheduled, a Model Code of Conduct for the parties comes into effect which greatly restricts what they can do. The Code consists of "rules" regarding general conduct, meetings, processions, behavior on polling day, the polling booth, and observers, and it restricts the use by the party in power of its official position for the election. Although vote buying, "booth capturing," and other violations of the Code have occurred, the Commission and its officials have been increasingly successful in limiting corruption in the elections. The Code is applicable in both national and federal unit elections.

Elections occur at least every five years for the *Lok Sabha* and the Legislative Assemblies. Candidates for the *Lok Sabha* run in one of 543 single-member districts (the *Lok Sabha* has 545 members, but 2 are appointed as representatives of the Anglo-Indian community). No fewer than two weeks for campaigning is allowed, but the campaigns are very short compared with countries like the United States. Voting in national elections is held over at least three days because of the difficulty of supervising such a huge event. Legislative Assembly elections are often scheduled for more than one day for similar reasons. Election to the *Rajya Sabha* and the

Legislative Councils is by a complex system of voting by elected officials.

Because of the inability of national parties to win majorities in the *Lok Sabha*, electoral alliances are often developed with regional parties prior to an election. In these cases, the parties come to an agreement on which districts each will run candidates so they do not compete against each other. The bargaining is often difficult and sometimes defections occur when the likely candidate of a party is not allowed to run in a district because his or her party has allotted the district to its alliance partner. A deposit is required of each candidate, amounting to about $225 for those running for a *Lok Sabha* seat. As is the case in the United Kingdom, the deposit is returned to the candidate if he or she gets a certain proportion of the vote.

One relatively unique feature of elections in India is that the proportion of the poorer sections of the population who vote seems to have increased over time relative to that of the wealthy. Some observers see this trend as indicative of a deepening of democracy. At a minimum, it shows that the poor are not as alienated as they are in many countries, including many democracies, believing that their participation can make a difference.

The 2004 general election surprised the ruling National Democratic Alliance led by the BJP. The BJP called the election early because it thought circumstances were favorable for a victory. Yet, INC received over 103 million votes of the nearly 390 million votes cast (and won 150 districts), while the BJP got only 86 million votes across the country (and won 130 districts). These figures highlight the strength of regional parties, the seat-sharing electoral alliances, the necessity of coalition government, and the scale of the democratic electoral event in India.

Nigeria

Nigeria's electoral rules are rather straightforward, particularly in the case of the National Assembly. Candidates for the lower house, the House of Representatives, run in single-member districts and are selected on the basis of FPTP. For the Senate, each of the thirty-six federal territorial units selects three senators, by dividing each territorial unit into three districts and using FPTP rules in each district without a threshold requirement. The Federal Capital Territory, home to the country's capital city of Abuja, selects only one senator.

The People's Democratic Party (PDP) did well in the 1999 elections that marked the reestablishment of democracy, winning a majority of the governorships, a significant number of seats in the National Assembly, and the presidency under Olusegun Obasanjo. Obasanjo received over 62 percent of the vote in 1999 and nearly 62 percent in 2003. Even more than in 1999, the 2003 elections demonstrated that ethnic and regional divisions had not been purged from Nigerian electoral politics. Obasanjo's challenger, Muhammadu Buhari, was a former military ruler of Nigeria in the mid-1980s, an ethnic Fulani, and a Muslim. Not surprisingly, Buhari's support was heavily concentrated in the north.

In 2003, the PDP received over 54 percent of the popular vote in the House of Representatives elections and gained control of well over 200 of its 360 seats. It also took a similar portion of the national vote in the Senate elections and won 76 of the 109 seats. The All Nigeria Peoples Party (ANPP) earned a little more than 27 percent of the national vote and won 96 seats in the House of Representatives and 27 seats in the Senate. The ANPP's support was concentrated in the north of the country. Support for the Alliance for Democracy (AD) was even more concentrated, in the southwest of the country, limiting its potential to gain a significant number of seats.[48] In the 2003 national legislative elections, the AD received less than 9 percent of the national vote and controlled only 34 seats in the House of Representatives and only 6 seats in the Senate.

The PDP increased its control of the legislative branch as a result of the elections in 2007. Although almost a year after the elections Nigeria's electoral commission had still not posted the official results, others estimated that the PDP won over 70 percent of the seats in both the House of Representatives and the Senate.[49] The 2007 vote also highlighted the deepening regional concentration of party support, at least for the smaller parties. Following the elections, representatives from the Action Congress (AC), the successor to the AD, held every House seat from the region of Lagos (as well as all three of its Senate seats). The AC had much less success in other parts of the country, ending up with only around thirty total seats in the House and six in the Senate. The ANPP performed only a little better, taking 27 percent of the national vote in the House elections by sweeping some regions across the north of the country and gaining over sixty House seats and holding more than twenty seats in the Senate.

The campaign for the presidency in 2007 was even more controversial than the legislative elections. The campaign was also a long one in many ways. Major candidates had announced their intentions to run a year or more before the election, but by the fall of 2006 they had not used the campaign to take a programmatic approach to gaining office. Detailed policy proposals, particularly those addressing the question of how to spread out more of Nigeria's wealth to those in severe poverty, were generally absent.[50]

The May 29, 2007, presidential vote that brought President Umaru Yar'Adua to power marked an important moment in Nigeria's history. It offered an example of what consolidated democracies take for granted: a sitting democratically-elected president peacefully turning over the reins of power to a newly elected president. Yet, this event almost did not happen. In 2006, President Olusegun Obasanjo discussed pursuing a third term. The "third term project" became a major distraction, both to others' campaign efforts and to governance in Nigeria.

The discussion appeared designed to block the presidential aspirations of the sitting vice president, Atiku Abubakar, and weaken the move in various parts of the country to reconsider the idea that the president should come from the north.

By the end of the summer, Obasanjo had backed down from the "three term project," but the PDP then "suspended" Abubakar from the party for three months in late September 2006.[51] Since the party's primary vote was held on December 16, 2006, the suspension ended his chances to be the PDP's nominee. Abubakar then defected to the AC. After the Independent National Electoral Commission (INEC) initially declared him ineligible to run, the Nigerian Supreme Court unanimously ruled that he must be allowed on the ballot. He was, but he finished a distant third.

Elections in the Hybrid Electoral Systems of Germany and Mexico, and the SMD-MMD System in Iran

Germany and Mexico provide examples of how PR and FPTP approaches can be combined in unique ways, while Iran demonstrates other variants of the traditional FPTP-SMD format. The rules for election to the lower house in Germany, the *Bundestag,* are complicated. The system gives some seats to candidates on the basis of FPTP-SMD rules, and others through PR rules. In Mexico, both the Chamber of Deputies and the Senate are elected through a combination of FPTP and PR. The rules for dividing up the seats for the lower house are less complicated than Germany's, though the rules for the Senate elections are complex. In its *Majles* elections, Iran combines the SMD and MMD approaches, with many districts having only one corresponding legislative seat but others having as many as thirty. The electoral rules also require a candidate to receive above a percentage threshold of the votes in the district to win a seat. The most important rule in these elections, however, is the requirement that candidates be approved by the unelected Guardian Council in order to appear on the ballot.

Germany

Germany employs a mixed electoral system combining FPTP and PR for *Bundestag* elections. Voters get two votes, one of which is a vote for the representative of their electoral district and the other is a vote for a political party. Many voters make tactical choices and accordingly split their votes between two different parties in the hope of securing a desired coalition government. Half of the 598 *Bundestag* seats are distributed based on single-member districts and a simple plurality (FPTP) of the votes for individual candidates. The other 299 seats are filled by party lists on the basis of the party vote. Threshold rules prevent small splinter parties from winning representation. Thus, a party must win at least 5 percent of the party vote nationally or three single-member districts in order to win any seats.

The number of seats that a party wins in the FPTP district vote is deducted from its percentage of seats won by PR, although this is calculated based on the party's performance in each of the *Länder* rather than nationally. The overall effect of the electoral system is to allocate seats, roughly, as if it were a PR-only system. This provision helps smaller parties, who typically fail to win in the FPTP district races but finish above the 5 percent threshold in the PR vote. One of the more interesting rules of this system concerns this effort to distribute the total number of seats in the *Bundestag* as if it was a PR system rather than a hybrid one. A party that secures more seats through the FPTP district vote in any of the *Länder* than it would have earned if the electoral system were PR-only is not required to forfeit these "extra" seats. Instead, the number of these "overhang" seats are added to the total number of seats in the *Bundestag.* As a result, following the 2005 elections the *Bundestag* had 614 total seats.

Germany's complex hybrid electoral system produces a multiparty system and coalition governments.[52] As discussed in Chapter 7, the head of the largest party in the coalition becomes the German chancellor.[53] Most of the time, a coalition is forged among one of the larger parties and one of the smaller parties. However, there have been two instances of grand coalitions between the two largest parties, the CDU and SPD. The first grand coalition formed in response to Germany's first postwar recession, which the political elite perceived as an economic crisis, and lasted from 1966–1969. The second grand coalition, headed by CDU chancellor Angela Merkel, has been in office since 2005. Grand coalitions tend to be unstable because they force former electoral enemies together and because they threaten to drain support from the participants to parties at the extremes.

Mexico

The presidential election in Mexico is an FPTP national vote. While the Mexican political system resembles the American one in a number of ways, there is no electoral college and no *estado*-by-*estado* winner take all approach. The national election and the emerging multiparty system means that, as happened in 2006, a candidate could be elected president with less than 40 percent of the national vote.

Elections for the bicameral Congress are more complex. The 500-member Chamber of Deputies is selected through a combination of FPTP and PR. Of the 500 members, 300 are elected through FPTP arrangements and 200 through PR.

Senate elections also combine FPTP and PR arrangements. The 128 senators are selected based on a tally of votes within the 31 *estados* and the Federal District, as well as the country as a whole. Parties nominate a two-person slate in each state, and voters select their preferred pair. The pair that receives the most votes wins two senate seats from the *estado* (and the Federal District). An additional senate seat from each *estado* (and the Federal District) is given to the party that finishes second in the voting in that *estado*. This **second past the post (SPTP)** rule is also known as the **principle of the first minority**. It is designed to address the situation where a party finishes second in many FPTP races and gets no seats from them. Finally, thirty-two more senators are chosen based on the total votes across all the states. Divided on the basis of PR, these remaining senators are not linked to a particular state but are considered "senators-at-large."

Electoral results hinted at problems for the PRI throughout the 1980s and 1990s. In 1997, the PRI lost majority control of the Chamber of Deputies and, at least as important, control of the local government of the Federal District of Mexico City. This process culminated with the PRI losing control of the presidency in 2000. Mexico's most recent federal elections took place on July 2, 2006. Voters selected a new president to replace Vicente Fox and the 500 members of the Chamber of Deputies. There were a number of other local and regional elections, including for the important position of leader of Mexico City.

As presidential elections in many countries do, the 2006 vote for the Mexican president highlighted the country's regional divisions. The winner, Felipe Calderón of the PAN, defeated Andrés Manuel López Obrador, who represented an alliance that included the PRD. López Obrador, riding the wave of electoral success by left-of-center politicians in Latin America in the past decade, barely lost the election. The official vote count gave Calderón 35.9 percent to López Obrador's 35.3 percent. Despite López Obrador's claims of massive irregularities—claims challenged by European Union election monitors[54]—and protests by López Obrador's supporters when he was not declared the winner, Calderón succeeded Vicente Fox at the end of 2006. Calderón's support came largely from the north of Mexico, while López Obrador's support was concentrated in the south. Regional divisions in Mexico are nothing new, but the 2006 presidential election did show how much things had changed in Mexican politics in one respect. The PRI candidate, Roberto Madrazo Pintado, finished a distant third.

In the elections for the Chamber of Deputies, PAN candidates won the most districts (137). Receiving around 33.5 percent of the vote, the party also picked up nearly 70 more based on

The **second past the post (SPTP)** rule is also known as the **principle of the first minority**. It reserves seats in a particular body for the party that finishes second in a district election. This rule is used in Mexican senate elections.

Supporters of presidential candidate Andrés Manuel López Obrador, from the Party of Democratic Revolution (PRD), take part in a protest against the inauguration of Mexican President Felipe Calderón on December 1, 2006, in Mexico City. In the center, one supporter holds up a sign reading "Andrés Manuel López Obrador: The Real President of Mexico."

(©Yuri Cortez/AFP/Getty Images)

the results of the PR voting. The PRD-led Alliance for the Welfare of All won almost 100 of the district races. Receiving around 29 percent of the vote, it secured another 60 seats based on PR. Showing its weakening popularity and organizational strength, the PRI-led Alliance for Mexico won only 64 seats from the FPTP district races. However, it picked up almost 60 additional seats from the PR vote, after gaining over 28 percent of the vote nationally. These results again show the dramatic move away from the former one-party dominant system. The 2006 elections cut the presence of the PRI-led Alliance for Mexico in the Chamber of Deputies almost in half. Two small parties, the New Alliance Party and the Social Democratic and Peasant Alternative Party, won 9 and 4 seats, respectively, all from the PR portion of the vote.

In the senate, PAN ended up with 52 seats (32 from FPTP, 9 from SPTP, and 11 from PR). The PRD's Alliance for the Welfare of All won 36 seats (22, 4, and 10), while the PRI's Alliance for Mexico won 39 seats (10, 19, 10). Mexico's second past the post rule benefited the PRI greatly, with nearly half of its alliance's senate seats

earned through SPTP. The New Alliance Party gained the remaining senate seat on the basis of the PR arrangement.

Iran

Iran is an authoritarian system, and the level of electoral contestation for the *Majles* (the national legislature) and the presidency is significantly curtailed through the prohibition against certain types of candidates making it on the ballot. At the same time, elections matter in Iran. A more moderate legislature, particularly if combined with a moderate president, can put pressure on the more conservative unelected components of the government. Success of pro-reform candidates also points out to the government, to the broader population, and to observers outside Iran that many citizens continue to support a less hard line approach to politics and social policies.

After candidates register to stand for election to the *Majles*, there is a two-month period of review, during which their "legitimacy" to stand as candidates is ultimately determined by the Guardian Council, following initial screening by two other unelected bodies. Those who are approved to appear on the ballot run in electoral districts and vie for 285 of the 290 *Majles* seats, while the remaining 5 seats are set aside for religious minorities. Many of these districts have only one *Majles* seat associated with them, but the district of Tehran has thirty. Showing the size of Tehran compared with other cities in the country, no other electoral district in Iran has more than six seats.

In the first round of voting, a candidate must clear a certain threshold (currently 25 percent) to win a seat. If more candidates clear this threshold than the number of seats from the district, the top vote getters receive the seats. If not enough candidates clear the threshold to fill a district's seats, a second (runoff) round of voting takes place to fill the remaining seats. Twice as many candidates as open seats compete in the second round, with the candidates getting the most votes in the first round being the ones who face off in the second round.

Moderates did well in elections during Khatami's two terms as president, gaining control not only of the presidency but also of the *Majles* from 2000 to 2004. The pragmatic conservatives and hardliners, on the other hand, have done particularly well since 2004. The Guardian Council's decisions to bar many reformist candidates from seeking legislative or presidential office have played a role in the hardliners' successes. These actions of the Guardian Council were controversial both inside and outside the country, and reformers organized a boycott that drove down turnout in 2004. The Guardian Council repeated its efforts to keep reformers off the ballot in the 2008 *Majles* elections, helping conservatives maintain control despite growing disenchantment with President Ahmadinejad.

In the 2005 presidential race, Ahmadinejad was a surprising finalist, finishing in the top two in the first round of voting despite receiving less than 20 percent of the vote. In the runoff, Ahmadinejad won handily, gaining nearly 62 percent of the vote against his opponent, Akbar Hashemi-Rafsanjani. Rafsanjani had been president of the country from the late 1980s to the mid-1990s. At that time, some Western observers saw Rafsanjani as a hardliner—a view reinforced by Khatami's subsequently more moderate positions—but today most see him as a pragmatic conservative. He has worked to improve the Iranian economy and, during his time as president, had supported closer ties with the West.

Ahmadinejad portrayed Rafsanjani as a supporter of the corrupt, wealth-concentrating status quo and himself as a supporter of policies designed to help ordinary Iranians.[55] Western observers have tended to focus on Ahmadinejad's anti-U.S. and anti-Israel statements and his more hardline interpretation of social and cultural practices in the country. In the end, however, the 2005 election was as much about economics as about Islam or Israel.

(Local) Elections in China

Though China is a one-party state, not all elections are meaningless. The government has resisted pressures to liberalize politically at the national level, but it does give some voters a say at the local level. The practice of allowing more genuine elections in small towns began in 1980, when village elders in two rural counties sought greater control over practices they saw as hostile to traditional, Communist farming practices. The result was "villagers' committees" (also called village committees), bodies that did not control state resources but did set certain policies within their communities.[56] Within two years, villagers' committees were in the constitution, though open elections to determine who held positions on them took longer.

While understandably unpopular with many existing local government officials, leaders in the central government were also divided about the wisdom of allowing genuine self-government. Far from all of China's 930,000 villages participated in open villagers' committee elections during the 1990s. Many village leaders resisted implementing the reform entirely, and even in the villages that have instituted competitive elections, many have met the bare minimum official government requirement of one more overall candidate than open position to fill.[57]

Still, the long-term importance of these elections should not be dismissed.[58] Just as the large, urban special economic zones had been experiments with capitalism before its more general acceptance, the selection of village officials through competitive elections is an experiment in self-government. While the CCP tightly controls the nomination of officials for the indirect election of leaders at higher levels of government, candidates for village elections are not always those preferred by local CCP officials. For now, this experiment is seen as helpful to the government's maintenance of political power.

Topic in countries

COMPARATIVE EXERCISE

Duverger's Law and Canadian Elections

Maurice Duverger believed that electoral systems have two basic consequences, which he labeled psychological and mechanical. Psychological consequences relate to how voters and candidates behave in light of electoral rules; mechanical consequences concern how the votes in an election actually translate into seats in the legislature.[59] One of Duverger's claims, that FPTP systems encourage two-party systems, has so much logical and empirical support behind it that it is known as **Duverger's Law**.[60] Even Duverger argued that the idea that a FPTP system encourages a stable two-party system "approaches . . . a true sociological law."[61]

Why would FPTP arrangements encourage a two-party system? For a multiparty system to remain in place over time, smaller parties must be able to translate votes from the general public into at least some seats in the national legislature. With FPTP rules, small national parties tend to get votes across a large number of electoral districts but win the election in few or even none of those districts. As a result, voters become increasingly reluctant to "waste their votes" on third parties, deciding instead between the two main parties.

Duverger first proposed his ideas about the relationship between electoral systems and party systems in the early 1950s, and it is certainly possible that evidence since then would call his theory about FPTP systems into question. To test Duverger's argument in more recent times, one could conduct a case study, a comparative study, a large N statistical analysis, or a combination of these approaches. The comparative exercise here focuses on a case study of a FPTP system. A case study is particularly appropriate, since Duverger himself suggested his theory's universal nature. In other words, it was supposed to hold in all cases, and finding a counter example would call the "lawlike" nature of his argument into question.

The earlier discussion of the United Kingdom's two-and-a-half party system cast some doubt on Duverger's Law. Like the United Kingdom, Canada combines a parliamentary system with a FPTP district electoral system. Over the last two decades, Canadian elections have provided interesting evidence regarding Duverger's Law.

Overview of the Canadian Case

Prior to parliamentary elections in 1993, Canada was a two-and-half party system. In 1988, the Conservative Party, which had recently renamed itself the Progressive Conservative Party, won a majority (169) of the 295 district races for seats in the Canadian House of Commons. As a result, its leader was prime minister and it controlled the Canadian federal government. The Liberal Party, a moderate to left-of-center party, was a strong second place party with 83 seats, while the New Democratic Party (NDP), a social democratic party, had 43 seats.

For a variety of reasons, including a number of scandals involving the party and the emergence of regional parties, the Conservatives suffered one of the most massive electoral defeats in history in 1993. Following this election, the Conservatives held *only two seats in the parliament*, failing to gain enough seats even to be recognized as an official party in parliament under Canadian rules. Many observers viewed the 1993 elections as not only the death knell of the Conservative Party but also possibly of the two-and-a-half party system as well.

The main beneficiary of the Conservatives' collapse was the Liberal Party. The Liberals won 177 seats in 1993, over 120 more seats than their closest rival in parliament. The party went on to control the Canadian government for more than a decade and looked at first to be poised to be the

Duverger's Law is the term used to describe Maurice Duverger's argument that FPTP electoral systems generate two-party systems.

dominant party in a one-party dominant system. The second place party was a new player on the scene, the Bloc Quebecois, a nationalist party supporting independence for the province of Quebec. Though it ran candidates in only 75 of the 295 districts, it won 54 of those seats. The third-place party was another newcomer, the Reform Party, a right-of-center party with strong support in the west of the country. It ran in 207 districts and won 52 of them. Though not as dramatically as the Progressive Conservatives, the NDP was also a big loser in 1993, gaining only 9 seats and falling to less than 7 percent of the national vote.

The Liberal Party remained the majority party following elections in 1997 and 2000. The Reform Party entered into an alliance with former Conservative Party members in 2000 (forming the Canadian Alliance party) but made few inroads into the Liberals' dominance. In June 2004, however, new elections took place. By then, the Canadian Alliance had completely disbanded, replaced by a revived Conservative Party. The Liberals won the most seats in 2004 (135), but they fell well short of the 155 seats needed to control the (now 308-seat) parliament. The revived Conservative Party of Canada was right on the heels of the Liberals, winning 99 seats. The Liberals entered into a coalition agreement with the NDP, but its 19 seats only took the coalition to 154 seats, and a number of important measures failed to pass. The resulting minority government was fragile, and a vote of no-confidence brought new elections in January 2006.

In 2006, the pendulum continued to swing toward its pre-1993 form: the Conservatives won the most seats (124), the Liberals were relegated to the number two party, and the NDP recovered to gain twenty-nine seats on 17.5 percent of the national vote. Thus, the 2006 elections marked a *possible* revival of the two-and-a-half party system. However, the Conservatives did not gain a majority of the seats in parliament in 2006. They secured only around 36 percent of the national vote, and their roughly 40 percent of parliamentary seats was the lowest percentage ever by a ruling party.

This pattern continued when Prime Minister Stephen Harper called for early elections in October 2008. The Conservatives received the most votes (38 percent) and seats, but they still controlled only 46 percent of the seats in the House of Commons. Harper remained prime minister, overseeing his second consecutive minority government.

Discussion

Along with similar traits in the United Kingdom, Canada's combination of FPTP electoral arrangements and two-and-a-half party systems calls into question Duverger's Law. What explains the ability of smaller parties to garner notable vote totals in Canada? Part of the answer lies in the powerful regional divisions, sometimes fueled by ethnic nationalism. The importance of regionalism in Canada points to the need to amend Duverger's Law to consider the role of identity divisions that break down along regional lines.

Because supporters of smaller parties are concentrated in particular parts of the country, candidates from these small parties can actually win a majority of the vote (and thus a seat) in a number of electoral districts. The Bloc Quebecois is a party based in only one of Canada's provinces, but its ability to win around one-sixth of the seats in the parliament clearly disrupts Duverger's calculus about FPTP arrangements. In addition, the Liberals tend to do well in the eastern part of the country, while the Conservatives do better in the west. Whichever of these two large parties is better able to move into the other's territory is likely to win the most seats.

Unlike the United Kingdom, however, Canadian elections have not even perpetuated the two-and-half party system. In light of Duverger's Law, electoral results in Canada have been simply chaotic. There is little in Duverger's Law to explain a majority party being wiped out, reconstituted, and coming back to lead a minority government.

It will be interesting to watch future Canadian elections. Like two-party systems, the two-and-a-half party variant appears to be able *either* to perpetuate itself *or*, in the aftermath of a significant shock, at least to reconstitute itself in relatively short order. But if future elections continue to give neither of the two main Canadian parties majority control of parliament, the country would fall into the multiparty system category. This would require more than an "amendment" to Duverger's Law to include two-and-half party systems. It would require a fundamental restatement of

Duverger's Law: FPTP systems encourage two-party systems *except in countries with strong regional divisions*.

Think and Discuss

Does the existence of regionally-strong third parties in the United Kingdom and Canada have implications for the United States? Could American third parties be successful if they adopted a regional strategy rather than trying to run as national parties?

CONCLUSION

Comparativists interested in mass participation and elite-mass linkage commonly examine political parties and elections in democratic political systems. In democracies, parties and elections are part of a complex relationship. Parties and their candidates compete for office through elections. Yet, electoral rules partially determine which (and how many) parties and candidates are successful. As discussed in this chapter, Germany's parliamentary system employs a complex set of electoral arrangements. The direct elections to the lower house, the *Bundestag*, use a hybrid electoral system combining elements of FPTP and PR. The result is a multiparty system, with two relatively large parties and a number of smaller ones. Because the two larger parties fail to secure a majority of the seats in the *Bundestag*, coalition governments are the norm.

In addition, changes in patterns of a country's electoral outcomes, as well as changes in its party system, can represent other fundamental changes in its political structure. No part of Mexico's transition to democracy has been more visible than the move from a one-party dominant system controlled by the Institutional

Revolutionary Party (PRI) to a system based on genuine multiparty competition.

Finally, social divisions in many democracies affect the nature of parties and party systems, but the practice of voting can also deepen those social divisions. In new democracies in particular, electoral politics and identity politics frequently become intertwined. In Nigeria, the PDP's control of the national government masks strong regional showings by other parties, which increasingly turn to identity-based appeals to head off the PDP's growing dominance.

Nondemocratic systems also generally incorporate both political parties and elections. China shows how a dominant political party can be the vehicle for authoritarian political control, although other nondemocratic leaders appear increasingly compelled to hold national elections. As countries such as Iran (and, increasingly, Russia) demonstrate, however, political leaders often work both openly and behind the scenes to prevent these elections from being genuine contests that threaten the ruling government's control of the state.

Think and Discuss

The previous chapter discussed nonelectoral mechanisms for linking elites and masses. This chapter focused on political parties and elections. Which of these sets of mechanisms are more important for understanding how mass participation and masses are linked to elites? Why?

The next chapter focuses more closely on individuals and their political decisions. Up to this point, there have been various accounts of the way that individual leaders matter to a political system, how elites and masses interact, and some of the factors that influence individuals' decisions to participate (or not participate) in collective political activities. At the same time, the starting point for these discussions has been the concern with structures: economic, cultural, identity, and political. Chapter 11 moves squarely to the "choice" side of the structure versus choice framework, focusing on individuals and their decision making.

Key Terms

Catch-all parties, p. 372
Cleavage structure theory of party systems, p. 378
Critical elections, p. 375
Duverger's Law, p. 400
Election, p. 383
First past the post (FPTP), p. 385
Hybrid electoral system, p. 387
Majority (majoritarian) system, p. 386
Multi-member district (MMD), p. 386
Multiparty system, p. 367
One-party dominant system, p. 365
One-party system, p. 365
Open list proportional representation, p. 388
Party identification, p. 364
Party organization theory, p. 381
Party system, p. 364
Political parties, p. 363
Preference system, p. 386
Primary election, p. 385
Principle of the first minority, p. 397
Proportional representation (PR), p. 384
Realignment theory, p. 375
Runoff, p. 386
Second past the post (SPTP), p. 397
Single-member district (SMD), p. 385
Single transferable vote (STV) system, p. 386
Threshold, p. 384
Two-and-a-half party system, p. 366
Two-party system, p. 366

Learning Objectives

After reading this chapter, you should be able to:

- Describe the basic features of the choice approach.

- Discuss the differences among leadership traits, skills, and style.

- Discuss the strengths and weaknesses of focusing on leadership as a way of understanding political outcomes.

- Provide examples from the chapter about the importance of specific individuals in shaping political outcomes.

- Explain rational choice theory and propose criticisms of it.

11

Leadership and Individual Political Choices

During World War II, the country of Bulgaria was under the leadership of King Boris III. Hoping to be able to regain territories in Macedonia, Greece, and Serbia that Bulgaria had lost in earlier wars, the king agreed to an alliance with Nazi Germany. As part of dealing with Nazi Germany, the Bulgarian government secretly agreed to send at least 20,000 Jews to Poland, where they were to be placed in concentration camps. The majority of these were to come from the regions Bulgaria had seized from neighboring countries, but between 6,000 and 8,000 were to come from Bulgaria itself.

As the deportation process was about to begin in Bulgaria, the vice president of the Bulgarian National Assembly, Dimitar Peshev, went public about the secret plan.[1] Forty-two others in the legislature signed a letter to the king and Prime Minister Bogdan Filov, asking that the deportations be stopped. His actions led leaders of the Orthodox Church

Look for this icon to point you to **Deepening Your Understanding** features on the companion website www.college.cengage.com/politicalscience/barrington, which provide greater depth for some key content.

in Sofia to speak out, and mass demonstrations broke out in opposition to the plan. While some in the Bulgarian government began discussing a new plan to deport all of the nearly 50,000 Jews in Bulgaria,[2] the king instead ordered Bulgaria's Jews to be put into internal exile, many in labor camps, within Bulgaria rather than being turned over to the Nazis. Although more than 10,000 Jews from Bulgarian-controlled neighboring regions had already been deported, the king's refusal to follow through with the plan to begin deporting the Jews inside Bulgaria as well—a decision sparked by Peshev's courageous choice to speak out against the deportation plan—saved the lives of thousands of Bulgarian Jews. ■

To this point, much of this textbook has focused on the economic, social, and political settings within which political outcomes occur. As important as these socioeconomic and political structures can be, political outcomes are, most directly, the result of political choices. Those choices are made by individuals—many by political leaders such as Dimitar Peshev and King Boris III, others by ordinary citizens. Political scientist Eric Selbin, highlights the importance of both elite and mass choices in revolutions:

> Leaders play a unique role in social revolutions, organizing the population, and perhaps most importantly, articulating the vision—the ideas and ideals—around which they rally. The population, in turn, responds to these entreaties or not; if they do, it is they who determine how far and how fast the process unfolds and often shape the efforts of the leaders to their reality. We need fundamentally to refocus the discussion of profound change or transformation on the power and possibility of individuals to control their destiny.[3]

This chapter addresses the importance of individuals in politics. Most history textbook accounts of specific political events (revolutions, wars, dramatic policy reforms, etc.) emphasize the individuals and their decisions, but structural explanations typically receive more attention in comparative politics.[4] In this book, the concentration on individuals and their decisions is referred to as the **choice approach**. In other books, it is known as focusing on "agency," referring to the idea of individuals as agents of political change.[5]

Other terms comparativists use to refer to the choice approach include elite-focused explanation, micro-approach, intentionalism, voluntarism, and decision-making analysis.

Individual-based explanations of political outcomes spotlight two somewhat distinct ideas. The first holds that the traits of individual political figures make a big difference in determining political outcomes and centers on the concept of leadership. History is often taught through an examination of the actions of great leaders. Of course, bad leaders are no less important, and not all political decisions are good ones. Government leaders' misperceptions can play an important role in political outcomes. Given the importance that the focus on leadership places on the background and style of political leaders, the first set of Topic in Countries discussions in this chapter highlights these characteristics of the countries' current and important recent leaders.

Arguing that individual leaders' traits are crucial to political outcomes, however, is problematic. How can one develop and test theories about unique individual leaders at different points in time and in varying settings around the world? The choice approach anchors itself to individuals, but it does not stop there. The

The **choice approach** explains political outcomes by looking at the effects of individuals and their political decisions. Theories based on the choice approach tend to focus on general concepts such as leadership and decision making.

ultimate goal of most scholars employing choice theories is to understand political action in a general sense. The discussion of a particular leader, for example, is placed in the context of broader understandings of leadership.

This is also true of those who focus on the second half of the choice approach's dual nature: individual decision making. Theories about decision making seek to explain how individuals, in general, approach the process of making a political decision. Such theories are based on generalizable ideas (e.g., that humans act rationally to maximize the likelihood of realizing their personal interests). Explanations of specific political events—such as democratization in a particular country—might highlight the role of individual action, but *theorizing* about democratization moves choice into the more generalizable realm of decision making. In addition to presenting a number of theories about decision making, this chapter's second set of Topic in Countries sections examines the role of individuals in shaping important political events in each country, by analyzing an event or decision in light of how rational it appears to have been.

Leadership and the Importance of Individuals in the Political Process

The traits of individuals making political decisions have an impact on the form those decisions take. One of the key ways that political decision makers in positions of power differ from one another is in their ability as leaders. Thus, a great deal of work across social science disciplines has been conducted on **leadership**.

Leadership is the ability to influence members of a particular group to achieve a set of defined goals, ideally without making them feel forced to do so. Successful leaders hold positions of authority but also have the ability to convince or inspire those they lead to take certain actions. This ability might come from the leader's captivating style— psychologist Howard Gardner states that leaders must be good "storytellers"[6]—or it may result

from an effective argument about the necessity of the task at hand.

Political scientists utilize a number of concepts and perspectives on leadership, including many that were originally developed in other disciplines like psychology and business administration. Across these different perspectives, one can identify three important themes: successful leaders have certain common character traits, successful leaders develop certain skills that contribute to their effectiveness, and successful leaders tend to have particular leadership styles that help them to reach their goals.

Those who emphasize **leadership traits** view the ability to lead as driven by particular in-born traits such as general intelligence as opposed to learned skills. Trait theory proposes that an individual possessing these traits can more effectively achieve key policy goals. Although this view of leadership has been around since the early 1900s, it has failed to gain wide acceptance. In addition to recognizing that leadership may involve more than innate features, scholars have not been able to agree on the exact list of essential traits or how to identify and measure them.

Rather than search for natural and rather fixed characteristics, other social scientists turned their attention to **leadership skills**—focusing on attributes of leaders that can be learned and developed. These include technical knowledge about the subject in question, the ability to work well with people, and the capacity to grasp a problem conceptually and express a vision about addressing it. These individual attributes create "competencies" that drive leadership outcomes.[7]

Leadership is the ability to influence a group to achieve goals through the combination of a position of authority, effective argumentation, and charisma.

Leadership traits are innate personal qualities that make for a successful leader.

Leadership skills are qualities that can be developed, such as technical expertise and the ability to work with others.

The concept of **leadership style**, connected to arguments from psychology about the importance of personality, considers how leaders approach relationships with colleagues and subordinates. One can consider, for example, the extent to which a leader is relationship-oriented or task-oriented. Leaders who combine both orientations are more likely to be successful at achieving their policy goals than those who possess one or neither. This view of leadership is a common approach to examining leaders in studies of business management, educational administration, and health care.

> **Leadership style** emphasizes the approaches leaders take, including task-oriented behaviors and relationship-oriented behaviors.

Leaders in the United Kingdom

With its monarchs of the past and its often charismatic prime ministers in more recent times, the United Kingdom is a country where individuals have had a tremendous influence on the evolution of the political system. In recent decades, these leaders have included controversial and persuasive prime ministers such as Margaret Thatcher and Tony Blair, as well as more workmanlike prime ministers such as John Major and the current British leader, Gordon Brown.

Current Leader: Gordon Brown

Inheriting the reins of power from Tony Blair, a politician he both admired and clashed with, Gordon Brown became the United Kingdom's prime minister in 2007. Born in Glasgow, Scotland, in 1951, Brown grew up in the industrial city of Kirkcaldy, just north of Edinburgh. His seat today in the House of Commons represents the district of which Kirkcaldy is a part.

Influenced by his minister father and his industrial surroundings, Brown developed an interest in economics with a focus on such problems as unemployment, which the British working class faced in the latter decades of the twentieth century. Having excelled in school, Brown started at Edinburgh University at the age of sixteen. At the university, Brown began his political career, a career that would see him rise quickly through the ranks of the Labour Party.

Brown earned a seat in the House of Commons at the age of thirty-two, sharing an office

Tony Blair (Right) accompanied by Gordon Brown speaks during a campaign visit to Bristol, England on April 25, 2005. At the time, Blair was British Prime Minister, while Brown was the Chancellor of the Exchequer.
(© Matt Cardy/Getty Images)

with another new MP, thirty-year-old Tony Blair. Labour Party leader Neil Kinnock eventually promoted both of them into the Labour shadow cabinet. The two also became rivals. In the mid-1990s, Blair and Brown struck a deal, involving Brown's support of Blair for party leader and Blair's promise to give Brown significant control over domestic policy if Labour were to become the governing party.

In 1997, the Labour Party won parliamentary elections by an unexpectedly large margin, and Brown joined Blair's first cabinet. He held the powerful position of chancellor of the exchequer, somewhat equivalent to a minister of finance or the treasury and seen in the United Kingdom as the most powerful domestic political position after the prime minister. For the next decade, Blair and Brown had a tense relationship. After the Labour Party's narrow victory in 2005, the stage was set for Brown to take control from Blair, something that finally happened in June 2007. Whether Brown will be able to continue the Labour Party dominance of British politics remains to be seen. While he lacks Blair's charisma, Brown is known as a driven and tireless worker, a tough negotiator, and, as evidenced by his rise to the top of British politics, someone not to be underestimated.

Important Recent Leader: Tony Blair

Tony Blair rose to become one of the more influential prime ministers in British history through a combination of a vision to reform the British political system, his charisma and eloquence, and the sizeable majority that his Labour Party held in the House of Commons. Becoming head of the Labour Party at the age of forty, Blair led Labour to landslide electoral victories in the 1997, 2001, and 2005 House of Commons elections. With sizeable majorities, he was able to enact many policies with ease and even begin to tackle problems many thought impossible to resolve, such as the makeup and role of the House of Lords.

Though less controlling in cabinet meetings than previous prime ministers, such as Margaret Thatcher, Blair developed a reputation for micromanaging—a change from the way the prime minister before him, John Major, let his ministers run their ministries with significant autonomy. Blair became less popular during his second term, partly due to opposition among the British public to the United Kingdom's participation in the Iraq War. He faced his biggest electoral challenge in the 2005 elections but again delivered, becoming the only Labour Party leader in history to win three straight elections.

Important Recent Leader: Margaret Thatcher

The daughter of a shopkeeper, Margaret Thatcher was elected to parliament in her mid-thirties and became a part of the cabinet (education minister) in her mid-forties. When she led the Conservatives to victory and became prime minister in 1979, she did so on a platform of controlling labor union influence and limiting the growth of government spending. Arguing forcefully for the superiority of the market and the dangers of excessive government intervention in the economy, she privatized large government-run companies such as British Airways and British Steel.

Thatcher had a great deal of success in introducing significant political and economic reforms, certainly more than many people expected when she first proposed them. Her success was due in part to her strong personality and almost dictatorial control of her cabinet. The Soviet government gave her the nickname the "Iron Lady," which certainly fit her leadership style. Not only was she the first female prime minister in Europe, Thatcher became the first British prime minister to hold the position for three consecutive terms.

Margaret Thatcher on the May 14, 1979, cover of Time Magazine.

(©Time & Life Pictures/Getty Images)

Her leadership style also played a role in her ultimate undoing. Members of the Conservative Party grew tired of her iron hand, and when her popularity waned among the public as well, other top Conservative Party officials turned on her and removed her as party leader. By replacing her as party leader, John Major also became the country's prime minister. Major was more of a coalition builder in the cabinet, listening to the advice of his ministers rather than telling them what to do. At the same time, he lacked Thatcher's vision and charisma, which helped pave the way for the resurgence of the Labour Party and the rise of Tony Blair to the forefront of British politics.

Leaders in Germany

Germany's political system disperses executive power through coalition governments, federalism, and a policymaking process that grants key interest groups a strong voice in negotiating and implementing policy. Still, some chancellors have proved to be strong leaders. Their personalities and their skill have transformed the political system's structural constraints into opportunities.

Current Leader: Angela Merkel

Chancellor Angela Merkel heads the grand coalition of the Christian Democrats (CDU) and Social Democrats (SPD) formed in 2005. Hardworking and with a formidable intellect, she rose quickly through the ranks of the CDU to become party chair in 2000.[8] She is Germany's first female chancellor and the first chancellor of the Federal Republic from the east. Merkel is not a typical CDU politician in other respects—she is Protestant, divorced, without children, and a scientist with an advanced degree in physics.

Many believed that the chancellor would have great difficulty enforcing discipline on the two rival parties turned governing partners, and that the grand coalition would be short-lived. But, at least for the few first years of the coalition, this was not the case. In fact, Chancellor Merkel brought problem-solving skills that she honed in her earlier career as a physicist to her leadership of the coalition. She developed a reputation as a good listener who allows all sides to air their views before pursuing a consensus

German Chancellor Angela Merkel gestures during a press conference on July 23, 2008, in Berlin, Germany.
(©Andreas Rentz/Getty Images)

decision.[9] Moreover, Merkel took advantage of commanding majorities in the *Bundestag* and in the *Bundesrat* to focus her energy on forging agreements among top party leaders in her coalition and to bypass the usual influence of interest groups.[10] With a *Bundestag* election looming in 2009, however, the grand coalition may become more fractious as the CDU and SPD regard each other as rivals rather than partners. If so, it will severely test Merkel's domestic leadership skills.[11]

In addition to her domestic political successes, Merkel has also shown herself to be a strong leader in foreign policy matters. European leaders viewed favorably her tenure as president of the European Union's Council of Ministers. She was also able to repair relations between

Germany and the United States, which had been badly strained by the Iraq War.

Important Recent Leader: Helmut Kohl

Helmut Kohl is most famous for his role in German unification and for being the chancellor with the longest tenure in office. Kohl assumed the chancellorship of the newly formed coalition government of the Christian Democrats and Free Democrats (FDP) in 1982 following the FDP's abandonment of its previous coalition with the Social Democrats. Kohl led his party to four consecutive election victories until the Christian-Liberal coalition's defeat in the 1998 *Bundestag* elections.

Kohl was not a charismatic leader. He was from Rhineland-Palatinate, a largely rural *Land* in West Germany. He was provincial rather than worldly and did not know languages other than his own German tongue. Yet, these traits masked considerable political skills. He was an astute manager who rewarded loyalists and

kept ambitious CDU *Land* party leaders in line. Moreover, he proved to be attuned to the mood of the majority of Germans who yearned for unification at the end of the 1980s. He pushed forward the process of German unification and was rewarded with a decisive victory in the first all-German parliamentary elections in 1990.

Helmut Kohl's achievements were strongest in the area of foreign policy, but his record in domestic policy, especially on economic management, was less stellar. Becoming chancellor in 1982 amid a deep recession, Kohl was unable to overcome subsequent sluggish growth and high unemployment in the West German economy.[12] The collapse of the eastern economy in the mid-1990s belied his earlier election promises of eastern prosperity and no new taxes. Finally, a scandal over party financing marred the end of his chancellorship. He left office with a mixed reputation, despite being one of post–World War II Germany's most important political figures.

Leaders in France

French governance is the product of expertise and ideology. But a predilection for populist leaders and the ongoing role of "notables" within the circles of high politics place a great deal of weight on the strengths and personalities of individual leaders. With its dual executive at the national level, and a quasi-parliamentary system at the local level where mayors are elected by municipal councils, the president and the local mayor have come to embody the nation, the city, or town—and so the French Republic as well.

Current Leader: Nicolas Sarkozy

Elected in 2007, President Nicolas Sarkozy in many ways represents a profound break with the elite leadership of the Fifth Republic. Unlike his predecessors, who include two alumni of the *École Nationale d'Administration*, Sarkozy was never a stellar student and failed to graduate from one of the *grandes écoles*. Though he was

born into a solidly bourgeois family, his father was a Hungarian immigrant, and his maternal grandfather was a Jewish immigrant. While Mitterrand was well known to have a mistress, Sarkozy himself was the first president of France to be divorced, having left his first wife and married a former fashion model. His second marriage ended in divorce only a few months after he was elected president, and he has since remarried. Unlike his predecessors, Sarkozy is also known for what many French consider an unusual fondness for American culture.

Sarkozy came to be known as a talented and adept politician. In 1983, when he was not even thirty years old, Sarkozy became the youngest person ever elected mayor of a major city in France. Five years later, he was elected to the National Assembly. In his early years, he was a protégé of Gaullist leader Jacques Chirac, mayor and leader of the RPR. But Sarkozy turned his back on Chirac to serve as budget minister in the government of his mentor's chief rival, Édouard Balladur. Despite Chirac's victory over Balladur in the 1995 presidential election, Sarkozy became party leader in 1999. With the stunning success of the 2002 election, Sarkozy forced himself into the government, overseeing the powerful Interior Ministry. Though he would later serve in the more prestigious position of finance minister, Sarkozy, preferring law and order issues, as well as the influence of the Interior Ministry, returned as interior minister in 2005. While establishing a Muslim Council and appointing the first Muslim to serve as prefect, he also expelled undocumented immigrants and cracked down on crime.

Two violent encounters mark Sarkozy's image as an advocate of law and order. The first was a 1993 hostage taking at a kindergarten in Neuilly. As mayor of the city, Sarkozy entered the school to negotiate directly with the hostage taker who had strapped explosives to his body. The incident ended in a police assault and the death of the hostage taker. In 2005, Sarkozy was condemned and praised for his response to rioting in the poor housing projects on the outskirts of Paris, after a police pursuit ended with the deaths of two boys who were hiding in an electrical substation. In the first days of the unrest, Interior Minister Sarkozy called the rioters "scum."[13] Further angered by Sarkozy's words and the actions of the police under his direction as interior minister, the demonstrators continued the violence for twenty nights.

France's Most Important Local Leader: Bertrand Delanoë

Socialist Bertrand Delanoë could be Sarkozy's chief rival for president in 2012. While "important leaders" are typically found in national government, the position of Mayor of Paris, the capital of France, carries with it significant standing. Like Sarkozy, Delanoë has an unusual pedigree and is part of the new generation of French leaders who rose to prominence without the benefit of an elite education. He was born and raised in

what is now Tunisia, and his father is a native of the two small islands off the Atlantic coast of Canada that remain part of France. Delanoë was also the first openly gay man elected mayor of a major city anywhere in the world.

Delanoë followed Mitterrand's rise to power, joining the Socialist Party in 1971, advancing to a position of leadership as part of a new generation around future Prime Minister Lionel Jospin. Elected first to the Paris municipal council and then the National Assembly in the Socialist landslide of 1981, he was named spokesperson for the party. But Delanoë ultimately grew unhappy in politics after he was passed over in the next elections, instead turning to business in 1986 and maintaining only a foothold in public life on the Paris municipal council.

In 1993, he became leader of the Socialist opposition in Paris and was elected senator by the electoral college for the capital in 1995, working to forge a local coalition between the Socialists, the Communist Party, and the Greens. With the debate over public recognition for same-gender relationships, Delanoë again grew frustrated with the tenor of politics, and came out informally as part of an interview on a national televised news show in 1998. But he did not embrace full marriage rights, as many gays and lesbians wanted, instead arguing that marriage was a heterosexual institution.[14] Considered bland, Delanoë had to fend off potential rivals as the city geared up for an electoral contest pitting the Left, out of city hall for a century, against the Right that had been marred by a variety of corruption scandals. Nevertheless, Delanoë was elected mayor with a clear majority and a call for greater citizen participation in governance and a new emphasis on the diverse cultures of Paris. He has been criticized by the opposition for popular but flashy programs such as the annual "Paris Plage" festival, where sand and palm trees make the banks of the Seine into a tropical beach, and by the Left for favoring mere window dressing instead of real reforms.

Topic in Countries

Leaders in India

All of India's top leaders since independence in 1947 have achieved office through elections. For the first thirty years, the principal leaders came solely out of the Indian National Congress (INC). Although the INC has remained a key provider of such leaders in the years since, other parties have successfully challenged the monopoly. Today, the top leadership comes either from the INC or from the Bharatiya Janata Party (BJP), yet they rule through coalitions, which means that the leaders of many other parties hold ministerial positions.

Within the INC, there has been a strong tendency toward what many observers call "dynastic rule." This began with the first prime minister, Jawaharlal Nehru. His daughter, Indira Gandhi, held the same office, as did her son, Rajiv Gandhi. Rajiv's wife, Sonia Gandhi, is currently the leader of the INC and its parliamentary party. Rajiv and Sonia Gandhi's son, Rahul Gandhi, is now a general secretary in the INC. This tendency for "inheriting" leadership positions recurs in other parties and in the governance of many of the federal units.

Current Leader: Manmohan Singh

When the INC won more *Lok Sabha* seats than any other party in the 2004 general elections, the party leader, Sonia Gandhi, decided against becoming prime minister and endorsed Dr. Manmohan Singh for that position. A Sikh born in 1932 in a part of the Punjab that is now in Pakistan, much of the story of Dr. Singh's background involves education and the development of technical expertise. He earned a B.A. and M.A. in economics from Panjab University in Chandigarh, another undergraduate degree from Cambridge University, and a Ph.D. from Oxford. He moved quickly through the professorial ranks at Panjab University, and he published widely on economic issues.

Manmohan Singh's career took him to a variety of positions in academia, the United Nations, the International Monetary Fund, and with the Indian government as a governor of the Reserve Bank of India and in a variety of other positions. When INC's Narasimha Rao became prime minister in 1991, he selected Singh as his finance minister. Responding to serious balance-of-payment problems, Singh instituted economic reforms that initiated a significant shift to a liberalized economy. Unlike most of his predecessors, he was elected to the *Rajya Sabha*, rather than the *Lok Sabha*, in 1991 and reelected since 1995 from the federal unit of Assam. He became prime minister on May 22, 2004. As prime minister, he is widely viewed as honest, intelligent, and—befitting his background—more of a technocrat than a politician.

India's Other Current Leader: Sonia Gandhi

The leader of the INC parliamentary party and of the ruling United Democratic Alliance, Sonia Gandhi was born Sonia Antonia Maino in a village near Vincenza, Italy, in 1946. In 1964, she went to study English at The Bell Educational Trust language school in Cambridge, where she met Rajiv Gandhi, who was at Cambridge University (Trinity College). He was Hindu and she was Roman Catholic. They were married in India in 1968.

Rajiv Gandhi did not want to enter politics, but was drawn in after his mother, Indira Gandhi, was assassinated by her Sikh bodyguards in 1984. Following his assassination by a Sri Lankan Tamil in 1991, Sonia Gandhi initially refused to enter politics. Nevertheless, following persistent pressure, she joined the INC six years later and became its president the following year. In 1999, she was elected to the thirteenth *Lok Sabha* and chosen leader of the Opposition. Three senior INC leaders, who subsequently resigned from the party, challenged her selection because of her foreign birth. (In fact, she was the third person of foreign birth to lead the Congress Party.) When the INC gained a plurality of seats in the *Lok Sabha* in 2004 and she refused to become prime minister, she was widely praised for the selfless act. Her decision shielded her from strong BJP opposition to a foreign-born person assuming the prime ministership. In 2007, *Forbes* magazine ranked her as the sixth most powerful woman in the world.

Important Recent Leader: Atal Bihari Vajpayee

The prime minister who preceded Manmohan Singh was Atal Bihari Vajpayee. Unlike Singh, Atal Vajpayee had been a political leader almost his whole life. Born in the Princely State of Gwalior, a part of what is now the federal unit of Madhya Pradesh, he was drawn into politics at an early age. A high caste Brahmin (and respected poet), he became involved with the Hindu nationalist Rashtriya Swamyamsevak Sangh (RSS) and was a founding member of its associated political party, the Bharatiya Jana Sangh (BJS) in 1951.

First elected to the *Lok Sabha* in 1957, Vajpayee was a member of the *Lok Sabha* or the *Rajya Sabha* for almost fifty years. He was a founding member and first president of the successor to the BJS, the BJP, founded in 1980.

When the BJP won the most seats in the 1996 *Lok Sabha* election, he was appointed prime minister but was unable to form a majority coalition. After the 1998 elections, the BJP was again asked to form a government. This time, Vajpayee succeeded in putting together a majority government, but the coalition was brought down the next year. Following the 1999 elections, in which the BJP won a plurality of seats, he was able to put together a coalition that lasted until 2004.

Vajpayee's moderate leadership was criticized from the right and the left. His critics in the *Hindutva* movement complained about his efforts to regularize relations with Pakistan, to gain Muslim support, and his failure to build the Ram Temple at Ayodhya. His critics on the left condemned his failure to help the poor in India's villages and towns. To many Indians, however, he was a respected political leader, whose experience generated a degree of stability in the government during a difficult period in Indian national politics.

Leaders in Mexico

The struggle for independence from Spain and the subsequent Mexican Revolution involved some of the more colorful individuals in history. For those interested in revolutionary uprisings, Mexico provides a wonderful case. It is ironic, therefore, that more recent Mexican history involves a long period of stable governance under relatively bland leaders. But lacking flair does not mean one is weak or unimportant. Some of the most important individuals in shaping Mexico in recent years were presidents not known for their charisma.

Current Leader: Felipe Calderón

When he became Mexico's president at the end of 2006, Felipe Calderón faced a mountain of challenges: a sizeable portion of the population being suspicious about the legitimacy of his election, a contentious legislature with the majority of seats

held by parties other than Calderón's National Action Party (PAN), and an anti-immigration mood in the United States—represented by the U.S. House of Representatives voting to authorize construction of a seven hundred–mile fence along a portion of the border with Mexico in the fall of 2006. These early tribulations provided a strong test of Calderón's leadership abilities.

Calderón is the son of a devout Catholic, Luis Calderón Vega, who helped found the PAN before leaving it in 1980 because he believed the party had abandoned its Catholic roots in favor of a big business bent.[15] Consequently, some feared that Felipe Calderón might turn away from the PAN's probusiness positions. For the most part, however, his Harvard education in law and business and former position as head of the national development bank won over Mexican professionals at the same time his campaign successfully struck blue-collar themes, including proposals to get tougher on crime, improve education, and expand public health programs.[16] Particularly given what most consider a lack of charisma, how well Calderón is able to win over his numerous doubters will depend on how successfully he institutes these policies, how well the economy performs, and how well he can work with U.S. political leaders.

Important Recent Leader: Vicente Fox

Vicente Fox was president of Mexico during 2000–2006. His victory in 2000 was surprising, not because he was unpopular (he was quite popular), but because he defeated a candidate from the Institutional Revolutionary Party (PRI)—the party that had dominated Mexican politics for the previous seven decades. Born in 1942, Fox was raised on a ranch in the state of Guanajuato. Educated at an American university in Mexico, Vicente Fox attended Harvard Business School. He eventually became the president of Coca-Cola's Mexican division in 1979. After being elected to the national legislature in 1988, he ran for governor of Guanajuato in 1991 as a member of the PAN. Though some thought Fox won the election, the PRI candidate opposing him was declared the winner. Fox tried again in 1995, this time successfully securing the governorship. As early as 1997, he began discussing a run for president.

His brash style and frank discussion about the problems of the political system won him the support of many in the general population. As president, however, this style led him to clash with members of other political parties who controlled a majority of the seats in the Congress. He responded by attempting to reach out to his opponents—even putting a number of members of the other main political parties in his cabinet. Many of his successful activities were a continuation of trends begun under the previous presidents, Zedillo and Salinas, but his political opponents in the legislature frustrated Fox's other attempts to reform Mexican politics.

Important Recent Leader: Ernesto Zedillo Ponce de Leon

Ernesto Zedillo was the last president of a seven-decade reign of the PRI over the office. In 1994, he won a race that was close and that observers of Mexican politics considered fairer than previous presidential elections. Continuing some reforms of his predecessor, Carlos Salinas, Zedillo also proposed and implemented many of his own. Zedillo attended public schools, received an economics degree in Mexico, and went on to earn a Ph.D. in economics from Yale.

Zedillo's path to the presidency was somewhat accidental. He had been viewed as a technocrat by many observers—competent in his field of economics but far from inspiring and lacking the political sophistication of other PRI officials. Under President Salinas, Zedillo had overseen planning and budgeting, prior to becoming secretary of education in 1992. In March 1994, the PRI candidate for the presidency was assassinated. Zedillo emerged as the replacement candidate and won a tough electoral victory with unusually high voter turnout. The election was relatively free from fraud, marking the ongoing and dramatic shift in the Mexican political system over the previous decade.

Zedillo mostly continued the economic policies of Salinas but also played a major role in continuing the transformation in Mexico toward a legitimate democracy. It was one of his final acts as president that forever solidified Zedillo's reputation as a political reformer. When Vicente Fox won the 2000 presidential election, Zedillo made a public statement of congratulations to Fox. That he did this before Fox's PRI opponent angered some in the PRI, but it also paved the way for a smooth transition of power from one set of ruling elites to another. Establishing the precedent of a peaceful transfer of power following an election is one of the most important events for the long-term consolidation of a new democracy.

Leaders in Brazil

As previous chapters have noted, the weakness of most Brazilian political parties puts a premium on individual leadership characteristics. The problem with relying on leadership skills is that while you may get excellent leaders, you may also get spectacularly bad ones. How systems cope with bad leaders is just as important as whether they offer room for good leaders to emerge, especially from outside the traditional political class.

Current Leader: Luiz Inacio "Lula" da Silva

Luiz Inacio "Lula" da Silva is one of those leaders who did not come from a traditional background for a president. One of eight children, he was born to a poor peasant family. His father left the family when Lula was a baby, and his mother later moved them to the large industrial city of São Paulo in search of work. Lula did not learn to read until he was ten years old and attended formal school only through the fourth grade. By the age of twelve, he was working as a shoeshine boy on the streets. By nineteen, he was working in an auto parts factory, where he lost a finger on his left hand in an industrial accident. This accident—and the indifference with which factory owners treated his injury—turned him toward union organization, as did the influence of his older brother, a Communist Party member. His charismatic leadership and willingness to take risks propelled him to the head of the local steelworkers' union in 1978, when he was just thirty-three years old.

Over the next several years, Lula and the steel workers' union led a wave of protests against the authoritarian military regime and its repression of independent unions. They were joined in this effort by many civil society associations, neighborhood associations, and progressive Catholic activists. Pressure from

President Luiz Inacio "Lula" da Silva speaks as he is sworn in for his second term
(© CityFiles/WireImage)

Lula's radical leftist supporters helped convince the military to turn over power to what they hoped would be a much more moderate political party system in 1985. But Lula did not give them that luxury. Declining to join the centrist antimilitary coalition, he led the way in founding both the Workers' Party (PT) and the main independent union federation, the CUT. He ran for president for the first time in 1989 and came within an inch of winning the election, demonstrating the potential popular appeal of a candidate who not only spoke for common people, but also was actually one of them. It was largely the hope of electing Lula that kept his diverse coalition together. Without the personal leadership of Lula, it is unlikely that the PT would have been created or held together as a party for over twenty years.

Lula was finally elected president in October 2002—his fourth try at the office—and subsequently reelected in 2006. His tenure as president has been much less radical or revolutionary than many of his supporters hoped. He has largely kept to the terms of

Did You Know? The nickname "Lula" means "Squid" in Portuguese. While he seems to have used the nickname from childhood—probably a diminutive of his first name, Luiz—his fans and critics later used it to refer to his uncanny ability to wriggle out of tight spots, including military prisons.

IMF deals signed by his predecessors, although when they expired, he declined to sign another deal with the IMF. He has distributed some land, but not as much as the Landless Workers' Movement (MST) wanted. He has attempted to reorient public spending toward the poor, but without totally alienating the business class. In short, he has been a pragmatist, understanding that Brazil needs foreign investment and trade even as he tries to change the terms in favor of Brazil. As a result, the Brazilian economy has remained stable, but less change has occurred in the structures of economic and political power than he originally advocated.

The worst stains on his presidency have been self-inflicted: a series of corruption scandals involving close collaborators, some of which have been mentioned in previous chapters. Lula will no doubt end his mandate with a mixed legacy. On the positive side, he has demonstrated that a leftist president need not mean economic or social collapse. On the negative side, he has disappointed millions of Brazilians, who had voted for his party because they saw it as different—an honest alternative for real change.

Important Recent Leader: Fernando Henrique Cardoso

In sharp contrast to Lula, Fernando Henrique Cardoso was born into the political elite, the son and grandson of generals. As a young boy, Fernando Henrique knew presidents and governors. He lived a comfortable upper-middle-class life. Determined to avoid what he called "the family business"—that is, politics—Cardoso got a Ph.D. in sociology and became a professor.[17] He would later establish a worldwide reputation as a neomarxist and a founder of dependency theory (see Chapter 3), which argues that poverty and underdevelopment in lesser developed countries is the result of exploitation by the advanced industrial democracies.

Like Lula, Cardoso opposed the military regime, but his opposition took a very different form. Shortly after the 1964 military coup, he fled the country with his family to exile in Argentina, Chile, and France. When he returned to Brazil in 1968, he helped create a Brazilian think tank, CEBRAP, which produced sociological and economic analyses critical of the military regime's policies, particularly its neglect of the needs of Brazil's poor majority. The CEBRAP headquarters was bombed, and Cardoso was arrested and interrogated, but the prominence of his family protected him from summary execution or jail. In 1978, Cardoso ran for the Senate as a protest candidate. Though he lost, it was at this time that he first met Lula, who endorsed his candidacy. Five years later, both men participated at the head of their respective movements—Cardoso with the centrist Brazilian Democratic Movement Party (PMDB), and Lula with the radical-left PT—in the "Direct Elections Now" campaign that finally brought the military government down.

Despite his history as a leftist intellectual and critic of market capitalism, Cardoso as president was best known for stabilizing the economy and ushering in a series of economic reforms designed to embrace markets and reduce state regulation. In other words, he downplayed as president the negative consequences of capitalism that he once emphasized as an academic. Cardoso himself sees this apparent about-face as a natural outgrowth of his previous arguments that Latin American countries could develop by working within the capitalist system.

Important Recent Leader: Fernando Collor de Mello

The greatest contribution Fernando Collor de Mello made to the consolidation of Brazilian democracy may have been getting impeached. Collor was elected president in 1989, the first directly elected president in twenty-nine years and the youngest in Brazilian history. Collor was handsome, athletic, a bit of a playboy, and married to a beautiful second wife. He campaigned on a platform emphasizing his public reputation as an effective governor of the rural state of Alagoas, where he had earned the nickname "Maharaja-Hunter" for his efforts to eliminate the payment of exorbitant salaries to top government officials (the Maharajas). He promised as president to reduce inflation and fight corruption. In the 1989 presidential election, he won the support of middle-class and conservative sectors of society worried about the prospects of a Lula presidency.

Former Brazilian President Fernando Collor de Mello waves to reporters on December 30, 1992, after a press conference where he spoke about his resignation. The Brazilian Senate voted 76–3 to charge him with misconduct and banned him from political life for eight years.

(©Julio Pereira/AFP/Getty Images)

However, just two years into his presidential term, his younger brother Pedro went public with accusations of rampant corruption. According to Pedro, Collor set up a scheme to collect millions of dollars in bribes and kickbacks from private companies in exchange for government contracts and inside information on privatization bids. Corrupt and eccentric presidents are nothing new in Brazil (or elsewhere), but as more information became public, massive student-led public demonstrations increased the pressure on Collor. The Congress launched a formal investigation. Four months later, in September 1992, the Chamber of Deputies voted to impeach him. In December—as the Senate met to remove him from office—Collor resigned. He was condemned by the Senate anyway, and lost all political rights for eight years.

The story of Collor is notable less for what *did* happen than what did *not* happen. Protests did not (directly) force Collor out. The military did not stage a coup. Instead, the problem of removing Collor was resolved by legal procedures. Despite the fact that Brazil's new constitution was barely four years old, Collor's enemies and friends alike committed themselves to abide by its rules. The Collor scandal was the first major test of Brazil's new democratic institutions—and they passed.

Thus, Collor's story highlights the limits of leadership as a way of explaining political outcomes. As a leader, Collor sought to use his position for his own enrichment. He was held accountable by politicians who invested in a system of institutional rules. Brazil thus provides an important lesson: Democracy can survive bad leaders *if* other politicians, voters, interest groups, and the military see more long-term advantages in playing by the same set of rules than in breaking the rules for personal, short-term gain.

Leaders in Nigeria

Since independence, leadership in Nigeria has involved the military in one way or another. Much of the period since independence has been under military rule. Even the democratic interludes have produced elections of former military leaders. This includes Nigeria's first president of the Fourth Republic, Olusegun Obasanjo: a dictator turned democratizer, who twenty years later reemerged to win the presidency by way of a relatively free and fair election.

Current Leader: Umaru Yar'Adua

Umaru Yar'Adua is the current president of Nigeria. Elected in the spring of 2007, Yar'Adua became the first civilian leader to succeed another civilian leader since independence. Many Nigerians and outside observers criticized his path to power, labeling the 2007 presidential election one based on both blatant intimidation and other less overt forms of manipulation. Because he was the handpicked successor of former President Olusegun Obasanjo, skeptics inside and outside of Nigeria assumed he would be little more than a puppet of Obasanjo, who would pull the strings of the Nigerian government from the background. Such skeptics appear to have underestimated Yar'Adua.

Yar'Adua is, in many ways, a unique politician, particularly in a region of the world known for its flamboyant military leaders. Relatively unknown nationally before Obasanjo chose him as his successor, Yar'Adua is a Muslim from Nigeria's north. A former chemistry teacher (and the first Nigerian leader in more than four decades to have a university education),[18] he is described as soft-spoken and thoughtful but also tough and independent.

While some expressed concerns over his adoption of *Shari'a* (Islamic Law) while governor of Katsina, several months after his election he had already won over many non-Muslims who liked his unassuming personality and came to believe his conciliatory approach

Nigerian President Umaru Yar'Adua addresses the 62nd session of the United Nations General Assembly on September 26, 2007.
(©Don Emmert/AFP/Getty Images)

toward different groups in the country was genuine.[19] While this initial evidence was promising, Yar'Adua continues to face a large number of significant challenges, including tackling corruption, curtailing violence in the oil-rich Niger Delta region, and, perhaps most important, emerging from the shadow of his predecessor, Obasanjo.

Important Recent Leader: Olusegun Obasanjo

Often portrayed as a reluctant leader, Olusegun Obasanjo was Nigeria's elected president from 1999–2007. Well before this, however, he had become a central figure in Nigerian politics. In 1976, General Obasanjo took over control of the military-led government following the assassination of the military leader at the time, Murtala Mohammed. Obasanjo won the support of many in the country by following through, as others had not, with a pledge to step down from power in favor of a democratically elected president. He oversaw a transition to democracy in 1979 and stepped out of the political limelight. He gained further notoriety and popular sympathy in 1995 when he was arrested, charged with plotting to overthrow the military leader at the time, General Sani Abacha, and jailed. In 1999, after Abacha's death, Obasanjo was released from prison and successfully sought the presidency via democratic elections.

A Christian of Yoruba ethnic identity, Obasanjo cultivated support in Nigeria's Muslim north, helping him win sizeable victories (around 62 percent both times) in 1999 and 2003. Some questioned his leadership approaches and abilities on divisive issues, such as the *Shari'a* debates, and accused him of worrying more about his image abroad than about solving domestic problems. Still, his central role in Nigeria's transitions to democracy in both 1979 and 1999, particularly his decision not to try to hold on to power after his second term expired in 2007, make him one of the most important figures in Nigerian politics since the country's attainment of independence.

Important Recent Leader: General Sani Abacha

From 1993 until his death in 1998, Sani Abacha ruled Nigeria with an iron fist. Abacha first gained note as a participant in a military coup that overthrew democracy in Nigeria in 1983. In 1993, Nigeria tried democracy again, but the military president at the time, General Ibrahim Babangida, nullified election results. Out of the chaos that followed, Abacha seized power.

Abacha became the symbol of everything wrong with Nigerian politics in the 1990s. He oversaw massive human rights violations, targeted political opponents, and disregarded the country's constitution. Corrupt even by African military leader standards, Abacha accumulated as much as $4 billion in foreign assets before his death in 1998. His quick burial and the absence of an autopsy fueled various rumors about the cause of his death, from poisoning by political rivals to a heart attack during sex with multiple Indian prostitutes.

Leaders in the Russian Federation

There are a large number of events in Russian history that highlight the role of individuals in political outcomes. Going back to the tsarist period, various tsars' decisions to get involved in wars (e.g., the Crimean War), to respond to defeat in such wars (the emancipation of the serfs), and to stay in unpopular wars (Tsar Nicholas II and, later, Prime Minister Alexander Kerensky staying in World War I) radically altered the social, economic, and political landscape of the country. Even Communist leaders' early decisions, such as Lenin and Stalin's decision to accept an ethno-federal system as the Soviet Union was formed, continue to have implications for present events. Since the collapse of Communism, two of the main domestic politics issues have been economic reform and political liberalization. Key decisions by Presidents Boris Yeltsin and Vladimir Putin moved Russia away from its Soviet-era economics but failed to move Russia toward consolidation of democracy. Instead, under Putin, the Russian Federation moved sharply away from democracy during almost a decade of "creeping authoritarianism."

Current Leader: Vladimir Putin

Following Boris Yeltsin as president of Russia at the end of 1999, Vladimir Putin placed his stamp on both the office and the entire Russian political system. In 2008, Putin completed his second term as president. Through a deal arranged with his handpicked successor, Dmitry Medvedev, Putin slid seamlessly from the office of president into the prime ministership. This change simultaneously transformed the Russian political system, shifting at least some power away from the presidency, and guaranteed that Putin would remain one of the system's central figures.

Born in Leningrad (now St. Petersburg), Putin received his university education at

Leningrad State University, studying civil law. Putin made his way into politics only after a long period of service in the Soviet KGB. Spending five years in West Germany, Putin was exposed to Western economic and political ideas. He joined the administration of the St. Petersburg mayor—and his former law professor—Anatoly Sobchak in 1991.

From there, Putin rose quickly through the Russian political system at the end of the 1990s. Having received a federal government appointment in 1997, Putin got a major promotion when Yeltsin made him head of the Federal Security Service (the successor organization to the KGB). Yeltsin promoted Putin two more times. In August 1999, Yeltsin made him one of a string of new prime ministers. A few months later, Putin found himself the acting president of the country when Yeltsin suddenly and unexpectedly resigned on New Year's Eve. Yeltsin apparently liked what he had seen in Putin. By elevating him to acting president, Yeltsin all but ensured that Putin would be elected in the presidential elections held in March 2000.

Putin is the kind of president Russians had been craving during the Yeltsin years. He is perceived as strong and energetic (he is skilled in judo and the sport of sambo, which combines judo and wrestling), decisive and confident. As president, Putin has placed high importance on gaining control of the breakaway region of Chechnya while restoring a sense of respect for the country around the world. His tendency to favor those who share his St. Petersburg ties has concerned some in Russia, while Putin's efforts to reestablish Russian greatness and authoritarian political practices have troubled many outside observers. By the early stages of Putin's second term, it was clear that he was focused on consolidating power further in the central government and into his own hands. The Yeltsin-led experiment in democracy was facing a full-fledged assault from Putin—an assault that culminated not with him seeking an (unconstitutional) third consecutive term but rather by his resourceful move to shift power to the other half of Russia's dual executive system.

Russia's Other Current Leader: Dmitry Medvedev

In late 2007, a number of political parties loyal to then-President Vladimir Putin, including United Russia, and Putin himself announced their intention to support Dmitry Medvedev in the March 2008 presidential elections. The move ended speculation that Putin would seek a third term as president. However, when Medvedev announced the following day that he would support Putin to be prime minister, what some had envisioned as a *possible* route to Putin maintaining a firm grip on control of Russian politics became reality. In the context of what many considered to be, de facto, a "hyper-presidential" political system in the 1990s and during Putin's two terms, it seems strange to discuss the current Russian president, Medvedev, as secondary to the current prime minister, Putin. Yet, few inside or outside Russia believe that Medvedev is Russia's supreme political leader.

With Putin needing a reliable ally to sit alongside him, Medvedev made a great deal of sense. Medvedev was part of Putin's St. Petersburg inner circle his former chief of staff, and managed his successful 2000 presidential campaign. He is also used to serving in a position of power but letting Putin pull the strings; during Medvedev's time as chairman of Russia's massive energy company, Gazprom, many believed Putin was actually the one "calling the shots."[20] His last

Russian President Boris Yeltsin stands with a clenched fist during the August 24, 1991, funeral of three men killed during the coup attempt against former Soviet leader Mikhail Gorbachev days earlier.

(©Andre Durand/AFP/Getty Images)

name is even derived from the Russian word for bear, *medved'*, the Russian symbol of national identity and power in the way the bald eagle is to Americans. At the same time, he is someone who may be able to smooth over strained relations with the United States, given his support of free market economics and his vocal criticism of Russian governmental corruption.[21]

Important Recent Leader: Boris Yeltsin

Boris Yeltsin was Russia's first post-Communist president. His rise to power during the Soviet period was long and rocky. Following years working in construction in the city of Sverdlovsk, he was appointed Communist Party secretary of Sverdlovsk in the mid-1970s. This led to a position on the party's Central Committee in the early 1980s, his appointment as Moscow party boss in 1985, and a position in the powerful Politburo the following year. Once on the Politburo, Yeltsin made a name for himself when he publicly criticized perks and privileges for Communist Party officials.

This action, and other disagreements with Gorbachev, led to Yeltsin's removal from the body in early 1988 but won the hearts of many ordinary Soviet citizens. Yeltsin translated this popularity into electoral victories for a seat in the newly created Congress of People's Deputies in 1989, for a seat (and chairmanship) of the Russian union republic's parliament in 1990, and for the position of president of the Russian republic in mid-1991. The collapse of the hardliner-led coup against Gorbachev in August 1991 solidified Yeltsin's rise to prominence. He emerged as the most powerful figure in the Soviet Union and played a central role in negotiating its dismantling.

When the Soviet Union was relegated to history at the end of 1991, Yeltsin's position as president of the Russian republic of the USSR was transformed into president of an independent country, the Russian Federation. Governing a country with a failing economy and secessionist movements in some of its regions, Yeltsin faced a number of hardships, including a struggle with the parliament in 1992 and 1993.

His leadership style combined toughness and occasionally fiery rhetoric with an ability to broker political compromises at key moments. As a result, Yeltsin was the consummate survivor. He won reelection in the middle of 1996 despite very low popularity numbers early in the year. Yeltsin rejected discussions about seeking a third term, and resigned from the presidency on his own terms on New Year's Eve of 1999. His record as a leader is mixed, but he remains one of the most dynamic and important figures of the late twentieth century.

Leaders in China

The importance of individual leaders is as evident in China as any of the other countries examined in this textbook. Mao Zedong remade China, and his successor, Deng Xiaoping, remade it again. As discussed in previous chapters, one of Chinese Communist rule's stranger elements has been how an individual can be recognized as a leader without holding the official positions that one might associate with leadership. This has changed, but the importance of leadership and the role of individuals in Chinese politics has not.

Current Leader: Hu Jintao

Even more than Jiang Zemin's replacement of Deng Xiaoping, the emergence of Hu Jintao (pictured at the opening of this chapter) marked the transition to a new generation of Chinese leaders. Born in 1942, Hu went on to study hydroelectric engineering. He joined the Communist Party as a student in 1964 but did not receive a significant party position until the early 1980s. He gained attention later in the 1980s as party leader in Tibet, where he imposed martial law. Hu became vice president of the country in 1998. When Jiang Zemin stepped down as party general secretary in 2002 and president of China in 2003, Hu Jintao replaced him. Over the next two years, Hu solidified his control of the political system by succeeding Jiang as head of the party and state military commissions.

Hu's leadership style is that of a "soft-spoken technocrat,"[22] and although pro-reform Chinese initially expressed hope that he was open to ideas of political liberalization, the first years of his tenure as leader of China indicate that he is firmly opposed to significant political reforms. In addition, his past actions to stifle Tibetan independence are consistent with his more recently expressed position on independence for Taiwan. In early 2005, he told a party gathering that the people of Taiwan were "our flesh-and-blood brothers" and that the Chinese will "never compromise in opposing the 'Taiwan independence' secessionist activities."

Important Recent Leader: Jiang Zemin

Jiang Zemin was the first preeminent leader of Communist China who had not been a central figure in the Communist Revolution. Born in 1926, he joined the Communist Party in 1946 while in college. An electrical engineer, his initial work was in the automobile sector. He worked his way up the ranks of various research institutes and eventually into the state and party bureaucracy related to oversight of the electronics industry. Following a stint as mayor of Shanghai, he rapidly earned positions in upper levels of the party and state hierarchy, including the positions of party general secretary in 1989 and president of China in 1993. In 1989 and 1990, he also came to head the state and party military commissions. His replacement of Deng Xiaoping in these positions marked his rise to political power, as much or more than the other two positions did.

Unlike Deng Xiaoping before him, Jiang Zemin did not radically alter the direction of Chinese politics or economic policy. He expanded the development of a market economy, and allowed private business owners into the Communist Party for the first time. He also shared Deng's reluctance to engage in similar reforms in the political arena. Jiang once stated, "The theory of relativity worked out by Mr. Einstein, which is in the domain of natural science, I believe can also be applied to the political field. Both democracy and human rights are relative concepts—and not absolute and general."

Leaders in Iran

The overthrow of the shah in 1979 marked a dramatic shift in Iran's domestic politics and international relations. The United States had played a role in the shah coming to power in 1954, and the friendly relationship between the United States and Iran ended with the shah's departure from the country. While moderates in Iran had hoped the shah's removal would bring democracy to the country, the emergence of Ayatollah Ruhollah Khomeini as the symbol of opposition to the shah set the stage for the rejection of democracy and the development of Iran's current theocracy.

Current Leader: Ayatollah Ali Hoseini-Khamenei

Born in 1939, Ali Hoseini-Khamenei became a religious leader and ally of Ayatollah Ruhollah Khomeini. Imprisoned by the shah, he played an important role in the 1979 Revolution. Khamenei became commander of the Revolutionary Guard in 1979 and was elected president of Iran in 1981. The Council of Experts selected Khamenei to become *Rahbar-e Moazam* ("Supreme Leader") following the death of Khomenei in 1989. As Supreme Leader, he holds tremendous power in the Iranian theocratic political system. He opposed efforts by Iran's moderate president in the late 1990s and early 2000s, Mohammed Khatami, to liberalize the country.

Iran's Other Current Leader: Mahmoud Ahmadinejad

Iran's other chief executive is its elected president. The election in 2005 to replace Khatami brought Mahmoud Ahmadinejad to power as Iran's new president. Ahmadinejad won a run-off election against a less conservative candidate, Akbar Hashemi-Rafsanjani, the former president of Iran from 1989 to 1997. Ahmadinejad faces reelection in 2009.

Ahmadinejad studied civil engineering in college but after the 1979 Revolution became more active in political affairs, joining the Islamic Revolutionary Guards and participating in covert operations against Iraq during the Iran-Iraq War. He served in local and regional political positions, before being appointed the mayor of Tehran in 2003. Partly because of his efforts as Tehran mayor to roll back reforms in the city, he is seen as a religious conservative. Ahmadinejad's victory solidified the reestablishment of control of the elected positions of government in Iran by conservative clerics and marked the end, for the moment, of serious prospects for significant political reform.

Ahmadinejad ran a largely populist campaign, emphasizing the need to fight against corruption and support the interest of the poorer segments of society. The approach worked. While reformers issued claims of vote rigging and intimidation, his victory in the run-off was large enough (Ahmadinejad received nearly 62 percent of the vote) that it was hard to believe the run-off election was stolen. More legitimate criticism related to the role of the Guardian Council in banning a huge number of potential candidates from running, and the possibility that Ahmadinejad's vote totals in the first round of voting were inflated to get him into the runoff.

Adding to the controversy surrounding his election, some of the former American hostages that had been held in Iran from 1979 to 1981 accused Ahmadinejad of being involved in the hostage taking. The Iranian president denied this claim, as did the leader of the hostage takers, Abbas Abdi. Still, the controversy only deepened the divide between the new president and the United States, a divide already significantly increased by the events surrounding the 2004 parliamentary elections and Iran's pursuit of nuclear technology and materials with the capacity to be converted into nuclear weapons. Criticisms from the United States seemed only to embolden Ahmadinejad. Feeding the divisions further, Ahmadinejad unleashed particularly harsh comments against the United States and Israel in late October 2005, including recycling words first uttered by Ayatollah Khomeini that Israel should be "wiped off the map."

His tendency not to compromise unless absolutely necessary has been evident domestically as well. Ahmadinejad dislikes consulting with others before making appointments, and in 2005 he and the parliament disagreed over who should become Iran's oil minister. Ahmadinejad wanted a "fresh face," someone who would not be controlled by the "mafia" running the oil sector.[23] After his first three nominations ended in failure, Ahmadinejad finally relented and nominated a former deputy oil minister for the position.

Important Recent Leader: Ayatollah Ruhollah Khomeini

Born in 1900, Ruhollah Khomeini studied religion throughout his life, becoming an ayatollah in the 1950s. An ardent opponent of the shah, he criticized the shah's connections to the West. He was arrested in 1963 and exiled from Iran in the mid-1960s. He first went to Turkey and then lived in Iraq until forced out by Saddam Hussein in 1978. Khomeini settled in Paris, where he emerged as a leader of the opposition that drove the shah from power.

Democracy might have taken hold following the ouster of the shah were it not for one of his own decisions: to strike out against Ayatollah Khomeini while Khomeini was in exile. A prominent Tehran daily newspaper ran a fabricated letter attacking Khomeini. Instead of discrediting him, the letter's publication turned religious members of society more sharply against the shah's regime and vaulted Khomeini into the status of head of the political opposition.[24] One cannot know how events in Iran would have transpired had the decision to run this letter not been made. By placing Khomeini above middle-class opponents of the shah, however, it is plausible that this action both sped up the demise of the shah's regime and set the stage for Iran's theocratic system to emerge in place of a viable democracy.

Khomeini became Supreme Leader after the 1979 Revolution until his death in June 1989. He oversaw Iran through the American Embassy hostage crisis and the Iran-Iraq War. Khomeini also issued a famous *fatwa* in February 1989, calling for the killing of Salman Rushdie, author of *The Satanic Verses*, which Khomeini deemed blasphemous.

Important Recent Leader: President Hojjatoleslam Seyed Mohammed Khatami

From 1997 to 2005, Iran's president was Mohammed Khatami. Born in 1943 to an important religious leader, Khatami moved back to Iran from West Germany with the 1979 Revolution. He became minister of culture and Islamic guidance in 1982 but, in a hint of things to come, resigned from that position after clashes with conservatives in the government who viewed Khatami as too moderate on social and cultural issues. Khatami became president in 1997, after he won a surprisingly decisive electoral victory. He was reelected even more comfortably in 2001. As president, Khatami supported a more open society, greater freedoms for the population, and greater respect for women. His initial cabinet included a female minister.

Many in Iran became disillusioned with President Khatami—and with politics in general—because of his failure to deliver on his vision of a prosperous, democratic Iran. Seeing him as unwilling or unable to prevent the religious conservatives from dominating the political system, even former supporters soured on Khatami as a leader before his second term came to an end.

Think and Discuss

To what extent do the backgrounds and leadership styles of the current and past political leaders highlighted in the TIC sections explain their successes and failures?

Decision Making: Rational and Otherwise

In addition to emphasizing concepts such as leadership and the traits of successful leaders, political science research based on the choice approach often concentrates on features of the decision-making process. Within this body of political science research, decision making is generally viewed as a largely rational process. However, aided by insights from disciplines such as psychology, a growing number of political scientists have become skeptical of the idea that individuals routinely employ rational calculations to make their political decisions.

Rationality

Rationality is arguably the most important, and most controversial, concept related to political decision making. Rationality is a condition in which people base their decisions on reason and logic, taking logical steps in an effort to maximize their interests. Comparativists who emphasize rational decision making generally contend that rational decision makers are self-interested, and their interests are concrete and material, such as gaining more economic wealth, although some contend that they may be less objective things such as power or even emotional well-being. Whatever the specific interests, individuals operating in a fully rational manner determine and rank their goals, assess their options' costs and benefits, and choose the option that they believe maximizes

the likelihood of achieving their most important goals with the fewest costs.

The idea of rational political decisions makes a fair amount of sense when thinking about political elites, though it is less clear that the masses engage in rational calculations as they formulate their political choices. In political science studies that focus on rational decision making, rationality is typically assumed rather than empirically tested. Most actual tests of the idea of rational decision making do not inspire confidence that individuals, particularly the mass public, in fact make rational political decisions.

Scholars who emphasize individual rationality are often interested in understanding collective political outcomes. Such collective decisions include voting and joining political organizations. The approach of examining collective outcomes via individual rational decisions came to political science by way of economics, which is one of the reasons that interests are often defined in economic terms.[25] Voters, for example, are assumed to make their assessments about candidates on the basis of their own economic well-being, a process usually referred to as **pocketbook calculations**. These are either **retrospective calculations**—"Am I better off than I was four years ago?"—or **prospective calculations**—"Will I be better off in the future?" Other voters may take into account the well-being of society as a whole,

---

Rationality is a condition under which people base decisions on reason and logic, leading them to act in ways that they believe will maximize their personal interests.

Pocketbook calculations are assessments by voters about their personal economic well-being.

Retrospective calculations consider recent performance by the government.

Prospective calculations mean choosing on the basis of which politician or political party is expected to perform best in the future.

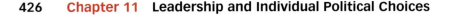

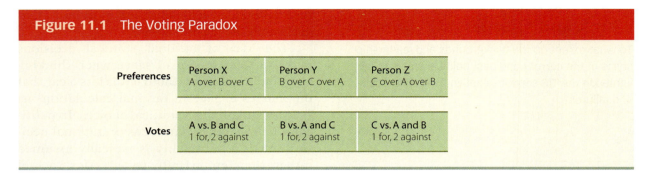

Figure 11.1   The Voting Paradox

Preferences	Person X A over B over C	Person Y B over C over A	Person Z C over A over B
Votes	A vs. B and C 1 for, 2 against	B vs. A and C 1 for, 2 against	C vs. A and B 1 for, 2 against

which is known as making **sociotropic calculations**. Sociotropic calculations can also be prospective or retrospective.

Collective outcomes based on the aggregation of individual choices may develop over time. For those who emphasize the importance of individuals acting in their rational self-interest, a series of individual decisions often results in an **equilibrium**. The equilibrium point occurs when no further improvement in the interests of the collective is possible through changes in individual positions. Outcomes in line with the equilibrium point would indicate that the individual rational calculations have led to a rational collective decision as well.

Scholars have long understood that a collection of individual rational choices is not the same thing as a rational collective outcome. Kenneth Arrow was one of many scholars to consider how individuals acting rationally can result in groups of individuals acting irrationally. Arrow's **impossibility theorem** holds that there is no method of aggregating preferences for three or more alternatives that meets a set of minimum criteria for fairness which Arrow outlined.[26] Arrow is best known for an example of the impossibility theorem known as the **voting paradox** (sometimes called "Arrow's paradox"). The voting paradox involves three individuals or groups choosing from among three policy options—A, B, and C. The three people order their preferences in the following way: A-B-C, B-C-A, C-A-B (see Figure 11.1). Not only is there no majority for any of the outcomes, but each outcome considered is secondary to at least one other outcome: A is secondary to C for two of the people; B is secondary to A for two people; but C is secondary to B for two people. The consequences of the impossibility theorem and the voting paradox are significant. For example, the voting paradox explains why most voting decisions in political bodies are simple yes or no votes on a single policy choice. It is also why amendments, supported by a majority of members of a legislature, can ultimately sabotage the passage of a bill.

Bounded Rationality

In addition to difficulties in making rational *collective* decisions, a number of social

---

Sociotropic calculations take into account the well-being of society as a whole.

In theories that seek to understand collective outcomes through examining individuals and their interests, **equilibrium** is the point at which no improvement in the collective interests of the individual actors is possible.

Kenneth Arrow's **impossibility theorem** demonstrates that, given certain rules about equality and fairness, it is impossible to reach acceptable collective decisions among three or more alternatives.

A specific example is the **voting paradox**, in which three individuals choose among three alternatives and no two of them can agree on which alternative is best.

scientists have challenged whether fully rational *individual* decisions are possible. In the late 1940s, for example, political scientist Herbert Simon proposed the concept of **bounded rationality** as a challenge to the dominance of "comprehensively rational" models in economics.[27] Simon's notion of checks on full rationality, which earned him the Nobel Prize in economics, emphasizes the extent to which individuals are constrained in their decision making, particularly by cognitive limitations.

The bounded rationality concept does not hold that people are stupid. Rather, it asserts that there are greater demands placed on, and more information available to, decision makers than they can possibly digest in a fully rational manner. Short-term memory, computation skills, and attention are finite. These limits are more important the more difficult the decision-making task. Simon is particularly known for the idea of **satisficing**, a decision-making model that states humans select the first option they find that *satisfies* their aspirations rather than—as an "ideal" rational decision maker would—conducting an exhaustive search for the *best* choice.

Irrational Choices: Cognitive Dissonance, Groupthink, Mood, and Emotion

Some political scientists contend that even "bounded" rational decisions are few and far between. Influenced by psychology more than economics, they focus their study of political decision making on situations and settings in which individuals might act less than rationally.

Cognitive dissonance is a psychological concept with important political implications. People do not like to hold obviously contradictory positions or engage in obviously inconsistent

Did You Know? While many people associate the voting paradox with Kenneth Arrow and his impossibility theorem, the paradox was actually first described in detail by a French social scientist, Marquis de Condorcet, in the late 1700s.

behaviors. The dissonance between these incongruous positions or behaviors—like playing a white and black key that are next to each other on a piano at the same time—is hard for many people to tolerate, particularly over time. So far, this sounds like rational thinking, but it may not be. Evidence from psychological experiments shows that people's initial position on an issue influences their interpretation of evidence about that issue. If this desire to be consistent leads people to interpret information a certain way or outright reject it, it is fair to ask how rational their thought process really is.

Another concept highlighted by those who question the idea of fully rational individual decision making involves the dynamics of making a decision in a group. Since politics involves interactions among individuals, how individuals behave in groups is an important question. **Groupthink**, for example, occurs when individuals succumb to pressure from the group of which they are a part. Their positions on an issue, and even how they come to view

Bounded rationality holds that humans are cognitively limited in important ways that restrict their ability to process information in a comprehensively rational manner.

As a result of bounded rationality, decision makers will employ short-cuts such as **satisficing**—choosing the first acceptable solution rather than searching for a best solution.

Cognitive dissonance is an idea from psychology that people do not like to hold obviously contradictory positions, leading them to reject evidence that may run counter to their initial beliefs about a particular topic.

Groupthink occurs when individuals, due to a desire to "fit in," quietly go along with the apparent decision of the group even if they disagree with it.

the issue, can be shaped greatly by the arguments of others in the group. They fear standing out and instead go along with the crowd. Like more extreme forms of mob mentality, groupthink typically has little in common with fully rational thought.

Imagine you are having a conversation with four of your classmates about where to go out tonight. One by one the other four have all expressed a preference for a place that you really dislike. You become apprehensive and agree with their choice. A fully rational person would have proposed other ideas that would have maintained the friendships while being more individually satisfying, but you would rather fit in than stand out by challenging your friends' decision.

While both cognitive dissonance and groupthink still imply some element of conscious thought, other concepts, such as **mood** and **emotion**, involve processes that operate at a less conscious level but also interfere with the ability to make rational choices. Although people often use the terms interchangeably, psychologists generally distinguish between mood and emotion. Emotions are more intense, short-lived responses to specific events or objects.

Moods are less intense but deeper and longer lasting feelings, which may not be tied to particular events. Such feelings, what psychologists often call "affective states," include joy, surprise, fear, anger, and shame. Empirical research supports the view that conditions of fear, anger, or shame do not foster rational thought. Studies have shown that those in mildly positive moods not only make more positive judgments about things they confront but are also better at processing information than those in mildly negative moods. Fear can lead to interpreting events as more threatening.

Finally, scholars working in psychology and related fields are increasingly recognizing the extent to which past events and experiences shape how individuals view what is happening to them in the present. At one level, this might be a conscious act. For example, one might take into account the reputation of a rival—based on that individual's past behavior—when trying to interpret current conduct.

On the other hand, concepts such as **transference** highlight the unconscious, and thus nonrational, role of past experiences in present behavior. The process of transference is like a lens that filters initial experiences through past contacts or relationships with similar settings or individuals. As a 2007 *Science News* article put it, "A variety of evidence now suggests that the brain continually maps current experiences, such as interactions with new people, onto prior ones—namely, the thoughts, feelings, motivations, and relationship styles associated with important people from the past."[28] As a result, transference can significantly affect an individual's first impressions and behaviors, both inside and outside of the political arena.

A **mood** is less intense than emotions but deeper and longer lasting feelings, which may not be tied to particular events.

An **emotion** is an intense, short-term response to a specific event. Like moods, emotions can affect the ability of individuals to make rational decisions.

Transference is a concept from psychology that highlights the extent to which contact or experiences are filtered through past contacts or relationships with similar individuals or settings.

Important Political Decisions and Their Rationality in the United Kingdom, Germany, France, and India

An examination of the past and present leaders of the ten TIC cases provides a large number of examples of important political decisions. Adding important decisions by ordinary citizens into the mix increases exponentially the possible decisions that one could highlight. This section highlights just a few of those decisions, one per country, starting with decisions by former British Prime Minister Margaret Thatcher, former German Chancellor Helmut Kohl, French farmer José Bové, and Indian Prime Minister Manmohan Singh.

The United Kingdom: Margaret Thatcher and the Falklands Islands War

While most known for her domestic policy changes related to privatization and contraction of the size of the national government, Margaret Thatcher also carved a place for herself in British history with her strong leadership in the arena of foreign policy. When Argentina seized the Falkland Islands in 1982, Thatcher had a number of options. Her own Foreign Office (the British equivalent of the State Department in the United States), British defense advisors, and even the U.S. government counseled her against trying to retake the islands. Without someone like Thatcher as prime minister, the United Kingdom would likely not have fought to regain the Falklands.[29]

How can one understand Thatcher's decision to use violence to regain control of the Falklands? While not denying that mood and emotion played a role, the Falklands decision may be a good example of rational decision making. Thatcher weighed the costs of the war to the benefits of reclaiming the islands, maintaining the British reputation as a military power, and bolstering her domestic standing if the conflict ended successfully. Although she expected to receive criticism from the rest of Europe, she knew she could count on support from British Commonwealth countries and on the United States to at worst remain quiet; indeed, the United States did more than that, providing useful intelligence to the British military.

Thus, once Thatcher came to believe that diplomatic efforts had little chance of success, she turned to what she considered to be the best, albeit unpopular, decision: to pursue a military response. Against the mountain of advice to continue to negotiate—and public opinion, which was against military action—Thatcher mobilized the military. The ultimate British victory confirmed her international reputation as Britain's "Iron Lady." It also elevated her status domestically, helping lock up a sizeable Conservative Party electoral victory in 1984.

Germany: The German Currency Union

Following the fall of the Berlin Wall on November 11, 1989, the process of German unification proceeded at a dizzying pace. On October 3, 1990, German Unity Day, the German Democratic Republic (East Germany) ceased to exist, and its five *Länder* were incorporated into the Federal Republic—what had previously been West Germany, now the name of the reunified country of Germany. One of the major decisions surrounding unification concerned the question of merging the two very different economies of east and west. Not only had East Germany been a centrally planned economy, but also the living standards of its citizens had been far below those of the citizens of West Germany. The greater economic opportunities and political freedoms enjoyed in the Federal Republic had triggered a substantial exodus of East Germans to the west beginning in the summer of 1989. East Germans took holidays in neighboring Hungary to take advantage of that country's recently opened borders with the West—the result of Soviet leader Mikhail Gorbachev's decision to let Eastern Europe decide its own political destiny—and cross over into West Germany. Other East Germans sought asylum at the West German embassies in Czechoslovakia and Poland.[30]

With the disintegration of the Berlin Wall and the open border between East and West Germany, the specter of continued mass migration to the west haunted Chancellor Helmut Kohl and other West German politicians. Indeed, eastern emigration was running at nearly fifty thousand easterners a month in the first two months of 1990.[31] The process of unifying the West German *deutschmark* with the East German *ostmark* thus became of paramount importance in staunching the flow of easterners.

In the weeks after the opening of the Wall, the *ostmark* had rapidly devalued to 20:1, down from 2.5:1 in 1980 and 10:1 at the end of 1988.[32] A formal currency union between the two Germanys at a 20:1 rate would have left easterners with vastly reduced purchasing power, wiped out their savings, and given them a strong incentive to flee to the more prosperous western regions. In order to encourage easterners stay put, the Kohl government implemented the currency union that valued the East German and West German marks at a rate of one-to-one (up to a set amount of savings) in May 1999.

The economic wisdom of this decision was suspect. West German economists and members of the *Bundesbank*, the country's central bank, opposed such a move, arguing that East German goods would be overvalued and that mass unemployment would follow. Such a currency union would also provide pressure for wage equalization between western and eastern workers, as easterners would now have to pay for goods at western prices. But politicians argued that attaining parity between eastern and western living standards was necessary to prevent political unrest and ensure a smooth process of unification. In the end, the central bank yielded to the Kohl government, while insisting on preserving its ability to set economic policy for united Germany free from subsequent political interference.

The dire economic predictions following currency union were largely borne out. The currency union certainly helped eastern pensioners and those with savings, but it did so at the cost of unemployment and economic decline in the east. After unification, labor unions demanded wage parity between east and west, and the competitiveness of eastern industry, which was far below that of the west, consequently suffered. As government subsidies and welfare state spending rose to absorb the costs of unification, the *Bundesbank* compensated for the ballooning federal deficit by raising interest rates. This induced a severe recession and accelerated the collapse of the economy in the eastern part of the country.[33]

The currency union decision demonstrates one of the difficulties in assessing a political decision's rationality. This decision was clearly questionable—perhaps even irrational—on economic grounds. But politicians have to worry about more than their choices' economic rationality. Although it generated significant economic problems that had been predicted well in advance of the policy, the choice to pursue a currency union across the newly unified Germany was, arguably, the most *politically* rational decision available to the German government.

France: José Bové and McDonald's

In the late 1990s, the United States and the European Union became involved in a trade dispute. The EU, despite pressure from the United States and a World Trade Organization ruling supporting the American position, refused to allow the importation of American beef from cattle raised with the aid of growth hormones. In retaliation, the United States slapped a high tariff on imported Roquefort cheese made from ewe's milk.

José Bové, a farmer and activist from the Larzac in France, had become increasingly concerned about the globalization and industrialization of agriculture. In 1999, he helped organize a group of farmers around the town of Millau, in the region famous for Roquefort cheese. Under Bové's leadership, the Millau farmers dismantled a half-completed new McDonald's in the small French town. Along with several other farmers, Bové was arrested for vandalism, even though they did not damage any of the prefabricated materials used in the construction. The action at the McDonald's was both a local and national act, giving the farmers who were suffering the loss of a lucrative market the ability to express their outrage and to raise awareness—to fight for public support—to strengthen the resolve of national governments in resisting industrial agricultural practices. The event also drew international attention, and Bové later admitted that the effort was more successful than the farmers had expected.[34]

Some might consider the actions of the Millau farmers a simple expression of emotion, even outright hate or fear, but certainly not rational behavior. Increasingly, however, scholars have come to challenge the dichotomy between emotion and rationality in politics, considering symbolic and moral actions as, in part, the focus of political struggle and the formation of political identities.[35] Indeed, the target of the farmers' actions had particular symbolic importance. Despite the popularity of McDonald's in France and across Europe, it is widely regarded as not just fast food, but bad food. So the attack of the farmers and cheese makers pitted an artisan product that is an inherent part of the French culinary heritage against the clearest manifestation of mass produced and uniform industrial food they could find. When he refused to post bail and instead languished in prison, Bové became a symbol himself, the internationally known "French Farmer" fighting for the rights of family farmers or, as Bové explained, for "proper food against *malbouffe* (junk food), agricultural workers against multinationals."[36]

India: "Freezing" and "Unfreezing" the Indo-U.S. Nuclear Agreement

In 1974, India exploded a nuclear weapon. In view of that event, the United States imposed sanctions on India. Consequently, India had not been able to acquire from abroad the nuclear technology and uranium it needed to expand its nuclear power generation plants to provide it with the electricity essential to the maintenance of its rapidly developing economy. In July 2005, Indian Prime Minister Manmohan Singh and U.S. President George W. Bush met and issued a joint statement about building a global partnership. Subsequent negotiations led to the Indo-U.S. Nuclear Agreement, made public in August 2007. For the agreement to come into operation, India had to negotiate safeguards with the International Atomic Energy Agency (IAEA) and the Nuclear Suppliers Group (NSG). The Bush Administration initially sought to finalize the deal and get it to the U.S. Congress by the end of 2007. But, Singh faced major obstacles within India, which delayed progress and forced extensions of the "deadline."

Singh devoted more energy and political capital to getting the Indo-U.S. Nuclear Agreement adopted than to getting any other policy adopted during his tenure as prime minister. He viewed the agreement as something that would better the lives of Indians and India's position in the world—much as had the economic liberalization reforms he had initiated in 1991 when he was finance minister. Yet, in October 2007, he appeared to have been defeated and announced that his government would "freeze" further consideration of the agreement.

The explanation had to do with political calculations. To prevent its collapse, Singh's United Progressive Alliance (UPA) government needed the support of a group of parties on the left that was not a formal part of the Alliance, primarily the CPI(M) and CPI. Both parties opposed the closer ties with the United States that the nuclear agreement seemed to imply.[37] The UPA was unable to get the Left to give up its opposition. The government feared that losing its domestic political allies would force new elections, a situation widely thought to benefit the fortunes of the Bharatiya Janata Party (BJP).

Although the BJP had sought to foster close relations with the United States in the previous government, it opposed the nuclear agreement, complaining that it would undermine India's sovereignty. While BJP leaders may have truly held this belief, they also may have concluded that bringing down the government and holding new elections would increase their standing in the parliament and the odds that they would form the next Indian government. Because they feared they might lose elections held in the near future, neither Manmohan Singh nor Sonia Gandhi wanted to risk the government's collapse over the Indo-U.S. Nuclear Agreement. Consequently, in October 2007 they decided not to move forward with it. Prime Minister Singh justified his retreat by saying that his government was not a "single-issue government." "Freezing" progress toward the adoption of the nuclear agreement had political costs, too. As one commentator observed, "The loss of face" suffered by Singh and the INC (the main party of the UPA coalition government) was not "taken lightly by advocates of liberalization."[38]

The success of the Left in blocking the agreement, though, was a temporary one. Believing the Indo-U.S. Nuclear Agreement was no longer a possibility and wanting to give Singh a face-saving exit, the Left allowed the UPA to go to the IAEA to work out a safeguard agreement to facilitate access to nuclear fuel. By the end of June 2008, when the UPA-Left coordination committee again met, it became very clear to the Left parties that Singh was determined to move forward and "unfreeze" the nuclear agreement with the United States.[39] Indeed, on July 9, 2008, the Indian government submitted the proposed deal to the IAEA, initiating a process that culminated with the U.S. Senate approving the Indo-U.S. Nuclear Agreement on October 1, 2008.

In response to Sinhg's actions, the Left publicly withdrew its support for the UPA government. Following the loss of the Left's support, Singh scheduled a confidence vote for July 22, 2008. After a period of intense lobbying for support, Singh won on a vote of 275 to 256, although charges of vote-buying tarnished the UPA's success.

Manmohan Singh's "nuclear freeze" shows the extent to which political leaders will weigh the short-term political consequences of a major policy initiative. When Singh believed that the nuclear agreement threatened the survival of his government, he backed off. When it subsequently appeared that he could survive moving forward with the agreement, he "unfroze" it, forged ahead, and ultimately won the battle. However, short-term victories can sometimes carry negative long-term consequences. The break with the secular Left that occurred in route to the passage of the Indo-U.S. Nuclear Agreement may make it more difficult for Singh's government to win future confidence votes. If so, Singh's pursuit of the Indo-U.S. Nuclear Agreement may look less rational in the future than it appeared to be in the fall of 2008.

IN THEORY AND PRACTICE

India and Incrementalism

The theoretical approach that emphasizes **incrementalism** highlights how decision makers use a particular short-cut in setting government policy. The theory is most closely associated with Charles Lindblom, who argued that rational politicians do not start from scratch when formulating policy.[40] "New" policy is rarely new, but rather involves small, incremental changes to an existing policy.

While a theory related to the choice approach, incrementalism leaves little role for individual

Incrementalism is a theory of decision making which assumes, short of a crisis, that government officials will make small changes to existing policy rather than start from scratch when making policy decisions.

initiative. It assumes that most leaders will operate in a similar manner, regardless of who the individuals in question are.

Take the example of local government budgeting. A local city council must pass a budget, usually annually. This budget is broken down into various sections, and committees may formulate recommendations for the whole council about spending amounts for each of these sections. In making these recommendations, policymakers rarely ask if an existing program is actually needed, and they rarely spend a great deal of time assessing the best possible budget amount for that program given their goals and the program's costs and benefits. Instead, they take the previous year's budget amount for that program and change the figure by some percentage downward or, more often, upward. In keeping with the idea of incremental policy adjustments, this change is usually fairly small, at least in percentage terms.

In crisis situations, significant policy changes sometimes occur quite quickly, but incrementalism explains policymaking well when no crisis or new problem has emerged. It clarifies, for example, why government programs are rarely eliminated entirely. It also helps one understand the growth in government spending over time. Though changes from year to year are usually made in small increments, small increments add up. Over a long period of time, incremental alterations can result in dramatic changes in the scope of a government program.

Although incrementalism guides economic policy development in some parts of the world, India's basic economic policies have developed in "fits and starts." For fifteen years after independence, public sector development was emphasized; some liberalization followed in the mid-1960s; this was followed by a return to an emphasis on the public sector and to nationalization of industries in the late 1960s and early 1970s; in the remainder of the 1970s and 1980s, limited and sporadic liberalization occurred; when the National Front government took power in 1989, it was divided on

which way to take the economy and major economic problems began to develop.

Then, in 1991, came the worst economic crisis India had faced since independence, including a serious balance of payments deficit. This was also the year when a new INC government came to power. In order to get the financial resources the government needed, it was forced to turn to the International Monetary Fund (IMF) which demanded serious liberalization of the economy. The government responded positively to the demand, and that year is widely viewed as the start of real economic liberalization.

The liberalization process has been less incremental than it has been a series of steps, both large and small. In the late 1990s, two governments were brought down shortly after they were elected. Political forces on the right have fought fully opening the economy to "outsiders," while those on the left have fought privatization. Nevertheless, by the end of the term in office of the BJP-led National Democratic Alliance (NDA) government in 2004, the economy was growing at a rapid rate. To the surprise of many observers, the NDA lost the election. The victory of the INC-dominated United Progressive Alliance was attributed, in part, to poorer segments of the population not benefiting much from the economic growth occurring in the liberalizing economy—a situation that favored a greater economic role for the state.

Thus, India provides two important caveats to the use of incrementalism to explain domestic policy choices around the world. First, incrementalism is less likely to hold immediately following a major policy shift, such as the IMF-inspired Indian emphasis on economic liberalization, than in periods of "normal politics." Second, when consecutive governments come to power under the control of rival political parties, incrementalism is likely to take a backseat to ideological (and electoral) considerations. This certainly appears to be the case in India, where the democratic struggle for political power has contributed significantly to the "fits and starts" of liberalization.

Important Political Decisions and Their Rationality in Mexico, Brazil, and Nigeria

The decisions examined in the cases of Mexico, Brazil, and Nigeria are very different yet all important. In Mexico, former president Ernesto Zedillo decided to make, and follow through with, promises to liberalize the political system, setting the stage for the establishment of democracy. In Brazil, Fernando Henrique Cardoso faced the daunting task of devising a plan to curb Brazil's runaway inflation. In Nigeria, a series of decisions paved the way for the Nigerian civil war. Each of these cases shows how elites can make decisions, in part at least, as the result of rational calculations. Each also shows, however, the extent to which the setting in which the decisions occur—external pressure, previous policy failures, and growing frustrations alongside increasing tensions—can make rational decision making more or less likely.

Mexico: Ernesto Zedillo and Liberalization

When Ernesto Zedillo replaced Carlos Salinas de Gortari as president in 1994, he faced a number of serious adversities: Mexico's currency, the peso, was threatening to collapse, and the uprising in Chiapas struck at Salinas's vision of closer ties to the United States on the basis of economic liberalism. Arguably his most serious challenge, however, was to fulfill his promise to limit the power of the presidency and liberalize Mexico's authoritarian political system. Zedillo could have backtracked on significant transformation of the regime. Instead, he set out to alter Mexican politics in three ways: creating a greater balance of power in practice between the presidency and the other two branches, reforming the electoral system, and devolving power to the state governments. For these actions to work, he also had to reform the PRI itself and make it accustomed to not controlling Mexican political life.[41]

Following a pledge in 1996 that the following year's state and national legislative elections would be free and fair, Zedillo surprised some observers by following through on his promise. The 1997 elections demonstrated that Zedillo was serious about letting power slip from the PRI's hands. For the first time in decades, PRI candidates for the lower house of the national legislature did not win a majority of the votes. The powerful position of mayor of Mexico City also went to a non-PRI candidate.

No single decision-making perspective can explain Zedillo's decision to push forward with political liberalization, partly because this choice actually involved a series of decisions. The process of liberalization that culminated under Salinas had been underway for many years. Thus, Zedillo inherited a Mexican system engaged in *incremental* choices by the ruling elite—see the "In Theory and Practice" box on India for a discussion of incrementalism—which had built up to the point that the country reached a crossroads: turn liberalization into democratization or turn back and reestablish authoritarian rule.

Zedillo's final decisions, particularly to allow the PRI to lose the presidential election, however, may be understood as examples of rational calculations in response to increasing domestic and international pressure. The PRI leadership had been under significant pressure, including from the United States, to honor the results of the 2000 presidential election. A failure to do so risked a significant strain between Mexico and the United States, a relationship that Salinas and Zedillo had done much to cultivate. In addition, when the PRI openly stole the 1988 presidential election, it sparked protests and did significant damage to the legitimacy of PRI rule. Stealing another election, when it was so clear to most observers that Fox would win if the election were fair, might have unleashed violent social protest and threatened to eliminate the PRI as a viable party in whatever system emerged from the chaos. Instead, the PRI's acceptance of defeat allowed it to remain a significant political force in the newly democratic Mexico.

Brazil: Cardoso and the *Plano Real*

After Fernando Collor de Mello resigned in late 1992, he was replaced by his vice president, Itamar Franco, in the midst of an ongoing economic crisis. Since the transition to democracy, inflation had skyrocketed to over 1,000 percent per year. In 1993, the year after the Collor scandal, inflation more than doubled, to nearly 2,500 percent.[42] Despite efforts to restrain the rampant inflation—Brazil went through seven different currencies in eight years—nothing seemed to help. As Fernando Henrique Cardoso would later note, "By the time Itamar took office, many economists believed that Brazil's inflation problem could not be solved . . . it *was* tempting to just give up. However, Itamar did not have that luxury. . . . All of us had nightmares about people running around with suitcases full of worthless cash. This would cause unimaginable riots and social unrest."[43] After going through three finance ministers in seven months, Franco in desperation turned to Cardoso, his minister of foreign relations. Cardoso tried to refuse. His less-than-delighted reaction when the press printed reports of his appointment as finance minister was, "Oh my God, I'm ruined. . . . What am I supposed to do now?"

Cardoso was not a professional politician; nor did he have training in economics. He approached his problem more like a professor than a politician, thinking that he "needed a clear diagnosis of the problem, a plan to end it, and then the political support to carry such a plan through." He found a team of economic advisors with the training he lacked. Remembering it later, Cardoso describes an intense debate: "Untold gallons of coffee went into the making of the *Plano Real* [the 'Real Plan']. We spent countless nights poring over economics textbooks, scribbling equations on chalkboards, and arguing until four in the morning. . . . For months we met secretly in people's homes and back offices. . . . Finally, by December 1993, we took a collective deep breath and announced a course of action."[44]

The plan would create a new currency (the *Real*), initiate a round of steep budget cuts, and reduce the practice of tying raises to inflation. "Naturally," says Cardoso, "almost everybody hated it." Cardoso spent the next few months campaigning for the plan on talk shows, at business conventions, in city council meetings, and—most important—among congressmen. Ultimately, the Real Plan passed, in his view, because "none of these congressmen had any better ideas of their own. [And] it dawned on them that they would lose their jobs unless they met society's demands to end inflation."[45]

Not only did the Real Plan work, dropping inflation below 20 percent in two years, but the process itself was eminently rational. Cardoso brought together a team of experts, determined logically that he had to take the politically unpopular but necessary step of drastically cutting the budget, and then sold it to reluctant congressmen on the basis of their own self-interest. The fact that seven previous plans had failed worked in Cardoso's favor: with each failure, more people became convinced that the hard choice was the only viable choice to resolve a serious problem.

Nigeria: The Rationality of the Nigerian Civil War

The Nigerian civil war of the 1960s had important structural causes—most notably, the country's ethno-federal political structure which made violence more likely. This ethno-federal arrangement itself, however, was the result of decisions by political leaders. The British established the system, and the post-independence Nigerian leadership chose to continue it. These decisions indirectly produced the civil war. More important were a series of other decisions at various levels of the Nigerian government. The leadership of the southeastern province of the country could have sought greater autonomy short of independence, but it instead chose to pursue independence. The leadership of the federal government had numerous alternatives in response to the demands, but it chose to confront them violently.[46]

It is tempting to argue that the Ibo nationalists' decision to pursue independence was rational.

Nationalist elites are often portrayed as conniving and self-serving, and in the case of Ibo ethno-nationalist leaders, they did indeed likely weigh the costs and benefits of pursuing independence. At the same time, decisions leading to or in response to ethno-national violence are often made under conditions in which emotions drive decisions as much as rational calculations. Frustration at the inability of an ethnic group to control its own affairs can trigger aggressive responses.

As violence becomes a real possibility, and as the crisis makes pressure mount, the use of information short-cuts such as stereotypes and historical analogies sometimes replaces cautious, reasoned decision making. Often, this results in misunderstandings about the other side's intentions, incorrect assessments of threat, and a rush to violence to defend the nation. The Nigerian Civil War was no exception.

Important Political Decisions and Their Rationality in the Russian Federation, China, and Iran

The examples of decision making in the Russian Federation—in this case actually, the Soviet Union just prior to its collapse—China, and Iran highlight how key figures in nondemocratic systems sometimes make choices designed to bolster their own position or save the nondemocratic system itself. In the case of the Soviet Union, hardliners in the Soviet government chose to attempt an overthrow of Soviet leader Mikhail Gorbachev, whom they saw as having become too supportive of political liberalization. In China, Mao Zedong made two choices, designed to shake up the Communist system and mold it even more in his image, which ended up having negative consequences for him and his legacy. (The China section also includes a discussion of Deng Xiaoping's decision to use violence against the Tiananmen Square protesters as an example of "elite learning.") The example from Iran—the Guardian Council's decision to reject a large number of moderate candidates from the ballot for the 2004 *Majles* elections—is more recent. Unlike the coup against Gorbachev or Mao's great reforms, it is also one that appears to have succeeded in its goals, at least for the time being.

Russia (During the Soviet Period): The Coup Against Mikhail Gorbachev

As events spiraled out of Mikhail Gorbachev's control in 1990 and 1991, he began to backtrack on some of his liberalization efforts. He appointed hardliners (those opposed to reform of the Soviet system) to key positions in the government. By mid-1991, however, Gorbachev tried once again to get ahead of the wave of reform and proposed a new treaty to hold the Soviet Union together. The agreement to grant significant powers to the republics was the last straw for the hardliners, who placed Gorbachev under house arrest while he was vacationing in Crimea (in the USSR's Ukrainian union republic). Initially announcing that Gorbachev had requested that he be removed from power, the coup leaders quickly made clear that they were acting to restore order to the country.

The coup leaders were, arguably, acting in a classic rational choice manner. By August 1991, Gorbachev had clearly abandoned the conservatives and thrown his support behind a revamped, and much less Soviet, Soviet Union. Seeking to protect both the Soviet Union and, consequently, their personal political power, the coup leaders weighed the costs and benefits of doing nothing against the option of seeking to restore order through removing Gorbachev. Despite the costs of something as dramatic as a coup, they believed it offered them the best chance of maximizing their goal of hanging onto political power.

In the end, the coup leaders made a number of mistakes and showed poor leadership skills. The mistakes included allowing Boris Yeltsin, a chief opposition figure, to rally the masses in Moscow against the coup. Giving rousing speeches, at times standing on tanks that had been ordered into the streets by the coup leaders, Yeltsin won over much of the population of Moscow and, more important, much of the military supposedly acting on behalf of the coup leaders.

The coup fell apart in a matter of days, and the fate of the Soviet Union was sealed. Gorbachev tried to maintain control of the country and save some sort of Soviet state, but his efforts to win the support of those in the middle failed to recognize the absence of a political middle. Yeltsin replaced Gorbachev as the de facto leader of the country, part of a process that would culminate with the dissolution of the Soviet Union at the end of 1991.

China: Mao, the Great Leap Forward, and the Cultural Revolution

Mao Zedong will be remembered in China and around the world as one of the great leaders of the twentieth century, yet two of his most important policy decisions ended in failure. In 1958, Mao launched the Great Leap Forward. Designed to speed up China's economic development and reach Marx's vision of a communist utopia before the Soviet Union, peasants—still the majority of the population—were organized into massive communes. Each community was expected to be as self-sufficient as possible, which led to the practice of installing backyard blast furnaces on communes so that each collective could produce its own steel. Within a year,

Mao backed down. The fiasco even led him to resign as president, but he kept the all-important position of party chairman.

Less than a decade later, Mao encouraged the young to rise up against the country's establishment in the Great Proletarian Cultural Revolution. The youth of China responded, setting up Red Guard units that terrorized the country. University professors and high school teachers were particularly targeted. Many were killed or committed suicide; many more were sent to the countryside to work as peasants. Once more, Mao eventually came to realize that he had made a mistake, although the policy remained officially in place until Mao's death. Mao had to use the army to regain control of the situation, but not before a great deal of damage had been done.

It is hard to say that either of these major decisions was made in a fully rational manner; Mao clearly failed to think through all the possible consequences. Instead, it is likely Mao was making decisions based on his view of Marxist ideology and his desire to apply Marxism in a more pure manner than the Soviet government. Already by the time of the Great Leap Forward, and certainly during the Cultural Revolution, cracks had developed in China's relationship with the Soviet Union. Personal rivalry between the leaders of the countries at times shaped policy decisions, leading to rushed decisions, clouded judgment, and decisions based more on emotion than rational calculation.

IN THEORY AND PRACTICE

Deng Xiaoping, Tiananmen Square, and Elite Learning

One important theory related to the concept of rational decision making is that of **elite learning**. Elite learning theory holds that elites make adjustments based on previous political experiences. Simply put, elites learn. They remember their past decisions (and the context of those

decisions) that led to success, and they remember those that led to failure. They adjust their

Elite learning is a theory that political leaders learn from previous successes and failures and adjust their behavior accordingly to maximize the likelihood of future successes.

behavior accordingly to maximize the likelihood of success at present and in the future. In countries with unsuccessful democratization experiences, for example, mistakes made the first time can be corrected in subsequent democratization opportunities. This theory can be applied to decision makers' use of historical analogies or recent experiences in other countries.

In 1989, as Communism was faltering across Eastern Europe, students in Beijing began protesting economic conditions in the country. As their numbers grew and time went on, demands for political reform moved front and center. The Chinese government, under the leadership of Deng Xiaoping, initially tolerated the protests, centered in Beijing's Tiananmen Square. Once they began to draw as many as a million people in Beijing and spread to other major Chinese cities, Deng decided to listen to those in the government calling for a crackdown against the protesters. On June 4, 1989, the Chinese military regained control of Tiananmen Square and surrounding areas of the city, killing hundreds (perhaps thousands) of protesters and injuring thousands more in the process.

Another leader might have handled the Tiananmen Square incident differently, but it is a solid example of elite learning. Although the Berlin Wall would not fall until November 1989, already by early that summer, the Communist leaders of China had seen Communist parties lose power in several Central and Eastern European countries and Soviet troops had completed their withdrawal from Afghanistan. Although one cannot attribute the exact timing of the crackdown to the Chinese leaders' following of events as they unfolded in Eastern Europe, it is at least ironic that the Tiananmen Square crackdown came on the same day as Eastern Europe's first free election (in Poland) in four decades. What is clear is that the decision to suppress the protesters was not made in a domestic vacuum. The Chinese elites had learned: protests were rapidly bringing down Communist governments in Europe, and without a significant show of force the Chinese Communist Party was in real danger of suffering the same fate.

Iran: The Choice to Bar Reformist Candidates in the 2004 *Majles* Elections

Tensions between then–President Mohammed Khatami and conservative clerics came to a head in 2004. Since the elections in early 2000, Khatami had had a pro-reform majority in the national legislature, the *Majles*. In the lead-up to the 2004 *Majles* elections, the legislature sought to pass laws strengthening presidential power. The Guardian Council sprang into action. It announced that a large portion of the candidates (including most reformers currently in the legislature) were disqualified. Ayatollah Khamenei ordered the Guardian Council to reconsider its decision, but many initially banned politicians remained off the ballot for the 2004 elections.

President Khatami also faced a decision in response to the actions of the Guardian Council. Having promised not to endorse the holding of a fraudulent election, he backtracked in the hope of clinging to what little power he had left. Instead, the elections sealed the fate of the reform movement, at least in the near term. Even those pro-reform candidates who were allowed to run did poorly, though this was partly because of the election's low turnout.

The actions of the Guardian Council can be effectively explained from a rational choice perspective. By 2003, only through the unelected government positions, such as the Supreme Leader and the Guardian Council, were conservatives still able to shape national political outcomes. It is not hard to imagine discussions among the top conservatives about their goals, their options, and especially the costs of blocking pro-reform candidates versus allowing them to run. Given the successes of the reformer movement—gaining the presidency under Khatami for two terms, gaining control of the national legislature in 2000, and making major inroads in many city governments—the costs of allowing reform to continue were too great at the time.

In the short run at least, the decision by Iran's hardliners worked. For all intents and purposes, the first post–Islamic Revolution "reform era" in Iran ended in 2004. Hopes for any serious steps toward democratization in the near term were dashed, and the theocratic nature of Iran's regime was solidified. In 2005, Mahmoud Ahmadinejad's election as president further deepened religious conservatives' political control of Iran.

COMPARATIVE EXERCISE

The Mexican Government's Support of NAFTA

This chapter's comparative exercise uses rational choice theory to examine the Mexican government's support of the North American Free Trade Agreement (NAFTA). The goal of this case study is a deeper understanding of the event. In doing so, however, one should also consider the challenges of understanding decision making as rational without thinking carefully about factors shaping perceptions of interests, costs, and benefits.

Rational Choice Theory

The primary assumption of **rational choice theory** is that humans act rationally when making decisions, seeking to maximize the likelihood of attaining their interests by weighing the costs and benefits of particular actions. The approach typically understands collective political outcomes as flowing from a set of individual decisions. The interest that an individual seeks to maximize need not be egoistic self-interest, though that is a common starting point for models of rational behavior. Note that rationality is more than just conscious thought. Being conscious of one's actions is not enough to make those actions rationally based.

Overview: Carlos Salinas and the NAFTA Agreement

As president of Mexico from 1988 to 1994, Carlos Salinas de Gortari solidified a new path for Mexico in its relationship with the United States and its attitude toward economic openness. In 1988, Salinas opposed a proposed free trade agreement with the United States. After witnessing the success of an agreement between the United States and Canada and the collapse of socialist governments in Central and Eastern Europe, however, he chose to aggressively pursue the idea of extending that agreement, both in scope and to include Mexico. (Salinas had also taken a trip to Europe early in his presidency, in which his efforts to expand economic connections with Western European countries garnered only a lukewarm reception.) This led to an agreement in 1990 to negotiate a new trade pact involving the entire North American continent. The North American Free Trade Agreement (NAFTA) was born.

This action went against a tradition of economic protectionism and a tightly controlled domestic economy in Mexico, though this tradition had already been breaking down by the eve of Salinas's 1988 election.[47] Salinas dramatically changed the face of Mexican economic policy by extending this emerging trend and by successfully using his position as Mexican president to convince other officials to support his vision.

Rational choice theory is a wide-ranging theoretical perspective used to explain both individual political behavior and collective actions. It assumes that individuals make rational decisions to maximize their interests.

A Rational Choice Explanation of Salinas's Decision?

What drove Salinas to increase ties with the United States and Canada through NAFTA? Can NAFTA be explained as a rational choice? Rational choice explanations commonly assume that politicians seek to maximize the likelihood of reelection, taking popular policy positions, particularly for their political "base." There was little public support for NAFTA when negotiations began. In addition, unlike Thatcher's initially unpopular reforms which were at least beneficial to her electoral base, NAFTA would hit farmers—a core component of the PRI's base—harder than any other economic sector.

One might conclude that Salinas acted irrationally, especially if one fails to look beyond the decision itself and bring institutions into the story. Chapter 6 discussed the extent to which political rules can constrain or create opportunities for political leaders. For this comparative exercise, one of Mexico's key institutional provisions, the single-term president, is particularly crucial. Because Mexican presidents serve only one term, Salinas had no electoral concerns to take into account.

Rather, it was in Salinas's self-interest to maximize his personal authority during his term in office. Salinas had come to power under allegations of vote fraud, faced a troubled economy, and led an increasingly unpopular PRI. He had little to lose in shaking up Mexican economic approaches but much to gain if new investment in the country sparked an economic turnaround. Salinas pursued a number of economic reforms—dubbed "Salinastroika," after the *perestroika* reforms under Mikhail Gorbachev in the Soviet Union. These reforms included the privatization of most state-owned companies in Mexico.

One could certainly argue that NAFTA was in Mexico's overall economic interests. Able to produce manufactured products more cheaply than the United States, Mexico's exports should have expanded significantly under NAFTA.[48] Perhaps as important, Salinas likely believed that NAFTA would make the United States even more willing to offer economic assistance to Mexico[49]—something it indeed did do in the mid-1990s in an effort to stabilize the value of the peso. Even considering Salinas as self-interested rather than having sociotropic interests, his personal fate was tied to maximizing Mexico's economic performance. If he believed a trade agreement like NAFTA would improve Mexico's economic performance—and especially if he had come to realize that closer economic ties with Europe were unlikely—his decision to support NAFTA was rational.

Discussion

This discussion of Salinas's interests has already gone beyond the realm of the choice approach, bringing in political structure. Asking *why* Salinas believed that NAFTA maximized the likelihood of strong Mexican economic performance further complicates the application of rational choice theory in this case. Here one must consider Salinas's background and experiences. Born in Mexico City, Salinas had little direct knowledge of rural life. In addition, Salinas attended graduate school in the United States, studying economics and politics at Harvard University. Finally, the world that Salinas saw around him was very different in 1990 than it had been only two years earlier. The collapse of Communism in Europe led many political figures to consider American-style economic neoliberalism as their only option.

Thus, rational choice theory provides some help in understanding Salinas's decision to encourage NAFTA, but this examination also raises questions about applying rational choice perspectives to particular settings. Traditional assumptions of political self-interest involving reelection do not apply to this case, requiring an adjustment of the assumption about Salinas's interests to fit the situation in question.

This reconsideration of Salinas's interests makes it necessary to take into account various structural and leadership-related issues: institutional arrangements in Mexico, Salinas's education in the United States, and even the transformation of international politics with the collapse of Communism.

This case study demonstrates how rational choice theory is easily adapted to capture the nuances of particular leaders and settings. This is one of its strengths. It is also a potential weakness, although bending the theory to fit the events is less of a problem in this case than it might be in others. The goal of this case study was not to test the theory but rather to use the theory to understand Salinas's decision to pursue Mexico's participation in NAFTA.

Think and Discuss

What else, not examined in the comparative exercise, might explain Carlos Salinas's decision to support the North American Free Trade Agreement?

CONCLUSION

The choice approach, with its emphasis on individuals and their decisions, stands in stark contrast to structural approaches in the field of comparative politics. As Jack Goldstone writes about the study of revolutions, "In the 1970s and 1980s, scholars studying revolutions focused their attention on long-term characteristics of states and societies that heighten their risk of revolution. . . . in focusing on these 'macro' or large-scale structural causes, scholars seemed to lose an appreciation for the critical role of ideas, and the decisions of key individuals, as elements that make revolutions happen."[50]

Over the next two decades, the pendulum swung away from structural approaches and toward an emphasis on choice. Though some scholars believe that rational choice theory solves the levels of analysis problem (allowing one to explain both collective events and those at the individual level), one must be careful not to underestimate the extent to which structures provide constraints on political decision makers. Although these constraints do not shape every individual political decision in the same way, one should not ignore them when looking at a given individual political decision.

Think and Discuss

This idea that leadership matters is a strong challenge to structural arguments discussed in previous chapters. At this point, which seem more important, structural arguments or choice arguments? Why?

Information problems also should be taken seriously. Scholars have addressed information problems in "amendments" to rational choice such as satisficing or incrementalism, both of which were discussed in this chapter. The idea that humans are creatures of emotion poses perhaps the greatest challenge to rational choice. Human emotions are something that rational choice scholars cannot easily co-opt into their models. Taking emotion into account does not mean one must assume that all political decisions are irrational. It does mean that one must consider the conditions under which political decisions are likely to be more rational or less rational.

This chapter's comparative exercise was a simplified version of what a scholar would do seeking to understand Salinas's support for NAFTA. A real case study would include a much more detailed account of the decision-making process and the factors that shaped Salinas's views of increased economic integration with the United States. Yet even the exercise's simplified discussion involved economics, political institutions, and international factors. While it is very important to consider the role of individual leaders and how rational these leaders are, a full understanding of broad patterns of political behavior and of particular political outcomes benefits from finding ways to integrate structural and choice-based explanations, a recognition that appears to be gaining momentum among comparative politics scholars.[51]

Integrating choice and structure requires one to understand them both. Previous sections of the book introduced the political consequences of various economic, cultural, identity, and political structures. This section of the book, and this chapter in particular, has emphasized individuals and their choices. It is now time to bring structures and choices together more systematically. The next chapter integrates structure and choice arguments in the examination of the important comparative politics topic of democratization.

Key Terms

Bounded rationality, p. 427
Choice approach, p. 405
Cognitive dissonance, p. 427
Elite Learning, p. 437
Emotion, p. 428
Equilibrium, p. 426
Groupthink, p. 427
Impossibility theorem, p. 426
Incrementalism, p. 432
Leadership, p. 406
Leadership skills, p. 406
Leadership style, p. 407
Leadership traits, p. 406
Mood, p. 428
Pocketbook calculations, p. 425
Prospective calculations, p. 425
Rational choice theory, p. 439
Rationality, p. 425
Retrospective calculations, p. 425
Satisficing, p. 427
Sociotropic calculations, p. 426
Transference, p. 428
Voting paradox, p. 426

12
Regime Transitions

Learning Objectives

After reading this chapter, you should be able to:

- Define key concepts such as regime transition, liberalization, and democratization.

- Discuss why democratization can be destabilizing for a country.

- Describe characteristics of a consolidated democracy.

- Summarize the major explanations that focus on structures and choices of democratization.

- Outline the historical and recent experiences with regime transition in the United Kingdom, Germany, France, Mexico, Brazil, Russia, China, India, Nigeria, and Iran.

Over the last two decades, Benin, a French-speaking country located just to the west of Nigeria, has been one of Africa's democratic success stories. In 1991, the country held multiparty elections, and the sitting president—Mathieu Kérékou, the military leader of the country from 1972 to 1991—lost to an economist, Nicéphore Soglo. In one of many important moments in the development of democracy in Benin, Kérékou accepted the results and stepped down, albeit partly in exchange for immunity from prosecution for his actions during the nondemocratic period. Kérékou defeated Soglo in the presidential election five years later, and again the transition went smoothly. Following Kérékou's reelection in 2001, discussions eventually turned to the 2006 vote, when voters in Benin would choose Kérékou's successor.

Look for this icon to point you to **Deepening Your Understanding** features on the companion website www.college.cengage.com/politicalscience/barrington, which provide greater depth for some key content.

Because the constitution prohibited a third term (as well as forbidding presidential candidates from being over seventy years old), the two-term president and seventy-two-year old Kérékou could not run again in 2006—unless, of course, the constitution was amended. The practice of amending the constitution to accommodate sitting presidents is not uncommon (remember, former Nigerian President Olusegun Obasanjo considered a similar idea to allow him to seek a third term and extend his rule beyond 2007). In Benin, however, when the idea was floated in 2005 to amend the constitution so Kérékou could run again, it met with significant resistance from the general population. In addition to stories of ordinary citizens threatening violence if the constitution was changed,[1] a group of nongovernmental organizations in Benin organized an informational campaign against the potential move. The centerpiece of this campaign was the use of signs and billboards that read "Touche pas ma constitution!" ("Don't touch my constitution!"). The slogan resonated with citizens of Benin, particularly after government officials initially responded by tearing down the signs.[2] Kérékou backed off, the election went ahead without him, and in March 2006, economist Thomas Yayi Boni won the presidential contest. ■

Regime transition is one of the central topics of comparative politics, arguably serving as the dependent variable in as many comparative politics studies as any other political outcome. Some instructors design their introductory comparative politics courses entirely around regime transition because it provides an effective anchor for the discussion of central comparative politics concepts, theories, and debates. It is, therefore, appropriate that this first chapter of the final section of the book is devoted to a discussion about how analyzing structures and choices can help one to understand regime transitions, such as the successful democratization in Benin.

Understanding the causes and consequences of different political regimes is crucial to understanding politics. If political systems matter, it is a good idea to know what influences their creation, consolidation, or collapse. The topic of regime transition also highlights the connections between comparative politics and other political science fields such as international relations, as well as other social science disciplines. Moreover, in the last several decades, both the architects of American foreign policy and the leaders of international organizations such as the European Union have placed an emphasis on fostering regime change in certain countries in order to achieve various national and international political goals.

Comparative politics research regarding regime transitions focuses more on transitions to democracy than on the collapse of democracy. Likewise, this chapter centers more on democratization than on democratic breakdown. There are several justifications for focusing on democratic establishment and consolidation. A number of normative and empirical arguments hold that democracy is a superior form of government. They argue for the inherent good of people having a say in running their own lives; that consolidated democratic systems are more politically and socially stable than their counterparts;[3] and that, because democracies tend not to go to war against other democracies, increasing the number of democracies promotes peace.[4]

Democratization can have pitfalls, too. While mature democracies are politically quite stable, periods of transition to democracy can be chaotic, leading elites and masses alike to look back fondly to times of relative order and stability under a nondemocratic system.[5] Elections in new democracies may also produce awkward results. In 2006, for example, Hamas—a group the U.S. government labeled a terrorist organization—won elections in the Palestinian territories. In prior decades, democratic elections in a variety of settings increased ethnic tensions and brought ethnic nationalists to power.[6] Additionally, although democracies rarely fight each other, they fight plenty of wars against nondemocracies. A world in which every political system were democratic might indeed be much more peaceful than it is today, but recent history suggests that one should expect a number of civil wars and international conflicts along the way to that point.

Even claims of the moral superiority of representative government can be challenged. As cases such as Nigeria demonstrate, the establishment of democratic government does not guarantee an end to corruption, economic hardship, or ethnic violence. Moreover, in times of social chaos, people may struggle to enjoy democratic freedoms. While most Iraqis were happy for the chance to select their political leaders after the American-led occupation of their country, subsequent instability made many afraid to engage in daily activities that American citizens take for granted.

Comparativists today also have a superb opportunity to discover generalizable patterns regarding democratization. There have been a large number of democratizations over the last several decades. These recent regime transitions provide fertile ground for comparison.

Regime Transition

A **regime transition** occurs when one type of political system changes into another. Figure 12.1 displays a continuum of regime types, ranging from authoritarian to democratic. (Totalitarian systems are excluded from the figure, though as some of this chapter's Topic in Countries discussions point out, transitions can begin from or end in totalitarianism as well.) A regime transition involves movement, in either direction, from one category to another on this continuum.

Regime transitions vary in pace and extent. Some happen relatively quickly, such as the collapse of Eastern European Communist regimes in the late 1980s. In other cases, the process is more protracted. Mexico moved from authoritarianism to democracy over several decades. Some transitions are also more sweeping than others. Mexico's spanned the entire spectrum in Figure 12.1, but Russia's recent retreat from democracy has been less wide-ranging. Though increasingly less democratic, many observers do not yet consider Russia a full-fledged authoritarian system.

Because real-world political systems differ from ideal-type regimes, gauging when a country has moved from one regime type to another can be difficult. Those studying transitions often disagree about how best to measure a particular regime type or where a certain country falls

A **regime transition** is the process of changing from one type of political system to another.

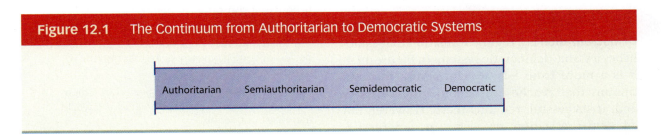

Figure 12.1   The Continuum from Authoritarian to Democratic Systems

Authoritarian   Semiauthoritarian   Semidemocratic   Democratic

on the continuum in Figure 12.1. While one comparativist might view a country as authoritarian, another looking at the same country might see it as having already made the transition from authoritarian to semiauthoritarian.

Liberalization

Liberalization occurs when a nondemocratic system becomes politically more open and less repressive. The government expands individual rights and freedoms, often through official changes to the country's constitution or the enforcement of previously ignored constitutional provisions. Nondemocratic leaders may pursue liberalization for a number of reasons. They may seek to boost their legitimacy and believe that they can maintain control of the reform process. Some, such as China's Communist leadership, are able to maintain control while loosening some restraints over people's daily lives. Others, as in the case of Soviet leader Mikhail Gorbachev, are unable to contain the politically destabilizing forces that can surface during periods of liberalization.

There are degrees of liberalization. A country undergoing significant liberalization would move from left to right in Figure 12.1, but liberalization does not necessarily alter the category in which a comparativist would place the regime. Reforms that liberalize a nondemocratic system *might* move the country from one regime type (authoritarianism) to another (semiauthoritarianism), but they might also simply make an authoritarian system less authoritarian without clearly moving it out of the authoritarian category.

Democratization

Democratization is a regime transition that establishes a stable democratic system. In Figure 12.1, it is a move from left to right across the continuum that reaches the democratic category and, if successful, remains there. However, not all democratization processes are successful.

Incomplete democratization occurs when a democracy exists for only a short time and then collapses or slowly regresses. Examples of incomplete democratizations are plentiful, particularly among less economically developed countries or countries with a history of repeated military involvement in domestic politics.

Like regime transitions in general, the pace of democratization varies. A nondemocracy may collapse in a matter of days, or it may evolve into a more democratic system over a lengthy interval, with liberalization ultimately leading to the establishment of a system recognized as democratic. The successful consolidation of a democracy, however, is nearly always a protracted process, typically occurring in decades rather than years.

Waves of Democratization

Just as democratizations can vary from one case to the next, the global spread of democracy varies over time. A noticeable surge in global democracy over a particular period of time is known as a **democratization wave**. Although Samuel Huntington was not the first to discuss the idea of democratic surges and retrenchments globally, the concept of waves of democratization is most closely associated with his 1991 book, *The Third Wave*.[7]

Liberalization is the process of making a nondemocratic political system more open and less repressive.

Democratization is a regime transition that establishes a democracy. A successful democratization produces a consolidated democracy.

A transition in which a democracy is established but the democracy does not last for an extended period of time is known as an **incomplete democratization**.

A **democratization wave** is a period in which the number of democracies around the world increases noticeably.

Table 12.1   Waves and Reverse Waves of Democratization

Wave/Reverse Wave	Examples	Period
First Wave	American and French democracy; expansion of the franchise in Western democracies.	1820s–1920s
First Reverse Wave	Rise of fascism in Europe, especially in Germany, Italy, and Spain, but also in Eastern Europe.	1920s–1940s
Second Wave	Post–World War II occupation and decolonization in Africa and Asia.	1940s–1960s
Second Reverse Wave	Resurgence of bureaucratic and military authoritarianism in Latin America, Africa, and Asia.	1960s–mid-1970s
Third Wave	Southern European, Latin American, and post-Communist democratizations.	Mid-1970s–1990s
Third Reverse Wave ???	Creeping authoritarianism in Peru under Fujimori and some post-Communist states (e.g., Belarus); Military coups in Africa (e.g., Niger and Gambia).	1990s–2000
Fourth Wave ???	Mexico's 2000 presidential election; the "Color Revolutions" (Serbia, Georgia, Ukraine, Kyrgyzstan, and Lebanon); U.S.-led efforts at regime change in Afghanistan and Iraq	2000–present

Source: Modified from Samuel Huntington's *The Third Wave* (1991)

During a democratization wave, the number of new democracies exceeds the number of democratic breakdowns. Eventually the balance may shift, bringing an unmistakable contraction in the number of democracies. This reduction in democratic systems is known as a **reverse wave**. Huntington points out that, even when reverse waves have occurred, they have still left behind more democracies than had existed prior to the original wave.[8] While a great number of new democracies have developed in the last three decades, Huntington's historical framework implies that not all of the "third wave" democracies will survive. One can expect a number to be swept away in a subsequent reverse wave. As Table 12.1 indicates, one could claim a reverse wave already occurred in the 1990s, followed by a new, "fourth wave" of democratization.

Stages of Democratization

Democratization in a particular country occurs in stages. Some comparativists argue that these stages can overlap, while others see them as more distinct. Assorted democratization studies

A **reverse wave** occurs when there is a sizeable reduction in the number of democracies globally.

use different labels for these stages and even disagree about the number of stages. For the most part, however, there is agreement that democratization entails a nondemocratic regime breaking down, a democracy being instituted, and that democracy becoming stable and secure. As presented in Figure 12.2, comparativists often label these three stages the **breakdown of nondemocracy**, **establishment of democracy**, and **consolidation of democracy**. Although successful democratization involves movement through all three stages, it is not always easy to identify when a country has completely left one stage and moved into the other.

Arriving at one stage of democratization also does not guarantee that a country will reach the next stage. Regime transitions are times of great uncertainty. When a nondemocratic system collapses, a new leader might reestablish that system or form a different nondemocratic system. Even when the population perceives the old nondemocratic government as very corrupt, government change without regime change is a distinct possibility. Likewise, the founding of a democracy does not guarantee its consolidation. Just as established nondemocracies can break down, so too can established democracies.

The Breakdown of the Nondemocratic System

The first stage of democratization involves the slow liberalization or rapid collapse of a nondemocratic system. Dankwart Rustow has called the breakdown of the nondemocracy the "preparatory" stage of democratization.[9] This label captures the idea that the disintegration of the nondemocracy makes the emergence of democracy possible.

Nondemocratic systems can break down in a variety of ways. Comparativist Terry Lynn Karl distinguishes between "transitions from above," where the ruling elite liberalizes and effectively controls the political reform process, and "transitions from below," where opposition leaders successfully organize unconventional mass participation in resistance to the existing nondemocracy.[10] Comparativist Scott Mainwaring adds a middle category, where the old rulers do not fully control the process but are able to participate in negotiations and protect themselves from retribution following the establishment of the new democracy.[11] This is, in many ways, the story of the democratization of post-Apartheid South Africa.

Establishment of the Democratic System

During the second stage, political elites establish the institutional framework for the new democratic system. The country typically adopts a new constitution, often through a national referendum. Because of the importance of the choices and decisions elites make during this stage of democratization, Rustow

> Comparativists emphasize three stages of democratization: the **breakdown of nondemocracy**, the **establishment of democracy**, and the **consolidation of democracy**. Nondemocratic breakdowns do not always lead to democracies, and established democracies do not always become consolidated. A democracy becomes consolidated when elites and masses alike see no viable alternative to the democratic system.

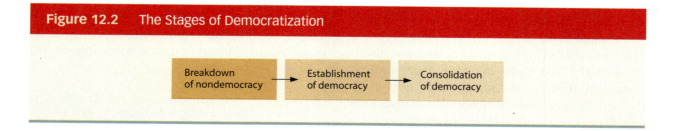

Figure 12.2   The Stages of Democratization

Breakdown of nondemocracy → Establishment of democracy → Consolidation of democracy

labels it the "decision stage."[12] By emphasizing decisions, Rustow highlights the choice side of the structure versus choice framework. Consequently, his label fails to convey the extent to which the existing socioeconomic and political structures affect the decisions about the new institutional arrangements. It also fails to capture that these new democratic institutions themselves become a central part of the country's political structure, constraining and providing opportunities to government officials in the new democracy.

The composition of the new institutions matter a great deal. A presidential system with FPTP electoral arrangements might work in one country but be disastrous in another. As a result, those designing a new constitution ideally look not only at examples of other democratic systems but also take into account their own country's unique challenges and needs. Similarly, those outside the country providing advice about the new system should study the country in question in great detail and consider the possible consequences of their suggestions before making them.

Consolidation of Democracy Democratic consolidation is one of the more thought-provoking concepts in comparative politics. Comparativists disagree on its causes and even how to determine when it exists. In defining consolidation, scholars such as Lawrence Whitehead and Juan Linz stress the lack of viable alternatives to the democratic system.[13] Both the government leaders and their political opponents expect democracy to endure and accept it as the "only game in town."[14] Accordingly, a consolidated democracy is one that is very unlikely to break down and be replaced by a nondemocratic system. Such a breakdown would require a fundamental change in the political setting—such as the development of massive corruption or a severe economic crisis—to eliminate democracy's status as the "only game in town" and make the transition to a nondemocratic system a viable alternative.

APPLYING CONCEPTS

When Is a Democracy Consolidated?

Like many political science concepts, the concept of democratic consolidation generates debates over its definition, as well as over its measurement. Comparativists have identified a number of indicators that one could use to measure consolidation:

- *Holding repeated free and fair elections.* When free and fair elections become routine, it is a strong sign that democracy has become the "only game in town."
- *Peaceful transfer of power through elections.* Some believe that elections alone are not enough. A number of scholars suggest looking for a successful and peaceful transfer of power from one set of rulers to another. If democracy is, as Adam Przeworski claims, "a system in which parties lose elections,"[15] it cannot only be opposition parties that lose such elections. If an election results in a president or ruling party losing control of the government *and* the rulers peacefully hand over power to those who defeated them, democracy would appear to be entrenched. But even this is not enough for some scholars, who need to see repeated transfers of power before labeling a democracy as consolidated. Samuel Huntington, for example, prefers a "two-turnover" criterion, where those who peacefully replace the sitting government later turn over power to another set of leaders.[16]
- *Surviving a "test."* A consolidated democracy can endure various threats or "tests." Such tests include an attempted coup (e.g., Spain in 1981), a very close election (e.g., Mexico in 2006), or severe economic hardship (e.g., a number of 1980s Latin American countries, when democracy actually expanded despite a regional economic crisis).[17]
- *Adherence to the "rule of law."* Following the constitution and accepting that no one is above the law—principles at the heart of the
(continued)

concept of "rule of law"—are also features of a consolidated democracy. It is not always easy to determine when the rule of law has taken hold in a country, but the more one sees what Lawrence Whitehead calls "durable compliance with rules and procedures,"[18] the more likely democracy is consolidated.

- **■ *Legitimacy.*** Chapter 1 discussed legitimacy, the population's acceptance of the political system as having the right to produce binding rules over society. It makes sense that the development of legitimacy would signal a democratic system's consolidation, but it is unclear how much legitimacy is necessary—that is, the portion of the population that needs to accept the system as legitimate for it to be called consolidated.

- **■ *Survival for a lengthy period of time.*** Surviving for a period of time is not the same thing as stability, nor does it guarantee that democracy has become the "only game in town." Still, the longer a democracy survives the more likely that it will continue to survive.

The idea that even a consolidated democracy can possibly break down at some point in the future has led some scholars to emphasize an additional stage of democratization, maturation. According to this view, a "mature" democracy is one that has lasted so long and survived so many tests that it is unthinkable that it could collapse even in the face of economic or political crises.[19] The vast majority of democratization scholars, however, discuss only three stages of democratization, considering "mature" democracies as simply more consolidated than others.

Think and Discuss

Which of the conditions highlighted in the "Applying Concepts" box would most convincingly indicate that a democracy is consolidated? Why?

Democratic Breakdown

It is not unusual for an established democracy to break down and be replaced by some form of nondemocratic political system. **Democratic breakdown** can happen over time, as in the cases of "creeping authoritarianism" discussed earlier in the book, or it can happen rather abruptly. Sometimes, a democracy may exist for a lengthy period, appear to be consolidated, and still collapse. This is much less common, however, than instances of incomplete democratization where the democracy is never consolidated.

The seminal study of democratic breakdowns is a 1978 book edited by Juan Linz and Alfred Stepan that covers cases from Europe to Latin America, including Germany and Brazil.[20] In the book's introduction, Linz proposes that, like democratization, democratic breakdown occurs in stages. Linz labels the first the **crisis stage**, where a democratic government fails to address one or more pressing social problems. When a crisis is severe enough that it undercuts not just support for the government but the legitimacy of the system itself, the typical result is the **breakdown stage**. According to Linz, this stage is reached when the sitting government, faced with mounting instability and diminishing legitimacy, chooses among dramatically strengthening the executive, surrendering power to the military, or attempting to co-opt opposition forces that are uncommitted to democracy. These actions often fail to save democracy, transforming the system instead into one form of nondemocratic system or another. The nondemocratic period that

Democratic breakdown occurs when a democracy collapses or slowly transforms into a nondemocratic system. Juan Linz identifies three stages of democratic breakdown: the **crisis stage**, the **breakdown stage**, and **reequilibration**.

The **crisis stage** occurs when a crisis emerges that threatens an existing democracy.

The crisis stage can lead to the **breakdown stage**, when the democratic system collapses.

follows democratic breakdown may be a brief interlude, or it may last decades or more.

Alternatively, the crisis stage may lead the current democratic government to transform without a regime transition. Democracy survives, although it generally looks quite different from its previous incarnation. Linz calls this the process of **reequilibration**. It requires a leadership untainted by the preceding crisis and able to win over important political, economic, and social groups; the willingness of former leaders to turn over power to the new rulers and accept new policy directions; and a high level of passivity among the general population.[21] Such conditions do not frequently intersect. Consequently, reequilibration is far from guaranteed, and severe crises commonly result in a period of nondemocratic government.

Think and Discuss

Could democracy possibly break down in the United Kingdom? In the United States? How?

Understanding Regime Transitions

Over the past five decades, most of the comparative politics research on regime transition has focused either on specific structural conditions or on elite choices. Works studying democratization, for example, initially tended to emphasize economic structure as part of comparativists' "search for the necessary conditions and prerequisites for the emergence of a stable democracy."[22] Later, identity and culture took center stage among those emphasizing structure, while other researchers increasingly focused on the role of elites. Indeed, both structural and choice factors help explain regime transitions. Unfortunately, there appear to be no necessary or sufficient causal factors that determine the outcome of democratization in all cases. Consequently,

causal theories of democratization are, as a rule, probabilistic (see Chapter 1). They emphasize factors that make democratic establishment and consolidation more likely.

It is important to distinguish between causal factors that make democracy more likely and criteria that one can use to measure whether a system is democratic. Citizens' strong belief in the practice of free and fair elections is a causal factor that facilitates democratic consolidation. Likewise, the development of values such as tolerance of differing opinions increases the prospects that a democracy will survive. Actually holding repeated free and fair elections or establishing and enforcing the right to engage in controversial speech, on the other hand, are indicators that democracy has indeed taken hold. To avoid tautological explanations of democratization, mass values such as tolerance cannot be included in definitions of what democracy is, nor can practices such as free and fair elections be considered causal factors that influence democratization.

Structure Versus Choice and Internal Versus External

The overall set of causal factors related to regime transition can be divided two ways: structure versus choice and factors within a country versus those outside that country. At times throughout the text, discussions of the structure versus choice framework have emphasized this second dividing line. For example, the overview of economic and cultural structures underscored the role of globalization in domestic economic development and political culture. Even the previous chapter's coverage of elite decision making pointed to how elites in a particular country can learn from the decisions of leaders in neighboring countries, or how an important global

---

The crisis stage can also lead to **reequilibration**, when the crisis stage brings an overhaul of the democratic system rather than a nondemocratic system.

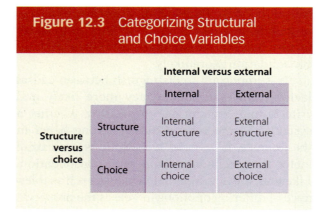

Figure 12.3   Categorizing Structural and Choice Variables

		Internal versus external	
		Internal	External
Structure versus choice	**Structure**	Internal structure	External structure
	Choice	Internal choice	External choice

leader's decisions can directly affect that country's political outcomes.

Taking the difference between internal and external factors into consideration aids in the application of the structure versus choice framework. The result is four sets of factors—internal structure, external structure, internal choice, and external choice—presented in Figure 12.3.

Internal Structural Explanations of Democratization

This book's general discussion of internal structure is divided into economic, cultural, identity, and political structure. Likewise, when considering how internal structural factors might influence democratization, it is useful to distinguish among these four types of structural factors.

Economic Structure Modernization theory and its emphasis on capitalist economic development influenced initial democratization studies. In 1959, political scientist Seymour Martin Lipset published a seminal article on what he believed to be the social and economic requisites for democracy.[23] Lipset's claim that economic development is associated with democracy remains a central topic within the democratization literature. Even rough indicators of such development—for example, per capita

GDP—reveal a strong relationship between development and democratization. Especially if one excludes states prosperous due to oil wealth, most stable democracies are much wealthier than most nondemocracies. Excluding the oil states improves the relationship largely because oil states generally lack another key economic structural factor, a sizeable middle class, which many democratization scholars believe makes successful democratization more likely.

Scholars discuss the development-democracy relationship in terms of both direct and indirect effects. Direct effects include economic power being spread out across the general population, which makes it more difficult for the government to engage in repression. Scholars such as Barrington Moore have also pointed to the importance of specific development patterns and alliances between particular economically powerful groups. For Moore, a certain form of commercial agriculture—the presence of free farmers rather than a labor-repressive agricultural system—and especially the existence of a bourgeois middle class make democracy possible.

Economic structure's indirect effects on democratization include conditions generated by economic development like urbanization and education. Economic development also provides a sense of security that makes it possible for people to value voting rights. When people are struggling to find food for themselves and their families, whether or not they had a say in the selection of their country's political leaders is often far from their top priority.

Political Culture Chapter 4 presented five key components of political culture. Three of them—beliefs about authority, values regarding security versus liberty, and national identity—are particularly relevant to democratization. The other two political culture components are of less importance for understanding democratic transitions. Beliefs about the political system's legitimacy are important for the stability of *any* regime, and political cultures that highlight the collective over the individual are not necessarily harmful to democracy, although they are more conducive to a democratic system stressing majority rule and equality over individual rights.

Existing beliefs about authority, such as deference to social elites and a strongly vertical social hierarchy, can make democracy difficult to establish. At the same time, Gabriel Almond and Sydney Verba argue in *The Civic Culture* that a certain degree of deference to authority (as in British political culture) increases stability in an established democracy, since the masses are not regularly challenging the system's outputs and legitimacy.[24]

Cultures valuing security over liberty pose a challenge to democracy. As a system of "institutionalized uncertainty" and one that emphasizes personal liberty, democracy is not necessarily conducive to social order, especially in its early years. If people prefer order over freedom, new democracies are vulnerable both to creeping authoritarianism and to a rapid breakdown as in the case of a military coup d'état. Consequently, some comparativists turn to cultural explanations, such as Ronald Inglehart's postmaterialism theory, that address the emergence of values supporting personal self-expression and freedom from government control.[25]

Cultures emphasizing national identity and attachment to the central government as the primary political unit enhance prospects for democracy. Without national unity, democratic practices can deepen divisions rather than overcome them. When the population is detached from the central government, government policies may not be respected or enforced at the local level. Nondemocratic systems can overcome these challenges through force, something democracies use only in rare cases. In his seminal piece on democratic transitions in 1970, Dankwart Rustow goes so far as to call national unity a precondition of any democratic transition.[26]

Identity Structure Explanations of identity structure and democratic transition often center on the form of identity diversity, or what Chapter 5 called cleavage structure theory. According to this perspective, when social divisions cut across one another, democracy is plausible. In contrast, when deep social divisions complement one another—for example, when two ethnic groups speak different languages, have different religions, are concentrated in different parts of the country, and differ in terms of each group's collective wealth—democracy is tenuous. Democratic practices like elections foster candidates and parties that emphasize and reinforce these social divisions. Preventing the "other" from gaining control of the political system becomes a stimulus for participation. Programmatic differences between parties give way to identity politics.

Other comparativists interested in identity structure and democracy explore whether certain collective identities are incompatible with democracy. Much of this work turns the spotlight on religion, most recently scrutinizing the relationship of Islam to democracy. When considering the role religion plays in a particular country's democratization prospects, one should ask three questions. First, since *any* strain of fundamentalism is arguably hostile to democracy, how prevalent is fundamentalism? Fundamentalists take religious texts literally, see religion as essential to society's proper functioning, and are commonly intolerant of opposing viewpoints. Listening to others' views and seeking compromise and cooperation are inconsistent with belief in an absolute "Truth" that should guide all political, economic, and social relations.

Second, have events possibly made past arguments about a particular religion less relevant at the present? Prior to the third wave of democratization, many believed that Catholicism was less compatible with democracy than Protestantism. Yet, partly because of the changes in the Catholic Church associated with Vatican II, most of the democratizations of the first half of the third wave took place in Catholic countries.

Third, to what extent does a country's main religion correlate with its overall culture? A dominant religion shapes a society's culture, but existing political cultural values about authority, security, and national identity may be distinct from that religion. Disputes over whether Islam is conducive to democracy bring to light the factor of attitudes toward women. When women are seen as second-class citizens, individuals may use elements of Islam to perpetuate those views, even if Islam itself did not create them.

Political Structures: The Institutional Arrangements of the New Democracy Political structures affect democratization in several ways. The form of a nondemocratic regime can influence the nature and speed of that regime's dissolution. In addition, when a nondemocracy breaks down, its institutional structures can leave lasting legacies with which the new democracy must contend. Each of the independent states that emerged from the collapse of the Soviet Union, for example, began independence with the constitutions and institutional composition the state had used as a USSR union republic.

Democratization specialists also pay a great deal of attention to the design of new democratic institutions and the implications that different arrangements have for stability and consolidation. Such design options include some of the major divisions discussed in Chapters 6 through 10: federal versus unitary systems, presidential versus parliamentary systems, judiciaries with constitutional review powers versus those without, pluralist versus corporatist interest group arrangements, and first past the post (FPTP) versus proportional representation (PR) electoral systems. A particular country may employ any combination of these arrangements as it launches its new democracy, including semipresidentialism and a FPTP-PR hybrid electoral system.

Some comparativists see federalism, including ethno-federal approaches, as beneficial for democracy. Others worry that it can deepen divisions and potentially lead to the breakdown of the state itself. Nancy Bermeo argues that federal systems provide greater long-term stability for a new democracy, since they spread out power across more layers of government, creating more arenas for political bargaining and giving regional political elites a greater stake in the survival of the democracy.[27] Others, such as Henry Hale and Donald Horowitz, take a more cautious view. Hale discusses how certain ethno-federal systems can contribute to the territorial breakdown of the state (Yugoslavia) or civil war (Nigeria).[28] Horowitz advocates federal systems in deeply divided societies when the federation's internal territorial boundaries cut across identity group boundaries, but he opposes ethno-federal systems, which he sees as reinforcing the already-deep identity group divisions.[29]

Arguments over the relative merits of presidential and parliamentary systems have been among the most lively in comparative politics. Chapter 7 contrasted Juan Linz's theory of parliamentary superiority with Donald Horowitz's theory of presidential system design. Linz proposes that presidential systems are unstable and inhibit democratic consolidation by creating dual legitimacy problems and making it too difficult to remove a corrupt or incompetent leader. Horowitz counters that parliamentary systems have been unstable as well, and argues that the careful design of presidential system rules can address the weaknesses Linz identifies.

Comparativists have done less work on the role of judicial review powers or the implications of corporatist versus pluralist arrangements for successful consolidation. The concept of civil society, however, has garnered significant attention. In addition to definitional problems with the term (see Chapter 9), causal claims have been plagued by questions of tautology, causal direction, and contrary evidence. Some scholars, such as Robert Putnam, see civil society activities as crucial to the development of "social capital"—values such as tolerance and interpersonal trust that make democracies more stable in the long run. Others point to the value of civil society as a "counterweight" to the state, making creeping authoritarianism or other forms of democratic breakdown less likely.[30] In contrast, work by comparativists such as Sheri Berman challenges the idea that civil society is a crucial aid to democratic consolidation. Berman's case study of Weimar Germany (the democratic system between World War I and the Nazi seizure of power) demonstrates not only that civil society did not save the Weimar democracy, but also that it actively subverted it.[31] Extremists on both ends of the political spectrum used civil society groups to spread their messages and mobilize their supporters. Comparativists also disagree about the benefits of different electoral arrangements, though there is general agreement that rules which create a vast number of small parties can add to the instability of the early years of democratic transition.

External Structural Explanations of Democratization

Just as international relations scholars sometimes downplay the importance of domestic causes of foreign policy and international affairs, comparativists are often reluctant to regard external influences as playing a key role in domestic policy and other national political outcomes. Research on democratization, however, is one arena in which scholars have taken international influences very seriously. These external factors include structural conditions, such as the nature of the international "polar system," direct imposition of democracy via military conquest, global economic processes, pressure from international organizations, and examples provided by neighboring states or states with similar demographic features.

The Importance of the International Polar System For many international relations scholars, one of the starting points in determining the effects of the international political system is to examine its poles. A **pole** is a dominant state in the international system. The number and type of poles at a certain point in time forms the **polar system**. Those emphasizing the importance of polar arrangements—in the political science field of international relations, they are usually called "neorealists" or "structural realists"—accept political scientist Kenneth Waltz's claim that the form of the polar system shapes the actions of states in the international system.[32] These scholars distinguish between four types of polar systems: unipolar, bipolar, tripolar, and multipolar.

The existence of a unipolar or bipolar system would have the greatest impact on global democratization. A bipolar world has two poles, each of which dominates a large bloc of countries. While nonaligned countries are possible, they are typically much fewer in number than the number of countries that fall into one bloc or the other. If one of the two poles is hostile to democracy, other countries in its bloc are unlikely to be democratic. This was true of the Communist countries during the Cold War, most of which were allies of and strongly influenced by the Soviet Union. However, the Cold War also shows that a democratic pole in a bipolar system may tolerate nondemocracies in its bloc if it prevents them from falling under the sphere of influence of the other pole. During the Cold War, the United States supported a sizeable number of authoritarian governments, largely in the name of fighting the spread of Communism into those countries.

Scholars examining international structural effects sometimes focus on the existence of a **pole**, a dominant state in the international system.

The international **polar system** is the arrangement of poles—unipolar, bipolar, tripolar, or multipolar—at a certain point in time.

In the unipolar case, a single pole dominates globally, imposing its will on all other countries. If that unipolar country were a democracy, it is possible that it would encourage democratic systems in other countries as well, though the main feature of the unipolar system is that the dominant pole will not tolerate challenges to its rule. Thus, the democratic pole in a unipolar world may look on quiet nondemocracies more favorably than vocal democracies. If the dominant pole were a nondemocracy, however, it is hard to imagine that it would tolerate the global spread of democracy. The accompanying free speech and political organization in democratizing countries would almost certainly facilitate challenges to its global rule. There has never been a truly unipolar world. Some believe the current international system is as close to it today as ever before, though most international relations scholars consider today's polar system to be an unusual hybrid of a unipolar and multipolar arrangement. A large number of powerful states exist, but the United States is much more powerful than the others.

Imposition Through Conquest A second external structural factor has been important both historically and recently. Regime change is not always a home-grown process, driven by the structural conditions and elites of the country undergoing the transition. A huge number of democratizations have been the result of military conquest and the conquering power's desire to establish a democratic system. These include the often-discussed cases of West Germany and Japan after World War II, a large number of colonial states—particularly British colonies—that were given democratic systems before independence, and a number of countries in which the United States fostered regime change through military action. In the last few decades, this latter group includes Grenada (during the Reagan administration), Panama (George H. W. Bush administration), Haiti (Clinton administration), and Iraq (George W. Bush administration).

Many imposed democracies fail, partly because the domestic structural conditions identified in the previous section are lacking. British colonies have fared better than those of other European states, partly because the British tended to spend more time working closely with the successor government during the transition period to independence. Yet, even the democratic record of former British colonies is far from stellar.

In his book, *Democracy in the Third World*, Robert Pinkney proposes that "imported democracy" generally results in one of three responses—perversion, adaptation, or rejection—in which the externally created democracy is either altered to fit domestic circumstances or the system becomes something less than democratic.[33] It is interesting to note what is missing from Pinkney's list: acceptance of an imposed, Western-style democracy. Nancy Bermeo's work on federalism and democracy echoes Pinkney's concerns. While generally supportive of federal approaches in new democracies, Bermeo warns about the fragile nature of "imposed federalism."[34]

Global Economic Structure By the 1970s, some scholars began to respond to modernization theory with criticisms that came to be labeled dependency theory (see Chapter 3). Dependency theorists emphasized aspects of the global capitalist economic structure which discouraged democratic development. These arguments provided a solid explanation of the "second reverse wave," when democracy retreated, particularly in Latin America and Africa. But just as modernization theory does not explain the lack of democracy in some relatively developed states, dependency theory has little to offer when developing states successfully democratize. With the onset of global democratization's third wave, those looking for external structural explanations began to turn away from dependency theory and toward arguments about the increasing importance of international organizations and "demonstration effects."

International Organizations and Their Membership Rules One of the most noticeable markers of increasing globalization and regionalization has been the explosion in the number and authority of international organizations. International relations scholars distinguish between international **intergovernmental organizations (IGOs)**, made up of internationally recognized states, and international **nongovernmental organizations (NGOs)**, whose members are individuals and/or groups. Many international NGOs advocate democratization, reduced corruption, and the spread of respect for human rights. As political scientist Hans Peter Schmitz argues, such NGOs "diffuse democratic principles, support domestic allies, and exert pressure on authoritarian regimes."[35]

Of the two types of organizations, however, NGOs have been less effective at pressuring countries to liberalize and democratize than IGOs. The reason is relatively straightforward: IGOs can offer rewards and punishments not available to NGOs. One of the major rewards is membership in the organization itself. The use of standards for membership in an IGO is known as **conditionality**. Receiving and maintaining membership is conditional on a country meeting the existing standards of the organization. The best example of the use of membership as a reward for democratization is the European Union. Becoming an EU member is a long and difficult process involving both negotiation and demonstration of changes required by the organization. For the EU, such standards include Western democratic practices.

Demonstration Effects ("Contagion") A final external structural effect involves states providing models of democratization for other

similar states. Democratization scholars typically refer to this process as **demonstration effects** or "contagion." Many nondemocratic governments successfully resist pressures to liberalize and democratize, often by stressing to their populations the chaotic nature of such transformations and proposing the idea that the country is not yet ready for democracy. This becomes much more difficult when neighboring or otherwise similar countries democratize. As a result, it is most difficult to be the first country of a particular region or group of similar states to democratize. Once the threshold is crossed by that first country, pressure increases on the others to follow this lead. In such cases, nondemocratic system collapse can "snowball"[36]—with each successive collapse taking less time than the previous one—as happened in Eastern Europe in 1989. The countries need not be neighbors. Spain and Portugal's democratization in the 1970s was important for subsequent democratization in Latin America because it challenged the idea that democracy is difficult to establish in predominantly Catholic countries.

Demonstration effects can help explain both democratizations in specific countries and broader global patterns. The fact that democratization in one country plays a role in fostering democratization in another is part of

Among the external forces that can shape regime transitions in a given country are international **intergovernmental organizations (IGOs)**, whose members are internationally recognized states, and international **nongovernmental organizations (NGOs)**, whose members are individuals and/or groups.

Conditionality is the process of IGOs creating and enforcing standards for organization membership. Such standards can include the establishment of a democratic system.

Demonstration effects, also known as "contagion," occur when regime transition in one country sparks a parallel regime transition in a neighboring or otherwise similar type of country.

the story of the tendency for democratization to occur in waves. Likewise, demonstration effects can play a role in reverse waves. As democratic systems break down in neighboring countries, a particular state's elites and masses are less likely to consider democracy "the only game in town." Particularly if the new nondemocracies are successful in their stated policy goals (restoration of order, turning around the economy, redistributing wealth), a floundering democracy looks increasingly unattractive by comparison.

Internal Choice Explanations of Democratization

Traditionally, structural explanations were more common in democratization research than theoretical perspectives emphasizing individual and collective choices. One reason for this is the difficulty in generalizing choice-based explanations. But as tests of structural theories failed to generate a widely accepted, single theory of democratization, the choice approach became more prevalent. Studies of specific cases of democratization seemed to confirm that the actions of individual decision makers were central to the breakdown of the nondemocratic system, the form of the democratic system that replaced it, and the prospects for democratic consolidation. As political scientist Michael McFaul puts it:

> Inert, invisible structures do not make democracies or dictatorships. People do. Structural factors such as economic development, cultural influences, and historical institutional arrangements influence the formation of actors' preferences and power, but ultimately these forces have causal significance only if translated into human action.[37]

The study of individuals generally focuses on four types of political elites that play important roles in different stages of democratization: the ruling elite in the nondemocratic system prior to its breakdown, the opposition leaders in the nondemocracy prior to its collapse, the rulers of the new democratic system, and the leaders of institutions like the military that must side with the new democracy in times of crisis in order for it to become consolidated.

Leadership and Elite Choices in the Nondemocratic System Breakdown Stage Structural factors and changes in them can create favorable conditions for the breakdown of a nondemocracy, but it is the decisions of particular individuals that turn this potential into reality. A leader may decide to liberalize; the head of the opposition may choose to organize mass protests. When the nondemocratic elites are dominated by those who support liberalization, a gradual opening of the political system can set the table for democratization. Such elites are typically called **reformers**, though comparativists also refer to them as moderates or "softliners."

If, on the other hand, the nondemocracy is controlled by individuals committed to the maintenance of the nondemocracy at all costs—whom comparativists typically call **hardliners** or "standpatters"—liberalization will not occur. Thus, many democratization scholars point to the importance of a split in the ruling elite between moderates and hardliners, particularly when moderates gain the upper hand. When hardliners continue to dominate a nondemocratic system, democratization is unlikely but not impossible. If it comes, it will typically be swift and violent, such as in the overthrow of Nicolae Ceaușescu in Romania in December 1989.

Rulers are not the only important individuals in a nondemocracy. When opposition

---

Reformers, also known as moderates or "softliners," are members of the nondemocratic political elite committed to liberalization and possibly to democratization.

Those who oppose such reforms and prefer to maintain or strengthen the current nondemocratic system are known as **hardliners**.

forces contest the rule of a nondemocratic government, the leaders of those forces make decisions and take actions to enhance prospects for removing the nondemocratic leaders from power. Here again, comparativists distinguish between types of opposition elites. **Moderates** are those that favor working with the ruling elite to facilitate a gradual transition to democracy, while **radicals** are unwilling to work with nondemocratic rulers. Radicals may support placing the rulers on trial once they are no longer in power, and may even prefer another form of nondemocracy. Prospects for a smooth and peaceful transition to democracy are enhanced when reformers dominate the government and moderates dominate the opposition.

Splits in the ruling elite make liberalization possible, and moderate opposition elites make a smooth transition to consolidated democracy more likely. Sometimes, however, elites have to learn to be moderate. Previous and unsuccessful attempts at radical-led democratization can encourage opposition elites to be more moderate the second time around.

Yet, it may not only be prodemocratic elites who learn and calculate a more effective strategy. A nondemocratic system may also *fail* to collapse because of elite learning and rational calculations on the part of authoritarian leaders. In an intriguing 2005 article, Bruce Bueno de Mesquita and George Downs proposed that the relationship between economic development and the breakdown of nondemocracies has become weaker in recent decades because the leaders of these systems have learned to adapt to development and its consequences.[38] Authoritarian governments have grown more sophisticated, realizing how to limit public goods useful to a democratic opposition, such as a free press, while still supporting economic development.

Leadership and Elite Choices in the Establishment and Consolidation Stages
A relatively small number of individuals can play a large

role in establishing a new democracy, including crafting its initial institutional arrangements. Their influence can be long-lasting. (Think about how often Americans focus on the intentions of the U.S. democratic system's founders.) Likewise, the leadership and choices of the initial leaders can be very important for a new democracy's consolidation. Work by political scientist Shale Horowitz on post-Communist transitions points out that the people who lead new democracies can be more important than the democracies' institutional design. Horowitz argues that strong presidential powers can improve a new democracy's prospects for consolidation *if* these powers are in the hands of a leader committed to the democracy. If, on the other hand, the leader is ambivalent or hostile to democracy, a strong president can promote creeping (or rapid) authoritarianism.[39]

Because the choices that elites make during the establishment and consolidation of democracy are so important, a number of comparative politics works on democratization focus on decision-making topics such as bargaining and elite learning. New democracies are often the result of bargaining between reformers in the old government and moderates in the opposition, which produces a **pact** between the differing sides. In democratization, a pact is an official agreement about the rules of the game for the new democratic system and certain policy approaches it is expected to take. Pacts typically address

In a nondemocratic system, **moderates** are members of the opposition who support cooperating with the government to encourage liberalization and democratization.

Radicals are opponents who are unwilling to work with the nondemocratic rulers, sometimes even supporting another form of nondemocracy under their control rather than democratization.

A **pact** is a negotiated agreement during democratization that often establishes the institutional arrangements of the new democracy as well as specific policy approaches the democratic government will adhere to following the democratic system's establishment.

specific issues, including economic and social policies. The pact-making process often excludes the most radical and most conservative political groups. The negotiations that created Venezuela's Pact of Punto Fijo in 1958, for example, excluded the Communists. Pacts are helpful to democratization because they reduce the uncertainty surrounding elections and their aftermath. They assure the various sides involved in the negotiations that their interests will be protected even if they lose at the ballot box.

Think and Discuss

Pacts are, in many ways, undemocratic. They involve a small group of individuals deciding both the institutional arrangements of a new democracy and key economic and social policies. Is it good to build a new democracy in such an undemocratic fashion? Why or why not?

When comparativists study bargaining and pact-making during democratization, they often employ many of the decision-making theories discussed in the previous chapter. During negotiations, individuals on each side pursue institutional arrangements that they believe work to their own benefit. Thus, rational calculations are likely during bargaining over the new system, though these calculations need not take the form of full-blown rational choice. Bounded rationality options like satisficing are common, especially if the various sides feel pressure to reach decisions in short order. Comparativists also often make use of the elite learning perspective to understand pact making. In his study of Venezuelan democratization, for example, Daniel Levine emphasizes that opposition leaders learned from their mistakes and were more willing to compromise than they had been in an earlier, unsuccessful attempt at democratization. During the bargaining process, elites also learned to work together and to trust each other.[40]

The possibility of irrational decision making, discussed in Chapter 11, should also not be overlooked. Egos and emotions can interject themselves into bargaining during the process of democratization. Negotiators looking at those across the table from them see not only future rivals but also past opponents. Even more moderate opposition leaders may have spent time in jail, while reformers in the current government may have felt threatened by past opposition undertakings, such as the organization of unconventional mass political participation.

External Choice Explanations of Democratization

The final set of causal factors associated with democratization is external choice. The leadership and decisions of elites outside a country can support or deter its democratization. Like their domestic counterparts, external elites who want a particular country to democratize face choices about if and how to intervene in the democratization process. These choices can include whether to support sanctions against the nondemocratic government, to provide military support to prodemocracy forces, to engage in more direct intervention through military invasion, or to provide significant economic support once a new democracy is established. Elites making such decisions ordinarily weigh the costs and benefits of their actions carefully, taking the "national interest" of their own country into account more than that of the democratizing country. As with other choices, however, these leaders are subject to limitations—including ego, emotion, and wishful thinking—on their ability to reach these decisions in a rational manner.

One ongoing debate about external choice concerns the collapse of Communist states in 1989, as a wave of liberalization and democratization spread across Eastern Europe. Who is most responsible for the downfall of these Communist systems remains relevant for a number of reasons, including its implications for the enduring

American foreign policy goal of fostering democracies in heretofore undemocratic regions of the world. Those who emphasize the role of external leaders usually point to one of three individuals as most central to European Communism's demise: Soviet leader Mikhail Gorbachev, U.S. President Ronald Reagan, and Pope John Paul II.

Political scientist Joseph Nye emphasizes the importance of Gorbachev. The first Soviet leader born after the Bolshevik Revolution, Gorbachev instituted major domestic reforms. Even more important for events in 1989, he announced a policy of "new thinking" in Soviet foreign policy that included abandonment of the Brezhnev Doctrine, a guiding principle that had maintained the USSR's right to intervene in support of threatened Communist governments. Nye also points out the importance of Gorbachev's miscalculations.[41] He did not, after all, set out to destroy Communism in the region, but rather to revitalize the Soviet economy and society.

Andrew Busch and Elizabeth Spalding give the credit for ending European Communism to President Reagan, emphasizing his rhetoric and policies. They praise his famous speech labeling the Soviet Union an "Evil Empire," and they credit his increase in defense spending and strategic defense initiative (SDI) with forcing the Soviets to overspend on their own military.[42] They also contend that Reagan's domestic policies generated an economic recovery in the United States that stood in stark contrast to the stagnation of the Communist economies.

In his book, *Man of the Century*, Jonathan Kwitny gives credit for the fall of the Communist states to Pope John Paul II. Kwitny discusses how the Pope's anti-Communist beliefs and the fact that he came from a Communist country made him a symbol of the struggle against Communism in Poland and other Eastern European countries. Kwitny labels the Pope's 1983 trip to Poland "a turning point in history," and he points out that even Gorbachev has said, "Everything that happened in Eastern Europe during these past few years would have been impossible without the Pope, without the political role he was able to play."[43]

Triggering Events

The structural factors discussed to this point can provide solid explanations of *why* a nondemocratic government might break down or a new democratic system might be established. They are less effective, however, at predicting *when* a transition will occur. Even focusing on leaders and their decisions provides, at best, a rough sense of the timing of a regime transition.

As a result, a complete understanding of regime transitions requires not only a sense of underlying causes but also of **triggering events**, the happenings that provide the spark which ignites the fuel the underlying causes have provided. Triggering events are occurrences that directly affect the timing of a movement from one stage of the democratization process to another. In Ronald Inglehart and Christian Welzel's book on the causes and consequences of changes in political culture, the authors distinguish between slow, underlying changes that they refer to as "culminating variables" and more rapid changes that they call "break variables."[44] Triggering events are break variables; they come quickly and can have an immediate impact. Without the underlying causal factors, triggering events cannot generate a regime transition. At the same time, democratizations without any major triggering event are few and far between.

One could point to a large number of possible triggering events, but in the study of regime transitions, three stand out. The first is the death of the nondemocratic system's

As opposed to underlying causal factors, **triggering events** are incidents that spark political transitions and thus affect their timing. Examples include the death of an authoritarian leader or a severe economic crisis.

leader. An authoritarian system based on the rule of a single, charismatic leader often becomes associated with that leader to such an extent that it may not survive the leader's death. In Spain, a number of underlying causal factors had emerged during the rule of Francisco Franco that provided potential fuel for a regime transition. Franco's death in 1975 provided the spark.

Another common triggering event is a severe economic crisis, particularly one that emerges quickly. An economic crisis can be the result of domestic forces alone, including poor government decision making, or could result from the effects of other countries' economic problems. They also result from a crisis in one country triggering similar crises in neighboring countries. In the late 1990s, economic difficulties in Asia spread quickly and pressured nondemocratic governments to liberalize in countries such as Indonesia, Malaysia, and Singapore.

Protests and government responses to them can also trigger a regime transition. Once a sizeable protest develops, nondemocratic governments face a difficult choice. If they violently repress the protests, what may already be shaky legitimacy can evaporate; if they allow them to continue, protests can spread to other parts of the country and give protesters time to better organize and coordinate their activities. Sometimes, orders to crack down on a protest are not followed, or one component of the state security apparatus (e.g., the army) defends the protesters from attacks by another (e.g., the police). Though such events need not result in a democratic political system, they often signal the end of the existing nondemocratic government.

Structural and Choice Explanations of Democratic Breakdown

The various structural and choice-based factors related to democracy's establishment and consolidation can also play a role in its breakdown. According to Juan Linz, unresolved internal structural problems "are rarely the immediate cause of the breakdown" unless these problems lead the situation to deteriorate quickly.[45] When that happens, all bets are off. An opposition unsupportive of democracy may be able to mobilize large numbers of people, and the military may be unwilling to stand by and watch social order crumble. More often, internal structural factors slowly eat away at democratic legitimacy, making an eventual crisis more likely.

Socioeconomic and political structural features can challenge democratic consolidation in several ways. Economic development followed by a severe economic downturn can frustrate citizens. In a new democracy, they may associate the economic failures with the democratic system.

A political culture inconsistent with democracy may not prevent a democracy from being established, but it can certainly play a role in its termination. Lacking mass values supportive of democracy, elites favoring abandonment of democracy may anticipate the population to be passive, or even supportive, of actions to overthrow the democratic system. Democratic leaders, in such a case, may see little reason to fight to protect the democratic system.

In terms of identity divisions, democracy can be fragile when ethnic, religious, or linguistic identity divisions run deep. Consistent with cleavage structure theory (see Chapter 5), when complementary social divisions exist, a regionally concentrated minority may favor its region's secession from the state rather than working through that state's existing democratic system. As Juan Linz puts it, "democracy does not provide an easy answer to the question of under what conditions secession is legitimate, inevitable, and viable."[46]

On the issue of political structures, comparativists point to the relative merits of presidential versus parliamentary systems for democratic stability (e.g., the Linz-Horowitz debate discussed in Chapter 7). Democratization scholars also emphasize the importance of whether the military accepts civilian rule, and the extent to which the judiciary is free from corruption and dominance by the executive branch. Finally, scholars argue that electoral rules make democracies less likely to break down when they foster party cooperation and prevent party systems that are both polarized and contain a large number of major parties.[47]

Just as individuals and their decisions are important to the breakdown of a nondemocracy, they are also central to the survival or demise of a democracy. Following Francisco Franco's death, for example, King Juan Carlos became head of the Spanish government. He oversaw a transition to democracy, eventually surrendering rule and appointing Adolfo Suárez as prime minister. In 1981, a group of military leaders in Spain staged a coup against the democratic government and sought to reinstall Juan Carlos as head of the government. Instead, the king chose to oppose the coup, publicly ordered the rest of the military not to support the coup leaders, and became a crucial factor in saving the fledgling Spanish democracy.

In other cases, especially those where there is no figurehead monarch to oppose the coup, military takeovers are successful. Chapter 8 presented the new professionalism theory that comparativists use to understand the potential for the military to overturn a democratic government. When the military is content that the democratic system does not threaten it or in cases where the military's central goals involve protection against external threats, the military is less likely to overthrow a democracy.

Combining Structural and Choice Arguments

Perhaps more than any other political outcome comparativists seek to understand, getting a handle on democratization requires an openness to combining structural and choice-based arguments. There are numerous possible combinations, such as the way economic development shapes political culture, which then affects elites' calculations about possible political reform.

One case of democratization provides an especially useful example. An earlier section of the chapter highlighted Levine's contention that pact making in Venezuela's second effort at democratization is a classic example of elite learning. Terry Lynn Karl's study of the same case emphasizes how changing structural conditions aided that pact making.[48] While accepting the importance of elite bargaining and compromise, Karl argues that a significant increase in oil revenue prior to the democratic transition was the key to its success. The discovery of new oil deposits meant there were more government revenues to go around. Rather than having to fight over how to divide up the same "pie," the pie had grown bigger. This structural change made pact making easier, though it still took the actions of elites to secure the Venezuelan democracy.

Regime Transitions in the United Kingdom, Germany, and France

The ten TIC countries have a wide range of experiences with democratization. As a result, these cases provide comparativists with a variety of lessons about the role of structures and choices in regime transitions. The case of India is particularly compelling. As a result, it serves as the topic of this chapter's Comparative Exercise.

Three of the TIC cases—the United Kingdom, Germany, and France—are considered long-consolidated ("mature") democracies. The United Kingdom's democracy emerged through slow, evolutionary change. Germany's consolidated democracy still deals with legacies of past totalitarian rule. In France, the current system is the latest in a long line of attempts at different approaches to democratic governance.

The United Kingdom

The drawn-out nature of British democratization stands in stark contrast to many of the other TIC countries. Over centuries, the British political system evolved—away from a strong monarchy and toward expanded political rights and voting privileges for an increasing portion of the population. As political scientist Vernon Bagdanor argues, even the British Constitution is the result "not of deliberate design but of a long process of evolution."[49] The development of the British political system coincided with other slow and evolutionary processes, including economic development, an increasingly prodemocratic political culture, and the emergence of an overarching British national identity.

While a casual glance at the evolution of the British political system portrays a slow and deliberate march forward, a closer look reveals fits and starts. Though scholars point to the Magna Carta (1215) and the Glorious Revolution of 1688 (when William of Orange oversaw a monarchy further restrained by parliament) as important events in limiting the power of the British monarchy, at the end of the eighteenth century, Britain remained largely a system dominated by the Crown, the aristocracy, and the Anglican Church. Serious movement toward democracy began only in the 1800s. Reforms included important acts of parliament in 1832, 1867, 1884, 1918, and 1928, which collectively expanded the franchise from less than 10 percent of the population to universal adult suffrage. As political scientists John Freeman and Duncan Snidal put it, while a country like Finland moved to universal suffrage essentially in one step, reaching that point took the British "five separate reforms and a century."[50]

The Industrial Revolution brought capitalist development to the British Isles earlier than anywhere else in the world. The result was a large middle and working class and a comparatively prosperous population. (The United Kingdom is, in per capita terms, the wealthiest of the ten TIC countries.) Although periods of economic downturn sparked the acts of parliament that expanded the franchise in the 1800s and early 1900s, economic inequality as a whole declined during this period.[51] In addition, economic development had important spill-over effects on urbanization and education. In the arena of political culture, British society was rather slow to embrace mass participation. Working-class deference meant ordinary citizens did little beyond voting, and even the makeup of the electorate was limited for much of the nineteenth century and into the twentieth century. During that same period, however, the United Kingdom did develop a significant civil society. With a general acceptance of an overarching national identity and complementary cleavages less prominent than in the other TIC countries, the United Kingdom's identity structure is conducive to democracy. Finally, though one might question how well the United Kingdom's Westminster political system would work in other countries, it has been effective, stable, and a source of pride for the British.

The United Kingdom is the model of slow liberalization and democratization. Ruling elites worked with opposition forces during the nineteenth and early twentieth centuries to exchange an expansion of political rights for commitment to the system and social stability. While the United Kingdom does not have a single pact like Venezuela's Pact of Punto Fijo to point to, its history demonstrates how bargaining, cooperation, and concessions can facilitate a peaceful transition toward consolidated democracy, even if such cooperation emerges haphazardly rather than as part of a conscious plan for long-term democratization.[52] As in other European countries, rulers extended political rights when socioeconomic changes and legitimacy crises pushed them to reach out to those who had previously been excluded.

It is hard to believe that the United Kingdom's evolutionary democratization can serve as a model at this point in history. The general populations of most nondemocratic countries today are unlikely to tolerate a century-long process of regime transition. Yet, it is equally unlikely that British democracy could be threatened, even by significant economic or social crises. The system is well engrained, with the public used to participating in elections and the military accepting of civilian rule. This stability and legitimacy notwithstanding, the Labour Party felt the need to revamp key aspects of the system through its attempts at constitutional reform in the late 1990s and early 2000s. Such efforts demonstrate that even leaders of a long-consolidated democracy may look for ways to improve the system's policy performance and representation of public opinion.

Germany

Germany has undergone a number of regime transitions since its establishment as a nation-state in 1871. The short-lived democracy of the Weimar Republic after World War I was superseded by the Nazi regime, one of the most brutal dictatorships in human history. Following World War II, a divided Germany experienced democracy and communist totalitarianism. Yet, democracy proved to be the stronger regime, taking firm root in the Federal Republic in the years after 1949 and extending to the east in 1990. Since then, it has withstood substantial economic and political challenges. Both structural and choice explanations can help us make sense of Germany's turbulent path of multiple regime changes.

Explaining the failure of the Weimar Republic (1919–1933) has occupied many scholars of comparative politics. In seeking to understand democratic breakdown, political scientists have asked how a modern country—a leading industrial power with a middle class and one of the most progressive political systems of the time—could have slid so quickly and thoroughly into such a brutal dictatorship, and done so by legal means and with substantial popular support.

The character of Germany's class structure played an important role in Weimar's collapse. Under the "marriage of iron and rye," the industrial bourgeoisie in the west and the Prussian landed aristocracy in the east modernized Germany following its establishment as a nation-state in 1871. Rapid industrialization created a large working class and a substantial middle class, but the state outlawed the working class–based Socialist Party while the middle classes "exchang[ed] the right to rule for the right to make money" and let the antidemocratic industrial and agrarian elites run the country.[53] Conservative elites survived into the Weimar period and supported the Nazi Party's rise. At the same time, many on the political left rejected democracy and supported the Communist Party that attempted to overthrow the nascent Weimar Republic's democratic system in 1919 and subsequently refused to cooperate with the more moderate Social Democratic Party. Class polarization grew more noticeable at the ballot box. In the regime's last years, antisystem parties of the Left and the Right—particularly the Nazi and Communist Parties—received the majority of votes, leaving democratic parties occupying a shrinking middle space.

In addition, although the Weimar political system was democratic, a political culture supportive of democracy was not broadly shared. Existing authoritarian values were deepened by experiences following Germany's defeat in World War I, including the humiliating and punitive terms of the Versailles Treaty that set the peace. Germans then had to endure two periods of severe economic hardship in less than a decade—the hyperinflation of 1923 that wiped out the savings of the middle classes, followed by the Great Depression of 1929 that ushered in mass unemployment and destroyed numerous businesses and farms. These events soured many Germans on democracy. Small farmers and the lower middle class especially found Hitler's message of economic security and a restoration of national greatness appealing.[54] In short, German society and politics during Weimar were highly polarized, and antidemocratic forces on the right and left became stronger as economic misery deepened during the Depression.

The Weimar Republic's political structures also contained flaws that paved the way for antidemocratic elements to take power. The constitution's provision for a dual executive granted the president too much power and the parliament too little. The electoral system also fostered fragmentation among numerous splinter parties that made for unstable governing partners.[55]

Finally, triggering events combined with the deeper structural features of German society to tip the regime into dictatorship. These events included the intentionally set fire at the *Reichstag* (the Weimar system's parliament building) in 1933. Hitler used the fire—which many historians believe the Nazis had a hand in—as an excuse to request sweeping emergency powers. The resulting decree, which President Paul von Hindenburg authorized, read:

> Restrictions on personal liberty, on the right of free expression of opinion, including freedom of the press; on the rights of assembly and association; and violations of the privacy of postal, telegraphic and telephonic communications and warrants for house searches, orders for confiscations as well as restrictions on property, are also permissible beyond the legal limits otherwise prescribed.[56]

The Third Reich was born.

Germany's second attempt at democracy arose from occupation, as the Allied powers of Britain, France, and the United States invited Germany's democratic elites to draw up the Constitution of the Federal Republic. Rather than simply an external imposition, the construction of democracy was the result of conscious choices by German political elites to overcome the social divisions and mistakes that had destroyed the Weimar Republic. Konrad Adenauer, Germany's first postwar chancellor (and one of its longest-serving), built the Christian Democratic Union (CDU) into a quintessential catch-all party that successfully bridged regional, religious, and class divisions. Adenauer also worked with union leaders and employers to forge a system of "Social Partnership" involving corporatist negotiations among them and legally sanctioned employee participation in the management of firms.[57] Moreover, the CDU's creation of the social market economy, (see Chapter 13) which guaranteed private property alongside a generous welfare state, reconciled German conservatives and Social Democrats to democracy and capitalism.[58]

In terms of political structure, German elites fashioned the political system in ways that structured conflict within democratic channels and encouraged bargaining and compromise. The proportional representation effects of the German electoral system produce coalition governments that require governing parties to negotiate solutions. Federalism requires the chancellor to bargain with the *Länder* to ensure passage of the government's legislative program. In addition, the 5 percent electoral

The fire at the Reichstag in Berlin that aided the Nazi Party's ascent to power in Germany.

(©Fox Photos/Getty Images)

threshold rule has prevented extreme splinter parties from gaining parliamentary representation. Along with the constructive vote of no confidence requirement to remove a chancellor (see Chapter 7), these political institutional designs have made governments in the Federal Republic more durable than they were in the Weimar Republic.

Important structural elements have also strengthened democracy in the post–World War II era. West Germany's "economic miracle" of the 1950s and 1960s helped legitimize democracy. A democratic political culture took root, particularly after the passing of the Nazi-era generation. Finally, the partition of Germany after 1945 eliminated the conservative landed aristocracy's deleterious influence on politics. The landed elite found themselves in East Germany, where the Communist regime wasted no time confiscating their land and stripping them of political power.

Today, Germany is a consolidated democracy, and its political system has been able to contain difficult challenges. East German voters in 1990 elections essentially opted for unification under the democratic institutions of the Federal Republic. To be sure, surveys since then have registered lower levels of support for democracy and capitalism among easterners than among their western compatriots. But this disillusionment is understandable, given frustrated expectations of immediate prosperity in the face of mass unemployment in the east following unification, easterners' relatively brief experience with democracy, and the correspondingly short time for a democratic political culture to take firm root there. Despite the difficulties of economic stagnation and the strains associated with German unification, majorities throughout Germany still support democracy, and the differences between easterners and westerners have narrowed, particularly among younger cohorts.[59]

The legitimacy of Germany's democracy has proven ample and resilient. Far right parties have entered some *Land* parliaments where unemployment is high, but they have not cleared the threshold to win representation at the national level. The privatization of East German state enterprises, the settlement of thorny questions of property claims in the east, and the opening up of the secret police (*Stasi*) files on citizens have all advanced under the rule of law. The fact that the current chancellor is from the east provides further evidence of democracy's consolidation.

Germany's turbulent political history provides several important lessons about the process and prospects of democratization and challenges some of the core assumptions of democratization models. First, the Weimar Republic's fate demonstrates that the middle class is not always a force for democracy. Capitalist elites and small businesspersons opted for Hitler's promises of order and economic security rather than democracy. Second, the destruction of the Weimar Republic and the subsequent consolidation of the Federal Republic point to the importance of such structural factors as class, general economic conditions, and political culture that may buttress or undermine the broader legitimacy of any regime. Finally, successful democratization under the Federal Republic underscores the importance of elite decisions to settle their differences through negotiation and compromise and their ability to develop robust democratic institutions, designed in large part to avoid repeating the mistakes of the past.

France

In drawing lessons from the European path to democracy, comparativist Barrington Moore wrote the famous line, "No bourgeois, no democracy." He contrasted the early democratizers (Britain and France) with those states where fascism would rise, and identified a strong urban merchant and capitalist class as the key ingredient in the turn away from absolutism and aristocratic authority and toward liberal governance.[60] But one must be careful about assuming the British and French cases are synonymous. The fits and starts of British democratization pale in comparison with the French back and forth between liberal democratic regimes and aristocratic and authoritarian ones. In addition, France, like Germany, provides lessons about possible causes of democratic breakdown.

Moore is correct that the French Revolution marked a fundamental break with the royal past, while at the same time establishing the conditions and principles of French democracy. The Declaration of the Rights of Man and the Citizen was adopted by the first French National Assembly a month before the U.S. Congress submitted the American Bill of Rights for ratification by the states in 1789. Nevertheless, French democracy was not consolidated until after 1878, and as we have seen, it would still suffer one more reversal and several strong challenges through the twentieth century. Today, well past the two hundredth anniversary of

the Revolution, many in France believe the compromised nature of the French system falls short of the promise of democracy.

The Revolution itself remains an object of intense study and debate in both history and political science, certainly in an effort to locate its causes, but also over its meaning. While previous generations, often holding romantic notions of revolutionary struggle, believed the French Revolution was just the kind of break with the past that Barrington Moore described, recent scholarship has pointed to the decades before the Revolution as the epoch during which the historic break actually occurred.[61] In that sense, the rise of democratic principles, the rupture with a religious worldview in favor of rational thought, and sentiments of equality and patriotism were the result of both radical change and evolutionary development before 1789. The monarchy and the church were under attack not only from a few philosophers such as Voltaire and Rousseau, but also from within the institutions of the state, where the courts became an arena to contest the power of the king and aristocracy.[62] Finally, the American Revolution of 1776 provided a model of change and a reason to do so, as French financial and military support for America exhausted the royal treasury.[63]

The promise of democracy would not last long after the early days of the revolution, however, with the first decade closing as Napoleon Bonaparte seized power in a coup d'état. His goal was not reactionary, but to use increasingly authoritarian means to consolidate the gains of the revolution and curtail the radical challenges to the emerging moderate leadership. Fifteen years later, defeated at Waterloo, France would return to royal rule—albeit with an elected legislature and limited suffrage—for another thirty-three years until the July Revolution in 1830. The next break occurred with the Revolution of 1848 and universal suffrage for men, but ended with the election of Napoleon's nephew, Louis Napoleon, as president and his own coup d'état in 1852. The Second Empire came to an end in 1870, and though monarchists won the first elections under foreign occupation, they could not settle on a candidate for the throne. Ultimately, a democratic majority prevailed at the end of the decade; the Third Republic lasted until the German invasion at the start of World War II and the establishment of a fascist government at Vichy under Nazi supervision.

If the transition to democracy was the consequence of a rising bourgeois class and the transformation of values, as well as the slow unsettling of the aristocracy brought about by a break with the past, the *consolidation* of democracy after 1878 resulted from different causal factors. Key to this transformation was the "middle peasantry"—land-owning small farmers who gained from the confiscation of feudal land during the Revolution—who ultimately decided to join forces with the urban bourgeoisie.[64] The bourgeoisie themselves, relatively conservative and uninterested in substantial alteration, negotiated what has been called "a stalemate society,"[65] which sought to preserve the social status quo despite industrialization while also securing a democratic approach to politics. Workers were marginal to this system, which stifled more revolutionary demands until the Depression and the rise of fascism united mainstream and radical working-class parties in the polarized atmosphere of the 1930s.

The French experience with democratization and regime change, and ultimately the consolidation of a hybrid presidential system, provide some important analytical insights about democratization, as well as striking lessons about the threats to democracy. Analytically, the important role of the bourgeoisie and the peasantry points to the necessity of cross-class alliances in forging democratic consensus. It also highlights the significance of a major portion of the peasant class taking on an active political role. While not unique to the French case, the reexamination of democratization and class politics in the 1970s and 1980s moved the peasantry to a central place in research, in contrast to the dismissive characterization offered by Karl Marx: "a sack of potatoes" ancillary to political struggle.[66] This is especially important today, as democratization occurs in lesser developed countries. The French case also suggests that, while a break with the past might be necessary, that break can occur over a period of gradual reform and transformation—a lesson particularly for countries such as China, where gradual but persistent social and economic changes might become the foundation for a transition to democracy.[67]

At the same time, France stands as a warning to democratizers. Alongside other countries that suffered challenges and outright reversals on the path to democracy, the French experience suggests that *intra*class politics—highlighting divisions within a particular class—and how a given regime responds to the politicization of new movements and interests are potentially crucial factors leading to the breakdown of an established democracy. The different experiences in countries that have adopted the French dual executive are also telling. The creeping authoritarianism in countries such as Russia points to the dangers inherent in a semipresidential system (see Chapter 7), particularly when one party controls the legislative and executive branches and key leaders value democratic principles less than others such as unity and stability.

Topic in countries

Regime Transitions in Mexico, Brazil, and Nigeria

Mexico, Brazil, and Nigeria have all existed as established democracies since 2000. While Mexico passed an important consolidation test in 2006, it remains too early to consider its democracy consolidated. Of the three, Brazil comes closest to meeting the criteria of a consolidated democracy. Because Brazil seeks to consolidate its democracy in the shadow of a military that historically has been deeply involved in politics, however, scholars are reluctant to declare Brazilian democracy consolidated. At the other extreme from Brazil is Nigeria, which increasingly appears to be drifting away from the established democracy category. Launched in 1999 after repeated and unsuccessful previous attempts, Nigeria's most recent democratic undertaking has faced structural conditions inconsistent with a strong likelihood of consolidating its democracy. Significant questions about the legitimacy of the 2007 national elections, for example, made many ask whether the appropriate question was not how Nigeria would consolidate its democracy but rather if it was still a democracy at all.

Mexico

Over its history, Mexico has had limited experience with democracy. Of the 685 years since the founding of the Aztec Empire, the three periods of democratic rule total only a little more than two decades. Mexico's recent transition is a case of economic development and related changes altering its socioeconomic structure, setting the stage for government leaders to choose liberalization and the eventual establishment of democracy. In addition, a large part of the story of Mexico's democratization involves the role of external factors—both demonstration effects from democratizations across Latin America and pressure from the United States.

Mexico's liberalization and ultimate democratization mirrored underlying economic and social developments. At the time of the 1910

Revolution, the Mexican population was largely rural and illiterate. By the 1980s, the population had been transformed into a more urban and educated one, capable of and desiring a greater say in the country's political affairs. Mexico's citizens were less accepting of the dominance of the Institutional Revolutionary Party (PRI) than they had been in the past, particularly when the economy failed to keep up with their rising expectations in the 1980s. When the PRI's supremacy finally came to an end in 2000, Mexico had a more industrial, globalized economy and a more visible civil society than ever before.

Government and opposition officials' decisions and leadership were also crucial to Mexican democratization. Individuals such as Presidents Carlos Salinas and Ernesto Zedillo chose the liberalization path. Zedillo's presidency marked the final victory of the technocrat wing of the PRI—those leaders of the party committed to economic reform and increased connections with the United States and willing to engage in political liberalization to achieve those goals. His presidency also brought some semblance of stability to Mexico, after the chaotic 1994 campaign that saw the PRI's original candidate, Luis Donaldo Colosio, assassinated.

As Mexico liberalized in the 1980s and 1990s, elections became more important. The public joined opposition elites in believing that elections should be free and fair. Controversy and protests over the 1988 presidential elections were important triggering events. They pushed the government to back up its commitment to liberalization with an independent body to oversee elections and by allowing non-PRI candidates to win a larger number of local, regional, and national races. This set the stage for the 2000 elections, the Mexican democracy's "founding elections," which marked the point at which liberalization gave way to established democracy.

The 2006 presidential election provided a strong test for Mexico's fledgling democracy. The results were close, disputed, and led to large-scale protests involving blockage of major streets and government buildings in Mexico City. Despite threats from Andrés Manuel López Obrador and his allies in the Party of the Democratic Revolution (PRD) to form an alternative government, the protests eventually died down and Felipe Calderón of the National Action Party (PAN) was sworn in as president. In the year following the election, Calderón worked to reach out to those who had opposed him. A large number of López Obrador's former supporters disapproved of his tactics, and his popular support declined. In 2008, Obrador faced a strong challenge for leadership of the PRD by moderates within the party.

Mexico was a late-comer to Latin American democratization, and it took a different path. Rather than the rapid democratization, democratic collapse, and renewed democratization efforts of other Latin American countries, Mexico's transition was more cautious and deliberate. Mexico reveals how committed reformers in the government, who are willing to allow the potential of underlying economic development to transform into the reality of democratic change, can play a decisive role in a successful, and relatively nonviolent, transition. It also supports Samuel Huntington's contention that sustained economic growth followed by a short-term economic downturn is a formula for transition from authoritarianism to democracy.[68]

The Mexican case also demonstrates the importance of removing corruption from the electoral process as much as possible. A series of reforms from 1986 to 1996 resulted in nearly three hundred separate legal stipulations governing the electoral process. The reforms included the creation of Mexico's Federal Election Institute (FEI), an independent body that oversees elections from the training of poll workers to the counting of votes, and the creation of rules allowing political parties to engage in careful surveillance of the casting and counting of votes.[69]

Mexico's elections have improved so much that in 2001 the head of the FEI was invited to write an article for the *Journal of Democracy* on lessons from Mexico for the problems with the American presidential election in 2000![70] Though its democracy is not yet consolidated, Mexico's democratization process has been impressive. Its electoral process is, by most standards, free and fair. Accordingly, the country was able to weather the storm of the very close 2006 presidential elections and the protests that followed, and with the passing of this test, the consolidation of Mexico's democracy appears increasingly likely.

Brazil

Brazil's democratic transition was largely managed from above by authoritarian elites, a form of democratization that comparativist Terry Lynn Karl calls "imposition."[71] Only at the very end did the military government find itself giving up more power than it had intended. Nevertheless, Brazilian democracy has since survived a presidential impeachment, years of economic crisis and high inflation, and high levels of poverty and inequality. It also passed what political scientist Samuel Huntington considers a telling test for a democracy—two alternations of the ruling elites in power—just over ten years after the ratification of its newly designed democratic constitution in 1988.

The seeds of Brazil's democratic transition in 1985 were present from the moment of the military coup in 1964. Faced with a somewhat erratic president, some military officers thought the army's interests would be better served by staying out of politics and protecting the military's institutional autonomy, while others felt it was necessary for national security to remove him. The hardliners won this battle, but when no civilian replacement for President João Goulart could be found that was acceptable to all sides, the military took over directly. In order to appease the softliners within the military, Brazil's military junta never entirely scrapped the façade of democratic elections, though it strictly regulated who could participate in them and which offices were subject to election.

By 1974, six years in a row of record growth (on average, 8.5 percent per year) had strengthened the position of moderates in the military coalition. With the country doing so well, they argued, the military was popular. There would be little risk in opening up the political system, in preparation for an eventual transition back to civilian control. Thus, in 1974, President/General Ernesto Geisel began a process of *distensão* (liberalization). By the late 1970s, however, the position of the military had deteriorated. The oil shocks and world recession of the 1970s had slowed the growth of the Brazilian economy. Workers who had seen their incomes rise during the golden years of 1968–1974 now watched their wages erode under growing inflation.

Brazilian civil society began to mobilize. In 1977, the Movement against the High Cost of Living coordinated efforts of neighborhood associations and church-related grassroots organizations to petition the federal government to freeze the prices of basic foodstuffs and transportation. Simultaneously, metalworkers, led by future president Luiz Inacio Lula da Silva, pushed for a 34 percent wage increase after the military government admitted misrepresenting the inflation rates on which salary adjustments were based. In 1978, the metalworkers went on strike and won a 24.5 percent raise, sparking a wave of strikes in other sectors during 1978 and 1979. The Catholic Church openly supported these strikes. Increasingly, moderates within the official parties, intellectuals, and business sided with this broad, multiclass coalition and demanded political liberalization.

Moderates within the military responded to this growing pressure by implementing a liberalization process, known in Brazil as the *abertura*, which they hoped they could control. At the end of 1979, the military abolished the two official parties and permitted the registration of multiple parties in order to divide the opposition. Most of the opposition refused to take the bait,

and in the 1982 legislative and municipal elections the opposition parties together received a majority of the seats in the Chamber of Deputies. Hardline military factions fought further liberalization, launching a series of fierce attacks on perceived "Leftist enemies."

Just at this juncture, however, the Latin American debt crisis hit, creating a severe economic recession across the entire region. In lieu of economic progress, further democratization was virtually the only thing the military could offer to appease the protesters. The battle for direct elections failed to win enough votes in Congress, but the existing indirect system, through which the Congress elected the president, refused for the first time to endorse the military's nominee. Instead, they chose a respected moderate named Tancredo Neves. Although Neves died before he could be inaugurated, his successor Jose Sarney called for a constitutional assembly, which wrote the 1988 Constitution that completed the transition to an established democracy.

Although the Brazilian economy grew during the military regime, economic growth did not trickle down to the poor or create a large middle class. Inequality increased above its historically high levels. Political culture was not dramatically different in the late 1970s than it had been in the 1960s. The United States supported the military coup of 1964, and although the Carter administration (1976–1980) criticized human rights abuses by the Brazilian military government, that largely ended with the election of Ronald Reagan. Some pressure to democratize did result from the fall of the military regime in Brazil's neighbor and trading partner Argentina, in 1983, but other military governments, like that of General Pinochet in Chile, remained strong. So why did Brazil democratize in 1985 and, more important, why has it remained democratic?

Up until the early 1980s, the existence of divisions within the military largely drove the pace and the extent of the transformation. Because hardliners and softliners had to compromise with one another to avoid splitting the military, Brazil's military government stayed in power, but always had at least some limited space for political opposition to organize. Tancredo Neves spent most of the military regime as a member of the legal Movement for Brazilian Democracy (MDB), even getting elected senator in 1978 and governor of the state of Minas Gerais in 1982. Lula became head of an independent union during military rule, and Fernando Henrique Cardoso published reports critical of the regime. However, these internal divisions existed from the start of the military government. Space for opposition even, in some ways, enhanced the stability of the regime. Although key leaders of the military intended to transfer power to civilians—someday—they lacked the strength to overcome hardline resistance.

The factor that *triggered* the Brazilian transition, more than any other, was the increasing failure of the military government to provide economic stability and growth, and the resulting explosion of opposition from civil society. When hardliners in the military attempted to roll back liberalization in the early 1980s, one of the reasons they failed was the 1982 debt crisis, which caused many former supporters of the regime, such as business, to change sides and back those who wanted a democratic transition.

Neither of these factors explains the survival of Brazilian democracy, a survival that, at first glance, poses a significant puzzle. After all, democracy endured an agonizing decade of continued economic crisis, followed by a second decade of relatively slow growth. What had changed from earlier periods was that civilians— political elites, but also the general public—had become reluctant to call upon the military to step in during moments of crisis. During the painful impeachment of President Collor, for example, his allies did not ask the military to protect him, and his opponents did not ask the military to overthrow him. Instead, they handled the conflict using constitutional procedures.

Several factors explain this change. First, civilians of many different ideological persuasions had learned from the experience of twenty-one years of military government that, simply put, they did not like military rule. Although Brazil's military was less repressive than some, it still tortured, imprisoned, and murdered hundreds of its own citizens. Second, the 1988 Constitution provided a place within the system for most of the significant societal elites, including influential conservatives who were overrepresented in the Brazilian federal structure codified in the new democratic system. Along with other arguably undemocratic features of Brazilian democracy—some of which have been discussed in previous chapters of this book—the federal arrangements helped appease conservatives. Finally, the world began to be a much less friendly place for military governments, especially after the Cold War. At the same time that officials from countries such as the United States were pushing for neoliberal economic reforms in the 1990s, they were also encouraging that such reforms take place within a democratic political structure. Such "encouragement" played a less direct role in Brazil's democratization than in Mexico's. Yet, like Mexico, Brazil serves as a reminder that external factors can undermine democracy on occasion, but they can also sometimes be a key part of the story of its establishment and consolidation.

Nigeria

Long considered by many analysts a country with great potential, Nigeria has disappointed its advocates both politically and economically. Endowed with abundant natural resource wealth, oil in particular, the country has failed to effectively use its resources to develop a vibrant economy with a sizeable middle class. Its political system, which began independence as a democracy, has spent more years under military rule than under representative government and has seen more successful and unsuccessful military coups than free and fair presidential elections. Thus, Nigeria is a fascinating case for comparativists interested in democratization. In its fourth democratization attempt and its third established democracy in less than half a century,[72] the country provides an abundance of evidence about causal factors related to democratization and democratic breakdown.

Even a quick look at Nigeria's socioeconomic structures helps one to understand the country's unstable and unsuccessful experiments with democracy since independence. It remains relatively poor, economically unequal, and largely rural, with barely a majority of the population literate and the middle class few and far between. High population growth rates and a fate closely tied to the world price of oil has made the crafting of economic policy a challenge, a situation made much worse by the country's lingering and significant corruption. Its deep identity divisions pose hurdles to democratic consolidation and help foster a deeply divided political culture, in which the different cultural groups often seem to have only an acquiescence to corruption in common. If Dankwart Rustow is correct that national unity is a precondition of democratization, it is no wonder that Nigerians have struggled to consolidate their democratic republics.

To make matters worse, elites in the government and military have placed maintenance of the democratic system below other priorities, including social stability, economic performance, and, unfortunately, personal gain. Nigeria's past experiences with democracy provide ample room for elite learning, and some lessons from past failures have generated transformations (e.g., the evolution of the Nigerian federal system) in the institutional arrangements of subsequent democratic systems. But the potential for elite learning has been more than canceled out by a history of military involvement in politics and the failure to successfully promote a culture of civilian rule and military noninterference in political disputes. Given this history, a military overthrow of the democratic system in the face of a severe crisis—perhaps with significant support from the Nigerian population—would not be surprising.

Still, the country has had three brief periods of democratic rule. Nigeria's colonial power, the United Kingdom, wanted as many of its colonies as possible to begin independence as functioning democracies. The British worked with the Nigerians to conduct elections prior to independence, and they played a significant role in the design of the initial Nigerian democracy with its ethno-federal and Westminster parliamentary features. In addition, while many Nigerian elites have not demonstrated a commitment to democracy, others have. President Olusegun Obasanjo oversaw a transition to democracy in 1979 and won presidential elections in 1999 and 2003. These elections contained irregularities, but they were relatively free and fair, and Obasanjo's victories were large enough that these irregularities did not ultimately affect the outcome. Obasanjo also rejected the use of unconstitutional means to remain in office beyond a second term and worked to save the Fourth Republic, as the looming 2007 elections led to renewed political and social instability. For all his faults, Obasanjo will deserve at least some of the credit if the latest attempt at Nigerian democracy succeeds for an extended period of time.

The Nigerian case shows the importance of tackling corruption following the establishment of a democracy. Not only can continued corruption sap a new democracy of much of its legitimacy, but also, as stressed in Chapter 8, it provides the military with an excuse to intervene in domestic politics. Like many other African states, political office in Nigeria is seen as the gateway to both direct and personal economic wealth. The direct wealth comes from skimming government funds before their distribution. The indirect wealth is a consequence of the ability to target state resources to loyal clients, which deepens an office holder's political power and opens the doors to bribes and kickbacks. Neither is helpful to democratic stability.

Another Nigerian lesson is the importance of addressing social divisions in the design of a democratic system. One could argue, with the structural and choice chips stacked against successful democracy, that it is a miracle the Second and Fourth Republics survived as long as they did. An important part of the reasons for their relative success was the design of the Nigerian federal system, which scuttled the initial ethno-federal approach in favor of one that used internal political boundaries to cross-cut the country's deep social divisions. The tensions over the 2007 presidential election demonstrated that these efforts have not been fully successful. Identity divisions remain strong and correspond to broad regions, but at least the elections have not reinforced these divisions to the extent that they did in the past.

Regime Transitions in the Russian Federation, China, and Iran

Russia, China, and Iran are the three TIC cases furthest away from being considered established democracies. By 2008, the last year of former President (and current Prime Minister) Vladmir Putin's second presidential term, Russia had turned well away from its democratic experiment. Both China and Iran are countries without any significant experience with democracy, yet countries that intrigue comparativists with their potential to move in a more democratic direction in the years ahead.

The Russian Federation

The collapse of the Soviet Union resulted in fifteen new countries. The experience with democracy in these countries has varied greatly, from consolidated democracies in the Baltic region to the failure to seriously consider democracy in most of the Central Asian states. The largest of the fifteen successor states, Russia, has itself run the gamut of democratic experiences. Boris Yeltsin's action in October 1993—when he used the military to put down opponents in the parliament—was an undemocratic action yet created the stability necessary for the establishment of democracy. The new democracy functioned, if not perfectly, in the 1990s. Significant turnover among prime ministers, disputes between Yeltsin and the new parliament, and questionable campaign practices during national elections pointed to areas of weakness. Since 2000, Russia has backtracked from a deepening of its democracy, placing order above freedom and pursuing that order through a strong central government controlled by a formidable executive.

For comparativists interested in democratization, Russia provides two puzzles: why the country established a democratic system, and why this system appears to have fallen apart. It is necessary to consider both structural and choice factors in answering these questions. While some elements of socioeconomic and political structure and certain decisions by political leaders made democracy possible, other socioeconomic and political conditions and decisions by subsequent leaders have prevented its consolidation.

One can make a case that structural changes caused the liberalization and democratization in the late Soviet and early post-Soviet periods. Over the previous fifty years, the economy had developed dramatically—cultivating urbanization and increases in education—only to suffer a period of stagnation in which people's expectations for a better life were unmet. Soviet political structures also made liberalization difficult to control. The ethno-federal arrangement, created partially to address identity diversity and placate minority groups, created opportunities for provincial leaders to engage in political reforms beyond those sanctioned at the center.[73]

These structural conditions may have made reform more likely, but Soviet leader Mikhail Gorbachev still had to decide to pursue liberalization. Gorbachev's inability to foresee the destabilizing consequences of his political (*demokratizatsiya*), economic (*perestroika*), mass communication (*glasnost'*), and international relations ("new thinking") reforms was what ultimately undid the Soviet authoritarian system and similar systems across Eastern Europe. Gorbachev expected greater legitimacy for the system, and for himself. Instead, the reforms allowed people to see that many others in the country were as unhappy as they were. Soviet authoritarianism's collapse brought an establishment of democracy, rather than another form of nondemocracy, largely because of the commitment of such Russian leaders as Boris Yeltsin.

During Yeltsin's tenure as president, there were hints that democracy might be in trouble, even if there was no sense that a sharp move away from democracy was a foregone conclusion. Yeltsin allowed media censorship and attacks against political opponents, though both in lower levels than appeared after 2000. In addition, the system Yeltsin designed, which had few genuine checks on the president, made further concentration of power in the hands of the executive a distinct possibility.[74] Yeltsin also never built a strong political party committed to democracy during the 1990s, instead believing that the president should be above party politics. Parties like the Communists and Liberal Democrats initially filled this void, followed by, even more effectively, Putin's United Russia Party.

Socioeconomic structural factors in Russia also hinted at incomplete democratization. Economic development under the Soviets did not produce a middle class, and the economic ups and downs of the 1990s generally did not either. Many associated the period of economic decline in the first half of the 1990s, and again in 1998, with Russia's new democracy. In addition, Russian political culture, never historically conducive to democracy, did not change overnight once democracy was established. As Russians watched Putin consolidate power rather than democracy, they mostly liked what they saw.[75] In 2005, fewer than 30 percent of Russians felt democracy was preferable to a strong leader.[76] Even those who supported democracy in the early 1990s, such as

younger residents of big cities, began to sour on it in the subsequent decade.

While socioeconomic structures in Russia gave Putin the opportunity to move Russia in a more authoritarian direction, the political system that he inherited provided further tools for such a move. In a system with a weaker president, those in other branches of government might have had a greater stake in protecting the democratic system. In a system in which the institutional arrangements allowed Putin to govern nearly unchecked, however, elites supportive of democracy were constrained and had little self-interest in opposing his further consolidation of power.

In some ways, the Russian case mirrors the Mexican one. A long period of economic development ran headlong into a period of economic hardship, leading governing elites to support economic and political liberalization. In other ways, the two cases differ noticeably. Gorbachev was a reformer challenged by hardliners, but unlike the PRI leaders in Mexico, he did not intend to democratize the Soviet Union. Russian history's late Soviet period is consistent with the idea that the combination of economic development followed by economic downturn and a split in the ruling elite fosters liberalization, but it also provides a glaring example of the challenges facing a reformer who only wants to partially reform a nondemocratic system.

The late Soviet and early post-Soviet periods were times of great division among political leaders, but Russia provides a counterexample to the idea that such situations automatically lead to bargaining and pact making. Yeltsin's successful attack against his opponents in October 1993 made bargaining unnecessary. Yeltsin certainly does not deserve all the blame for the lack of compromise. His opponents in the 1993 conflict did little to pursue a new system based on negotiation. Whichever side is more to blame for the 1993 events, the Russian political system that emerged was a political structure that made creeping authoritarianism possible. Because they decisively won against their opponents in 1993, Yeltsin and his advisors were able to impose their vision during the final design of the new Russian Constitution without serious challenge. Yeltsin's successor, Vladimir Putin, used the resulting dual executive system with its substantial presidential powers to escort Russia along the path to authoritarianism.

China

Unlike the other TIC cases discussed so far, China has no significant experience with democracy. Thus, one could argue it makes little sense to discuss Chinese democratization, especially since the timing of a particular instance of democratization is so difficult to predict in advance. Many comparativists agree, focusing instead on the factors that have, to date, allowed China to maintain its authoritarian system. China specialist Bruce Gilley, however, argues that comparativists have a professional obligation to use their knowledge of general theories and particular cases to explain why democratization in China is or is not likely.[77] He adds, given the extent to which global changes and transformation of socioeconomic structures in China are consistent with comparative politics explanations of democratization, that the "burden of proof" is on comparativists who believe China will not democratize.[78]

In addition to examining China itself, transitions in Asian countries and other parts of the world in recent years provide evidence about the kinds of factors that might influence Chinese democratization. For comparativists, Taiwan's democratization provides particularly strong evidence. Both governments have aggressively fostered economic development, though the resulting middle class is arguably a larger portion of the population in Taiwan than in China. The political cultures of the two countries are similar, with both heavily influenced by Confucianism and their authoritarian pasts. Both face ethnic tensions. In the case of Taiwan, ethnic divisions have largely been between the native population of the island and those who came from the mainland, while in China's case the divisions are

mainly between the Han majority and minority groups on the periphery of the country. Sharp ethnic divisions can make democracy difficult to consolidate, but as the late Soviet period demonstrated, regionally concentrated minorities can also push for liberalization and play a role in the breakdown of the nondemocratic system.

China has, so far, avoided the demonstration effects from nine major Asian states—Bangladesh, Indonesia, Mongolia, Nepal, Pakistan, the Philippines, South Korea, Taiwan, and Thailand—that established democracies from the mid-1980s to the late 1990s.[79] Korean political scientist Junhan Lee points out that in all of these cases except Pakistan, the establishment of democracy followed mass protests, typically led by university students. Once again, China defied this regional trend. Its most conspicuous instance of such protests, Tiananmen Square in 1989, ended not in liberalization and democracy but in a successful military crackdown.

Another interesting comparative case is Mexico. From the 1960s to the 1990s, Mexico lagged behind regional democratization trends. Unlike other authoritarian systems around it, Mexico's nondemocratic system concentrated political power in the hands of a single political party, using that party to penetrate into society and mobilize the population in support of the government. It also repressed a significant student protest by force and experimented with more legitimate elections at the local level before considering the liberalization of national politics.

While a comparison of Chinese conditions to those that sparked transitions in Taiwan and Mexico uncovers a number of parallels, there are also important dissimilarities. These help explain China's lack of democratization to date and provide lessons for comparativists about the potential for political reform in China and other nondemocracies. For example, China appears to lack a significant split in the ruling elite. If anything, by 2007 the CCP leadership was more unified about the current approach, wedding economic openness and political authoritarianism, than at any point since Deng Xiaoping launched his economic reforms at the end of the 1970s.

In addition, though technocrats like Hu Jintao have gained China's top leadership positions, their impact has been quite different from their counterparts' emergence in Mexico. Unlike technocrats in Mexico, who accepted political liberalization, the Chinese leaders have leaned on economic growth to provide performance legitimacy in their quest to maintain authoritarian rule. China has managed to avoid the economic downturn that sparked liberalization in Mexico. Consequently, no large gap between economic performance and aggregate popular expectations has occurred, although increasing inequality, including the novelty of noticeable urban poverty, poses a threat to the regime's ability to use economic growth to buy popular support. Perhaps as a hedge on its bets on economic growth, China's leaders have also appealed to nationalism. But just as history shows that high levels of economic growth cannot be sustained forever, nationalism does not always have a long shelf life.

China also demonstrates how some authoritarian leaders recognize the dangers that economic development poses to their rule and take steps to contain its effects. The country is an excellent example of Bruce Bueno de Mesquita and George Downs's idea, discussed earlier in the chapter, about authoritarian governments learning to blunt economic development's political consequences. The CCP government has taken steps to prevent support for democracy from taking deep hold. The crackdown against protesters in Tiananmen Square demonstrated the will of the CCP leadership to maintain control through force if necessary, but the CCP has also used more subtle methods. Agreements with software companies Google and Microsoft limited the possibilities for the Chinese population to access English-language news sites or use words such as "freedom" and "democracy" on Internet web logs.[80] Whether such actions will be enough to maintain China's authoritarian system, or at least limit the transformation of its system to one

that is semidemocratic, is one of the key questions about the next decade of Chinese politics.

Iran

The success of moderate reformers such as former president Mohammed Khatami, limited as it was, encouraged many who desire sustained liberalization in Iran. From 2004 to 2006, such views were tempered as hardliners successfully grabbed all of the reins of Iranian political power. While moderates can point to past electoral successes, and while socioeconomic structural changes over the past three decades have made democratization more likely, it does not appear to be on the immediate horizon. The design of Iran's current nondemocratic political system has allowed leaders opposed to political reform to block liberalization efforts.

Khatami's tenure as president proved that reformers existed and could mobilize significant political support in Iran. What many scholars identify as the first step in democratization, the split in the ruling elite between hardliners and reformers was in full view in the late 1990s and early 2000s. Since 2004, the hardliners have retaken control of the political stage. It is not hard to imagine a Khatami-like figure emerging in the future, though hardliners will use their institutional powers, which are sizeable, to try to prevent it.

If reformers are allowed to run in Iranian elections, there are a number of reasons in addition to Khatami's past success to expect them to do well. Iran's demographic changes since 1979, discussed in earlier chapters, are consistent with liberalization and democratization. The Iranian population is young, increasingly urban, and much better educated than in the past. Within two decades of the Revolution, the population changed from one in which the majority lived in rural areas to one well over 60 percent urban. With population growth hitting its peak in 1986, large numbers of these urban Iranians are now in their twenties, the age at which unemployment and other economic problems can become intolerable.[81] Adding to the frustration of the younger cohorts, although literacy and education have improved in past decades, only around 10 percent of high schoolers are admitted to Iranian universities.[82] These younger Iranians are generally more politically liberal and supportive of reform than older generations. At least prior to the American-led invasion of Iraq and open tensions with the United States over Iran's nuclear program, they also supported an improvement in ties with the West in general and the United States in particular.

Iran provides a telling example of how a split between reformers and hardliners does not always result in significant reform. While former president Khatami and others supportive of liberalization have had significant public support in the recent past, Iran's institutional arrangements allow hardliners to trump most pro-reform efforts. The banning of reformist candidates and the resulting conservative transformation of the elective Iranian political offices strengthened the hardliners' control over Iranian politics, at least in the short run. But all is not well for the hardliners' vision. The success of moderate candidates in the 2006 elections for the Assembly of Experts made a dent in the hardliners' hold on power. Whether this dent marks the start of another pro-reform period remains to be seen.

As discussed previously, nondemocratic leaders in some countries appear to have learned from the experiences of others and found ways to limit the impact of desires among the general population for greater political openness. Iran is no exception. President Mahmoud Ahmadinejad has effectively used populist appeals and nationalist rhetoric to deflect attention away from the regime's antidemocratic characteristics. But such efforts never make leaders fully immune from desires for greater political participation. The various structural changes in Iran since the 1979 Revolution are inconsistent with long-term, stable authoritarian governance. Thus, whether soon or whether decades from now, Iranian hardliners are likely to face renewed challenges from groups championing political reform.

COMPARATIVE EXERCISE

The Classic Democratic "Outlier"—A Case Study of India

This chapter's Comparative Exercise again involves one of the TIC countries, in this case India. Because this exercise is a detailed case study of India's democratization, there was no Topic in Countries entry for India in the preceding section. Why focus so intently on India's democratization? It is a regional military power, a potential economic powerhouse, and has a booming population—on pace to overtake China as the world's most populous country over the next couple of decades. It is also a democracy, a feature of India that is almost certainly its most surprising. Many argue that, given its socioeconomic structures, India has little business being a democracy, not to mention a consolidated democracy. But other than a very brief period of authoritarian rule in the mid-1970s, India has been governed by a democratic system since its independence from the British.

India is, therefore, the definition of a deviant case. As discussed in the opening chapter of the book, a deviant case is one that differs greatly from the general pattern that one sees when looking at a large number of countries. It is, in statistical terms, an "outlier." One knows going into the study of a deviant case that the dominant theories will not produce hypotheses that fit the case. As a result, comparativists do not study deviant cases to test existing theoretical perspectives. Rather, they examine the case in detail to seek insight into what the existing dominant explanations have missed. Such studies are useful not only for understanding the particular case—and understanding a country as important as India is certainly valuable in its own right—but they may also uncover one or more variables that scholars had previously neglected. Subsequent examinations of such variables in other cases may indicate that they were more important than previously thought.

An Overview of Indian Democracy

The British ruled over colonial India with a combination of coercion and compromise, emphasizing the latter. While it is tempting to give the British credit for such compromise, the enormity of the territory, sheer size of the population, and complexity of the society gave the British little choice. To rely on coercion alone would have required a continuous, massive, and costly display of force. Yet, being forced to compromise is a different matter from encouraging democratic practices. The British do deserve credit for their support of certain democratic procedures during colonial rule. They allowed localities and some regions degrees of self-rule as early as the late 1800s, a process that accelerated in the first half of the twentieth century.

This acceleration of self-rule coincided with the emergence as a national political force of the Congress Party (also referred to as the Indian National Congress, "INC"). The INC became a mass political party, reaching into all corners of India. While many attribute the INC's success to Mahatma Gandhi, it is important to remember that Gandhi was president of the party for only one year, during 1924 and 1925, while Jawaharlal Nehru was its president six times starting in 1929. Yet, Gandhi's impact on the party was substantial. His personal views and rational calculations about what was best for the INC and its goal of independence led the party to stress nonviolent resistance. This made it even more difficult for the British to justify coercive control.

Inspired by Gandhi and reinforced by Nehru, the party's openness to a diverse collection of leaders and supporters from across India's territory and social divides also fostered political cooperation and tolerance for identity and policy differences. The diversity of the party played a role in creating an overarching and largely civic Indian national identity, which helped India to achieve independence and institute a functioning, postindependence democracy.[83] Independence came in 1947, the same year that a partition of India removed a significant portion of Muslim-majority territory, the western portion of which is now Pakistan and the eastern portion of which is now Bangladesh.

Jawaharlal Nehru became India's first prime minister. Continuing the Gandhi-inspired vision of broad and diverse membership in the INC, the party remained popular, indeed dominant, in Indian politics for the next several decades. Nehru did as well, remaining prime minister from 1947 until his death in 1964.

The first of the greatest challenges to India's democracy came in the mid-1970s. In 1975, widespread protests and strikes demanding Prime Minister Indira Gandhi's resignation followed an Allahabad High Court finding that she had misused government machinery in her election campaign in 1971. Although the court acquitted her of more serious charges, it ruled that as a result of her conviction the election was null and void, she had to vacate the seat, and she was banned from running for office for six years. In response, Prime Minister Gandhi asked President Fakhruddin Ali Ahmed to declare a state of emergency and suspend the democratic system. The official justification was that a threat to national security had arisen. Following nearly two years of authoritarian rule, Indira Gandhi held elections in 1977 that she thought the INC would win. Instead, the Janata Party won. Indira Gandhi surrendered power to her political opponents, and Indian democracy was reestablished.

More recently, a form of nationalism posed a second challenge to India's democracy. The Bharatiya Janata Party (BJP), in a coalition with a number of smaller parties, gained control of the government in 1998, and again in 1999, through appeals to Hindu nationalism, criticism of policies designed to protect and give preference to minority groups, and a tough stance against India's neighbor, Pakistan. The BJP's approach concerned Indian supporters of secularism, as well as outside observers, since it challenged India's past commitment to civic nationalism and an inclusive, overarching national identity. However, again showing the extent to which India's democracy is consolidated, when the BJP called early elections in 2004 and lost, it peacefully turned over control to a coalition headed by the INC.

Discussion

India is only one case. As democracy continues to spread into countries lacking the conditions generally thought to promote democracy, considering cases where such conditions are absent and yet democracy has flourished becomes increasingly important. Scholars who emphasize the importance of choice factors in democratization point to the impact of India's leaders and their commitment to democracy in the face of social and economic challenges. The presence of a ruling elite committed to democratic norms is an important part of the story of the establishment and initial stability of India's democracy, and it is certainly what many casual observers of the country and its history emphasize.

Focusing on the role of individual leaders alone, however, is overly simplistic in the Indian case. Structural conditions in India are more complicated than they first appear, and choices and structures interacted in important ways in the years before and after independence. India's middle class, for example, is smaller in percentage terms than in many other consolidated democracies. But in a country of more than one billion people, a small percentage can equal a large absolute number. It is possible that the effect of an emergent middle class may be as much about absolute numbers as about percentages.[84]

In addition, India is a deeply divided society, but one in which cross-cutting divisions are as prevalent as complementary ones. In terms of religion, Hindus are the vast majority (80 percent). But Hindus are linguistically and economically diverse, and even the religion itself has many manifestations across the country. The caste system in India—officially outlawed though still important—adds another dimension to social divisions, again cutting across linguistic lines and dividing Hindus from one another. Even ethnic divisions in the country are more localized than national, helping contain conflicts when they flare up.[85]

Finally, the partition is a valuable example of the intersection of choices and structures in India. According to political scientist Ashutosh Varshney, the choice to partition India and create Pakistan allowed India's British-style majoritarian system to work.[86] While perhaps not the intention of those supporting the partition, it weakened the Hindu-Muslim divide in India enough to allow the cross-cutting divisions to have an effect. Without it, identity divisions between Hindus and Muslims might well have been too deep for such a democratic system to survive.

Thus, even India, which at first appears to be a prime example of a country in which the role of leadership and choices trump structural factors, demonstrates how both structural and choice factors can be important and play off one another. The structure of Indian society helped foster cooperation under British rule, but choices such as the partition, the Congress Party's inclusive approach, and Mahatma Gandhi's commitment to nonviolence also had lasting effects on the country's identity and cultural structures.

Think and Discuss

What lesson can be learned from India to better understand democratization? Is this lesson applicable to other cases?

CONCLUSION

No other comparative politics topic highlights the importance of structure and choice as clearly as regime transition. The three stages of democratization—the breakdown of a nondemocratic system, the establishment of a new democracy, and the consolidation of that democracy—result from the complex interplay of underlying structural factors and the decisions of political agents, both domestically and internationally. Economic development and the emergence of a middle class, for example, can both challenge the power monopoly of a nondemocratic government and lead to changes in the general population (e.g., education) that make them more accepting of democratic principles.

Certain cultural features of the population can make democracy more or less likely. These include not only values directly tied to democracy, such as a comparative desire for freedom over a strong leader, but also related beliefs such as tolerance for differing opinions, interpersonal trust, and the desirability of social equality over a strongly hierarchal society. For example, an increasing body of comparative politics research points to a strong relationship between beliefs about women's equality to men and the establishment and consolidation of democracy.

There is also general agreement that deep identity divisions in a country pose challenges to democratic consolidation. The already unstable period of regime transition can be even more chaotic in such cases, particularly when the new democratic institutions have not been designed to encourage groups to reach across identity group boundaries. Finding ways to overcome deep social divisions gives democracy a better chance to survive.

There is less consensus about whether particular identities make democracy less likely. For example, some contend that Islam is not conducive to democracy, but one should not blindly accept such claims. Even if one believes elements of Islam contrast with democratic ideals, Islam is not the only source of identity for Muslims. Individuals can have strong religious identities but still identify themselves in other ways, such as through their national, ethnic, racial, linguistic, regional, or class identities. Also remember that many questioned Catholicism's compatibility with democracy prior to the "third wave" democratizations in majority-Catholic countries.

Political institutional arrangements also affect democratization. The experiences of Nigeria demonstrate the importance of institutional design. Debates continue about the effects of unitary versus federal systems, presidential systems versus parliamentary ones, and FPTP versus PR electoral arrangements on democratic consolidation. There is little debate, however, that the fit between a country's political structure and its socioeconomic structure matters.

The decisions and leadership of certain individuals also have a significant impact on democratization. Some argue that choice factors, being closer to the process of democratization, are more directly related to democratization than structural ones. Indeed, after heavily focusing on structure from the 1950s to the 1970s, comparative studies of regime change have more to the role of leaders and their choices. Individuals and their decisions can drive a country toward democracy, but they can also prevent democratization. As democracy specialist Larry Diamond argues, "The principal obstacle to the expansion of democracy in the world is not the people of the remaining authoritarian states. The problem is the ruling elites who have hijacked the structures of state power and barricaded themselves inside."[87]

Structural and choice-based factors, both internal and external, also intersect. Domestic socioeconomic structures and international conditions shape leaders' abilities to consolidate new democracies, and affect whether nondemocratic ruling elites choose to liberalize or remain "barricaded" in their nondemocratic systems. But structures alone do not fully determine this process. Comparativist Sheri Berman puts it nicely: "Structural developments may be necessary to create an environment favorable to democratization and eventual consolidation, but unless powerful and determined local actors step up to lead the way, even weakened authoritarian regimes may find themselves with an extended lease on life."[88] In turn, these individuals' choices can alter the socioeconomic and political structures and their effects on regime transition. Thus, a full understanding of democratization and democratic breakdown, even in a single country, requires an examination of internal and external structures, choices, and their interaction.

Key Terms

Breakdown of nondemocracy, p. 448
Breakdown stage, p. 450

Conditionality, p. 457
Consolidation of democracy, p. 448
Crisis stage, p. 450
Democratic breakdown, p. 450
Democratization, p. 446
Democratization wave, p. 446
Demonstration effects, p. 457
Establishment of democracy, p. 448
Hardliners, p. 458
Incomplete democratization, p. 446
Intergovernmental organizations (IGOs), p. 457
Liberalization, p. 446
Moderates, p. 459
Nongovernmental organizations (NGOs), p. 457
Pact, p. 459
Polar system, p. 455
Pole, p. 455
Radicals, p. 459
Reequilibration, p. 451
Reformers, p. 458
Regime transition, p. 445
Reverse wave, p. 447
Triggering events, p. 461

13

Public Policy and Government Performance

Learning Objectives

After reading this chapter, you should be able to:

- Explain the differences between domestic, foreign, and "intermestic" policy.

- Discuss the differences among first, second, and third order policy change and explain why third order changes are relatively rare.

- Describe the major indicators of successful government performance.

- Explain how socioeconomic structures, political structures, and leadership can affect policy outcomes and discuss the extent to which policy is made through a process of rational decision making.

- Discuss major policy debates and measures of government performance in the United Kingdom, Germany, France, Mexico, Brazil, Russia, China, India, Nigeria, and Iran.

In 1985, Mikhail Gorbachev became General Secretary of the Communist Party of the Soviet Union (CPSU), the position that signaled him as the political leader of the Soviet Union. Gorbachev initiated a number of significant policy reforms, many of which did not bring the results he had intended. While he eventually turned to more significant policy changes aimed at "restructuring" the Soviet economic and political systems, his initial reforms sought to jump-start the economy. At the center of these initial efforts was an undertaking to reduce Soviet citizens' unparalleled consumption of alcohol. There were reasons for Gorbachev to embark on such a campaign. Spending on alcohol was estimated to be as much as 20 percent of disposable household income, and drunkenness contributed up to 90 percent of absences from work.[1]

Look for this icon to point you to **Deepening Your Understanding** features on the companion website www.college.cengage.com/politicalscience/barrington, which provide greater depth for some key content.

The antialcohol policy, launched in May 1985, combined an increase in the drinking age, a ban on the sale of alcoholic beverages at many locations in the country, a prohibition against the sale of hard liquor on weekends, and steep price increases on beer, wine, and liquor when and where it could be sold. On the face of it, the policy appeared to work. By October 1985, *Time* magazine was reporting that hard liquor sales had already fallen by 15 percent, and wine and champagne sales had decreased by 25 percent.[2]

Unfortunately, like many policy initiatives, the antialcohol program had unintended consequences. Stores began running short of sugar and inexpensive cologne. The former disappeared as individuals began making their own alcohol, while the shortage of the latter came about as some alcoholics substituted cologne and other similar solutions for the suddenly more expensive liquor. The Soviet government also began running a significant budget deficit, brought about by a sharp decline in government revenue from alcohol sales in state-run liquor stores. In 1988, the Soviet government ended the campaign. ■

If politics is the struggle for "who gets what," understanding it requires knowledge about how and why governments seek to address social and economic problems. Rarely do efforts to alter "who gets what" take the form of a single, revolutionary change. Instead, they are the result of a government making a large number of small decisions over time. These decisions concern how to address what government leaders, and often the general public, perceive to be problems—such as alcoholism in the Soviet Union in the 1980s—in need of a solution.

Policies are important political outcomes, and their study has become a central component of comparative politics over the last several decades. As a result, **comparative public policy** is treated as a key subfield of comparative politics. Comparative public policy seeks to understand the causes and consequences of policy decisions, including why some governments act to solve certain problems that other governments refuse to address. As one public policy textbook puts it, comparative public policy is the "study of how, why, and to what effect different governments pursue particular courses of action or inaction."[3] Because many of the most important government policies relate in one way or another to the economy, there is significant overlap between the study of public policy and the study of political economy.

Given its focus on policy creation and implementation, comparative public policy looks closely at the inner workings of government institutions. This focus that is often given its own label, **public administration**. While public policy scholars seek to understand policies, including the factors, political institutions or otherwise, that affect variation in policy approaches, the study of public administration centers on the nuts and bolts of the government institutions that produce such policy.

The first of public policy scholars' two main tasks is to understand why particular policies are adopted. As Figure 13.1 indicates, this first task centers on the causal link between the structural and choice factors that comparativists believe influence policy and patterns in the resulting policies. Similar to other comparative politics topics, the study of policy adoption sometimes takes the form of a detailed analysis of a single case. One might, for example, examine the

Comparative public policy is a subfield of comparative politics that examines the causes and consequences of policy decisions.

Public administration is a subfield of political science that studies the inner working of government institutions that produce public policy.

Figure 13.1   Understanding the Policy Process and Its Consequences

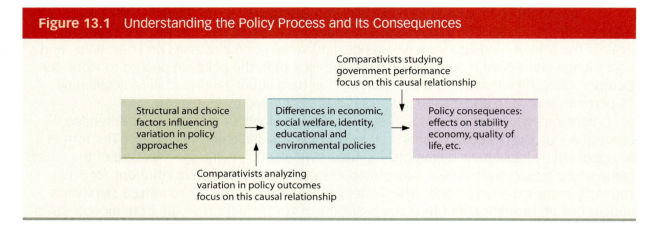

development of taxation policy in Russia after the collapse of the Soviet Union. While this type of study is very helpful for those interested in that case, it can also generate ideas that scholars may use to examine other cases.

Case studies of policy are common, but they are far from comparativists' only option. Other comparativists look at multiple cases but restrict their analysis to a single policy area, such as education policy or spending on transportation. Those seeking to develop a more generalizable explanation of policy adoption may choose to compare a number of policies in one or more countries, through use of the comparative method. The comparative exercise in Chapter 6, for example, looked at major policy changes that occurred in the United Kingdom and China through the lens of veto point theory. Still others may choose to engage in the study of a large number of cases, using statistical techniques to test theories about what factors influence variation in policy adoption. These studies often analyze a large number of policies in a variety of countries over a long period of time. Some of the most persuasive comparative politics research on public policy combine one or more of these approaches, uniting qualitative and quantitative analyses.

In addition to studying what influences policy adoption, many comparative public policy scholars focus on the consequences of policy implementation. As indicated in Figure 13.1, this second side of public policy examines whether general policy approaches and particular government programs actually work. Do the individual programs examined achieve the specific goals of the officials who designed them? Do they solve what was identified as a problem? In addition to their specific goals, do the policies in question achieve broad goals such as stability and prosperity? Do they improve the lives of ordinary people?

How well government policies achieve broad goals such as stability and narrower goals related to a specific program is a key part of what comparativists label governmental or regime "performance." When governments in democratic systems perform badly over time, voters often remove the leaders or ruling party at election time. Populations of authoritarian systems do not have that luxury, although ongoing poor performance by an authoritarian government can lead to popular uprising, which may trigger military action to overthrow the sitting government.

Studying government performance is one way that comparative politics has practical applications. Indeed, the topic of government performance links comparative politics and the actual practice of politics more directly than many other topics. As discussed in Chapter 1, over the last decade, political science has placed a greater emphasis on making its research "policy relevant" (of value to political leaders). Furthering the understanding of which policy approaches appear to work and which ones do not can contribute, over time, to better public policy.

Public Policy

Public policy is a commonly-used political science term. The *public* modifier in the term emphasizes that political scientists are generally interested in policies created by governmental entities rather than those of other social organizations such as corporations or religious bodies. But what are policies? Policies are outputs of a political system that are created with the objective of altering some aspect of political, economic, or social conditions. Policies are broader than laws. Laws are specific acts of a government that alter the rules for individual and collective behavior. All laws are part of one or more policies, but not all parts of a particular policy are laws. Policies also include specific government programs and implementation strategies.

While a policy is a purposive government act, the term can also refer to a government's *lack of effort* to address a problem. Not *everything* governments fail to do is a policy. Those who study public policy consider inaction to be a policy when it occurs over time and in the face of pressure on the government to act.[4] In other words, such inaction must be a conscious choice to be a policy. For example, by the start of the twenty-first century, the absence of a significant government approach to rising health care costs in the United States had become a policy. The American people's support for a greater federal role in addressing health care costs and the existence of national health insurance or health care programs in other economically developed countries indicated that the United States' lack of such programs was the result of political leaders—or at least key leaders with the ability to block major policy proposals—choosing not to address to the problem.

Foreign Versus Domestic Policy

Political scientists distinguish between three broad categories of policy. The first two, domestic and foreign, likely sound familiar. **Domestic policy** is the set of programs and directives that seek to improve economic, social, and political conditions *within* a country. **Foreign policy**, on the other hand, typically refers to all policies concerning that country's international relations, national security, and defense.

Note that one labels a policy as foreign or domestic based on the *target* of the policy rather than its causes. Causal factors from outside the country can affect domestic policies. Likewise, internal considerations may drive foreign and defense policy. Work by political scientist Geoffrey Pridham highlights situations where internal and external topics are "linked" in the study of policy. For Pridham, **inner-directed linkage** is when external factors influence domestic policy; **outer-directed linkage** occurs when domestic factors shape foreign policy.[5] Figure 13.2 captures how internal and external causes intersect with domestic and foreign policy.

Public policy is an output of a political system designed to alter some aspect of political, economic, or social conditions.

Domestic policy is the set of government approaches designed to improve economic, social, and political conditions within a country.

Foreign policy is the set of approaches related to international relations, national security, and defense.

Inner-directed linkage occurs when external factors influence domestic policy.

Outer-directed linkage involves domestic factors shaping foreign policy.

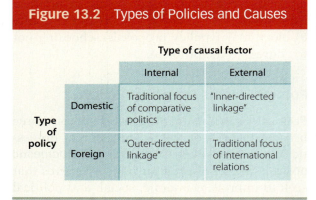

Figure 13.2   Types of Policies and Causes

Intermestic Policy

Although differences between domestic and foreign policy are clear in principle, it is not always easy in practice to place particular policies in one category or the other. As globalization and regionalization connect countries to one another more and more, the boundaries between domestic and foreign policy are increasingly unclear. Perhaps the best example is trade policy. A particular country's trade policies seek to improve economic conditions within that country, but they also affect international relations between that country and others. Immigration policy also has both domestic and international targets. The difficulty of labeling such policies as either domestic or foreign has led to the creation of a new category, **intermestic policy**.

Similarly, factors influencing policy creation cannot always be neatly labeled internal or external. Is pressure over a trade policy proposal from a multinational corporation that is based in the United States but has most of its factories overseas an internal or external factor? Is a protest by U.S. citizens with ties to groups outside the country who are targeted by a proposed immigration policy an internal or external factor? Comparative politics has yet to adopt a label such as "intermestic" for such causal factors, but they are important to consider.

Major Types of Domestic and Intermestic Policy

Within comparative politics, public policy studies span domestic and intermestic policy arenas. The types of policies comparativists examine include economic strategies, regulatory practices, social welfare programs, education programs, and identity-related policies.

Economic Policy: Fiscal, Monetary, Developmental, and Trade

Of the various types of government policies, a large number—and many of the most important ones—fall under the category of economic policy. These include policies concerning government spending, initiatives to alter government revenue through taxation and other means, efforts to reduce budget deficits caused by more spending than revenue, approaches to the supply of money in the economy including the setting of interest rates, programs aimed at improving economic development, and practices involving foreign trade.

Fiscal Policy   Fiscal policy relates to the set of government decisions affecting taxing and spending. Government programs cost money, and governments spend money on almost every policy decision they make. In federal systems, it is also possible for a government to command that lower levels of government take certain actions without providing the necessary money to those lower levels of government. Such dictates are known as **unfunded mandates**. These policies require spending, but the spending does not take place at the federal level.

Intermestic policy is the set of government policies that share the traits of domestic and foreign policy. Examples include trade and immigration policy.

Unfunded mandates are commands from higher levels of government to lower levels of government to take certain actions without providing the money necessary to cover the expense of those actions.

In most countries, the national government budget is a source of ideological and partisan conflict. How much and on what programs money is spent comprises the heart and soul of the "who gets what" nature of politics. Because most national government budgets are passed annually, the budget process is an opportunity to review and adjust policy priorities. As scholars who emphasize incrementalism point out, however, government programs are rarely eliminated and budgets rarely decrease. In most countries, the national government budget has consistently increased in recent decades. In percentage terms, annual increases are often well above both the rate of inflation and growth in gross domestic product. For example, Canada's GDP grew significantly from late 1960s to the early 1990s. Yet, spending by Canada's federal and provincial governments *as a percentage of GDP* doubled over the same period.[6]

The other side of fiscal policy is the collection of revenues through taxation and other sources of income. In most countries, taxes fall into a handful of categories: personal income taxes, corporate income taxes, value added taxes, sales taxes, excise taxes (tariffs), and property taxes. Americans are most familiar with personal income taxes, sales taxes, and property taxes, since these generate much of the revenue for the various levels of government in the United States. Sales taxes add a certain percentage to the cost of a product, which a seller must turn over to the government. Property taxes are based on a percentage of the value of personal property—often restricted only to the value of one's home and land.

Income taxes extract a portion of money based on an individual's income. In a few countries, the tax rate (the percentage of income paid is tax) is constant across all levels of income. This is known as a **flat tax**. Most countries, including the United States, use some form of **progressive tax**, where the tax rate increases as one's income increases. The top tax rates can be very high, although individuals in the top tax bracket usually still take home a lot of money. Sweden used to have a top tax rate of nearly 90 percent. Over the last few decades, top tax rates have fallen in most advanced industrial countries. Sweden's top tax rate dropped to a little more than 50 percent in the early 1990s before again creeping upward. At the start of 2007, it was nearing 60 percent.

People also pay different amounts of tax based on the number and type of deductions and credits for which they qualify. A **tax deduction** is a reduction, based on some criterion, in the portion of taxable income. For example, if a married couple with three children live in a country with a $5,000 deduction per child on national income taxes, the deduction for these children would *reduce their taxable income* by $15,000. A **tax credit** is a reduction in the amount of tax paid rather than in the amount of taxable income. If the same couple with three children lived in a country with a child tax credit of $1,000 per child, this credit would *reduce their tax bill* by $3,000. The array of credits and deductions used around the world is immense, partly because they are a way to reward political allies or politically important groups.

Corporate taxes secure a portion of a particular business's revenues. Like personal income taxes, there may be a large number of deductions which reduce the amount of taxable revenue or credits that reduce the amount of tax owed. Governments employ a vast assortment of deductions designed to protect domestic

A **flat tax** is a form of income tax in which individuals pay the same percentage of income in tax regardless of their level of income.

A **progressive tax** is one in which the percentage of income paid in taxes increases as one's level of income increases.

A **tax deduction** is a criterion that reduces the portion of an individual's income that is subject to tax.

A **tax credit** does not affect the amount of taxable income but instead reduces the amount of tax an individual owes on that income.

companies, encourage investment in domestic facilities, and spur job creation. Again, because these deductions can be used to reward political allies or to win political support from powerful economic groups, their number tends to grow over time and some individual deductions may be very narrow, benefiting only a single large company.

The final aspect of fiscal policy falls at the intersection of spending and taxing. When governments secure more revenue than they spend in a given year, they run a **budget surplus** for that year. If they spend more than they take in—as is often the case—they run a **budget deficit**. Running deficits over time can lead to a large **government debt** (also known as the public debt). While a deficit is an annual shortfall in revenue compared to spending, the debt is the sum of money owed when governments repeatedly run deficits. Running a deficit forces a government to borrow money, typically by issuing government bonds.

Monetary Policy   While fiscal policy concerns taxing and spending, monetary policy relates to the supply of money circulating in the economy and the interest rates associated with lending the money in circulation. In most countries, the government's **central bank** officially controls the money supply and affects interest rates across the country by altering the interest rate on loans it makes to private banks. However, a central bank's *actual* independence from the chief executive and legislature varies. In some countries, including the United States and the United Kingdom, decisions regarding money supply and credit conditions are not made by elected officials but rather by a small group of bureaucrats who run the central bank. In the United States, the central bank is known as the **Federal Reserve System**, while the **Federal Reserve Board**, commonly called the "Fed," sets monetary policy. In many other countries, however, top government officials not only have control over fiscal power but also can put significant pressure on the

central bank or even completely control monetary policy decisions.

A country's money supply and prevailing interest rates can have a dramatic impact on its economic performance. Too little money in circulation can make investment difficult and stifle economic growth, while too much money weakens the value of the country's currency and can fuel significant increases in inflation. Effective monetary policy helps achieve the central goals of fiscal policy (maintaining economic growth and reducing unemployment), but it also keeps inflation in check and stabilizes the currency's value.

Developmental Policy   Much of what government does with its fiscal and monetary policies is meant to foster stable economic growth. But governments also take a large number of additional steps to encourage economic development. These activities are known broadly as **development policy**, but they vary greatly. One type of development policy is the construction of the country's physical and communication infrastructure: its roads, bridges, railway systems, electricity and energy systems, telephone

A **budget surplus** occurs when a government takes in more revenue than it spends in a given fiscal year.

A government that spends more than it takes in runs a **budget deficit**.

The **government debt,** also known as the public debt, is the sum of annual budget deficits over time.

A **central bank** is a governmental entity that controls the supply of a particular country's money and affects interest rates in the country though changes to the rate it charges to private banks.

The **Federal Reserve System** is the central bank of the United States.

The **Federal Reserve Board** (the "Fed") sets U.S. monetary policy.

Development policy is the set of programs and activities designed to encourage economic development in a particular country.

systems, and radio and television broadcasts. Particularly in the early stages of a country's economic development, none of these activities is typically left solely to the private sector. Not only are they too vital to run the risk that they will not be developed, but their almost universal benefit to the population makes them attractive to politicians. As countries develop, some or all of these activities may fall to the private sector, though the government typically keeps a close watch on them through regulation by components of the bureaucracy.

Development policy also involves programs that target particular industrial sectors or businesses. A government may provide a **subsidy**, a tax break, or other incentives to a company that it deems crucial to the country's economy and its future development. Subsidies are payments to a company that allow it to sell its product less expensively and may encourage the company to employ more people. Tax incentives or low-interest loans can enable companies to invest in new technology that they otherwise would not have been able to afford.

In addition to the question of how to target particular companies, broader development questions include how much the government should directly control industries in the name of developing the country's economy. There are two approaches to dramatically altering the presence of the government in economic development. The first is known as **nationalization**, a process where the government takes over existing private companies and runs them as state-owned enterprises or produces its own companies, often with monopoly status in a major sector of the economy. Nationalization efforts might target a domestic company, though the target is often a foreign-owned company. The energy sector remains a popular venue for nationalization policies today, although in the past the practice also included the heavy industry-manufacturing sector. Proponents of nationalization argue that it greatly increases the government's ability to guide economic development, by not only controlling a significant source of revenue but also by controlling the production of key goods.

The opposite approach from nationalization is **privatization**. Privatization takes place when government-owned enterprises are sold to the public. Those who support privatization as a development strategy argue that nationalized companies tend to be inefficient and prone to corruption (see the discussion of types of economic systems later in the chapter). However, the privatization process itself is also vulnerable to corrupt practices. As the TIC section on Russia will discuss in some detail, the privatization of Russia's economy benefited those with political connections tremendously but did little for ordinary Russian citizens.

Trade Policy   There is no better example of an intermestic policy than trade. The provisions of trade policy affect how products produced outside a country are handled within it, as well as how products produced within that country compete as exports into foreign markets. It is also at the heart of theoretical debates in comparative politics such as the divergent views of trade contained in dependency theory and modernization theory (see Chapter 3).

Trade policies include the use of tariffs and quotas on imports. A **tariff** is a tax on an imported product. Tariffs serve a dual purpose, providing the government with additional revenue while helping protect domestic businesses

A **subsidy** is a government disbursement to a company that allows the company to sell its products less expensively, both domestically and abroad.

Nationalization is a process in which the government takes over existing private companies or develops its own companies which are often given monopoly status.

Nationalization is the opposite of **privatization**, the process where government-owned enterprises are sold to the general public or to foreign investors.

A **tariff** is a tax on an imported good or service.

by making foreign products more expensive. A **quota** is a more extreme trade policy measure. It sets a limit on the number or value of a certain product that can be imported, either from a particular country or across all imports. As with tariffs, a quota can encourage the purchase of a domestic product, but it also tends to increase the cost of that product for consumers. The widespread combination of high tariffs and restrictive quotas can fuel inflation. Thus, politicians considering new trade policy provisions must consider not only the impact on domestic businesses but also on domestic consumers.

Regulatory Policy

Regulatory policies place restrictions on individuals or groups. Although one typically thinks of regulations on businesses, laws defining criminal acts or civil rights rules can also be thought of as regulatory policies.[7] Of those affecting business, some regulatory policies set standards for products, others require certain disclosures, and still others limit certain companies from engaging in practices that give them something close to a monopoly of a particular market.

One of the best examples of regulatory policy is the set of rules governing the physical environment. Environmental policies establish and enforce regulations for individuals and businesses, setting rules against and punishments for polluting the soil, water, and air. Environmental policy is one of the newer areas of public policy. While governments have been involved in matters related to education for centuries, the environment became a widespread concern only after World War II, when states in Europe and North America began to measure "quality of life" with more than economic statistics such as growth, inflation, and unemployment.[8]

This does not mean the approaches to environmental policy are identical across Western countries. Compared with most European countries, environmental regulations in the United States are more detailed, U.S. enforcement of

environmental policies is much more confrontational, and the American judicial system is involved in environmental regulation to a much greater extent.[9] If one looks beyond Western EDCs, variation in environmental policy increases dramatically. As a basic rule, the less developed the country, the less restrictive the environmental regulations.

Social Welfare Policy: Retirement, Health, Unemployment, and Antipoverty Policies

One of the most controversial public policy arenas addresses problems of economic hardship, or potential hardship, among a country's general population. These policies include pension and other retirement programs or disability programs; health programs for the elderly, disabled, and poor; unemployment compensation and job training programs; and antipoverty programs. Social welfare policies differ across countries both in scope (how much the program expects individuals to contribute to their own welfare) and universality (the portion of the population eligible for the program).

Old Age and Retirement Policy

Most governments take some responsibility for caring for the elderly. In many cases, this is done through a **state pension**, a payment the government makes, typically monthly, to individuals after they retire. In some countries, workers may also receive pension payments from their employers, as well as income from private retirement funds to which they made payments while employed. Old age and retirement policies vary from country to country according to whether state pension programs are designed to be universal or targeted at the most poor members of the elderly

A **quota** is a limit on the number or value of a certain product that can be imported.

A **state pension** is a regular payment from the government to individuals after they reach retirement age.

and whether individuals are expected to contribute to private funds that would supplement the retirement income from the government. The United States, for example, assumes that retired workers will receive some compensation (from employer pension programs or private individual retirement accounts) in addition to their social security payments. Switzerland requires workers to contribute to private retirement funds.

Retirement policies become more difficult to manage as the overall population ages and, in some cases, declines in overall numbers. The combination of longer life expectancy and declining birthrates eventually means a smaller portion of the population in the workforce and a larger portion of the population retired from it. If retirement systems actually collected revenues from individuals and held onto them until they retired, the problem would be less severe. In most countries, however, the current funds for retirement programs come from the present workforce. In such cases, an aging population places significant stress on the retirement system, as more and more retirees must be supported by a proportionately smaller number of workers.

In Europe, the problem of a high portion of the population reaching retirement age has already arrived, though it will become significantly worse over the next several decades. By 2050, the number of people over age 65 will approach 50 percent of the number between 20 and 64. In the United States, the problem is on the immediate horizon, as the "baby boomers" begin to reach their mid-sixties. The problem is less severe in the United States than in parts of Europe, mostly because of the combination of higher birthrates and higher levels of immigration. The contributions of younger immigrant workers are crucial for the longer-term prospects of the American retirement system. China faces its own problem related to its one child policy. A significant portion of the population— born before the one child policy—are over sixty, with a comparatively smaller number of people entering the workforce than in the past.

Health Policy At earlier times in history, few political leaders considered health care a policy matter. Today, health care has been "elevated" and is a public policy issue around the world.[10] Many countries, including the United Kingdom, have national health care systems, where individual medical outlets are run by the central government bureaucracy rather than by private companies. Even in countries where medical care is largely provided privately, such as the United States, segments of the population have their health care costs covered, fully or in part, by the government. While the United States has neither a nationalized health care system nor universal health insurance coverage, health care still makes up a significant portion of government spending. American federal health care expenses, including Medicare, Medicaid, and medical care for veterans, have risen from $7.5 billion (or less than 1 percent of GDP) in 1967 to more than one hundred times that level (and well over 5 percent of GDP) in 2008.[11]

Despite the different approaches and levels of spending, certain problems related to health care are shared by all countries. First, the need for health care—and for increasingly expensive care per visit—increases with age. Thus, it is precisely at the time when most individuals are retired and often struggling to make ends meet that health care costs spike. The increased health care needs of the elderly are one of the central justifications for government involvement in the provision and funding of health care. Second, the poor are often in worse health than members of the middle and upper classes, who tend to eat better, exercise more, and see doctors more frequently for preventive care. Finally, doctors tend to be concentrated in large cities. Even in countries without a general shortage of doctors, the rural population may have a difficult time receiving health care services.

Unemployment Compensation While most governments pursue policies to encourage high levels of employment, most also implement programs designed to protect those who lose their jobs. The existence of unemployment benefits, and how generous such benefits are, varies from country to country. In some cases, unemployed workers receive a large portion of their original salary for months while they search for a new job. Existing unemployment programs are less generous today than they had been in the past, particularly in the countries of Western Europe.

In addition to payments to unemployed workers, many governments have established worker training programs. This government-funded training provides the unemployed with additional skills, which are sometimes related to their previous jobs and sometimes in a completely different field of work. Job training programs are not an alternative to unemployment compensation, but they are designed to make it easier for workers to find new jobs and less likely that those workers will be laid off in the near future.

Antipoverty Policies Another major goal of social welfare programs is to redistribute wealth in society to help address poverty. As a result, policies aimed at reducing the portion of the population living in poverty and improving the living conditions of those remaining in poverty are sometimes known as **redistributive policies**. This broad policy category can also include progressive tax systems, discussed earlier, since they take money from wealthier individuals for use in government programs that may, but do not always, benefit the poor.

In the United States, antipoverty policies such as aid to families with dependent children (AFDC) came under attack in the 1990s, amid concerns about their fairness and effectiveness. Despite the existence of such programs for several decades, a high percentage of single-parent families remained poor. (At the beginning of the 1990s, the figure was over 50 percent.) In addition to not solving single parent family poverty, critics argued that programs such as AFDC

provided no incentives for single parents to find work and instead made them dependent on government assistance.

Education

Education policy could be incorporated into existing categories above like economic development policy or even social welfare policy. Yet, the issues related to education policy are important enough and evolving to such an extent that education deserves consideration as its own policy category. Education is at the heart of efforts to create greater equality of opportunity, a topic discussed in detail later in the chapter.

According to political scientists Arnod Heidenheimer, Hugh Heclo, and Carolyn Teich Adams, education policies vary globally in four basic ways.[12] The first is the extent to which the government maintains something approximating an education monopoly by discouraging private educational institutions such as those run by religious organizations. The second is the scale of the educational system's centralization, ranging from those largely overseen by a national government to those almost entirely managed by local governmental bodies. The third is the way in which educational opportunities are available to the general population. In many European countries, secondary education is quite specialized and based on performance in earlier grades or on national exams. In the United States, such distinctions between elite academic institutions and technical schools do not appear until the level of postsecondary education. Finally, higher education approaches differ in their expectations for years to completion of a degree, types of degrees available, and the extent to which admissions decisions are based solely on applicants' academic abilities.

Redistributive policies are those policies aimed at reducing poverty by making the wealth in a particular society less unequal.

Identity-Related Policies: Citizenship, Immigration, Integration, and Diversity Programs

Another broad set of policies relate to identity and identity diversity. Such policies include citizenship, immigration, integration of minority groups, and other programs designed to address social divisions and cultural diversity. Approaches to such identity policies differ around the world as much as any other policy area.

Citizenship Chapter 2 introduced the concept of citizenship, a status held by a large portion of the population of every internationally recognized state that designates such individuals as the state's "official members."[13] In addition to being a form of status, citizenship is a policy. Government officials must determine rules for naturalization—the process through which noncitizens become citizens—as well as the rights and obligations reserved for citizens and whether or not to allow individuals to be dual citizens. In the case of newly independent states, the government must determine the initial base of citizens to which naturalization will add over time.

Citizenship practices vary significantly around the world. In some countries, it is relatively easy for noncitizens who have been long-time residents to gain citizenship. In other countries, the naturalization rules are exceedingly restrictive. Because citizenship is a form of identity, carries with it rights and obligations, and presumes a certain degree of loyalty to the state, decisions regarding citizenship policy can be quite controversial.

Immigration Immigration is the process of entering a country with the intention of residing there for a significant period of time. Immigrants typically seek residence in a new country that they feel offers opportunities for employment, education, and a better life for their families. They may also provide a number of benefits to the country to which they immigrate, such as

typically working for lower wages than domestic workers. Because immigrants pursue employment and sometimes participate in government-funded social welfare programs, immigration is also a highly controversial policy area around the world. In both the United States and the United Kingdom, survey data has indicated around half of the countries' citizens believe that immigrants "take jobs" and around two-thirds support reducing the number of immigrants.[14]

Countries differ greatly on their rules for official immigration, the extent to which they are targeted as a place of residence by illegal immigrants, and their responses to such illegal immigration. Even within a particular country, different groups may have decidedly different ideas about the proper approach to the topic of immigration. Policy can change significantly depending on which party or coalition controls the government.

Integration and Other Programs Designed to Address Cultural and Identity Diversity Chapter 5 included a discussion of various government options for dealing with significant racial, ethnic, and cultural divisions. These include efforts to eliminate minority identity groups (genocide, ethnic cleansing, and assimilation), to accept the minority identity (integration), and to cultivate the minority identity (accommodation, ethno-federalism, and recognition of claims for territorial independence). Most countries with sharp identity divisions choose one of the approaches near the middle of the spectrum of policy options—assimilation, integration, and accommodation—though even these "middle ground" policies represent very different ideas about the role of government in fostering minority cultures.

Integration policies are perhaps the most interesting policy option because they involve a delicate balancing act. The minority group recognizes that its culture is subordinate to an overarching culture in the country, often largely overlapping with the culture of the majority group. On the other hand, the majority group recognizes that the minority has a right to protect its culture and unique practices. While this seems an appropriate balance in theory, implementing policies consistent with the concept of integration can be difficult in practice. Even though nearly all Americans now support some form of racial integration in educational institutions, fewer than 50 percent of Americans supported it as recently as World War II,[15] and even today there is disagreement about practices such as forced busing to alter the racial makeup of the student body of individual schools. Since 2000, Latvia has been aggressively pursuing integration programs for its Russian-speaking minorities. The programs have been, at best, a mixed success, both because some Latvians continue to oppose the presence of so many Russian speakers in the country and because many Russian speakers have shown little interest in learning Latvian and taking other steps to integrate more fully into Latvian society.

Degrees of Policy Transformation: First, Second, and Third Order Change

In addition to studying different types of policies, many comparativists focus on changes to particular government approaches over time. Both changes in existing policies and the creation of entirely new policies share a common feature: they tend to result from vocal demands for change. But the degree of the resulting change can differ significantly. In an article looking at changes to economic policies in the United Kingdom, comparativist Peter Hall provides a useful framework for considering policy modifications. Hall distinguishes among first, second, and third order policy changes. A **first order policy change** is one in which the details of the policy change, but the "overall goals and instruments of policy remain the same."[16] Such changes include small alterations in fiscal and monetary policy, such as changes in marginal tax rates or interest rates.

A **second order policy change** occurs when the goals behind a particular policy remain the same, but the techniques used to achieve these goals change. For example, the switch in environmental policy from one that punishes companies that exceed pollution limits to one that allows companies to sell pollution "credits" to each other is a second order change. The goal of reducing pollution remains the same, but the instrument used to achieve that goal is altered.

A **third order policy change** takes place when the goals behind a given policy take a dramatic shift. According to Hall, third order changes are rare. They generally occur only when an examination of past experiences indicates that the policy has failed to meet its goals or has created unintended, negative consequences that far exceed its intended effects. Welfare reform in the United States in the 1990s was a third order change. A perception that existing approaches had created a dependency among welfare recipients led to a change in the goal of the policy, from enhancing the economic standing of single parents living in poverty to improving the prospects for such individuals to gain long-term employment.

Understanding Policy Outcomes

Given the range of policy areas studied by comparativists—economic policies, social welfare programs, education programs, and

A **first order policy change** occurs when the details of the policy change, but the general approach to the policy remains the same.

A **second order policy change** takes place when the policy's underlying goals are unchanged, but significant changes are implemented in how the goal is pursued.

A **third order policy change** occurs when the goals behind a policy are dramatically altered. Examples include welfare reform in the United States during the 1990s.

identity-related policies—it may not be surprising to learn that not all policies have the same causes. The same policy may have come about for different reasons in one country than in another, and looking at different policies within the same country can also lead to different causal stories. As discussed in the previous chapter, however, the various possible causal factors can be fairly well organized into four categories: internal structure, external structure, internal choice, and external choice.

As with other aspects of comparative politics, comparativists have typically paid more attention to internal factors than external ones. Internal choice factors are often called the **policy process**, highlighting the role of analysis, calculations, and the ultimate decision about which policy approach to take. Comparativists commonly label internal structural factors the **policy environment**, capturing that the policymaking process occurs within an economic, cultural, identity, and political context. Social and economic structures shape interest group and broader public demands, while political structures privilege some policy approaches and hinder others.

Internal Structural Factors Influencing Policy Outcomes

Throughout this book, various types of structural features—economic, cultural, identity, and political—have been highlighted. Understanding policy outcomes requires one to consider these various structural factors. However, examining the policy process also entails thinking about a particular combination of two structural features that, to this point, has not been taken up as a distinct factor. So far in the book, economic and political structures have been treated as separate entities. Discussions of economic structure focused on elements of the economy—level of economic development, class structure, and globalization—that can be addressed separately from the topic of government intervention into the economy. Likewise, discussions of political

institutions have had little to do with economics. But particularly when seeking to understand public policy, one cannot ignore a structural factor that unites economic and political structure: differences in the type of economic system based on the scope of government intervention.

The Economic System There are two ways that one can categorize economic systems. The first is to focus on development and mode of production, which was the approach taken in Chapter 3. The second is to look at the extent to which the government plays an active role in the economy of the country. Conceptualized in this second way, the type of economic system is, in many ways, the starting point for examinations of the policy environment. Using this second approach to the concept of economic systems, scholars have generally identified three ideal types of economic systems: capitalist, socialist, and mixed. Policy changes to "reform the economy" in any significant way typically mean moving away from one of these types and toward another. Because these economic systems are anchored in ideas about the most appropriate approach to economic activity, they are also at the center of the different political ideologies discussed in Chapter 4.

Free-Market Capitalism **Capitalism** is an economic system based on three fundamental ideas: the belief in private ownership of property and business, the principle that economic activity should take place within the **market**, and the

---

Comparativists sometimes refer to the internal choice factors influencing policy outcomes as the **policy process**.

The set of internal structural factors influencing policy outcomes is known as the **policy environment**.

Capitalism is an economic system based on private ownership of property and business and economic activity taking place within the **market**—a system of economic exchange where suppliers and purchasers find each other and agree to the terms of the transaction.

view that economic decisions should be made by individual companies and consumers. A market is a system of economic exchange in which those supplying goods and services and those seeking to purchase such goods and services find each other and come to agreement about the terms of the transaction. If one side is unhappy with the terms and an agreement cannot be reached, no transaction will occur. **Market forces** such as supply and demand determine many of the terms of economic exchanges, the most important of which is the asking price for goods or services. The ideal type capitalist system, often referred to as **free market capitalism**, is one in which the state plays little or no role in economic activity. This economic approach rejects state involvement in setting standards for the workplace (including minimum wages), in coordinating retirement benefits through a social security system, and in guarding against sharp divisions in wealth created by market activities.

In practice, countries used as examples of this system do interfere in their economies. This takes the form of protection from formation of a **monopoly** (when an individual company controls all or nearly all of the market for a particular good or service), regulations to protect consumers and the environment, creation of government-controlled retirement systems, and establishment of at least limited worker's rights regarding wages and working conditions. But such countries engage in economic intervention much less than other countries.

Although Americans often view the United States as the model of free market capitalism, other countries have even less government involvement in the economy than the United States. Still, among wealthy, postindustrial countries, the United States has one of the most free market approaches. As such, it may provide lessons about the free market approach. It is the wealthiest country in the history of the world and one with a strong tradition of entrepreneurial activity and innovation. Yet, it is also a country with a relatively large gap between rich and

APPLYING CONCEPTS

Microsoft the Monopoly?

Political scientists interested in economic policy sometimes work with concepts that, while relatively straightforward in principle, can be challenging to apply in practice. A monopoly is one such concept. In the late 1990s, the government of the United States pursued a case against Microsoft, accusing it of monopolizing the web browser market by bundling Internet Explorer to its Windows operating system. At a Senate hearing in 1998, the CEO of Netscape, James Barksdale, asked those in attendance how many used PCs rather than Macintosh computers. When a large number of hands went up, he then asked how many of those people used an operating system other than Windows on their PCs. As all the hands went down, Barksdale turned to the members of the Senate panel and declared, "Gentlemen, that is a monopoly."

Despite Barksdale's assertion, many who studied the case against Microsoft were unconvinced that the government had proven Microsoft's monopoly status. Indeed, following an initial court ruling in 2000 that Microsoft would have to be split into two companies, the federal government and Microsoft ultimately agreed to a settlement, which involved Microsoft agreeing to share information with third-party companies to make other web browsers more compatible with Microsoft Windows.

poor, and a country in which a sizeable portion of the population lacks basic health insurance coverage.

Market forces such as supply and demand drive the terms of transaction in capitalism.

Free market capitalism is another name for the capitalist ideal type, in which there is minimal government involvement in regulation of the economy and little social welfare spending.

A **monopoly** is a situation in which a single company controls all or nearly all of the market for a given good or service.

Socialism At the opposite extreme from the ideal type of free market capitalism is **socialism**, often called the **central planning** approach. This approach to economics involves government ownership of the means of production. The state owns the physical capital, and the workers are thus employed by the state. In addition to state ownership of the means of production, the socialist approach places most of the decisions about production and distribution in the hands of the state. The state decides what products the country's various factories manufacture, how many of each item are produced, and at what prices these products are sold. While some of the small decisions may be made at the level of the firm, more fundamental decisions about targets for production are made by government bureaucrats, far removed from the factory floor.

The Soviet Union prior to 1991 provides an example of a government deeply entrenched in economic decision making. Soviet government officials created economic plans and determined the terms of economic transaction from the supply of products to setting prices. Heavy industry production was privileged at the expense of the production of consumer goods. An example of government involvement can be found in the artificial prices which were set for certain goods. While consumer goods were generally low quality and expensive, the price for food and energy was kept low for political gain.

One thing Soviet central planners could not do was force consumers to buy the products they supplied at the quality and prices they offered. When the demands of consumers were not met through the state-run economy, a **black market** economy emerged. Black market economies are those in which products and services are bought and sold illegally. In the Soviet case, the black market became most noticeable under Mikhail Gorbachev, as the Soviet Union began to introduce limited market economic features. The confusion, corruption, and distributional difficulties that existed in this era of partial reforms

allowed those with political connections, those who participated in the growing organized crime sector, and those who were particularly creative and daring to make sizeable amounts of money selling products illegally.

The Soviets also had a difficult time getting workers to work hard on the job, especially prior to Gorbachev's reforms. Since there was little monetary incentive for hard work, Soviet workers developed a poor work ethic. As Soviet citizens liked to say at the time, "We pretend to work, and they pretend to pay us." Absenteeism and overly long lunch breaks—related to increasing problems of alcoholism in Soviet society—became the norm.

As a result of these problems, The Soviet "experiment"[17] and other real world socialist systems showed that one of the inherent problems of central planning systems is a lack of economic efficiency. Centrally planned systems also lack the entrepreneurial spirit and innovation found in capitalist systems. The result in the Soviet Union was slower economic growth than in the capitalist West, especially as the world economy became more technology-dependent. The Soviet Union became the world's leading steel producer at the moment in history when no one cared which country was the world's leading steel producer. It was becoming much more important to be the world's leading producer of consumer electronics.

On the other hand, the socialist systems that emerged in the twentieth century tended to produce less inequality than capitalist systems. They were also, arguably, better able to direct economic resources to address pressing national needs. Finally, they avoided the ups and downs

Socialism or **central planning** is an economic approach that emphasizes government ownership of the means of production and government control of economic decisions such as the supply and prices of particular products.

A **black market** is a market in which goods and services are bought and sold illegally.

of the "business cycle" commonly found during the same period in the West. Though economic growth had come to a standstill by the middle 1980s, the Soviet and Eastern European economies did not collapse until the economic and political reforms unleashed by Gorbachev.

Mixed Systems Some approaches, often lumped together under the heading of **mixed economies**, fall in between the ideal types of capitalism and socialism. Because these are not outright socialist systems employing central planning, political scientists and economists usually discuss these and the more free market approach as "varieties of capitalism." These varieties take the form of ideal types but are also often associated with particular countries. Lester Thurow provides a useful starting point for discussing varieties of capitalism by highlighting differences among the more free market approach of the United States, the welfare-state system of Europe, and the leadership role of the state in Japan.[18] Employing Thurow's vision of a tripartite categorization, David Coates has called free market capitalism *market-led capitalism*, while describing two categories of mixed systems as labor-led and state-led.[19]

The approach of **labor-led capitalism**, or what some refer to as a **social democratic system**, accepts many of the general principles of capitalism, including private ownership and the belief that most economic activity should be based on market principles of supply and demand. Yet, this approach to capitalism allows for extensive government intervention and even government ownership of particularly important, large industries and is bound together with a social democratic culture. Social democrats believe that governments have a responsibility to regulate economic activity—heavily, if necessary—to protect consumers, laborers, and the environment. As a result, individual rights and personal responsibility are balanced by collective benefits and the responsibility of society to protect vulnerable individuals.

This approach is consistent with the concept of a **welfare state**, where government provides welfare benefits and services. In most countries, social welfare is protected through a combination of government policies, private interests, and individual responsibility. The more numerous and expensive the welfare provisions enacted by the government, the more substantial a particular country's welfare state is. Countries in northern Europe, Sweden in particular, are most associated with social democracy and welfare state systems.

A system of **state-led capitalism** accepts the principle of private ownership and, to a lesser extent, individual decision making. However, it also emphasizes the good of the group over the individual and is associated with a more conservative, nationalistic culture.[20] As a result, the approach allows for significant government intervention in the economy. This intervention takes the form of guiding investment into growing sectors of the economy and in turn phasing out nonprofitable businesses and economic

Mixed economies are those with significant elements of capitalist and socialist practices.

Labor-led capitalism, also known as a **social democratic system**, involves a substantial role for government in the regulation of the economy and the establishment of social welfare programs. Its underlying activities are still based on capitalist principles, but it deviates significantly from the free-market ideal type in the level of acceptable government intervention in the economic structure.

Welfare state policies are a set of government programs that provide significant welfare benefits and services.

State-led capitalism is a system in which the government intervenes in the economy to guide economic activities in an effort to foster economic growth. This intervention generally does not take the form of large social welfare programs but rather concentrates on policies which support growing industries, help phase out dying industries, and increase the competitiveness of national companies in the global marketplace.

sectors. In countries such as Japan and South Korea, governments have used their power to control credit and to grant licenses to favor certain sectors of the economy and specific companies within particular sectors.[21] There are fewer social welfare protections than in labor-led economies, but often more than in market-led ones.

State-led capitalism is also consistent with **mercantilism**. A mercantilist approach to capitalism accepts the general principal of free market economics within the domestic sphere. However, it rejects the idea of free market competition internationally. Instead, mercantilism (also known as protectionism) supports government involvement in the economy to protect domestic economic interests, particularly employment, through subsidies of particular industries and businesses and tariffs and quotas on imports. This encourages the purchase of domestic products, but it also increases the cost of products for consumers.

In addition to the labor-led and state-led mixed systems, political economists have identified a relatively new mixed-system, which they call **state capitalism**. Particularly in many former Communist countries of Eastern Europe and Eurasia, the state neither heavily regulates nor creates large social welfare systems. Rather, it participates in the economy alongside private businesses through full or partial ownership of large individual companies.

Compared with social democratic capitalism, state capitalism involves a greater role for state ownership of economic entities but less of a role in regulation and social welfare protection. Thus, the economy functions more like a free market economy than social welfare capitalist economies do, but with the state as a major economic player in the market. This approach has been increasingly evident in the Russian Federation where the privatization of state-run enterprises led many enterprises to come under private control but the most lucrative ones—for example, large oil companies—to remain or come back under state control.

Other Economic Structural Factors Comparativists have long argued that economic development affects the amount of money that a government spends and the kinds of policies it funds. Economic development creates a larger "pie" from which the government is able to extract and redistribute. In addition, it is associated with other changes—education improvements, urbanization, and, eventually, an aging population—that both give citizens skills to participate in the political process and alter the current situation in ways that can increase anxiety. The emergence of this combination of skills and grievances leads democratic governments to spend money on new programs.[22] As a result, economic development creates conditions that lead governments of countries with quite different cultural and political backgrounds to take similar policy approaches.[23]

Different class structures can have disparate effects on policy approaches. As discussed earlier, leveling the economic playing field is a central goal of many government programs. Since policies are in part a response to demands placed on the political system, the existence of visible poverty in an otherwise wealthy society can also trigger demands for programs targeting such poverty from the poor and wealthy alike.

The final element of economic structure is how interconnected a country's economy is with other economies. In the 1970s, political scientist David Cameron's landmark study pointed out the important role of economic interdependence in the growth of government spending.[24] Because

Mercantilism is a form of capitalism that accepts the general principal of free market economics but allows significant government involvement in the economy in order to protect domestic economic interests. It is also known as protectionism.

State capitalism is a system in which the government neither engages in economic planning nor oversees an extensive welfare state. Instead, it owns certain individual enterprises, which are typically in lucrative industries such as energy.

economic openness made their economies more vulnerable to external economic shocks and because open trade policies are often opposed by domestic interest groups, governments oversee-ing economies with high levels of imports and exports developed more elaborate social welfare policies to protect their workers. In addition, the more "globalized" a country's economy is, the more certain policy areas such as education must reflect that reality. While much of the focus on education revolves around the idea of making life chances more equal for a country's citizens, globalization also encourages a well-educated, technologically literate population.

Political Culture and Ideology Policies are also the result of ideas. A particular society's values and system of meaning shape how much indi-viduals in that society view a certain situation as a problem and influence the range of alterna-tives available to policymakers to address some-thing that is perceived to be a problem. Social scientist Karl Deutsch argued that people's tendency to look to the past, present, or future plays a great role in differences in broad policy approaches across societies.[25] Ronald Inglehart's postmaterialism theory, discussed in Chap-ter 4, posits that economic development brings shifts in values away from survival and security and toward quality of life issues like the envi-ronment. It is probably not a coincidence that environmental policy became a matter of con-cern for Western governments around the same time that the "culture shift" supportive of envi-ronmental protections that Inglehart identifies began to emerge. Political culture is, therefore, important to consider when seeking explana-tions for variation in policies from one type of country to the next, such as differences in envi-ronmental policies between Western EDCs and non-Western LDCs.

It is also helpful in understanding policy approaches within the EDCs. A number of com-parative public policy works have sought to explain why public policies in the United States are less expansive and intrusive than those in Western Europe. Back in the early 1970s, British political scientist Anthony King proposed that this divergence is largely the result of a different political culture on the two sides of the Atlantic, arguing that government "plays a more limited role in America than elsewhere because Ameri-cans, more than other people, want it to a play a limited role."[26] More than thirty years later, even scholars who contend that the European social welfare systems have noticeably contracted see them as remaining more encompassing than the American approach, and many of them have continued to argue that cultural factors largely shape the difference.[27]

Just as with other types of political out-comes, there are limitations to using political culture to understand policy outcomes. The degree to which a given society's culture is uni-fied can influence the effect that culture has on products of the political system. In addition, while cultural differences can explain why two countries take very different general approaches to a similar problem, they are less helpful in explaining policy changes, especially dramatic policy changes, within the same country over a short period of time. If political culture is indeed "sticky" (see Chapter 4), then policy approaches should be as well if political culture is the driv-ing force behind policy selection.

An existing official ideology also provides policymakers with opportunities and constraints. If the general population accepts this ideology, then they will support policies consistent with it, at least initially. However, policy alternatives that contradict the ideology are difficult for a government to implement, requiring it to engage in logical gymnastics to justify their adoption.

Identity Structure Policies regarding identity differ greatly across countries based on policy-makers' different choices about how best to address identity diversity. But these differences are also driven greatly by the extent to which a given country has significant ethnic, religious, linguistic, or other cultural minorities in the first place. Where such minorities exist, the country's identity structure forces the government to consider how best to address this identity diversity. As they make policy decisions designed to address identity diversity, officials must also take into account the extent to which the minorities are self-aware, territorially concentrated, or politically mobilized, or otherwise have the resources to cause problems if they are unhappy.

At the same time, leaders must consider the views of the majority of the population. While a minority group may support adopting particular group rights approaches or affirmative action programs, the majority of the population may strongly oppose such policies. The dilemma facing governments of states with deep identity divisions is significant. The deeper the social divisions, the more pressing the need to address the concerns of the minority group. However, deep identity divisions also mean that the majority is likely to vehemently oppose policies it sees as unfairly favoring the minority.

Political Structure   Political structures are the part of the policy environment closest to the actual policy decisions. As a result, the design of the political system—its general regime type and its specific institutional arrangements—greatly affect the policies that system produces. Political scientist E. E. Schattschneider provocatively labels political organization "the mobilization of bias," arguing that "some issues are organized into politics while others are organized out."[28]

One of the reasons it is important to understand political systems and the transition from one type of system to another is that regime type can influence policy approaches to a particular problem. In some cases, authoritarian systems have a wider range of policy options than democracies, such as the ability to use coercive force against the population in order to enact what government leaders see as a necessary

policy. Democratic leaders, on the other hand, fear voters' ability to remove them from office if their policies produce short-term costs just prior to an election, even if these same policies will ultimately produce long-term benefits. At the same time, electoral mechanisms in democratic systems favor the development of new programs. Candidates make policy promises to secure the support of segments of the population, and successful candidates pursue at least some of these promises after the election.

The form of policies may also vary between countries that share the same general regime type but differ in specific governmental arrangements.[29] As discussed in Chapter 6, the more veto points a political system has, the more difficult it is to adopt substantial policy initiatives, particularly those designed to reallocate economic wealth. The fear that a proposal to greatly alter an existing policy approach will never make it past the numerous veto points means government officials in such systems are often reluctant to introduce such proposals in the first place.

Within democratic systems, the institutional options discussed in Chapters 6 through 8 affect policy outcomes. Federal systems make certain policy issues the prerogative of lower levels of government. Even in policy areas not reserved for lower levels, federal officials must take into account the potential for regional or local governments to obstruct policy implementation. Presidential systems with checks and balances place a premium on policy compromise. In democracies with strong judicial review provisions, the threat that a certain policy will be viewed as unconstitutional or in violation of existing statutes constrains policymakers.

Existing approaches to elite-mass linkage also matter. In nearly every country, interest groups are a hugely important part of the story of public policy. Yet, these groups share a common challenge—the "collective action problem" discussed in Chapter 9—of acquiring members and mobilizing support. The environment is a classic collective action problem, since the costs of improving the environment are targeted while the benefits of ecological improvement are shared collectively across society. The exception is the case of protecting against or cleaning up highly localized environmental damage. Because the benefits of such environmental action are more concentrated, NIMBY ("not in my backyard!") interest groups often deal with environmental matters, and they are typically quite successful in their endeavors.

While interest groups have many features in common across different countries, how they are brought into the policy process and their ability to shape particular proposals can vary greatly. A corporatist approach to bringing interest groups into the policy process may require more compromise up front but also generate fewer disputes over the final policy once the major peak associations are on board. Systems in which iron triangles are common may produce quite different policies from ones in which interest groups compete more openly for policymakers' attention. The ability of a group to affect policy can also differ from group to group within the same country based on each group's resources (membership size, financial assets, etc.) and its relative strength compared to other groups working in the same policy area.

The electoral and party systems matter as well. Two-party systems are likely to produce more moderate policies than multiparty systems, especially if the bulk of the country's population falls in the middle of the political spectrum. Electoral systems that encourage numerous parties to hold seats in the national legislature—thus necessitating coalition governments—can lead to certain policy options receiving more attention than they might in a two-party system. Policies regarding agricultural subsidies, for example, can be a central topic of discussion in a coalition government that includes a small farmers' party.

External Structural Factors: Existing Policy Models, Policy Imposition Through Conquest, and Pressure from International Organizations

The discussion of regime change in the previous chapter highlighted three important external factors—demonstration effects, imposition through conquest, and conditionality—that comparativists also emphasize in public policy studies. These three factors not only influence the broad form of the political system but also the specific policies that system produces. Like other structural factors, they provide political leaders with both opportunities and constraints.

A program adopted in one country can serve as a model for another country. Similar to how government officials assess the performance of policies in their own country, leaders evaluate policy results in other countries. Policies in other countries provide leaders with a menu of policy options complete with evidence about how successful or unsuccessful each option may be. Political leaders, seeing the successful implementation of the policy in the first country, may emulate the policy in their own country. Such emulation is a conscious process.[30] Other states' policy approaches and experiences provide political leaders with opportunities to learn about the effectiveness of the policies that they would not have had otherwise.

As a result, comparativists frequently examine policy trends across countries. Often, these analyses center on a number of states within a distinct global region, such as the EDCs of Western Europe. At other times, the focus is more global, looking at how pervasive and rapid is the spread of general approaches to certain types of policy around the world.

When policy approaches become similar over time globally or regionally, comparativists often label the phenomenon **policy convergence**.

Policy convergence exists when policies become similar over time globally or in a particular region.

Others use the term **policy diffusion**, particularly when tracing the spread of a new policy from an initial country to others. Just as the policy process is complex, involving various stages and practices, convergence can take different forms. Increasingly similar policy goals, content, instruments, outcomes, and "style"—the latter term applying to broad approaches such as consensual versus conflictual, incremental versus more fully rational, and corporatist versus pluralist— are all signs of policy convergence.[31] Of interest to comparativists for decades, the topic of policy convergence has become increasingly prominent in recent years because of the growing importance of globalization and regional integration, particularly in Europe, North America, Latin America, and Asia.

Sometimes, external structures constrain government leaders more than they provide them with opportunities. The most extreme example of this is when a country is occupied militarily by another country. As discussed in Chapter 12, such instances can lead the occupied country to establish a regime favorable to the occupying power. The occupying forces may also dictate to the new government a wide range of policy approaches during the occupation.

External policy constraints need not be so blatant. Leaders of states pursuing membership in a particular international organization, for example, must meet conditions for membership that include adopting new policies or significantly amending existing ones. Chapter 2 included a brief discussion of how, when their statehood was restored in the late Soviet period, Estonia and Latvia faced decisions regarding whom should receive automatic citizenship, whom should be required to naturalize, and how difficult naturalization should be. Both countries chose to exclude large portions of their Russian-speaking minority populations from their citizenries. A variety of international organizations put pressure on them to amend these policies, and they made certain changes over the next few years. The most dramatic changes, however, took

place in the late 1990s and early 2000s, when European Union membership became a real possibility for the first time. The EU required the two countries to adopt more inclusive citizenship policies and institute policies to better integrate their Russian-speaking minorities.

Internal Choice Factors: Leadership and Rational Policymaking

Policymaking is a process in which individuals make decisions, and these decisions are often made in public. As a result, like many comparativists who study democratization, those who study public policy place a strong emphasis on internal choice explanations of differences across countries or across time within the same country. The focus on internal choice includes an examination of leaders and their leadership skills as well as a consideration of how rational particular leaders' decisions tend to be.

Leadership While the structure of the political system determines who has the authority to make policy decisions, not all those who hold institutional powers are equally adept at using them. When a president or prime minister gets behind a particular proposal, the leader may choose to "go public," making speeches or issuing press releases in support of the policy.[32] The leader may also work behind the scenes, using persuasion, trading promised support for other policy initiatives, and at times accepting compromises in the proposal in order to see it pass. In either case, the ability of the leader to lead— to influence others to achieve a set of defined goals—can be decisive for the adoption of a particular policy.

Effective leadership skills are even more important in the case of controversial or unpopular policies that the leader believes are necessary.

Policy diffusion is another term for the process of a new policy approach spreading from one country to another over time.

In such cases, the leader may need to persuade many people who are initially quite hostile to the proposal. In democracies, efforts to pass such policies typically involve the leader making public statements about the policy, since without some increase in support among the general public, the leader is likely to fail to convince skeptical members of the legislature. Early in Bill Clinton's first term as U.S. president, he attempted to win support for a major overhaul of the American health care system. His efforts included a number of speeches on the topic, and a series of events involving the First Lady, Hillary Rodham Clinton. Ultimately, these efforts were unsuccessful, and the vision of a third order change in health care policy failed.

It is also possible for an individual citizen to emerge as a high profile advocate for a particular policy. Such individuals' efforts are sometimes aided by the news media. In many cases, such individuals are celebrities, used to the media glare and how to use it to their advantage. During 2006 and 2007, for example, actor George Clooney used his celebrity status to help mobilize support in the United States for international action to address the genocide in the Darfur region of Sudan. Other celebrities across the world have engaged in similar efforts to address domestic problems in their countries.

How Rational Was the Decision-Making Process? Much of the work on public policy uses decision-making theories to explain particular policy initiatives or examines policy outcomes to test existing decision-making theories. Much of this research centers on the question of how rational policy choices are. Do policymakers act as fully rational actors by identifying the problem, ordering their goals, weighing the costs and benefits of every policy alternative in light of their goals, and choosing the best policy? Do they take short cuts but still operate within the broad domain of rational decision making? Or, are many policy decisions the result of irrational decisions?

Comparative policy studies tend to reject the idea that policymakers regularly engage in full-blown rational efforts involving ranking goals, identifying all possible alternatives, and considering the costs and benefits of these alternatives. Instead, comparativists point to theoretical perspectives like satisficing and incrementalism, introduced in Chapter 11. When a new policy is introduced, the proposal is likely to be the first one on which all the decision makers involved could agree, rather than the result of an exhaustive effort to produce the best possible policy.[33] Likewise, when old policies are modified, the alterations rarely involve innovative, third order changes. Controlling for a variety of other possible explanations, the strongest predictor of expenditures on particular government programs is the previous amount spent on that program—a finding highly consistent with incremental policymaking.[34]

In addition, over the last two decades comparativists have paid increasing attention to the notion of policymaking as a form of learning. This idea of learning also links together what are sometimes thought of as separate stages of the policymaking process: the creation of a policy and the assessment of whether or not the policy worked. While political leaders look abroad for policies to possibly emulate, they pay even more attention to past policy experiences in their own country. They evaluate the performance of past and current policies, and they take these evaluations into account when they consider changes to existing policy or entirely new policy approaches. As Peter Hall puts it, "Policy responds less directly to social and economic conditions than it does to the consequences of past policy."[35]

Think and Discuss

Are most government policies the result of rational calculations? Which particular kinds of policies are most likely not to be made in a rational manner?

External Choice Factors

Decisions leaders make in one state can affect policy decisions in other states. As important as the concept of policy diffusion is, it is important to remember that, for diffusion to occur, government leaders somewhere must first decide to adopt the policy. Only then can the existence of the policy and experiences with its adoption in one state affect the policies adopted in another.

Likewise, while the role of international organizations also must be taken into account when examining particular domestic policies, individuals within an international organization decide how that organization should become involved in a country's domestic politics. Funding from international institutions like the World Bank and the International Monetary Fund can have a significant impact on a particular state's economic performance, but a relatively small number of individuals decide how to distribute these funds. The United Nations can have a significant impact on domestic policies in a particular country. Once again, however, it is individuals such as the representatives of the UN member states, officials in the UN bureaucracy, and sometimes the UN secretary general alone who decide how and for what purposes the UN interacts with that country.

Sometimes ordinary people from outside a country rise to the occasion and successfully advance a cause they passionately support. Jody Williams, a former teacher of Spanish and English as a second language in the United States, played a crucial role in the creation and success of the International Campaign to Ban Landmines (ICBL). Partly because of her efforts, an international treaty banning landmines was signed in Ottawa, Canada, in 1997. As a result, Williams and the ICBL were awarded the 1997 Nobel Peace Prize.

Public Policy and Government Performance

Scholars who study government performance emphasize the importance of proper design and implementation of government policies. If government policies had nothing to do with how social and economic problems are solved, there would be little reason for a government. Indeed, different policy approaches lead countries at similar levels of development and facing similar kinds of problems to have varying degrees of success solving those problems. Policy design and implementation are thus crucial factors in government performance.

These are far from the only factors. Many additional factors mirror those discussed in the previous section. Countries at lower levels of development have fewer resources to address pressing national problems. On the other hand, more economically developed countries, with political cultures that have become more postmaterialist (see Chapter 4), will hold the government to a different standard about quality of life issues such as the environment. Countries with deep social divisions place governments in a very difficult position. Failing to address the concerns of a minority group risks political instability, violence, and territorial secession. Addressing the concerns through programs that favor the minority over others deepens identity divisions and can lead the majority group to turn on the government.

Internal political structures play an additional role in government performance. Because fewer people are involved in the policy creation process in a nondemocracy than in a democracy, nondemocracies may be able to respond more quickly to a problem when it emerges. However, the limited input may also increase the likelihood that the policy will fail to achieve its goals or have unintended consequences requiring another round of policy responses.

Factors outside a country can also affect government performance. Assuming the aid does not end up in the pockets of corrupt government officials, a government receiving foreign aid suddenly has a bigger "pie" with which to address particular problems. Loans and other forms of support from organizations like the World Bank and IMF can help a country tackle its economic problems. Yet, because such aid is the result of decisions—rational or otherwise—by individuals outside the country, if those individuals do not understand the domestic context of that country, their "support" can cause as many problems as it solves.

Public Policy and Policy Debates in the United Kingdom, Germany, and France

As discussed earlier in the chapter, a great deal of the comparative study of public policy has taken place in the context of Western Europe. This is partly because these countries' relatively long experience with democracy provides a significant public record regarding the development and reform of major government policies. These public policy studies have pointed to themes across countries such as the United Kingdom, Germany, and France, including the adoption of a strong set of welfare state provisions after World War II, and the criticism of and attempts to reform those policies since the late 1970s. At the same time, important differences can be seen across the three cases, particularly in which policy questions prompt the greatest debate at the present time. In the United Kingdom, for example, it is ongoing struggles over the question of health care, while in France, it is the perceived threat that immigration and European integration poses to French identity and state sovereignty.

The United Kingdom

The relatively early development of the British economy had important policy implications. The emergence of a sizeable working class, for example, led to the creation of the Labour Party at the start of the twentieth century. Particularly after World War II, the large working class and its Labour Party allies pushed it in the direction of a mixed economy, leading to the creation of a large welfare state. The United Kingdom never developed the kind of full-blown, labor-led economic system found in other parts of Europe. But, the emergence of a politically powerful working class played an important role in its

decision to join much of Western Europe in adopting the **postwar settlement**, a compromise that insured a largely capitalist economic system but one with significant social welfare protections. Even the Conservative Party, Britain's major political party on the right of the political spectrum, accepted the significant social welfare protections, at least until the reforms instituted by Margaret Thatcher beginning in the late 1970s.

Thatcher's attempt to unravel the welfare state was, in part, a policy decision based on her views about social welfare policy. Thatcher saw social welfare policies as both inefficient and generating dependency on the state, and she believed that a third order change in the approach to such policies was needed. But her decisions were also based on considerations of fiscal policy. The Conservatives had pledged to cut government spending and reduce taxes. The Thatcher government was modestly successful in such efforts, including, controlling for inflation, a 1 percent cut in spending by government departments in her final year in office.[36]

After coming to office in 1997, the Labour Party presided over three major policy debates: devolution and other constitutional reforms, immigration, and health care. As touched on earlier in the book, Tony Blair's government sought major constitutional reforms, but the reforms ended up being less ambitious in practice. Devolution was begun, but even the record

The **postwar settlement** is a term for the compromise in Western European countries like the United Kingdom after World War II between those who wanted a socialist system and those who desired a more free market capitalist one. The result was a largely capitalist economic system with significant social welfare protections.

on this reform was mixed, with a particularly bumpy road in Northern Ireland, at least until 2007. The House of Lords was reformed, but far less than the Labour Party had planned.

Immigration remains a thorny issue. Asylum rates increased under Blair's government until 2002, when the government began to scale back acceptance of new immigrants. The July 7, 2005, terrorist bombings altered the immigration debate. Already a concern for many in the working class, immigration became fused with national security at a previously unseen level. Conservatives have tried to make immigration a major campaign issue, and they clearly pulled some support from Labour in the most recent elections because of the immigration issue.

Perhaps no issue appears more frequently during Question Time than health policy. When sitting in opposition, Labour and Conservative MPs alike have attacked the performance of the British National Health Service (NHS). When in power, both parties have simultaneously defended the NHS's general performance and sought to reform it.[37] Since the late 1970s, these reforms have emphasized the idea that government services may be more efficiently administered by giving officials at lower levels of the government, as well as at the regional and local levels, greater autonomy to implement policy approaches.[38]

During their time in power in the 1980s and 1990s, the Conservatives searched for a "politically managed market" approach to health care with significant local autonomy but maintained the government-run approach to health care.[39] Blair's Labour government accepted the idea of greater autonomy, but its approach differed from the Conservatives' in important ways. While Conservatives supported decentralization of operational control, they increased central government monitoring and regulating activities, and they desired a greater separation between those making policy and those delivering government services.[40] In contrast, the Labour government has allowed greater regional and local autonomy on a variety of fronts and encouraged greater cooperation between policymakers and administrators, all while dramatically increasing government financial support for certain programs, such as health care and education. In the decade leading up to the 2005 elections, the Labour government has tripled spending on health care.[41]

Germany

Germany's **social market economy** (SME) is a distinctive variety of capitalism with a comprehensive conservative corporatist welfare state. Conservative social forces created the SME, and its institutions and practices reflect traditional values.[42] This variety of capitalism and welfare state thus differs from the labor-led social democratic welfare state, in which unions and social democratic parties were the key architects, and free-market capitalism and its residual welfare state were at categories of the population deemed the "deserving poor."

The political elites who created West Germany's social market economy in the post–World War II period did so to forge a "third way" between the free-market capitalism that had yielded the mass unemployment and insecurity during the Great Depression, and the socialist command economy that thwarted individual freedom in the Soviet Union (and East Germany). The social market economy preserves private property and generally views the market as the best way to allocate resources and generate economic growth. But it does not see the market as a legitimate means to distribute the proceeds of economic growth. In practice, the SME has entailed a small state sector, the state working through market actors rather than engaging in

The **social market economy** (SME) is the economic approach that developed in Germany, which united corporatism and welfare state protections with traditional social values. It stands as a counter to both socialist and free market capitalist economic approaches.

detailed planning to guide the economy, and a comprehensive cradle-to-grave welfare state to compensate the losers in the market.[43]

Germany's conservative corporatist welfare state is the oldest modern welfare state in the world. It dates from the social insurance legislation that Chancellor Bismarck enacted in the 1880s, which introduced compulsory pensions, accident insurance, unemployment insurance, and health insurance to the working class. These programs withstood a number of political regime changes in the twentieth century and today comprise the welfare state in the Federal Republic. The major social force behind the (re)creation of the welfare state in the post–World War II era was the Christian Democratic Party (CDU) under Chancellor Adenauer. The Social Democratic Party (SPD) and its union allies later came to accept the contours of the social market economy, with its generous welfare state in exchange for the preservation of private property, but have generally worked to expand the generosity and scope of social benefits.[44]

The core values underpinning the welfare state and the broader SME are decidedly conservative. First, the principle of solidarity envisions a community that cares for its less fortunate members. But this community is one marked by class, status, and occupational hierarchies that are reflected in the design of social insurance programs, which means that some categories of employees enjoy more generous benefits than others. On the whole, however, the German welfare state is marked by the comprehensiveness of benefits such as national health insurance, universal child allowances, and relatively generous social assistance (welfare).

Second, the subsidiarity principle (see Chapter 4) requires that individuals look first to the family for social assistance; then to natural social groups like unions, employers, or churches; and, finally, to the state as a provider of last resort. Rather than directly providing social programs, the state acts as the guarantor of social welfare by setting out the broad goals and parameters of the welfare state in framework legislation and then granting wide latitude to corporatist groups to implement the laws and deliver welfare state services under the principle of self-governance. At the same time, the state possesses the authority to sanction these actors, or in some cases to intervene directly in their social welfare domain if they refuse to fulfill the law.

Finally, the welfare state embodies a strong dose of social Catholicism, which champions human dignity, work, and a traditional family structure. Thus, the social market economy institutionalizes worker consultation in industry (codetermination) and the welfare state promotes traditional gender roles by allotting generous family allowances and leave time to allow women to stay at home and care for children.[45]

The SME delivered outstanding economic growth rates (the *Wirtschaftswunder* or "economic miracle") until the 1980s that were well above other EDCs in this period. It also provided the population with a comprehensive welfare state. Furthermore, the SME's "social partnership" between labor unions and employers delivered high wages and peaceful industrial relations. But the model ran into serious trouble in the 1990s. Persistent high unemployment, exceeding 9 percent of the workforce, became a regular feature of the German economy.

The unsustainability of the current approach has sparked serious debate over labor market reform in Germany, but the policy debate has also extended to the viability of the welfare state itself. Simply put, there are too few workers contributing payroll taxes to finance the welfare benefits of those who are not working. Germany's low fertility rate and aging population exacerbate the situation and threaten a severe shortfall in welfare state financing in future decades. The heavy reliance on payroll taxes to finance welfare state programs is particularly perilous, given the shrinking numbers of those in work and the burgeoning of those reliant on welfare state benefits. Moreover, high payroll taxes raise overall labor costs, discouraging job creation and leading to a vicious cycle of "welfare without work."[46] This trend is only beginning to be reversed as a result of the Schröder government's Agenda 2010 and the so-called Hartz reforms of the welfare state. These reforms have encouraged the creation of part-time, low-wage employment by changes in labor market rules and stricter access to less generous unemployment benefits. The Merkel government has, by and large, continued these reforms.[47]

An additional concern is that the conservative corporatist welfare state's programs, which assume a traditional family structure and gender division of labor between a full-time breadwinner husband and a wife staying at home full time to care for children, no longer reflect the realities of German society. The growth in single-parent families and the rising number of women in paid employment have generated new demands for child care and parental leave that the welfare state is only beginning to address.[48]

France

Since the emergence of industrial capitalism in Euope, much of the debate about economic policy in France centered on **dirigisme**. *Dirigisme* is an approach to economic development based on centralized authority in the hands of state bureaucrats that is rooted in the aspirations of seventeenth and eighteenth-century monarchs. Under Louis XIV, for example, Finance Minister Jean-Baptiste Colbert directed resources to key industrial sectors to raise revenues and fight wars; bolstered by additional mercantilist provisions, these industries flourished at the onset of the Industrial Revolution. In modern France, it has come to mean the application of rationality to decision making and policy in pursuit of progress, stability, and the needs of the state.

The French Revolution legitimized *dirigisme* through the Jacobin state, while Napoleon consolidated the aspirations of the Revolution and extended protectionism across the continent through the Continental Blockade against Britain. Starting in the 1830s, social scientists,

doctors, and engineers, known as Saint-Simonians, advocated for economic development that would lead to social development under the tutelage of an enlightened elite.[49] With the elaboration of scientific statistics, this new movement would find support in the mechanisms of the state that sought to combat illness and disease, and provided a foundation for a social *dirigisme* promoting stability, human development, and modernization.[50] Public education became the hallmark of the Republican state, governed from Paris with the explicit goal of forming the next generations of citizens.

At the end of World War II, governments had a tradition of economic intervention and new tools to enhance the authority of bureaucrats in the central state. Relatively autonomous ministries adopted a series of five-year plans, directed public and private support to key industrial sectors and giant firms, gradually substituting the state trained elite for private management. At the same time, governments of the Left and Right promoted social welfare, known as "solidarity," as a social imperative as well as a tool to achieve stability.

By the 1980s, however, a variety of linked foreign and domestic factors necessitated a change of direction. The newly elected Socialist Party in 1981 faced an economic environment characterized by the oil crisis, inflation, and stagnation that affected all industrial democracies in the 1970s. At first, they attempted to strike out on their own against Thatcher in the United Kingdom and Reagan in the United States, stimulating the economy through an expansion of government interventions and the nationalization of key banks, but were soon forced to reverse course because of external pressures on the currency and financial system.[51] Since 1984, governments

> **Dirigisme** is a term used to describe the economic approach commonly used in France since the Industrial Revolution, which is based on the principle of rational direction by government bureaucrats with the goal of protecting the interests of the state.

of the Left and Right have moved to liberalize aspects of economic activity, reduce the direct authority of the central state, and provide greater autonomy for local and private initiative. These reforms included freeing finance and banking of much regulation, the privatization of state companies in whole or in part, and the promotion of a stock market culture. At the same time, fiscal and policy authority have been transferred to local and regional agencies outside of the hands of the bureaucracy in Paris. Today, debates about economic reform focus on the cost of pensions and other benefits as well as regulation of the labor market and employment.

As indicated in previous chapters, citizenship and identity remain central to French politics and policymaking. As a country with many immigrants but a history of silencing the foreign born,[52] debates over citizenship focus on exclusion at the borders and assimilation (or "integration," as its moderate variant) within them. But no amount of assimilation has cooled the often heated rhetoric. In 1991, then Mayor of Paris (and later President) Jacques Chirac portrayed Muslim immigrants as a threat to the nation, culturally for what he considered an un-French "noise and the smell" and demographically, as he alleged they often had "three or four wives and 20-odd kids."[53] Today, immigration continues from former colonies in Africa, as well as from Asia, Latin America, and Eastern Europe. Many of these immigrants form an almost clandestine society and economy, driven further underground by policies of automatic expulsion enforced by Socialist governments as well as those of the Right.

Finally, the expansion of the European Union has been contentious. Some nations question the curtailment of sovereignty. Others are concerned that the EU will not protect solidarity and social welfare or are bothered by the democratic deficit in the institutions of the EU.

Public Policy and Policy Debates in Mexico, Brazil, Nigeria, and India

An overview of major policy issues in Mexico, Brazil, Nigeria, and India highlights the challenges of policymaking in developing countries. In Mexico, policy debates have centered on fiscal, monetary, and trade policy. Forces outside the country—including the diffusion of economic ideas from Mexico's northern neighbor and the global collapse of Communist systems—encouraged policy reforms in these areas as much as forces within Mexico did. The history of policymaking in Brazil highlights the contrast between *making* policy and *implementing* policy. Brazilian domestic policy has become increasingly intermestic—aimed at influencing foreign investors and lending agencies as well as domestic economic actors—and has also become increasingly driven by external influences. Nevertheless, its domestic capacity to enforce and implement policy remains a stumbling block to effective public policy. In Nigeria, the economic structure includes high levels of poverty but also oil wealth that could aid in its development. Identity divisions also pose a great challenge. The lingering affliction of corruption negatively affects both specific policy developments and general government performance. In India, the types of public policies adopted at the various levels of government differ, not only from differences in their relative constitutional powers, but also from differences in party control of those legislative bodies and from the varying demands of a heterogeneous population in a large country with diverse topography and a complex history.

Mexico

Since Mexico became an established democracy, the country's citizens have paid increasing attention to government policies and performance. Well before this, however, a number of significant policy reforms had occurred. Indeed, economic development has been a central concern of Mexican policymakers since independence. The state became heavily involved in the economy partly because of the late start in industrialization—a pattern shared by many Latin American countries—but also because it complemented the party authoritarian system by tying the working class to the ruling party.[54] While the PRI nationalized major industries throughout its rule (including the telecommunications sector as late as 1972), the debt crisis of the 1980s encouraged the government to consider privatization as a way to address the country's debts without significant cuts in government spending.

In the years leading up to the establishment of democracy, debate swirled not only around the political reforms but also economic policies such as NAFTA and questions about the stability of the Mexican currency. In early 1995, newly inaugurated President Zedillo took measures to prop up the peso, the value of which had fallen 40 percent. His fiscal and monetary policy included steep spending cuts and drew on a U.S. credit package to help stabilize the peso.

Most scholars and policy analysts recognize the importance of education and adequate health care to a country's long-term economic development. While the government has attempted to reform the country's educational system, these efforts have been criticized as haphazard and half-hearted.[55] The most ambitious effort at improving education was the PROGRESA program, a set of reforms launched in 1997 to address rural poverty. The program included cash incentives for parents who kept their children in school, serving the dual purpose of reducing poverty in the short run and improving the families' long-term financial prospects.

Health care system reform has been more notable. PROGRESA also included financial

As part of a visit to Mexico in April of 2007, New York City Mayor Michael Bloomberg, center, walks through the city of Toluca. Bloomberg visited Toluca to see firsthand the implementation of Mexico's *PROGRESA* Program, now known as *Oportunidades*, on which he modeled the Opportunity NYC initiative.
(©AP Photo/Mario Vazquez de la Torre-Agencia MVT)

incentives for receiving preventive health care treatments such as vaccinations. But the centerpiece of health care reforms is the national health insurance program launched in 2004. Designed to provide universal coverage by 2010, the cost of the insurance is covered through national and state governments as well as individuals and is progressive, with wealthier families being required to contribute more than poorer ones.[56] It is too early to tell whether the new program will lead to a significant improvement in Mexican health, and far too early for an evaluation of its benefits versus its significant costs. But the universal nature of the program, consistent both with the ideals of the Mexican Revolution and the claim in Mexico's Constitution that health care is a human right, has helped it earn support across the political spectrum.[57]

Brazil

Economic development has long been the most salient policy problem in Brazil. The First Republic's proclamation of goals—order and progress—saw progress principally in economic terms, and order as a prerequisite to the achievement of progress. Like many Latin American countries in the late nineteenth century, the First Republic was dominated by *positivists*, a group of educated elites who believed that ordinary people were not really capable of making decisions about public policy; they were too stupid, too ignorant, too short-sighted, or too likely to be persuaded to give their votes to demagogues. Instead, well-trained experts—in science, technology, and industry—should have authority to decide public policy on the basis of technical criteria. Later versions of this approach would refer to rule by *technocrats*.

The main problem with rule by technocrats is that someone must decide what the goals of policy should be before the "technically appropriate" policy can be applied. Fiscal and monetary policies, for example, can be designed to favor lending or to encourage savings. In the case of Brazil, the main conflict involves trade-offs between policies designed to maximize macroeconomic growth and policies designed to reduce Brazil's staggering levels of inequality. Countries that began the development process with more equal incomes, such as South Korea, Taiwan, or Japan, often do better in economic development because they have larger domestic markets and higher average levels of health and education, more evenly spread across the population. Obviously, a sick, malnourished and uneducated workforce is less productive.

Achieving greater average levels of health, education, and consumption capacity—especially when one starts from a position of highly unequal distribution of resources—typically requires some redistribution of wealth and assets through progressive taxation or land reform. However, high tax rates and redistribution of real property are likely to arouse opposition among the propertied classes and potential investors, which in turn reduces the amount invested in the creation of new jobs. Much of Brazil's historical political instability can be attributed at least in part to pendulum swings between governments that emphasized equality and redistribution and governments (often the product of military coups) that emphasized economic growth, privileging the property rights of the ruling class in order to stimulate investment.

The emergence of the so-called "Washington Consensus," which favors the free market model of capitalism, has tended to resolve this conflict in favor of economic growth over equality, particularly in countries such as Brazil where the management of a massive public debt has put the state in the hands of international lending agencies. These agencies, such as the IMF, typically require adoption of market-oriented policies as a condition for emergency loans. Within this context, substantial redistribution becomes more difficult. Even a leftist president like Lula has found himself constrained by the terms of deals with the IMF to keep state spending low and to cut subsidies of goods consumed by the poor. There still are some alternatives: Lula has used moral persuasion (among other tactics) to launch a program called *Fome Zero* ("Zero Hunger"), which provides poor families with a monthly food subsidy. Similar programs (Zero Thirst, and Light for All) aimed to provide poor Brazilians with clean water and electricity. In the area of education, new affirmative action programs created opportunities for black Brazilians (often among the poorest) to attend college.

Nigeria

The importance of tackling corruption remains the central policy issue in Nigeria, as it affects the effectiveness of initiatives in all other policy arenas. Until corruption is successfully attacked, Nigeria's great potential is likely to remain unrealized. The government of Olusegun Obasanjo took a number of steps to address the corruption problem—or at least appear to be addressing it—during his two terms as president. These included the arrest of high profile government officials, including regional governors, federal government ministers, and the inspector general of the police.[58] The extent to which President Umaru Yar'Adua will be any more serious, and any more effective, at addressing the corruption problem remains to be seen. Some of his initial actions are promising, such as demanding that ministries return any unspent funds in 2007 and then firing two ministers in March 2008 who defied the order. Yet, local organizations such as the Coalition against Corrupt Leaders have criticized the Yar'Adua Administration for delays in trials of officials charged with corruption, which have "undermined public confidence in the anti-corruption efforts."[59]

Beyond corruption, the government faces other pressing issues. One is how to better distribute and invest the country's oil wealth while working to get its fiscal house in order. Some of Nigeria's foreign debt was forgiven in 2005. A "fiscal responsibility bill" with significant economic reforms remained stalled in the national legislature throughout Obasanjo's second term[60] before it was finally passed and signed into law after Yar'Adua took office.

Another vital problem is the deepening of identity divisions in the country. Nigeria's policy approaches related to identity have been uneven. It has tried to emphasize a strong overarching identity and worked to minimize religious and ethnic divisions, but its federal system allows regional governments say over many cultural matters. A number of regional and local politicians have exploited this, working to inject identity divisions into the political process.

India

India's efforts to liberalize the economy, especially after 1991, have stimulated intense debate on several issues such as the speed of privatization, the sectors in which privatization should take place, the degree of openness to foreign

capital, the sectors of the economy that should be "out of bounds" to foreign capital, and the subsidies that should be removed or added. The creation of Special Economic Zones to lure private business has given rise to a great deal of debate between those championing the rights of farmers whose land was to be acquired and those championing the transition to an industrialized economy.

The majority of the rural population has not shared in the economic progress of the country as a whole.[61] Partly as a result, debates over how to deal with this problem occur regularly, especially at the federal unit and *panchayat* levels and as elections approach. The debate centers around issues such as those related to the provision of water, power, fertilizer, seeds, prices, and subsidies.

Debates over policies to supply electricity and water to both urban and rural populations are perennial. Proponents of the Indo-U.S. nuclear agreement (see Chapter 11) contend that one reason to support it is to increase the availability of electricity through nuclear power. The rapidly growing industrial sector requires more and more electricity. Farmers need electricity to pump irrigation water.

Indeed, a regular supply of water is one of India's great problems. If the monsoon does not arrive regularly, drought often results. Yet, when it comes, flooding frequently follows. Dams, such as on the Narmada River, have been built to offset both problems, but they produce political tensions, including the displacement of residents and disputes over the use of the water between upriver and downriver communities.[62] When rivers flow between federal units, for example, Karnataka and Tamil Nadu, the disputes take on an India-wide significance. In some areas of the north where melting glaciers in the Himalayas contribute to the river flow, debates over the consequences of global warming and what to do about it have developed. One solution to

Social activist Medha Patkar, right, speaks at a rally in Bangalore, India in June of 2006. The rally occurred at the end of the three-day convention of the National Alliance of People's Movements (NAPM), a network of over two hundred movements in India with an ideology against globalization, caste discrimination, and religious fundamentalism.

(©AP Photo/Gautam Singh)

the water problem that has been widely discussed is the interconnecting of India's rivers, both within federal units and among major rivers throughout the country.

In a country with as much identity diversity as India, policy debates concerning identity are expected to be vigorous. The role of religion in India, that is, whether the government of India should be secular or communal, is a contentious topic. The debate focuses on the appropriateness of using *Hindutva* (Hindu nationalism) as the set of ideas guiding the governance of India.[63] It pits the Bharatiya Janata Party (BJP), which advocates *Hindutva*, against the Left, which advocates secularism. The INC leans toward secularism, but sometimes uses communalism in its struggle for power. Advocates of *Hindutva* say that it is a set of ideas inclusive of most of the people and religions of India, though it excludes some of the ideas associated with Islam and Christianity.

Policies aimed at creating a greater sense of inclusion among many groups have also aroused considerable debate. A key policy has been that of "reservations," that is, reserving a certain percentage of places in public educational institutions and public employment for individuals from groups that are deemed to have been excluded.[64] The debates center on which groups should be given reservations and whether reservations should be extended to private sector schools and jobs. Particularly intense debate has arisen over whether Muslims should be accorded reservation. Alongside the calls for new reserved positions and categories, opposition to such reservations has grown. Opponents often use the argument that only a few people within these groups, referred to as the "creamy layer," seem to benefit. Women have also been pushing to overcome their under-representation in legislative bodies.[65] The 73rd and 74th Constitutional Amendments reserved 33 percent of seats in local government for women. Yet they constitute only about 9 percent of the elected members of the *Lok Sabha*. Thus, women's groups have been arguing for reservations in the central legislatures to increase their numbers.

The controversies over economics and identity are fueled by India's frequent terrorist incidents. Some of these are instigated by militant domestic groups like the Naxalites or Maoists, who assert they are fighting to improve the lives of the rural poor. Others are fomented by communally based groups to stir conflict especially among Muslims and Hindus, and still others are inspired by pro-Pakistani groups or those associated with Pakistan's Interservices Intelligence (ISI). In the northeast and northwest there is secessionist violence and terrorism. The debates over how to deal with terrorism frequently involve the extent to which the policy should allow infringement of civil liberties—a topic of significance to many Indians.

Public Policy and Policy Debates in the Russian Federation, China, and Iran

Like the other TIC cases, economic concerns have driven many policy debates in Russia, China, and Iran. In Russia and China, policy challenges have included the proper approaches to making a transition from a planned economy to a more market-based economy. Although both appear to have settled on their respective approaches, the limited veto points in both countries make additional, dramatic policy changes down the road feasible. In addition to economics, major policy debates in Iran surround the role of the government in controlling Iranians' daily lives and identity divisions in the country. These various debates are shaped by factors discussed throughout this text—Iran's oil-based economy, its complex political culture, its religious and ethnic makeup, its institutional arrangements, and its specific leaders at any given time.

The Russian Federation

The two most important domestic policy debates in Russia since 1991 have been broad economic policy—how to remove the state from the economy through privatization and the extent to which the state has reentered the domestic economy as a major player—and policy questions related to identity, including the conflict in Chechnya. More than Soviet leader Mikhail Gorbachev had done, President Boris Yeltsin introduced elements of capitalism into the Russian economy. The Russian government privatized most state-owned enterprises during the 1990s but maintained some large state-owned companies. A number of analysts of Russia labeled the 1990s economic system **oligarchic capitalism**, with a handful of incredibly wealthy individuals dominating the economy and using their political weight to guide Yeltsin's policy decisions.

Since Putin's ascendancy to the presidency, Russia has moved away from oligarchic capitalism and into an era of state capitalism. Russia has become the model in practice for the state capitalist ideal type. The system is much more capitalist than socialist, but it is a Russian brand of capitalism, with political connections and state power visible underneath the façade of free market liberalism. Entrepreneurs are encouraged to create new, profitable entities, but they are often forced to compete with enterprises connected to or run by the state or forced to work with state bureaucrats, making themselves vulnerable to "political shakedowns."[66] According to Russian specialist Stephen Sestanovich, the only hope that the Russian government will take less of a role in the economy would be a significant economic downturn.[67] As long as world oil prices remain high, such a downturn seems unlikely.

Another central domestic policy question in Russia is how best to address its identity diversity. The Russian government has struggled to forge an overarching identity that would unite ethnic Russians with the sizeable number of Russian Federation citizens who are ethnically non-Russian. Policy approaches have varied since 1991. Russia has maintained its ethno-federal system, but the central government has taken steps to weaken the autonomy of ethnic republics. Indeed, the one consistent position has been the opposition to the idea of granting independence to territorially concentrated minority groups. In the case of the Chechens, both presidents, Yeltsin and Putin, supported military action to prevent Chechnya from seceding from Russia.

China

After Mao Zedong's death in 1976, Deng Xiaoping emerged as China's leader. He emphasized the importance of "practice"—finding economic approaches that worked—over theory and ideology, and his consolidation of power in 1978

Oligarchic capitalism was a term some analysts of Russian politics used to describe the Russian economic system of the 1990s, a system they believed benefited a small number of economically and politically powerful individuals.

set the stage for a dramatic shift in Chinese economic policy. A 1981 statement by the party Central Committee strongly denounced the Cultural Revolution. The question was no longer whether there would be important economic reform but rather how considerable it would be. It turned out to be very considerable.

The decision by Deng to institute radical economic reform was one of monumental consequence and risk. By abandoning the economic principles of Marxism-Leninism-Maoism, Deng was basing the legitimacy of Chinese Communist Party rule largely on economic performance. Chinese agricultural and industrial production soared in the 1980s, but the downsides of market-based economic growth—inflation, unemployment, inequality, and, perhaps most important, rising expectations—created new challenges.

As a result of Deng's policies and their impact on China's economic development, the country became a symbol of the **Asian economic model**, a combination of mercantilism, other state-led development measures, and a less-than-democratic approach to governing. The model, which was often viewed as the means for LDCs to become EDCs, began to unravel in the 1990s. Not only did growing prosperity lead to pressures to democratize, but also the Asian economic crisis of the late 1990s called into question the economic components of the approach taken by countries like China. Still, China has retained a role for state intervention in the economy even as it continues further liberalization of its formerly socialist economy.

Related to the broad arena of economics, one of the most important, and controversial, policy questions in China concerns the relative autonomy of the regions versus the center. As discussed earlier in the book, China has granted regional and local governments a greater degree of autonomy to administer government policy. Thus, in contrast to Russia—a federal system in which the lower levels of government are less powerful than they had been a decade earlier—China remains a unitary system, but one in which lower levels of government are increasingly assertive and the central government is increasingly acquiescent.

Iran

Both before and after the Islamic Revolution, Iranian governments have stressed a goal of improving the country's economy and ordinary citizens' lives. From 1989 to 2005, the government proposed three successive "development plans." Like most sets of goals attached to a significant new government policy, the goals in each of the three plans were a combination of efficiency and equity, associated with economic growth and a reduction in poverty. They also reflected tensions over how best to use the country's oil money. Like other oil-rich countries with significant poverty, some in Iran favor a more dramatic, short-term redistribution of wealth, while others favor a longer-term strategy based on investment and diversification of the economy. Also similar to other oil-rich countries, too often neither goal has been achieved in Iran, thanks to clientelism and the presence of significant corruption in both the public and private sectors.

The other major areas of debate concern social life and identity. Initially, the rhetoric of Iran's hardline president, Mahmoud Ahmadinejad, had little impact on most Iranians' daily lives. By the latter part of 2006, however, Ahmadinejad's vision for Iranian society had begun to materialize. The changes were most evident in the arena of gender relations, already a touchy subject in Iran. New policies led to the segregation of previously co-ed classes, bans on women smoking in cafés in Tehran, and new restrictions on women's clothing stores and the public performance of music by women.[68] Other controversial identity policy questions surround the question of Iran's sizeable ethnic minority population, a topic highlighted in Chapter 5.

The **Asian economic model** was a combination of state-led development measures and authoritarian political practices from the 1970s through the 1990s.

Assessing Policy Performance: Do the Policies Work?

Because policies are the central output of the political system, they attract a great deal of attention from government officials, interest groups, the general public, and political scientists.

Policy Evaluation by Government Officials

Peter Hall anchors his discussion of degrees of policy change to an important point: government officials often look to how past policies have performed for guidance about what to do at present. Once a policy has been in place for a period of time, members of the legislative and executive branches evaluate its performance. They then decide if the policy should be maintained, altered slightly, or overhauled entirely.

Whether a particular policy or set of policies work depends on what they were intended to do, what they cost, and what unintended consequences they have generated. For the same policy, the particular goals may differ from country to country and from government to government within the same country. Two governments implementing a flat tax at the same time, for example, might have quite different expectations. One may simply hope that citizens who have paid little in taxes to that point actually begin to pay taxes and become accustomed to doing so. The other might believe that the flat tax will provide a specific increase in revenue, necessary for approaching a balanced national budget the following year. In some cases, governments use the evaluation stage as a delay tactic rather than a legitimate effort at performance assessment. Creating commissions to study a problem and the existing approaches to solving it is a common strategy to delay implementing any new policies or revise existing ones.

Policy Assessment by Others

Government officials are not the only ones evaluating policy performance. Similar evaluations of particular policies take place among scholars, interest groups, and members of the general public. Citizens expect their political leaders to take steps to address existing social, economic, and political problems. They also expect these efforts to be successful. Interest groups evaluate existing policies, and make recommendations for changes, based on their own goals. Comparativists interested in the study of public policy typically look for patterns of policy effectiveness across countries. Sometimes, however, they analyze the consequences of a particular policy in a particular country by answering the same question that government officials do: Do the policies *actually* work? These analyses are, hopefully, more systematic and objective than many of those by government officials, interest groups, or ordinary citizens.

Assessing Government Performance

At the same time that they consider specific policy initiatives, members of interest groups, ordinary citizens, and scholars engage in another, broader form of assessment. They evaluate a government's *overall performance* at addressing pressing problems. For members of interest groups, this overall assessment is colored by the issue or issues about which they care deeply. The same is also true for ordinary citizens. As discussed in Chapter 11, in democracies general evaluations of government performance play a role in voters' decisions about which parties or candidates to support. But different individuals care about different issues and are likely to give a few issues much more weight than others in their performance assessments.

Comparativists studying government performance look more broadly for their evidence.

Some focus on the general public's perceptions. They analyze survey data to understand why some individuals believe the government is doing a better job than others. One must be careful about assuming that citizens accurately recognize when a government's performance has improved. Their partisan affiliations, the news outlets they turn to for political information, or a general lack of interest in politics can all bias how members of the general public evaluate government policy and its effects. As a result, comparative public policy researchers generally do not rely only on public opinion.

Instead, comparativists attempt to measure government performance more objectively. Measuring whether a government's general approaches have been a success, however, is difficult. Analyzing performance involves decisions about the period of time to analyze. Some policies may have short-term effects that differ greatly from their long-term ones. It also requires information about the recent and current situation, the changes over that period, evidence that the changes were the result of government actions, and evidence about the effects of governmental activities on different groups in society. Most important, it requires comparativists to agree on a broad set of goals by which to judge government performance.

Common Goals of Public Policy: Increased Political and Social Stability, Economic Performance, Improved Quality of Life, and Greater Equality

Other things being equal, scholars consider social and political stability and effective national security to be signs of positive performance. Fostering social stability is a central task of any government. Few governments, democratic or otherwise, can survive being unable to gain control of a chaotic situation—be it sustained and large scale strikes or recurring violent protests. Another vital government task is defending the

state from an external threat. Here, however, one must think in relative terms. Although Israel is the scene of a sizeable number of small terrorist attacks on an ongoing basis, taking into account what one might expect Israel to face may lead one to assess the government as highly effective at protecting its population from such threats.

Government and regime legitimacy relate to its stability. A government that must continually resort to violence to maintain order may sustain its rule for a significant period of time, but it is hard to call such a government successful. On the other hand, when governments preside over stable situations without resorting to repression, it is a sign that the citizens of the country accept the existing political rules of the game.

Most comparativists also accept improvement in economic conditions like employment and inflation as positive signs of a successfully functioning government. What this improvement should look like again depends on the context of the case. If a country's economy is stagnant, growth would be a sign of improvement. If it has experienced a severe economic crisis, however, simply stabilizing the economy would be an important step. Clearly, government performance is not easily measured across cases without a fairly deep understanding of each case.

In addition, measuring quality of life with economic statistics like GDP, unemployment, and inflation tells an incomplete story. Other circumstances associated with the well-being of the population, such as education, health care, crime, and ecological conditions—and improvements in them—must also be taken into account. For example, a comparativist might put side by side country rankings for per capita GDP-PPP (see Chapter 3) and those of the United Nations Human Development Index (HDI), which also takes into account factors such as education and life expectancy. The two sets of rankings are far from identical. A conspicuous case is the United States, which is the second most developed country in the world in per capita GDP-PPP, but only held the eighth spot in the 2006 HDI rankings. By contrast, Sweden has the world's sixteenth highest per capita GDP-PPP but is in the top five on the HDI.[69]

Finally, many comparativists also take into account the government's efforts to promote greater social and economic equality. When considering how policies might improve economic or social equality, it is important to consider the distinction between **equality of opportunity** and **equality of result**. Equality of opportunity is the idea that individuals should, as much as possible, begin a particular process with a level playing field. While recognizing that individuals have different natural abilities, those emphasizing equality of opportunity would look for people to have jobs reflecting their effort and acquired skills rather than their family name or inherited income. Concerns with equality of opportunity in the United States, for example, lead policymakers to support education funding schemes that provide greater aid for school districts in economically poor areas, educational programs such as Head Start designed to assist disadvantaged children, and tax provisions such as the inheritance tax, which targets income destined for family members not directly involved in the earning of that income.

The concept of equality of result focuses on leveling income differences among income earners and on providing increased opportunities for historically disadvantaged groups in the hiring of employees or awarding of contracts. Equality of result policies include progressive taxation systems and other redistributive policies, as well as affirmative action programs. Redistributive policies that provide financial support to the poor are based on the principle of **means-tested income maintenance**. Means-tested programs are not universal but rather require individuals to demonstrate a need for assistance.

Equality of result efforts such as affirmative action are often more controversial than equality of opportunity programs. At least in the United States, many see both welfare programs and affirmative action programs as rewarding individuals for traits other than ability or effort. Progressive taxation systems do not face the same kind of opposition, largely because they take only a step toward equality of result (as opposed to giving an entire job or contract) and because many believe that the wealthiest individuals in society already earn significantly higher levels of income than their talents or abilities dictate.

Think and Discuss

What is the most important indicator of successful government performance? Why is that indicator more important than others?

Think and Discuss

Former U.S. Vice President Hubert H. Humphrey claimed, "It was once said that the moral test of government is how that government treats those who are in the dawn of life, the children; those who are in the twilight of life, the elderly; and those who are in the shadows of life, the sick, the needy, and the handicapped." Do you agree with his portrayal of this moral test for a government? Why or why not?

Equality of opportunity is the concept that individuals should have a fair chance of acquiring goods such as a quality education and employment.

Equality of result is the idea that income differences should be leveled through significant redistributive efforts and through preferential treatment for members of historically disadvantaged groups.

Means-tested income maintenance is an approach in which a program is available only to those individuals who can demonstrate a need for financial assistance.

Government Performance in the United Kingdom, Germany, and France

As in other democracies, the existence of free and fair elections in the United Kingdom, Germany, and France provide an effective measure of government performance. For example, while the FPTP, district electoral system in the United Kingdom links electors to a particular representative to a certain extent, swings in the electoral fortunes of the major parties have more to do with voters' views about the current government's performance than they do with voters' connections to their local representatives. Likewise, the 2005 election in Germany registered the public's dissatisfaction with government performance. Election results in France over the past several decades point to a longer pattern of frustration, with sitting governments rarely winning reelection.

The United Kingdom

Because its elections are free and fair, the British government works hard to demonstrate to the population that its policies are performing adequately. In an example of its efforts to convince the public it was trying to improve government performance, Tony Blair's government produced a major public statement titled "Modernising Government" in early 1999. It continued several of the ideas of the previous Conservative Party government, and marked a major departure from past Labour Party proclamations. The document stated that the aims of the Labour government's approach to providing service included a combination of high quality and efficiency, while shifting the focus from the providers of services to the users of them.[70]

As part of its initiatives to modernize government services, the Labour Party–controlled government has also stressed the idea of **evidence-based policymaking (EBP)**. EBP is based on the principle "what matters is what works," stressing the need to adjust existing policies that fail to produce even if such changes go against the traditional ideological positions of the party.[71] This idea is consistent with the more centrist position of the Labour Party, evidenced by the decision in 1995 to remove the wording in Clause Four of the party's constitution, which had declared a commitment to collective ownership of the means of production in the economy.

How successful have efforts to improve government performance been? One could point to the resounding defeat of the Conservatives in 1997 as a sign of ineffective performance, but it is important to note that this election followed successive Conservative Party victories under Margaret Thatcher. Although Thatcher was increasingly unpopular at the end of her tenure in office, she had introduced a large number of significant reforms, many of which remain in place today.

Likewise, one must be careful not to assume that the three successive Labour Party victories mark broad happiness with the party's governance of the country. Granted, the British economy has outperformed many of its European counterparts over the last decade, and survey data indicate that many recognize this success. Only 11 percent of those surveyed in 2006, for example, indicated that unemployment is the United Kingdom's most pressing problem,

Evidence-based policymaking (EBP) is an approach championed by the Labour Party under Tony Blair, which emphasizes the need to abandon policies that fail to produce even if such changes are in contrast to the traditional ideological positions of the party.

which compares with more than 70 percent of German respondents who viewed unemployment as the most important problem in their country, and small numbers of Britons are concerned about economic inequality compared with citizens of other European countries such as Germany.[72]

However, survey data also show that British citizens are concerned about crime, health care, and immigration, and have little confidence in their head of government. Compared with other EDCs, such as the United States, Germany, France, Italy, and Spain, the population in the United Kingdom has by far the lowest levels of confidence in their government leaders to solve the country's major problems. It is possible that the British population does not believe that noneconomic issues are easily addressed by the government. But the fact that Britons held these views not long after returning the Labour Party to power should be of comfort neither to members of the Labour Party nor to the Conservatives who were unable to wrest power from them.

Comparativists studying the United Kingdom have also conducted their own analyses of policy effectiveness and political performance. An analysis of the British health care system, for example, paints a mixed picture about its performance leading up to the latest round of reforms under Tony Blair. While the strong central control of the system prior to Thatcher's reforms succeeded in improving equity in access to health care and modernizing hospital facilities, implementation of national policies and quality of health services varied significantly at the local level. The Conservative Party's approach of combining local autonomy with increased central government oversight led some of the worst performing facilities to improve, but it fell far short of the goals for improved service that the designers of the policy had envisioned.[73]

Since Tony Blair came to office, the access to health care has improved. Many patients waited up to eighteen months for an operation in the 1990s, a problem that showed noticeable improvement during the following decade. Wait times did not, however, reach a level that most people in the United Kingdom saw as satisfactory. In addition, given the large increase in spending under Blair, scholars wondered whether the improvements reflected structural improvements or whether the increased funding simply made an inefficient system look somewhat better.

Germany

Germany's social market variant of capitalism has delivered economic growth and a generous welfare state for much of the postwar period. This widely-shared prosperity has, in turn, helped legitimate the democratic regime. Since the mid-1990s, however, the social market economy has come under strain, particularly from high unemployment and concerns over the financial viability of the welfare state.

While some of this was due to the collapse of the eastern economy after unification, much of it was due to the way that the welfare state was intertwined with the broader labor market. Payroll taxes provide the bulk of financing of welfare state programs. Coupled with high wages, these payroll taxes render German labor the most expensive in the world. Labor costs also increased as employers shifted unemployment onto the welfare state by granting early retirement pensions for older workers.

This practice served as a remedy for the deindustrialization in the former GDR after unification, as easterners thrown out of work received generous unemployment insurance and early retirement pensions. Paying for this required higher payroll taxes on those Germans still in work. The high labor costs combined with employment protection rules that make it difficult to dismiss permanent full-time workers in a recession and that sharply limit the hiring of temporary or part-time labor. Taken together, they have discouraged job creation among German employers.[74] The result has been what some have termed "welfare without work" and a kind of labor market dualism of "insiders and outsiders." The "insiders" are those in secure full-time employment with high wages and the promise of generous pensions when they retire. The "outsiders" are those excluded from the labor market, especially the long-term unemployed who are generally women, immigrants, and the unskilled.[75]

The SPD-Green government of Gerhard Schröder began to tackle these issues. The Schröder government introduced a pension reform to reduce the generosity of the state pension and encourage private supplemental pensions. The so-called Hartz reforms of the labor market sought to reduce long-term unemployment by allowing for more temporary work and easing dismissal rules on small businesses. They also introduced incentives for the jobless to get back into work by drastically shortening the duration of unemployment insurance, curbing the generosity of financial assistance to the unemployed, and requiring them to actively seek work and accept an offer of a job.[76] The Hartz reforms appear to have succeeded in bringing down unemployment, but the cost has been a new form of social exclusion, with rising poverty among those in low-paid, temporary work. Germany now faces the problem of the "working poor," a phenomenon that used to be the sole preserve of more free-market capitalist economies such as that of Britain and the United States.[77]

The political system has registered the public's fears over Germany's future. The public's unhappiness with the Hartz reforms led to early elections in 2005, which yielded a "hung parliament" in which the SPD and CDU were virtually tied. This result signaled the deep ambivalence in the electorate, which recognized that Germany had to undertake major reform of the welfare state and labor market, but at the same time dreaded the pain that such changes might bring.[78] Neither party could muster a governing majority with a preferred coalition partner among the smaller parties, so the CDU and SPD finally agreed to form a "grand coalition." This constellation has provided the government with an enormous majority in both houses of the legislature, making it easier to enact its reform program, but it has also necessitated tortuous negotiations among the coalition partners to build consensus on controversial policies.[79]

The messy 2005 electoral result also reflected the failure of the corporatist channel of policy-making to forge a consensus on reform among the social partners. The Schröder government's Alliance for Jobs roundtable talks with the peak associations of employers and labor unions deadlocked on labor market and welfare state reform. In response, the chancellor turned to the legislative channel to pursue his reform program, with some success. Schröder overcame the usual veto points of the semisovereign state and reached a compromise with the CDU-dominated *Bundesrat* to enact Agenda 2010, his broader welfare state and labor market reform program of which the Hartz reforms were a part. Chancellor Merkel's grand coalition has subsequently formalized this cross-party cooperation. Her government has maintained the Hartz labor market reforms, enacted expansions of child care and parental leave for working parents, and passed a law that will provide state subsidies to national health insurance as a way to ease the burden on payroll taxes.[80]

Reform of Germany's welfare state and social market economy has been a slow and tortuous process. These piecemeal steps are increasingly viewed by analysts as necessary changes in the financing and scope of benefits of the conservative corporatist welfare state that will help it meet the challenges of the twenty-first century.

France

In addition to assessing the performance of democratic governments in France through elections, French performance has been measured against the stated intent of government in enacting specific programs and the consequences of such policies as they diverge from stated goals. Such analytical measures of policy are especially important for the elite French bureaucracy, with its emphasis on expertise and effectiveness in the pursuit of modernization. But politics is more than the delivery of economic progress, and in France performance is judged as much on creating stability, solidarity, and a unified national identity as on generating economic growth and low unemployment.

Regardless of how government performance is measured, the results of economic and political reform in France have been mixed. Elite bureaucrats held on to power in the newly privatized industries,[81] the privatization process included a high degree of corruption,[82] and neither the central nor the local authorities have been able to encourage the kind of autonomy that leads to innovation.[83] The bureaucracy remains large and powerful. Unemployment has been in the high single digits, even surpassing 10 percent at times, for the better part of two decades, and remains above the double digit mark among suburban youth.

Reforms in management and firm level initiative, however, have transformed the French economy and produced a set of successful industries in key sectors of the global economy. Until the global financial crisis of late 2008, inflation was low, economic growth continued at a solid pace, and French leadership on the Euro currency was an unparalleled success, as the U.S. dollar slid internationally and European states, by and large, maintained fiscal stability.

At the same time, the riots of 2005 and 2007, when angry youth responded to police with increasing violence in the poor suburban housing projects outside Paris, indicate that policies of social and economic integration have not succeeded. Inflammatory rhetoric such as that of former President Jacques Chirac, now often employed by President Nicolas Sarkozy, has reinforced social divisions, while an elite debate over the right of young women to wear headscarves symbolized for many a detachment from the real needs of the poor. Economic reform proposals have been met with larger and larger demonstrations. They were so massive in 2006 that the government was forced to withdraw the proposed reform of labor law.

Electoral results indicate a widespread frustration with the government's mixed record—a pattern of dissatisfaction that some call a "malaise"—on the part of voters reflecting deep-seated feelings of declining performance.[84] Since the 1970s, every government but one has failed to win reelection, the extreme right-wing National Front party has flourished, and a variety of new parties has emerged as voters are turned off by the mainstream Right and Left.[85] Only Sarkozy's party was reelected in 2007, but as its leader, the new president promised a change in policies from those of the outgoing government. Even the success of the Euro could not dispel the malaise, leading to the 2005 rejection of the proposal for an EU constitution considered by many voters to be too great a sacrifice of sovereignty to the power of capitalist markets or "Brussels bureaucrats."

Government Performance in Mexico, Brazil, Nigeria, and India

While the United Kingdom, Germany, and France demonstrate how voters' frustrations with government officials can lead sitting governments to lose power, dissatisfaction with government performance is hardly threatening to the legitimacy of the regime itself. In nondemocratic systems and newer democracies, however, poor government performance can threaten the entire system. As the cases of Mexico, Brazil, and Nigeria point out, this is particularly true in developing countries, where periods of economic success can raise expectations and subsequent periods of economic hardship—particularly under a government the population views as corrupt—can foster significant levels of frustration that can shake the foundations of the political system. India, however, also highlights not only that broad economic success does not automatically generate successes in other policy arenas but also that economic success is not even necessarily the result of the government fully achieving its economic reform goals.

Mexico

As the previous chapter highlighted, there are many factors that explain the breakdown of authoritarian rule under the PRI. One of the more important factors is the sense, on the part of a growing portion of the population, that PRI governments had become corrupt and ineffective. Americans are often surprised at how many citizens of other countries will tolerate government corruption *if* the government's policies are seen as successful. Few individuals in any country, however, are satisfied with a government that is corrupt *and* ineffective. While the end of PRI rule brought hope on both fronts, the Mexican government has continued to struggle to adopt effective policies and tackle corruption since 2000.

As the person whose election signaled the firm establishment of Mexico's new democracy, former President Vicente Fox enjoyed an extended honeymoon period with the Mexican population. However, he quickly ran afoul of the Mexican Congress, a minority of which was made up of members of his National Action Party (PAN). Consequently, much of his six-year term was spent trying—with great effort but little success—to get the national legislature to adopt a number of reform proposals. The government's failure to get a lot done fed some of the anger of the voters in 2006, who came close to stripping the PAN of control of the presidency.

Of Fox's many proposed reforms that Mexico's Congress blocked, one of the most important was an effort to unify the police force and create a national code for criminal procedure. Crime strikes at the heart of a population's sense of day-to-day personal security. As a result, the inability of a government to address effectively a marked increase in crime can be devastating to perceptions of its performance. Mexico is no exception.

As President Felipe Calderón took office late in 2006, the Mexican population was increasingly unhappy about crime, especially crime related to drug trafficking and corruption within the ranks of the police.[86] When violent crime rose significantly in 2006, the government's response was seen as ineffective. It spent more on policing, but police forces lacked coherence, there was a significant annual turnover in uniformed officers, and an estimated 75 percent of crimes went unreported.[87]

Comparative studies also point to Mexico having a long way to go to improve on its poor past performance. At the start of Vicente Fox's term as president, Mexico lagged behind other middle-income Latin American countries on a number of social indicators. The percentage of school age children attending high schools in Mexico was higher than Brazil, but lower than Argentina, Uruguay, Chile, and Venezuela. While other countries were improving in this area, Mexico's figures were stagnant across the 1980s and 1990s.[88] With the exception of a handful of top universities, the higher education system Fox and Calderón inherited was seriously deficient.

Mexico was performing equally poorly in the area of health care. It has fewer hospital beds per capita than nearly all Latin American countries, while having one of the region's highest child malnutrition rates.[89] Whether the new health reforms implemented after Fox took office will improve the country's relative standing in the long run remains to be seen.

Brazil

The results of President Lula's recent initiatives, discussed earlier in the chapter, have been disappointing. They have been ineffective most of all to the poor and marginalized citizens of Brazil, who expected much more from Lula. Moreover, Lula has done relatively little to change the structures of power in Brazil. Even the *Fome Zero* program relied more on voluntary contributions from the private sector than compulsory tax contributions.

Another example of Lula's reluctance and/or inability to confront the wealthy can be seen in the slow progress of land reform. According to the Brazilian Census Bureau,

> "1% of landowners currently control 45% of the nation's farmland, while approximately 37% of Brazil's 184 million citizens hold less than 1% of land. Meanwhile . . . about 4.8 million landless farmers struggle to survive with temporary or part-time work, on meager wages, and under conditions, as reported by the U.S. State Department Human Rights Bureau, as being analogous to slavery."[90]

Lula sought the support of the landless workers' movement (MST) in his 2002 presidential campaign by promising to settle 400,000 families on land seized by the government and redistributed, but during his first term he resettled only about half that number.[91]

More generally, the Brazilian state has suffered from widespread perceptions that it is at the same time excessively bureaucratic and exceptionally inefficient and corrupt. Indeed, its Byzantine bureaucracy feeds both corruption and inefficiency. It becomes simply impossible to comply with all of the many and contradictory rules imposed by the bureaucracy. Either nothing gets done, or one has to bribe a bureaucrat to help. Efforts to simplify and streamline the state bureaucracy have been weak or ineffective because so many people profit from the current system. Corrupt officials need the state to be impossible to navigate in order to extract bribes. Businesses who want to evade government regulations, such as labor codes or environmental standards, need a state that cannot effectively enforce these rules. And people who want employment—even if their job duplicates half a dozen others—are unlikely to support trimming the state employment rolls in the name of efficiency.

Such a government system has costs, albeit mostly for ordinary Brazilians who have to pay bribes or endure poor performance in the provision of public services. Some recent studies also indicate that it may hamper economic growth, especially for small entrepreneurs who lack the state connections to get around regulations. Many of these entrepreneurs wind up in the informal economy. They therefore do not pay taxes, which can be a benefit, but they also are excluded from systems of credit and vulnerable to breaches of contract by buyers or suppliers, since their businesses don't officially exist. As Hernando de Soto documents, the informal sector is less profitable overall than the formal sector, and working conditions are worse. He argues that a clear system of property rights, enforced by the government, would contribute significantly to economic growth.[92] Nevertheless, informal businesses account for an increasingly large percentage of economic activity in Brazil, as in many other developing countries.

Nigeria

Despite the high-profile displays of concern about government corruption, the problem remains. Given previous Nigerian government actions, when declared attacks on corruption became thinly veiled attacks on political opponents, it is not surprising that many Nigerians remained skeptical about the true motives of Olusegun Obasanjo's government. Stories of the ongoing corruption, including one in *The Economist* by a correspondent kicked out of the country for refusing to pay a bribe to an information ministry official,[93] also tarnished the reputation of the government outside the country during Obasanjo's reign.

The government's failure to address key social problems becomes harder to justify as oil income continues to flow into government coffers. Neither short- nor long-term fixes for problems such as the country's poor health care and education have appeared. Studies of Nigeria's health care institutions have indicated that the "supply of essential drugs was inadequate . . . and facilities for emergency care were lacking."[94]

It will also take able leadership to handle ongoing ethnic and religious hostilities. Even Obasanjo, seen by many as both a strong leader and a president acceptable to a variety of identity groups in Nigeria, struggled to contain such violence. The traits and background of Obasanjo's successor, Umaru Yar'Adua (see Chapter 11) have inspired some hope for the years ahead.

India

As discussed in Chapter 7, legislatures in India are hampered increasingly by disruption and coalition governments. Both factors make normal democratic policymaking more difficult. Governments have worked to address many of the issues involved in the major policy debates in India discussed earlier in the chapter, though the effectiveness of these efforts is open to debate.

By 2008, the Indian economy was growing at the rate of about 9 percent per year, one of the highest rates in the world. That did not mean that the government, that is, the INC-dominated United Progressive Alliance (UPA), was succeeding in making progress liberalizing the economy. Since the coalition depended on the "outside" support of the Left, and the Left often opposed privatization, little took place. Additionally, in several parts of the country, politicians capitalized on the unhappiness of many peasants with

their loss of land to the Special Economic Zones to place serious limits on its use.

India's overall economic success since the early 1990s has also not translated into policy successes on other issues. Effective response to the water supply problem, for example, has not materialized. Governments have studied the interlinkage of India's rivers, but due to the magnitude of the project and financial constraints, progress on the proposed connecting of rivers has been minimal. Similarly, the central government has not solved the perennial problem of rural poverty, though at the federal-unit level there have been a number of efforts to respond, such as subsidies for electricity.

Policies designed to address identity divisions have had a similarly mixed record. Controversy over the efforts to extend educational and occupational reservations to Muslims has been so intense as to make a solution at the national level impossible. Again, regional governments may have to lead the way. While they have gained quotas for local government representation, women continue to seek reserved seats in the *Lok Sabha* without success. They were, however, able to get a domestic relations bill passed in 2007, which provided much needed protections for many women.

Communalism remains an important political tool used to halt construction projects, influence elections, and affect political positions on a variety of issues. Yet the fears many had that it would seriously affect government actions during the BJP-dominated coalitions (1998–2004) were not substantiated. The prime minister at the time, Atal Bihari Vajpayee, seemed to recognize that to hold his coalition together and to prevent chaos in India, restraint was required.

Discussions about security and terrorism have failed to secure the former or prevent the latter. Serious terrorist attacks have continued across India. In 2007, bombs exploded in mosques and courts, killing many people, while activities by radical Maoist groups generated a seemingly unstoppable "war" between them and the police in many parts of the country.

Government Performance in the Russian Federation, China, and Iran

As the least democratic of the TIC cases, the Russian Federation, China, and Iran provide valuable examples of how government leaders in nondemocratic systems still worry about their political performance. They also highlight that, even when other policy arenas get more attention outside the country, economic successes (or shortcomings) can greatly affect a population's willingness to tolerate poor performance in those other arenas. Buoyed by high world oil prices, Russia's economy appeared strong during Putin's second term. While the economy lacked the diversity and considerable middle class found in a typical economically developed country, its dramatic turnaround in the decade since the mid-1990s is a significant part of the story of Putin's popularity. China's economic performance has been even more impressive. Yet, arguably much more than in Russia, the government has also been self-critical, openly discussing the problems of corruption and inefficient policy implementation. In Iran, the performance record is mixed. Like Russia, the high price of oil has been a catalyst for any economic successes that the country has had in recent years.

The Russian Federation

In the 1990s, Russian leaders, including President Yeltsin, had little public support. Although there were many reasons for the dissatisfaction with the government's performance, economic performance was a central one. With the exception of 1997—a year in which the economy officially grew slightly, but for which many observers believe the official statistics were overly optimistic—1999 was the first year of Russian economic growth since the collapse of the Soviet Union in 1991. Taking into account gross domestic product declines in the late Soviet period, Russia had faced a decade of significant reductions in GDP, with double-digit declines in many of these years. Inflation was also a huge

problem, particularly early in the decade when triple-digit inflation was common, and 1992 saw consumer prices rise over 2,000 percent. (Inflation in the month of January 1992 alone was almost 250 percent!) By comparison, the year 1998, with a GDP decline of around 5 percent and inflation barely above 25 percent, should have been welcomed by Russians. Instead, it was particularly damaging to perceptions about the Yeltsin government's performance, since the previous year had looked so promising.

Drawing on a well-known framework developed by Albert Hirschman, Anchrit Wille's study of Russian responses to such dissatisfaction considers the options of exit, voice, and loyalty.[95] While many Russians chose to "voice" their dissatisfaction, others chose to "exit" from politics. Severing their bond with the political system and essentially giving up on the idea that any of their political leaders could solve Russia's problems, Russian citizens increasingly viewed the government as having the worst possible combination of traits: corruption and incompetency.

It is in this context that Vladimir Putin assumed the presidency at the end of 1999. Since Putin took office, the Russian government has enjoyed broad public support. It has varied some from year to year, but within a range most American presidents would greatly desire. Compared with the 1990s, the period from 2000 to 2008 was one of dramatic economic growth, with annual growth in Putin's second term averaging around 7 percent. Inflation also improved greatly. Although it was above 20 percent in some of the years early in the decade, the average was closer to 10 percent from 2004 to 2008. By the end of Putin's second term, more Russians had opted for "loyalty," a passive support for the political system and a hope that things will continue to get better. While Russia's political conditions would concern the populations of many countries, many Russians are content with a concentration of policymaking power in exchange for a stable and robust economy.

China

The Chinese government has highlighted the country's GDP growth as evidence of the benefits of its decades-old economic reforms. At the same time, it has publicly emphasized improvements in efficiency of government services and openly admitted to certain deficiencies. It adopted an index of thirty-three criteria for assessing local governments, including efficiency and performance of duty. Surprisingly to some, in 2006 the Chinese government declared that it had received over 100,000 complaints about the performance of government officials and departments and punished more than 11,000 government workers in "efficiency-related cases."[96]

Have China's public efforts at improving government performance translated into better performance? The views of scholars and analysts outside the country are mixed. Some research based on analysis of survey data from China has pointed to public approval of the government's economic development policies,[97] and annual growth rates in the economy have been impressive. In 2006, the Chinese government pointed to an analysis by the Switzerland-based International Institute of Management Development showing that China's international competitiveness ranking jumped from thirty-one to nineteen,[98] but the country was also one of the sixty-one ranked countries that the researchers labeled as having a government with a negative impact on competitiveness.[99]

One indicator of how well China's government is performing outside the economic arena comes from an assessment of its handling of the SARS outbreak. Different regional governments in China handled the crisis—spawned by the outbreak of a deadly respiratory virus in late 2002 and early 2003—differently, but the authorities in Hong Kong were much more open about the extent of the problem than those from other regions. In addition, the central government initially tried to portray the situation as under control and labeled claims about an epidemic as false, before finally publicly intervening once the story broke in Hong

People wear surgical masks while walking through Hong Kong's business district on April 1, 2003, to try to reduce the chance of infection from Severe Acute Respiratory Syndrome (SARS).

(©Christian Keenan/Getty Images)

Kong. The politburo then ordered regional governments to be open about the epidemic and the prime minister threatened to punish those who underreported rates of infection.[100]

Iran

The nature of the Iranian political system makes gauging support for the government difficult. Elections are far from free and fair. Comparativists seeking to collect accurate survey data or conduct focus groups or in-depth personal interviews with ordinary Iranians face a number of challenges. These include both government resistance to public opinion research and a certain degree of public apprehension about openly opposing government policies.

That said, there are clues to how the Iranian people view their government. While the Guardian Council restricts the range of candidates, how the relative moderates perform compared with hardliners can be telling, assuming those supporting reform bother to turn out to vote. The 1997 and 2001 presidential elections pointed to significant support for moderate reform. At the same time, the 2005 presidential elections represented both discontent with the failure of President Khatami to take Iran in a new direction and support for Ahmadinejad's populist vision of greater economic equality. The December 2006 local elections and elections for the Assembly of Experts pointed to anger at the increasingly conservative social policies. Taken as a whole, recent elections in Iran lead one to conclude that a considerable portion of the population is unhappy with some of the hard line government policies, while a number of others are concerned about the lingering corruption and economic inequality.

As in the other TIC cases, comparativists have conducted their own analyses of government performance, as well as examined reports from IGOs like the World Bank. Such assessments of Iran's development efforts paint, at best, a mixed picture.[101] The "Third Development Plan," which ran from 2000 to 2005, included three dozen objectives, nearly half of which dealt specifically with the economy.[102] In the case of some of the goals, such as unemployment and inflation, it is difficult to tell how the government performed because—as with many nondemocratic, developing countries—the official government statistics are notoriously unreliable.

Where its performance was ascertainable, the government exceeded some specific targets and failed to deliver on a number of others, including the downsizing of the government bureaucracy, curtailing government spending, and expanding privatization efforts. Despite robust economic growth, the percentage of GDP associated with government spending rose during the plan. Although the government tried to privatize a number of state-owned enterprises, its efforts were less successful than it had hoped they would be, with few private buyers and many state firms simply transferred to other state-run organizations and funds.

Like in Russia, to the extent the Iranian government's economic programs were successful, one of the most important reasons was the high price of oil during the first decade of the twenty-first century. The Third Plan had (strangely) assumed oil would remain around $12.50 per barrel; in reality, it was several times that during portions of the plan's five years and generated more than twice the $64 billion in export revenue anticipated in the plan.[103] Thus, while the outgoing government of President Khatami claimed the results of the plan were strongly positive, long-term successes will continue to depend on oil prices until the government can more effectively use the oil revenues to better diversify the country's economy.

Think and Discuss

When examining government performance in the ten TIC cases, what themes emerge across these otherwise very different countries?

COMPARATIVE EXERCISE

9/11, Hurricane Katrina, and Political Performance in the United States

In many places throughout this book, introductory discussions of key concepts drew on the United States for real world examples. This was done not only because of a general familiarity of the United States by many comparative politics students but also because the United States is, increasingly, recognized as a valuable case for comparativists to take into account. This chapter's comparative exercise examines the performance of former American President George W. Bush in response to two significant challenges: the September 11, 2001, terrorist attacks and 2005's Hurricane Katrina.

These two events pose a puzzle. The American public and most political observers viewed

Exercise

the Bush Administration's domestic response in the days and weeks that followed the terrorist attacks on September 11 as a success. Even many of his political opponents gave him credit for his handling of the crisis, particularly in New York City where the attacks did the greatest damage. His support among the American general population reached all-time highs. The administration's response to Hurricane Katrina, which devastated the city of New Orleans, was much less favorable. This response was quickly and roundly criticized, decreasing President Bush's approval ratings, which had already been in decline over his handling of the Iraq War.

Research Question, Hypotheses, Variables, and Cases

This puzzle leads us to a specific research question: What explains the different performance outcomes following these two events? The events lend themselves to a limited most similar comparative method study. The country and president are the same, but the dependent variable differs across the two cases. The similar nature of the two cases allows one to rule out certain variables. For example, as discussed in Chapter 11, scholars seeking to understand successful decision making often start by examining the leadership traits and skills of the top decision makers in question. In the cases of September 11 and Hurricane Katrina, however, the leader was the same.

Fortunately, there are other theoretically-relevant independent variables one might examine to understand variation in success of the initial presidential response to a national crisis. One possibility concerns the federal nature of the American political system. In the American system, the diffusion of power includes not only the checks and balances of the federal institutions, but also the decision-making power of lower levels of government. In a federal system, these lower levels may act as veto points to slow down federal action. While the federal system

was the same in both of the cases examined in this exercise, the parties in control of the offices of the lower levels differed. They were the same as the president in the case of September 11, with the New York governor and mayor both being Republicans. But in the case of Hurricane Katrina, the governor of Louisiana and the mayor of New Orleans were both Democrats. State and local governments are most likely to exercise their power as veto points when these levels of government are controlled by members of a political party different from that of the president. This argument can be called the *party-federalism hypothesis*.

Given these particular cases, it also seems important to consider the nature of the disasters. According to political scientist Bert Rockman, foreign policy crises often generate a sympathetic public reaction to the president's response, at least in the short run.[104] In addition, the events of September 11 were not simply a foreign policy matter. The United States was attacked, and there was an identifiable target (Al-Qaida) for a response. This made September 11 much different from Hurricane Katrina, which "attacked" a New Orleans that lacked the ability to launch a counteroffensive. This is the *nature of the disaster* hypothesis.

Results

Table 13.1 summarizes the results of the relationship between the dependent variable and the two main independent variables. In this study, both independent variables changed in accord with the dependent variable. The nature of the disasters differed, in a pattern consistent with the possibility that responses to natural disasters are generally less likely to be successful compared to responses to terrorist attacks. In addition, the party-federalism hypothesis was supported. When the president, governor, and mayor were of the same party, the president's response was successful. When the governor and mayor were from a

Table 13.1	George W. Bush's Handling of 9/11 and Hurricane Katrina		
Case	**Dependent Variable**	**Independent Variables**	
	Success of Response	Nature of Disaster	Political Party in Control of Federal Executive, State, and Local Governments
9/11 Response	Successful Response by the Executive	Terrorist Attack	Same
Katrina Response	Unsuccessful Response by the Executive	Natural Disaster	Different

different party from the president, the president's response was perceived to be unsuccessful.

Thus, as sometimes occurs in comparative method studies, one cannot find only one variable that appears to tell the entire story of the pattern in the dependent variable. Rather, at least in the case of the quick look taken in this exercise, it appears that both independent variables played a role in influencing how successful President Bush's responses were. In such situations, a researcher might consider additional cases, which could point to one of the two variables as varying more consistently with the dependent variable than the other.

Think and Discuss

This Comparative Exercise examined the party-federalism hypothesis and the nature of the disaster hypothesis to explain the different levels of successful response to September 11 and Hurricane Katrina. What other local or national factors might help explain the difference?

CONCLUSION

In any country, policymaking is complex. It involves the identification of a problem, the crafting of a policy solution to that problem, and the implementation of that policy. Policy changes are often incremental but occasionally dramatic. The policy approach to a particular problem is affected by socioeconomic factors, governmental institutions, and the leadership and choices of a number of individuals. The constellation of these factors differs from country to country and sometimes from situation to situation within the same country.

Policies are created by individuals, but those individuals are dispersed across economic, social, and political configurations. These structures provide the socioeconomic and political setting for the decision-making process. As a result, differences in these structures can affect policy outcomes. An examination of policy and government performance demonstrates that while individuals make political choices, they do not make them in a structureless vacuum.

The comparative study of public policy also demonstrates how difficult it can be to categorize particular features of the policy environment. The extent of government intervention into the economy can have a tremendous impact on economic and other policies. But differentiating among economic systems based on government involvement in the economy unites the categories of economic and political structure, making it difficult to neatly label the type of economic system as a purely economic factor. Likewise, the extent to which the economy is interconnected with other economies through spreading globalization can be thought of both as an internal economic factor and part of that country's external economic structure.

Consideration of policy and government performance also highlights interconnections between structural and choice factors. In the case of a large number of veto points, incrementalism is not only a rational strategy for reducing information costs during the process of policy creation but also a response to the institutional setting in which such policy creation takes place. Likewise, choices within a country are affected by existing policies in other countries. These existing policies serve as an external structural factor, providing opportunities for political elites to craft policies, in part at least, by learning from other countries' experiences. Thus, while elite learning is typically treated as an *internal choice* factor, policy diffusion and convergence often occur through political elites searching for *external lessons*.

Finally, the comparative study of public policy highlights the extent to which the political outcomes of interest to comparativists—in this case, public policies—themselves have consequences, including their ability to shape the structural "environment." While economic development affects policy options, many policy initiatives are designed to stimulate economic development. Cultural factors influence how people perceive pressing problems and potential solutions to them, but policy successes and failures can alter a society's values

and system of meaning. The identity structure in a given society generates challenges for governments to address and affects the range of policy options, while identity-related policies can alter how individuals view their membership in identity groups. Political institutions, the part of the policy environment closest to the actual policy decisions, create incentives for certain policy approaches and disincentives for others. Yet, many policy initiatives alter also the institutional rules of the game, changing the political structure in which future policy decisions are made.

Key Terms

Asian economic model, p. 518
Black market, p. 499
Budget deficit, p. 490
Budget surplus, p. 490
Capitalism, p. 497
Central bank, p. 490
Central planning, p. 499
Comparative public policy, p. 485
Development policy, p. 490
Dirigisme, p. 511
Domestic policy, p. 487
Equality of opportunity, p. 521
Equality of result, p. 521
Evidence-based policymaking (EBP), p. 522
Federal Reserve Board, p. 490
Federal Reserve System, p. 490
Flat tax, p. 489
First order policy change, p. 496
Foreign policy, p. 487
Free market capitalism, p. 498
Government debt, p. 490
Inner-directed linkage, p. 487
Intermestic policy, p. 488
Labor-led capitalism, p. 500
Market, p. 497
Market forces, p. 498
Means-tested income maintenance, p. 521
Mercantilism, p. 501

"People's thoughts and actions—even if haphazard and spontaneous—are the mediating link between structural conditions and social outcomes."
Eric Selbin[1]

"Politics is more difficult than physics."
Albert Einstein

In a book called the *The Thinking Game*, political scientist Eugene Meehan argues that structures and choices come together in all aspects of life:

> (T)he quality of human life is a function of two major factors: (1) the content of the natural environment; and (2) human capacity for molding or shaping that environment. The natural environment sets limits to what can be accomplished, positive or negative. . . . The channel through which human knowledge is applied to the environment is the choice or action.[2]

Meehan's point is consistent with this textbook's approach to the comparative study of politics. The existing structures provide political decision makers with certain opportunities while at the same time constraining their ability to do whatever they want. These structures have been molded by individuals in the past, and some of them continue to be shaped by other individuals' choices and actions. Though comparativists often see structure and choice as rival perspectives, the reality of domestic politics around the world is that structures and choices are very much intertwined.

Admittedly, contemplating how structures and choices interact produces explanations of political outcomes that are less tidy than those relying on only one theoretical perspective. But that is not all bad. After all, politics is not easily captured with simple, bumper-sticker explanations. It is messy and complex. As long as the more complex explanations generated by combining theoretical perspectives are more accurate but also not so complex that they become impossible to apply, a little complexity can be a good thing.

Examining Structural Factors in Combination

Getting a handle on this complexity requires one first to think about how different structural features relate to one another. Having a fuller understanding of the impact of economic forces, for example, requires us to consider the way in which these forces both influence and are influenced by political institutions. The topic of regime transition in Chapter 12 points out how economic structure can shape government institutions, but the pre- and post-transition institutions also make certain economic approaches more or less likely. As Chapter 13 made clear, the intersection of economic and political structure can also lead to new, hybrid categories. It is impossible to discuss capitalism, socialism, and mixed economies without taking into account the extent of government penetration into and control of the economic system. Not all economic concepts involve government, but the ideal types of an economic system certainly do.

Likewise, the discussion of political culture is rarely isolated from the ideas of economic development. Indeed, one of the major comparative politics theories of political culture discussed in Chapter 4 of this book, Ronald Inglehart's theory of postmaterialism, takes economic development as its starting point. While a number of comparativists have challenged Inglehart's specific formulation of the concept of postmateralism, few would argue with the idea that economics plays a role in the development of political culture.

Another valuable pairing of structural theories is culture and identity. Most scholars who look at identity understand culture's significance, but it is important not to completely subsume identity within the cultural approach. Culture is part of what makes identity powerful, but there are other features (humans' desire to belong to groups, for example) that cannot easily be forced into our understanding of culture. As stated by comparativist Marc Ross, "It should be stressed that culture is only one basis for linking individual to social identity."[3]

Culture and political structures may also be tightly interconnected. New institutionalists, discussed in Chapter 6, like to emphasize the importance of one set of rules compared to another. But without a deep understanding of culture, questions such as why that set of rules was adopted rather than another and why the rules, once adopted, are actually obeyed can be difficult to answer. New institutionalists seeking answers to such questions often turn to rational choice rather than cultural structure, but it is often "beliefs and shared meanings that prevent institutional chaos."[4]

Additional structural intersections could be highlighted. Economic structure can shape and reinforce identity. Identity structure can affect the design of a country's political institutions. The different components of political structure can affect each other. Thus, while putting structural factors into the categories of economics, culture, identity, and political institutions can help one to make sense of their possible effects on political outcomes, it is important to remember that in practice they rarely operate in isolation.

Structures, Choices, and "Structured Choices"

The elements of the choice approach—leadership and individual decision making—can also be united with an examination of particular structural factors. The idea that the decisions of political leaders such as Mexico's Felipe Calderón or Nigeria's Umaru Yar'Adua are important is compatible with an emphasis on economics, culture, identity, and political institutions. After all, structural conditions such as identity are unlikely to be fully politically salient without some degree of leadership from intellectual, social, or political elites. For example, studies of electoral behavior have shown that people often vote for candidates that share a similar ethnic, linguistic, or religious identity,[5] but political candidates also sometimes go to great lengths to highlight their identity characteristics—particularly when speaking to a crowd of potential supporters who are "their own" people. As a result, understanding electoral behavior requires one to consider not only the identity traits of the general public but also the actions of candidates that provide the spark that turns the fuel of identity into what can become an inferno of "identity politics."

The "structure versus choice" framework allows one to separate and make sense of the various factors that affect particular political outcomes. Using these factors to develop a comprehensive understanding of such outcomes, however, requires a willingness to think about how structures *and* choices combine in various ways. In short, it requires a move from "structure versus choice" to "structured choices."

The structured choices approach recognizes *both* the importance of individuals *and* the crucial nature of context. It acknowledges that humans have created the settings in which they make political decisions. But it also takes into account that existing structures affect how new people make new decisions and that these existing structures may have emerged decades or centuries before and been relatively fixed over that period of time.[6] This approach accepts that individuals are often rational political agents, but it also appreciates that their ability to act in a fully rational manner is constrained by limited information and emotion, and the economic, cultural, identity, and political settings of which they are a part.

This is true whether the individuals in question are members of the elite or part of the masses. The idea that a voter in the general population agonizes for months over a voting decision, while collecting all possible information about the candidates and considering all conceivable costs and benefits of the voting decision, is hard to take seriously. You have spoken to enough of your friends and family members about politics to know this is not how most people make their decision. Yet, the stereotype that masses always blindly and irrationally follow elites also doesn't hold up to scrutiny. Ordinary citizens are sometimes rational, sometimes not.

The image of members of the political elite as always being fully rational, manipulative, and able to construct mass identity in any way they see fit is likewise flawed. Elites can be both rational actors and true believers. They are able to shape their economic, social, and political environments (usually gradually, occasionally rapidly). But their environment also affects their actions, sometimes hampering them and at other times providing them with new opportunities. Elites cannot construct structures out of thin air in any way they want, and they do not make decisions in a structureless vacuum.

Understanding comparative politics therefore, requires a comprehensive perspective. As a comparative politics student, you need to understand economic development, the importance of economic class, and arguments about economic inequality. You need to consider the importance of underlying values and ways of thinking in various societies, while understanding the diversity of thought within each. You need to recognize the power of identity as something that both unites and divides people. You need to be aware of the various institutional arrangements in political systems around the world. You need to be aware of the ways in which all these structural forces interact. And, of course, you need to understand how individuals make political decisions—often rationally, but at times far from rationally—within this complex structural context, and how these choices themselves can, at times, alter that structural context.

Think and Discuss

How can you apply the idea of "structured choices" to other courses you are taking?

Think and Discuss

In addition to using examples from American politics from time to time, the spotlight in this textbook was largely on the United Kingdom, Germany, France, Mexico, Brazil, Russia, China, India, Nigeria, and Iran. If you were asked to propose one additional country that should be covered in detail in this book, which one would you suggest? Why? What central concepts or theories discussed in this book does it help illustrate?

Conclusion

There are times when the comparative study of politics is as puzzling as it is invigorating. Realizing that members of the political elite are not always fully rational and that economic, social, and political structures both close *and* open doors to individuals can lead one to think that comparative politics is too complicated, too messy, and too difficult. Since you have made it to the end of this book, however, you are apparently not someone who is ready to give up on comparative politics so easily. This leaves three possible responses.

The first possibility is to abandon the effort to explain across time and place and to instead engage in thick descriptions of single cases. Indeed, such descriptions play a valuable role in our understanding of individual cases and are incorporated into comparative research. Too often, however, they stop at the stage of description and have little to say to those interested in broader understandings of politics. In short, although they are studies of politics, they fail to be *comparative* politics studies.

Think and Discuss

Is having a broad understanding of the possible effects of structures and individual choices on political outcomes truly more valuable than being able to describe the politics of a country in significant detail? Why or why not?

The second approach is to filter out much of the messiness—engaging in a form of tunnel vision—through the exclusive use of a single approach or method. This is not uncommon in comparative politics, with individual comparativists clinging to one theoretical or methodological perspective, such as only engaging in comparative studies of the effects of economic structure or conducting solely "Large N" research on policy outcomes based on rational choice assumptions.

The final option is the approach of this textbook: to embrace the messiness, while simultaneously finding a way to organize and make sense of it. This book's mixture of concepts, theories, and country-specific details provides a roadmap for your ongoing journey toward a more complete understanding of politics around the world. As the quotation from Albert Einstein at the beginning of the Epilogue claims, politics may indeed be more difficult than physics. By recognizing how different types of structures and choices influence political outcomes, however, *understanding* politics is not as hard as Einstein's declaration implies.

While you may not believe it at the moment, as a student at the end of an introductory comparative politics course, you are among a privileged few. You know more about other countries than most people, but also you know more than just the background traits of those countries. You know how to make sense of new economic, social, and political information that you will encounter long after this course is done. You know how to place these details into the "boxes" of structure and choice. Most important, you know how to take them back out of those boxes and bring them together to explain new political outcomes you will encounter in the future. Enjoy the road ahead!

Photo Captions and Credits

p. 1, An Iranian girl casts her mother's ballot at a polling station in Tehran during the second round of parliamentary elections on April 25, 2008.(©Behrouz Mehri/AFP/Getty Images); **p. 24,** Façade of the Faculté de Droit building of the Paris 1 Panthéon-Sorbonne University, Paris, France.(©www.fotalia.com); **p. 62,** Women in Nigeria dry cassava by an oil refinery gas flare. (©George Steinmetz/Corbis); **p. 101,** Members of the Cao Dai Sect at Prayer, Tay Ninh, Vietnam (© Christophe Boisvieux/Corbis); **p. 144,** An Ulster Volunteer Force (UVF) mural is seen in north Belfast, Northern Ireland, in January of 2007.(©AP Photo/ Peter Morrison); **p. 189,** Afghan President Hamid Karzai, right, with Afghanistan's former king Mohammed Zaher Shah, signs the decree implementing Afghanistan's first democratic constitution, on January 26, 2004 in Kabul, Afghanistan. (©AP Photo/ Ed Wray); **p. 231,** Queen Elizabeth II, sitting with Prince Philip, Duke of Edinburgh, reads the annual address, written for her by the prime minister's government, during the State Opening of Parliament, which marks the new session of parliament in the United Kingdom. (© Pool Photograph/Corbis); **p. 279,** Chinese soldiers march in front of a crowd in Hong Kong on August 1, 2004, to mark the 77th anniversary of the creation of the Peoples' Liberation Army (PLA). (©Mike Clarke/AFP/Getty Images); **p. 321,** German health professionals and pharmacists protest in Erfurt, Germany, on December 4, 2006, against the government's efforts to overhaul Germany's healthcare system. More than 40 healthcare organizations engaged in street demonstrations, panel discussions, and informational campaigns in hospitals.(©AP Photo/Jens Meyer); **p. 362,** Residents stand in line to cast their vote in Shilla Koraibari, located in the Indian state of Assam on Thursday, May 10, 2001. The day was marked by violence, as voters selected representatives to the legislatures of five of India's federal territorial units. (©AP Photo/Amit Bhargava); **p. 404,** Venezuelan President Hugo Chavez (left) toasts Chinese President Hu Jintao as they attend a signing ceremony at the Great Hall of the People on August 24, 2006 in Beijing, China. (© Adrian Bradshaw-pool/Getty Images); **p. 443,** A sign used by protesters in Benin to oppose efforts to amend the constitution to allow then-President Mathieu Kérékou to remain in power. (©USAID, www.usaid.gov/bj/images/constitution.jpg); **p. 484,** Thousands of students and union members march through Paris and dozens of other French cities on February 7, 2006, to denounce the CPE (*Contrat Premiere Embauche*, or First Job Contract), a government plan to cut youth unemployment, saying the measure would instead leave young people more vulnerable to job instability. (©AP Photo/Remy de la Mauviniere).

Notes

Chapter 1

1. Mark I. Lichbach and Alan S. Zuckerman, "Research Traditions and Theory in Comparative Politics: An Introduction," in *Comparative Politics: Rationality, Culture, and Structure*, ed. Lichbach and Zuckerman (Cambridge: Cambridge University Press, 1997), 4.
2. Though a difficult article, a classic work that raises the issue of "conceptual stretching" is Giovanni Sartori, "Concept Misformation in Comparative Politics," *American Political Science Review* 64, no. 4 (December 1970): 1033–1053.
3. Harold Lasswell, *Politics: Who Gets What, When, and How* (New York: McGraw-Hill, 1936).
4. Max Weber, *From Max Weber: Essays in Sociology*, trans. and ed. H. H. Gerth and C. Wright Mills (New York: Oxford University Press, 1946), 78.
5. See Clifford Geertz, *The Interpretation of Cultures* (New York: Basic Books, 1973).
6. Bent Flyvbjerg, "Five Misunderstandings About Case-Study Research," *Qualitative Inquiry* 12, no. 2 (April 2006): 230; italics added.
7. Ibid., 231.
8. Evelyne Huber, "Letter from the President: The Role of Cross-regional Comparison," *APSA-CP Newsletter* 14, no. 2 (Summer 2003): 1.
9. This is a point made by Evelyne Huber. She also comments on Giovanni Sartori's concern about the "stretching" of a concept by scholars trying to examine it in different regions. Rather than stretching concepts to their breaking point, however, Huber contends that cross-regional studies might allow researchers to refine their concepts based on their analysis of cross-regional data. See Ibid., 1–2.
10. Mark I. Lichbach, "Social Theory and Comparative Politics," in *Comparative Politics: Rationality, Culture, and Structure*, ed. Lichbach and Zuckerman (Cambridge: Cambridge University Press, 1997), 243.

Chapter 2

1. Slavenka Drakulic, "Destined to be a Croat," *Yugofax*, no. 6, October 31, 1991.
2. See Anthony Richmond, "Ethnic Nationalism: Social Science Paradigms," *International Social Science Journal* 39, no. 111 (February 1987): 3–18.
3. For a discussion of ethnic boundaries, see Fredrick Barth, ed., *Ethnic Groups and Boundaries: The Social Organization of Cultural Difference* (London: Allen and Unwin, 1969).
4. Carl-Urlik Schierup, Peo Hansen, and Stephen Castles, *Migration, Citizenship, and the European Welfare State* (Oxford: Oxford University Press, 2006), 148–149.
5. "Population," summary statistics from the "Facts about Germany" website, http://www.tatsachen-ueber-deutschland.de/en/inhaltsseiten-home/zahlen-fakten/bevoelkerung.html (accessed August 1, 2007).
6. François Xavier Verchave, *La Françafrique: La plus long scandal de la République* (Paris: Sock, 1998).
7. See John Gledhill, "Liberalism, Socio-economic Rights and the Politics of Identity: From Moral Economy to Indigenous Rights," in *Human Rights, Culture and Context: Anthropological Approaches*, ed. Richard Wilson (London: Pluto Press, 1997), 70–110.
8. See p. 4 of Glynn Custred, "North American Borders: Why They Matter," *Backgrounder*, Center for Immigration Studies, May 2003, http://www.cis.org/articles/2003/back803a.pdf (accessed July 12, 2008).
9. See Ludwig Lauerhass Jr., "A Four-Part Canon for the Analysis of Brazilian National Identity," in *Brazil in the Making: Facets of National Identity*, ed. Carmen Nava and Ludwig Lauerhass Jr. (Rowman & Littlefield, 2006), 1–14.
10. Jeffrey Lesser, "To Be a Brazilian?: Immigration and National Identity in Brazil," *Harvard International Review*, May 06, 2006, http//:www.harvardir.org/articles/1361/ (accessed February 9, 2008).
11. Pavan K. Varma, *Being Indian: The Truth About Why the 21st Century Will Be India's* (New Delhi: Penguin Books, 2004).
12. Alessio Loreti, "More Authentic, or Less?," *The Iranian*, August 27, 2002, http://www.iranian .com/Opinion/2002/August/Identity/index.html (accessed July 15, 2008).
13. Nayereh Tohidi, "Iran: Regionalism, Ethnicity and Democracy," an Open Democracy-Democracy and Iran article, June 29, 2006, http://www.opendemocracy.net/democracy-irandemocracy/regionalism_3695.jsp (accessed July 11, 2008).
14. See Lowell W. Barrington, "The Making of Citizenship Policy in the Baltic States," *Georgetown Immigration Law Journal* 13, no. 2 (1999): 159–199.
15. The population figures presented in this chapter are based on 2009 estimates from the United States Census Bureau's International Data Base (IDB), www.census .gov/ipc/www/idb/ (accessed July 21, 2008).
16. See "Population."
17. See Gérard Noiriel, "Immigration: Amnesia and Memory," *French Historical Studies* 19, no. 2 (Fall 1995): 367–380.
18. An excellent source of factual information on the states of India is *The Penguin Guide to the States and Union Territories of India*, 2nd ed. (New Delhi: Penguin Books, 2007).
19. Sources from the United States, such as the Census Bureau's International Data Base that provides the population estimates for the other countries in this chapter (see note 17), place the figure at around 66 million. Other sources, such as the United Nations, estimate Iran's population at closer to 75 million. Population estimates for Nigeria also vary between American and international sources, but not to the extent of those on Iran.
20. Linda Weiss, "Introduction: Bringing Domestic Institutions Back In," in *State in the Global Economy: Bringing Domestic Institutions Back In*, ed. Linda Weiss (Cambridge, UK: Cambridge University Press, 2003), 20.

21. Max Weber, *From Max Weber: Essays in Sociology*, trans. and ed. H. H. Gerth and C. Wright Mills (New York: Oxford University Press, 1946), 78.

22. Ibid., 82.

23. Peter J. Katzenstein, *Policy and Politics in West Germany: The Growth of a Semisovereign State* (Philadelphia: Temple University Press, 1987).

24. Philippe Roger, "Global Anti-Americanism and the Lessons of the French Exception," *The Journal of American History* 93, no. 2 (September 2006): 448–451; Tony Chafer and Emmanuel Godin, eds., *The French Exception* (New York: Berghahn Books, 2005).

25. Ezra Suleiman, *Elites in French Society* (Princeton: Princeton University Press, 1978).

26. Michel Crozier, *La Société Bloquée* (Paris: Seuil, 1967).

27. Among texts addressing the political system of India are Ramesh Thakur, *The Government and Politics of India* (New York: St. Martin's Press, 1995) and Robert Hardgrave Jr., and Stanley A. Kochanek, *India: Government and Politics in a Developing Nation*, 7th ed. (Boston: Thomson Wadsworth, 2008).

28. Local government is described and assessed in Girish Kumar, *Local Democracy in India, Interpreting Decentralization* (New Delhi: Sage, 2006).

29. "European Union Election Observation Mission, Federal Republic of Nigeria, Presidential, Gubernatorial, National and State Assembly Elections: 14/21 April 2007: Statement of Preliminary Findings and Conclusions," a press release of the European Union Election Observation Mission to Nigeria, April 23, 2007, http://ec.europa.eu/external_relations/human_rights/eu_election_ass_observ/nigeria/preliminary_statement_23_04_07.pdf (accessed July 21, 2008).

30. See "Eurobarometer 65: Public Opinion in the European Union," Standard Eurobarometer 65 report, January 2007, http://ec.europa.eu/public_opinion/archives/eb/eb65/eb65_en.pdf (accessed June 22, 2008).

31. See Claes H. de Vreese, "Why European Citizens Will Reject the EU Constitution," Center for European Studies Working Paper, no. 116, 3, http://www.ces.fas.harvard.edu/publications/deVreese.pdf (accessed June 25, 2008). The work by Inglehart that de Vreese mentions is Ronald Inglehart, "Cognitive Mobilization and European Identity," *Comparative Politics* 3 (1970): 45–70.

32. Radoslaw Markowskia and Joshua A. Tucker, "Pocketbooks, Politics, and Parties: The 2003 Polish Referendum on EU Membership," *Electoral Studies* 24 (2005): 409–433.

33. "Citizenship and Sense of Belonging," report on Special Eurobarometer Wave 60.1, February 2004, http://ec.europa.eu/public_opinion/archives/ebs/ebs_199.pdf (accessed Jun 27, 2008).

34. David Miliband, "Perspectives on European Integration—A British View," MPIfG Working Paper 02/2, Max Planck Institute for the Study of Societies, March 2002, http://www.mpifg.de/pu/workpap/wp02-2/wp02-2.html (accessed June 24, 2008).

35. de Vreese, 5.

Chapter 3

1. Dulue Mbachu, "The Poverty of Oil Wealth in Nigeria's Delta," *ISN Security Watch*, a publication of the International Relations and Security Network, March 2, 2006, http://www.isn.ethz.ch/news/sw/details.cfm?id=14670 (accessed December 21, 2007).

2. Russell J. Dalton, *Citizen Politics: Public Opinion and Political Parties in Advanced Industrial Democracies*, 3rd ed. (New York: Chatham House, 2002), 147.

3. As Theda Skocpol characterizes Marx's argument, "For Marx, the key to any society is its mode of production or specific combination of socioeconomic forces of production (technology and division of labor) and class relations of property ownership and surplus appropriation." Theda Skocpol, *States and Social Revolutions: A Comparative Analysis of France, Russia, and China* (Cambridge: Cambridge University Press, 1979), 7.

4. This figure is based on a comparison of the percentage of non-Hispanic whites and African Americans in poverty, using the official U.S. government poverty measure. See "Annual Demographic Survey, March Supplement: The Effects of Government Taxes and Transfers on Income and Poverty," U.S. Census Bureau. Available at: http://pubdb3.census.gov/macro/032006/altpov/newpov01_000.htm (accessed October 20, 2008).

5. Abby Goodnough, "Census Shows a Modest Rise in U.S. Income," *New York Times*, August 29, 2007, http://www.nytimes.com/2007/08/29/us/29census.htm (accessed January 8, 2008).

6. Sources on class structure and economic equality include the Organization for Economic Cooperation and Development (OECD), the United Nations Human Development Index (UNHDI), and the World Bank's World Development Index. See http://www.oecd.org/, http://hdr.undp.org/, and http://www.worldbank.org/.

7. Class consciousness is related to a concept, alienation, which was at the center of Marx's early writings. See T. B. Bottomore, trans. and ed., *Karl Marx: Early Writings* (New York, McGraw-Hill, 1964).

8. Russell J. Dalton, *Citizen Politics: Public Opinion and Political Parties in Advanced Western Democracies*, 2nd ed. (Chatham, NJ: Chatham House, 1996), 174.

9. Herbert Kitschelt and Wolfgang Streeck, "From Stability to Stagnation: Germany at the Beginning of the Twenty-First Century," *West European Politics* 26, no. 4 (2003): 1–34. See esp. Table 6.

10. Average unemployment in the eastern *Länder* rose from 16.5 percent in 1991 to 18.3 percent in 2004. For both years, eastern unemployment was more than twice as high as in the western states. See Bertrand Benoit, "Growing Apart: 15 Years After the Wall's Fall, Germany's Two Halves Diverge," *Financial Times*, September 23, 2004.

11. Karl Marx, *The Eighteenth Brumaire of Louis Napoleon*, in *Karl Marx: Selected Writings*, ed. David McLellan (Oxford: Oxford University Press, 2000), p. 347.

12. Among those who discussed France's "200 families" was Leon Trotsky in his 1938 work, *The Death Agony of Capitalism and the Tasks of the Fourth International*. A copy of the text is available at: http://www.marxists.org/archive/trotsky/1938/tp/index.htm (accessed July 24, 2008).

13. David Hoffman, *The Oligarchs: Wealth and Power in the New Russia* (New York: Public Affairs, 2002).

14. Minxin Pei, "Contradictory Trends and Confusing Signals," *Journal of Democracy* 14, no. 1 (2003): 75.

15. An Chen, "The New Inequality," *Journal of Democracy* 14, no. 1 (2003): 55.

16. Naazameen Karmali, "India's Mega Rich: Old and New," *Forbes*, August 14, 2007, http://www.rediff.com/money/2007/aug/14forbes.htm (accessed August 26, 2007).

17. Pavan K. Varma, *The Great Indian Middle Class* (New Delhi: Penguin, 1998), xi and xii.

18. P. Sainath, *Everybody Loves a Good Drought: Stories from India's Poorest Districts* (London: Review, 1996).

19. François Bourguignon, "The Poverty-Growth-Inequality Triangle," paper prepared for the Conference on Poverty, Inequality and Growth, Agence Française de Développement / EU Development Network, Paris, November 13, 2003.

20. "The World Factbook: Brazil," https://www.cia.gov/library/publications/the-world-factbook/geos/br.html, July 15, 2008 (accessed July 31, 2008).

21. Benjamin Senauer and Linda Goetz, "The Growing Middle Class in Developing Countries and the Market for High-Value Food products" (paper prepared for the Workshop on Global Markets for High-Value Food Economic Research Service, USDA, Washington, DC, February 14, 2003) 5.

22. Lloyd Amaghionyeodiwe and Tokunbo Osinubi, "Poverty Reduction Policies and Pro-Poor Growth in Nigeria," *Brazilian Electronic Journal of Economics* 6, no. 1 (2004).

23. See "Country Summary: Nigeria," the United States Census Bureau's International Data Base (IDB) country page on Nigeria, http://www.census.gov/ipc/www/idb/country/niportal.html (accessed July 27, 2008).

24. Friedrich Schneider, "Size and Measurement of the Informal Economy in 110 Countries around the World," paper presented at a workshop of Australian National Tax Centre, ANU, Canberra, Australia, July 17, 2002, 3, http://rru.worldbank.org/Documents/PapersLinks/informal_economy.pdf (accessed October 20, 2008).

25. See *The Inequality Predicament: Report on the World Social Situation 2005* (New York: United Nations Department of Economic and Social Affairs, 2005), ch. 2, www.un.org/esa/socdev/rwss/media%2005/cd-docs/fullreport05.htm (accessed July 15, 2008).

26. Ibid., 33.

27. International Monetary Fund World Economic Outlook Database, April 2008, http://www.imf.org/external/pubs/ft/weo/2008/01/weodata/index.aspx (accessed August 8, 2008).

28. The GDP-related statistics in this chapter's Topic in Countries sections come from the International Monetary Fund World Economic Outlook database, http://www.imf.org/external/pubs/ft/weo/2007/02/weodata/index.aspx (accessed July 24, 2008).

29. Alexander Gerschenkron, *Bread and Democracy in Germany* (Ithaca, NY: Cornell University Press, 1943/1989).

30. Barrington Moore, *The Social Origins of Dictatorship and Democracy: Lord and Peasant in the Making of the Modern World* (Boston: Beacon Press, 1966), xxx.

31. Stephen Padgett, "Political Economy: The German Model Under Stress," in *Developments in German Politics*, ed. Stephen Padgett, William E. Paterson, and Gordon Smith (Durham, NC: Duke University Press, 2003), 123.

32. Charles S. Maier, *Dissolution: The Crisis of Communism and the End of East Germany* (Princeton: Princeton University Press, 1997), ch. 2.

33. Herbert Kitschelt and Wolfgang Streeck, "From Stability to Stagnation: Germany at the Beginning of the Twenty-first Century," *West European Politics* 26, no. 4 (2003): 1–34, Table 1.

34. Benoit.

35. Kitschelt and Streeck, 12–14; Philip Manow and Eric Seils, "Adjusting Badly: The German Welfare State, Structural Change and the Open Economy," in *Welfare and Work in the Open Economy: Diverse Responses to Common Challenges,* vol. 2, ed. Fritz W. Scharpf and Vivien A. Schmidt (Oxford: Oxford University Press, 2000).

36. Anton Hemerijck and Philip Manow, "The Experience of Negotiated Reform in the German and Dutch Welfare State," paper presented at the Varieties of Welfare Capitalism conference, Max Planck Institute for the Study of Societies, Cologne, June 11–13, 1998; Gøsta Esping-Andersen, *The Social Foundations of Post-Industrial Economies* (Oxford: Oxford University Press, 1999); Manow and Seils.

37. Pierre Rosanvallon, *L'État en France de 1789 à nos jours* (Paris: Seuil, 1992).

38. Alexander Gerschenkron, *Economic Backwardness in Historical Perspective* (Cambridge: Belknap Press, 1962).

39. Stanley Hoffmann, "The Effects of World War II on French Society and Politics," *French Historical Studies* 2, no. 1 (1961): 28–63.

40. Minxin Pei, "Contradictory Trends and Confusing Signals," *Journal of Democracy* 14, no. 1 (2003): 75. The IMF puts the bad debt figure for China at 40 percent, but that is still well above most other countries. The U.S. figure is well below 10 percent, while even Mexico is only slightly higher than 10 percent.

41. The work most often associated with post–World War II claims about economic development and democracy is Seymour Martin Lipset's "Some Social Requisites of Democracy: Economic Development and Political Legitimacy," *American Political Science Review* 53, no. 1 (March 1959): 69–105.

42. "World Gas: Mexico—Reform or Bust," *Petroleum Economist*, May 19, 2003, 23–26.

43. Mbachu.

44. For examples of dependency theory works, see Raúl Prebisch, "The Economic Development of Latin America and Its Principal Problems," *Economic Bulletin for Latin America* 7, no. 1. (1962): 1–22; Theotonio dos Santos, "The Structure of Dependence," *American Economic Review* 60, no. 2 (May 1970): 231–236; and Immanuel Wallerstein, *The Modern World System I: Capitalist Agriculture and the Origins of the European World-Economy in the Sixteenth Century* (New York: Academic Press, 1974). For a critical overview of the theory, see Robert A. Packenham, *The Dependency Movement: Scholarship and Politics in Development Studies* (Cambridge, MA: Harvard University Press, 1992). Reading various works by Brazilian sociologist Fernando Henrique Cardoso (who also served two terms as president of Brazil) is also an interesting exercise. Initially one of the leading proponents of dependency theory, by the 1970s Cardoso had become a critic of the dependency perspective.

45. Sanam Vakil, "Iran: The Gridlock Between Demography and Democracy," *SAIS Review* 24, no. 2 (Summer–Fall 2004): 45–53.

46. "Globalization Must Work for the Poor, Says New Research Report," a press release of the World Bank (number 2002/132/S), December 5, 2001, http://go.worldbank.org/DQP7G280Y1 (accessed June 12, 2008).

47. Wolfgang Streeck, "German Capitalism: Does It Exist? Can It Survive?" *New Political Economy* 2, no. 2 (1997): 237–256.

48. Michael Loriaux, "Socialist Monetarism and Financial Liberalization in France," in *Capital Ungoverned:*

Liberalizing Finance in Interventionist States, ed. Michael Loriaux, Meredith Woo-Cumings, Kent E. Calder, Sylvia Maxfield, and Sofia Perez (Ithaca: Cornell University Press, 1997).

49. Sarah Waters, "À l'attac: Globalization and Ideological Renewal on the French Left," *Modern and Contemporary France* 14, no. 2 (2006): 141–156. Members of this movement prefer the term "alter-globalization," rather than "anti-globalization," because they believe it better captures their aim of making sure that non-economic goals, such as human rights, are given priority in the globalization process.

50. Jean-Marie Guehenno, "Globalization and the International System," *Journal of Democracy* 10, no. 1 (1999): 31.

51. Ibid., 32.

52. "Free Trade on Trial: Ten Years After NAFTA," *Economist*, January 3, 2004, 13–16.

53. David Korten's work, *When Corporations Rule the World*, 2nd ed. (Bloomfield, CT: Kumarian Press, 2001), is a more readable but also more alarmist and less scholarly account of the topic compared with Dani Rodrick's *Has Globalization Gone Too Far?* (Washington, DC: Institute of International Economics, 1997).

54. For contrasting views of the race to the bottom idea, see Alan Tonelson, *The Race to the Bottom* (Boulder, CO: Westview Press, 2000) and Thomas L. Friedman, *The Lexus and the Olive Tree* (New York: Farrar, Straus, Giroux, 1999).

55. On corruption, however, a large amount of systematic research—both qualitative and quantitative—has been conducted. One leading source is Transparency International. See http://www.transparency.org.

56. Ross Perot, independent candidate for president of the United States in 1992 and 1996, was especially fond of the "giant sucking sound" phrase when arguing against the launch of NAFTA.

57. It is important to note that this emerging crisis was due only in part to economic issues. Investors were also concerned about political stability after the emergence of the Zapatista National Liberation Army (EZLN, see Chapter 9) and the assassinations of PRI presidential candidate Luis Donaldo Colosio and the PRI's secretary general Ruiz Massieu in 1994.

58. "Free Trade on Trial."

59. But, see Torben Iversen and Thomas R. Cusack, "The Causes of Welfare State Expansion: Deindustrialization or Globalization," *World Politics* 52, no. 3 (April 2000): 313–349. Iversen and Cusack emphasize that domestic economic changes, particularly the shift away from employment in industrial and agricultural sectors, creates demands for government policies independent of the effects of globalization.

Chapter 4

1. Mark Stevenson, "In Mexico, Woman Challenges Indian Rights, Runs for Mayor," *New York Sun*, January 28, 2008, http://www.nysun.com/article/70272 (accessed February 18, 2008).

2. Ibid.

3. Marc Howard Ross, "Culture and Identity in Comparative Political Analysis," in *Comparative Politics: Rationality, Culture, and Structure*, ed. Mark I. Lichbach and Alan S. Zuckerman (Cambridge: Cambridge University Press, 1997), 44.

4. Tom Christensen and B. Guy Peters, *Structure, Culture, and Governance: A Comparison of Norway and the United States* (Lanham, MD: Rowman & Littlefield Publishers, 1999).

5. Leonard Freedman, *Politics and Policy in Britain* (New York: Longman, 1996), 27.

6. Ibid.

7. Ibid., 293.

8. Gabriel A. Almond and Sidney Verba, *The Civic Culture: Political Attitudes and Democracy in Five Nations* (Princeton: Princeton University Press, 1963).

9. David P. Conradt, *The German Polity*, 8th ed. (New York: Pearson/Longman, 2005), 80–89.

10. Charles Maier, *Dissolution: The Crisis of Communism and the End of East Germany* (Princeton, NJ: Princeton University Press, 1997). See especially chs. 1 and 2.

11. Bertrand Benoit, "Growing Apart: 15 Years After the Wall's Fall, Germany's Two Halves Diverge," *Financial Times*, September 23, 2004; see also Conradt, 92.

12. François Furet, "The *Ancien Régime* and The French Revolution," in *Realms of Memory: Rethinking the French Past (Volume 1, Conflicts and Divisions)*, ed. Pierre Nora (New York: Columbia University Press, 1996), 79–108.

13. Pavan K. Varma, *Being Indian: The Truth About Why the 21st Century Will Be India's* (New Delhi: Penguin, 2004), 14.

14. Ibid., 208.

15. Dipankar Gupta, *Mistaken Modernity, India Between Worlds* (New Delhi: Harper Collins, 2000), 30.

16. Ibid., 211. Gupta answers the question about why there are so many "mahatmas" in India by observing that "(i)n societies which resist institutionalization, there is always a need for great people" (Ibid., 42).

17. Ibid., 52, 54.

18. Ibid., 61.

19. See "Geert Hofstede™ Cultural Dimensions: India," http://www.geert-hofstede.com/hofstede_india.shtml (accessed July 31, 2008).

20. Stephen D. Morris, "Corruption and Mexican Political Culture," *Journal of the Southwest* 23, no. 3 (2003): 671–708.

21. For more on the *jeito*, see Keith Rosenn, "The Jeito: Brazil's Institutional Bypass of the Formal Legal System and Its Developmental Implications," *American Journal of Comparative Law* 19, no. 3 (Summer 1971): 514–549.

22. Latinobarómetro 2007 Report ("Informe Latinobarómetro 2007: Banco de Datos en Línea,") November 2007, http://www.latinobarometro.org/ (accessed July 30, 2008), 102.

23. "Geert Hofstede™ Cultural Dimensions: Brazil," http://www.geert-hofstede.com/hofstede_brazil.shtml (accessed August 2, 2008).

24. Ibid.

25. Latinobarómetro 2007 Report, 81.

26. Ibid., 90.

27. Ibid., 93.

28. M. A. O. Aluko, "The Impact of Culture on Organizational Performance in Selected Textile Firms in Nigeria," *Nordic Journal of African Studies* 12, no. 2 (2003): 170.

29. See James T. Gire, "The Varying Effect of Individualism—Collectivism on Preference for Methods of Conflict Resolution," *Canadian Journal of Behavioural Science* 29, no. 1 (January 1997): 38–43.

30. Ronald Inglehart and Daphna Oyserman, "Individualism, Autonomy, and Self-Expression: The Human Development Syndrome," in *Comparing Cultures, Dimensions of Culture in a Comparative Perspective*, ed. Henk Vinken, Joseph Soeters, and Peter Ester (Leiden, Netherlands: Brill, 2004). 74–96, Figure 2.

31. See Ronald Inglehart and Christian Welzel, *Modernization, Cultural Change, and Democracy: The Human Development Sequence* (Cambridge: Cambridge University Press, 2005).
32. Inglehart and Oyserman, Figure 2.
33. Ibid.
34. Ibid.
35. Lyman Tower Sargent, *Contemporary Political Ideologies*, 12th ed. (Belmont, CA: Wadsworth/Thomson, 2003), 63.
36. Eugen Weber, *Peasants into Frenchmen: The Modernization of Rural France, 1870–1914* (Stanford: Stanford University Press, 1976); Laurence Wylie, *A Village in the Vaucluse: An Account of Life in a French Village* (Cambridge: Harvard University Press, 1972).
37. Sudhir Hazareesingh, "The Société d'Instruction Républicaine and the Propagation of Civic Republicanism in Provincial and Rural France," *Journal of Modern History* 71 (June 1999): 271–307.
38. Alejandro Moreno and Patricia Méndez, "Attitudes Toward Democracy: Mexico in Comparative Perspective," working paper, http://www.worldvaluessurvey.org/Upload/5_ArticleMorenoMendez.pdf (accessed August 2, 2008).
39. "Brazil: Statistics," http://www.unicef.org/infobycountry/brazil_statistics.html (accessed July 31, 2008).
40. Boris Lanin, "Putin and Culutre," in *Putin's Russia: Past Imperfect, Future Uncertain*, ed. Dale R. Herspring (Lanham, MD: Rowman & Littlefield, 2005), 81.
41. See "Geert Hofstede™ Cultural Dimensions: China," http://www.geert-hofstede.com/hofstede_china.shtml (accessed August 3, 2008).
42. Ronald Inglehart, *Culture Shift in Advanced Industrial Society* (Princeton, NJ: Princeton University Press, 1989).
43. George Ritzer, *The McDonaldization of Society* (London: Sage, 1993).
44. Samuel P. Huntington, *The Clash of Civilizations and the Remaking of World Order* (New York: Simon & Schuster, 1996).
45. Benjamin R. Barber, *Jihad Versus McWorld* (New York: Ballantine Books, 1995), p. 4.
46. Ibid., 9.
47. Ibid., 221.
48. Japanese business leaders first used the term "glocalization" (the uniting of global trends and local distinctiveness) in the 1980s. The term entered the social science lexicon in the West in the early 1990s.
49. Mahmood Sariolghalam, "Understanding Iran: Getting Past Stereotypes and Mythology," *Washington Quarterly* 26, no. 4 (Autumn 2003): 69–82.
50. Francis Fukuyama, *The End of History and the Last Man* (New York: Free Press, 1992).
51. Gaston V. Rimlinger, *Welfare Policy and Industrialization in Europe, America and Russia* (New York: John Wiley, 1971), 138–148; Gordon Smith, *Democracy in Western Germany: Parties and Politics in the Federal Republic* (New York: Holmes & Meier, 1986).
52. Michael J. Bosia, "Guilty as Charged: Accountability and the Politics of AIDS in France," in *The Global Politics of AIDS*, ed. Patricia Siplon and Paul Harris (Boulder, CO: Lynne Rienner, 2007).
53. Varma, 193.
54. Latinobarómetro 2007 Report, 75.
55. Vladimir Shlapentokh, *A Normal Totalitarian Society: How the Soviet Union Functioned and How It Collapsed* (Armonk, NY: M.E. Sharpe, 2001).
56. Lampton made this comment during an interview on PBS's *Frontline* show in the fall of 2001. See "Interview: David Lampton," *Frontline* interview transcript, http://www.pbs.org/wgbh/pages/frontline/shows/china/interviews/lampton.html (accessed July 21, 2008).
57. See David Graddol, *The Future of English: A Guide to Forecasting the Popularity of the English Language in the 21st Century* (London: British Council, 2000).

Chapter 5

1. Benedict Anderson, *Imagined Communities: Reflections on the Origin and Spread of Nationalism* (London: Verso, 1991).
2. David Laitin, *Identity in Formation: The Russian-Speaking Populations in ihe Near Abroad* (Ithaca: Cornell University Press, 1998).
3. Donald L. Horowitz, *Ethnic Groups in Conflict* (Berkeley: University of California Press, 1985), 12.
4. Ibid., 57.
5. This quotation is cited in Eric Dickson and Kenneth Scheve, "Social Identity, Political Speech, and Electoral Competition" (paper presented at the Eighth Meeting of the Laboratory in Comparative Ethnic Processes, University of Washington at Seattle, October 17, 2003), 1.
6. Kathleen Collins, "The Logic of Clan Politics: Evidence from the Central Asian Trajectories," *World Politics* 56, no. 2 (January 2004): 224–261.
7. Peter J. Schraeder, "From Irredentism to Secession: The Decline of Pan-Somali Nationalism," in *After Independence: Making and Protecting the Nation in Postcolonial and Postcommunist States*, ed. Lowell W. Barrington (Ann Arbor: University of Michigan Press, 2006), 107–137.
8. Thomas J. Reese, *Inside the Vatican: The Politics and Organization of the Catholic Church* (Cambridge, MA: Harvard University Press, 1996), 1.
9. See Ronald Inglehart and Pippa Norris, "The Developmental Theory of the Gender Gap: Women's and Men's Voting Behavior in Global Perspective," *International Political Science Review* 21, no. 4 (2000): 441–463.
10. On relations among the Canadian provinces, see Stephen Brooks, *Canadian Democracy: An Introduction*, 4th ed. (New York: Oxford University Press, 2004).
11. "Population," summary statistics from the "Facts about Germany" website, http://www.tatsachen-ueber-deutschland.de/en/inhaltsseiten-home/zahlen-fakten/bevoelkerung.html (accessed August 25, 2008).
12. Elaine R. Thomas, "Keeping Identity at a Distance: Explaining France's New Legal Restrictions on the Islamic Headscarf," *Ethnic and Racial Studies* 29, no. 2 (March 2006): 237–259.
13. Comte de Clermont-Tonnerre, quoted in Pierre Birnbaum, *Anti-Semitism in France* (Cambridge: Blackwell, 1992), 30.
14. Henry Rousso, *The Vichy Syndrome: History and Memory in France Since 1944* (Cambridge, MA: Harvard University Press, 1991).
15. Alice Conklin, *A Mission to Civilize: The Republican Idea of Empire in France and West Africa 1895–1930* (Stanford: Stanford University Press, 2000).

16. Patricia M.E. Lorcin, *Imperial Identities: Stereotyping, Prejudice and Race in Colonial Algeria* (London: I.B. Tauris, 1999).

17. See Cécile Pelletier, "Minorités particulièrement (in)visibles," *L'Internaute*, June 2007, http://www .linternaute.com/actualite/politique/assemblee-nationale/ portrait-robot-nouvelle-assemblee/5-minorites-invisibles .shtml (accessed August 24, 2008).

18. Fernando Henrique Cardoso, with Brian Winter, *The Accidental President of Brazil: A Memoir* (New York: Public Affairs, 2006), 4.

19. R. Andrew Chesnut, *Born Again in Brazil: The Pentecostal Boom and the Pathogens of Poverty*, (New Brunswick, NJ: Rutgers University Press, 1997), 158.

20. Ibid, 60.

21. Cardoso, 4.

22. Eduardo Telles, "Racial Ambiguity among the Brazilian Population," Working paper series of the California Center for Population Research, May 1, 2001, http:// repositories.cdlib.org/ccpr/olwp/CCPR-012-01 (accessed August 20, 2008).

23. On the question of Muslims in Russia, see Dmitri Glinski, "Russia and Its Muslims: The Politics of Identity at the International-Domestic Frontier," *East European Constitutional Review* 11, nos. 1–2 (Winter/Spring 2002): 71–83.

24. Some associate primordialism with Anthony Smith, one of the world's leading scholars on national identity, though he might be better labeled as a proponent of the "radical middle position." See the discussion in Soren Rinder Bollerup and Christian Dons Christensen, *Nationalism in Eastern Europe* (New York: St. Martin's Press, 1997), 36–38.

25. John L. Comaroff, "Ethnicity, Nationalism, and the Politics of Difference in an Age of Revolution," in *The Politics of Difference: Ethnic Premises in a World of Power*, ed. Edwin N. Wilmsen and Patrick McAllister (Chicago: University of Chicago Press, 1996), 165.

26. Ronald G. Suny, "Nationalism, Nation Making, & the Post-Colonial States of Asia, Africa, & Eurasia," in *After Independence: Making and Protecting the Nation in Postcolonial and Postcommunist States*, ed. Lowell W. Barrington, (Ann Arbor: University of Michigan Press, 2006), 280. Stephen Cornell and Douglas Hartmann offer the label "constructed primordiality," although their description of this approach is still strongly anchored in constructivism's contention that perceptions such as shared blood ties are only powerful because they have been constructed to be powerful. Stephen Cornell and Douglas Hartmann, *Ethnicity and Race: Making Identities in a Changing World* (Thousand Oaks, CA: Pine Forge Press, 1998), 89.

27. Dru C. Gladney, "China's National Insecurity: Old Challenges at the Dawn of the New Millennium" (paper presented at the "2000 Pacific Symposium: Asian Perspectives on The Challenges of China" conference, Washington, DC, March 7–8, 2000).

28. Dru C. Gladney, "China's Ethnic Divisions Are Showing Up and Could Cause Trouble," *International Herald Tribune*, February 22, 1995, www.iht.com/articles/1995/02/22/ eddru.php (accessed August 24, 2008).

29. "Nigeria: International Religious Freedom Report 2004," a publication of the Bureau of Democracy, Human Rights, and Labor of the U.S. Department of State, September 15, 2004, http://www.state .gov/g/drl/ rls/irf/2004/35376.htm (accessed August 14, 2008).

30. For an overview of Azeri identity and implications for Iran, see Brenda Shaffer, *Borders and Brethren: Iran and the Challenge of Azerbaijani Identity* (Cambridge, MA: MIT Press, 2002).

31. See Amy G. Mazur, *Theorizing Feminist Policy* (Oxford: Oxford University Press, 2002).

32. For example, Christina Hoff Sommers has criticized the use of anecdotes in the landmark work of social psychologist Carol Gilligan (including in Gilligan's 1982 book *In a Different Voice*). See Amy Benfer, "Battle of the Celebrity Gender Theorists," *Salon.com*, March 9, 2001, http://archive.salon.com/mwt/feature/2001/03/09/ sommers/index.html (accessed July 25, 2008).

33. Jon Jeter, "Affirmative Action Debate Forces Brazil to Take a Look in the Mirror," June 16, 2003, A01, http://www .washingtonpost.com/ac2/wp-dyn/A62685-2003Jun15 (accessed June 17, 2008).

34. Arend Lijphart, *Democracy in Plural Societies: A Comparative Exploration* (New Haven, CT: Yale University Press, 1977).

35. Horowitz, *Ethnic Groups in Conflict*.

36. Elizabeth Fromberg, "Ethnic Conflict, Secession, and Political Violence in Tatarstan and Chechnya: The Role of the Russian State" (paper presented at the IREX Caucasus Regional Policy Symposium, Shepherdstown, WV, March 25–28, 2004), 1–3.

37. Mark Cichock, *Russian and Eurasian Politics: A Comparative Approach* (New York: Longman, 2003), 143.

38. Fromberg, 2–3. Because their birthrates are higher than those of ethnic Russians, Tatars have since become a majority of the republic.

39. Ibid., 2.

40. Dru C. Gladney, "The Chinese Program of Development and Control, 1978–2001," in *Xinjiang: China's Muslim Borderland*, ed. S. Frederick Starr (Armonk, NY: M.E. Sharpe, 2004), 118.

41. Pradeep K. Chhibber and John R. Petrocik, "The Puzzle of Indian Politics: Social Cleavages and the Indian Party System," *British Journal of Political Science* 19, no. 2 (April 1989), 191.

42. Ernst B. Haas, *The Dismal Fate of New Nations*, vol. 2 of *Nationalism, Liberalism, and Progress*, (Ithaca, NY: Cornell University Press, 2000), 158.

43. The term "bargain" has especially been applied to the integrationist approach taken in Malaysia. See Diane Mauzy, "From Malay Nationalism to a Malaysian Nation?" in *After Independence: Making and Protecting the Nation in Postcolonial and Postcommunist States*, ed. Lowell W. Barrington (Ann Arbor: University of Michigan Press, 2006), 45–70.

44. "No 10 Plays Down 'Ethnic Rebrand,'" BBC News, online edition, August 8, 2005, http://news .bbc.co.uk/2/ hi/uk_news/4130594.stm (accessed August 24, 2008).

45. Carl-Ulrik Schierup, Peo Hansen, and Stephen Castles, "The 'Migration Crisis' and the New European Diversity," in *Migration, Citizenship and the European Welfare State* (Oxford: Oxford University Press, 2006), 30–32.

46. Veysel Oezcan, "Changes to German Law Help Boost Naturalization Numbers," *Migration Information Source*, a publication of the Migration Policy Institute, August 2003, http://www.migrationinformation.org/Feature/display.cfm?id=152 (accessed July 23, 2008).

47. Ludwig Siegele, "Thinning blood," in "Waiting for a Wunder: A Survey of Germany," *Economist*, February 11, 2006, 12–14.

48. J. Christopher Soper and Joel S. Fetzer, "Explaining the Accommodation of Muslim Religious Practices in France, Britain, and Germany," *French Politics* 1, no. 1 (March 2003) 47-48, 51-52.

49. Siegele, "Thinning Blood," 13.

50. See "Decision n° 2007-557 DC November 15ᵗʰ 2007," http://www.conseil-constitutionnel.fr/langues/anglais/a2007557dc.pdf (accessed February 28, 2008).

51. Joan Wallach Scott, "French Universalism in the 1990s," *Differences* 15, no. 2 (Summer 2004): 32–53.

52. See Lea Sgier, "Discourses of Gender Quotas," *European Political Science* (online version) 3, no. 3 (Summer 2004) http://www.essex.ac.uk/ecpr/publications/eps/onlineissues/summer2004/research/sgier.htm (accessed July 23, 2008).

53. Éric Fassin, "The Politics of PaCS in a Transatlantic Mirror: Same Sex Unions and Sexual Difference in France Today," in *Beyond French Feminisms: Debates on Women, Politics, and Culture in France, 1981–2001*, ed. Roger Célestin, Eliane Françoise DalMolin, Isabelle De Courtivron (New York: Palgrave Macmillan, 2003).

54. Franz Fanon, *A Dying Colonialism* (New York: Grove Press, 1994).

55. At the same time, the Chinese government has refused to address the question of whether certain groups are "indigenous" to the territories in which they presently reside. See Gladney, "The Chinese Program," 102.

56. Dru C. Gladney, "Prisoner's Release Does Not Herald a Xinjiang Spring," *YaleGlobal*, March 30, 2005, http://yaleglobal.yale.edu/display.article?id=5497 (accessed June 19, 2008).

57. "Nigeria: International Religious Freedom Report 2004."

58. "Nigeria," *Policy Focus*, a publication of the United States Commission on International Religious Freedom, Washington, DC, August 2004, 2.

59. "Ethnic Minorities Singled Out for Attack in Iran," *Wire* 35, no. 9 (October 2005), http://www.amnesty.org/en/library/asset/NWS21/009/2005/en/dom-NWS210092005en.html (accessed August 24, 2008).

60. Larry Diamond, "Nigeria: Pluralism, Statism, and the Struggle for Democracy," in *Politics in Developing Countries: Comparing Experiences with Democracy*, ed. Larry Diamond, Juan J. Linz, and Seymour Martin Lipset (Boulder, CO: Lynne Rienner, 1990), 358.

61. Indeed, a number of such book-length studies exist. See, for example, John De St. Jorre, *The Nigerian Civil War* (London: Hodder and Stoughton, 1972); Frederick Forsyth, *Biafra Story: The Making of an African Legend* (New York: Penguin, 1977); and Alfred Obiora Uzokwe, *Surviving in Biafra: The Story of the Nigerian Civil War* (Lincoln, NE: iUniverse, Inc., 2003).

Chapter 6

1. Borscht is a Russian beet soup.

2. Thomas A. Koelble, "The New Institutionalism in Political Science," *Comparative Politics* 27, no. 2 (1995): 231.

3. Karen Orren and Stephen Skowronek, "Beyond the Iconography of Order: Notes for a 'New Institutionalism,'" in *The Dynamics of American Politics: Approaches and Interpretations*, ed. Larry Dodd and Calvin Wilson (Boulder, CO: Westview Press, 1994), 325.

4. Robert A. Dahl, *Polyarchy: Participation and Opposition* (New Haven, CT: Yale University Press, 1971).

5. See Robert A. Dahl, *A Preface to Democratic Theory* (Chicago: University of Chicago Press, 1956), esp. ch. 1.

6. See Arend Lijphart, "Dimensions of Democracies," *European Journal of Political Research* 31, nos. 1–2 (February 1997): 193–204.

7. Robert Dahl, *On Democracy* (New Haven, CT: Yale University Press, 1998).

8. Carl J. Friedrich and Zbigniew K. Brzezinski, *Totalitarian Dictatorship and Autocracy* (Cambridge, MA: Harvard University Press, 1956) and Hannah Arendt, *The Origins of Totalitarianism* (New York: Harcourt, Brace, 1951).

9. Linz and O'Donnell are the scholars most associated with developing the core ideas surrounding authoritarianism in comparative politics. See Juan Linz, "An Authoritarian Regime: Spain," in *Mass Politics: Studies in Political Sociology*, ed. Erik Allardt and Stein Rokkan (New York: Free Press, 1970), 252–283; and Guillermo O'Donnell, *Modernization and Bureaucratic Authoritarianism: Studies in South American Politics* (Berkeley: University of California Press, 1973).

10. Arend Lijphart, *Patterns of Democracy* (New Haven, CT: Yale University Press, 1999).

11. Stephen Ingle, "Overview: A Wilderness Year," *Parliamentary Affairs* 58, no. 2 (2005): 199.

12. V. R. Berghahn, *Modern Germany: Society, Economy and Politics in the Twentieth Century*, 2nd ed. (Cambridge: Cambridge University Press, 1987), 18–22.

13. Ibid., 93–95.

14. Peter J. Katzenstein, *Policy and Politics in West Germany: The Growth of a Semisovereign State* (Philadelphia: Temple University Press, 1987).

15. Ibid. See also the discussion of German corporatism by Wolfgang Streeck and Philippe C. Schmitter, "Community, Market, State—and Associations? The Prospective Contribution of Interest Governance to Social Order," *European Sociological Review* 1, no. 2 (September 1985): 119–138.

16. Ezra Suleiman, *Elites in French Society* (Princeton, NJ: Princeton University Press, 1978).

17. Andrew Knapp, "Prometheus (Re-)Bound? The Fifth Republic and Checks on Executive Power," in *Developments in French Politics*, ed. Alistair Cole, Patrick Le Galès, and Johan Levy (New York: Palgrave Macmillan, 2005).

18. Orren and Skowronek, "Beyond the Iconography of Order," 313.

19. See "Combined Average Ratings: Independent Countries, 2008," Freedom House, http://www.freedomhouse.org/template.cfm?page=410&year=2008 (accessed September 6, 2008).

20. See p. 7 of Ellen Immergut, "The Theoretical Core of the New Institutionalism," *Politics and Society* 26, no. 1 (March 1998): 5–34.

21. Adam Przeworski, "Institutions Matter?" *Government and Opposition* 39, no. 4 (2004): 527–540.

22. Thomas A. Koelble, "The New Institutionalism in Political Science," *Comparative Politics* 27, no. 2 (1995): 232.

23. Vernon Bogdanor, "Constitutional Reform in Britain: The Quiet Revolution," *Annual Review of Political Science* 8 (2005): 73–98.

24. Matthew Flinders, "Majoritarian Democracy in Britain: New Labour and the Constitution," *West European Politics* 28, no. 1 (January 2005): 61–93.

25. Bogdanor.
26. See Flinders, 64.
27. Ibid., Table 3. Flinders points out, for example, that although the reforms of the House of Lords were supposed to pave the way for a more representative and powerful upper house, the elimination of most of the hereditary peers in the House of Lords has weakened its role as a check on the House of Commons.
28. Gaston V. Rimlinger, *Welfare Policy and Industrialization in Europe, America and Russia* (New York: John Wiley, 1971), 139.
29. *Basic Law for the Federal Republic of Germany,* Promulgated by the Parliamentary Council on May 23, 1949 (Bonn: Press and Information Office of the Federal Republic, March 1995), 22.
30. Rimlinger, 138–148, esp. p. 139.
31. Douglas Johnson, "De Gaulle and the Founding of the Fifth Republic," *History Today* 33, no. 6 (June 1983): 5–11.
32. William Safran, *The French Polity*, 6th ed. (New York: Longman, 2003).
33. Ministry of Law and Justice, Government of India, *Constitution of India (Updated up to 94th Amendment Act)*, http://indiacode.nic.in/coiweb/welcome.html (accessed September 9, 2008).
34. Chappell Lawson, "Fox's Mexico at Midterm," *Journal of Democracy* 15, no. 1 (January 2004): 149.
35. Fernando Henrique Cardoso, *The Accidental President of Brazil: A Memoir* (New York: Public Affairs, 2006), 166.
36. See "Title VIII: The Social Order," Federative Republic of Brazil, Constitution of 1988 with 1996 reforms in English, http://pdba.georgetown.edu/Constitutions/Brazil/brtitle8.html (accessed September 3, 2008).
37. Ingle, 207.
38. Ibid., 208.
39. Ibid., 209.
40. Katzenstein, *Policy and Politics in West Germany*, 45–50; Gordon Smith, *Democracy in Western Germany*, 3rd ed. (Aldershot: Gower, 1986), xx.
41. Katzenstein, 16.
42. David P. Conradt, *The German Polity*, 8th ed. (New York: Pearson/Longman, 2005), 199.
43. Hugh Williamson, "Germany to Make Big Changes to Constitution," *Financial Times*, July 1, 2006, 2.
44. Jonah Levy, *Tocqueville's Revenge: State, Society, and Economy in Contemporary France* (Cambridge: Harvard University Press, 1999).
45. Harvey B. Feigenbaum, "Centralization and National Integration in France," *Mediterranean Quarterly* 8, no. 1 (Winter 1997): 60–76.
46. Levy.
47. Patrick Le Galès, "Reshaping the State? Administrative and Decentralization Reforms," in *Developments in French Politics*, ed. Alistair Cole, Patrick Le Galès, and Johan Levy (New York: Palgrave Macmillan, 2005).
48. Robert Hardgrave Jr. and Stanley A. Kochanek, *India: Government and Politics in a Developing Nation*, 7th ed. (Boston: Thompson Wadsworth, 2008), 84.
49. The total number of members cannot exceed one-third of the total number of members of the Legislative Assembly; one-third is elected every two years; and they cannot be dismissed by the dissolution of the Legislative Council.
50. Hardgrave and Kochanek, *India*, 129–136.
51. R. Andrew Nickson, *Local Government in Latin America* (Boulder, CO: Lynne Rienner Press, 1995), 118.
52. Ibid., 52
53. Ibid., 44.
54. Ibid.,121–122.
55. See Gabriella Montinola, Yingyi Qian, and Barry R. Weingast, "Federalism, Chinese Style: The Political Basis for Economic Success in China," *World Politics* 48, no. 1 (October 1995): 50–81.
56. See Yahong Li, "The Law-Making Law: A Solution to the Problems in the Chinese Legislative System?" *Perspectives* 2, no. 2, http://www.oycf.org/Perspectives/8_103100/lawmakinglaw.htm (accessed September 6, 2008).
57. Kian Tajbakhsh, "Political Decentralization and the Creation of Local Government in Iran: Consolidation or Transformation of the Theocratic State?," *Social Research* 67, no. 2 (Summer 2000): 377-404.
58. Ibid.
59. The definitive work on veto points is George Tsebelis, *Veto Players: How Political Institutions Work* (Princeton, NJ: Princeton University Press, 2002).
60. Ibid., ch. 1.
61. Comparativist Duane Swank states that the changes under her watch were "notable." See Duane Swank, "Withering Welfare?: Globalisation, Political Economic Institutions, and Contemporary Welfare States," in *State in the Global Economy: Bringing Domestic Institutions Back In*, ed. Linda Weiss (Cambridge, UK: Cambridge University Press, 2003), 71.
62. Przeworski, 530.
63. Ibid., 528.

Chapter 7

1. Some have labeled this trend "presidentialization." See Thomas Poguntke and Paul Webb, eds., *The Presidentialization of Politics: A Comparative Study of Modern Democracies* (Oxford: Oxford University Press, 2005).
2. The concept of separation of powers is found in the works of John Locke and the *Federalist Papers*, especially those by James Madison. See John Locke, *Two Treatises of Government*, ed. Peter Laslett (Cambridge, MA: Harvard University Press, 1960) and Clinton Rossiter, ed., *The Federalist Papers* (New York: Mentor Books, 1961).
3. See Juan J. Linz, "The Perils of Presidentialism," *Journal of Democracy* 1, no. 4 (Winter 1990): 51–69; Donald L. Horowitz, "Comparing Democratic Systems," *Journal of Democracy* 1, no. 4 (Winter 1990): 73–79.
4. Horowitz.
5. Stanley Hoffmann, "The Effects of World War II on French Society and Politics," *French Historical Studies* 2, no. 1 (Spring 1961): 29.
6. Hoffmann notes that within two years, there were at least six books on the new republic in English. Stanley Hoffmann, "de Gaulle's Republic," *Political Science Quarterly* 75, no. 4 (December 1960): 554–559.
7. See Gary W. Cox and Matthew McCubbins, *Legislative Leviathan: Party Government in the House* (Berkeley: University of California Press, 1993).
8. David P. Conradt, *The German Polity*, 8th ed. (New York: Pearson Longman, 2005), 199.

9. Hugh Williamson, "Germany to Make Big Changes to Constitution," *Financial Times*, July 1, 2006.

10. "Frayed Tempers Cost Parliament Dear: Report," *Deccan Herald*, January 20, 2006, cited by Social Watch India, http://www.socialwatchindia.net/news_page1.asp?newsid=35 (accessed September 5, 2008).

11. Both the *Lok Sabha* and the *Rajya Sabha* have websites with considerable current and historical information. See http://loksabha.nic.in/, http://rajyasabha.nic.in, and http://parliamentofindia.nic.in/ls/intro/introls.htm (accessed September 8, 2008).

12. See Howard Handelman, *Mexican Politics: The Dynamics of Change* (New York: St. Martin's Press, 1997).

13. Stephen Haber, "Mexican Gridlock," *Hoover Institution Weekly Essays*, August 26–September 22, 2002.

14. "Mexico Lawmakers Stop Fox Speech," BBC News report, September 2, 2006, http://news.bbc.co.uk/1/hi/world/americas/5307038.stm (accessed September 4, 2008).

15. Much of the analysis here draws from Barry Ames's excellent book, *The Deadlock of Democracy in Brazil* (Ann Arbor: University of Michigan Press, 2001).

16. The Jospin government vacillated on the PaCS law (see Chapter 5), with some ministers encouraging dissension, though it never opposed the law. The proposal was originally introduced in the National Assembly by deputies from the leftist parties that would come together in a coalition to win the 1997 election, and reintroduced and passed after the new coalition took office. See Eric Fassin, "The Politics of PaCS in the Transatlantic Mirror," in *Beyond French Feminisms: Debates on Women, Politics, and Culture in France, 1981–2001*, ed. Roger Célestin, Eliane DalMolin, and Isabelle de Courtivron (New York: Palgrave Macmillan, 2003).

17. Clinton Rossiter uses this term in his book, *The American Presidency* (New York: Mentor, 1960).

18. Conradt, 219.

19. This scenario has also been repeated in subsequent elections within the *Länder*. See Hugh Williamson, "Defiant Beck Sees Links With Left as SPD's Salvation," *Financial Times*, March 11, 2008, 2.

20. Soutik Biswas, "India's Architect of Reforms," BBC News, October 14, 2005, http://news.bbc.co.uk/go/pr/fr/-/1/hi/world/south_asia/3725357.stm (accessed March 24, 2008).

21. Denise Dresser, "Mexico: From PRI Predominance to Divided Democracy," in *Constructing Democratic Governance in Latin America*, ed. Jorge I. Domínguez and Michael Shifter, 2nd ed. (Baltimore, MD: Johns Hopkins University Press, 2003), 321–347. See p. 325.

22. "Mexico's Fox Vows to Block 'Irresponsible' Budget," *Washington Post*, November 20, 2004, p. A11.

23. Samuel Kernell, *Going Public: New Strategies of Presidential Leadership* (Washington, DC: CQ Press, 1997).

24. Others, such as George Edwards, challenge the idea that presidential efforts to use the bully pulpit actually change public opinion or lead to policy successes. See George C. Edwards III, *On Deaf Ears: The Limits of the Bully Pulpit* (New Haven, CT: Yale University Press, 2003).

25. Press Conference, January 31, 1964, quoted in Jean V. Poulard, "The French Double Executive and the Experience of Cohabitation," *Political Science Quarterly* 105, no. 2 (Summer 1990): 248.

26. The president also appoints the representatives to the seven federal districts. See Mark Chicock, *Russian and Comparative Politics: A Comparative Approach* (New York: Longman, 2003), chs. 5–6.

27. Andrea Chandler, "Presidential Veto Power in Post-Communist Russia, 1994–1998," *Canadian Journal of Political Science* 34, no. 3 (September 2001): 487–516.

28. See Thomas F. Remington, *Politics in Russia*, 3rd ed. (New York: Pearson Longman, 2004), ch. 3.

29. See, e.g., Claire Bigg, "Does Russia Care What The West Thinks?," a *Features* article of Radio Free Europe/Radio Liberty, August 29, 2008, http://www.rferl.org/content/Article/1194876.html (accessed September 9, 2008) and "Who Rules Russia: Putin or Medvedev?," *The Daily Telegraph* online edition, September 5, 2008, http://www.telegraph.co.uk/opinion/main.jhtml?xml=/opinion/2008/05/09/dl0902.xml (accessed September 9, 2008).

Chapter 8

1. Sanjeev Sabhlok, "Reform the Bureaucracy," *Times of India*, July 30, 2007, http://timesofindia.indiatimes.com/Editorial/Reform_the_bureaucracy/articleshow/2242779.cms (accessed September 12, 2008).

2. J. K. Rowling, *Harry Potter and the Deathly Hallows* (New York: Arthur A. Levine Books/Scholastic, Inc., 2007).

3. Benjamin H. Barton, "Harry Potter and the Half-Crazed Bureaucracy," *Michigan Law Review* 104, no 6 (2006): 1525.

4. C. Neal Tate, "Past, Present, and Future with the 'Comparative Advantage': Part I, 1892–1989," *Law and Courts* (newsletter of the Law and Courts Section of the American Political Science Association) 12, no. 2 (Spring 2002): 1, 3–10.

5. Christopher Wolfe, "The Rehnquist Court and 'Conservative Judicial Activism'" in *That Eminent Tribunal: Judicial Supremacy and the Constitution*, ed. Christopher Wolfe (Princeton, N.J.: Princeton University Press, 2004), 199–224.

6. Laurence H. Tribe, Jeremy Waldron, and Mark Tushnet, "On Judicial Review," *Dissent*, Summer 2005, http://www.dissentmagazine.org/article/?article=219 (accessed September 4, 2008).

7. Tom Ginsburg, *Judicial Review in New Democracies: Constitutional Courts in Asian Cases* (Cambridge: Cambridge University Press, 2003), 3.

8. Ibid., 4.

9. Gaston V. Rimlinger, *Welfare Policy and Industrialization in Europe, America and Russia* (New York: John Wiley and Sons, 1971), 139.

10. David P. Conradt, *The German Polity*, 8th ed. (New York: Pearson Longman, 2005), 251.

11. Ibid., 252.

12. Ibid., 249. See also Douglas Webber, "Die Kassenärztlichen Vereinigungen zwischen Mitgliederinteressen und Gemeinwohl," in *Verbände zwischen Mitgliederinteressen und Gemeinwohl*, ed. Renate Mayntz, (Gütersloh: Verlag Bertelsmann Stiftung, 1992).

13. Peter J. Katzenstein, *Policy and Politics in West Germany: The Growth of a Semisovereign State* (Philadelphia: Temple University Press, 1987), 58–60, 74–76.

14. Reported by Cécile Prieur, "Une dizaine de ministres ont été condamnés depuis la Révolution française: Le principe de la responsabilité pénale des ministres remonte à 1789," *Le Monde*, March 11, 1999.

15. Maurice Agulhon, *The French Republic 1879–1992* (Oxford: Basil Blackwell, 1993).

16. Jacques Vergès, *La Justice est un jeu* (Paris: Albin Michel, 1992), 98.

17. Michel de S.-O.-l'E. Lasser, "Judicial (Self-) Portraits: Judicial Discourse in the French Legal System," *Yale Law Journal* 104, no. 6 (April 1995): 1325–1410.

18. Doris Marie Provine, "Courts in the Political Process in France," in *Courts, Law, and Politics in Comparative Perspective*, ed. Herbert Jacob, Erhard Blankenburg, Herbert M. Kritzer, and Doris Marie Provine (New Haven: Yale University, 1996), 177–248.

19. Ibid.

20. Jodi Finkel, "Judicial Reform as Insurance Policy: Mexico in the 1990s," *Latin American Politics & Society* 47, no. 1 (Spring 2005): 87–113.

21. Jose Antonio Caballero Juarez and Hugi A. Concha Cantu, "The Elements of Judicial Reform: A Multidisciplinary Proposal for Studying Mexican State Courts," *Mexican Law Review* 1 (January–June 2004), http://info8.juridicas.unam.mx/cont/1/arc/arc1.htm (accessed September 16, 2008).

22. However, Brazilian law requires all judges to retire at the age of seventy.

23. "Economic Effects of Legal Infrastructure: Effect of Brazilian Restructuring," *Emerging Market Strategies* 3, no 3 (June 25, 1999), http://www.emergingmarketstrategies.com/brazil.htm (accessed September 3, 2008).

24. Ibid.

25. "Brazil — Supreme Court," http://www.v-brazil.com/government/judiciary-branch/supreme-court.html (accessed September 6, 2008).

26. See, for example, "Brazil: Investment Climate Assessment, Volume I: Executive Summary and Policy Recommendations," a World Bank document, December 6, 2005, http://www.enterprisesurveys.org/documents/enterprisesurveys/ICA/Brazil_Volume%20I.pdf (accessed September 12, 2008).

27. "Nigeria: Time for Justice and Accountability," *AI Index*, AFR 44/014/2000 (December 21, 2000), http://www.amnesty.org/en/library/asset/AFR44/014/2000/en/dom-AFR440142000en.html (accessed August 23, 2008).

28. Somnath Chatterjee, "Foreword," in *The Supreme Court Versus the Constitution: A Challenge to Federalism*, ed. Pran Chopra (New Delhi: Sage Publications, 2006), 12–13.

29. Soli Sorabjee, "The Ideal Remedy: A Valediction," in *The Supreme Court Versus the Constitution: A Challenge to Federalism*, ed. Pran Chopra (New Delhi: Sage Publications, 2006), 204.

30. An example of the reactions is the editorial appearing in *The Hindu*: "Constitutionally Off-Track," *The Hindu*, October 3, 2007, http://www.thehindu.com/2007/10/03/stories/2007100353901000.htm (accessed October 2, 2007).

31. M. V. Kamath, "Justice Delayed Is Justice Denied," *News Today*, June 5, 2006, available on Sify News at http://sify.com/news/fullstory.php?id=14225041 (accessed October 6, 2007).

32. "Putin Approves Move of Russia's Constitutional Court to St. Petersburg," *International Herald Tribune*, February 5, 2007, http://www.iht.com/articles/ap/2007/02/05/europe/EU-GEN-Russia-Court-Move.php (accessed March 15, 2008).

33. John Ferejohn, "Judicializing Politics, Politicizing Law," *Law and Contemporary Problems* 65, no. 3 (June 2002): 63.

34. Cornell W. Clayton, "The Supply and Demand Sides of Judicial Policy-Making (Or, Why Be So Positive About the Judicialization of Politics?)," *Law and Contemporary Problems* 65, no. 3 (June 2002): 72.

35. Ibid.

36. Shannon Ishiyama Smithey and John Ishiyama, "Judicial Activism in Post-Communist Politics," *Law & Society Review* 36, no. 4 (January 2002): 719–742; Erik S. Herron and Kirk A. Randazzo, "The Relationship Between Independence and Judicial Review in Post-Communist Courts," *Journal of Politics* 65, no. 2 (May 2003): 422–438.

37. "Russian Federation, Attacks on Justice 2002," an International Commission of Jurists report, Geneva, August 27, 2002, http://www.icj.org/news.php3?id_article=2690&lang=en (accessed September 6, 2008).

38. Philip P. Pan, "In China, Turning the Law into the People's Protector," *Washington Post*, December 28, 2004, A1.

39. Ibid.

40. Mei-Ying Gechlik, "Judicial Reform in China: Lessons from Shanghai," *Columbia Journal of Asian Law* 19, no. 1 (Spring–Fall 2005): 97–137.

41. Ibid, 98.

42. Hootan Shambayati, "A Tale of Two Mayors: Courts and Politics in Iran and Turkey," *International Journal of Middle East Studies* 36, no. 2 (May 2004): 253–275.

43. According to Amnesty International, there were at least ten executions of individuals under the age of eighteen from 1990 to 2005. See "Iran: Amnesty International Outraged at Reported Execution of a 16 Year Old Girl," *Amnesty International Public Statement*, AI Index News Service No: 210 (August 23, 2004), http://www.amnesty.org/en/library/asset/MDE13/036/2004/en/dom-MDE130362004en.html (accessed September 18, 2003).

44. Ibid.

45. Stephen Brooks, *Canadian Democracy: An Introduction*, 4th ed. (Oxford: Oxford University Press, 2004), 239.

46. John Ferejohn and Charles Shipan, "Congressional Influence on Bureaucracy," *Journal of Law, Economics, and Organization* 6 (1990): 3.

47. Ibid, 2.

48. See Scott N. Schools, "An Overview of the General Counsel's Office of the Executive Office for United States Attorneys," *The United States Attorneys' Bulletin* 55, no. 3 (May 2007): 2–3.

49. James Q. Wilson, *Bureaucracy: What Government Agencies Do and Why They Do It* (New York: Basic Books, 1989), 334–335.

50. Ibid., 317–325.

51. Ibid., 326–327.

52. Roger D. Masters, *The Nature of Politics* (New Haven: Yale University Press, 1989), 204.

53. Wilson, 221.

54. Leonard Freeman, *Politics and Policy in Britain* (New York: Longman, 1996), 154–155.

55. Terry M. Moe, "The Politics of Structural Choice: Toward a Theory of Public Bureaucracy," in *Organizational Theory: From Chester Barnard to the Present and Beyond*, ed. Oliver E. Williamson (New York: Oxford University Press, 1990) 116–153.

56. Ibid., 145.

57. Freeman, 154–156.

58. Ibid.

59. Alexander Gerschenkron, *Economic Backwardness in Historical Perspective* (Cambridge, MA: Belknap Press, 1962).

60. Conradt, 232.

61. Katzenstein, 19–22; Conradt, 229–231.

62. Conradt, 229; Katzenstein, 19–22.

63. Statistics in this section are from Patrick Le Galès, "Reshaping the State: Administrative and Decentralization Reforms," in *Developments in French Politics 3*, ed. Alistair Cole, Patrick Le Galès, and Jonah Levy (New York: Palgrave Macmillan, 2005).

64. Ezra Suleiman, *Elites in French Society: The Politics of Survival* (Princeton, NJ: Princeton University Press, 1978).

65. Michael Loriaux, "France: A New Capitalism of Voice?" in *States in the Global Economy*, ed. Linda Weiss (New York: Cambridge University Press, 2003).

66. Andy Smith, "The Europeanization of the French State," in *Developments in French Politics 3*, ed. Alistair Cole, Patrick Le Galès, and Jonah Levy (New York: Palgrave Macmillan, 2005).

67. Kristopher Mendez, "Mexico's New Hope: Vicente Fox and a Vision for Reform," *Harvard International Review* 22 , no. 4 (Winter 2000), http://www.harvardir.org/articles/876/ (accessed September 4, 2008).

68. George W. Grayson, "Mexico Prefers to Export Its Poor, Not Uplift Them," *Christian Science Monitor*, March 30, 2006, http://www.csmonitor.com/2006/0330/p09s02-coop.html (accessed September 3, 2008).

69. See "Corruption Perceptions Index 2007," Transparency International, http://www.transparency.org/policy_research/surveys_indices/cpi/2007 (last modified July 10, 2008; accessed September 16, 2008).

70. Kim R. Holmes, Edwin J. Feulner, Mary Anastasia O'Grady, et al., *2008 Index of Economic Freedom* (Washington, DC: The Heritage Foundation, 2008).

71. The data are available at http://info.worldbank.org/governance/wbes/questions3.asp (accessed September 17, 2008). Data are not provided for Iran.

72. M. A. O. Aluko and A.A. Adesopo, "An Appraisal of the Two Faces of Bureaucracy in Relation to the Nigerian Society," *Journal of Social Science* 8 no. 1 (2004): 18.

73. Ibid., 19.

74. Robert Hardgrave Jr. and Stanley Kochanek, *India: Government and Politics in a Developing Nation*, 7th ed. (Boston, MA: Thomson Wadsworth, 2008), 108–109.

75. Ibid., 110.

76. Ibid., 109.

77. Bimal Jalan, *Future of India: Politics, Economics and Governance* (New Delhi: Penguin, 2006), 105.

78. For more on the *nomenklatura*, see Dmitriy Gershenson and Hershall I. Grossman, "Cooption and Repression in the Soviet Union," *Economics and Politics* 13, no. 1 (March 2001): 31–47.

79. Peter Finn, "Tycoon Decries Russia's 'Criminal Bureaucracy' as Trial Ends," *Washington Post*, April 12, 2005, A15.

80. *Anti-Corruption in Transition #3: Who is Succeeding . . . And Why?* (Washington, DC: World Bank, July 2006).

81. Suzanne Maloney, "Islam and Iran's Postrevolutionary Economy: The Case of the Bonyads," in *Gods, Guns, and Globalization: Religious Radicalism and International Political Economy*, ed. Mary Ann Tetreault and Robert A. Denemark (Boulder, CO: Lynne Rienner Publishers, 2004), 201.

82. "Iran: Special Report on Bam—One Year after the Devastating Earthquake," UN Office for the Coordination of Humanitarian Affairs, January 4, 2005, http://www.irinnews.org/Report.aspx?ReportId=24530 (accessed August 24, 2008).

83. Samuel P. Huntington, "Reforming Civil-Military Relations," *Journal of Democracy* 6, no. 4 (1995): 9–17.

84. See, for example, Dale R. Herspring, "Civil-Military Relations in Post-Communist Eastern Europe: The Potential for Praetorianism," *Studies in Comparative Communism* 25, no. 2 (1992): 99–122.

85. Ian Herbert, "Are British Troops at Breaking Point in Iraq?" *Independent*, October 18, 2005.

86. Conradt, 207.

87. Ibid., 208.

88. Ronald E. Ahnen, "The Politics of Police Violence in Democratic Brazil," *Latin American Politics and Society* 49, no. 1(Spring 2007): 141–164.

89. "Brazil: 'They Come in Shooting': Policing Socially Excluded Communities," AI Index: AMR 19/033/2005, December 2, 2005, http://www.amnesty.org/en/library/asset/AMR19/033/2005/en/dom-AMR190332005en.html (accessed August 22, 2008).

90. One such scholar was Claude Welch, who wrote in 1995 that "were the armed forces of Nigeria to disengage, they would, in fact, be equally likely to hasten back." Claude E. Welch Jr., "Civil-Military Agonies in Nigeria: Pains of an Unaccomplished Transition," *Armed Forces and Society* 21, no. 4 (Summer 1995): 593–614. The quotation is on pages 593–594.

91. Ibid.

92. Alfred Stepan, "The New Professionalism of Internal Warfare and Military Role Expansion," in *Authoritarian Brazil: Origins, Policies, and Future*, ed. Alfred Stepan (New Haven, CT: Yale University Press, 1973).

93. Anthony H. Cordesman and Martin Kleiber, "The Asian Conventional Military Balance in 2006: Overview of Major Asian Powers," working draft paper, Center for Strategic and International Studies, June 26, 2006, http://www.csis.org/media/csis/pubs/060626_asia_balance_powers.pdf (accessed July 14, 2008).

94. Ramesh Thakur, *The Government and Politics of India* (New York: St. Martins, 1995), 198.

95. See Brian D. Taylor, "The Soviet Military and the Disintegration of the USSR," *Journal of Cold War Studies* 5, no. 1 (Winter 2003): 17–66.

96. Claire Bigg and Victor Yasmann, "Russia: Can Sergei Ivanov End Hazing?" *RFE/RL Features*, February 14, 2006, http://www.rferl.org/content/article/1065769.html (accessed June 18, 2008).

97. Harlan W. Jencks, "Civil-Military Relations in China: Tiananmen and After," *Problems of Communism* 40 (May–June 1991): 14–29.

98. Rebecca Cann and Constantine Danopoulos, "The Military and Politics in a Theocratic State: Iran as a Case Study," *Armed Forces and Society* 24, no. 2 (1997): 269–288.

99. Ibid.

100. Ibid., 280–283.

101. Ginsburg, *Judicial Review in New Democracies*, 3.

102. Ibid., 9–10.

Chapter 9

1. Philippe C. Schmitter and Terry Lynn Karl, "What Democracy Is . . . and Is Not," *Journal of Democracy* 2, no. 3 (Summer 1991): 75–87.
2. For example, Russell J. Dalton, *Citizen Politics in Western Democracies: Public Opinion and Political Parties in the United States, Great Britain, West Germany, and France* (Chatham, NJ: Chatham House Publishers, 1988).
3. Ibid., 59.
4. Samuel P. Huntington, *Political Order in Changing Societies* (New Haven, CT: Yale University Press, 1968).
5. Unless otherwise specified, turnout rates are based on percentage of registered voters and come from the International Institute for Democracy and Electoral Assistance (IDEA) Voter Turnout Website, http://www.idea .int/vt/ (accessed March 22, 2008).
6. Dalton, 48.
7. David Broughton, "Participation and Voting," in *Developments in West European Politics 2*, ed. Paul Heywood, Erik Jones, and Martin Rhodes (Basingstoke and New York: Palgrave, 2002), 97.
8. David P. Conradt, *The German Polity*, 8th ed. (New York: Pearson Longman, 2005), 95.
9. On far-right parties and movements in Germany, see Piero Ignazi, *Extreme Right Parties in Western Europe* (Oxford: Oxford University Press, 2003), esp. ch. 4, and Cas Mudde, "Extremist Movements," in *Developments in West European Politics 2*, ed. Paul Heywood, Erik Jones, and Martin Rhodes (Basingstoke and New York: Palgrave, 2002), 135–148.
10. Conradt, 29–31; and Charles S. Maier, *Dissolution: The Crisis of Communism and the End of East Germany* (Princeton, NJ: Princeton University Press, 1997), esp. ch. 4.
11. Andrew Appleton, "Associational Life in Contemporary France," in *Developments in French Politics 3*, ed. Alistair Cole, Patrick Le Galès, and Jonah Levy (New York: Palgrave Macmillan, 2005), 54–69.
12. Rémy Herrera, "Three Moments of the French Revolt," *Monthly Review* 58, no. 2 (June 2006): 13–25.
13. Dean E. McHenry Jr., "The Numeration of Events, Studying Political Protest in India," in *Interpretation and Method, Empirical Research Methods and the Interpretive Turn*, ed. Dvora Yanow and Peregrine Schwartz-Shea (Armonk, NY: M.E. Sharpe, 2006), 187–202.
14. See Joseph L. Klesner, "Social Capital and Political Participation in Latin America" (paper presented at the XXV International Congress of the Latin American Studies Association, Las Vegas, Nevada, October 7–9, 2004).
15. Ronald F. Inglehart et al., eds., *Human Beliefs and Values: A Cross-Cultural Sourcebook Based on the 1999–2002 Values Surveys*. (Mexico City: Siglo XXI, 2004), tables E025–E029.
16. The government did not release official turnout rates for the 2007 elections, so this figure is based on the reported number of votes for the various candidates and the estimated number of registered voters prior to the vote. Many observers believe the reported number of votes cast were greatly inflated.
17. Peter Maass, "Niger Delta Dispatch: Road to Hell," *New Republic*, January 31, 2005, 15–17.
18. Ian McAllister and Stephen White, "Political Participation in Postcommunist Russia: Voting, Activism, and the Potential for Mass Protest," *Political Studies* 42, no. 4 (December 1994): 593–594.
19. Samuel H. Barnes, "The Changing Political Participation of Postcommunist Citizens," *International Journal of Sociology* 36, no. 2 (Summer 2006): 76–98.
20. "Russia Elects Putin Successor in Tarnished Poll," Agence France-Presse, March 2, 2008, http://news .ph.msn.com/topstories/article.aspx?cp-documentid= 1271515 (accessed September 21, 2008).
21. "Ingush Oppositionist Sheds Light on Low Turnout Figure," *RFE/RL Newsline* 12, no. 43 (March 4, 2008), http:// www.rferl.org/newsline/2008/03/040308.asp (accessed March 26, 2008).
22. William M. Reisinger, Arthur H. Miller, and Vicki L. Hesli, "Public Behavior and Political Change in Post-Soviet States," *Journal of Politics* 57, no. 4 (November 1995): 941–970.
23. Ronald Inglehart and Gabriela Catterberg, "Trends in Political Action: The Developmental Trend and the Post-Honeymoon Decline," *International Journal of Comparative Sociology* 43, no. 3 (2002): 300–316.
24. Murray Scot Tanner, "China Rethinks Unrest," *Washington Quarterly* 27, no. 3 (2004): 137–156.
25. Herbert Kitschelt, "Linkages Between Citizens and Politicians in Democratic Polities," *Comparative Political Studies* 33, nos. 6–7 (2000): 845–879.
26. Ibid., 845.
27. See Jacek Tarkowski, "Poland: Patrons and Clients in a Planned Economy," in *Political Clientelism, Patronage and Development*, ed. S. N. Eisenstadt and Rene Lemarchand (Beverly Hills, CA: Sage Publications, 1981), 173–188.
28. Kitschelt, 849.
29. Ibid.
30. Rene Lemarchand, "Comparative Political Clientelism: Structure, Process and Optic," in *Political Clientelism, Patronage and Development*, ed. S. N. Eisenstadt and Rene Lemarchand (Beverly Hills, CA: Sage Publications, 1981), 7.
31. Otto Kirchheimer, "The Transformation of West European Party Systems," in *Political Parties and Political Development*, ed. Joseph LaPolombara and Myron Weiner (Princeton, NJ: Princeton University Press, 1966).
32. Maier, 39–40.
33. Jonathan Fox, "The Difficult Transition from Clientelism to Citizenship: Lessons from Mexico," *World Politics* 46, no. 2 (1994): 153.
34. Tina Hilgers, "The Nature of Clientelism in Mexico City" (paper presented at the Canadian Political Science Association Annual Conference, June 2–4, 2005, London, Ontario).
35. On this point, see Barry Ames, *The Deadlock of Democracy in Brazil* (Ann Arbor: University of Michigan Press, 2001).
36. Brian Wampler, "Can Participatory Institutions Promote Pluralism?: Mobilizing Low-Income Citizens in Brazil," *Studies in Comparative International Development* 41, no. 4 (Winter 2007): 57–78.
37. See also Rebecca Abers, "From Clientelism to Cooperation: Local Government, Participatory Policy, and Civic Organizing in Porto Alegre, Brazil." *Politics & Society* 26, no. 4 (December 1998): 511–537.
38. Wampler, 74.

39. See Larry Diamond, "Nigeria: Pluralism, Statism, and the Struggle for Democracy," in *Politics in Developing Countries: Comparing Experiences with Democracy*, ed. Larry Diamond, Juan J. Linz, and Seymour Martin Lipset (Boulder, CO: Lynne Reinner Publishers, 1990), 351–409.
40. See Alena Ledeneva, "Continuity and Change of *Blat* Practices in Soviet and Post-Soviet Russia," in *Bribery and* Blat *in Russia: Negotiating Reciprocity from the Middle Ages to the 1990s*, ed. Stephen Lovell, Alena Ledeneva, and Andrei Rogachevskii (New York: St. Martin's Press, 2000), 183–205.
41. See, for example, J. C. Oi, "Communism and Clientelism: Rural Politics in China," *World Politics* 38, no. 2 (1985): 238–266.
42. Snejina Michailova and Verner Worm, "Personal Networking in Russia and China: *Blat* and *Guanxi*," *European Management Journal* 21, no. 4 (2003): 509–519, see Table 2.
43. Ibid.
44. Kazem Alamdari, "The Power Structure of the Islamic Republic of Iran: Transition from Populism to Clientelism, and Militarization of the Government," *Third World Quarterly* 26, no. 8 (2005): 1285–1301.
45. Ibid., 1288.
46. Charles Tilly, *From Mobilization to Revolution* (Reading, MA: Addison-Wesley, 1978).
47. Friedhelm Neidhart and Dieter Rucht, "The Analysis of Social Movements: The State of the Art and Some Perspectives for Further Research," *Research on Social Movements: The State of the Art in Western Europe and the USA*, ed. Dieter Rucht (Boulder, CO: Westview Press, 1991), 451.
48. See Robert A. Dahl, "Pluralism Revisited," *Comparative Politics* 10, no. 2 (January 1978): 191–203.
49. For a classic work on the difference between state and societal corporatism, see Philippe C. Schmitter, "Still the Century of Corporatism?" in *The New Corporatism: Sociopolitical Structures in the Iberian World*, ed. Fredrick B. Pike and Thomas Stritch (Notre Dame, IN: University of Notre Dame Press, 1974), 85–131.
50. Phillipe Schmitter, "Modes of Interest Intermediation and Models of Societal Change in Western Europe," *Comparative Political Studies* 10, no. 1 (April 1977): 9.
51. Compare this to Phillipe Schmitter's characterization of state corporatism as involving the "imposition of a symbiotic relationship between such 'semivoluntary' associations and the central bureaucracy." See Philippe Schmitter, "The Portugalization of Brazil," in *Authoritarian Brazil*, ed. Alfred Stepan (New Haven, CT: Yale University Press, 1973), 16.
52. On voluntary association membership in the United Kingdom, see Peter A. Hall, "Social Capital in Britain," *British Journal of Political Science* 29, no. 3 (July 1999): 417–461.
53. Fred Attewill, "Police Allow Anti-war March to Parliament," Guardian Unlimited, October 8, 2007, http://www.guardian.co.uk/antiwar/story/0,,2186367,00.html (accessed November 11, 2007).
54. See Kate Nash, "A Movement Moves . . . Is There a Women's Movement in England Today?" *European Journal of Women's Studies* 9, no. 3 (2002): 311–328.
55. The tension between feminists and Margaret Thatcher's Conservative Party is highlighted in Joni Lovenduski and Vicky Randall's *Contemporary Feminist Politics: Women and Power in Britain* (Oxford: Oxford University Press, 1993). The authors contend that although the women's movement appeared to be in decline during the 1980s, feminists became more involved in less visible outlets, such as working directly with state agencies.
56. For an excellent analysis of corporatism, see Peter J. Katzenstein's classic work, *Policy and Politics in West Germany: The Growth of a Semisovereign State* (Philadelphia: Temple University Press, 1987). See also Wolfgang Streeck and Philippe C. Schmitter, "Community, Market, State—and Associations? The Prospective Contribution of Interest Governance to Social Order," *European Sociological Review* 1, no 2 (1985): 119–138.
57. Conradt, 20; Maier, 12–14.
58. On the Greens, see Andrei S. Markovits and Philip S. Gorski, *The German Left: Red, Green and Beyond* (Cambridge, UK: Polity Press, 1993).
59. See Wolfgang Streeck and Anke Hassel, "The Crumbling Pillars of Social Partnership," *West European Politics* 26, no. 4 (October 2003): 101–124.
60. Alex Gordon and Andy Mathers, "State Restructuring and Trade Union Realignment: The Pensions Struggle in France," *Capital and Class* 83 (Summer 2004): 9–18.
61. Cornelia Woll, "National Business Associations Under Stress: Lessons from the French Case," *West European Politics* 29, no. 3 (May 2006): 489–512.
62. Appleton.
63. Nick Hewlett, "New Voices, New Stage, New Democracies?" *Modern & Contemporary France* 12, no. 1 (2004): 9–22.
64. Karen Offen, "Depopulation, Nationalism, and Feminism in Fin-de-Siècle France," *American Historical Review* 89, no. 3 (June 1984): 648–676.
65. Mark Blasius and Shane Phelan, *We Are Everywhere: A Historical Sourcebook of Gay and Lesbian Politics* (New York: Routledge, 1997).
66. José Bové and François Dufour, *The World Is Not For Sale: Farmers Against Junk Food* (New York: Verso, 2001).
67. Robert Hardgrave Jr. and Stanley Kochanek, *India: Government and Politics in a Developing Nation*, 7th ed. (Boston: Thomson and Wadsworth, 2008), 196–202.
68. Ibid., 225.
69. For example, Jonathan Rosenberg, "Mexico: The End of Party Corporatism?" in *Political Parties and Interest Groups: Shaping Democratic Governance*, ed. Clive Thomas (Boulder, CO: Lynne Rienner, 2001), 247–268.
70. See James G. Samstad, "Corporation and Democratic Transition: State and Labor During the Salinas and Zedillo Administrations," *Latin American Politics and Society* 44, no. 4 (Winter 2002): 1–28.
71. For an excellent discussion of both the student movement and the peasant rebellions, see Dolores Trevizo, "Between Zapata and Che: A Comparison of Social Movement Success and Failure in Mexico," *Social Science History* 30, no. 2 (2006): 197–229.
72. David B. Truman, *The Governmental Process: Political Interests and Public Opinion* (New York: Alfred A. Knopf, 1951).
73. Omar Encarnación, *The Myth of Civil Society: Social Capital and Democratic Consolidation in Spain and Brazil* (New York: Palgrave Macmillan, 2003), 178.
74. Charles Gore and David Pratten, "The Politics of Plunder: The Rhetorics of Order and Disorder in Southern

Nigeria," *African Affairs* 102, no. 407 (April 2003): 211–240.

75. Clifford Bob, "Political Process Theory and Transnational Movements: Dialectics of Protest among Nigeria's Ogoni Minority," *Social Problems* 49, no. 3 (August 2002): 395–415.

76. Paul Kubicek, "Variations on a Corporatist Theme: Interest Associations in Post-Soviet Ukraine and Russia," *Europe-Asia Studies* 48, no. 1 (January 1996): 27–46.

77. Andrei Illarionov, "When the State Means Business," *International Herald Tribune*, January 25, 2006, http://www.iht.com/articles/2006/01/25/opinion/edandrei.php (accessed August 24, 2008).

78. For an interesting recent work on Russian social movements, see Graeme B. Robertson, "All They Need Is Someone to Organize It: Protest and Politics in Post-Communist Russia" (Ph.D. diss., Columbia University, 2005).

79. Bruce Dickson, "Cooptation and Corporatism in China: The Logic of Party Adaptation," *Political Science Quarterly* 115, no. 4 (Winter 2000–2001): 520–521.

80. Ibid., 533.

81. James Q. Wilson, *Bureaucracy: What Government Agencies Do and Why They Do It* (New York: Basic Books, 1989), 251.

82. "Weapons Proliferation and the Military-Industrial Complex of the PRC," Commentary, a Canadian Security Intelligence Service publication, No. 84, August 23, 2003, http://www.fas.org/nuke/guide/china/com84.html. (accessed November 12, 2008).

83. Richard Bitzinger, "The PRC's Defense Industry: Reform Without Improvement," *China Brief* 5, no. 6 (March 15, 2005): 5–7.

84. Ronald Inglehart and Gabriela Catterberg, "Trends in Political Action: The Developmental Trend and the Post-Honeymoon Decline," Institute for Social Research working paper, University of Michigan, http://www.worldvaluessurvey.org/Upload/5_Partapsa.pdf (accessed September 17, 2008).

85. Sidney Verba and Norman H. Nie, *Participation in America: Political Democracy and Social Equality* (New York: Harper & Row, 1972).

86. Eric M. Uslaner, "Bowling Almost Alone: Political Participation in a New Democracy" (paper presented at the ECPR Joint Sessions of Workshops, "Emerging Repertoires of Political Action: Toward a Systematic Study of Postconventional Forms of Participation," Uppsala, Sweden, April 13–18, 2004). See esp. Table 4.

87. C. Wright Mills, *The Power Elite* (London: Oxford University Press, 1956), 324.

Chapter 10

1. "Khomeini's Grandson Quits Iran Race After Slurs: Report," AFP, March 2, 2008, http://afp.google.com/article/ALeqM5ijcHx_rywt3GwWI8AiN5cLqJ_t-g (accessed September 22, 2008).

2. Anthony Downs, *An Economic Theory of Democracy* (New York: Harper & Row, 1957), 25.

3. Maurice Duverger, *Political Parties: Their Organization and Activity in the Modern State*, 3rd ed., trans. Barbara North and Robert North (London: Methuen, 1967), 17.

4. See Richard Gunther and Larry Diamond, "Species of Political Parties: A New Typology," *Party Politics* 9, no. 2 (March 2003): 167–199.

5. E. E. Schattschneider, *Party Government* (New York: Farrer and Rinehart, 1942).

6. Gunther and Diamond, "Species of Political Parties."

7. Giovanni Sartori, *Parties and Party Systems: A Framework for Analysis*, Volume I (Cambridge: Cambridge University Press, 1976), 222.

8. Ibid., 230.

9. Jean Blondel, "Party Systems and Patterns of Government in Western Democracies," *Canadian Journal of Political Science* 1, no. 2 (June 1968): 180–203.

10. Ibid.

11. Duverger, 228.

12. "Iran: Country Reports on Human Rights Practices, 2004," a publication of the Bureau of Democracy, Human Rights, and Labor of the United States Department of State, February 28, 2005, http://www.state.gov/g/drl/rls/hrrpt/2004/41721.htm (accessed September 24, 2008).

13. Ali R. Abootalebi, "Iran's 2004 Parliamentary Election and the Question of Democracy," *Iran Analysis Quarterly* 1, no. 3 (Winter 2004): 2–6.

14. "Iran: Time for a New Approach," a report of an independent task force sponsored by the Council on Foreign Relations," 2004, http://www.cfr.org/content/publications/attachments/Iran_TF.pdf (accessed August 20, 2008).

15. Kazem Alamdari, "From Populism to Pluralism: The Islamic Republic in Transition," *The Iranian*, May 8, 1998, http://www.iranian.com/Opinion/May98/Power/index.html (accessed September 26, 2008).

16. Mu Feng, "Communist Party Strengthens Its Role in Business; Will the Old Way Work?" Voice of America, February 2, 2005, http://en.epochtimes.com/news/5-2-2/26202.html (accessed September 4, 2008).

17. Pita Ogaba Agbese, "Party Registration and the Subversion of Democracy in Nigeria," *Issue: A Journal of Opinion* 27, no. 1 (1999): 63–65.

18. On Kirchheimer, see Andre Krouwel, "Otto Kirchheimer and the Catch-All Party," *West European Politics* 26, no. 2 (April 2003): 23-40. He described such parties as *Volksparteien*, or "people's parties," which are essentially catch-all parties.

19. A. Sat Obiyan, "Political Parties Under the Abubakar Transition Program and Democratic Stability in Nigeria," *Issue: A Journal of Opinion* 27, no. 1 (1999): 41–43.

20. See, for example, Ben Rawlence and Chris Albin-Lackey, "Briefing: Nigeria's 2007 General Elections: Democracy in Retreat," *African Affairs* 106, no. 424 (2007): 497–506.

21. Duverger, 208–210.

22. Blondel.

23. See Theodore Rosenof, *Realignment: The Theory That Changed the Way We Think About American Politics* (Lanham, MD: Rowman & Littlefield, 2003).

24. Chris Bryant and Gerrit Wiesmann, "Reformers at Helm as SPD Prepares for Poll," *Financial Times*, September 8, 2004, 4; Gerrit Wiesmann, "Merkel Strikes First Blow at Rival," *Financial Times*, September 9, 2008; "Steinmeier at Helm," *Financial Times*, September 10, 2008.

25. Sudhir Hazareesingh, "The Société d'Instruction Républicaine and the Propagation of Civic Republicanism in Provincial and Rural France, 1870–1877," *Journal of Modern History* 71, no. 2 (June 1999): 271–307.

26. Both the Republican and traditional Right are associated with dynasties, including Bonapartists with their nostalgia for charismatic leaders and anti-Republican "legitimists" such as the extreme right-wing National Front who support a return to traditional authority. See René

Remond, *The Right Wing in France from 1815 to de Gaulle* (Philadelphia: University of Pennsylvania Press, 1969).

27. Jocelyn Evans, *The French Party System* (Manchester: Manchester University Press, 2003).

28. Seymour Martin Lipset and Stein Rokkan, "Cleavage Structures, Party Systems and Voter Alignments: An Introduction," in *Party Systems and Voter Alignments: Crossnational Perspectives*, ed. Seymour Martin Lipset and Stein Rokkan (New York: Free Press, 1967), 1–64.

29. Donald L. Horowitz, *Ethnic Groups in Conflict* (Berkeley: University of California Press, 1985).

30. Peter Katzenstein, *Small States in World Markets: Industrial Policy in Europe* (Ithaca, NY: Cornell University Press, 1985).

31. A good source of further information on political parties in India is Robert Hardgrave Jr. and Stanley Kochanek, *India: Government and Politics in a Developing Nation*, 7th ed. (Boston: Thomson and Wadsworth, 2008), 259–369.

32. Sartori, 235.

33. On the 2000 election, see Joseph L. Klesner, "The End of Mexico's One-Party Regime," *PS: Political Science and Politics* 34, no. 1 (March 2001): 107–114.

34. See Joseph A. Schlesinger, "On the Theory of Party Organization," *Journal of Politics* 46, no. 2 (May 1984): 369–400.

35. Ibid., 380.

36. Schlesinger borrows this term from Robert Salisbury. See Robert H. Salisbury, "An Exchange Theory of Interest Groups," *Midwest Journal of Political Science* 13, no. 1 (February 1969): 1–32.

37. Schlesinger, 390.

38. Adam Przeworski, *Democracy and the Market* (Cambridge: Cambridge University Press, 1991), 10.

39. David M. Farrell, *Comparing Electoral Systems* (London: Prentice Hall, 1997), ch. 6.

40. Ibid., 151.

41. For a discussion of the role of money in early post-Soviet Russian elections, see Daniel Treisman, "Dollars and Democratization: The Role and Power of Money in Russia's Transitional Elections," *Comparative Politics* 31, no. 1 (October 1998): 1–21.

42. See Byron J. Moraski and William M. Reisinger, "Explaining Electoral Competition Across Russia's Regions," *Slavic Review* 62, no. 2 (Summer 2003): 278–301.

43. "Blair: I've Listened and Learned," *BBC News Election 2005* report, May, 6, 2005, http://news.bbc.co.uk/1/hi/uk_politics/vote_2005/frontpage/4521627.stm (accessed September 24, 2008).

44. "Kennedy Hails 'Party of Future,'" *BBC News Election 2005* report, May, 6, 2005, http://news.bbc.co.uk/1/hi/uk_politics/vote_2005/frontpage/4518803.stm (accessed September 24, 2008).

45. Roger F. S. Kaplan, "Elections and Ideologies in France: 2002," *Society* 40, no. 1 (November/December 2002): 86–91.

46. Sharif Gemie, "Anti-Le Pen Protests: France, April–May 2002," *Journal of Contemporary European Studies* 11, no. 2 (November 2003): 231–251.

47. The Indian Election Commission provides a very complete report of information about past and present elections in India, including election results at: http://www.eci.gov.in/index.asp.

48. See Obiyan.

49. The unofficial estimates of the legislative election results vary greatly, depending on the source. In March 2008, however, an examination of the party affiliations of members of the House of Representatives and the Senate, according to the two bodies' official web pages, put the total seats for the PDP at 257 in the House and seventy-eight in the Senate.

50. Roland Ogbonnaya, "Nigeria: Politicians Urged to Market Their Programmes," *This Day*, July 9, 2006, http://allafrica.com/stories/200607100475.html (accessed October 23, 2006).

51. Bolaji Adebiyi and Oke Epia, "PDP Edges out Atiku," *This Day*, September 29, 2006, http://allafrica.com/stories/printable/200609290062.html (accessed October 23, 2006).

52. See David P. Conradt, *The German Polity*, 8th ed. (New York: Pearson Longman, 2005), 162–166.

53. German parties often designate a person to lead the party in the *Bundestag* elections, serving as the chancellor-candidate. This person may not necessarily be the same person as the chairman of the party.

54. See "EU Says Disputed Mexico Vote Fair," BBC News report, July 8, 2006, http://news.bbc.co.uk/2/hi/americas/5160188.stm (accessed September 27, 2008).

55. Kamal Nazer Yasin, "Election Landslide in Iran May Moderate President-Elect's Domestic Policies," *Eurasia Insight*, June 29, 2005, www.eurasianet.org/departments/insight/articles/eav062905.shtml (accessed September 24, 2008).

56. See Kevin J. O'Brien and Lianjiang Li, "Accommodating 'Democracy' in a One-Party State: Introducing Village Elections in China," *China Quarterly* 162 (June 2000): 465–489.

57. Ibid.

58. See Robert A. Pastor and Qingshan Tan, "The Meaning of China's Village Elections," *China Quarterly* 152 (June 2000): 490–512.

59. For a summary of Duverger's discussion of these two types of consequences, see Andre Blais and Louis Massicotte, "Electoral Systems," in *Comparing Democracies: Elections and Voting in Global Perspective*, ed. Lawrence LeDuc, Richard G. Niemi, and Pippa Norris (Thousand Oaks, CA: Sage Publications, 1996), 49–82.

60. See, for example, William H. Riker, "The Two-Party System and Duverger's Law," *American Political Science Review* 76, no. 4 (December 1982): 753–766.

61. Duverger, 217.

Chapter 11

1. Details of Peshev's actions are available at Norbert J. Yasharoff, "Bulgaria's Schindler," www.peshev.org/yashar.htm (accessed March 23, 2008).

2. "Transports from Macedonia and Thrace," A publication of the Aktion Reinhard Camps project (www.Deathcamps.Org), June 2, 2006, http://www.deathcamps.org/reinhard/macedonia%20thrace%20transports.html (accessed March 23, 2008).

3. Eric Selbin, "Agency and Culture in Revolutions," in *Revolutions: Theoretical, Comparative, and Historical Studies*, ed. Jack A. Goldstone (Belmont, CA: Wadsworth/Thomson Learning, 2003), 79.

4. Of course, this is not true of all political science works. William Riker contends that, above all else, decision making is the subject of political science. See William Riker, *The Theory of Political Coalition* (New Haven, CT: Yale University Press, 1962), 10.

5. Writing about revolutions, for example, Jack Goldstone states, "'Agency' implies that not all aspects of a revolution are predetermined by macro-social, structural factors. The decisions of key actors (or 'agents') make a difference in whether a revolution will be successful and how it evolves." Jack A. Goldstone, "Introduction," in *Revolutions: Theoretical, Comparative, and Historical Studies*, ed. Jack A. Goldstone (Belmont, CA: Wadsworth/Thomson Learning, 2003).

6. Howard Gardner (in collaboration with Emma Laskin), *Leading Minds: An Anatomy of Leadership* (New York: Basic Books, 1995).

7. See Peter G. Northouse, *Leadership: Theory and Practice* (Thousand Oaks, CA: Sage, 2004), ch. 3.

8. Bertrand Benoit, "New Kid from the Bloc," *Financial Times*, September 10–11, 2005, W1–W2.

9. Benoit, "New Kid from the Bloc"; "Waiting for a Wunder," Survey on Germany, *Economist*, February 11, 2006, 5–6.

10. Bertrand Benoit, "Cold Shoulder: How Merkel's Coalition Is Spurning Lobbyists in Reform Push," *Financial Times*, August 3, 2006, 11.

11. See Gerrit Wiesmann, "Merkel Strikes First Blow at Rival," *Financial Times*, September 9, 2008, 4.

12. David P. Conradt, *The German Polity*, 8th ed. (New York: Pearson Longman, 2005), 33–39, 214–217.

13. Michel Wieviorka, "Violence in France," *SSRC Online Forum: Riots in France*, November 18, 2005, http://riotsfrance.ssrc.org/Wieviorka/ (accessed September 28, 2008).

14. Wendy Michallat, "Marions-nous! Gay Rites: The Campaign for Gay Marriage in France," *Modern & Contemporary France* 14, no. 3 (August 2006): 305–316.

15. Kevin G. Hall, "Calderón's Views Rooted in Devotion to the Church," *Miami Herald*, July 22, 2006, http://www.miami.com/mld/miamiherald/news/world/americas/15096651.htm (accessed March 14, 2008).

16. "Profile: Felipe Calderon," *BBC News*, September 5, 2006, http://news.bbc.co.uk/2/hi/americas/5318434.stm (accessed September 29, 2008).

17. Fernando Henrique Cardoso, with Brian Winter. *The Accidental President of Brazil: A Memoir* (New York: Public Affairs/Perseus Books, 2006).

18. "Profile: President Umaru Yar'Adua," BBC News, May 29, 2007, http://news.bbc.co.uk/2/hi/africa/6187249.stm (accessed on December 5, 2007).

19. Lydia Polgreen, "After Rocky Election, Nigerians Warm to New Leader," *New York Times*, October 4, 2007, www.nytimes.com/2007/10/04/world/africa/04nigeria.html?n=Top/Reference/Times%20Topics/People/Y/Yar'Adua,%20Umaru (accessed December 3, 2007).

20. See p. 1 of Ariel Cohen, "Russian Succession: Putin Prime Minister, Medvedev President," *Web Memo*, a publication of the Heritage Foundation, no. 1731 (December 11, 2007): 1–3.

21. Ibid., 1–2.

22. Joshua Eisenman, "A Shift in China's Leadership Style?" *Straits Times*, May 8, 2003, http://www.nixoncenter.org/EISENMAN%20PUBLICATIONS/Straits%20Times%20May%208,%202003.htm (accessed September 29, 2008).

23. "Iranian MPs Approve Oil Minister," BBC News, December 11, 2005, http://news.bbc.co.uk/2/hi/middle_east/4518300.stm (accessed October 1, 2008).

24. See Jerrold D. Green, "Countermobilization in the Iranian Revolution," in *Revolutions: Theoretical, Comparative, and Historical Studies*, ed. Jack A. Goldstone (Belmont, CA: Wadsworth/Thomson Learning, 2003), 238.

25. The previous chapter discussed one of the classic works that takes an economic approach to understanding voting, Downs's *An Economic Theory of Democracy*. See Anthony Downs, *An Economic Theory of Democracy* (New York: Harper, 1957).

26. Kenneth Arrow, *Social Choice and Individual Values* (New Haven, CT: Yale University Press, 1951).

27. For an overview of Simon's arguments, see Bryan D. Jones, "Bounded Rationality," *Annual Review of Political Science* 2 (1999): 297–321; and "Herbert A. Simon: Political Scientist," *Annual Review of Political Science* 6 (2003): 433–471.

28. See p. 364 of Bruce Bower, "Past Impressions: Prior Relationships Cast a Long Shadow over Our Social Lives," *Science News* 171, no. 23 (June 9, 2007): 363–365.

29. Daniel L. Byman and Kenneth M. Pollack, "Let Us Now Praise Great Men (and Women): Restoring the First Image," *International Security* 25, no. 4 (Spring 2001): 107–146.

30. John Tagliabue, "In a Dizzying Day, 2,500 More Seek Refuge in Prague," *New York Times*, October 3, 1989, http://query.nytimes.com/gst/fullpage.html?res=950DE6D6103AF930A35753C1A96F948260 (accessed September 29, 2008).

31. Charles S. Maier, *Dissolution: The Crisis of Communism and the End of East Germany* (Princeton, NJ: Princeton University Press, 1997), 227.

32. Ibid., 228.

33. Ibid., 227–244.

34. José Bové and François Dufour, *The World Is Not for Sale: Farmers Against Junk Food* (London: Verso, 2001).

35. James M. Jasper, *The Art of Moral Protest* (Chicago: University of Chicago Press, 1997).

36. "A Farmer's International," *New Left Review* 12 (November–December 2001): 89–101.

37. In late 2006, the U.S. Congress passed the Hyde Act that was interpreted by the Left as undermining India's sovereignty and requiring coordination of foreign policies. The Bush Administration's international behavior also produced deep concerns among parties on the left.

38. Venkitesh Ramakrishnan, "No-Win Situation," *Frontline* 24, no. 21 (October 20–November 2, 2007), http://www.frontlineonnet.com/stories/20071102501803000.htm (accessed October 28, 2007).

39. Venkitesh Ramakrishnan, "On the Brink," *Frontline* 25, no. 14 (July 5–18, 2008). http://www.hinduonnet.com/fline/fl2514/stories/20080718251400400.htm (accessed September 27, 2008).

40. Charles Lindblom, "The Science of 'Muddling Though,'" *Public Administration Review* 19 (Spring 1959): 79–88; David Braybrooke and Charles Lindblom, *A Strategy of Decision* (New York: Free Press, 1963). Incrementalism is also associated with Aaron Wildavsky, especially in the arena of government budgeting.

41. For more on what Zedillo set out to do, see Stephen Fidler, "Mexico: What Kind of Transition?" *International Affairs* 72, no. 4 (1996): 713–725.

42. Rogério L. F. Werneck, "Meeting the Challenge of Setting up a Modern Macroeconomic Policy Framework: Brazil, 1993-2004," a publication of the Comission on Growth and Development Workshop on Country Case Studies, Washington, DC, April 12–14, 2007, http://www.growthcommission.org/storage/cgdev/documents/

CaseStudies/Presentation%20Werneck%20on%20Brazil .pdf (accessed October 1, 2008).

43. This section is based on Cardoso's own recollections of these events, in Cardoso, esp. ch. 9.

44. Ibid.

45. Ibid.

46. Nicholas Sambanis expands on this point in "Using Case Studies to Expand the Theory of Civil War," CPR Working Paper No. 5, Social Development Department, Environmentally and Socially Sustainable Development Network, May 2003, http://www.forecastingprinciples .com/Conflicts/PDF%20files/Using_Case_Studies.pdf (accessed September 29, 2008).

47. The points are made by Carolyn Rhodes in *Pivotal Decisions: Selected Cases in Twentieth-Century International Politics* (Fort Worth, TX: Harcourt Brace, 2000), 110–111.

48. This was indeed the case. Even in real terms, Mexican exports tripled in the years following NAFTA's introduction.

49. William A. Orme Jr., "NAFTA: Myths Versus Facts," *Foreign Affairs* 72, no. 5 (November/December 1993): 2–12.

50. See Goldstone's introduction to the excerpt from Eric Selbin ("Agency and Culture in Revolutions") in *Revolutions: Theoretical, Comparative, and Historical Studies*, ed. Jack A. Goldstone (Belmont, CA: Wadsworth/Thomson Learning, 2003), 76.

51. See, for example, James Mahoney and Richard Snyder, "Rethinking Agency and Structure in the Study of Regime Change," *Studies in Comparative International Development* 34, no. 2 (1999): 3–32; Katherine Adeney and Andrew Wyatt, "Democracy in South Asia: Getting Beyond the Structure-Agency Dichotomy," *Political Studies* 52, no. 1 (2004): 1–18.

Chapter 12

1. A returned Peace Corps volunteer from Benin shared a story in which a conversation he had about the plan to amend the constitution prompted a local resident to proclaim that if Kérékou tried to change the constitution, he would take his pistol, round up his neighbors, march to the capital, and go to war. Throughout the man's impassioned declaration, which went on for quite some time, other locals nodded and interjected their approval.

2. "Achieving Transformational Democracy in Africa: Benin Strikes Again," USAID-Benin "Governance Success Stories," available at: www.usaid.gov/bj/democracy/ election.html. Accessed: March 27, 2008.

3. For a recent look at the question of stability and political openness, see Ian Bremmer, *The J-Curve* (New York: Simon & Schuster, 2006).

4. There is a body of literature in international relations about what is called the "democratic peace" theory. For an overview of the argument, see James Lee Ray, "The Democratic Path to Peace," *Journal of Democracy* 8, no. 2 (April 1997): 49–64.

5. Ian Bremmer argues that consolidated democracies are more stable than consolidated nondemocracies but also points out that consolidated nondemocracies are more stable than the transitional periods of increasing political openness. See Bremmer.

6. Jack Snyder, *From Voting to Violence: Democratization and Nationalist Conflict* (New York: W. W. Norton and Co., 2000); Edward D. Mansfield and Jack Snyder, *Electing to Fight: Why Emerging Democracies Go to War* (Cambridge, MA: MIT Press, 2005).

7. Samuel Huntington, *The Third Wave: Democratization in the Late Twentieth Century* (Norman: University of Oklahoma Press, 1991).

8. Ibid.

9. Dankwart A. Rustow, "Transitions to Democracy: Toward a Dynamic Model," *Comparative Politics* 2, no. 3 (April 1970): 337–365.

10. Terry Lynn Karl," Dilemmas of Democratization in Latin America," *Comparative Politics* 23, no. 1 (October 1990): 1–21.

11. See Scott Mainwaring, Guillermo O'Donnell, and J. Samuel Valenzuela, eds., *Issues in Democratic Consolidation: The New South American Democracies in Comparative Perspective* (Notre Dame, IN: University of Notre Dame Press, 1992).

12. Rustow.

13. See, for example, Juan Linz, "Transitions to Democracy," *Washington Monthly* 13 (Summer 1990): 143–164.

14. A number of democratization scholars have used the "only game in town" phrase to describe consolidation. See, for example, Adam Przeworski, *Democracy and the Market: Political and Economic Reforms in Eastern Europe and Latin America* (Cambridge: Cambridge University Press, 1991), 26.

15. Przeworski, 10.

16. Huntington.

17. On the Latin American cases, see Karen Remmer, "The Political Impact of Economic Crisis in Latin America in the 1980s," *American Political Science Review* 85, no. 3 (September 1991): 777–800.

18. Lawrence Whitehead, *Democratization: Theory and Practice* (Oxford: Oxford University Press, 2002), 28.

19. Doh Chull Shin is one scholar who emphasizes the maturation stage. See p. 143 of Doh Chull Shin, "On the Third Wave of Democratization: A Synthesis and Evaluation of Recent Theory and Research," *World Politics* 47, no. 1 (October 1994): 135–170.

20. Juan J. Linz and Alfred Stepan, eds., *The Breakdown of Democratic Regimes* (Baltimore, MD: Johns Hopkins University Press, 1978).

21. See Juan J. Linz, "The Process of Reequilibration," in *The Breakdown of Democratic Regimes*, ed. Juan J. Linz and Alfred Stepan (Baltimore, MD: Johns Hopkins University Press, 1978), 87–97.

22. Shin, 139.

23. S. M. Lipset, "Some Social Requisites of Democracy: Economic Development and Political Legitimacy," *American Political Science Review* 53 (1959): 69–104.

24. See Gabriel A. Almond and Sidney Verba, *The Civic Culture: Political Attitudes and Democracy in Five Nations* (Princeton, NJ: Princeton University Press, 1963).

25. See, for example, Ronald Inglehart and Christian Welzel, *Modernization, Cultural Change, and Democracy: The Human Development Sequence* (Cambridge: Cambridge University Press, 2005).

26. Rustow.

27. Nancy Bermeo, "The Import of Institutions," *Journal of Democracy* 13, no. 2 (April 2002): 96–110.

28. See Henry E. Hale, "Divided We Stand: Institutional Sources of Ethnofederal State Survival and Collapse," *World Politics* 56 (January 2004): 165–193.

29. Donald L. Horowitz, *Ethnic Groups in Conflict* (Berkeley, CA: University of California Press, 1985).
30. See M. Foley and B. Edwards, "The Paradox of Civil Society," *Journal of Democracy* 7, no. 4 (1996) 38–52.
31. Sheri Berman, "Civil Society and the Collapse of the Weimar Republic," *World Politics* 49, no. 3 (April 1997): 401–429.
32. Kenneth Waltz, *Theory of International Politics* (New York: McGraw-Hill, 1979).
33. See Robert Pinkney, *Democracy in the Third World*, 2nd ed. (Boulder, CO: Lynne Reinner Publishers, 2003).
34. Bermeo 107–108.
35. See p. 408 of Hans Peter Schmitz, "Domestic and Transnational Perspectives on Democratization," *International Studies Review*, vol. 6 (2004): 403–426.
36. Samuel Huntington uses the term "snowballing" in *The Third Wave.*
37. See p. 214 of Michael McFaul, "The Fourth Wave of Democracy and Dictatorship: Noncooperative Transitions in the Postcommunist World," *World Politics* 54, no. 2 (January 2002): 212–244.
38. Bruce Bueno de Mesquita and George W. Downs, "Development and Democracy," *Foreign Affairs* 84, no. 5 (September/October 2005): 77–86.
39. Shale Horowitz, "Sources of Post-Communist Democratization: Economic Structure, Political Culture, War, and Political Institutions," *Nationalities Papers* 31, no. 2 (June 2003): 119–137.
40. Daniel H. Levine, "Venezuela Since 1958: The Consolidation of Democratic Politics," in *The Breakdown of Democratic Regimes: Latin America*, ed. J. Linz and A. Stepan (Baltimore: Johns Hopkins University Press, 1978), 82–109.
41. See Joseph S. Nye, "Mikhail Gorbachev and the End of the Cold War," a *Project Syndicate* commentary, http://www.project-syndicate.org/commentary/nye31/English (accessed October 1, 2008).
42. Andrew E. Busch and Elizabeth Edwards Spalding, "1983: Awakening from Orwell's Nightmare," *Policy Review* 66 (Fall 1993): 71–75.
43. Jonathan Kwitny, *Man of the Century: The Life and Times of Pope John Paul II* (New York: Henry Holt, 1997), 592.
44. See Inglehart Welzel.
45. Juan J. Linz, "The Process of Breakdown," in Juan J. Linz and Alfred Stepan, *The Breakdown of Democratic Regimes* (Baltimore, MD: Johns Hopkins University Press, 1978), 54.
46. Ibid., 63.
47. Ibid., 66–69.
48. Terry Lynn Karl, "Petroleum and Political Pacts: The Transition to Democracy in Venezuela," *Latin American Research Review* 22, no. 1 (1987): 63–94.
49. See p. 73 of Vernon Bogdanor, "Constitutional Reform in Britain: The Quiet Revolution," *Annual Review of Political Science* 8 (2005): 73–98.
50. See p. 300 of John R. Freeman and Duncan Snidal, "Diffusion, Development, and Democratization: Enfranchisement in Western Europe," *Canadian Review of Political Science* 15, no. 2 (June 1982): 299–329.
51. See M. Justman and M. Gradstein, "The Industrial Revolution, Political Transition, and the Subsequent Decline in Inequality in 19th-Century Britain," *Explorations in Economic History* 36 (1999): 109–127; John Garrard, "Democratization in Britain," in *European Democratization since 1800*, ed. John Garrard, Vera Tolz, and Ralph White (New York: St. Martin's Press, 2000), 29–49.
52. John Garrard makes the point that the British transition was more ad hoc than a conscious effort aimed at total enfranchisement of the population from the start. See Garrard, "Democratization in Britain," 29.
53. Barrington Moore Jr. *Social Origins of Dictatorship and Democracy* (Boston: Beacon Press, 1966), 437.
54. Ibid., 448–450.
55. Gordon Smith, *Democracy in Western Germany*, 3rd ed. (Aldershot: Gower, 1986), 16–20.
56. "The Reichstag Burns," The History Place, 1996, http://www.historyplace.com/worldwar2/riseofhitler/burns.htm (accessed March 27, 2008).
57. Peter J. Katzenstein, *Policy and Politics in West Germany: The Growth of a Semisovereign State* (Philadelphia: Temple University Press, 1987), esp. ch. 3. In the early years of the Federal Republic, business elites were discredited by their prior collaboration with the Nazi regime while labor leaders found legitimacy in their resistance to Hitler. As a result, labor made gains in the industrial relations arena.
58. Gaston V. Rimlinger, *Welfare Policy and Industrialization in Europe, America and Russia* (New York: John Wiley, 1971), pp. 138–148; Katzenstein, *Policy and Politics in West Germany*, chs. 2 and 4.
59. Bertrand Benoit, "Growing Apart: 15 Years After the Wall's Fall," *Financial Times*, September 23, 2004; David P. Conradt, *The German Polity*, 8th ed. (New York: Pearson Longman, 2005), 80–85, 92–94.
60. Moore.
61. Simon Schama, *Citizens: A Chronicle of the French Revolution* (New York: Knopf, 1989).
62. Sarah C. Maza, *Private Lives, Public Affairs: The Cause Célèbre of Pre Revolutionary France* (Berkeley: University of California Press, 1993).
63. Theda Skocpol, *States and Social Revolutions* (New York: Cambridge University Press, 1979).
64. Gregory M. Leubbert, *Liberalism, Socialism, or Fascism: Social Class and the Political Origins of Regimes in Interwar Europe* (New York: Oxford University Press, 1991).
65. Stanley Hoffmann, "The Effects of World War II on French Society and Politics," *French Historical Studies* 2, no. 1 (Spring 1961), 28–63.
66. Karl Marx, *The Eighteenth Brumaire of Louis Napoleon*, in *Karl Marx: Selected Writings*, ed. David McLellan (Oxford: Oxford University Press, 2000).
67. Bruce Gilley, *China's Democratic Future: How It Will Happen and Where It Will Lead* (New York: Columbia University Press, 2004).
68. See Huntington, 72.
69. José Woldenberg Karakowsky, "Lessons from Mexico," *Journal of Democracy* 12, no. 2 (April 2001): 151–156.
70. Ibid.
71. Terry Lynn Karl," Dilemmas of Democratization in Latin America."
72. Nigeria's Third Republic never got off the ground, as its founding elections were immediately invalidated by the ruling military government.
73. See Carol Skalnik Leff, "Democratization and Disintegration in Multinational States: The Breakup of the Communist Federations," *World Politics* 51, no. 2 (January 1999): 205–235.
74. On the role of the design of the Russian system in its democratic breakdown, see M. Steven Fish, *Democracy Derailed in Russia* (Cambridge: Cambridge University Press, 2005).

75. On the way in which the views of the more conservative masses toward democracy constrained Russia's liberal elites (and thus gave opportunities to the conservative elites), see Judith S. Kullberg, "Liberal Elites, Socialist Masses, and the Problems of Russian Democracy," *World Politics* 51, no. 3 (April 1999): 323–358.

76. See "Russia's Weakened Democratic Embrace," Pew Global Attitudes Project Report, 2006, http://pewglobal.org/reports/display.php?ReportID=250 (accessed October 2, 2008).

77. See Bruce Gilley, "Should We Try to Predict Transitions to Democracy: Lessons for China," *Whitehead Journal of Diplomacy and International Relations* 6, no. 1: 113–128.

78. Ibid., 124.

79. See p. 821 of Junhan Lee, "Primary Causes of Asian Democratization: Dispelling Conventional Myths," *Asian Survey* 42, no. 6 (November/December 2002): 821–837.

80. De Mesquita and Downs, "Development and Democracy."

81. See Sanm Vakil, "Iran: The Gridlock Between Demography and Democracy," *SAIS Review* 24, no. 2 (Summer-Fall 2004): 45–53.

82. Ibid., 49.

83. Ashutosh Varshney, "Why Democracy Survives," *Journal of Democracy* 9, no. 3 (1998): 36–50.

84. In his book, *The Great Indian Middle Class* (New Delhi: Penguin Books, 1998 p. xiii), Pavan Varma refuses to define the size of the middle class. On the other hand, he argues that "disproportionate to its size, [it] has played a pivotal role in the making of modern India."

85. Varshney, 42.

86. Ibid.

87. Larry Diamond, "Universal Democracy?" *Policy Review* 119 (June 2003), http://www.hoover.org/publications/policyreview/3448571.html (accessed October 1, 2008).

88. See p. 459 of Sheri E. Berman, "Modernization in Historical Perspective: The Case of Imperial Germany," *World Politics* 52 (2001): 431–462.

Chapter 13

1. See Martin McKee, "Alcohol in Russia," *Alcohol and Alcoholism* 34, no. 6 (1999): 824–829.

2. John Moody, "Soviet Union Fighting the Battle of the Bottle," *Time*, October 21, 1985, http://www.time.com/time/magazine/article/0,9171,960191,00.html (accessed March 28, 2008).

3. Arnod J. Heidenheimer, Hugh Heclo, and Carolyn Teich Adams, *Comparative Public Policy: The Politics of Social Choice in America, Europe, and Japan*, 3rd ed. (New York: St. Martin's Press, 1990), 3.

4. Ibid., 5–6.

5. Geoffrey Pridham, "The International Dimension of Democratization: Theory, Practice, and Inter-regional Comparisons," in *Building Democracy? The International Dimension of Democratization in Eastern Europe*, ed. Geoffrey Pridham, Eric Herring, and George Sanford (New York: St. Martin`s Press 1994), 7–29.

6. See "Making Sense Out of Dollars 2002–2003: Trend in Government Spending by Level," March 16, 2005, website of the Canadian Department of National Defence, http://www.admfincs.forces.gc.ca/financial_docs/Msood/2002-2003/intro_e.asp (accessed March 28, 2008).

7. James E. Anderson, *Public Policymaking: An Introduction* (Boston, MA: Houghton Mifflin, 1990), 12.

8. See Heidenheimer, Heclo, and Adams, *Comparative Public Policy*, 308–309.

9. Ibid., 323.

10. Ibid., 13.

11. These statistics are available at: http://www.gpoaccess.gov/usbudget/fy07/sheets/hist16z1.xls (accessed October 5, 2008).

12. See Heidenheimer, Heclo, and Adams, ch. 2.

13. See Lowell W. Barrington, "The Making of Citizenship Policy in the Baltic States," *Georgetown Immigration Law Journal* 13, no. 2 (1999): 159–199.

14. Russell J. Dalton, *Citizen Politics: Public Opinion and Political Parties in Advanced Industrial Democracies*, 3rd ed. (New York: Chatham House Publishers, 2002), table 6.4.

15. Ibid., figure 6.1.

16. See p. 278 of Peter A. Hall, "Policy Paradigms, Social Learning, and the State: The Case of Economic Policymaking in Britain," *Comparative Politics* 25, no. 3 (April 1993): 275–296.

17. This term is borrowed from the title of the best book available on the history of the Soviet Union: Ronald G. Suny, *The Soviet Experiment: Russia, the USSR, and the Successor States* (Oxford University Press, 1998).

18. Lester Thurow, *Head to Head: The Coming Economic Battle Among Japan, Europe, and America* (New York: William Morrow, 1992).

19. David Coates, "Models of Capitalism in the New World Order," *Political Studies* 47, no. 4 (1999): 643–661.

20. Ibid.

21. Francis Fukuyama and Sanjay Marwah, "Dimensions of Development," *Journal of Democracy* 11, no. 4 (2000): 80–94.

22. On the issue of industrialization fostering an aging population that demands more government programs, see Harold L. Wilensky, *The Welfare State and Equality: Structural and Ideological Roots of Public Expenditures* (Berkeley: University of California Press, 1975).

23. Ibid.

24. See David Cameron, "The Expansion of the Public Economy: A Comparative Analysis," *American Political Science Review* 72 (1978): 1243–1261.

25. See Karl W. Deutsch, *Politics and Government* (Boston, MA: Houghton Mifflin, 1970).

26. See p. 418 of Anthony King, "Ideas, Institutions and the Policies of Governments: A Comparative Analysis, Part III," *British Journal of Political Science* 3, no. 4 (October 1973): 409–423. The text of this quotation in the original article is in italics.

27. See, for example, Wim Van Oorschot, Birgit Pfau-Effinger, and Michael Opielka, eds., *Culture and Welfare State: Values and Social Policy in Comparative Perspective* (Edward Elgar Publishing, Inc., 2008).

28. E. E. Schattschneider, *The Semi-Sovereign People* (New York: Holt, Rinehart, and Winston, 1960), 71.

29. See, for example, Giuliano Boloni, "Political Institutions, Veto Points, and the Process of Welfare State Adaptation," in *The New Politics of the Welfare State*, ed. Paul Pierson (Oxford: Oxford University Press, 2001), 238–264.

30. See p. 220 of Colin J. Bennett, "What Is Policy Convergence and What Causes It?" *British Journal of Political Science* 21, no. 2 (April 1991): 215–233.

31. Ibid., 218.

32. See, for example, Andrew W. Barrett, "Gone Public: The Impact of Going Public on Presidential Legislative Success," *American Politics Research* 32, no. 3 (2004): 338–370.

33. While such policy is usually the result of satisficing, Breena Coates argues that in the case of certain policies, such as the USA Patriot Act (2001), the result may not even be one of satisficing but rather a policy that is "sufferable." See Breena E. Coates, " 'Sufferable' or Satisficing?: Hard Policy Choices Within the USA Patriot Act of 2001," *Public Administration & Management: An Interactive Journal* 7, no. 3 (2002): 211–228.

34. See p. 216 of Roger Friendland, Frances Fox Piven, and Robert R. Alford, "Political Conflict, Urban Structure, and the Fiscal Crisis," in *Comparing Public Policies: New Concepts and Methods*, ed. Douglas E. Ashford (Beverly Hills, CA: Sage Publishers, 1978), 197–225.

35. See Hall, "Policy Paradigms, Social Learning, and the State," 277.

36. See p. 586 of Norman Flynn, "Modernising British Government," *Parliamentary Affairs* 52, no. 4 (October 1999): 582–597.

37. On the NHS, see Gwyn Bevan and Ray Robinson, "The Interplay Between Economic and Political Logics: Path Dependency in Health Care in England," *Journal of Health Politics, Policy and Law* 30, nos. 1–2 (February–April 2005): 53–78.

38. For an interesting discussion on this topic, see Mike Marinetto, "Governing Beyond the Centre: A Critique of the Anglo-Governance School," *Political Studies* 51, no. 3 (October 2003): 592–608.

39. See Chris Ham, "Managed Markets in Health Care: The UK Experiment," *Health Policy* 35, no. 3 (March 1996): 279–292.

40. Flynn, 588, 590.

41. Karen Allen, "Election Issues: Health," a BBC News analysis, http://news.bbc.co.uk/1/hi/uk_politics/vote_2005/issues/4337851.stm (accessed October 3, 2008).

42. Gosta Esping-Andersen, *The Three Worlds of Welfare Capitalism* (Princeton, NJ: Princeton University Press, 1990); Gosta Esping-Andersen, *The Social Foundations of Post-Industrial Economies* (Oxford: Oxford University Press, 2000).

43. On the origins of the social market economy, see Gaston V. Rimlinger, *Welfare Policy and Industrialization in Europe, America and Russia* (New York: John Wiley, 1971), 138–148; Peter J. Katzenstein, *Policy and Politics in West Germany* (Philadelphia: Temple University Press, 1987), esp. chs. 1, 2, and 4; and Gordon Smith, *Democracy in Western Germany*, 3rd ed. (Aldershot: Gower, 1986), 211–213.

44. Katzenstein, ch. 4.

45. On the influence of the Catholic Church in social policy, see Kees van Kersbergen, *Social Capitalism: A Study of Christian Democracy and the Welfare* State (London and New York: Routledge, 1995); Esping-Andersen, *The Three Worlds of Welfare Capitalism*. The Catholic Center Party was a key actor in enacting social welfare legislation in the Bismarckian and Weimar eras. Social Catholicism, as embodied in papal encyclicals of the nineteenth and twentieth centuries, championed social policy as a way to humanize capitalism.

46. Esping-Andersen, *The Social Foundations of Post-Industrial Economies*; Philip Manow and Eric Seils, "Adjusting Badly: The German Welfare State, Structural Change, and the Open Economy," in *Diverse Responses to Common Challenges*, vol. 2 of *Welfare and Work in the Open Economy*, ed. Fritz W. Scharpf and Vivien A. Schmidt, (Oxford: Oxford University Press, 2000), 264–307.

47. Achim Kemmerling and Liver Bruttel, "'New Politics' in German Labour Market Policy? The Implications of the Recent Hartz Reforms for the German Welfare State," *West European Politics* 29, no. 1 (January 2006): 90–112; Bertrand Benoit, "A Temporary Solution? Germany's Labour Market Develops a Second Tier," *Financial Times*, Oct. 27, 2006.

48. Esping-Andersen, *The Social Foundations of Post-Industrial Economies*; Gerrit Wiesmann, "Germany's Career Women Look for a Lifeline from First Female Chancellor," *Financial Times*, October 13, 2005; Wolfgang Streeck, *Endgame? The Fiscal Crisis of the German State*, MPiFG Discussion Paper 07/7 (Cologne: Max Planck Institute for the Study of Societies, 2007).

49. Patricia M. E. Lorcin, "Imperialism, Colonial Identity, and Race in Algeria, 1830–1870: The Role of the French Medical Corps," *Isis* 90, no. 4 (1999): 653–679.

50. Pierre Rosanvallon, *L'État en France de 1789 à nos jours* (Paris: Seuil, 1992).

51. Michael Loriaux, *France After Hegemony: International Change and Financial Reform* (Ithaca, NY: Cornell University Press, 1991).

52. Gérard Noiriel, *The French Melting Pot: Immigration, Citizenship, and National Identity*. (Minneapolis: University of Minnesota Press, 1996).

53. See James Shields, *The Extreme Right in France: From Pétain to Le Pen* (London: Routledge, 2007), 238.

54. See p. 464 of Maria Victoria Murillo, "Political Bias in Policy Convergence: Privatization Choices in Latin America," *World Politics* 54, no. 4 (2002): 462–493.

55. Germán Álvarez-Mendolia, "Lifelong Learning Policies in Mexico: Context, Challenges, and Comparisons," *Compare: A Journal of Comparative Education* 36, no. 3 (September 2006): 379–399.

56. Harvey V. Fineberg, "Health Reform in Mexico: A Work in Progress," *Lancet* 368 (November 18, 2006): 1755–1756. See also Felicia Marie Knaul, Héctor Arreola-Ornelas, Oscar Méndez-Carniado et al., "Evidence Is Good for Your Health System: Policy Reform to Remedy Catastrophic and Impoverishing Health Spending in Mexico," *Lancet* 368 (November 18, 2006): 1828–1841.

57. Fineberg.

58. Ike Oguine, "War on Corruption," *New Internationalist*, December 2005, 29.

59. Gilbert da Costa, "Top Nigerian Officials Fired for Alleged Graft," VOA News, March 26, 2008, http://www.voanews.com/english/2008-03-26-voa36.cfm?rss=africa (accessed March 29, 2008).

60. "The Lady Was for Moving," *Economist*, July 6, 2006.

61. P. Sainath, *Everybody Loves a Good Drought, Stories from India's Poorest Districts* (Delhi: Penguin Books India [P] Ltd., 1996).

62. M. V. V. Ramana, *Inter-State River Water Disputes in India* (Madras: Orient Longman Ltd., 1992); S. N. Sadasivan, *River Disputes in India, Kerala Rivers Under Siege* (New Delhi: Mittal Publications, 2003).

63. Thomas Blom Hansen, *The Saffron Wave, Democracy and Hindu Nationalism in Modern India* (Princeton, NJ: Princeton University Press, 1999).

64. Ashghar Ali Engineer, ed., *Mandal Commission Controversy* (Delhi: Ajanta Publications, 1991); Anirudh Prasad, *Reservation Policy and Practice in India, A Means to an End* (New Delhi: Deep and Deep Publications, 1991); Sagar Preet Hooda, *Contesting Reservations* (Jaipur: Rawat Publications, 2001); A. K. Lal, *Protective Discrimination, Ideology and Praxis* (New Delhi: Concept Publications, 2002).

65. Asha Ramesh and Bharti Ali, *33 1/3% Reservation Towards Political Empowerment* (Bangalore: Books for Change, 2001).

66. Stephen Sestanovich, "Force, Money, and Pluralism," *Journal of Democracy* 15, no. 3 (2004): 36.

67. Ibid.

68. Azadeh Moaveni, "Iran's Hard Line Begins at Home," *Time*, September 4, 2006, http://www.time.com/time/magazine/article/0,9171,1376212,00.html (accessed October 5, 2008).

69. *Human Development Report 2006* (United Nations Development Programme, 2006), table 1, http://hdr.undp.org/en/media/HDR06-complete.pdf (accessed October 2, 2008).

70. See Flynn.

71. See Ian Sanderson, "Is It 'What Works' That Matters?: Evaluation and Evidence-Based Policy-making," *Research Papers in Education* 18, no. 4 (December 2003): 331–345.

72. Bobby Duffy and Rea Robey, "A New British Model," An Ipsos-Mori report, June 2006, http://www.ipsos-mori.com/researchspecialisms/publicaffairs/socialresearchinstitute/istu/britishmodel.ashx (accessed October 5, 2008).

73. See Chris Ham, "Improving NHS Performance: Human Behaviour and Health Policy," *British Medical Journal* 319 (December 4, 1999) 1490–1492.

74. Manow and Seils, "Adjusting Badly"; Wolfgang Streeck and Christine A. Trampusch, "Economic Reform and the Political Economy of the German Welfare State," *German Politics* 14, no. 2 (June 2005): 174–195.

75. Esping-Andersen, *The Three Worlds of Welfare Capitalism*, chs. 7 and 8; Esping-Andersen, *The Social Foundations of Post-Industrial Economies*, chs. 8 and 9.

76. Kemmerling and Bruttel.

77. Benoit, "A Temporary Solution?"; Bertrand Benoit, "Germany Prepares to Vote," *Financial Times*, September 16, 2005; Bertrand Benoit and Richard Milne, "Election Deadlock in Germany," *Financial Times*, September 19, 2005, 1.

78. Benoit, "Germany Prepares to Vote"; Benoit and Milne, 1.

79. On internal coalition politics, see Bertrand Benoit, "Cold Shoulder: How Merkel's Coalition Is Spurning Lobbyists in Reform Push," August 3, 2006, p. 11.

80. Streeck, *Endgame?*; Hugh Williamson, "Healthcare Reform Deal Gives Boost to Merkel's Coalition," *Financial Times*, October 6, 2006, 9.

81. Michael Loriaux, "France: A New Capitalism of Voice," in *States in the Global Economy: Bringing Domestic Institutions Back In*, ed. Linda Weiss (New York: Cambridge University Press, 2003).

82. Jim Wolfreys, "Shoes, Lies, and Videotape: Corruption and the French State," *Modern & Contemporary France* 9, no. 4 (2001): 437–451.

83. Jonah Levy, *Tocqueville's Revenge: State, Society, and Economy in Contemporary France* (Cambridge: Harvard University Press, 1999).

84. Sophie Meunier, "Free Falling France or Free Trading France?" *French Politics, Culture, & Society* 22, no. 1 (Spring 2004): 98–107.

85. J. G. Shields, "Political Representation in France: A Crisis of Democracy?" *Parliamentary Affairs*, vol. 59, no. 1 (2006): 118–137.

86. See "Policing the Police," *Economist*, November 18, 2006, 14–15.

87. Ibid.

88. "Mexico: A Statistical Evaluation of Government Performance," a report of the World Policy Institute Americas Project, April 2000, http://www.worldpolicy.org/projects/globalrights/mexindex.html (accessed October 4, 2008).

89. Ibid.

90. Christine Crowley, "Lula No Long Ball Hitter When it Comes to Land Reform," Council on Hemispheric Affairs analysis, April 7, 2006, http://www.coha.org/2006/04/07/lula-no-long-ball-hitter-when-it-comes-to-land-reform/ (accessed October 2, 2008).

91. Ibid.

92. Hernando de Soto, *The Other Path: The Invisible Revolution in the Third World* (New York: Harper Collins, 1989).

93. See "A Reporter's Tale," *Economist*, February 28, 2004.

94. See p. 181 of J. E. Ehiri, A. E. Oyo-Ita, E. C. Anyanwu et al., "Quality of Child Health Services in Primary Health Care Facilities in South-east Nigeria," *Child: Care, Health & Development* 31, no. 2 (March 2005): 181–191.

95. See Anchrit Wille, "Political Responses to Dissatisfaction in Russia," *Journal of Happiness Studies* 2, no. 2 (June 2001): 205–235.

96. "China's Supervisory Bodies Receive 100,000–Plus Complaints About Government Performance in 2006," *People's Daily Online*, December 27, 2006, http://english.people.com.cn/200612/27/eng20061227_336295.html (accessed October 5, 2008).

97. Zhengxu Wang, "Explaining Regime Strength in China," *China: An International Journal* 4, no. 2 (September 2006): 217–237.

98. "China's Competitiveness Improves: IMD," May 11, 2006, http://english.peopledaily.com.cn/200605/11/eng20060511_264725.html (accessed September 13, 2008).

99. "China Leaps in Competitiveness Ranking," Chinadaily.com, May 11, 2006, http://www.chinadaily.com.cn/china/2006-05/11/content_587174.htm (accessed October 5, 2008).

100. Baopu Liu, "Containing SARS: A Case Study of China's Bureaucracies," *China Brief* 3, no. 11 (June 3, 2003), http://www.jamestown.org/publications_details.php?volume_id=19&issue_id=676&article_id=4739 (accessed October 2, 2008).

101. For an analysis of the First Development Plan (1989–1993), see Hooshang Amirahmadi, "Iran's Development: Evaluation and Challenges," *Third World Quarterly* 17, no. 1 (1996): 123–147.

102. See Jahangir Amuzegar, "Iran's Third Development Plan: An Appraisal," *Middle East Policy* 12, no. 3 (Fall 2005): 46–63.

103. See pp. 50 and 62 of Jahangir Amuzegar, "Iran's Third Development Plan: An Appraisal," *Middle East Policy*, vol. 12, no. 3 (Fall 2005): 46–63.

104. Bert Rockman, "The American Presidency in Comparative Perspective: Systems, Situations, and Leaders," in *The Presidency and the Political System*, ed. Michael Nelson (Washington, DC: Congressional Quarterly Press, 2003), 65.

Epilogue

1. Eric Selbin, "Agency and Culture in Revolutions," in Jack A. Goldstone, ed., *Revolutions: Theoretical, Comparative, and Historical Studies* (Belmont, CA: Wadsworth/Thomson Learning, 2003), 78.
2. Eugene Meehan, *The Thinking Game: A Guide to Effective Study* (Chatham, NJ: Chatham House Publishers, 1988), 130.
3. Marc Howard Ross, "Culture and Identity in Comparative Political Analysis," in *Comparative Politics: Rationality, Culture, and Structure*, ed. Mark I. Lichbach and Alan S. Zuckerman (Cambridge: Cambridge University Press, 1997), 48.
4. Joel S. Migdal, "Studying the State," in *Comparative Politics: Rationality, Culture, and Structure*, ed. Mark I. Lichbach and Alan S. Zuckerman (Cambridge: Cambridge University Press, 1997), 214.
5. If one treats partisanship as a form of identity, of course, the pattern of voting for "one of your own" is even stronger.
6. As Andreas Bieler and Adam Morton remind us, structures do not change with every individual choice, and the most important structures are those which are the "most deeply embedded ones" and the "most unlikely ones to change." Andreas Bieler and Adam D. Morton, "The Gordian Knot of Agency-Structure in International Relations: A Neo-Gramscian Perspective." *European Journal of International Relations*, vol. 7, no. 1 (2001): 10.

Index